EARLIEST CHRISTIANITY

VOLUME II

HARPER TORCHBOOKS

Augustine/Przywara	AN AUGUSTINE SYNTHESIS TB/35
Roland H. Bainton	THE TRAVAIL OF RELIGIOUS LIBERTY TB/30
Karl Barth	THE WORD OF GOD AND THE WORD OF MAN TB/13
Nicolas Berdyaev	THE BEGINNING AND THE END TB/14
Martin Buber	ECLIPSE OF GOD: *Studies in the Relation Between Religion and Philosophy* TB/12
Martin Buber	MOSES: *The Revelation and the Covenant* TB/27
Jacob Burckhardt	THE CIVILIZATION OF THE RENAISSANCE IN ITALY [Illustrated Edition]: *Vol. I,* TB/40; *Vol. II,* TB/41
F. M. Cornford	FROM RELIGION TO PHILOSOPHY: *A Study in the Origins of Western Speculation* TB/20
G. G. Coulton	MEDIEVAL FAITH AND SYMBOLISM TB/25
G. G. Coulton	THE FATE OF MEDIEVAL ART IN THE RENAISSANCE AND REFORMATION TB/26
Adolf Deissmann	PAUL: *A Study in Social and Religious History* TB/15
C. H. Dodd	THE AUTHORITY OF THE BIBLE TB/43
Johannes Eckhart	MEISTER ECKHART: A Modern Translation TB/8
Mircea Eliade	COSMOS AND HISTORY: *The Myth of the Eternal Return* TB/50
Morton S. Enslin	CHRISTIAN BEGINNINGS TB/5
Morton S. Enslin	THE LITERATURE OF THE CHRISTIAN MOVEMENT TB/6
Austin Farrer, *ed.*	THE CORE OF THE BIBLE TB/7
Ludwig Feuerbach	THE ESSENCE OF CHRISTIANITY TB/11
Harry Emerson Fosdick	A GUIDE TO UNDERSTANDING THE BIBLE TB/2
Sigmund Freud	ON CREATIVITY AND THE UNCONSCIOUS: *Papers on the Psychology of Art, Literature, Love, Religion* TB/45
Edward Gibbon	THE END OF THE ROMAN EMPIRE IN THE WEST [J. B. Bury Edition; Illustrated] TB/37
Edward Gibbon	THE TRIUMPH OF CHRISTENDOM IN THE ROMAN EMPIRE [J. B. Bury Edition; Illustrated] TB/46
Charles C. Gillispie	GENESIS AND GEOLOGY TB/51
Edgar J. Goodspeed	A LIFE OF JESUS TB/1
Herbert J. C. Grierson	CROSS-CURRENTS IN 17TH CENTURY ENGLISH LITERATURE: *The World, the Flesh, the Spirit* TB/47
William Haller	THE RISE OF PURITANISM TB/22
Adolf Harnack	WHAT IS CHRISTIANITY? TB/17
Edwin Hatch	THE INFLUENCE OF GREEK IDEAS ON CHRISTIANITY TB/18
Karl Heim	CHRISTIAN FAITH AND NATURAL SCIENCE TB/16
F. H. Heinemann	EXISTENTIALISM AND THE MODERN PREDICAMENT TB/28
Stanley R. Hopper, *ed.*	SPIRITUAL PROBLEMS IN CONTEMPORARY LITERATURE TB/21
Johan Huizinga	ERASMUS AND THE AGE OF REFORMATION TB/19
Soren Kierkegaard	EDIFYING DISCOURSES: A Selection TB/32
Soren Kierkegaard	THE JOURNALS OF KIERKEGAARD TB/52
Soren Kierkegaard	PURITY OF HEART TB/4
Alexandre Koyré	FROM THE CLOSED WORLD TO THE INFINITE UNIVERSE TB/31
Emile Mâle	THE GOTHIC IMAGE: *Religious Art in France of the 13th Century* TB/44
H. Richard Niebuhr	CHRIST AND CULTURE TB/3
H. Richard Niebuhr	THE KINGDOM OF GOD IN AMERICA TB/49
Josiah Royce	THE RELIGIOUS ASPECT OF PHILOSOPHY TB/29
Auguste Sabatier	OUTLINES OF A PHILOSOPHY OF RELIGION BASED ON PSYCHOLOGY AND HISTORY TB/23
George Santayana	INTERPRETATIONS OF POETRY AND RELIGION TB/9
George Santayana	WINDS OF DOCTRINE *and* PLATONISM AND THE SPIRITUAL LIFE TB/24
F. D. E. Schleiermacher	ON RELIGION: *Speeches to Its Cultured Despisers* TB/36
Henry Osborn Taylor	THE EMERGENCE OF CHRISTIAN CULTURE IN THE WEST: *The Classical Heritage of the Middle Ages* TB/48
Paul Tillich	DYNAMICS OF FAITH TB/42
Edward Burnett Tylor	THE ORIGINS OF CULTURE TB/33
Edward Burnett Tylor	RELIGION IN PRIMITIVE CULTURE TB/34
Evelyn Underhill	WORSHIP TB/10
Johannes Weiss	EARLIEST CHRISTIANITY: *A History of the Period* A.D. *30–150* *Vol. I,* TB/53; *Vol. II,* TB/54
Wilhelm Windelband	A HISTORY OF PHILOSOPHY I: *Greek, Roman, Medieval* TB/38
Wilhelm Windelband	A HISTORY OF PHILOSOPHY II: *Renaissance, Enlightenment, Modern* TB/39

EARLIEST CHRISTIANITY

A History of the Period A.D. 30-150

VOLUME II

JOHANNES WEISS

Completed after the author's death by Rudolf Knopf

Translation edited by Frederick C. Grant

HARPER TORCHBOOKS

HARPER & BROTHERS, PUBLISHERS

New York

EARLIEST CHRISTIANITY, VOL. II

This translation of *Das Urchristentum* was originally published in 1937 under the title *The History of Primitive Christianity* and is reprinted by arrangement with Mrs. Rufus Rockwell Wilson.

First HARPER TORCHBOOK edition published 1959

Library of Congress catalog card number: 59–6651 *Vol. II*

LIST OF ABBREVIATIONS

Translated works are referred to by their English titles.

BC—*The Beginnings of Christianity,* Part I, 5 vols., ed. by F. J. Foakes Jackson and Kirsopp Lake, 1920–33.

PRE—*Realenzyklopädie für Protestantische Theologie und Kirche* (Protestant Encyclopaedia of Theology), 3d ed., 1896–1909.

RGG—*Die Religion in Geschichte und Gegenwart* (Religion in Past and Present), 1909–1913. A second edition, entirely rewritten, has since appeared (1927–32); but Weiss's references are to the first.

Schürer—*Geschichte des Jüdischen Volkes* (History of the Jewish People), 4th ed., 1901–09. Where possible, reference is added to the English translation of the second edition; but the fourth contains much material not found in the second.

SNT—*Die Schriften des Neuen Testaments* (The Writings of the New Testament), 2d ed. (1907). A much enlarged third edition has appeared since, Weiss's references are to the second.

Additions by the translators, or by the editor, are enclosed within square brackets.

CONTENTS TO VOLUME II

Book III

Paul the Christian and Theologian

XIII. The Writer
1. His Literary Directness 399
2. Epistolary Forms 401
3. Extravagance of Style 402
4. Homiletic Tone 405
5. Artistry of Expression 406
6. Antithesis 411
7. His Versatility 416

XIV. The Theological Thinker
1. Religion and Theology 422
2. Inherited Concepts 424
3. Linguistic Antecedents: Septuagint Greek 431
4. Patterns of Thought 433
5. Dialectic Forms 435
6. Proof from Scripture 436
7. Hellenistic Elements 440
8. The Proof from Experience 441
9. The Theology of Conversion and of Mission 442

XV. The Christ-Faith
1. The Eschatological Messiah-faith 446
2. The New Conception of the Messiah 448
3. Paul and the Historical Jesus 452
4. The Names of Christ 455
5. The Lord 458
6. Christ-mysticism 463
7. Faith in Christ and Faith in God 471
8. Christological Speculation 475
a. The Son of God 476
b. The World Soul 478
c. The Heavenly 'Man' 484
d. The Incarnation 488
e. Christ's Death and Resurrection 491

XVI. The New Relationship to God
1. Reconciliation 497
2. Justification 498
3. Adoption 504
4. Election 506
5. Faith, Love, Knowledge; God-mysticism 508

XVII. The New Creation
1. Redemption 514
2. Freedom from the Power of Sin 515
3. The Enthusiastic Anticipation of Perfection, Here and Now 518
4. Death and Resurrection with Christ 520
5. The New Life in its Physical Aspect 523

XVIII. The Hope
1. The Longing for Christ 526
2. The Victory of God over the World 526
3. The Dominion of the Saints 528
4. Life, Salvation, Glory 529
5. Resurrection 531
6. The Transformation of those who Survive to the Resurrection 537
7. The Judgment 540
8. Further Details of the Apocalyptic Drama 543

XIX. The Pauline Ethic
1. Its Norms:
   a. Relation to the Law 546
   b. The Words and Example of the Lord 554
   c. The Spirit 556
   d. Limits to Liberty 557
2. The Motifs of the Pauline Ethic
   a. The Eschatological Motif 559
   b. The Religious or Holiness Motif 563
   c. The Fellowship Motif 564
   d. The Personality Motif 566
3. Applications of the Ethical Ideal
   a. Love 569
   b. Truth 573
   c. Self-examination 574
   d. Education and Training 576
   e. Courage and Loyalty 577

f. Possessions, and Problems of Life in the World .. 580
(1) Sex 580
(2) Slavery 585
(3) The State 590
(4) Labor 592

XX. The World-View of Paul
1. The Universe and its Several Parts 595
2. Conflicting Estimates 597
3. Angels and Satan 599
4. The Two Aeons 603
5. Anthropology 605
6. Human Nature 611

XXI. The Church
1. The Church of God 615
2. The Community and the Spirit 622
3. The Sacraments 629
a. Baptism 630
b. The Eucharist 639

Summary 650

Book IV

The Missionary Congregations and the Beginnings of the Church

Prefatory Note 655

XXII. The Expansion of Christianity During its First Hundred Years (A.D. 30–130)
1. The Mission Field 657
2. Judaism and the Gentiles 660
3. The Leaders in the Mission: the Apostles 673
4. The Earliest Gospel: *Mark* 687

Book V

The Separate Areas

XXIII. Judaea
1. Persecutions 707
2. The Death of James 709
3. The Flight of the Christians beyond the Jordan 712
4. The Brethren of the Lord 716
5. The Monarchical Episcopate 719

6. Bar-Kochba 722
7. The Later Christians in Palestine 723
8. The Heretical Jewish Christianity 729

XXIV. Syria
1. The Churches 740
2. *The Epistle of James* 743
3. *The Gospel of Matthew* 751
4. The Samaritan Gnosis 756
5. The Church of Antioch 766
6. Ignatius of Antioch 767

XXV. Asia Minor
1. The Provinces 774
2. Chief Sources 775
3. Cappadocia, Galatia, Cilicia, and Cyprus 775
4. Asia 776
5. Bithynia-Pontus 780
6. Phrygia 781
7. Paulinism in Asia 782
8. *The Gospel of John* 786
9. Persecutions. *First Peter, The Apocalypse of John,* the Letter of Pliny 803

XXVI. Macedonia and Achaia
a. Macedonia
1. Foundation 818
2. The Sources: *The Epistle of Polycarp* 818
3. The Church of Philippi 820
4. Church Organization 820
5. Heresies 822
6. Paulinism 825
7. Christian Macedonia 826
b. Achaia
8. Corinth and the Rest of the Province 827
9. Church Organization 830

XXVII. Rome
1. Paul 837
2. Peter 838
3. The Persecution under Nero 839
4. Influence of the Christian Community 844
5. Piety and Theology: *First Clement* 849
6. Final Summary 863

Index 867

Book III PAUL THE CHRISTIAN AND THEOLOGIAN

Translated by Paul Stevens Kramer

CHAPTER XIII

The Writer

THE biographer of Paul is, it seems, very well provided with material, because he possesses in the letters of the Apostle infinitely rich documents of his innermost being. Paul is one of those few personalities of the past who appear before us clearly because he has not intentionally pictured himself in these sources, but without any thought of posterity has given himself to it as he was. Certainly we should not be ungrateful for this. There are few autobiographical monuments so valuable as the genuine letters of Paul. However we must note one limitation. Between us and the real Paul there stand all kinds of hindrances to a true understanding. There are not only the strange language and the difficulties of interpretation which in many places are almost too great to be overcome. With this problem we are finally compelled to struggle when we study all the great writers of the past; and every 'translation' into the speech and thought of today always means, in spite of every precaution, some falsification. Between us and the real person we are seeking there stands also his literary form and method, inculcated by education and by his traditional points of view, through which he must pour out the contents of his personality.

1. *His Literary Directness.* Recently one of our greatest philologists, who has at his command the material for comparison of the whole of Greek literature, has honored Paul as follows: "It is certain that Hellenism is a preliminary condition for him; he reads only the Greek Bible, he also thinks only in Greek. It is certain that unknowingly he is the executor of the will of Alexander the Great, in that he brings the Gospel to the Hellenes. But he himself is carved out of a different kind of material, he is a Jew, as Jesus is a Jew. But that this Jew, this Christian thinks and writes in Greek, for all the world, and yet first of all for the brethren whom he addresses; that this Greek of his is related to no school and follows no model, but clumsily, in a continual topsy-turvy manner, flows directly from the heart, and yet is still just Greek, not a translated Aramaic (like the sayings of Jesus), this makes him one of the classicists of Hellenism. At last, at long last, one speaks again in Greek of a new experience of life. This is his faith; in it his hope is sure, and his

burning love embraces all humanity. In order to bring salvation to it, he joyously sacrifices his life, but new life of the soul springs up everywhere, wherever his feet carry him. It is as a substitute for personal action that he writes his letters. This epistolary style is Paul, no one but Paul. It is not the style of a private letter and it is not literature; it is an inimitable although often mutilated 'medium' . . . ."[1]

The directness which is here so strongly emphasized as the distinguishing and essential characteristic of Paul's writings impresses every perceptive reader so strongly that it appears almost like calumny if one dare to assert that the eminently personal style of Paul is nevertheless often fettered by a certain practice and by certain traditional forms. We are not at all convinced that the ability of great personalities in modern times to reveal themselves with entire directness in conversation or by letter, to disclose the inner man completely, is an acquisition of the spiritual development of the last few centuries. If we disregard the incommensurable individuality of Luther, it was really Pietism, Rousseau, and the classical period of literature that were the first through which self-expression and the psychological exploration of the individual soul, free from stereotyped models, were born. It was in this period that language first became the fine instrument for true individual expression. The stripping off of rhetorical convention is a great advance over the ancient method. In this respect Paul also belongs to antiquity and his directness is thus not as free as the first impression would lead one to assume. Again in the most personal and intimate parts of his letters we can find a rhetorical form-element which we now no longer perceive at first sight, because we are too much accustomed to it. This is perhaps due to the fact that Paul dictated his letters and always visualized the restricted public he addressed. He speaks to the majority, he does not pour out the fulness of his soul into the bosom of a friend. And even when he writes to an individual like Philemon, he does not free himself from certain forms of rhetorical style.

In itself this is in no way a defect. Form is only there a dead incrustation, or an empty tinkling of a hand bell, where the speaker is not able to animate it, and the modern rejection of time-tested art forms on the plea of individual liberty is often only a sign of impotence. To it these formations have nothing more to say, because they cannot express anything through it. But the true artist shows

[1] Von Wilamowitz, in *Kultur der Gegenwart* (Culture of the Present), i. 8, p. 159.

just in this, that it is given to him to breathe a new life into the inherited form, which for a genuinely artistic reason is just what it is, and thus he is able to develop it further organically. Now it is in this respect that the individuality of Paul reveals itself; that he understands how to handle freely the forms with which he is familiar, and can play upon this instrument as he wills. But there are always the manifold pre-formed methods of revealing inner experience by which he is guided; and to a certain degree they produce a reactionary influence upon the expression of his thought and feeling.

2. *Epistolary Forms.* Among these fixed forms is, e.g., the epistolary introduction. Paul knows how to vary and enliven the beginning of his letters in various ways in order to avoid monotony and to awaken interest. One may compare the simple form of address of II Cor. 1:1f with one which has been expanded to announce a program or with one which is filled with a deep religious pathos, as in the Epistles to the Romans and to the Galatians. But one can also see in the customary thanksgiving, which is not lacking even in Philemon, although certainly here it is expressed rather stiltedly, how he always modifies the particular form of address to suit the different circumstances. In Col. 1:3ff and in I and II Thess. 1 he builds on the recognized triad, faith, hope, and love; in Phil. 1:3ff he points to the alms which they had so freely given; in Rom. 1:8ff he tells of his desire to visit them. Again in I Cor. 1:4-9 he refers with conscious partiality only to the rich gifts of the congregation, so that other deficiencies must be read between the lines. Again in II Cor. 1:3ff he speaks without any reference to the congregation, and in Gal. 1:6 such reference is obviously omitted or is at once slurred over by the inserted reproof. With the strong emotional expression in these fixed forms is of course bound up a certain 'stylistic' method, e.g. a certain exaggeration of praise (as in I Cor.).

The *captatio benevolentiae* found in different forms plays a great rôle, but we must not overlook the conventional element here. Not only the Thessalonians (I Thess. 2:19; II Thess. 1:4) but also the Philippians are called his 'joy' and 'crown of glorying' (Phil. 4:1), and even the Corinthians (II Cor. 1:14), after the saddest period of his relations with them. Not only is the faith of the Romans praised in all the world (Rom. 1:8), but everyone knows also that of the Thessalonians (I Thess. 1:7f) and of the Corinthians (II Cor. 3:2). Paul almost goes too far in his commendation of the Corinthians to the Philippians and of the Philippians to the Corinthians as mutual examples to follow in the matter of the collection for the saints (II Cor. 9:2; 8:1ff). Necessary blame is often modified by previously bestowed praise (I Cor. 11:2); extended exhortation through earlier personal acknowledgments (II Cor. 8:7f,10f; Phil. 1:7). The somewhat strong exhortation of Rom. 15:14f is weakened by the declaration that the readers themselves are able now to correct one another. The oft-repeated phrase, 'as ye yourselves know,' becomes almost monotonous in face of the ever-necessary exhortation and warnings, as in the Thessalonian epistles.[2] In other places very strong implications and assertions are almost completely withdrawn (I Cor. 4:14; II Cor. 7:3), or are limited through acknowledgments or expressions of hope (Phil. 2:12; Col. 2:5; II Cor. 1:14; II Thess. 3:4; I Cor. 1:9; 5:7). Almost too eagerly the writer misrepresents himself or acknowledges mistakes which the readers themselves would scarcely perceive; certainly in Second Corinthians, where he must weigh every word,[3] or where he is dealing with the ticklish matter of money, e.g. Phil. 4:10f,17; I Cor. 9:15. Often there is the fear of making himself obnoxious to his readers through self-praise or of becoming despicable in their sight (II Cor. 3:1; 5:12; 12:19; 11:1,16), or of lessening his humility towards God (I Cor. 15:10; II Cor. 3:5; 4:1), or through severity of casting doubt upon his love (II Cor. 1:24; 2:4; 13:7). Who would dare say that this was not really genuine with Paul? But a conventional and all too smooth connection which makes a somewhat uneasy impression cannot be overlooked, especially in Second Corinthians, where an occasion for this sort of thing is found. It is to be noted that all these urbanities are lacking in the Epistle to the Galatians.

3. *Extravagance of Style*. This leads us to consider the exaggerated manner of expression which is found in all the letters, the bulky individual hyperboles and the exalted expression of feeling as a whole. If he assures every congregation that he thinks of it unceasingly and particularly refers to it in his prayers[4] (although this is not mentioned in Galatians, where nevertheless he has them

[2] 1:5; 2:1f,5,11; 3:3; 4:1; 5:1. Cf. also C. C. Douglas, *Overstatement in the New Testament*, New York, 1931.

[3] Expressive of this are the formulas: *οὐχ ὅτι, οὐχ ἵνα, οὐ λέγω*; II Cor. 1:24; 2:4; 3:5; 7:3,9; 13:7; Phil. 3:12; 4:11,17; II Thess. 3:9.

[4] *ἀδιαλείπτως* Rom. 1:9; I Thess. 1:2; 2:13.

πάντοτε Rom. 1:10; I Cor. 1:4; Phil. 1:4; Col. 1:3; I Thess. 1:2; II Thess. 1:2; Phm. 4. *μνείαν ποιοῦμαι* Rom. 1:9; I Thess. 1:2; Phm. 4. *ἐπὶ πάσῃ τῇ μνείᾳ ὑμῶν* Phil. 1:3.

ἐπὶ τῶν προσευχῶν μου Rom. 1:10; I Thess. 1:2; Phm. 4. *προσευχόμενοι* Col. 1:3. *ἐν πάσῃ δεήσει μου* Phil. 1:3.

chiefly upon his heart in his prayers), it is clear that—without scrutinizing the Apostle too closely—there is a little exaggeration here, in no way different from that of the exhortation, 'Pray without ceasing' (I Thess. 5:17). One may read and analyse such extracts as I Thess. 2:17—3:13, with its exaggerated piling up of expressions,[5] or II Cor. 7:5-16, in which Paul cannot say enough about the happy change of mind on the part of the Corinthians, repeatedly introducing new expressions to describe the confidence and comfort which have filled him since the return of Titus.[6] One will believe the sincerity of Paul's feeling, not because of but rather in spite of the fulsomeness of these expressions. Here too belongs his purely stylistic fondness for reiterating the words 'many' and 'all,'[7] which does not in fact make a good impression upon us. One must not take too seriously the occurrence of such redundancies, as we might in view of the content of feeling expressed; and we cannot ask the question why Paul should express himself so strongly in these particular places. Naturally he would not have been inclined to such

[5] *περισσοτέρως* 2:17, *ὑπερεκπερισσοῦ* 3:10, *περισσεῦσαι* 3:12; *πλεονάσαι* 3:12. *ἐσπουδάσαμεν—ἐν πολλῇ ἐπιθυμίᾳ* 2:17; *ἠθελήσαμεν* 2:18; *μηκέτι στέγοντες* 3:1 (5); *ηὐδοκήσαμεν, ἐπιποθοῦντες* 3:6; *δεόμενοι εἰς τὸ ἰδεῖν ὑμῶν τὸ πρόσωπον* 3:10; *κατευθῦναι τὴν ὁδὸν πρ. ὑμᾶς* 3:11. *χαρά* 2:20; 3:9; *ἀγάπη* 3:6,12; *πίστις* 3:2,5f,8,10. *παρακαλέσαι* 3:2; *παρεκλήθημεν* 3:7; *στηρίξαι* 3:2,13. *ἔμπροσθεν τ. κυρίου (θεοῦ)* 2:19; 3:9; 3:13. *παρουσία* 2:19; 3:13.

[6] 7:7 *ἐπιπόθησις, ὀδυρμός, ζῆλος.*

7:11 *σπουδή, ἀπολογία, ἀγανάκτησις, φόβος, ἐπιπόθησις, ζῆλος, ἐκδίκησις.*

7:6f *ὁ παρακαλῶν . . . . παρεκὰλεσεν . . . . τῇ παρακλήσει, ᾗ παρεκλήθη*; 7:12ff *παρακεκελήμεθα . . . . παρακλήσει.* Cf. II Cor. 1:3ff.

7:7 *χαρῆναι*; 7:8 *χαίρω*; 7:13 *ἐχάρημεν . . . . χαρᾷ . . . . ἀναπέπαυται . . . .* 7:16 *χαίρω . . . . θαρρῶ.*

[7] Rhetorically this is called 'Parachesis'. Cf. Wendland, *Literaturformen* (Early Christian Literary Forms), p. 355; Diels, *Parmenides*, p. 60, Rom. 5:15ff *οἱ πολλοί . . . . εἰς τοὺς πολλούς . . . . ἐκ πολλῶν*; 19 *οἱ πολλοί . . . . οἱ πολλοί* always in contrast to *εἷς*, vs. 18 *πάντας—πάντας*; II Cor. 2:4 *ἐκ πολλῆς θλίψεως καὶ συνοχῆς καρδίας . . . . διὰ πολλῶν δακρύων*; 8:22 *ἐν πολλοῖς πολλάκις*; I Thess. 1:5ff. . . . *ἐν πληροφορίᾳ πολλῇ θλίψει*; the four times repeated *πολλάκις*. II Cor. 11:23,26f—I Cor. 1:5 *ἐν παντί . . . . ἐν πάσῃ*; 9:22f *τοῖς πᾶσιν γέγονα πάντα, ἵνα πάντως τινὰς σώσω, πάντα δὲ ποιῶ*; 13:2f *τὰ μυστήρια πάντα, πᾶσαν τὴν γνῶσιν, πᾶσαν τὴν πίστιν, πάντα τὰ ὑπάρχοντα*; II Cor. 1:3f *πάσης παρακλήσεως, ὁ παρακαλῶν ἡμᾶς ἐπὶ πάσῃ τῇ θλίψει ἡμῶν, εἰς τὸ δύνασθαι ἡμᾶς παρακαλεῖν τοὺς ἐν πάσῃ θλίψει διὰ τῆς παρκλήσεως, ἧς παρακαλούμεθα αὐτοὶ ὑπὸ τ.θεοῦ*; II Cor. 5:14f,18; 7:4f,14f; 9:8 *πᾶσαν χάριν . . . . ἐν παντὶ πάντοτε πᾶσαν αὐτάρκειαν ἔχοντες περισσεύητε εἰς πᾶν ἔργον ἀγαθόν*; 10:5f, Phil. 1:3f *ἐπὶ πάσῃ τῇ μνείᾳ ὑμῶν πάντοτε . . . . ὑπὲρ πάντων.* 7f *πάντων ὑμῶν . . . . πάντας ὑμᾶς*, 4:12 *ἐν παντὶ καὶ ἐν πᾶσιν μεμύημαι. πάντα ἰσχύω.* 19 *ἀπέχω δὲ πάντα καὶ περισσεύω. πεπλήρωμαι . . . . πληρώσει πᾶσαν χρείαν.* Col. 1:10f, *εἰς πᾶσαν ἀρέσκειαν, ἐν παντὶ ἔργῳ . . . . ἐν πάσῃ δυνάμει . . . . εἰς πᾶσαν ὑπομονήν . . . .* 1:28, *πάντα ἄνθρωπον*, three times.

a redundant style if he had not been outwardly a man of strong emotions: joy and sorrow, fear and hope alternate very frequently in him, and the heart-stirrings and the many tears (II Cor. 4:4) we must indeed believe and grant to him. Nevertheless, much of his language is still a habit of literary style, as is also his fondness for piling up synonyms where one word instead of two or three would suffice: e.g. 'deceit,' 'uncleanness,' 'guile' (I Thess. 2:3), 'flattery,' 'greed,' 'sycophancy' (2:5f), 'holily,' 'righteously,' 'unblameably' (2:10), 'exhorting,' 'admonishing,' 'entreating'—all in one chapter! [8] Such redundancy has often a noble pathos about it; e.g. the expressions, 'eternal power and Godhead' (Rom. 1:20), 'the riches of his goodness, and forbearance and the longsuffering of God' (Rom. 2:4), 'thy hardness and impenitent heart,' 'the day of wrath and revelation of the righteous judgment of God' (Rom. 2:5), 'glory,' 'honour,' and 'immortality' (Rom. 2:7), 'glory,' 'honour,' and 'peace' (Rom. 2:10); [9] but often there are fixed forms, such as 'grace and peace,' 'joy and peace,' (Rom. 15:13; Gal. 5:22), 'fear and trembling,' 'wonders and signs,' 'speech and understanding' (I Cor. 1:6; II Cor. 8:7), 'wisdom and understanding' (Rom. 11:33; I Cor. 12:8; Col. 2:3), or the almost conventional summaries, as the well-known catalogue of evils, for which there are Greek examples. Here also probably belong certain stereotyped designations of sorrows and needs, such as we find in Rom. 8:35 and I Cor. 4:11, and which also have parallels in Epictetus.[10]

To all this we must add the stylistic tendency, partly inherited from Judaism and partly learned in Hellenistic schools, to enhance the expression through the method of parallelism of members, often with the same beginning and the same ending. We are reminded of an Old Testament turn in Rom. 1:21,

> With their thoughts they have attached themselves to that which is not,
> And they have permitted their hearts to sink into darkness;

and in Rom. 9:2,

> I have great sorrow
> And unceasing pain in my heart.

[8] I Thess. 3:2, *στηρίξαι καὶ παρακαλέσαι*; 3:7, *ἀνάγκη καὶ θλίψις*; 3:12, *πλεονάση καὶ περισσεύση*.

[9] Cf. Rom. 4:20ff.

[10] Cf. Bultmann, *Der Stil der paulin. Predigt* (Style of the Pauline Preaching), p. 71.

The following sound far more like Greek:

I Cor. 10:21,
Ye cannot drink the cup of the Lord, and the cup of devils:
Ye cannot partake of the table of the Lord, and of the table of devils.

I Cor. 13:7,
Beareth all things, believeth all things,
Hopeth all things, endureth all things.[11]

4. *Homiletic Tone.* In such places it seems that the sermon tone strongly dominates the lesson taught. Almost everything is said in a far more intense and emphatic manner than one would expect to find in a quiet friendly conversation or monologue. In this way these 'letters' are distinctly marked off from the usual epistolary style, which is found in its purest form when presenting the dialogue of daily life, of course without vulgarisms and platitudes. Passages of this kind occur not infrequently in Paul,[12] but they are far less in evidence than one would expect in a literary bequest which consists only of letters. When they do appear they rise far above the complete artlessness of those private letters of antiquity which we now know in such large numbers. The papyrus letter which might really be compared with the letter to Philemon is yet to be found.[13] This is not only because the New Testament letter was written by such an outstanding personality as Paul, but also because Paul himself even in this purely private communication could not for an instant lay aside the 'pastoral-letter' form, and must use an elegant method of expression which is not at all the language of every-day life.

First we have the solemn thanksgiving (vv. 4-7), then the threefold earnest and intense turn (vv. 8f,14,21) that Paul certainly had the right to demand what he asked, though he would prefer the fulfilment of his request through the love of Philemon rather than be-

[11] Cf. my *Beiträge zur paulinischen Rhetorik* (Contributions to the Study of Pauline Rhetoric).

[12] Cf. for example, Phil. 2:19-30, concerning Timothy and Epaphroditus, or I Cor. 16:1-9.

[13] The reader who knows no Greek can understand such letters with the help of Deissmann's *Light from the Ancient East.* One may read the Letter from Caor, *Papas* of Hermupolis, to Flavius Abinnaeus, an officer at Dionysias in the Fayum, *c.* 346 A.D., papyrus from Egypt, now in the British Museum: "To my master and beloved Abinnaeus the Praepontus—Caor, Papas of Hermupolis, greeting: I salute thy children much. I would have thee know, lord, concerning Paul the soldier, concerning his flight: Pardon him this once, seeing that I am without leisure to come to thee at this present. And, if he desist not, he will come again into thy hands another time. Fare thee well, I pray, many years, my lord brother."

cause of this exhortation; the repeated and somewhat stilted word-play, Onesimus, 'the useful one,' who had shown himself 'useless' but now can be 'useful to you and to me'; 'I might use you a little' (vv. 11,20); then the twice-repeated charge: 'he that is my heart'; 'you owe me still more,' 'you owe me yourself' (vv. 12,19); the tender inference that the temporary separation of Philemon and Onesimus has really served this purpose, namely that a permanent reunion may follow and Onesimus will be received no longer as a slave but as a brother—in a double sense, as a freeman and a Christian (vv. 15f); finally we have the humorous and yet solemn 'note-in-hand' (vv. 18f). Here every word is carefully chosen and used for its particular purpose. What another would have said clearly, simply, and in a few words, is here, in view of the circumstances, filled in and expanded with expressions of love and tenderness, with spirit and skill. Certainly Paul would have had reason to express his request in this manner, for he demands much of a friend; but such a lavish expenditure of fine eloquence in a short letter to a friend seems rather unusual to us. One cannot deny that this letter-writer writes not only because it is necessary to do so, but also because he loves to produce polished literary pieces, and he certainly possesses the ability to do so.

5. *Artistry of Expression.* We have not only to reckon in the letters of Paul with the speaking element, which, by the grace of God, is natural to the speaker, but also with an artistic method of expression which occasionally leads him far beyond the practical purpose which lies at hand, in the creation of pictures which have a meaning all their own, and like independent mosaics project themselves out of the context. I call to mind in this connection the two great Christological excurses, Col. 1:14-20 and Phil. 2:5-11,[13a]

[13a] [E. Lohmeyer, *Kyrios Jesus: eine Untersuchung zu Phil. 2:5-11* (Heidelberg, 1928), looks upon this passage as an early Christian psalm in six strophes of three lines each. The strophes in turn fall into two groups, of three strophes each. He points out that its literary form is highly ornate and self-conscious (pp. 4-6). It is not rhetorical prose; instead it is a '*carmen Christi* in the strict sense;' and it is not a fragment of a larger composition, but complete in itself (p. 7). It contains a number of expressions not found elsewhere in St. Paul (p. 8), and the phrase *θανάτου δὲ σταυροῦ* is the Apostle's gloss. Its use of the aorist participle represents Semitic ways of speech, and Lohmeyer concludes that although it was written originally in Greek, the author's mother-tongue was a Semitic one, 'or in other words, it is a Jewish Christian psalm' (p. 9). Furthermore, it must have had for the Philippians the character of a *Kerygma Christi* and an authoritative place in their public worship (p. 13). Cf. also J. Weiss, "Beiträge zur paulinischen Rhetorik" in *Theol. Studien für Bernhard Weiss,* pp. 190ff; A. Deissmann, *Paulus* (2d ed.), p. 149; H. Lietzmann, *Messe und Herrenmahl,* p. 178. (S.E.J.)]

which it is believed should be removed from the text since they have been considered to be interpolations; or the wholly independent and rounded out closing refrain of the 'diatribe' concerning 'remaining in the state of the calling,' I Cor. 7:17-24, which stands in the midst of the chapter on marriage, although, obviously, in regard to subject matter, it passes far beyond that; or again when Paul (I Cor. 2:6-9) speculates on the nature of the divine wisdom, when he depicts (Rom. 7:14—8:2) the battle of the ego with the law of sin, or (Rom. 14:7ff) when he shows the dependence of the Christian upon his Lord. These all, indeed, hang together, but the writer permits himself for the moment to drop the thread of the exposition and loses himself in a by-way, which for a time becomes the chief subject of interest. In this connection we must mention the chapter on Love which fits so loosely into its real context (viz. the explanation concerning the charismata, I Cor., chh. 12,14) that one doubts whether it really belongs here, whether it was fashioned for this particular place, or whether it is not really an independent picture which carries its purpose in itself.[14] We need not safeguard ourselves against a foolish misunderstanding when we say that this gem of religious art is 'created.' Yes, 'created,' like a poem of Goethe or a song of Schubert, yet likewise created through the impulse of strong inner feeling. What we mean is that he did not 'shake it out of his sleeve,' or toss it off while dictating something relative to an entirely different matter; when Paul composed it he had forgotten all about the dispute concerning the speaking with tongues. This work of art came into existence as a result of the deepest reflection and through the impetus of an almost unconscious feeling for form and literary style. It is quite different in regard to the glorious confession of Rom. 8:31-39, which in a powerful way not only closes chapter 8 but the whole exposition which begins with Rom. 1:18, just as with the parallel passage Rom. 5:1-11 he closes the first part of the epistle. Here one must guard himself against any supposition of improvisation; such fruits do not fall except after long previous ripening. One will certainly form a false picture of the literary work of Paul if he imagines that such widely comprehensive works—for they really are small books—were in a few hours and without much reflection bubbled forth into a single stream. They are, for the most part, long, well thought-out, gradually-formed conceptions; and often many chapters, like, perhaps, I Cor. 7 or 15, or Rom. 1:18—

[14] Cf. my *Commentary* on The First Epistle to the Corinthians, *ad loc.*

3:20, or Rom. 9-11, represent the entire literary output of one or several days.

What we wish to say is this: Paul, in his letters, gives only now and then an impulsive improvisation, of the kind the ordinary letter writer gives us. He works rather like an author or artist, and often enough he embodies in his letters previously formed or prepared speeches, to the use of which he is led not only by the practical purpose of the moment, but also by the urge to give to his thought an all-embracing, complete, and rounded form. And indeed very often this has a simple though strongly marked artistic form, usually produced by the use of symmetrical parallelism, written down, as the occasion demanded, in free rhythmical cadence. For example we have Rom. 14:7ff,

For none of us liveth to himself	and none dieth to himself,
For whether we live, we live unto the Lord;	or whether we die, we die unto the Lord:

Whether we live therefore, or die, we are the Lord's.

For to this end Christ died,	and lived again,
That He might be Lord	of both the dead and the living.

Then again, with an almost refined development of the thought, I Cor. 9:19-22,

For though I was free from all men, I brought myself under bondage to all, that I might gain the more.

And to the Jews I became as a Jew,	that I might gain Jews;
to them that are under the law, as under the law—	not being myself under the law,

that I might gain them that are without law;

to them that are without law, as without law—	not being without law to God, but under law to Christ,

that I might gain them that are without law;

To the weak I became weak,	that I might gain the weak:
I am become all things to all men,	that I may by all means save some.

One will observe the consistently developed rhyme-scheme, a b c c b a, in which a and a, b and b, c and c correspond; further, the extension of the two middle sentences (through the two parentheses), the rounding-off by means of a return of the conclusion to the beginning. Such things are not produced of themselves, but only through reflection or masterly training. Here one must observe how the thought is developed in all directions beyond the particular occasion (which is here the consideration of the matter of his support by the congregation).

The discourse concerning the Heavenly Wisdom sounds almost like a strophic poem: I Cor. 2:6-9,

I. Howbeit we speak wisdom—among the perfect,
Yet a wisdom not of this world
Nor of the rulers of this world,
Which are coming to nought.

But we speak of God's wisdom—in a mystery,
The wisdom that hath been hidden,
Which God foreordained before the worlds
Unto our glory.

Which none of the rulers of this world knoweth;
For had they known it,
They would not have crucified the Lord of Glory—
But—as it is written:

'Things which eye saw not, and ear heard not,
And which entereth not into the heart of man,
Whatsoever things God prepared
For them that love him.'

II. For unto us God revealed them through the Spirit;
For the Spirit searcheth all things,
Yea, the deep things of God.

For who among men knoweth the things of a man?—
Save the spirit of the man, which is in him.
Even so the things of God none knoweth,
Save the Spirit of God.

But we received, not the spirit of the world,
But the Spirit which is of God,
That we might know the things that are freely given to us by God.

III. Which things also we speak—not in words
Which man's wisdom teacheth,

But which the Spirit teacheth,
Interpreting spiritual things to spiritual men.

Now the natural man receiveth not the things of the Spirit of God;
He cannot know them,
For they are foolishness unto him,
Because they are spiritually judged.

But he that is spiritual judgeth all things,
But he himself is judged of no man,
For who hath known the mind of the Lord, that he should instruct him?
But we have the mind of Christ.

Anyone who will take pains to analyse this picture carefully will gain an unforgettable impression of Paul's art. Of course the entire mystic charm of the whole discourse can only be really felt in the Greek words themselves. We have been rather bold in designating this discourse on Wisdom as a poem, though in fact we do recognize here certain refrains which one might call lyrical; but for the rest, nevertheless, lyric is just that genre which lies farthest from Paul's genius. In the letters known to us he has contributed nothing to the 'psalms, hymns, and spiritual songs' (odes) of which Col. 3:16 speaks. Again, the passages in Rom. 8:31ff and I Cor. 13 are incorrectly called psalms or hymns [15] in spite of the 'I' form which occurs. The chief characteristic of the lyric, the free out-pouring of entirely personal emotion, is entirely wanting. If one but compares with Rom. 8:31ff the hymn of Paul Gerhardt, "Ist Gott fur mich," he will see the difference; notice particularly the numerous rhetorical questions in the Epistle to the Romans. Nor is I Cor. 13 either a prayer or a hymn of thanksgiving and praise; the composer does not speak of his own love, for the 'I' is universal. The fact that he chooses the abstract word 'love' instead of intuitively saying whom and how and why he loves, is noteworthy. So inspired is he by love

[15] E. Norden, *Die griechische Kunstprosa* (Greek Prose Style), p. 509: "Only seldom does this tone appear, but when it does, the flame of his inspiration bursts into a devastating power; both of those hymns (?) of love to God and love to man (Rom. 8:31ff; I Cor. 13) have presented again to the Greek language that which for hundreds of years had been lost, the earnestness and enthusiasm of a man who has been inspired by union with his God, such as we only meet in Plato and finally Cleanthes. How such language must have struck into the hearts and souls of people who had been accustomed to listening to the absurd chattering of the Sophists! The diction of the Apostle here rises to the height of the Platonic *Phaedrus*."

that he desires to portray its nature and its works, and he does it in a discourse-form. Even here the real nature of Paul the thinker is revealed; certainly he is a thinker who is at the same time all feeling and intuition. The beauty of the passage lies in the choice of words, in the structure of the sentences, and in the figures of speech; in the design and rhythm of the whole.[16] We leave it to the reader to make a careful and detailed analysis of it, merely pointing out that here also the fundamental elements of Pauline composition are found, namely parallelism and antithesis.[17]

6. *Antithesis* is perhaps the most distinctive characteristic of his style. We may say, perhaps with some exaggeration, that all his speaking and thinking has an antithetical rhythm in it. There may be differences of opinion as to whether the reason for this lies more definitely in his method of thought and feeling, or in his habit of literary composition. A recent critic has remarked: "That antithesis dominates is easily understandable. As long ago as the fifth century B.C., when the reality of all natural phenomena was questioned, e.g. by Heraclitus, the mighty revolution of ideas was hypostasized in an antithetical manner of speech. We stand again now at a turning point; the denial of the reality of all that has existed up to this time is an exceedingly sharp one. Is it to be wondered that the man [Paul] who, eager for battle, set about to smash into ruins a world of beauty, should clothe his revolutionary ideas in antithetical forms; that the sharp opposition between heaven and earth, light and darkness, life in Christ and death in sin, spirit and body, belief and unbelief, love and hate, truth and error, being and appearance, yearning and fulfilment, past and present, present and future, should be strikingly set forth, at times almost to the point of obscurity, in monumental antitheses?" [17] Certainly we will agree with these words, and yet we must add something more. Paul's preference for antithesis is not to be explained only by reference to the general period of Hellenism. Later Judaism itself with its sharp dualism, clearly apparent in its belief in Satan (II Cor. 4:4), in its doctrine of the two ages and the new creation [18] (II Cor. 5:17), in

[16] In part one (vv. 1-3), there are three very different parallelisms, and yet they are bound together by an harmonious rhythm; in the second part (vv. 4-7), there are five parallel lines, which are nearly all again divided into two; in the third part (vv. 8.13), groups of three (vs. 8), three (vv. 9f), five (vs. 11), five (vs. 12), three again in v. 13. Cf. my Commentary, *ad loc.*

[17] Cf. E. Norden, pp. 507ff and 20ff, concerning the Gorgianic antitheses, e.g. in Heraclitus.

[18] Cf. IV Ezra 4:26-32.

its conception of the immense gulf between the supernatural God of heaven and man—'flesh and blood cannot inherit the Kingdom of God' (I Cor. 15:50)—represents religious thinking based entirely upon antithesis. Paul was clearly accustomed to this habit of thought and has brought it with him. Nor is it lacking in another sphere of life into which Paul may have entered in some way, that is, in the Hellenistic type of religion which we find in the Pseudo-Hermetic writings. In the apocalyptic discourse of Hermes to Tat,[19] a number of important chapters (κεφάλαια) are set down, in which the pious man—and he only who possesses the right philosophy can be considered as such—is given grounds for encouragement, as for example:

> There is nothing good on earth, nothing evil in heaven.
> God is good, man is evil.
>
> Everything in heaven is unchangeable, everything on earth is changeable.
>
> Nothing in heaven is servitude, nothing on earth is free.
>
> The immortal has no part in the mortal, but the mortal has a portion in the immortal.[20]
>
> The earthy has nothing to do with the heavenly, the only use of the heavenly is for the earthy.

Paul seems nearer, in form of composition, to this sphere of thought than he is to his Jewish sources.

To all this must be added the influence of his own experience. The two parts of his life are sharply separated, one from the other, by his conversion; on the one side there is only error, sin, and flesh; on the other, life, spirit, truth, and righteousness. Finally one must call to mind the entirely individual predisposition of Paul. Does he not belong to those choleric natures for whom there is an 'either-or,' who always observe things in their sharpest and most exclusive aspects? So he appears to us in the letters—even the more so on account of his strongly dominant tendency to use sharp and exclusive

[19] Cf. the Stobaeus Hermetica, i. 41. 1. (Tr. by Walter Scott, *Hermetica,* Oxford, 1924ff.)

[20] Wachsmuth has explained this passage in quite another way, wrongly it seems to me.

antitheses. The stylistic peculiarity seems to be grounded in the soul of this personality and in its wholly peculiar history. This is certainly true, and one may only wish that at all times theology had taken it seriously, and had not considered this deeply established antithetical view of the world as self-evident and binding upon every Christian.

Yet here we must propose still another consideration. A so deeply rooted habit and tendency of thought and speech, firmly imbedded in the very soul of a personality, reacts upon it as a compulsion to place everything which has been experienced and observed under the category of contradiction, even where such a method is not immediately suggested by the content of the experience. The speaker and the writer are to a high degree especially sensitive to the seductive charm of antithesis, for it is a very simple means of arranging thought and a very impressive figure for the speaker. There can lie here, moreover, a real danger for truth, particularly when the problem is that of the self-representation of individual inner experiences, which, under ordinary conditions, most people at least are not accustomed to set forth in antithetical sentences, but after an entirely different pattern. It must be described as nothing less than fateful that Paul has bequeathed to Christian theology and preaching the tendency to establish conclusions by the method of sharp contradiction, and to fail to take into consideration the transitions at hand and the apparent modifications—with the result that much confusion is furnished for those of fine feeling and tender conscience. In fact we may learn from a study of Paul that he could not himself carry through his world view, set in a completely antithetical frame-work, without coming into conflict with experience, and that the attempted portrayal of his own inner life through antithetical observation is thus shifted into a partly false perspective. He himself, indeed, has acknowledged that the present world is not only the Kingdom of the devil (II Cor. 4:4), but that in it also powerful forces for good are at work, e.g. in the submission to authorities (Rom. 13:1ff); he acknowledges that not all people are sinners, but that even among the heathen, the 'unrighteous' (I Cor. 6:1), and 'sinners' (Gal. 2:15), there are people who 'by nature' do the works of the Law (Rom. 2:14)—which according to his usual theory is really not at all possible. Moreover, if we honor truth, it is simply false to maintain that upon his conversion Paul became an entirely new man. In his thinking and feeling, and not the least in his acting, much unalloyed Judaism is still powerful with him, while, on the other hand, certainly not everything that he possesses of 'love, joy, peace, longsuffering, kindness, goodness, faithfulness, meekness, temperance' (Gal. 5:22) was received as a 'fruit of the Spirit.' How much of it was the result of his education in the Jewish Old Testament and in Hellenistic schools! How often he is obliged to modify his exclusively antithetical confessions! In one breath he says, "It is no longer I that live—but Christ that liveth in me," and adds "the life I now live in the flesh . . . ." (Gal. 2:20). It is thus stated in Rom. 8:9, "Ye are not in the flesh, but in the Spirit," and immediately adds (8:12), "Ye are debtors, not to the flesh, that ye should live after the flesh. For if ye live after the flesh, ye must die." We shall see later that this sharp change is not only a self-correction of the speaker's antithesis, but has a very deep religious and theological foundation; moreover it has about it a trace of literary and oratorical style. One sees that the rhetorical antithesis is frequently unable to cover the facts of real experience and must be corrected on the basis of the experience itself. One recognizes here especially clearly that the wonderful literary gift of Paul is not only a perfect means of expression, but that it also occasionally serves as a means of veiling the inner soul. Here we touch upon a problem that must further concern us, and one which will always furnish the explorer of the spiritual life, as well as the investigator in other spheres, much material for study, since it has been generally found that every man is bound by the thought-forms of his time, often entirely inadequate as they are to express his new experiences—so that in order to be just to him, we cannot simply judge by his words.

We were obliged first to consider the Pauline antithesis from this aspect; now we shall try to show, on the other hand, that it is a richly varied form of expression and has become for him an excellent method of self-representation.

Those main, recurrent antitheses, enumerated above (by E. Norden), are well known, and every chapter furnishes examples,[21] e.g. that unforgettable passage I Cor. 15:42f,

> It is sown in corruption, it is raised in incorruption;
> It is sown in dishonour, it is raised in glory;
> It is sown in weakness, it is raised in power;
> It is sown a natural body, it is raised a spiritual body.

[21] Compare the table of antitheses in Holtzmann's *New Testament Theology* (vol. ii, pp. 19, 56; 2d edition, pp. 21ff, 61ff) with my *Beiträge zur paulinischen Rhetorik,* pp. 176ff.

Or compare Rom. 14:7ff (page 408); I Cor. 12:3 and 26; II Cor. 9:6; Gal. 6:7f; II Cor. 4:16ff,

> Though our outward man is decaying,
> Yet our inward man is renewed day by day;
> For our light affliction, which is for the moment,
> Worketh for us more and more exceedingly an eternal weight of glory,
> While we look not at the things which are seen,
> But at the things which are not seen:
> For the things which are seen are temporal;
> But the things which are not seen are eternal.

We choose here a special group of antithetical sentences which show the inner life of the Apostle from an exceptionally direct and gripping point of view. There is in the faith of Paul, and also in that of primitive Christianity, especially in the proclamations of Jesus, a deeply engrained paradoxical and antithetical element: e.g. the joyfully defiant 'although'—'nevertheless' which is perhaps the really essential and eternal element in our religion. In Paul this element is strengthened by contacts with Stoicism, which in its own way, but in a similar manner, contrasts the true worth of existence with its illusory possession, the inner happiness with the outer lustre. We may here also grant that the paradoxical form of such considerations has produced a certain power of attraction; it always costs sacrifice and self-denial to grasp it fully—therefore we must consider it as an essentially true mirror of an inner emotional conception. It appears so often and in so many dfferent nuances in Paul that it must likewise be considered a fundamental element in his outlook upon life. One may call to mind the three following passages (not to mention I Cor. 4:12; Rom. 5:3; and others):

I Cor. 7:29f. In view of the nearness of the end, a Christian must lead his life thus:

> Those that have wives, as though they had none;
> Those that weep, as though they wept not;
> Those that rejoice, as though they rejoiced not;
> Those that buy, as though they possessed not;
> Those that use the world, as not using it to the full.

Here once more, the liberty which the Christian must always guard in his intercourse with the world, the inner distance and reserve, comes to clear expression. In the following passage is set forth the firm conviction that suffering cannot defeat him, that he is never completely 'done for.'

II Cor. 4:8,

> We are pressed on every side, yet not distressed;
> Perplexed, yet not unto despair;
> Pursued, yet not forsaken;
> Smitten down, yet not destroyed.

And again, II Cor. 6:4-10 expresses the feeling of the friend of God who, in spite of all sufferings and misunderstandings, has in his heart a hidden, costly treasure of innocence and blessedness.

> In much patience—
> In afflictions, necessities, and distresses,
> In stripes, imprisonments, and in tumults,
> In labors and watchings and fastings;
> In pureness and in knowledge,
> In long suffering and in kindness,
> In the Holy Ghost, in love unfeigned,
> In the word of truth, with the power of God,
> With the armour of righteousness on the right hand and on the left,
> By glory and dishonour, by evil report and good report;
> As deceivers, and yet true;
> As unknown, and yet well known;
> As dying, and behold, we live;
> As chastened, and not killed;
> As sorrowful, yet always rejoicing;
> As poor, yet making many rich;
> As having nothing, and yet possessing all things.

7. *His Versatility*. Paul the writer, whom, naturally, we are unable to picture completely without the help of the Greek, appears before us in varying aspects according to the subjects he is dealing with; indeed, it would seem that the various letters are written in very different ways, e.g. First Thessalonians differently than First Corinthians, which again differs much from Second Corinthians, which, in turn, is entirely different from Colossians. This may have its cause in the varied moods of the writer; but we cannot entirely rid ourselves of the suspicion that occasionally Paul's amanuensis, Silvanus or Timotheus, had a greater and a different kind of influence upon the formation of each of his letters than is ordinarily assumed. But aside from this differentiation, the investi-

gator and critic of the personality and teaching of Paul, viewing him from the standpoint of his literary style, must take heed to other causes. It is not legitimate to treat in the same manner the sharp, precise, and exactly measured doctrinal teachings, with an occasional argument about suffering or help, or a solemn liturgical formulation or tone, and the sober expression of practical, private views. Often a mistake is made in attempting to spread out the entire Pauline doctrine and religion upon one level, without observing the differences between height and depth—an effect produced by neutralizing the various emphases and values. The preliminary condition for a correct evaluation, and the needful protection against an all too strong systematization, is a proper feeling for the literary values—'values,' indeed, as the artist uses the word.

What strikes us next of all, in the light of our heritage from Greek literature, is Paul's affinity with the so-called Diatribe,[22] that elastic medium intermediate between tractate and sermon, monologue and dialogue, which is most clearly illustrated in the *Discourses* of Epictetus as preserved for us by his pupil Arrian.[23] Here an interlocutor is visualized—in the case of Paul it is usually the congregation, though often it appears in the form of a typical 'you,' to whom the writer addresses himself, to whose understanding he appeals,[24] with whom he shares in reflection,[25] and with whom he disputes. In this latter case he permits himself to raise objections [26]—which he often half-grants, only to reply in language so much the stronger to the contrary effect ('certainly, good—but'); but often enough he replies with a violent repulse: "God forbid . . ."; "Against this I say . . . ." Where this kind of rhetorical dialogue prevails, we usually find short sentences, which is something quite different from the method of the Attic period; often there is no closer connection between them than that of contradiction, expressed in a gracious, almost playfully elegant manner (as in I Cor. 3:5-9; Rom. 14:2-6); then again—according to the mood—it may be intensely forceful

[22] Cf. Wendland, *Hellenist.-Röm. Kultur*, pp. 75ff, and *Literaturformen*, p. 356; also R. Bultmann, *Der Stil der paulinischen Predigt und die kynisch-stoische Diatribe*, 1910.

[23] Cf. Hilty, *Gluck*, i; translations of Epictetus are common—the best is now the one in the Loeb Library. See also Wendland, *Kultur*, pp. 95f.

[24] Very frequently with Paul: "Do ye not know?" "Dost thou not know?" "I remind you;" "I will not leave you in uncertainty;" "Judge ye yourselves."

[25] For example, in the rhetorical question, with its deep reaching-back which brings to light a hidden obscurity, "Or are ye not at all clear about this, that . . . ?" Compare also the little retarding question, "What also?"

[26] "But someone will say;" "You will now say."

(Rom. 2:21ff; I Cor. 9:4-7), often with the opening sentence (*anaphora*) reiterated at the conclusion (*epiphora*). Here the unusual lightness and liveliness of expression always moves in a popular vein. Here the concrete particular expression and the sharply individualized case are the rule; general thoughts are unfolded, separated often by such expressions as 'it may be—it may be,' or similar terms. Especially noteworthy as characteristic of the diatribe is that peculiar form of premise which wavers between interrogation and condition, as in I Cor. 7:18,27,

> Was any man called being circumcised—let him not be circumcised;
> Hath any been called in uncircumcision—let him not be circumcised.
>
> Art thou bound to a wife—seek not to be loosed;
> Art thou loosed from a wife—seek not a wife.[27]

Here the concrete examples are taken from life (I Cor. 9:7,24), often from the same spheres as in the Hellenistic diatribe (the prize-fight, war-service, farming, body and members); they are frequently not the result of Paul's actual experience, as in the case of Jesus, but are taken from tradition; we therefore occasionally find such an unreal and unfortunate example as that of the olive tree (Rom. 11:23f). This loose dialogue-style is found especially in the ethical parts of Paul's letters, which are also the chief domain of the diatribe, where the practical convictions and a change in the point of view of the reader are really aimed at.

Not entirely unlike this, in point of style, are the dialectic sections in which Paul carries through either a message of instruction or a Scriptural proof, as in Rom. 4:2-5,10-16 or I Cor. 15:12-19, 44-47; Gal. 3:6-22). Here, evidently, we must reckon more with the Rabbinical than the Hellenistic school. Here also we observe the short sentences and the rhetorical questions; but here there is also lacking that indirect gracefulness, and all that quality which immediately charms. Appeal is very frequently made to the reason, to which under the circumstances much is attributed because—quite in the manner of the Rabbis—often many important middle terms are left out. Therefore our exposition stumbles around very much in the dark; particularly because the thought-forms used here are not easy for us, the exegetical method tends to become trivial, literal, and over-sophisticated. We shall see this again in particular cases.

[27] Compare my *Commentary* on The First Epistle to the Corinthians.

Now we must draw attention to the unusually frequent deductions from the general to the particular (or the reverse, e.g. II Cor. 3:7-11), and to the artistically developed parallelism between primitive times and the End, Adam and Christ (Rom. 5:12-20; I Cor. 17:21f).

Again, Paul writes in an entirely different manner when he desires to express his teaching positively, as in Rom. 1:19f and 3:21-26; here he forces his thoughts so closely together, overloads his sentences with so many irrelevances and misunderstandings of the foregoing clauses, that the result is far from what he intended. We are often obliged to draw out of a single word the teaching of a whole chapter. We can only assume that the first readers, because of their knowledge of the oral proclamation and of the preliminary conditions, which we lack, could understand these compact sentences better than we. What appears to us only as an intimation (as in that passage concerning the Mediator, or in the doctrine of the Cross), must have had for them a far more intimate connection and background. Here he finds every stylistic medium to his taste, since the Greek language permits the ready spinning out of sentences by means of participles, relatives, prepositions with the infinitive, causal phrases, and appositional clauses, which in German [or in English] we can reproduce correspondingly only by beginning a new sentence (e.g. Rom. 3:24ff; 4:18-21; Col. 1:15-20; 2:9-15).

That careless, easy-going manner of sentence-structure, produced by 'crowding in' clauses, and by which long, unwieldy, rambling sentences are constructed (which can by no means be compared with the finely divided and uniformly organized periods of the Greeks), rules so strongly in certain portions of the Epistles to the Thessalonians, Colossians, and Second Corinthians, that we can scarcely recognize here the skilled writer and speaker of other passages.

How entirely different, again, are the combat passages: the penetrating warnings (Gal. 5:1-12) with their short, loose sentences (vv. 4,7ff), the compassion towards adversaries (II Cor. 11:29ff), with the ever repeated, 'I also,' with the heaped-up enhancing particles (ὑπὲρ ἐγώ, περισσοτέρως, περισσοτέρως ὑπερβαλλόντως, πολλάκις, πεντάκις), with the eight-fold repetition of the word 'dangers.' One should write down the entire section, divided into short sentences, and then read it aloud in Greek, in order to receive the full impression of the somewhat over-wrought man, as he gradually becomes more and more angry; hence the bitter irony at the beginning (vv. 19ff), which is similar to the passionately painful outbreak in

I Cor. 4:8-13, which belongs to the most intensely emotional of all that Paul has written.[28]

Already ye are filled,
Already ye are become rich,
Ye have reigned without us;
Yea, and I would that ye did reign,
That we might also reign with you (I Cor. 4:8).

And:

For ye bear with the foolish gladly,
Being wise yourselves!
For ye bear with a man if he bringeth you into bondage,
If he taketh you captive,
If he devoureth you,
If he smiteth you on the face (II Cor. 11:19ff).

Then again:

We are fools for Christ's sake;
But ye are strong and wise!
We are weak,
But ye are strong;
Ye have glory,
But we have dishonour:
Even unto this present hour we both hunger and thirst, and are naked also;
We are buffeted, and have no certain dwelling-place:
And we toil, working with our own hands;
Being reviled, we bless;
Being persecuted, we endure;
Being defamed, we entreat:
We are made as the refuse of the world, the off-scouring of all things, even till now (I Cor. 4:10-13).

Then again, that intimate, tender wooing of those congregations that were about to fall away (Gal. 4:12-20, and II Cor. 6:11ff; 7:2-4). What expressions! What pictures he presents here! One cannot read such passages without emotion.

And again, the exalted, poetical, rhapsodic language which appears in those 'prophetic' pronouncements, as where he speaks of the secrets of the End (I Thess. 4:15ff; I Cor. 15:42ff,50-57;

[28] I call attention to the analyses in my *Beiträge zur paulinischen Rhetorik;* here I merely mention similar violent ironies.

Rom. 11:25ff), or in those mystical revelations concerning the Wisdom of God (I Cor. 2:6ff), concerning the groaning of the creature (Rom. 8:19ff), in the calls to action (Rom. 13:11ff; I Thess. 5:6f), in the confessions of faith (Rom. 5:1ff; 8:31ff), in the Song of Songs of Love, and in the glorious witness to the liberty of the Christian man (I Cor. 13:1; Rom. 3:21ff). Here also I merely draw attention to the story of his vision (II Cor. 12:2ff). How peculiarly tender and solemn all this is!—as though the words were spoken in a low voice with a strange emotion and with closed eyes. He never speaks of himself blatantly, but always as of another; only after a twice-repeated strophic introduction does he speak of that most sacred experience.

Truly, this writer has at his disposal many different means and modes of expression; thus an astonishingly rich and many-sided, spiritually elastic personality unfolds itself to us. And if we have stated before that the forms used, which were acquired by the author in his early education, and the whole rhetorical character of the letters, sometimes bar our entrance into his inmost thought, all this is richly compensated by the magnificent fulness and manifoldness, by the lightness and skill of expression, by the richness in beautiful and impressive changes of emphasis which are in the control of Paul, and by means of which the few clumsy and unwieldy parts, the overloaded obliquities and violences, are more than covered up. The study of Paul's literary art is not only necessary in order to do justice to him, but it is also highly suggestive, and the deeper one penetrates into it and the more one reads, not only with the eye but also with the ear, so much the stronger becomes the impression of an original and significant personality, of one who not only strives, after a wholly new manner, to express an overwhelming view of life, but who in a high measure succeeded in overcoming the obstacles which lie in the organs of speech.

CHAPTER XIV

The Theological Thinker

1. *Religion and Theology.* Just as earlier theology concerned itself chiefly with the teaching of Paul, and saw in him above all else the systematic thinker, and even, from a one-sided point of view, the dialectician of hair-splitting logic, so now lately, with no less partiality, it emphasizes the religious personality, the spiritual leader and mystic.[1] It is necessary to avoid both extremes, for they are both, in reality, errors. For the special characteristic of Paul is just this, that he does not distinguish between religion and theology, piety and thought, at least in that side of his personality which has been revealed to us. It is, naturally, at once to be assumed that he could be untheological, in prayer, in his loving care for the bodily and spiritual welfare of those given into his care, and in all the particular concerns of his daily work. But, if we may draw conclusions from his letters, the moments when he gave himself without reflection to consider concrete individual cases of life were far less frequent than those when he also through trivialities and purely personal concerns permitted himself to be led to the consideration of the greater fundamental thoughts of his inner being, and faced the individual under the general, the lowest under the highest point of view. And indeed, not only in the purely religious sense of *sub specie aeternitatis,* but in the theological sense that the individual becomes an especial example of the rule that from daily occurrences arguments may be drawn for the elaboration of the highest truths: the question of the meats offered unto idols is a problem of sympathy and love; the question of the marriage of virgins leads him to the wholly general exposition of freedom from the world; the question concerning circumcision, especially, forces him to think through the nature of faith and of religion as such. The predominance of general and ab-

[1] E.g. Deissmann in his *Paul.* "Paul is essentially and foremost a hero of religion. The theological element is secondary. Naïveté is stronger than reflection; mysticism stronger than dogmatism; Christ means more to him than Christology, God more than the doctrine of God. He is far more a man of prayer, a witness, a confessor and a prophet, than a learned exegete and close-thinking scholastic" (tr. by W. E. Wilson, London, 1926, p. 6).

stract concepts, the preponderance of dialectic forms of expression, serve sufficiently to show the essentially reflective manner of this thinker. Hardly has he begun to speak of the peace of God won through Justification (Rom. 5:1-5), than he entangles himself in a logical syllogism and contradiction (5:6-11)—the entirely scholastically suggestive relationship between Adam and Christ (Rom. 5:12-20) has for him a deep religious sense, and is, in fact, a confession of faith. In this way the dialectic explanation of the settling of the difficulty between himself and Peter (Gal. 2:15-18) passes over, unnoticed, into the tone of a confession of faith (Gal. 2:19ff), and the joyful witness to the Resurrection of Christ (I Cor. 15:20) becomes at once the medium of a theological deduction and exposition. The great Christological excursus (Col. 1:14-20) appears under the sign of thankfulness for God's benefits in salvation (Col. 1:12f), and the other similar one, in the letter to the Philippians (2:5-11), glows with admiration for the humility that serves. Thus, always, religious feeling and theological reflection are joined in him; yes, even prior to this, we could not even represent to ourselves the basic experiences of conversion without at the same time indicating at least the changes in his theological fundamentals. He who would attempt to separate the one from the other would do violence to the nature of Paul. With all his soul and with all the power of his will he belongs among those who can really rejoice in an experience only when they have found for it a satisfying theoretical formula for its expression, and for whom, on the other hand, a consistent logical sequence of thought produces not only intellectual peace and satisfaction but indeed, and especially, a religious inspiration. Salvation must be at the same time both true and the means of solving the world's riddle, if it is to set him free inwardly. He is the outstanding theologian of the Christian Church; since Paul, religion and theology have been so closely coupled together in Christianity that it has not been possible to break their alliance, even to the present day. It is very questionable whether this has been a blessing to Christianity. However necessary theology may be to the Church and her relationship to the surrounding world, it would still be very much to be desired if one could find in the life of the individual a religious form from which the theological might be entirely excluded. The modern cry, 'Away from Paul to Jesus,' the demand for 'undogmatic Christianity,' rests on the feeling of this necessity. The question as to whether the realization of this hope will be accomplished in our time or in the future, may be left in abeyance. But one means to this end is the knowledge of how in Paul the truly religious life is embedded in a hard shell of theological reflection.

The problem here is the same as with Paul the writer. It is certainly true that God gave to him as to few others the ability to express what he felt; but he is able to do so, for the most part, only by means of thought-forms inculcated by education, and which to us are strange and difficult. He does not always have at his disposal that impetuous directness and freedom of expression, which is a rare gift of genius. In this he differs from Jesus, whose simplicity, objectiveness, warmth speak to every child and have something of great value to say to the deepest thinker. Paul is rather to be compared with Luther, who for the expression of his deepest and warmest experiences had at his command only an inflexible scholastic instrument. However much he overcomes these hindrances, it must be deeply regretted that he had for the tenderest and finest of all that he had to say to humanity only that formula, for most people incomprehensible, 'Justification by Faith.' In a like manner, the thought of Paul, in the most important matters, is moulded in preformed concepts; he proceeds, for the most part, clad in an armour of theological ideas, even when he might speak to the heart of every age, and this at once discourages the approach of the interested reader who has no knowledge of Biblical language.

2. *Inherited Concepts.* There is, first of all, the word *'faith,'* which even up to this day has given cause for grave misunderstandings, whether one understands it as distinct from a well-founded 'knowledge' as a partial, uncertain kind of knowing or supposition, or a languid reliance upon or surrender to a strange incomprehensible teaching. The word, whose history we must know to understand it,[2] was not created by Paul; it lay before him as a ready-made stereotyped concept, in fact, a favorite expression, taken from certain intra-Jewish controversies; he took it over as a well-known and commonly accepted symbol in his environment, to which a whole series of different thought-sequences was attached. So it is the fixed expression for a reliable proof of the reality of things unseen (Heb. 11:1),[3] e.g. of the being of God (Jas. 2:19); in this sense also it

[2] A more important contribution is Schlatter, *Der Glaube im N.T.* (Faith in the N.T.); cf. also Bousset, *Rel. d. Judentums* (Religion of Judaism), pp. 176ff.

[3] The two paraphrases which the Epistle to the Hebrews chooses in its famous definition of faith, are highly significant: ὑπόστασις, really the fixed substance or foundation, is used in Hellenistic prose of the unshakable firmness of the will or the disposition, or of the convictions (LXX Ps. 39:8; Ruth 1:12; Ezek. 19:5). Thus especially significant is the description of the followers of Judas of Galilee, given by

appears in Paul (II Cor. 5:7). Thus 'faith in God' is the distinguishing mark of those Gentiles who have been converted by the missionary preaching (I Thess. 1:8; I Peter 1:21). This deeply religious sense is readily expressed in the terminology of the propaganda, in that the Jews or Christians, in contradistinction to the unbelievers (I Cor. 6:2; 7:12ff; 10:27; etc.) are designated as the 'believers' (I Cor. 14:22; I Thess. 2:10,13; II Cor. 6:15), and the whole new condition of life is simply called 'faith' (Rom. 1:8).[4] Here the original meaning of the word, viz. 'trust,' 'reliance,' 'faithfulness,' is almost entirely wiped out. It is, on the other hand, strongly present where 'faith' indicates the unshakable certainty that the promises of God will be fulfilled; in this sense the faith of Abraham was typical, 'who in hope believed against hope' and 'gave glory to God' in that he trusted His almighty power even in that which was unthinkable (Rom. 4:17f,20f). Paul uses the word in this sense when he speaks of faith in miracles, which removes mountains (I Cor. 13:2), and which he reckons among the special gifts of the Spirit (I Cor. 12:8). In this sense faith is a trust in the faithfulness of God (Rom. 3:3; I Cor. 1:9; II Cor. 1:18; I Thess. 5:24); so also Rom. 4:24; 10:11; II Cor. 4:13. But however much this is with him the kernel of the representation of Faith, there appears less often and less clearly than we should expect, another side to it. For, indeed, the difference between his religion and the religion of Abraham and of Judaism is that he no longer awaits the fulfilment of further outstanding prophecies, but proceeds upon completed facts; therefore he distinguishes between the concept of faith and that of hope; he turns backwards and relates himself essentially to the past and to the present. In regard to the past, there appears an altogether momentous change in the history of the concept. One would think that that fact of the near past, which appears so clearly in the bright light of history, viz. the death and resurrection of Christ, could by no means be brought into connection with that faith which has to do with the unseen and future. Nevertheless this is

---

Josephus (*Ant.* xviii. 1. 6; §§ 23ff). After he has spoken of their unconquerable love of liberty, and observed that they look upon God as their only Lord and ruler, and that they consider death and the loss of relatives and friends merely as a lesser evil in comparison with the acknowledgment of a human ruler, he speaks of their unbending (αμετάλλακτον) conviction. (So also Paul in II Cor. 9:4; 11:17). And ἔλεγχος is the 'carrying over', i.e. to certainty, of something which rests upon convincing proof or experience; in connection with the 'invisible things,' this expression is very forceful; the unseen is as certain as if one could seize it physically with the hand.

[4] This less emphatic use is especially frequent in the Book of Acts.

what has happened; the missionary term 'faith,' which in its really good sense expresses conversion to monotheism, has also been related to the fact of Salvation, announced in the Gospels, to which it does not at all apply. It has, naturally, a definite sense here, in so far as the hearers of the preaching must accept it in good faith and in the belief that such great things do occur; because they themselves have not witnessed the miracle of the resurrection they must therefore have 'faith' in the Apostle (I Thess. 4:14). Now, upon the basis of this so-called 'fact-faith,' something else is developed concerning which we must next speak. We may look upon it as momentous that the same word, which can have such a deep meaning, serves at the same time to designate the acceptance of stories, which in themselves may not be accompanied with any religious emotion or decision of the will. And since the first hearers believed the first message of the Apostle, because, in a certain measure, they held to their own faith and were carried away by it, so it may almost be called a calamity that for later ages, and especially for our own, the idea is suggested by the use of such language that the believing acceptation of those far-away, dark, yea even, to modern man, highly doubtful facts, is the inescapable narrow-gate to the sanctuary of religion! This is one result of the fact that Paul was forced to seize upon this ready-made, stereotyped concept and to turn it to a use for which at first it was not intended. Naturally it has gained even for him other meanings, more closely corresponding to the original sense. When he says in Rom. 10:9,

> "If thou shalt confess with thy mouth Jesus as Lord,
> And shalt believe in thy heart that God raised him from the dead,
> Thou shalt be saved,"

he is very far from meaning that the bare acceptance of the facts or even the profession of this 'faith' guarantees salvation; nevertheless he himself (10:11) adds this sentence: "Whosoever believeth on him shall not be put to shame," and faith in the resurrection of Jesus is indeed a reason for trust in God, who has performed this miracle and to whom one can entrust all else (Rom. 4:24; Col. 2:12). Faith 'in Christ' (Rom. 3:22,26; Gal. 3:22; Phil. 3:9; Col. 2:5), to which he has devoted himself, (Gal. 2:16), means that henceforth he expects salvation from *him*, for it is faith in him 'who has given himself for me' (Gal. 2:20), from whose grace and love he expects the boon. Hence the religious element of trust is not lacking; in truth, it completely predominates.

It is quite remarkable that Paul uses the word faith, in the great majority of cases, without an object, without any further determination of its content, as if much more depended upon the act of believing than upon what one believes. But this, the intellectual or doctrinal side of the concept forces 'fact-belief' almost entirely into the background. And here lies the real change of meaning in the old, favorite expression, which Paul has drawn from the fulness of his own religious experience. We have already seen what he means by this; here we wish only to make ourselves clear again as to the meaning of two Pauline words. After he has shown (Rom. 10:5ff) the nature of the righteousness of the Law, as a storming of Heaven, or a descent into Hades, in order to compel the coming of the Messiah and his Salvation, he characterizes the nature of faith (Rom. 10:8) through the Scriptural words, "The word is nigh thee, in thy mouth and in thy heart," that is to say there is no need of such superhuman exertion, what is demanded is something very simple and very easy, you must only give your assent to what is offered to you in the Gospel, you have only to seize and receive as a gift what God will give. Herein lies the fundamental thought, already described, of the experience of conversion: that Salvation which seems so far away in the heavens, and yet demands comprehensive preparations, is, strangely enough, already here and is offered for acceptance; only one thing is necessary, viz. that the one to whom it is offered does not refuse it.

Paul also represents (Rom. 4:5) 'believing' (πιστεύειν) in exclusive opposition to 'having works' or 'being concerned with works'—as Luther says, 'doing' (ἐργάζεσθαι), which is the meaning of the Greek word. 'Believing' here appears as the counterpart of that closely related activity, which, as Paul renders it in Gal. 1:14; Phil. 3:6; Rom. 9:31; 10:2f,6f, is the renunciation of 'doing' which would seem to be an attempt to force God into giving a reward or to grant a blessing. Occasionally Paul also calls this the 'obedience' of faith (Rom. 1:5; 16:26), as he conversely calls disbelief also disobedience (Rom. 15:31); by this it is indicated that faith is the renunciation of every personal desire and personal determination of the way of Salvation; one should not wish to know better than God that which serves to our peace, but should subject himself to a new order which he has now, once and for all, established. The same concept of faith also occurs in Judaism (e.g. *The Apocalypse of Baruch* 54:5, 'They who have subjected themselves by faith to you and to your Law'). So it is said of one who utters the daily confession of faith, the *Shema*, that he 'takes upon himself the yoke of the Kingdom of Heaven'—another expression for subjecting oneself to God in faith. The new faith-concept of Paul has doubtless a connection with Judaism, only it is for Paul an entirely different and unheard-of new order which one acknowledges by faith, to which one must yield himself in an obedient, childlike, and trustful manner. Certainly this beginning of faith in the life of the Christian (I Cor. 3:5; Rom. 13:11; Gal. 2:16) which requires that one 'resolve upon faith' at the time of his conversion, is not restricted to that moment but henceforth becomes the fundamental basis of the religious life: 'I live in faith' (Gal. 2:20), and in this meaning he includes an infinitely humble, childlike, and continually thankful yielding of oneself in love to him 'who has loved me and given himself for me;' it means to serve him alone, no longer to live for oneself (II Cor. 5:15; Rom. 7:4), to give oneself to his guidance, and to requite him with faithfulness, to ally oneself with him from the heart, so that sometimes one may even speak of faith 'in Christ' (Gal. 3:26). Thus 'faith' has definitely become the expression for the new form of Christ-devotion (I Thess. 3:2,5ff,10; Col. 1:23), for the new fundamental conviction from which the whole future Christian life flows (Gal. 5:6; Rom. 14:1, 23). In this way the word has received a content which extends far beyond its natural meaning; it is forcibly over-enhanced and broadened. Therefore one must have a heart-felt sympathy for Paul's entire point of view in order to understand what he means by 'faith,' and naturally our German [or English] word does not suffice to reproduce perfectly its content; we are therefore obliged to use all kinds of circumscriptions. Here one may clearly see how Paul had to put new wine into old bottles.

This is still more plainly seen in his new concept of *Righteousness* and of *Justification*. These words refer to a legal act of declaring right or just, that is to say innocent, acquitted. It is certainly clear that the acquittal of a 'sinner' (Rom. 4:5) is really a contradiction in itself; still more crass and almost blasphemous to a Jewish ear sound the words of Paul (Rom. 3:24), "We are acquitted without being worthy," or as the Greek has it, "It is a matter of a gift." A judge who, in his act of judging, presents and acquits, is no longer a judge; at least his action is no declaration of 'acquittal' but a pardoning. Really, then, one should never use the expressions 'to declare innocent' and 'righteousness' (Rom. 1:17; 3:21; Gal. 2:21), for they actually eliminate themselves in this connection. When Paul, instead of using for these the terms 'grace' and 'pardon,' retains the legal terminology, he does it because his thought runs along in this scheme of divine judgment, and because he is not able to find an entirely new terminology for the new experiences; his new method of thought remains bound up in the old forms, which now, nevertheless, have been wholly shattered. Thus a whole series of other Jewish concepts is made to serve the new lines of thought. Quite apart from the concept of 'Christ' (or Messiah), which in Gentile areas lost its national-political significance and was viewed as a proper name, *Salvation* (ἀπολύτρωσις), which also occurs occasionally in the New Testament in the Jewish sense of deliverance of the people from slavery (Luke 1:18; 2:38; 24:21),[5] was naturally conceived of in the eschatological sense; thus we read in Luke 21:28, "Lift up your heads, because your redemption draweth nigh"—the approaching Parousia brings 'salvation' to the Jewish-Christian community from its Jewish enemies and oppressors. As Paul uses the word, it loses every trace of political meaning (Rom. 8:21,23) and, as it stands in the context, indicates that Salvation, in the main, has for him already come to pass: we already have it 'in Christ' (I Cor. 1:30; Rom. 3:24; Col. 1:4). Out of the changed meaning of the word there arises now the difficulty that the involved relationships connected with the political idea (slavery, heathen, destruction, liberty) become uncertain; from whom, or from what, are the Christians saved? How and to what extent can the death of Christ accomplish this salvation? The idea here loses its original concrete aspect.

We must bear in mind especially, as regards Paul, more so perhaps than in the case of any other man, that his great fundamental religious concepts had already had a long and very involved history behind them when he came to use them for the expression of his wholly unique experiences and ideas. They are benumbed witnesses of life-processes which have been connected, often in primitive times, with entirely different points of view; many of them—in spite of all 'spiritualization' and abstraction—still retain something of the primitive 'ethnic' sense which they had in primitive times. Thus it is with the concept of holiness, which though apparently so spiritual and even on the way of becoming ethical (I Cor. 6:11) is still occasion-

[5] "The characteristic name which the Messiah bears is 'Redeemer' (גואל) in distinction from Moses, the first redeemer (גואל הארשון *Ruth Rabb.* on 2:14) גואל אחרון, e.g. *Beresh. Rabb.*, cap. 85. As Moses led Israel out of Egypt, so the Messiah shall complete the final redemption (גאלה) and lead Israel out of Exile (גלות) into its own land." "The redemption wrought by him is also called, e.g. in *Mechilta* to Ex. 15, תשועה (*σωτηρία*) Salvation" (Weber, *Jüd. Theol.* §79:2). Cf. my Commentary on I Cor. 1:30.

ally presented in the primitive heathen sense of a contagion attached to men and to things, which, without the participation of anyone's will, passes from the one to the other (I Cor. 7:14).[6] Here, above all, the representation of the 'spirit' is especially instructive;[7] its unusual many-sidedness and various meanings for Paul are understood only if we always keep in mind the former history of this concept. Thus it means, in various connections, the invisible inner life of man (I Cor. 5:3; Rom. 2:29; 1:9), heart and mind (I Cor. 16:18; II Cor. 2:13; 7:13), the self-consciousness of man (I Cor. 2:11; Rom. 8:16), and also, a lesser sense, the 'disposition' (I Cor. 4:21); it is that in man which is indestructible by death (I Cor. 5:5). The idea of soul is closely related to these usages, in that the spirit can, in a certain measure, leave the body and convey itself elsewhere (I Cor. 5:4), as for example in ecstasy (II Cor. 12:2,4; cf. Rev. 4:2). But the words are also used of the Spirit 'which comes out from God' (I Cor. 2:12), and is poured into the individual as a power (Rom. 15:19) or faculty of the understanding (I Cor. 7:40), merges itself with the will or reason of the individual, so that his entire being is ruled by it (Rom. 8:4-9); but then again, it is conceived of as dwelling together with the human spirit (Rom. 8:16; I Cor. 14:14): the Christian lodges within himself a double-being, as did those possessed of demons, and as also, for example, every prophet received his own peculiar 'spirit' from God (I Cor. 14:12,32). Here the ancient animistic representation breaks through, which otherwise was held in check by Paul's abstract thought; nevertheless the idea prevails that the Spirit (*pneuma*) which has penetrated into individuals is only an outflow of the penetrating power of God, present in the whole world, and into which the Christian is plunged by Baptism, or by which he is so saturated that he is fused with God or with the exalted Christ and transformed into a new being (I Cor. 12:13; 6:17). The same duality of representation is often effected when the Spirit appears as a gift of God or of Christ (Rom. 8:9; II Cor. 1:22), so that he can be called an independent being beside God and Christ (II Cor. 13:13; I Cor. 6:11); soon, however, he appears as in some sense identical with Christ (II Cor. 3:17). Especially noteworthy is the fact that the representation has a uniquely dual character, since Paul, in spite of all efforts cannot avoid thinking of spirit as the opposite of matter, as a kind of finest heavenly matter, out of which are formed the bodies of the angels, of Christ, and of the trans-

[6] Cf. my Commentary on I Cor. 7:14.

[7] Cf. Volz, *Der Geist Gottes* (The Spirit of God), 1910.

figured risen ones (I Cor. 15:44,46). This extraordinarily rich shading of meanings is the result of a long religious and philosophical development. In the same way the word 'psychic' corresponds to the 'pneumatic,' and has received an especial modification of its original meaning 'soulful,' which produces an entirely different sense; it means, exactly, the earthly-natural, that which is connected with the body and with flesh and blood (I Cor. 15:44,46; 2:14).[8] This same development must have occurred also in the use of the word 'body' (σῶμα), because it occasionally does not mean the literal body (as Rom. 4:29; 6:12; 8:13), but the 'form' of the personality, indestructible by death, which only serves the body as a spiritual framework (I Cor. 6:13,15; 15:44,46), and after the casting-off of the really corporeal (flesh and blood, I Cor. 15:50) can acquire a filling-out with an entirely different substantiality (Phil. 3:21; I Cor. 15:51).[9]

3. *Linguistic Antecedents: Septuagint Greek.* It is necessary to keep in mind, in connection with Paul, the historical development of the concepts through the history of the language, since he is the product of two language-areas. Certainly he speaks and thinks in Greek, but he speaks also the Greek of his Bible, the Septuagint. In this wonderful book there is an entirely new series of language-creations by which the translator has frequently to make the often magnificently successful attempt to bring into accord Hebrew and Greek concepts, each of which brings with it elements inherited from its own environment, and which by a mere pairing could not really be equated. So it is with the difficult concept of 'doxa.' In Greek it means, 'opinion,' 'view,' also 'teaching,' or in contradiction to truth, 'appearance,' and then 'fame,' 'honor.' From this last meaning of 'honor' it recommended itself as an equivalent of the Hebrew *Kabod,* which indeed has the meaning of 'honor' and 'lustre,' 'worthiness' and 'fame,' but now chiefly means the 'appearance' or 'revelation' of God bathed in fire and light. Therefore, 'doxa' indicates in the New Testament—what it could hardly mean in Greek—the bright revelation of divine being (Luke 2:12; Rev. 15:8; 18:1; II Cor. 3:7); by Paul, once, the lustre of the stars (I Cor. 15:41); then again the bright flash of light which he saw at the appearance of the Lord (II Cor. 4:6; Phil. 3:21), and which

[8] Cf. also Reitzenstein, *Hellenist. Mysterienreligionen* (Hellenistic Mystery Religions), pp. 42ff,112. The word and the idea have a Hellenistic background; cf. my Comm. on I Cor. 2:16 and 15:44a.

[9] Cf. my Commentary on I Cor. 6:13 and 15:44a.

is to appear to the elect at the Parousia (Rom. 8:18,21; Col. 3:4). Often we cannot say with any surety what the word really means with Paul, as for example when the husband is called the 'doxa' of God and the wife the 'doxa' of the husband (I Cor. 11:7, 'reflection'?); nor whether Rom. 3:23 must be translated, "They lack the 'honor' which they should have before God," or "They have not yet any part in the future 'divine radiance' of heaven," or "They have lost the 'divine splendor' or 'lustre' which Adam and Eve once had before the Fall, and which any man who has been made in the image of God should possess." So also the concept of the 'righteousness of God,' in many places, can in no way be fully understood either in the Greek or even in the German [or English]; one must remember that the Greek word was occasionally substituted for the concepts, 'love,' 'grace,' 'loving-kindness,' 'truthfulness'; it must also have had a special meaning for the Hellenistic Jew, who, indeed, could have expanded it into exactly its opposite. This peculiarity agrees with the entirely unique formation of the Old Testament concept of the 'righteousness of God': the Israelite who expects salvation from the 'righteousness of God' only because he belongs to his people, is inclined to place it upon the same level with truth and grace, love and loving-kindness. Thus many words have different meanings with Paul, according as the Hebrew or the Greek fundamental emphasis becomes the stronger; so the word for 'justifying' hovers between the meaning, 'declaring righteous' (Rom. 3:24), and the actual relieving from sin (I Cor. 6:11); so 'peace' is now (Greek) the opposite of 'strife,' 'enmity' (Rom. 5:1), now as if it were the same as (Hebrew) 'redemption,' 'happiness,' 'harmony of the soul' (so especially in the benedictions, 'grace and peace').

Thus the lexicon of Paul gives us a good many complicated problems, and we dare not hope that we shall ever find an answer to all of them. Above all we must realize that a German [or English] translation will always remain inadequate, because seemingly corresponding words never really completely cover each other; for the most part the Greek will always be richer, more diverse, many-sided and elastic than the German, so that we are often obliged, in order to reproduce one Greek word to use several German words or even a paraphrase (as for example the word *pistis:* 'faith' and 'faithfulness').

The Greek genitive offers a source of difficulty: What does 'love of God' mean? Love to God, or God's love to us? The 'righteousness of God'—a characteristic of God? or a legal term referring to man? (righteousness before God?). And what is meant by the 'glory of God,' 'faith of Jesus Christ,' 'the suffering of Jesus Christ?' Here many different meanings are possible, for the Greek genitive possessed at this time a far greater elasticity and meaningfulness than our own,[10]—we are often left in a dilemma as to how we shall understand and reproduce certain Greek purpose-clauses.[11] The rules of classical Greek are here of no help: a 'therefore' is often rather a 'so that,' or has become 'namely.' Of course the converse is also found; where everyday language would designate one event as the natural sequence from another ('so that'), the religious thinking of the Apostle sees rather the divinely connected purpose; hence he says, 'so that.'

4. *Patterns of Thought.* With this we come now to the Pauline thought-forms, with which we must become very familiar if we are correctly to evaluate the full import of his thought. Just there where he does not give an expressly, clearly-stated account of why he judges this way or that, we must heed the unexpressed hypothetical condition which forms the basis for his assertions and conclusions. His complete teleological manner of thought is especially to be noted. Also where he does not say, "It has pleased God" (as Gal. 1:15), but simply states facts, the thought must be supplied that 'this has happened according to the will of God.' In this way II Cor. 4:7 which reads, 'We have this treasure in earthen vessels,' must be supplemented by 'according to the will of God'; for it was the purpose of God that all the world should know that the spiritual power of the Apostle comes from God and not from himself. So the actual formation of the Corinthian community (I Cor. 1:26-29) indicates how little God considers the wise-men of this world; thus the 'foolishness' of the Gospel, by which God will save the world, shows how meanly he esteems this world's wisdom (I Cor. 1:20f). So the unbelief of the Jews must rest upon a divine plan (Rom. 11:11), so the missionary successes of the Apostle are a divine working (Gal. 2:7f), Paul's labor a work of grace (I Cor. 15:10).

We wonder at the assurance with which Paul makes assertions concerning the events of the End, which he knows accurately in their exact sequence (I Cor. 15:23-28; I Thess. 4:16f); whence does he know this? How can he claim such an exact knowledge of these things? The fundamental conviction here is that the entire

[10] Cf. also Deissmann, *Paulus*, pp. 94f.

[11] ἵνα and εἰς τὸ with the infinitive.

course of things to come has long since been firmly established; everything is foreseen and determined, and Paul is acquainted with the apocalyptic writings or traditions in which all of this is given. They are for him neither fantasies nor speculations of men, but prophetic predictions of the End, which certainly must be fulfilled. We are especially surprised by the definiteness with which Paul says: "For as in Adam all die, so also in Christ shall all be made alive" (I Cor. 15:22), and the recurring parallelism which he sets up in Rom. 5:11-20, between the efficacy of the work of Adam and Christ. Why must this be so? Because, in his way of thinking, there lies the presupposition that the events of primitive times—only in a reverse sense—must be repeated at the end of time; a conviction which elsewhere plays a great rôle in Apocalyptic. But here something else appears: What is the meaning here of 'in Adam,' 'in Christ?' There is concealed in this short word 'in,' a very strange but fundamentally important method of thought on the part of the Apostle: what has happened with or to Adam is not merely his own personal experience; he is a representative personality, and his fate (death) is, according to God's plan, that of all his descendants. For Adam is, in a certain sense, the archetype of humanity; what happens to him happens to all men. Here rules the ancient (in a certain Platonic sense) 'realism of universal concepts.' So that while for our manner of thinking, Adam would be a man beside other men, for Paul he is at the same time the universal archetype of man, and this is with him not merely a fancy but the reality. It is exactly thus, now with Christ; he also is an archetype: what he experiences is not only his own fate, but is reproduced and works in all who belong to him; in this case it is not because of a physiological descent but through another kind of relationship. This is especially true of the work of Salvation. When Christ died upon the Cross, not only did his body die, but in and with his flesh, 'flesh' in particular was put to death, and with the flesh the indwelling sin (Rom. 8:3). This is naturally only thinkable if 'flesh' and 'sin' are not merely abstract concepts, but realities, and so, for Paul, the flesh of humanity is a living organism into which Christ, by his becoming man, has entered, and which in his crucifixion receives the destroying death-thrust. Therefore Paul can say, "Ye were made dead to the Law through the body of Christ" (Rom. 7:4) or "I have been crucified with Christ" (Gal. 2:19).

In connection with this, sin appears again as a personal demonic being who 'seduces' man (Rom. 7:11)—it is as if Paul were thinking of the serpent in Paradise. The whole representation of the Fall, in fact (Rom. 7:7-11), sounds, even though Paul gives it in the 'I'-form, like paraphrase of the story of Paradise, and one may assume that he (like Philo) interprets the narrative of Genesis not only as a once-occurring historical event, but as a universally human psychological fact. This brings us to a very important thought-form.

Just as Philo loves to transform the persons of Old Testament history into universal types, as the Stoics, by their allegorical method, changed the gods of ethnic religion into natural events or abstract ideas, and as conversely, such concepts as 'Reason,' 'Logos,' 'Wisdom' in the Jewish-Hellenistic Gnosis assume personal forms, so especially, for the thought of this time, the change from personality to concept, and the converse, was so easily accomplished that only with difficulty can we imagine it. We observe this same thing also in Paul. As for him, flesh and sin, law and the world, are not only concepts or 'principles,' but highly real, almost personally-imagined powers, so he is able to equate the personality of the highest Lord with 'the Spirit': 'The Lord is the Spirit' (II Cor. 3:17). This forces the conclusion that the representation of Christ, in certain thought-connections, is to a certain degree depersonalized; it merges with that of the world-filling, all-penetrating Spirit.

5. *Dialectic Forms.* In another sphere we meet with certain dialectic forms which remind us of the Rabbinical. 'For the Law worketh wrath; but where there is no law, neither is there transgression' (Rom. 4:15)—from this it follows that when the Law is eliminated, the reason for wrath disappears, and grace becomes free. This conclusion, however, rests on an intermediate thought, that a sin can only be pursued by the wrath of God if it is represented as a 'transgression' of an announced commandment of God; in any other case it is indeed 'sin' but not 'transgression.' Therefore, sins committed since the elimination of the Law are far more grievous (5:20) than before, since while there was no Law there was not as yet any 'imputation of sin' (5:13). This is a sharp and definite rabbinical idea—since the thought of the Rabbis touches this question in a thousand ways, under what conditions one who has transgressed may still be considered as guilty or perhaps as 'free.' Upon this basis Paul builds up the idea, so important for his system, that the prohibitions contained in the Law had either 'slipped in' or 'had been added' (Rom. 5:20; Gal. 3:19), in order rightly to give to sin its real sinful character (Rom. 7:8), in order to make it appear as a punishable transgression. There is also a rabbinical intimation in

I Cor. 15:12-16, where the thought moves back and forth: if in the one case Christ is presented as the fact of the Resurrection then the general statement that the dead do not rise is contradiction; but if this general statement is correct then the resurrection of the one individual is not possible. Peculiar and not at all convincing sounds the assertion (I Cor. 15:44) that if there is a 'natural' body, so there is also a 'spiritual' body; if one replaces the word 'spiritual' by 'supernatural' he will perceive how far from convincing the logic is. Why, then, if one part of the contradiction be true, must the other be true also? Must one be 'hot' because the other is 'cold,' or 'dark' because it is 'light?' The 'either-or' which is here silently accepted is certainly not logical; here lies the fundamental persistent religious antithesis between the divine and the human, between heaven and earth, spirit and flesh.

6. *Proof from Scripture,* which is so important for Paul, is but little illuminated for anyone who is outside the circle of his faith. For him, 'it stands written' cuts off all discussion and objection. But the manner in which scripture-proof is established contradicts entirely our idea of scientific exactness. The fact that he depends upon the Greek translation of the text, instead of going back to the original Hebrew, it seems to us, cannot be harmonized with the certainty which we would wish. Worse yet, he is accustomed not to bother himself about the context and original meaning of the words under discussion, but values them only in the sense that suits him; so that he has set us not a good, if all too frequently imitated, example. Thus we have only to look at Deut. 30:14, the equivalent of Rom. 10:8, to see that the clause, 'the word is nigh thee and in thy mouth,' does not refer to the faith but to the observance of the Law; it means thus just the opposite of what Paul desires to prove by it. The emphasis on the singular 'the seed of Abraham,' and the attempt to establish thus the possibility of a reference to the one Christ (Gal. 3:16), are entirely contrary to the Hebraic and Greek use of language, for it is here naturally a collective for 'seed' and is thus related to all the descendants of the people: thus Paul's exposition is entirely surreptitious. He approaches the Holy Scriptures with a fundamental conviction that God has placed concealed secrets in them, which only the eye enlightened by the Spirit can discover; it is the task and the precious right of a Spirit-filled teacher (I Cor. 12:28) with 'all wisdom and spiritual understanding' (Col. 1:9) to draw out of them what they have to tell to this present generation. All this has been written 'for our sakes' (Rom. 15:4; I Cor.

10:11), who stand on the border-line of both aeons. In these last times, the veil, which still lies over the unbelieving Jews, should be lifted by the reading of the Old Covenant (II Cor. 3:14); they indeed hear the Word but do not understand it (Rom. 11:8). Only when Israel turns to the Lord will the veil be lifted (II Cor. 3:16). At the moment when one has perceived that all the predictions of God have found their fulfilment in Christ (II Cor. 1:20), that he is the real content of the Holy Scriptures (Rom. 1:2f)—then there also spreads out over all individuals a wonderful light; everything in Scripture seems to relate itself to him, all must be related to him; and if the Scripture does not at once illuminate, and there are still some who grumble, skill will be necessary for the solving of the mystery. Thus many places in which there is a question concerning the word 'Lord' appear in a new light: wherever the word may mean 'the Lord of Hosts,' the Christian refers it frankly and freely to his Lord Christ, as in the expression in Jeremiah: 'He who boasts, let him boast in the Lord' (Jer. 9:22f; I Cor. 1:31; II Cor. 10:17). Indeed Paul can apply the same word with equal conviction as well to God as to Christ: 'Who has known the mind of the Lord' (Isa. 40:13) is applied to God in Rom. 11:34 and to Christ in I Cor. 2:16.[12] It is especially the faith of Abraham which appears to Paul in an entirely new light, owing to his personal experiences and in view of his success in the mission to the Gentiles. In the words to Abraham that 'his faith was reckoned unto him for righteousness,' God had already revealed, centuries before, the great principle of Salvation, which certainly was not accepted by the Jews (Rom. 10:3). But now it becomes clear how the bold faith of Abraham in the God who can work life out of death was like the Christian faith in the resurrection of Christ (Rom. 4:19ff,24). Now for the first time we understand the full meaning of the expression, that in Abraham all Gentiles shall be blessed (Gen. 17:15; 12:3; 18:18). Now also such a little train of thought, that Abraham believed when he was yet uncircumcised, becomes clear (Rom. 4:10f)—by this it was made possible for him to become the 'father' of the uncircumcised (4:11). The sequence of the stories in the sacred narrative is also noteworthy. Not without reason, the circumcision appears two chapters later (Gen. 17) than the pronouncement of the faith (Gen. 15). It is of fundamental importance that the

[12] This Isaiah passage would have served Paul much better in this context (I Cor. 2:16), as he would have seen had he read the original, where instead of 'mind' (νοῦς) 'spirit' (רוח, πνεῦμα) is used—which is certainly the word Paul means here.

promise to Abraham was made 430 years before the mission of the Law (Gal. 3:17); the former pronouncement of God cannot be nullified by the latter. This not only has its deeply religious reason in the unchangeableness of God's will, but also in the historical, philosophical opinion that the older is the truer. The primitive age is nearer to the real and innermost being and will of God than the later development. Thus Jesus directly declared the institution of marriage in Paradise as indissoluble, the permitting of divorce, by Moses, a mitigation (Mark 10:1-9). Thus the revelation made to Abraham contains the real meaning of God, and the later Law 'added unto' it (Gal 3:19), or 'slipped in between' (Rom. 5:20), is farther from God's intention than the promise.

Here we have found a critical principle of great scope, in that Paul can distinguish between the eternal and the temporal, between that which has been fulfilled and that which has died out in the Old Testament. And now he finds indications everywhere that the Law gives information concerning itself: the rabbinical Haggada teaches him that it does not come directly from God, but is given through the mediation of angels (Gal. 3:19); and when Moses 'covers his face with a veil' (Ex. 34:33,35), to shield it against the glory of the deity directed upon him from Sinai, Paul does not hesitate to impute to him the motive that the Israelites should not be permitted to observe how this glory became gradually weaker and weaker; he wished to hide from them the fact that the splendor of the Old Covenant must pass away (II Cor. 3:13). Rabbinical also is the method by which he amplifies the statements of Scripture by adding explanatory additions of his own, and then, nevertheless, treats these as Scriptural; thus in Rom. 10:6f to the 'to ascend up into heaven' and 'to descend into the nether-world,' he adds, 'to bring down Christ from above' and 'to bring up Christ from the dead,' as if this were an integral part of the text. In the same manner Paul argues about the passage, Psalm 143:2 (Rom. 3:20; Gal. 2:16), as if this verse treated of Justification 'by works of the law' (cf. page 170); so he cites Gen. 2:7 as if it read, "The first man Adam was made a living soul, (the last Adam a life-creating spirit)," although the bracketed words are not found in the original text; but it is just upon these that Paul bases his argument, and his proof rests upon this, that they are words of Scripture, which they certainly are not. It is very plainly to be seen here that the scribal tradition, which is drawn out of Scripture by exegesis, is just as important and convincing to him as the word of Holy Scripture itself, which comes from the Spirit of God. For our critical thinking, this interpolation of one's own thoughts is unbearable arbitrariness; at best it is simply naïve—however often it may likewise be practised by Christian theologians. This method becomes understandable and endurable only if we remember that the Apostle believed himself possessed of the same 'Spirit' which rules in the Scriptures, so that his interpretation is found to be congenial. As once Daniel, by the instrumentality of the Spirit, was able to interpret dreams and visions, so he (Paul) is able by the Spirit to point out the mysteries of Scripture (I Cor. 2:13); this is in truth the 'wisdom' over which he has control (I Cor. 2:6), or the 'knowledge' (I Cor. 13:2) in which he is second to none.

By means of this wisdom he discovers and treats of facts which are not found in Scripture, least of all in the canonical books, as for example the mysterious teachings concerning the sequence of events at the End (I Cor. 15:23f; II Thess. 2:1ff; I Thess. 4:13ff). He is not only acquainted with the classical predictions of the prophets but also with the secret wisdom of Apocalyptic. He must have read books which we no longer possess; we may uncover a fund of these any day, all of which suggests that many assertions which today appear to us as the words of Paul, may be, in truth, citations. Thus the phrase, 'what eye hath not seen nor ear heard' (I Cor. 2:9) comes from an unknown apocryphal writing of Elijah.[13] Thus also the phrase concerning the 'groaning of the creature' (Rom. 8:22), which Paul introduced with, "We know," may belong to a Jewish apocryphon; or the other (Rom. 8:28), "We know that to them that love God all things work together for good," may be found in another Hellenistic document.[14] But much of this he need not to have learned out of books, but from oral tradition; here belongs, for example, all that he says of the spirit-world and its enmity toward the Messiah.[15] The great fundamental thought is that the

[13] Origen says this expressly of Matt. 27:9.

[14] Not only does the 'we know' lead to such an assumption; above all the wholly un-Pauline expression, 'those who love God;' Paul then explains it at once by 'they who have been called after his will.' Certainly it is characteristically Pauline that he should look upon the love of God as a mark of election; cf. I Cor. 8:3. This reminds us very strongly of the phrase in the *Corp. Hermet.* ix. 4: the *θεοσεβής*, who possesses *γνῶσις*, bears all things—*πάντα γὰρ τῷ τοιούτῳ κἂν τοῖς ἄλλοις ᾖ κακά, ἀγαθά ἐστιν, καὶ ἐπιβουλευόμενος πάντα ἀναφέρει εἰς τὴν γνῶσιν καὶ τὰ κακὰ μόνος ἀγαθοποιεῖ.*

"The pious man will endure all things (cleaving to his knowledge of God), for to such a man all things are good, even though they be evil to others; when men devise mischief against him, he sees all this in the light of his knowledge of God; and he, and none but he, changes evil into good."

[15] Cf. also, *Die Geisterwelt bei Paulus* (The Spirit-World in Paul) by M. Dibelius, 1909.

time of the End, when the 'new creation' is to appear, the conditions of primitive ages will recur but must be understood in their opposite sense; the interpretation of Psalm 8, where the 'son of man' to whom all things are subjected is no longer referred to men in general, but specifically to Christ (I Cor. 15:27), and much else, comes from rabbinical tradition. Thus one must recognize a fixed, stereotyped rabbinical method as forming the basis of all the Apostle's theological thinking, if we are correctly to evaluate the comprehensiveness of his thought.

7. *Hellenistic Elements*. Other things, again, are less rabbinical than Hellenistic. Although Paul may not have read Philo, his thinking occasionally shows that he is somewhat acquainted with him. Thus it is when he treats (Rom. 7:7ff) the history of the Fall, not as a particular event but as a typical representation of the beginning of sin in every man; but especially in that he consciously applies the method of 'allegorical' interpretation and even, indeed, uses the Greek word itself. Just as the Stoics harmonized the story of Homer with the enlightened thought of their day, in that they transformed the persons of the gods into cosmic or spiritual forces, and the all too-human myths into natural events or metaphysical doctrines; and just as in Philo the characters of the Old Testament narratives become ethical principles and psychological categories, so Paul spins out of the story of Hagar and Ishmael a hidden prophecy relating to the Jews and Gentile Christians (Gal. 4:21ff); the former are represented by Isaac, the latter by Israel; Hagar is the Old Covenant, Sarah the New. Noteworthy also is the meaning applied to the threshing oxen whose mouths shall not be muzzled. It would be offensive to think that God would have concerned himself with oxen (I Cor. 9:9)! There must be another meaning hidden in this word. Here we feel strongly the transparent unreality of this method, which so clearly shows a mistreatment of the text: that he even thinks of animals is the really beautiful thing in the Mosaic law-giver (Deut. 25:4), and whoever strikes this out questions a noble feature in the faith of the God of the Old Testament.

There are many thought-forms in Paul which are strange and unconvincing to us. Very often we are obliged to separate the really forceful religious or ethical motive from its theological shell in order to obtain a true relationship toward it. Thus, unfortunately, the fact remains that the noble and necessary truths which he has to tell us do not speak to us everywhere with full power of conviction: in order to gain their treasure for present-day religious life, much meditation, paraphrasing, and fitting together is required—a difficult but also a thankful task.

8. *The Proof from Experience.* As we have already mentioned, the procedure of drawing a conclusion from the general to the particular, or from that which is difficult to conceive, plays a great rôle. This is one of the chief inventions of rabbinical dialectic; it is often found in the sayings of Jesus (Matt. 6:30; 7:11). But, as Paul uses it, it has in the case of primitive Christianity a deeply founded pathos; what God has already done for the salvation of his own is, in comparison with what is yet to come, so overwhelmingly great, that that which is still lacking can scarcely be compared with it. "He who has not spared his own son, but has given him for us all . . . . how should he not with him give us all things!" By this brittle and scholastic type of thought, Rom. 5:6-11 receives a peculiar turn: when Christ died we were still sinners, but now we are reconciled with God, have again come near to him—so that we may so much the surer hope for final salvation! Here we touch upon the most important and fundamental Pauline method of thought, viz. proof from experience. Since he writes to Christians, argumentation concerning that which among them is granted as valid, on the ground of the common religious experience, plays a great rôle. So the first argument to the Galatians, who do not yet understand, is a reference to what they have already experienced through the blessings of the Spirit—an argument based simply on their faith (Gal. 3:2-5). So the entire chapter concerning the Resurrection (I Cor. 15) rests upon the unquestioned fact of the resurrection of Christ, which is in no way doubted: if this basis should weaken, the whole argument would break down. Very unscientific, and directed only to those who believe, whose heart is determined upon their salvation, is the argument: "If Christ be not risen then is your faith vain, then are ye still in your sins"; the conclusion is addressed to the emotions: "Then indeed are those who have fallen asleep in Christ, perished" (15:17f). These are sermon proofs, effective only for the faithful, whom Paul has in mind, without power of conviction for those who are seeking certainty or for those who are wrestling with doubt. Paul's whole theology is borne along by his enthusiasm for the faith, it rises directly out of religious experience; it does not attempt, primarily, either to prove or to justify the wonderful acts of God; rather, it is based immediately upon them. At heart, it is theology of experience, not a science possessing no presuppositions. Moreover, in so far as it is apocalyptic it is connected only with

human ideas in general, and becomes convincing, in the last instance, only to one who moves in the same circle of ideas as Paul.

9. *The Theology of Conversion and of Mission.* It is essentially a conversion and mission-theology. As Paul himself reached his conclusions through a break in his life, so also all his essential theological concepts are worked out for people who have passed from one religion to another. This immense 'cut' appears everywhere in his religious thinking. Salvation does not appear as a quietly bestowed condition into which a man is born and which takes a deeper root through education, but is a highly dramatic process which is begun at a distinct moment in life, rapidly reaches its peak, and after a short or long period of time finally reaches its full completion. In the dark past lies the period of time when man did not know God (Gal. 4:8) and lived under the rule of demons (Gal. 4:9; I Cor. 12:2) and was the slave of sin (Rom. 6:21; 7:5,7-25; I Cor. 6:10f). Then came the 'calling,' when men heard the preaching and believed (Gal. 3:2; Rom. 10:7; 13:11); then came baptism and its washing away of sins (I Cor. 6:11), and the sending of the Spirit, the sign of sonship to God and of his love (Gal. 4:6; Rom. 5:5), of justification and atonement (Rom. 5:1,10; I Cor. 6:11). It is essential for the Christian that he has experienced the 'calling' with all these distinguishing marks and related circumstances, that he has accomplished this mighty step from darkness to light. There lies in this a real difficulty for men of later times, in regard to Pauline theology: a difficulty out of which have arisen innumerable controversies and much confusion. Since the theology of Paul is looked upon by the Church as standard, the life of the Apostle and his converts is presented as the normal one which every Christian must follow, and everyone who is to be considered as 'believing' and 'converted' must imitate Paul; he is the model of the converted sinner, and his experiences must be duplicated. And yet the presupposed necessary conditions are not present among the majority of Christians. Most of us, in fact, have not passed over from Judaism or heathenism to Christianity; we have not first learned the Gospel upon the heights of a conscious life, after having lived in a period of darkness. We have grown up in the Christian community, been educated by Christian parents; have learned the message of the heavenly Father and of the Lord Jesus while we were still children, and have been educated in the normal way in the fundamental commandments of Christianity, so that we have never experienced, personally, the deep night of a heathenism sunk in sin. We were

always 'Christians,' however imperfect and sinful, and most of us could never experience anything of a conversion in the sense of that mission-theology of Paul. So there arises in the life of many this problem, What must I do in order to experience 'justification' and 'salvation?' When comes the great moment when I too become believing and am converted? It is usually just those who were most in earnest who have felt the holy responsibility to experience their day of Damascus, and in this endeavor have sought to bring about a crisis which would not appear of itself. This is especially the problem of Pietism; but even up to the present hour there have been ever-renewed endeavors to urge men to experience that 'conversion' which, according to the Bible, is the indispensable foundation every Christian must lay. Indeed, the statement is made that the Christian, although trained in a Christian way and reared in the consciousness of the fatherly grace of God, who daily and freely forgives him all his sins, is still an utterly lost and condemned sinner, who—like a heathen—can only first become deeply and fully conscious of his entire depravity when there has appeared to him the overpowering light of grace, making possible for him a quiet conscience and a new life. The result is that sensitive and devout natures put forth excessive efforts, attempting to exaggerate the consciousness of sin to the point of desperation. Many of them experience something which they call conversion, a more or less sudden realization of grace, a new lifting-up and an inner quieting of conscience by which they are blessed. This is certainly felt sincerely and honestly by many, and for such it may be helpful and suitable. But there are probably others who can experience such things only through unwholesome irritation and exaggeration, and thus fall into a very dangerous condition of self-deception; it may be that they are even false to themselves, and picture something which in reality they do not at all experience. Thus they succumb, more or less, to the suggestion contained in the biblical and pietistic phrases; and it may be that, after this unusual tension and exaltation of mind, they soon lapse into all the more aridity and weakness, or—what is still worse—into a stereotyped use of the empty phrases, which no longer correspond to any inner experience. Certainly there are many whose entire nature is opposed to the experiencing of any such method of conversion—in no way by reason of unrepentance or stubbornness, or selfishness, but just out of a deeply earnest and inner veracity. Because since childhood they have always had an earnest desire for the good, they cannot—in spite of all their conscious knowledge of weaknesses and imperfections—persuade themselves that they are completely lost and condemned sinners. From childhood, or under the influence of the Sunday sermon and instruction, they have had the fixed conviction that God intends to treat them well, that they need not fear his anger, and that they may always be sure of his forgiveness and help when they pray to him. They feel themselves to be the children of God, as Jesus taught his disciples; and they cannot understand that they must still pass through a deep detour of conversion, through the valley of self-extinction, in order to receive again as something entirely new the consciousness of their relationship to God, as Paul teaches (Gal. 4:5). Certainly, they know it well, their aim is to grow more and more deeply into the will of God, to let themselves be penetrated more and more intimately with the power from above, always more faithfully to remain in the 'favor of God' (Rom. 11:22); but this is a slow, altogether gradual process of growth and of education—on the other hand, they could only experience a 'conversion' by becoming untruthful to themselves. Therefore, for them, those expressions, 'justification,' 'salvation,' etc., which indicate an extraordinary individual experience, are extremely difficult; never having experienced justification or the forgiveness of sins, since they have lived in the grace of God from a very early age, to be reborn and become a 'new creature' appears to them organically impossible, for they know all too well that it can only be by a gradual process, accompanied by many struggles and retrogressions. This is perhaps the position of the normal member of the community, who has grown up under Christian family training, in regard to the Pauline doctrine of Salvation.

Of course there are other types of Christians, such as those who through deep misfortune or continual carelessness have fallen away entirely from all Christian training and communion with God. There are, again, millions today who, in spite of Church and school, have never had the least inner sympathy with the spirit of the Gospel. There is growing up within the Church a modern paganism, and it is not impossible that the conversion theology may become the means for winning over both these masses and those individuals—not to speak in a narrow sense of the mission preaching to the Gentiles. One must wait for that. But it is certain that for infinitely many people of today, the exalted, dramatic, formal expression of the Pauline Gospel is incomprehensible, and that it will remain impossible to forge it into their inner lives.

But our concern here is not with these practical problems, but only with the understanding of the historical Paul. And one must make clear to himself the particular, historically-conditioned character of his theology, in order to escape the danger of a minimizing modernization.

Finally, we recall what we said (page 192) in connection with the conversion of Paul. The faith of Paul differs from our religion in the dramatic, eschatological form of its point of view. The conversion is not only the all-motivating principle of his own life, it is an example in the great revolution in the world's history, to which Paul and his communities not only are witnesses but in which they are participants. They live, indeed, upon the dividing-line where the two ages meet (I Cor. 10:11), they are a chosen generation, for whose sake God has permitted the great acts of the End to take place, and what happens to them is only the beginning of a world-change and a new creation which is now coming into being. The grace of God, in which they are participating, is not the sun which always shines over the entire world, on the evil and on the good alike, but it is the first beam of day, which, after an endless night, has just reached it. The love of God is not always and only the active goodness and care of the never-resting Father of men and Keeper of Israel, but it is now the redeeming mercy of the entirely new self-revealing Salvation of God, who snatches many victims out of the world-conflagration, and saves a few. And what these now experience is only the beginning and the pledge of that perfect Salvation, shortly to be revealed. Therefore all religious feeling and thinking is characterized by the highest excitement and expectation, as is only natural to later Christianity in times of great crisis. This eschatological feeling is entirely lacking in the Church of today. Therefore she is not prepared to understand fully the unique piety of Paul, let alone imitate it.

We have purposely drawn attention to the difficulties which lie before the modern Christian for an intimate understanding of Paul. Much else might be mentioned, and it now becomes clear that a simple representation of his personality is not here possible, not to mention an exalted description by which the reader might be at once inspired to imitate him and to accept his doctrine. An intensive analysis would be necessary, coupled with a critical setting-aside of the historical and for us out-lived thought-forms, perhaps also an analysis of his own consciousness, distinguishing it from that which is so fruitful and ever-living in this mighty personality.

CHAPTER XV

The Christ-Faith

"Therefore if any man be in Christ, he is a new creature: old things are passed away; behold, all things are become new."

This declaration (II Cor. 5:17) might serve as a motto for the following chapter. Anyone who wishes to understand Paul must strive to gain a realization and a sympathetic apprehension of the vital principle which permeates his whole personality and upon which all else depends: what do 'to be in Christ,' and 'to be one with Christ,' mean?

Christ-faith, Christ-devotion, Christ-culture, Christ-mysticism—this is the one focal point in the Pauline religion, this is the particular manner in which he has lived Christianity, and has experienced it for future centuries; this individual form is, in the main, something new in religion, as over against the pre-Pauline, as well the Palestinian as the Hellenistic type of Christianity. But one would draw a wrong composite picture of Paul, if he did not take into account the fact that in his Christ-faith there is still present a general primitive-Christian, indeed an actual Jewish-Christian substratum, upon which is first developed the peculiarly Pauline Christ-devotion.

1. *The Eschatological Messiah-faith*. We have seen in discussing the conversion of Paul that its deciding result was the conviction that Jesus, the crucified one, whom the Nazareans accepted as the Messiah of Israel, is in reality the Messiah predicted by the prophets, the Son of God (Rom. 1:3). In reality of course this statement appears with him in its genetic psychological form; the heavenly Messiah who has appeared to me is truly none other than the Jesus of the Nazareans! The identity of the heavenly Christ and the man Jesus is the paradoxical knowledge which he from now on possesses. It contains in itself, from the very first, two statements; on the one hand, a joyful message: the Messianic age has begun; on the other hand, the important corollary: it is now necessary to think of the Messiah in terms which proceed from the fact that Jesus is he.

The appearance of the Exalted One in the splendor of the divine glory (II Cor. 4:6) was for Paul incontrovertible proof that the kingly rule of the Messiah (I Cor. 15:24f) has begun; that the

Messianic age of Salvation has dawned (II Cor. 6:2); that the end of the present age has come, and the new age has been inaugurated (I Cor. 10:11). This general pre-Christian conviction also forms for Paul the foundation of his new life. His faith, also, from now on, is an eschatological hope; he also belongs to those who wait for the reign of God (Mark 15:43) and hope to share therein (Gal. 5:21; I Cor. 6:10; 4:20; Rom. 14:17). But just as for the primitive community, so for him this is no longer a far-off, only to be yearned-for, condition; the beginning of the end has been moved forward into the closest proximity by the exaltation of the Messiah; it is assured, since the last conflict, which is yet to be endured, will certainly end with the victory of Christ and the complete rule of God (I Cor. 15:24-28). Paul also manifests that same keen faith in the future which runs through the whole of primitive Christianity, and is accompanied with a present mood of joy: after the great things which God has done, it is surely to be expected that he will also perform the unfulfilled predictions that still remain (Rom. 8:32).

The Christ-faith of Paul is in part—as with the Jews—still a hope, it is a yearning for the Messiah Jesus: the life of the Christian is a waiting for the 'revelation of our Lord Jesus Christ' (I Cor. 1:7), a great yearning for complete communion with the Son of God (I Cor. 1:9), for union with him for all time (I Thess. 4:17; Phil. 1:23), for seeing him face to face (I Cor. 13:12). Therefore the present is a 'walking by faith, and not by sight' (II Cor. 5:7); at least, the view obtained by faith is only a 'reflection in a mirror' (I Cor. 13:12; II Cor. 3:18).[1] Paul emphasizes very strongly at times the preliminary, the incomplete nature of the present conditions (Phil. 1:23; I Cor. 13:12); so securely is his life anchored in heaven (Phil. 3:20), so vividly does he feel himself a stranger here (II Cor. 5:6), that occasionally the feeling of separation from Christ outweighs everything else. But these are passing moods; on the whole, the feeling of joy prevails, that the Messiah has come and the fulness of the Messianic salvation with him. Let one try to feel what it means when Paul says, 'We have salvation in him' (Col. 1:14), 'The salvation which is in Christ Jesus' is at hand

[1] The point in the comparison in the figure of the mirror is, as I see it (according to Philo's use of language, for example), that the image is only a picture and not the reality (ct. SNT on I Cor. 13:12). Therefore to see the glory of the Lord as in a mirror (ct. SNT on II Cor. 3:18) is like what we would call 'seeing with the imagination.' In *Corp. Herm.* XVIII (Reitzenstein, *Poimandres,* p. 54) it is stated that things which appear as in a mirror are 'incorporeal bodies' (σώματα ἀσώματα). Cf. my Commentary on I Cor. 13:12.

(Rom. 3:24). This 'in' is not used here as in the mystical formula, 'in Christ'; it is a shortened expression for the statement: "Because of the fact that Christ has come, because of the fact that we have Christ, we have Salvation"; thus this 'in Christ' is the most concentrated expression for the actuality of the Pauline Messiah-faith: we have the Christ.

2. *The New Conception of the Messiah.* Above all he knows him; the Messiah concept, or the Messiah fantasy of his Jewish time of waiting, has been changed for him into a living reality, into a concrete perception; the Messiah has revealed himself to him (Gal. 1:12,15); he has 'seen' him (I Cor. 9:1). He has seen not an indeterminate concept, not a phantom, but the 'face' or 'person' (πρόσωπον) of Christ, illuminated by the glory of the splendor of God (II Cor. 4:6). Determinative for him was not so much the actual impression which appeared on his retina, as the explanation and interpretation of what he had already of himself conceived of him. Even though at that time nothing further had appeared in his field of vision, save the perception of a bright light, he has nevertheless compared it to a human form, to a face with human features. How far this picture was plainly carried out in detail, whether it was more schematic or individual, we cannot say. That depends upon this: whether he had seen Jesus earlier with his own eyes, or whether the impression made at that time had penetrated deeply enough, and the recollection was sufficiently powerful and distinct—or whether he had only heard of Jesus, and from indefinite, imperfect descriptions possessed a generally colorless picture of him. But even if he had really seen him before, we have still to take this into account, namely that even very indistinct features and outlines would have sufficed for him as a representation. All this is on the whole an unattractive speculation, which easily wavers between object and concept, picture and significance, person and idea, since probably the necessity was never felt for a 'realization' perfect in every detail or feature. It was of far greater importance for him that he could now represent to himself the inner being and consciousness of the Messiah, not only more plainly, but in an entirely different manner than before.

Yet there always hovers before him the form of the mighty ruler of the world. As the *Book of Enoch* speaks of the 'Son of Man' sitting on the throne of his glory,

> And the word of his mouth slays all the sinners,
> And all the unrighteous are destroyed from before his face. . . .

And all the kings and the mighty and the exalted, and those who rule the earth
Shall fall down before him on their faces,
And worship and set their hope on that Son of Man,
And petition him and supplicate for mercy at his hands,

so Paul likewise still thinks of Christ as the mighty ruler of the world, before whom all beings in the tri-partite universe bow the knee and confess that he is 'Lord' (Phil. 2:10f). The features of power (II Thess. 1:7ff; Rom. 1:4) and majesty, the judgment-throne of the Messiah (II Cor. 5:10) are not eliminated from his new concept of faith. But new features have been added which were not contained in the Jewish Messiah-picture.

In truth, it is not always self-evident that the 'Son of God' has appeared in human form on earth, even though the Jewish Messianic expectation of Paul had already contained this feature; now however, he has accepted this idea so precisely and concretely that the 'Son of God' has taken on the appearance of the man Jesus, who was born of the seed of David, of a woman, has submitted himself to the Law, to which, as the heavenly Son of God, he was not really subject. Here is the first harmonization of the Pauline Christology. We shall see, later, how difficult it becomes for him to harmonize the idea of the heavenly Son of God and the historical manner of the appearance of Jesus, how impossible it is for him to retain correctly the full humanity, the full sharing of Jesus in human nature (flesh, sin, Law, world) which still, on the other hand, is so important for his doctrine of Salvation. Here we perceive very plainly how the facts of the historical Jesus will not fit into the frame of his former Jewish transcendental conception of the Messiah—it is only with great difficulty that this idea can be correlated with history.

A second, entirely new feature is the giving over of the Messiah to death. According to one sequence of thought, it is God who has delivered his Son to death (Gal. 4:4; Rom. 8:32; with echoes in John 3:16; I John 4:9). According to this one might think of Christ as a passive victim (so one could understand II Cor. 5:21). This view is especially favorably received by those who believe that, for Paul, in the sacrificial death of Christ the juristic, factual element was the essential. But this is contradicted by the fact that in other and really impressive passages, the self-offering of Jesus is strongly emphasized (Gal. 1:4; 2:20; echoes in I Tim. 2:16; Tit. 2:14). This motive is frequently varied: the offering which he himself has brought (II Cor. 8:9; Phil. 2:7f) is more vividly represented than the loving act of God which took place in heaven. New, as over against Judaism, are the characteristic features of the one who despises the way of autocracy and dominion (Phil. 2:6; Heb. 12:2), freely divesting himself of his glory, suffering himself to descend into poverty, and to become a servant, mild and gentle (II Cor. 10:1), selfless, self-denying (Rom. 15:3; I Cor. 10:33; 11:1) [2] —such is Christ, who conceived the purpose of his life to be to serve men, to live for them, to suffer and to die for their sakes, to bear the curse for them; new, above, all are the characteristics of love and mercy in the picture of the Messiah. Even if the death of the Messiah had already been a pre-Christian, Jewish concept, even if before this, Isaiah 53 could have been applied to the Messiah, still, nevertheless, the thought would have been undreamed of that the giving-up of life and self-sacrifice was not only a divine necessity, but the freely accepted basic idea and end-purpose of his entire life. That the innermost will of the Messiah is not might and power, not a threatening of judgment and a hatred of sinners, but pity, love—and precisely love for the sinner—the service of love, mildness, gentleness, sympathy—this is all conceived in the most un-Jewish manner possible. The message of the self-revelation of Christ, who, although he was indeed in divine form, had renounced the enforcement of his God-like claim to rule, and who first, as by a detour, through the humiliation unto death had ascended the throne of the world, all this is foreign to Jewish Messianism.

Whence comes this correction of the vulgar picture of the Messiah, whence this re-valuation of Jewish dreams of glory? Some of it perhaps from echoes of the Greek mystery-cults? Let any one try to produce a myth in which there is present this feature of self-denying devotion, this serving love of sacrifice! It is lacking there, even as in Judaism. Those who think that Paul had remained untouched by the quality of the personality of Jesus are inclined to assume that here there is predicated an understandable conclusion, *a posteriori,* from the now once and for all established fact of the death of the Messiah. This indeed must have had some purpose, and hence the idea of a sacrificial or atoning death would easily suggest itself; this, in turn, could readily be supported by the accepted idea that Jesus had freely offered himself for this purpose. This idea would have been all the more acceptable to Paul, since he himself,

[2] The love of Christ. Rom. 8:35,37; II Cor. 5:14; Gal. 2:20; Eph. 2:4; 5:2,25; II Thess. 2:16. The grace of Christ, Rom. 5:15; II Cor. 8:9; 12:9; Gal. 1:6; and often in Benedictions; also Col. 3:13.

indeed, had had the experience of Christ calling him, in spite of his enormous sins, to become his property and his Apostle. What could have moved him to do this? From this point it would not have been a great step on to the conviction that the final motives for the human self-humiliation, suffering and dying of the Messiah were mercy and love.

Many attempts have been made to explain the existence of the Pauline gospel from such conclusions of religious dialectic, and if it were only a question here of religious thought-formation, one might proceed in this manner. But never can the strong, newly-felt, rock-firm confidence, and the blessed joyousness of the Apostle, be thus explained.

It is of course certain that the personal religious experience of the Apostle has strongly influenced his development of thought at this particular point. The paradox that he, and only he, the persecutor, was not despised, but called, the certainty: "By grace I am what I am" (I Cor. 15:8ff), the confession: "Who has loved me and given himself for me" (Gal. 2:20)—this surely provided the starting-point for everything which he afterwards said in particular of Christ. But how is this fundamental experience to be explained? How is it comprehensible that he could gain comfort and peace from the appearance of the heavenly Christ? Would one not suppose, rather, that it would have driven him to desperation, since it was really imparted to him at the time of the persecution? And, as the Book of Acts of the Apostles represents it (9:8ff), it had, indeed, overwhelmed him, struck him down. One must also assume that some disciple, perhaps Ananias, had represented to him the appearance of the Lord in a sense rich in comfort, had assured him from his knowledge of Jesus' personality that he would not reject a repentant sinner. If we assume that the appearance of the Lord had also immediately given him the certainty that he had been received by grace, we must likewise assume that he already had a conception of Jesus prior to the vision, which now and henceforth could give him the consciousness that the Lord would forgive him, since his inmost being is mercy. In any case, faith in the love of Christ is not to be deduced simply from the appearance; in some way, the picture of Jesus which the tradition of the community offered must have cooperated. It may be objected that just those features of the Gospels according to which Jesus wished to die in the service of the many, and which represent the purpose of his death as nothing else than sacrificial (Mark 10:45), are to be viewed as a carrying-back of the Pauline doctrine into the gospel picture; thus there is formed a *circulus vitiosus,* from which in turn the Pauline teaching must be again deduced. On the contrary, the older tradition, not yet influenced by Paul, would indeed clearly show that although Jesus had learned for himself that his death was to be the fulfilling of a divine purpose, in spite of a genuine human shrinking from this hard necessity (Luke 12:49f, and the Gethsemane scene; perhaps also the word on the cross about his abandonment by God); yet in no case had the real Jesus conceived of his death as Paul has described it. This objection cannot be denied. It would not be permissible to assert that Paul has gained his conception of the self-sacrifice of Christ, for the sake of sin and out of love for the sinner, simply from the words of the Lord. Nevertheless, the old tradition contains other features, which although they do not, taken alone, explain the change in manner of Paul's thinking, are not to be ignored. And must not the former Pharisee have known already that the Jesus whom he was persecuting, instead of associating with the pious, instead of being a Pharisee, was the companion of publicans and sinners, that he had actually proclaimed to such people the salvation of the Kingdom of God, and had denied it to the 'righteous,' the 'wise,' to those who were not of the 'poor' (cf. Matt. 5:3)? This was indeed an essential reason for the Pharisees despising and hating him. At the moment, now, when he has recognized Jesus as the Messiah, this feature of the picture, which must once have appeared strange to him, encourages him and saves him from desperation. Thus from this point on it is not difficult to understand how he has learned to conceive of the death of Jesus as an act of love.

However the existence of this new picture of the Messiah is to be explained—we can only set forth a conjecture—in some way, the historical fact of Jesus had corrected his former representations of the Messiah and helped him to gain new conceptions on the important points.

3. *Paul and the Historical Jesus.* We must here again recur (cf. pp. 115ff) to the question as to what the 'historical Jesus' means for Paul's religion. After all that we have said previously, there is no need to refute the purely academic theory that Paul had known nothing at all of Jesus. That the crucified one, the sufferer, the man obedient to God (Phil. 2:8), the righteous one (Rom. 5:18), who had not experienced sin (II Cor. 5:21), who lived not to please himself (Rom. 15:3), the gentle, the mild (II Cor. 10:1), who offers himself (Gal. 2:20), stands as the focal point of all his thought, is proof

enough that he has drawn the conception from the Jesus who lived upon the earth, and had a living picture of him. The miraculous fact upon which he bases his faith is the awakening and exaltation of one who had died and had been buried. Indeed, by the purely Jewish personal name of Jesus, he is always reminded that Christ was once a man.[3] It would be correct to say—although we cannot prove it—that the detailed life of Jesus, his wanderings, his teachings and healings, in short, every historical detail, has become overshadowed, yes, absorbed by the two great facts of the Incarnation and Death: beginning and end move so closely together (Phil. 2:5,11) that between them there scarcely seems to remain room for any broadly outlined picture of his life. Paul presumably had never had the impulse to write a Gospel; indeed, in the same measure that his Judaistic opponents had emphasized the Judaism of Jesus, his faithfulness to the Law and his teaching, Paul has declared with the one-sided paradox of the mystic that he wished no more to know Jesus after the flesh (II Cor. 5:16b)—for we are obliged to interpret in this way the words, "We know him no more." But just as he was not able to extinguish the memory of others whom he 'had known after the flesh,' and could only say (5:16a) that he had broken off all former human and natural relationships with them[4] —his relations, friends, and compatriots exist for him no more as such, but only either as Christian brothers or as unbelievers—so the 'no more' in relation to Christ does not indicate that he had known nothing of him, but that he had actually had some kind of a natural human relationship to him, similar to that of which the

[3] It is one of the most drastic assertions of radical criticism that 'Jesus' was originally a name of God, i.e. 'the help of Yahweh,' i.e. it simply means Yahweh. On the contrary, it rather states that the man who bears this name is entrusted to the help of Yahweh, and may confidently rely upon Him.

[4] It is the same use of language that we observe in Matt. 7:23; Luke 13:27. When Jesus says to those who 'have eaten and drunk in his presence,' and who have done miracles 'in his name,' "I know you not," or "I have never known you," it is only to be understood that he does not wish to have anything to do with them, not that they were actually unknown to him. In fact, this declaration of Jesus corresponds to that made by him concerning his relatives (Mark 3:33). The question how the premise is to be understood, "If we also have known Christ after the flesh," is doubtful. It would perhaps be linguistically possible that Paul, in the general statement, "We know no one any longer after the flesh," merely states the hypothesis in an enhanced manner: "Even if we had, let us say, known Christ after the flesh, we now wish to know him no longer in this way" (so perhaps Reitzenstein, *Hellenist. Mysterienrel.*, pp. 194ff). Though I should prefer to offer a closer analysis, I can only say here that this conception, though linguistically possible, will not be understood by the reader who does not proceed from a clear idea of Paul. He has no occasion to consider the 'knowing Christ after the flesh' in this particular passage as any less real than the former knowledge of people generally.

Judaizers boasted, but upon which he himself laid no weight at all, because he is so bound up through the Spirit with the Exalted One. And now since Jesus has become the exalted Lord, all the ties by which he had been related to his disciples 'after the flesh,' his Jewish descent, his Davidic sonship, his position under the Law (Rom. 9:5; 1:4; Gal. 4:4), are for him a long-past intermediate stage. Certainly Jesus is for him the Jewish Messiah; but he could not be the bringer of Salvation simply for this reason: he is exalted beyond this stage to be the ruler of the world. Certainly Jesus has lived under the Law; but for Paul his faithfulness to the Law is not exemplary, but belongs to the Servant-form which out of love he has assumed; and the decisive factor is this, that he has died to the Law, and overcome it. Again, the word and teaching of Jesus is important to Paul; but yet only in secondary degree—the essential thing is that he now creates a new life in those who are his, through the Spirit. Therefore it is for him the achievement of a new point of view, when a man considers himself to be a disciple of Jesus of Nazareth; he feels that he is the servant of the exalted Lord.

But all this does not exclude the fact that the life and work of the earthly Jesus was of the highest importance to Paul: that Christ became flesh, that he endured all the suffering of a weak and painful human life, and that, as a man, he had yielded himself, in obedience to the will of God, to suffer a bitter death—all this, indeed, constitutes the great fact to which he attributes salvation; therefore, that somewhat over-emphasized statement (II Cor. 5:16b) does not fully cover all that he really feels. Like so many others, it must be understood as a momentary statement, flung out in the midst of conflict.

The essential thing is that the heavenly Lord, whom hereafter he serves exclusively, is inwardly the same as the one who died upon the Cross; the same motive of love which led him to enter into humanity and to endure death still fills him. As the primitive community, as indeed the whole of Christianity, has vivified the picture of the exalted Lord through the lineaments of the earthly Jesus, so Paul views both together. Certainly there is present here an important shifting of accent. For Peter, the earthly remembrance will always be the foundation for the picture, though it will always be encircled by the glory of the Transfiguration. For Paul, the bright light of the Exalted One will be the foundation, to the exclusion, however, of certain other features. Although they may also be less numerous, less clear, less attractive, they remain, nevertheless, and are important enough. Since the heavenly Christ is for him not simply an abstract concept, but a personality whom he could trust, the result is that the heavenly Lord is at the same time the Jesus who had sacrificed his life upon the Cross. Further, it is quite evident that there arises out of the concept of Jesus which he had gained—even though it may have been an entirely general one—the strongly ethical impulse which afterwards floods his life. The statement, "We have the mind of Christ"—although in its context (I Cor. 2:16) it has another meaning—may also be written over the life of Paul; the 'love of Christ' is in the last analysis the animating motive of all his willing and doing (II Cor. 5:14f), and it is no accident that for him this love has become the sum of all ethics.

4. *The Names of Christ.* What Paul calls Jesus is not an unimportant thing, but in the highest measure significant. The fullest designation, which frequently occurs with him, chiefly in a liturgical sense:[5] 'Our Lord Jesus Christ,' because of its formal, solemn character was in all probability not invented by him but was taken over from the customary usage of the congregation—we shall be obliged presently to say, from the usage of the Hellenistic communities, though perhaps, after all, its final origin goes back to the primitive community, especially in view of the fact that in addition to this fuller form a shorter one, 'Our Lord Jesus,' also appears. It is noteworthy how often Paul uses the name Jesus, alone, more often than one should expect; and perhaps, originally, oftener still than appears in our present text.[6] Does it mean anything that the Epistles

[5] It appears often in solemn, exalted sentences and concluding sections (Rom. 5:11, 21; 6:23; 7:25; 8:39; 15:6; I Cor. 1:10; 15:37, often with διά); further, in the concluding blessing: the Grace of our Lord Jesus Christ (Rom. 16:20 [24]; I Cor. 16:23; II Cor. 13:13; Gal. 6:18; Phil. 4:25; I Thess. 5:28; II Thess. 3:17; Phm. 25), where the ἡμῶν is often lacking; also in the introductory blessing: Grace from our Father and the Lord Jesus Christ, where the ἡμῶν (contrary to the preceding) is always lacking (Rom. 1:7; I Cor. 1:3; II Cor. 1:2; Phil. 1:2; I, II Thess. 1:2). So also in the formula of confession: God the Father of our Lord Jesus Christ (Rom. 15:6; II Cor. 1:3; 11:31; Eph. 1:17; Col. 1:3), and at the close of the Christological confession, Rom. 1:4; in the standing connection: the day, or coming, or revelation of the Lord Jesus Christ (I Cor. 1:7f; 5:5; II Cor. 1:14; I Thess. 5:23; II Thess. 1:7; 2:1); in the formula, 'the name of the Lord Jesus Christ' (I Cor. 1:10; 5:4; 6:11; Col. 3:17; II Thess. 1:12; 3:6) and in the solemn 'exhortation through Christ' (I Thess. 4:2; II Thess. 3:12), often in the shorter form.

[6] For the traditional text usually displays the tendency to 'expansion.' Thus, often, ἡμῶν is added to ὁ κύριος and χριστός to Ἰησοῦς, and often also, the title to the name, and the name to the title. So much the more, then, must we consider those readings in which the name of Jesus alone appears, or 'the Lord Jesus,' to be original. Unquestionably Jesus or 'the Lord Jesus' appears in Rom. 4:24; 10:9; 14:14; I Cor. 12:2a and b; II Cor. 4:5b, 11a, 14a and b; I Thess. 1:10; 2:15; 4:1, 14a and b;

to the Thessalonians use the name Jesus almost exclusively? Is the influence of Silas here to be noted? I merely raise the question. The use of the name Jesus in passages like I Thess. 2:15; 4:14 (Jesus has died and risen again) is self-explanatory: Rom. 4:24 ('He who had awakened Jesus from the dead'; Rom. 8:11a; II Cor. 4:14)—here the historical Jesus is both subject and object; it is also natural that in I Cor. 11:23 ('in the night when the Lord Jesus was offered up'), that is in a passage of narrative, the personal name is used as in the Gospels. Again it is highly significant that Paul said, "I have seen Jesus, our Lord" (I Cor. 9:1)—he knows that he has not only seen the heavenly Christ but also Jesus. It is perfectly in accord with the primitive Christian practice when the confession in I Cor. 12:3 and Rom. 10:9 runs, 'Jesus the Lord.' Not entirely self-evident is it, on the other hand, when without any reference to his earthly life, Jesus, as present to the faith of the congregation, receives the historical personal name; especially striking is this in the chapter II Cor. 4, where the name Jesus appears seven times, and where also, doubtless, the exalted Christ is in mind; that Paul speaks of the 'putting to death' of Jesus (cf. Gal. 6:17) is understandable; but the expression 'the life of Jesus,' used of the supernatural heavenly life of the Exalted One, is at least strange (Gal. 4:10). We feel why he says, 'for the sake of Jesus' (II Cor. 4:5b,11), but it is not very easy for us to sympathize with him when he can say: "I am persuaded, in the name of Jesus," (Rom. 14:14) where, according to numerous parallels, we should rather expect the Christ-name. This manner of speech is to be explained only by the fact that for Paul, the Exalted One and the earthly one have been completely identified; he has always the feeling that it is the same personality in two phases. Therefore the reverse exchange can take place, so that the name Christ is used where, plainly, the earthly Jesus is in mind, as in Rom. 5:6,8; 14:9; 6:4,9; I Cor. 15:3,12,13ff: Christ has died and risen; the Cross of Christ (I Cor. 1:17,23; Gal. 6:12), the body (Rom. 7:4), the blood (I Cor. 10:16), the sufferings (II Cor. 1:5), the tenderness and gentleness of Christ (II Cor. 10:1). Therefore it is not surprising that the object of the

---

in the following it is questionable, but was most probably original: Rom. 8:11a; 16:20; I Cor. 5:4a and b; 9:1; 11:23 (in B); 16:23; II Cor. 1:14; 4:10a and b, 11b; 11:4,31; Gal. 6:17; Eph. 1:15; Phil. 2:10,19; Col. 3:17; I Thess. 2:19; 3:12f; 4:2; II Thess. 1:7f,12; 2:8(?). One might enlarge this list still further if he added those passages where Codex B independently offers only Ἰησοῦς (Rom. 5:11; I Cor. 1:8; II Cor. 8:9; 13:13; Col. 3:3; I Thess. 5:9; II Thess. 2:16); however, the irregularities of B deserve little confidence.

'knowing after the flesh' (II Cor. 5:16) is Christ, although, doubtless, the earthly Jesus is in mind. The use of the name Christ for both phases of the development outweighs numerically that of the name Jesus. This is not strange, but points out very clearly Paul's position. In the far greater number of passages Christ is simply a personal name, and the title it implies is no longer taken into account. This is especially plain in Phil. 2:11, where the confession to the world reads, "Jesus Christ is Lord." Here it seems that every remembrance of the fact that Christ was once a name of honor, parallel to the Kyrios-name (cf. Acts 2:36f), has been obliterated. It is the same with II Cor. 4:5, "We proclaim Christ Jesus as Lord" (cf. Col. 2:6). One sees how impossible it is in such a passage to translate 'Christus' by 'the Messiah.' There are only a very limited number of passages where this translation is suggested, and the definite article before Christus is no sure sign for it.[7] The titular meaning appears certain only in Rom. 9:5; in any case it lies in the background when Paul prefers to say, 'The Gospel of Christ'—a reminiscence of the Jewish-Christian Messiah message; it may also be possible in I Cor. 10:4; Rom. 10:6f; I Cor. 15:22; II Cor. 4:4; 5:10. But here also it is only very faintly suggested; even here the feeling prevails that the concept of the Messiah has been changed into a personal reality. How completely the titular meaning has been supplanted by the personal name may finally be perceived in this, that the oldest form of the name, 'Jesus the Christ' (Ἰησοῦς ὁ Χριστός), has entirely disappeared; there remain now only fragmentary survivals, as in the very infrequent form, 'the Christ Jesus'—on the other hand, 'Christ Jesus' has come into complete dominance and, less frequently, 'Jesus Christ' as a double name in which the titular element is no longer recognizable.

The place of the Messiah-title is now taken by the term, 'the Son of God,' and above all by 'the Lord' (cf. pp. 175ff). We shall speak later of this. The *Kyrios*-name takes its point of departure from the old formula, 'our Lord,' which is still echoed in the Aramaic *Marana tha* (p. 37). But in Paul's usage, the 'our' is innumerable times left off, and the simple 'the Lord,' and also the *Kyrios* without the article, often sound like a personal name, which can readily be exchanged with 'Christ,' as for example in the formula 'in Christ' or

[7] So I Cor. 1:13 changes *μεμέρισται ὁ Χριστός* and 1:17 *ἀπέστειλέ με Χριστός*; 1:17 *ὁ σταυρὸς τοῦ Χριστοῦ* and 1:23 *Χριστὸν ἐσταυρωμένον*, without any distinction which should be noted in translation; so *τὰ μέλη τοῦ Χριστοῦ* and *Χριστοῦ* in one sentence, I Cor. 6:15. Often it is only rhythmical reasons which occasion the insertion or omission of the article.

'in the Lord.' The reason for this phenomenon is, on the one hand, the exclusiveness with which the one Lord is contrasted with the many *Kyrioi* (I Cor. 8:6); though for the Christian there is still, nevertheless, only the one. On the other hand, something else plays a part in this connection: according to Phil. 2:9ff, God, at the time of the exaltation, conferred upon him the name which, according to Isa. 45:23, he had retained for himself: this is in fact the name 'Lord.' Now since in the Old Testament this word is used instead of the personal name, Yahweh, so that the form, 'Lord, the God' (κύριος ὁ θεός) appears to be a personal name in apposition, and since, further, in reading many Old Testament passages, Paul refers the *Kyrios*-name simply to Christ, so he must, clearly, still have had the feeling that this was less a designation of honor than a name. But aside from these suppositions, it lies in the very nature of things that an object or being who is unique, or comes into the consideration of a speaker under many forms of title, finally changes its particular characteristic designation into a name.[8]

5. *The Lord*. The *Kyrios*-name is the briefest expression for the new faith of Paul:

"If thou confessest with thy mouth that Jesus is Lord . . . .
Thou shalt be saved."

But he offers no individual or original modes of expression; he simply takes over the language of the Hellenistic community (I Cor. 12:2; II Cor. 4:5; Col. 2:6), and this, at least in form, goes back to the primitive community itself. But since already, in the Hellenistic area, something entirely different has developed from the Aramaic *Maran*—the designation for a divine being, contrasted with the many 'Lords' of the heathen (I Cor. 8:6)—so in the religion of Paul the *Kyrios*-faith is considerably enhanced and individually toned up. What it means in a practical religious sense will best be made clear through the correlative concept of 'servant' or 'slave' of Christ (Rom. 1:1; I Cor. 7:22f; Gal. 1:10; Phil. 1:1; Col. 4:12).

Now for the Hellenistic feeling this says nothing more than that he confesses to the religion of this God; it is the distinguishing mark of his religion. This method of expression is characteristic of a time when the individual is not born into a national religion, but must seek for himself a religion and a community satisfying to him, so that the confessor, differing from others, must call himself the

[8] So, for example, τὸ ἱερόν 'the Sanctuary'; according to my meaning also τὸ ἱλαστήριον, the perfectly definite place of expiation.

servant of his God. This is in any case something new as regards the old folk and national religions. It has been said that such religious terminology is not really Greek, but that a bit of Oriental emotional life has been transplanted to Hellenistic soil.[9] This may be true

[9] But cf. Euripides, *Bacchae* 366: τῷ Βακχίῳ . . . δουλευτέον. In any case, the representation is not lacking in Hellenistic religion, as Reitzenstein shows: especially instructive is the passage in Apuleius *Metam.* xi, according to which the mystic had vowed lifelong obedience or service to the deity: (6) 'the rest of my life, to the last breath, is given to you,' (15) 'to those whose life the majesty of our deity hath employed for his service, no misfortune can happen.' It is noteworthy that the expression, δοῦλος Θεοῦ, is lacking in Epictetus: instead, he often has διάκονος. But this is meant in a different sense. The question is not about the relationship of possession, as in the case of a slave, but concerns the task which the Cynic has to perform in the world, iii. 26,28: God, of course, will not neglect his creatures, his servants and witnesses, who are, as over against the unlearned, the only proof of his existence, his excellent governing of the world; iii. 22,69: the Cynic is ready to serve God without any restrictions whatsoever; iv. 7,20: I hold what God wills to be better than what I will; I will give myself to him as a servant and follower, to act with him, to strive with him, in short, to will the same as he.

Concerning the Semitic idea of the 'Servant of God,' cf. W. Robertson Smith, *Lectures on the Religion of the Semites,* London, 1901, pp. 68-69 (new edition, 1927).

"Where the god is conceived as a king, he will naturally be addressed as Lord, and his worshippers will be spoken of as his subjects, and so we find as divine titles Adon, 'lord,' and Rabbath, 'lady,' among the Phoenicians, with corresponding phrases among other nations, while in all parts of the Semitic field, the worshipper calls himself the servant or slave *('abd, 'ebed)* of his god, just as a subject does in addressing his king. The designation 'servant' is much affected by worshippers, and forms the basis of a large number of theophorous proper names. . . . At first sight this designation seems to point to a more rigid conception of divine kingship than I have presented, for it is only under a strict despotism that the subject is the slave of the monarch; nay, it has been taken as a fundamental distinction between Semitic religion and that of the Greeks, that in the one case, the relation of man to his god is servile, while in the other it is not so. But this conclusion rests on the neglect of a nicety of language, a refinement of Semitic politeness. When a man addresses any superior he calls him 'my Lord,' and speaks of himself and others as 'thy servants,' and this form of politeness is naturally *de rigueur* in presence of the king; but where the king is not addressed, his 'servants' mean his courtiers that are in personal attendance on him, or such of his subjects as are actually engaged in his service, for example, his soldiers. In the Old Testament this usage is constant, the king's servants are often distinguished from the people at large. And so the servants of Jehovah are sometimes the prophets who hold a special commission from him; at other times, as often in the Psalms, his worshipping people assembled at the Temple, and at other times, as in Deutero-Isaiah, his true servants as distinguished from the natural Israel. In short, both in the political and in the religious sphere, the designation *'abd, 'ebed,* 'servant' is strictly correlated with the verb *'abad,* 'to do service, homage, or religious worship,' a word which, as we have already seen, is sufficiently elastic to cover the service which a son does for his father, as well as that which a master requires from his slave. Thus, when a man is named the servant of his god, the implication seems to be not merely that he belongs to the community of which the god is king, but that he is specially devoted to his service and worship. Like other theophorous names, compounds with *'abd* seem to have been originally most common in royal and priestly families, whose members naturally claimed a special interest in religion and a constant nearness to the god; and

in some measure; at all events Paul had his moments when Greek and Oriental feelings met and mingled. If one considers the expression from the Greek view-point, the idea of 'slave,' i.e. a relationship of ownership, appears much stronger than one would feel it to be in the Semitic, where the absolute devotion to service, that is personal dedication, is outweighed by the feeling that the servant belonged to the family circle of the master. What appears in the Greek as ignoble or servile appears rather, in the Semitic, as a proud title. We can understand how Paul now and then, in order to remove what to the Greek was unworthy in the name, in his Stoical, paradoxical way designated slavery as a mark of liberty and nobility: "Ye were bought with a price; become not slaves of men" (I Cor. 7:23); "He who belongs to Christ, is lord of all, and is able to humiliate himself for the sake of the service of love to others."[10] One must take care not to over-emphasize the note of utter devotion and self-abnegation which, perhaps, appears at times in the expression. Certainly Paul also knows that his life does not belong only to himself, but to the Lord (Rom. 14:7; II Cor. 5:15). He describes with the greatest energy how all thought and disposition, all self-will, and all exalted self-consciousness must be taken captive in the obedience to Christ (II Cor. 10:4f); and Paul himself, with a never-forgotten remembrance of his own guilt and pardon, has certainly felt stronger that all that he still is in the flesh he owes to the Lord. Yet for him this is anything but a self-debasement and humiliation which casts him to the earth and slays the personal self, out of honor for his deity; rather, it is a joyful, thankful act of self-devotion. It is truly 'the love of Christ' which has seized hold of his life in its strong grip, and holds it in restraint so that it cannot stubbornly break out, of its own will, either to the right or to the left. So also his 'faith' in him 'who has loved me and given himself for me,' possesses something of the quality of an inspired mutual love. Very expressive of this feeling is the oft-recurring expression, which we translate, although very inadequately, as 'to boast in the Lord.' Certainly there lies in it the note of the

---

in later times, when a man's particular worship was not rigidly defined by his national connection, they seemed to specify the cult to which he was particularly attached, or the patron to whom his parents dedicated him. That the use of such names was not connected with the idea of slavery to a divine despot is pretty clear from their frequency among the Arabs who had very loose ideas of all authority, whether human or divine. Among the Arabs, indeed, as among the old Hebrews, the relation of the subject to his divine chief is often expressed by names of another class."

[10] Cf. I Cor. 7:23; 3:21ff and my Commentary on both passages.

proud self-consciousness of being the servant of an exalted, mighty Lord; but one should also note the tone of confidence, of reliance, and the joyous calm which accompanies it.[11] And this brings us to the discussion of the other side of the *Kyrios*-faith.[12]

The heavenly Lord has not only taken possession of the body and the life, of the thinking and willing of his servant—he is also a savior and helper[13] in every concern of soul and body. Since it has cost him a high price to ransom him from the powers of darkness and from the curse of the Law, and to make him his own property (I Cor. 6:19f; 7:23; Gal. 3:13; Rev. 5:9), since he has also given his own life for him (Gal. 2:20), so the believer can now rely upon him in every situation. He feels himself entirely in his hands and dependent upon his guidance; when he looks back upon his life's work (Rom. 15:18f), he has to confess that there is nothing in it but what Christ has brought to pass; it is he who has led him from East to West. That it is a purely religious relationship of dependence which is under consideration here, one also recognizes from this, namely, that in viewing such evidences and pouring out such confessions Paul readily alternates between Christ and God. Thus it depends upon the will of God whether he shall come to Rome (Rom. 1:10; 15:32), while he makes the success of his journey to Corinth (I Cor. 4:19; 16:7) depend upon the will of the 'Lord.' It is noteworthy that there can be a difference of opinion in such cases, whether Kyrios here means 'God' or 'Christ,' though it would appear that it is probably the latter. Nevertheless one cannot be

[11] II Cor. 5:14. It is here again not plainly to be understood whether the love of Christ to us, or our love to Christ, is meant; but the significant thing is just this, that the expression implies that love is the element which unites him with Christ.

[12] In both passages where Paul cites the expression: "He who boasts, let him boast in the Lord" (from Jer. 9:22f), it is opposed to bragging or being proud of all kinds of natural gifts or privileges; but the point lies in a slight change of meaning in the word καυχᾶσθαι, which is difficult to reproduce in translation: he who boasts of the Lord does not really 'boast himself,' but acknowledges that everything he has and is he owes to the Lord. Therefore Phil 3:3 has 'boasting in Christ Jesus' in opposition to 'having confidence in the flesh.' By καυχᾶσθαι is meant religious exaltation (Rom. 5:2; Jas. 1:2), the assurance of salvation (Heb. 3:6 'the boldness of our hoping'), the 'being proud' of God or of the Cross (Gal. 6:14); occasionally as in Rom. 5:2 we might translate 'we are blessed.' Cf. also Psalm 5:12, "But let all that trust on thee be glad in thee: they shall exult (boast) forever; and all that love thy name shall rejoice in thee;" and Psalm 48:6, "They that trust in their strength, and boast themselves in the multitude of their riches."

[13] The expression σωτήρ is Hellenistic. It is very significant, however, that this title so widely diffused in the environment of Hellenistic culture is not found in Paul (cf. Wendland, σωτήρ, in *Zeitschr. f. Neut. Wissenschaft,* 1904; and my article "Heiland" in RGG, II); the exception in Phil. 3:20 proves this rule.

very certain about this, since in such moments Paul himself has made no sharp distinction.[14] In other passages God and Christ appear together, side by side, as dispensers of the benefits of Salvation, as in the blessings of the letters: "Grace and peace from God the Father, and our Lord Jesus Christ." Often Paul describes with exactly the same expressions what God and Christ have done for him.[15] It is to be noted, how, in a few passages, the united work of God and Christ is expressed by a mediating formula: "The love of God in Christ Jesus our Lord" (Rom. 8:39), or "God was in Christ reconciling the world unto himself" (II Cor. 5:19),[16] and how the experience of conversion and baptism is referred both to the name of Christ and to the Spirit of God (I Cor. 6:11), how the Spirit of God and the Spirit of Christ alternate (Rom. 8:9), and how in Rom. 5:10f the mediation of Christ is emphasized along with the work of God. As the death of Christ is now depicted as a sacrifice of God, now as the self-giving of Jesus (Rom. 8:32; Gal. 2:20), so Paul feels that his own existence is a result of the grace of God as well as of the grace and love of Christ (I Cor. 15:10 and II Cor. 12:9).

The proof of this, that there is present an actual religious relationship, not only of discipleship and not only of hero-worship, in the modern sense, is the fact that Paul has prayed to the exalted

[14] He is thus the originator of that naïve 'Modalism' (as the historian of dogma says) which lives on even today, and of course not only in the Catholic but also in the Evangelical churches. For one might ask of whom does the Bible reader think when he reads in the 23rd Psalm, "The Lord is my shepherd" or when he follows it in prayer, or when the congregation responds to the versicle, "The Lord be with you?" The broadest results have developed from the use of Old Testament words referring to Yahweh-Adonai, but which, because of the Kyrios-name, have been referred to Christ (cf. I Cor. 1:31.)

[15] A few examples are: the grace of God and the grace of Christ (I Cor. 15:10 and II Cor. 12:9; Rom. 15:15f and 1:5; Rom. 5:11?; Gal. 1:15 and 1:6?); the love of God and the love of Christ (Rom. 8:39 and 35; I Thess. 1:4 and Gal. 2:20; Rom. 8:37; Eph. 2:4 and 5:25); the power of God and the power of Christ (II Cor. 4:7 and 12:9; Phil. 3:10; II Cor. 4:10f) life of God and life of Christ (Rom. 7:4; Gal. 2:19 and II Cor. 5:15; Gal. 2:20); servant of God and of Christ (Rom. 6:22; I Pet. 2:16 and 1:1; I Cor. 7:22; Gal. 1:10; etc.).

[16] Rom. 8:39 would lead us to think of later liturgical developments, as well as of 8:35, though the change was probably original. And also II Cor. 5:19 again creates a slight doubt of the genuineness of the ἐν Χριστῷ. In any case it is doubtful whether the words can be referred only to 'God was in Christ' or to 'was reconciling.' In the first case we should find ourselves rather in the Johannine than the Pauline sphere; in the second case, we should expect that Paul would prefer διὰ Χριστοῦ. On the other hand καθῶς καὶ ὁ Θεὸς ἐν Χριστῷ ἐχαρίσατο ὑμῖν (Eph. 4:32) is so much in the style of Ephesians that one might suppose that both passages are additions or developments in the very same style.

Lord. Of course this does not appear frequently, and, as we shall show later (pp. 471ff), it is not mere chance that as a rule his prayer is addressed to God. But at least in one passage it is witnessed that Paul calls on the Lord Christ (II Cor. 12:8f), and that he has received an answer from him. And it is indeed noteworthy that in one extraordinary case he did actually call on him for help against the angel of Satan. In a certain measure it belongs to his office (I Cor. 15:24) that he should combat 'principalities and powers'; it belongs to the task of the heavenly Advocate that he should drive away evil spirits and the enemies of God (Enoch 40:7), who prevent the salvation of the elect and desire to tear them away from the love of God and of Christ (Rom. 8:34ff). Speaking generally, he is the strong helper of his own in the struggles and sufferings of the last age, for it is indeed the sufferings of Christ which overflow upon his own (II Cor. 1:5; Col. 1:24; II Cor. 4:10); nothing else then is to be expected than that comfort, power, and eternal life shall stream from him into them (II Cor. 1:5; 12:9f; 4:10f). With this, we come now to the actual culmination of Paul's devotion to Christ, to what is called his

6. *Christ-mysticism*. We shall not quarrel here over the expression Mysticism, and its particular qualification, but shall attempt to understand the fact and its meaning for Paul. The problem concerns a series of expressions in which the relationship between 'Lord' and 'servant' is described; indeed, I might say, the 'I' and 'thou' relationship, as this more strongly expresses the still more intimate union between the Lord and his believers. This relationship begins at baptism. Paul here uses the strongest possible expressions: 'through the likeness of his death, have grown together with him (σύμφυτοι)' (Rom. 6:5), 'have put on Christ' (Gal. 3:27). These formulae, which are connected in some way with the language of the Hellenistic mystery cults, mean that a communion now exists which we might almost call 'corporeal,' if that expression were not too physical; perhaps, we might say an 'organic' or 'dynamic' relationship, a kind of 'symbiosis' in the sense that the same element of life, the Spirit, which the Christians have received at baptism, joins them with the exalted Christ, who has been freed from his body of flesh, 'in one spirit' (I Cor. 6:17). Thus the Exalted One is united with his own, who are still sojourning on earth (Col. 3:3), and thus it may be conceived that his death and resurrection are extended to include them; they must taste, to the full, the measure of his suffering, which has not been completed with

the death on the Cross (Col. 1:24; II Cor. 1:5; Phil. 3:10). Then again, the idea is developed more fully that all the faithful, because they all have the same Spirit within themselves, are joined together into an organism (I Cor. 12:13), into a harmonious personality (Gal. 3:28), which is the body of Christ, or Christ himself, whose heavenly nature embraces them as a broad mantle (3:27). Again the representation changes, in that—as in the Epistles to the Colossians and to the Ephesians—he appears as the head of this mystical body (Col. 1:18; Eph. 1:22; 4:15f; 5:23), from whom life-powers flow into all the members. And yet again the picture changes, and it is said of every individual that he is 'in Christ' and 'Christ is in him.' These conceptions, especially as regards their peculiar changes, can only be understood from the parallel modes of expression: 'The Spirit of God dwells in you'; 'if anyone has the Spirit of Christ'; 'ye are in the Spirit' (Rom. 8:9f). What is true of Christ is also true of the Spirit, and the reverse. Fundamentally, the reason for this representation lies in the fact that Christ and the Spirit are in some way identical, as it is expressly stated in II Cor. 3:17. Where the Spirit is, there Christ is also; Christ works through the Spirit into men.[17] And as in I Cor. 12:13, the picture changes almost in the same breath: 'We are baptized into one Spirit' and 'We are saturated with one Spirit,' so that the Spirit appears as a fluid which surrounds us and also penetrates us; thus is explained the strange idea that at one and the same time Christ can be in us, and we can be in Christ. The first expression implies certain primitive, animistic concepts (p. 429): the idea that one spiritual being can dwell in another. But we see at once that this stage has been overcome; for if it were really meant in this way, viz. that the

[17] This idea can best be made clear by that conception of Philo's in regard to the 'powers' (δυνάμεις) of God which extend into the world and to men. Cf. Zeller, *Phil. d. Griechen*, III. ii. 365: "In his teaching concerning the powers, two ideas cross each other, the religious, of the personal, and the philosophic, of the impersonal mediating beings; he joins both definitions without noticing their contradiction, indeed he cannot notice it at all, because, otherwise, at once the rôle of mediation, the double nature of the divine powers would be lost. They would, on the one hand, have to be identical with God, in order that it might be possible for the transitory to share in the divinity; on the other, they must be separated from him, so that the divinity may, in spite of this participation, remain out of touch with the world." One may illustrate this representation by that Egyptian conception (Gressmann, *Texte und Bilder*, p. 66, no. 118) where the king appears with the queen at the sacrifice, the disc of the sun over him and its beams flashing out from his hands, or one hand touching the sacrificial gifts (and in a certain sense taking them in possession) and the other hand reaching down to those who are sacrificing, penetrating into them and offering them the sign of life. Here the connection of the worshippers with the deity, the streaming of his strength into them, is naïvely and vividly represented.

daemon Christ lives in men, it would not, in fact, be possible—at least according to our method of thought—for him to dwell in others and at the same time for the faithful to dwell in him. This manner of thought is possible only upon the supposition that—at least at the moment when the formula was first conceived and expressed —the fixed outlines of the personality had been softened and dissolved, and replaced by the idea of a formless, impersonal, all-penetrating being. For the expert in the history of religion this is not strange; it frequently happens where 'mystic' formulae appear. At the moment when the yearning of the pious man is no longer satisfied to place his own ego over against the divine Thou, to honor him with reverence and humility, to pray to him, but now desires to be united with the divinity and gives himself wholly and at once to the quenching of self in order to flow into a unity—God in me and I in God—at that very moment the concept of God suffers of necessity a depersonalization, and by a certain logical inevitableness pantheistic forms of expression appear. This is the case with Paul, as we shall see more exactly later when we come to consider his Christology; here I only refer to Col. 1:17, 'In him all things consist'; here Christ takes exactly the same position which the World Soul has in the Stoic system; he is the innermost, animating, cohesive principle of power in the natural universe and in the realm of spirit, and therefore identical with the life-creating Spirit of God which penetrates the entire world and pours into the souls of men. It is clear that these modes of expression differ sharply from the background of the Old Testament and the primitive Christian religion, which is actually founded upon the personality of God and the exalted 'Lord' Christ. So much the more pertinent, then, is the question whether Paul himself has created this language, especially the formula 'in Christ,' or has taken it over from some other source.

Because this mystical language works strangely within the oldest primitive Christianity, it is easy to assume a borrowing or dependence upon Hellenistic modes of thought and feeling.[18] This prob-

[18] I refer here only to A. Dieterich, *Eine Mithras-Liturgie*, pp. 97ff, especially to the prayer to Hermes (London Papyrus in Kenyon, *Greek Pap.*, Brit. Museum, 1893, p. 116, Pap. 122,3.2ff): "For you are I, and I am you; your name is mine and mine is yours; I am your image." Further, the other prayer to the Αγαθὸς δαίμων = Hermes (in Reitzenstein, *Poimandres*, pp. 19ff): "Come into my spirit (νοῦν) and soul (φρένας) throughout my whole life, and do everything for me that my soul desires. For you are I and I am you; what I say, may it always come to pass; for I have your name as an amulet in my heart; no swinging fist (? δράξ κινουμένη) will ever overcome me; nor be able to withstand me (cf. Rom. 8:38f), neither a spirit nor a daemon, no

lem has a more than historical implication. Behind it lies the greater psychological problem, whether the corresponding religious emotions of Paul are primary and original, so that they would, as it were, spontaneously force out this expression. If Paul, on the contrary, had taken over a mode of expression already at hand, it would certainly be possible that he might have been influenced by it: the formulae, working retroactively, could have formed his emotional life, or he could have adapted himself to them. The question as to what feelings are fundamental in them, or are borne along with them, is not easy to answer.

Now it is clear that Paul would not have chosen these strange over-forced modes of expression, originally unknown to him, if he had not wished to express what were to him extraordinary, overwhelming feeling-values, and to do so in the most plausible, intimate manner possible. One feels this especially in such passages as Gal. 2:19f. Here he cannot do enough to express, as strongly as possible, the full break with his legal past; therefore he uses the expression, "I live no more . . . . Christ lives in me." Here also is involved the question of rhetorical hyperbole.[19] This is clear from the fact that he at once attempts to correct himself: "But what I now live in the flesh . . ." It is quite evident that it is no mere question of rhetorical exaggeration, but that a strong emotion lies at bottom. He must have had wholly strange and extraordinary inner experiences. An unknown force, which cannot have come from himself—so he feels—has overwhelmed him, just when his personal powers had become weak, when the sufferings of the body and the fears of the soul were greatest (II Cor. 4:7-11; 12:9). In order to describe this, he uses the wondrous figure of the power of Christ descending

---

occurrence (συνάντημα), nor any other evil coming from Hades—for the sake of your name which I have in my soul."

Again, another prayer runs (Reitzenstein, *Poimandres,* p. 20): "Come to me, Hermes, as the child in the body of a woman. . . . I know you, Hermes, and you me. I am thou and thou art me. [Come to me] and do everything for me. . . . " Cf. further, Reitzenstein, *Die hellenist. Mysterienrell.* pp. 45,202ff. Very important also is Poimandres V: διὰ τί δὲ καὶ ὑμνήσω σε; ὡς ἐμαυτὸς ὤν; ὡς ἔχων τι ἴδιον; ὡς ἄλλος ὤν; σὺ γὰρ εἶ ὃ ἂν ὦ, σὺ εἶ ὅ ἂν ποιῶ, σὺ εἶ ὃ ἂν λέγω ("And how shall I sing to thee? Am I my own, or have I anything of my own? Am I other than Thou? Thou art whatsoever I am; Thou art whatsoever I do, and whatsoever I say").

[19] Such hyperboles appear sometimes in Lucian, for example in the *Dial. Deorum,* 12, where the love-passion of Rhea for Attis is described in the words, ἡ 'Ρέα . . . . ὅλη οὖσα ἐν τῷ Ἄττῃ; or in *Hermotimos* 2, where it is said of an inspired adherent of philosophy: ὅλος εἶ ἐν τῷ πράγματι; cf. also Philostratus, *Apollonius of Tyana* III:28 Φραώτου μεστὸς ἥκεις. Cf. also Plutarch, *Amator.,* 759 c, Κάτων ἔλεγε τὴν ψυχὴν τοῦ ἐρῶντος ἐνδιαιτᾶσθαι τῇ τοῦ ἐρωμένου.

upon him; [20] or the dynamic expression, that in weakness, when the strength and resistance of man has declined, the divine strength becomes preponderant (ὑπερβολή): in weakness, the power of Christ is perfected (τελεῖται, τελειοῦται); when death has seized the languished body, there is revealed to him an indescribable 'life'—this is Jesus himself—and it makes him strong (Phil. 4:13; Rom. 8:37). Wonderful inner victories over the terrors of the soul; an enigmatical welling-up of joy and courage in the midst of deepest depression; an inconceivable increase of his strength when already, apparently, its last particle had been exhausted; surprising results, when nothing was to be hoped for—such experiences Paul must have had, to be able to say, "I can do all things through him who strengthens me" (Phil. 4:13; II Cor. 13:4). It is an inner reality he wishes to describe when he says, "I live no more, Christ lives in me." He feels, or thinks he feels, that he has become another; he has been freed entirely from himself, and Christ governs his thinking and willing, like a strange power. One must conceive this entirely personally: he stands as if under a compulsion; even if he would, he could no more continue living for his own purposes—these no longer exist; he has lost all pleasure in what was once valuable to him (Phil. 3:7ff), all human, natural relationships have been loosed (II Cor. 5:16; I Cor. 9:19, 'free from every man!'); instead he must evaluate and will what Christ wills. In this connection the memorable expression, 'We have the mind of Christ' (I Cor. 2:16), may be paraphrased, "I think so entirely differently from other people that no one can understand or rightly judge me; they are Christ's thoughts, which appear in me, they do not come from myself, Christ thinks in me." Here also belongs II Cor. 5:14, 'The love of Christ constraineth me;' he does not live a life which is his own, Christ rules in him. So this group of passages is, fundamentally, the most enhanced expression for the complete dependence and devotion of the servant of Christ to his master. But, certainly, these pictures, taken from the sphere of animistic thought-forms, would not have been chosen if he had not occasionally felt the servant relationship as an 'enthusiasm' in its real sense, whereby man becomes completely the organ of God, who 'possesses' him and lives in him.[21]

[20] *ἐπισκηνοῦν*; in the word there is a reminder of the Old Testament שכן, which signifies the descent, the dwelling of the deity upon earth (שכינה).

[21] The Greek expression *κατοχή* is not found in the New Testament; this meaning, however, is clear. The word *ἐνθουσιασμός* is derived from *ἔνθεος*, which does not

Another shade of feeling seems to present itself here. Paul's use of the formula 'in Christ' has often been understood of the blessed feeling of sinking one's ego into the depths of the divine, of the fusion or 'becoming one' of the personalities. But here we must raise a question. Paul, as it seems, entirely lacks the note of contemplation which is a necessary condition of that method of feeling. In this restless, active, powerful nature, always engaged in ethical tension, there is no room for a blessed resting in the Lord. Still more completely absent from the language of Paul is that—I might say, *musical*—revelling in mystical moods, which manifests itself in the piling-up and arrangement of mystical formulae and in playing variations upon them; the expression 'in Christ' appears, for one thing, to be so brief and compact, and on the other hand is used so often and in connection with so many less exalted moments, that one must often doubt whether it is still filled with a true mystical, ecstatic content of feeling.[22] It almost seems as if it

---

mean *ὁ ἐν Θεῷ ὤν*; but on the contrary, *ἐν ᾧ ὁ Θεός ἐστιν*. Cf. *Berliner Zauberbuch* (Abh. d. Berl. Akad.; 'Reports of the Berlin Academy,' 1865), p. 120,20: *ἔσται τι ἔνθεον ἐν τῇ σῇ καρδίᾳ*).

[22] It is, it seems to me, a mistake of Deissmann in his *Die neutestamentliche Formel 'in Christo Jesu,'* when he assumes that in all passages the phrase carries the same emphasis. Perhaps a brief review is demanded. Cf. my article in *Theol. Studien und Kritiken*, 1896, pp. 1-35, and my exposition, *Die Mystik des Paulus* (1914). In the 164 passages in which Deissmann finds the formula, and interprets it in the full mystical sense (he does not consider Colossians, nor Ephesians, nor the Pastorals), he distinguishes, first of all,

(1) a series, where the 'in' does not at all mean 'the existence of Christians in Christ;' rather it states in an objective manner that salvation, i.e. redemption, or the love or the will of God, is present 'in Christ,' a shortened mode of expression for the statement: 'because of the fact that Christ has come, redemption is here,' as e.g. in Rom. 3:24 (redemption in Christ Jesus); 8:39 (the love of God in Christ Jesus); here, perhaps, also belongs II Cor. 5:19 (God was reconciling the world to himself in Christ); I Thess. 5:18; Gal. 3:14; Phil. 3:14.

(2) Related to this is a second series, in which, as I take it, there appears a more comprehensive, more inclusive or representative use: I Cor. 15:22 (as in Adam all die, so in Christ shall all be made alive); I Cor. 7:14 (the unbelieving man is sanctified in the wife); here the translations 'in' or 'in and with' would both be right; so also Col. 1:16; 2:10f; the 'in' could here also be replaced by a 'through' (*διά*) as in Rom. 5:5; 7:4; and with this cf. Rom. 8:4; 5:21.

(3) In other passages the 'in Christ' is no independent formula at all, but the words depend as objects of such verbs as praising, hoping, trusting: I Cor. 1:31, cf. 3:21; II Cor. 10:17; Phil. 2:19,24; 3:3f: "boasting in Christ Jesus, and not being confident in the flesh, though I might have confidence also in flesh." Cf. here also Rom. 5:11, 'boasting in God;' I Thess. 2:2, 'we waxed bold in our God;' Gal. 6:14, 'to boast in the Cross.'

(4) Again, in other passages we must raise the question whether the 'in' is not purely instrumental, as if it were 'through.' Thus in I Thess. 4:1 he replaces *παρακαλοῦμεν ἐν κυρίῳ* 'Ιησοῦ with *παραγγελίας ἐδώκαμεν διὰ τοῦ κυρίου* 'Ιησοῦ (4:2);

sometimes denotes simply belonging to Christ, being bound together with him and the brethren.[23] I would raise the question whether Paul really had had the feeling that in this union with Christ his own individuality was completely fused with him. Can one really feel this? Does there not rather lie, in all mysticism, a suggestion

---

cf. further, II Thess. 3:6 and 12; Rom. 15:30.

(5) The full mystical sense, indeed, seems to be present in such passages as II Cor. 5:17 ('if any man is in Christ, he is a new creature') or I Cor. 1:30; I Thess. 3:8; Phil. 4:1; 4:13 ('I can do all things in him who makes me strong'). But when one observes that the formula also occurs frequently simply as an expression denoting to be a Christian, without any accompanying expression showing deep religious feeling, as in Rom. 16:11; Phil. 1:1; II Cor. 12:2; I Cor. 7:39, I ask myself the question whether it is necessary to assume here a mystical 'temperature?' Certainly, indeed, it is an elevated mode of expression when the disciple is designated as a child in the Lord (I Cor. 4:15,17), the companion as a fellow-worker in Christ (Rom. 16:3,9), Christians as brethren in the Lord (Col. 4:7), and nothing forbids one to add to all such passages Gal. 3:28, "Ye are all one in Christ"—but since this formula appears ten times in the section Rom. 16:1-16, it would seem to be an exegetical exaggeration to assume each time that it implies the full feeling of union with Christ. Here it seems to me necessary either to take the 'in' as perhaps depicting the spheres within which that which has just been described belongs; so that one might say, 'workers together in Christ' and 'workers together in the Gospel' (I Thess. 3:2); Phil. 4:3 'they who have striven with me in the Gospel' could also mean 'striven with me in Christ.' Or, perhaps, the 'ἐν' in Greek is simply an expression for the connection with Christ, or of the possession of Christ, just as it is stated that the Christian is 'in the Spirit,' i.e. is furnished with the Spirit, is in possession of the Spirit, is in deep sympathy with the Spirit.

In any case there are very many passages in Paul in which the formula seems almost to possess a polished, phraseological sense, as in later usage. From this it would follow either that Paul did not create the formula, but had taken it over; or if he is the creator of it he used it so frequently that in his hands it has become, so to speak, like a coin which has been thinned by handling. It must of course have had its origin, in some way, in a mystical circle of thought; presumably it has been derived from the baptismal formula 'into Christ' (εἰς Χριστόν; so further, Rom. 16:5). Originally, this was the expression for 'belonging to Christ' (complementary to Χριστοῦ εἶναι); then it received a deeper meaning in connection with the mystical significance of baptism; finally it was taken literally, and the idea appears: *every* Christian is 'in Christ' (Rom. 16:7; II Cor. 12:2). But then again it was frequently used in a really objective sense, no longer with any special feeling, as a designation for being Christ-like. However we may conceive of the origin of the meaning of the formula in individual passages, it is an unstable, exaggerated interpretation if it is understood generally as *expressivo* and *sforzato,* and accordingly Christ-mysticism is represented as the prevailing, characteristic mark of Pauline religion.

[23] This ἐν it seems to me would rather indicate that which is 'furnished,' 'prepared' or 'possessed with' something; parallels are not only the well known ἐν ὅπλοις, ἐν ῥάβδῳ, ἐν ἐσθῆτι, also δένδρα ἐν καρποῖς, but, above all, ἄνθρωπος ἐν πνεύματι ἀκαθάρτῳ Mark 1:23, where Luke says: ἔχων πνεῦμα. Just as ἐν πνεύματι, according to the analogy of Rev. 1:19; 4:2, and according to the interchange of ἐν πνεύματι and κατὰ πνεῦμα εἶναι simply means: to be in a pneumatic condition, so that πνεῦμα ἔχομεν and τὸ πνεῦμα ἐν ἡμῖν mean exactly the same; so also ἐν Χριστῷ εἶναι as well as Χριστὸν ἔχειν, Χριστὸς ἐν ἡμῖν, in the power and communion of Christ, very closely bound to him, is only a stronger mode of expression for Χριστοῦ εἶναι, as in Rom. 8:9f.

of intoxicating musical tones, strong in their mysterious charm, which, in fact, express a yearning and striving for that which is never a full reality? Can a man as completely free himself from his ego as is demanded by the language of mysticism? I merely raise these questions, but I give no answer. Could Paul have answered? Would he have wished to answer? It will always remain suggestive that the most impressive mystical statement upon which, as a matter of fact, all our knowledge of his mysticism is based (Gal. 2:20), is at once interpreted or qualified by a confession entirely in the spirit of the I-and-thou-religion. After he had said:

> My life I live no more, Christ lives in me,

he continues at once:

> But what I yet live in the flesh,
> that I live in the faith of him who has loved me and given himself for me.

It seems to me that this change in point of view is very significant. Not only in that both modes of expression and feeling appear of equal value and are equally serviceable—thus also, in Rom. 8:9 and 10, he exchanges the 'to be in Christ' for 'Christ in you,' as if both were of equal weight—but one still has the impression that Paul wishes with that second statement to make clear the first, to make it more plain to the reader; the 'life of faith in Christ' is, in any case, the more common point of view. Indeed, one may go so far as to say that it corresponds to experience and feeling, while the mystical manner of expression, in its exclusiveness and intensity, really outruns actual experience. In this case the formula would not simply have been taken over, but it was not fully assimilated to the experience. It is, indeed, very difficult to pass a judgment on the question as to how far a writer can share his feelings with the words he employs, and who would venture to attribute this to Paul, who is so far removed from us by the centuries, by difference of language, and by the whole temper of his ideas! Nevertheless, I cannot withhold the confession that there seems to be lacking in his language the real glow and magic of mysticism, and its express and developed terminology. Present investigators, it seems to me, have exaggerated the meaning of the Christ-mysticism; from the purely quantitative point of view it does not fill the place which is so liberally granted to it; but also—and this is essential—the relationship of the servant who serves his master with complete devotion and who depends in everything upon him, is expressed with such clarity, sincerity, and force that we have the right to believe in the statement: here lies the focal point of devotion to Christ, and not in the Christ-mysticism which remains to a certain degree secondary, yes, perhaps a completely strange element.

The meaning of the Christ-mysticism for Paul may, perhaps, have to suffer a further limitation, when, in conclusion, we raise the question of the relationship between

7. *Faith in Christ and Faith in God.* When one reads a great many recent expositions, he receives the impression that in the Christ-devotion or Christ-mysticism, the religion of Paul not only culminates but straightway exhausts itself, as if Christ had for him taken the place of God, and as if God were completely forced into the background. There are, in fact, certain passages in the Pauline epistles in which God the Father seems to be overshadowed by Christ, e.g. the great Christological excursus in the Epistle to the Colossians, in which even the 'almighty' formula, elsewhere applied to God (Rom. 11:36), is applied to Christ, "He is before all things, and in him all things hold together" (1:17); "that in all things he might have the preëminence" (1:18). According to many passages, such as II Cor. 5:17; Gal. 2:19f, and others, it would appear as if it were of the greatest importance to win a relationship to Christ, as if by this means one's whole salvation were determined, and as if there were nothing higher in salvation than 'to be in Christ.' But this is a false inference, for which Paul is not to blame. If we examine in detail the problem which opens up here, we shall certainly find, even upon this point, a certain lack of unity which must simply be acknowledged.

We have seen earlier (pp. 461ff) how Paul often mentions Christ and God the Father, side by side, as the dispensers of Salvation, e.g. in the blessings, where, on the other hand, he interchanges God and Christ, as when he derives the super-earthly power, which supports him in his sufferings, now from God and now from Christ (II Cor. 4:7; 12:9). We ask now whether we cannot find, in explanation of this apparently simple juxtaposition, with its naïve and not always clarified modalism, a clearly thought-out conviction of Paul as to the relationship of God and Christ, and their meaning for Salvation.

Even if the preaching of Paul to the Greeks might leave the impression that he was announcing, over against the one highest God, a second God (δεύτερος θεός), this would not correspond to his final purpose. He did not, of course, consciously face the possibility that through the honoring of the Kyrios-Christ pure monotheism might be prejudiced, but he has, indeed, by his modes of expression unconsciously erected a bar against all inferences in that direction; for him, even in the present, there is but one true God (I Cor. 8:4,6; I Thess. 1:9), as he says in harmony with the fundamental confession of Judaism. Therefore he carries through the gradation (I Cor. 8:5f), corresponding to the differences between 'gods and lords':[23a] 'God the Father and the Lord Jesus Christ'; he seems consciously and consistently to withhold the predicate 'God' from Christ.[23b] It is noteworthy that in Phil. 2:11, after he has described the God-like position of the exalted Christ (τὸ εἶναι ἴσα Θεῷ), and has even given to him the Old Testament proper name of God, he finally adds these words: 'to the honor of God the Father.' Important also is the oft-recurring expression (Rom. 15:6; II Cor. 1:3; Col. 1:3), 'the God and Father of our Lord Jesus Christ,' according to which Christ remains subordinate to the Father, not only as Son, but also as creature to his God (cf. also John 20:17); in Rom. 8:29 Christ appears only as the first-born among many brethren, in spite (8:34) of his place at the right hand of God, as advocate of men standing before God. All this is to be confirmed finally by the last act of the apocalyptic drama, in which Christ gives back his kingship to his 'God and Father' (I Cor. 15:24-28), and thus steps back into the rank of creatures, so that finally God is 'all in all.' Here it becomes perfectly plain that in spite of the exaltation of Christ to equality with God, in spite of all his worship of Christ, Paul finally stands fast by his Jewish standpoint, according to which the rule of the Messiah was a temporarily limited episode in the history of the world, not an eternal and permanent state (cf. the strongly out-spoken IV Ezra 7:28f).

To this theoretical sketch of his world-view, his practical religious point of view also corresponds. Fundamentally important for the salvation of the Christian as the work of Christ is (Gal. 2:20), Paul nevertheless carefully emphasizes the fact that 'all' ultimately comes 'from God' (II Cor. 5:18); he is the final source of Salvation (I Cor. 1:30); by his initiative redemption takes place (Gal. 4:4; Rom. 3:24ff; 8:3,32); ever and again, it is said with sharp emphasis that Christ was only the efficient organ, and his death only the means, in the inauguration of Salvation (Rom. 5:1,11; 3:24; II Cor. 5:18f—

[23a] Cf. my Commentary on I Cor. 8:5f.

[23b] Also Rom. 9:5, where the correct text reads ὧν ὁ ἐπὶ . . . .

διά and ἐν).[23c] The final aim of redemption does not rest in fellowship with Christ, but justification before God, reconciliation with him, peace with God (Gal. 2:16; Rom. 5:1,10f; II Cor. 5:19f), sharing in the Kingdom of God (Gal. 5:19ff; I Cor. 6:10; 15:50), participation in the eternity and splendor of the presence of God, of course in company with Christ (I Thess. 4:17; Phil. 1:23) though the most important thing is, surely, that hidden life with God (Col. 3:3; Rom. 5:17), the being assimilated to God (I Cor. 15:28). And even now the deciding factor is that 'God is for us' (Rom. 8:31), that he has called us (I Thess. 2:12), that he works in us both to will and to do (Phil. 2:13), that we may be called his children (Gal. 4:6; Rom. 8:15); in this respect Christ is only the first-born among many brethren (Rom. 8:29). There are many sincere confessions of Paul in which the name of Christ does not appear at all (I Cor. 13), or only in an entirely casual reference (Rom. 8:12-30), and there are enough pithy words in which the process of salvation is described as though the whole were carried out only between God and the individual soul. Indeed, so important is all that which Christ has done for us—so fundamentally had the salvation of the elect been established since their predestination and election (Rom. 8:29)—that under whatever conditions it must be realized and would be realized, even if—we must say it—Christ had denied the Father's work of redemption, or even if God out of the fulness of his love could have dispensed with the sacrifice of Christ. Obviously it is impossible to separate Christ and his work from the religion of Paul; it would be a crass mistake both from the systematic and the genetic psychological points of view. Strictly, also, even where Christ is not mentioned, we must have him in mind; Paul would say that God's act of adoption and all our certainty of salvation could not be apart from Christ. And yet according to many of Paul's utterances, Salvation is so deeply anchored in the nature and love of God that one must at least raise the question, on what grounds then was the work of Christ still necessary? The answer cannot possibly be to the effect that the necessity proceeded from God, or was founded on his nature. There is only one single passage in Paul (Rom. 3:25f) in which the idea is to be found, unexpressed, it may be, yet underlying, that for his righteousness' sake God could not waive the demand for an expiatory sacrifice. But even this idea is so casual and

[23c] Rom. 3:24, 'being justified freely by *God's* grace *through* the redemption that is in Christ Jesus;' 5:1, 'we have peace with God *through* our Lord Jesus Christ, *through* whom we have had our access;' 5:10, 'reconciled to God *through* the death of his Son;' 5:11, 'we rejoice in God *through* our Lord Jesus Christ;' 5:21; 6:11, 23; 7:25; 8:39, etc.

so indirectly expressed that it cannot have played any great rôle. To be honest, one must say that the necessity of sending Christ and of his work would not follow from the nature of God as Paul conceives it, even if the appearance and death of Christ were not facts for which he frequently seeks explanation. Because Paul believed himself forced to the conviction that the crucified one is the Messiah, he saw himself also forced to fit this Messiah and his work into his religious system, even though redemption through Christ cannot be harmonized, organically, with a pre-natal election and predestination to salvation.

The basis for this disharmony in the Pauline system of course lies, historically, much farther back, viz. in the Jewish Messianic belief. Since all eschatology finally leads to the thought that God and his people must triumph over other peoples and gods, why then is there really any need of a Messiah? This figure is important or necessary, where the concern is for the re-establishment of the Davidic dynasty. But where political-national features pass into the background and the religious note takes the foreground, there is, fundamentally, no compelling necessity that a representative of God upon earth should carry the work to completion in heaven. Hence the Messiah is missing in the Book of Daniel, which deals with the exaltation of the people to world-power. In fact the Messiah really has no place at all where the final goal is the kingdom or reign of God. Therefore Paul is obliged, also, to let the Messiah step into the background at that point in the apocalyptic drama when the universal rule of God is to be realized (I Cor. 15:28)—what then happens to him is not mentioned. So we may, with a little exaggeration, say that in the Jewish eschatological system, in so far as it has developed beyond the wholly limited national-political idea, the figure of the Messiah appears to be an intruder; he has, really, no particular task which God himself could not accomplish; therefore we have in Paul now God, now Christ, as judge of the world (Rom. 2:2-10,16; 3:6,19f; I Thess. 1:9f; II Cor. 5:10); he is even nothing else than a representative, in many respects the double of God. And this fact, again, has roots which lie far back; for the figure of a divinely appointed world-ruler and world-judge is ultimately, as we have seen (p. 35), a vestige of mythological thinking, which does not fit into the monotheistic framework of the Pauline and generally primitive Christian world-view. The Gentile-Christian conception that Christ is a 'second God' instinctively strikes the truth and illuminates an inner split in the

Paul was exceedingly slow to equate Christ and God.

Pauline thought, which, although he seems not to have perceived it, we cannot but feel very strongly.

Paul is not the actual author of this dilemma. He has found and taken over the Kyrios-faith in which it is involved. But in his detailed expositions the contradiction, indeed, finally appears. It still is and continues to be a fact of the greatest importance—if one will, a fateful dispensation—that Christianity did not straightway develop out of the prophetic preaching of Jesus concerning the kingdom of God into a religion of pure monotheism, but that the Messiah-idea, even in the life of Jesus and then more fully after his death, entered into an indissoluble connection with his person.

But one may over-emphasize this circumstance, in that he views the whole religion of primitive Christianity and that of Paul as a Christ-cult, and thus fails to perceive that it was nevertheless and above all a new form of knowledge of God and a new relationship to God. On the other hand, we must not minimize the problem and say that Christianity is only the relationship to God and knowledge of him as Christ has lived it and proclaimed it. We may, at the present, accept this as the essential and enduring element in Christianity, and practically strip off the other; but, historically, the new religion did not appear only as a faith in God—it was also the worship of Christ. Paul has won his new knowledge of God from the message and the life of Jesus, yet the most decisive factor for him was the Incarnation, the Death and Resurrection of Christ: from these facts he had learned what henceforth he had to say of the nature and the will of God.

8. *Christological Speculation*. What we wish to express by the word speculation, Paul would call 'gnosis.' What we mean by this are those statements concerning the being of Christ in relationship to God, to the world and to humanity, which do not actually touch the religious status of the individual in respect to Christ, but seek to penetrate into the secrets of the person itself, its origin and function in the world. But one must not make the mistake of supposing that these speculations spring out of a pure urge for knowledge, or that the grounds upon which they are based are in any sense scientific. We shall see that the statements concerning Christ are nothing more than an application of views of the Messiah, already held, and of religio-philosophical or 'metaphysical' concepts to Christ. After it was once established that Jesus was the Messiah, the transference of these predicates, titles, and honors to him took place of itself; he

simply entered into the status which pre-Christian speculation had prepared for a mediator between God and the world. It belonged to the completeness and reasonableness of the Christ-idea; but it also corresponds to a more or less apologetic aim of the Apostle: while it is shown that certain religio-philosophical postulates have been fulfilled in Christ, the proof is advanced that he stands for the highest and last, the concluding revelation of God, the fulfilling of all religion. The first of these names or titles to be considered is:

(a) *The Son of God*. We have already (pp. 446ff) seen that the Christ-faith of Paul had a common, early-Christian foundation. In certain statements an adoptionist Christology (pp. 118f) manifests itself plainly: through the exaltation (Phil. 2:9ff) Christ is 'super-exalted,' not only above his earthly condition, but even above his pre-earthly, since the God-like rank and the Kyrios name have been granted to him; he first *became* Kyrios at the exaltation. This is expressed in Rom. 1:4, "He was declared to be the Son of God with power, by reason of his resurrection from the dead"; the older thought still appears here, that he then first *became* Son of God, that is to say, he received the status of world-ruler (Psalm 2:7; Acts 13:33). Now Paul certainly fixes this thought more closely, in that he adds 'with power,' and thus suggests that Christ now first received the status which really belonged to him as the 'Son of God'; he was accordingly that already, and this too is plainly stated in Rom. 1:3, where the subject of the whole passage is 'the Son of God.' This is a continuation of the line which we have observed earlier (p. 122); as in the evangelical tradition the name, Son of God, is carried back into the life of Jesus (Mark 1:11; 5:7; 9:7; 14:61; 15:39; Matt. 4:3; 11:27; 14:33; 16:16, etc.), so it happens here, only it is said more plainly that he was already the 'Son of God,' even before his birth of the seed of David. By this, obviously, pre-existence is indicated; it is simply assumed by Paul (e.g. I Cor. 10:4), who had grown up with the conviction that the Messiah had for a long time been in heaven, where, indeed, Enoch in his wanderings had seen him 'under the wings of the Lord of Spirits' (Enoch 46).

But what does this name 'Son of God' mean? That it is not to be referred to any special manner of his human birth is clear. For in the first place, when Paul in Gal. 4:4 says, 'born of a woman,' he wishes to indicate a normal human birth (as Jesus spoke of the Baptist, Matt. 11:11); secondly, in Rom. 1:3 his birth from the seed of David is naturally meant to imply that humanly (κατὰ σάρκα) he is a direct descendant of David; and thirdly, he was already the

Son of God *before* he became man. If one ask now what it means when Paul calls him God's 'own' son (Rom. 8:3,32; Gal. 4:4; II Cor. 1:19) or 'the Son of his love' (Col. 1:13),[24] we must not weaken the meaning of the words and say that 'Son' is here only a figurative representation of the love of God for Christ. Certainly this special love for him is strongly enough emphasized, but it belongs to him just because he is the Son, not the reverse. Naturally the term does not mean, in this connection, the ruler instituted by God, but just this, the divine relationship or descent: that is its normal meaning in other passages. Seen from the view-point of historical development, a Son of God is always one begotten of God. This is the patently evident meaning of the word as used in Gentile religion, in which there are innumerable Sons of Gods. When the Babylonian god Marduk is called by Ea 'my Son,' no one doubts that he was begotten of him. And if in the Old Testament religion the idea of the 'sons of God' appears only once, and then refers to dim antiquity (Gen. 6:2), the suppression of this really mythological, polytheistic idea by a strongly monotheistic religion is not in the least surprising. But at the same time it cannot be denied that both the name and the concept of a Son of God are to be viewed, in their historical development, as the survival of mythological ideas. Nevertheless, when Paul unhesitatingly makes use of the term, this is possible only because its mythological character has already been wholly stripped away by him. One learns this from the fact that he either gives no thought at all, or allows only a very slight mythological tinge to his speculation, as to the manner of the coming into existence of this Son of God. He does not brood over his origin; of the 'begetting' he says nothing at all;[24a] this Son of God is already in existence, and is from the beginning present with God. We shall see later that he thought rather of a creation of Christ, than of a begetting (I Cor. 15:45). But on the whole his concept is more abstract, more ideal. He calls him the 'image of God' (εἰκών, II Cor. 4:4; Col. 1:15). Without anticipating a later more exact explanation, we must say here that there lies implicit in this term the idea that Christ is the reflection, the shining forth, the glory of the being of God. As the *Wisdom of Solomon* calls the Divine Wisdom 'a

[24] These expressions ἴδιος, τῆς ἀγάπης, beside which we can also place ἀγαπητός (Mark 1:11; 9:7) or μονογενής (John 1:18) and ἐκλεκτός (Luke 23:35), all go back to the Hebrew יחיד 'only' or also יקיר —Jer. 31:20, Aramaic חביב 'beloved,' 'dear;' cf. also Dalman, *Worte Jesu* i. 230ff. [Eng. tr., *The Words of Jesus*, pp. 276-280.]

[24a] In the expression 'firstborn of all creatures' (Col. 1:15), the emphasis usually lies not upon 'born' but upon 'first.'

breath of the power of God, and a clear effluence of the glory of the Almighty, an effulgence from everlasting light' (7:25f), so the Epistle to the Hebrews calls Christ 'the effulgence of his glory, the very image of his substance.' We are perhaps permitted to explain the Pauline idea of the Son of God in the same way. When in I Cor. 11:3 and 7 he depicts the ladder of gradation of human beings: God, Christ, man, woman, and says of man that he is 'the image and glory of God' (εἰκὼν καὶ δόξα), so we have, indeed, the same right to say this of Christ. The 'divine form' which he possessed before becoming man (Phil. 2:6), was nothing less than the divine *Doxa;* and may we not understand this statement to mean, in the Pauline sense: Christ was from the beginning no other than the *Kabōd,* the *Doxa* of God himself, the glory and radiation of his being, which appears almost as an independent hypostasis of God and yet is connected most intimately with God? As he was the Rock which followed the armies of Israel through the Wilderness (I Cor. 10:4), so also he will have been present in the pillars of cloud and fire. He was from the beginning no other than the Power of God (δύναμις) which pours itself throughout the whole world; therefore he can also, in fact, be identified with the Spirit of God (II Cor. 3:17); he was, indeed, as we shall see, the Logos of God. All this is contained in the name 'Son of God'; or, better said, this already traditional name for the Messiah Paul would have rightly explained in this 'dynamic' or conceptual manner, in that he combines it with the likewise traditional hypostatic representations, δόξα, δύναμις, πνεῦμα, λόγος.[25] But certainly, by this process, the personal concept of 'Son' was in principle eliminated; but it was not difficult for Paul to combine in his thinking these various kinds of representations. Moreover, this wavering between concept and personality, between a formless power and a close-knit central will (p. 435), was too deeply ingrained in his thinking and in the thought of the whole period. This manifests itself especially in this, that

(b) Christ is also conceived as a *world-creating* Power, in fact as *the World Soul,* in the Stoic sense. This thought is, indeed, already clearly present in I Cor. 8:6. In this anti-polytheistic confession, 'God the Father' and 'Our Lord Jesus Christ' are contrasted with the so-called 'gods and lords' (p. 472), and with conscious levelling of the expression, the status of both is exactly defined relative to the cosmos. Of God it is said, with a slight change of the Stoic

[25] Philo, *De Monarchia,* § 45, states. . . . *δόξαν δὲ σὴν εἶναι νομίζω τὰς περί σὲ δορυφορούσας δυνάμεις* ('I consider thy glory to be the powers which accompany thee').

'Almightiness-formula',[26] that 'from him are all things,' and we are created 'for him.' Of Christ, on the other hand, it is said that 'through him are all things, and through him we' were created or became.[27] According to the philosophical use of language which Paul follows here, Christ was the intermediary cause or the instrument in the creation—a thought which is formally repeated not only in Col. 1:16 but also in Heb. 1:2 and John 1:3 as an accepted Christian formula of faith. Moreover it is so obvious to Paul that he expresses it in a relative sentence as something well-known to his readers. Here Christ occupies exactly the place which in the Jewish wisdom

[26] E. Norden, *Agnostos Theos* (pp. 347ff) has treated this in a very learned manner: 'A Stoic doxology in Paul, History of an Almighty-formula.' He proceeds from Marcus Aurelius iv. 23, who thus addresses 'Nature': *ἐκ σοῦ πάντα, ἐν σοὶ πάντα, εἰς σὲ πάντα,* ('from thee are all things, in thee are all things, unto thee are all things'), and cites rich material for the formula from the Stoa; for example, Plutarch, *Plat. quaest.* ii. 2, p. 1001C *ἡ ψυχὴ . . . οὐκ ἔργον ἐστὶ τοῦ θεοῦ μόνον ἀλλὰ καὶ μέρος οὐδ' ὑπ' αὐτοῦ ἀλλὰ καὶ ἀπ' αὐτοῦ καὶ ἐξ αὐτοῦ γέγονεν*; ('the soul. . . . is not alone the work of God, it is also a part, not only has it come by him but also from him and out of him;' Aristides 1,5f: *δι' αὐτοῦ δὲ τὰ πάντα συνέστηκε* ('now through him are all things established'). The characteristic thing about all these formulae is the play on the prepositions. The thought is already found in Plato's *Timaeus;* and Stobaeus I, xiii. 1. Seneca, *Ep.* 65:8, touches upon it when he says: "Quinque ergo causae sunt, ut Plato dicit; id ex quo, id a quo, id in quo, id ad quod, id propter quod, novissime id quod ex his est. tamquam in statua. . . . id ex quo aes est, id a quo artifex est, id in quo forma est, quae aptatur illi, id ad quod exemplar est, quod imitatur is, qui facit, id propter quod facientis propositum est, id quod ex istis est ipsa statua est. Haec omnia mundus quoque, ut ait Plato, habet: facientem: hic deus est. . . . ex quo fit: haec materia est. formam: haec est habitus et ordo mundi quem videmus. exemplar, scilicet ad quod deus hanc magnitudinem operis pulcherrimi fecit. propositum, propter quod fecit" ("Accordingly there are five causes, as Plato says: the material, the agent, the make-up, the model, and the end in view. Last comes the result of all these, just as in the case of the statue. . . . the material is the bronze, the agent is the artist, the make-up is the form which is adapted to the material, the model is the pattern imitated by the agent, the end in view is the purpose in the maker's mind, and, finally, the result of all these is the statue itself. The universe, also, in Plato's opinion, possesses all these elements. The agent is God; the source, matter; the form, the shape and arrangement of the visible world. The pattern is doubtless the model according to which God has made this great and most beautiful creation. The purpose is his object in so doing"). Philo mentions these same categories (*De Cherubim* § 125; the common source will be Posidonius): for the actual creation of anything, many things must cooperate: the instigator, matter, agent, purpose (*τὸ ὑφ' οὗ, τὸ ἐξ οὗ, τὸ δι' οὗ, τὸ δι' ὅ*); applied to the world, the instigator is God, from whom it is; the matter is the four elements, out of which it is compounded; the agent is the Logos of God, by whom it is constructed; the basis and purpose of the creation is but the goodness of the Creator.

[27] Paul, in the words, 'from him are all things,' opposes both the Greek assumption and Philo's that God had created the world out of matter. The Almighty-formula is found in its original monotheistic form in Rom. 11:36, and it is observed by E. Norden that in I Cor. 8:6 it is divided between God and Christ, in Col. 1:16f it has been applied to Christ alone.

teaching is held by the 'Wisdom' of God,[27a] and in Philo by the Logos.[28] It is doubtful whether Paul had the former more in mind than the latter, or was thinking only of the life-creating Spirit (I Cor. 15:45; II Cor. 3:17) who at the beginning swept over the waters. It is not at all important to decide this question; perhaps he himself had not fully made up his mind with which of these hypotheses to identify Christ at this point. The essential thing is that he did complete the synthesis, and this is a very important occurrence in the history of religion. Herein lies a strong apologetic note, opposed as much to Hellenistic, and particularly to speculative, Judaism as to Hellenistic philosophy in general. No one doubted the existence nor the necessity of such a mediating being in that spiritual environment. For only in this way was it possible to maintain the transcendence of God over the world, and at the same time the relative divineness of the world in the face of pessimistic, dualistic despisers of matter. And it is further characteristic of Paul's many-sidedness that he can unite this optimistic view of the world, according to which something divine had cooperated at its genesis, with his usually very pessimistic thought of the cosmos, corrupted by the Fall and destined to destruction.

But not only has Christ cooperated in the genesis of the universe, as the Wisdom or Power of God, as his Spirit or Logos, but even in the present world he is active as its vitalizing, animating, uniting force. Paul makes this clear in the Christological excursus in the Epistle to the Colossians (1:15ff),

[27a] Proverbs 8:30 states that wisdom was present with God at the creation as the mistress set over all his works; Wisd. Sol. 9:2 adds, "Through thy wisdom thou hast created mankind". The rabbinic exegesis even read this into Gen. 1:1. 'In the beginning' (בראשית) meant, according to the Jerusalem Targum, 'through wisdom,' since according to Prov. 8:22 'wisdom' was 'the beginning of the ways of God.' According to Philo, *De Profugis* § 109, everything came into existence through wisdom (cf. *Quod Det. Pot.* § 54). Since on the other hand the Book of Wisdom identifies the wisdom with the Spirit of God, which moves through the world, and since Paul certainly knew this book, Paul may have similarly identified the two. See my Commentary on I Cor. 8:6.

[28] Philo *De Cherubim* § 127; *Leg. Allegor.* iii. 96: the shadow of God is his Logos which he has used as an instrument in the creation; *De Conf. Ling.* § 34: εἷς ὢν ὁ θεὸς ἀμυθήτους περὶ αὑτὸν ἔχει δυνάμεις ἀρωγοὺς καὶ σωτηρίους τοῦ γενομένου πάσας, αἷς ἐμφέρονται καὶ αἱ κολαστήριοι. . . . διὰ τούτων τῶν δυνάμεων ὁ ἀσώματος καὶ νοητὸς ἐπάγη κόσμος, τὸ τοῦ φαινομένου τοῦδε ἀρχέτυπον, ἰδέαις ἀοράτοις συσταθείς, ὥσπερ οὗτος σώμασιν ὁρατοῖς ("God is one, but he has around him numberless powers which all assist and protect. . . . through these powers the incorporeal and intelligible world was framed, the archetype of this phenomenal world, that being a system of invisible ideal forms, as this is of visible material bodies").

. . . . he is the image of the invisible God,
the firstborn of all creation;
(1) for in him were all things created
in the heavens and upon the earth,
things visible and things invisible,
whether thrones or dominions,
principalities or powers;
(2) All things have been created *through* him and *unto* him:
and he is *before* all things,
and in him all things hold together . . . .

In the second group of statements the opinion is expressed concerning the now-existing cosmos (note the perfect, ἔκτισται), and it is stated that this was wholly created by his mediation, and that even in the present it still owes its existence to him. The last expression reiterates (with a genuine Stoic expression)[28a] that he is the cohesive force, the enlivening soul of the world. This is the same thought which John 1:3f expressed, though somewhat differently:

All things were made by him,
And without him was not anything made;
What hath been made was life in him,
And the life was the light of men.[29]

If the last line states that men could and should have known God through his self-revelation throughout the world, through the Logos present in the cosmos, even this idea is not lacking in Paul: in I Cor. 1:21 it appears in the form that humanity should have known God

[28a] See the passage from Aristides quoted above in note 26, and compare *De Mundo* § 6 *ἀρχαῖος μὲν οὖν τις λόγος καὶ πάτριος πᾶσιν ἀνθρώποις, ὡς ἐκ θεοῦ πάντα καὶ διὰ θεοῦ πάντα καὶ διὰ θεοῦ ἡμῖν συνέστηκεν* ('a certain *logos*, primal, and fatherly toward all men, just as from God are all things, and through God are all things, and through God exist for us'). See also Ecclus. 43:26; Pap. Paris f.20, ll. 1748ff, 'I hail thee commander in chief of all creation . . . . the primal parent of all . . . . upholding all living things . . . . from whom all things are established;' Pap. Leiden ii. 32f: 'By thee are upheld the pole and the earth;' Galen xiv. 698, of Athenaeus. Cf. Zeller, *Philosophie der Griechen* iii. 1, 138ff: "The Stoics described the Godhead as the Soul or Spirit or Reason of the world, as the unified whole which contained within itself all developed forms, as the consistency of things, the universal law, the nature, the destiny, the providence [ruling the world], as the perfectly blessed, kindly, omniscient Being." Diogenes Laert. 138: *τὸν δὴ κόσμον οἰκεῖσθαι κατὰ νοῦν καὶ πρόνοιαν . . . . εἰς ἅπαν ἀυτοῦ μέρος διήκοντος τοῦ νοῦ καθάπερ ἐφ' ἡμῶν τῆς ψυχῆς* ('the cosmos to be indwelt rationally and with foresight . . . . its several parts administered by mind even as with us by the living soul'); Cicero, *Academ*. ii. 37, 'this world to be wise, to have a mind, by which it fashions itself and is controlled, moved, and quieted throughout'.

[29] Cf. also Heb. 1:13: "Who upholds all things through the word of his power."

'through the Wisdom of God'; again in Col. 1:15 it is expressed in another way: Christ is called the image of the invisible God, the firstborn of the whole creation.[30] The idea of the 'image' (εἰκών) is turned in a somewhat different direction than is usual. Emphasis is laid not so much on the fact that Christ is perfectly like God, but upon the fact that, as God's faithful representation, he must pass as the substitute for the invisible original (John 1:18). As, according to Rom. 1:19, it is not the eternal unknown essential nature of God but rather the humanly knowable side of his being which can be perceived in the works of creation, so Christ is here called the image of the invisible God, since in him the being of God can be recognized; he is the Revelation of God, because and in so far as he, the first-born of God, is closest to the essence of God. By this it is of course assumed that, to a certain degree, he is identical with the cosmos. This is expressed by the strangely chosen statement: "In him all things were created." This *in* (ἐν) has by no means the same meaning as 'through' (διά); it appears here in a comprehensive or representative sense, and is to be explained by the statement: In that he was created, all things were created; the best translation would be, 'With him all things were created.' Here it is exceedingly plain that the basis of the idea is the Logos-concept as used by Philo. The Logos as the essence of all world-creating beings, 'the idea of ideas,' already contains 'in accordance with the idea' the whole world in itself, certainly only the 'thought-world' (the *cosmos noëtos*). With Paul the idea is, indeed, thought out more concretely: the pre-mundane Son of God, the similarly 'life-creating' Spirit (I Cor. 15:45),

[30] Both these pictures appear also in the Babylonian religion (Jastrow, i. 296, 305), when the god Girru is called the first-born of heaven and the image of his father, or when Nusku is called the express image of his father, the first born of Bel. This manner of speech expresses as strongly as possible the likeness of the god to his father; that because he is the first-born, he is the express image, is in itself certainly a rather naïve thought. In Philo, *Leg. Alleg.* iii. 96, the Logos is called the εἰκὼν or the shadow of God. Σκιὰ δὲ θεοῦ ὁ λόγος αὐτοῦ ἐστιν, ᾧ καθάπερ ὀργάνῳ προσχρησάμενος ἐκοσμοποίει. αὔτη δὲ ἡ σκιὰ καὶ τὸ ὡσανεὶ ἀπεικόνισμα ἑτέρων ἐστὶν ἀρχέτυπον. ὥσπερ γὰρ ὁ θεὸς παράδειγμα τῆς εἰκόνος, ἣν σκιὰν νῦν κέκληκεν, οὕτως ἡ εἰκὼν ἄλλων γίνεται παράδειγμα, ὡς καὶ ἐναρχόμενος τῆς νομοθεσίας ἐδήλωσεν εἰπών "καὶ ἐποίησεν ὁ θεὸς τὸν ἄνθρωπον κατ' εἰκόνος θεοῦ" (Gen. 1:27), ὡς τῆς μὲν εἰκόνος κατὰ τὸν θεὸν ἀπεικονισθείσης, τοῦ δὲ ἀνθρώπου κατὰ τὴν εἰκόνα λαβοῦσαν δύναμιν παραδείγματος ("But God's shadow is His word, which he made use of like an instrument, and so made the world. But this shadow, and what we describe as the representation, is the archetype for further creations. For just as God is the pattern of the image, to which the title of shadow has just been given, even so the image becomes the pattern of other beings, as was made clear at the very outset of the law-giving, by the saying, 'And God made the man after the image of God' (Gen. 1:27), implying that the man was made after the image when it had acquired the force of a pattern").

the concentrated Power of God, who is the essence of his Wisdom, already contained within himself the energy and the substance of all existence, as the sprout contains the whole plant.[31] How Paul thought this out in detail is not known. But this identification, which appears to us so strange, of the Son of God with the Logos, and of the Logos with the cosmos, has a striking parallel in certain speculations of Philo, who in several passages designates the Logos-Cosmos as the Son of God.[32]

That Paul's Christology is bonded into the framework of the Logos idea is finally clear from the fact that he here ventures the statement: "All things were created in respect to him." In this statement he seems to contradict plain monotheism so strongly that attempts have been made to deny that he wrote the passage, or even the whole section in which it occurs, or indeed, the entire Epistle to the Colossians. And, in fact, there is here apparently a violent contradiction of the 'Almighty-formula' of Rom. 11:36, where it is not only stated that 'from God and through God,' but also, 'to God, are all things.' It is characteristic of the vivacity of Paul's thought that he seems here to have forgotten I Cor. 8:6, which however proves that the phrase 'through him' really refers to Christ. But these dogmatic statements are with him of such a vacillating weakness that they seem almost unbearable. In a still stronger degree the passages in Colossians conflict with I Cor. 15:28, according to which the end of the story is reached when God shall be 'all in all.' But it is right here that the difference in the method of thought is made clear. I Cor. 15:28 is conceived eschatologically, and in this sense Paul would never have said of Christ, but only of God, 'Through him all things are created.' In Col. 1:17, on the other hand, the 'through him'

[31] Hippolytus says, *Philos.* vii. 26: "The seed of the world contained everything in itself, as the mustard seed holds everything gathered together in the smallest place. Philo, *De Plant.* § 2: *φυτὸν δὲ αὖ περιέχον ἐν ἑαυτῷ τὰ ἐν μέρει φυτὰ ἅμα παμμυρία καθάπερ κληματίδας ἐκ μιᾶς ἀναβλαστάνοντα ῥίζης ὅδε ὁ κόσμος* ("It is the world that is a plant containing in itself the particular plants, all at once in their myriads, like shoots springing from a single root").

[32] *De Ebriet.* § 30: *τὸν γοῦν τόδε τὸ πᾶν ἐργασάμενον δημιουργὸν ὁμοῦ καὶ πατέρα εἶναι τοῦ γεγονότος εὐθὺς ἐν δίκῃ φήσομεν, μητέρα δὲ τὴν τοῦ πεποιηκότος ἐπιστήμην, ᾗ συνὼν ὁ θεὸς οὐχ ὡς ἄνθρωπος ἔσπειρε γένεσιν. ἡ δὲ παραδεξαμένη τὰ τοῦ Θεοῦ σπέρματα τελεσφόροις ὠδῖσι τὸν μόνον καὶ ἀγαπητὸν αἰσθητὸν υἱὸν ἀπεκύησε, τόνδε τὸν κόσμον* ("[For instance, we should rightly say] that the architect who made this universe was at the same time the father of what was thus born, while its mother was the knowledge possessed by its maker. With this knowledge God had union, not as men have it, and begat created being. And knowledge, having received the divine seed, when her travail was ended, bore the only beloved son who is perceptible to the senses, the world which we see"). Cf. also *De Monarch.* § 41; *De Sacerdot.* § 96; Plut., *Is. et Osir.* 54; Reitzenstein, *Poimandres,* pp. 39ff.

is acceptable, since it is not thought out eschatologically but logically; i.e. the Logos-concept is fundamental, and it was his intention to say: "The whole creation exists to realize the creative thoughts of God, which are concentrated in the Logos; the Logos unfolds himself in the creation, so that accordingly it was created 'unto him.'

Whether Paul was now thinking more of the Stoic Logos, or of the more Jewish hypostases of Wisdom, or of the Word, or of the Spirit, it is certainly a fundamental condition of his speculation that Christ, in some way, is identical with the 'Spirit of God.' Although the passage in which this identification is expressly stated (II Cor. 3:17) may be more or less an exegetically opportunistic argument,[33] the thought is very often presupposed by Paul, especially where he exchanges, at will, the mystical formulae 'in Christ' and 'in the Spirit,' 'Christ in us' and 'the Spirit in us' (Rom. 8:9f). This would not be possible if Christ had not been conceived of as a fluctuating power, almost as a penetrating divine fluid entering into men. We have seen earlier that this really is the case, and how this mode of representation was made possible for Paul by his particular spiritual environment. But this view is always held in check by another: Christ is not merely a Power, not merely the divine Pneuma, whose waves of energy flow through the universe, but he is also, and above all, the definite personality in all three phases of his existence, as the exalted one, as the earthly one, and as the pre-existent one. And in this complex fact lies hidden a series of questions for the Pauline speculative gnosis, to which he gives some important answers.

(c) *The Heavenly 'Man.'* If Christ is the Son of God, after his exaltation, superior to all spiritual forces, all angels, principalities, and powers (Phil. 2:11f; Col. 1:16; 2:10; Eph. 1:10,21), but even before his appearance upon earth standing closer to God than other beings, and honored before them, because he participates in their creation—to what category of being then does he belong? Is he God, is he an angel, is he man?

We have seen earlier (p. 472) that Paul either purposely or instinctively withholds from him the name 'God,' although his religious attitude toward him is that of a man to his God, although in Gentile-Christian circles there must have always been a tendency to look upon him as a 'second God,' although he had even received the Old Testament personal name of God 'Kyrios,' ceded to him by God (Phil. 2:10f). But it would have been impossible for Paul to trans-

[33] According to *Ber. rabba,* 2, R. Simeon said, "The Spirit of the Messiah was the Spirit who hovered over the waters."

fer the name 'God' (ὁ θεός) to Christ, since it is the prerogative of the one, the Father.

But neither does he reckon him among the angels; in the Epistle to the Colossians he has an eager desire to lift him above the realm of angels, nor is there even an enrollment as *primus inter pares,* for not even that would be a position worthy of him, and the expression 'head' (2:10) means more than the first among many.

So much the more striking does it seem, then, that Paul places him in the only remaining category of 'man,' and in doing this, of course, speaks not only of the earthly Jesus but also of the Pre-existent One. This theory, of course, has been bitterly attacked. Reference is made to Phil. 2:6ff, where apparently it is undoubtedly said that he took upon himself the 'form of a man' when he appeared on earth, and that previously he had been 'in the form of God.' How can it be asserted that he was previously in a certain sense 'man?' In order to ward off this objection—in Phil. 2:6ff, 'man' is naturally taken in its usual sense: a man of flesh and blood, a man even as we are men. But Paul's method of thought, his 'realism of general concepts,' provides him an alternative use of language. Just as the word 'body' (σῶμα) designates not only the earthly body but is also a universal concept under which heavenly, pneumatic 'bodies' are classified, such as those of the risen and glorified, the angels, the stars, so likewise the concept 'man' contains several possibilities; heavenly 'men' are possible, in addition to earthly. And Christ was, as pre-existent, a heavenly or rather *the* heavenly Man. Paul makes him identical with the heavenly 'Son of Man' of the Books of Daniel and Enoch. This assertion also is vigorously denied: Paul, it is said, was entirely unacquainted with the concept of the Son of Man, with which the Gospel tradition was concerned. But this assertion cannot be proved; indeed, it is false. It cannot be proved: for it is perfectly evident that Paul could not simply transcribe the words, 'the Son of Man' (ὁ υἱὸς τοῦ ἀνθρώπου), by a slavish adherence to a Semitic expression (בראדם or ברנשא)—to Greek ears the phrase was barbarous; he could only Hellenize it, as 'the Man' (ὁ ἄνθρωπος). In this form we find it emphatically used (Rom. 5:15; I Cor. 15:21). But that Paul knows of the transference of the concept of 'the Son of Man' to Christ is fully proven by I Cor. 15:27f. Again, he would not have referred the words taken from Psalm 8:7, "He hath put all things under his feet," to Christ (instead of to men) if he had not already found a reference to him in Psalm 8:5, "What is man that thou art mindful of him, and the Son of Man that thou visitest him," as is clearly assumed in Heb. 2:6ff. He therefore knew that the title 'Son of Man' was given to Christ, and also, along with this, the teaching that the heavenly 'Son of Man' prophesied in the Books of Daniel and Enoch, and in other Apocalypses, was none other than Christ. Whether or not he knew the Book of Enoch, in any case it serves as an explanation of Pauline Christology, in that we read there how the Seer Enoch, in the gray dawn of time, saw the Son of Man in heaven and thus described him (46:1ff)—

> And there I saw One, who had a head of days,
> And His head was white like wool,
> And with Him was another being whose countenance had the appearance of a man,
> And his face was full of graciousness, like one of the holy angels.
> And I asked the angel . . . . concerning that Son of Man, who he was, and whence he was, (and) why he went with the Head of Days? And he answered and said unto me:
> This is the 'Son of Man' who hath righteousness,
> With whom dwelleth righteousness,
> And who revealeth all the treasures of that which is hidden,
> Because the Lord of Spirits hath chosen him,
> And his lot hath the pre-eminence before the Lord of Spirits in uprightness for ever.

It is very significant that the Apocalyptist, although he describes him as being like a man, also pictures him like the angels, as if he did not know in which category of being he belongs.[34] This Son of Man is then placed upon the throne of glory (61:8; 62:2,5; 69:27) and assumes the functions of the Messiah. Paul also has a similar view of the pre-existent state of Christ. This is recognizable from the strange section, I Cor. 15:45ff. Here Paul differentiates the first man, Adam, and the second man, Christ, whom he also calls the 'last Adam.' In this there is really nothing different from the somewhat pointedly expressed form of the contradiction Adam-Christ, which we also find in Rom. 5:12-20; I Cor. 15:22. When we read, "The second man (comes, or has his origin) from heaven," this could either be referred to the Parousia or simply indicate in a general way the coming of Christ from heaven. It does not yet mean that Christ, in the pre-existent state, was the 'heavenly Man.' But this is doubt-

[34] The enigmatical 'form of a man' in Daniel and Enoch, Bousset (*Rel. d. Judentums*, pp. 405ff), Gressmann, and Reitzenstein have traced to a very ancient, half-forgotten myth of primitive man. [But contrast Montgomery, *Commentary on Daniel*.]

less implicit in the Scripture-proof (vs. 45). Paul wishes to prove from Gen. 2:7 that there are two kinds of bodies, earthly and heavenly, fleshly (psychic) and pneumatic. But how can the passage prove this? The text simply states, "And the man became a living soul." Paul here goes beyond the meaning of the text, in that he says: 'The first man, Adam,' or as a recent happy emendation will have it, 'The man, the first Adam, became a living soul.' We observe here simply the method of the Targums; in the act of translation from the original Hebrew text into the vulgar tongue (Aramaic or Greek), a number of explanatory words were added to the text as if they belonged to the whole sacred original. One supposes that these expansions took place in a wholly bona fide manner, in order to reproduce the meaning of the Scripture words (p. 438). But Paul goes still further when he adds the second statement: "The last Adam (became) a life-creating Spirit." There is wholly lacking here any textual foundation; and yet, for Paul, these words are a part of Scripture; for only by means of this second part does the Scripture prove what it should prove, that there are also 'pneumatic' beings (bodies). But how does Paul discover that the creation or becoming of the 'last' or 'second' Adam is proved by Scripture, since only the creation of the first is actually narrated there? We can understand this from a similar sequence of thought in Philo of Alexandria. He conceives the two narratives of the creation of man, not as two parallel accounts of the same occurrence, but as two different acts of creation. As God had first created the idea of the world, the *cosmos noëtos* as an image or model, and afterwards this world, fashioned according to it and perceptible to the senses, so also man was made first 'in the image of God' and then, afterwards, one was created who was perceptible to the senses. The former was the 'idea' of man, the latter the real individual man.[35] While the Platonic doctrine of ideas suffices here for Philo, and the concept of man 'after the image' hardly passes beyond an impersonal idea, in another passage he speaks exactly of a heavenly and of an earthly man as if not only the latter but also the former really possessed actual existence; it really seems that Philo knew of a myth or a doctrine of a heavenly primitive

[35] *Op. Mundi* § 134: ". . . . a vast difference exists between the man thus 'formed' (Gen. 2:7) and the man (Gen. 1:27) who came into existence earlier 'after the image of God.' For the man so 'formed' is an object of sense-perception (αἰσθητός), partaking already of such or such quality, consisting of body and soul, man or woman, by nature mortal. He that was 'after the image' was an idea or type or seal [an emblem or symbolic sign], and object of thought [only], incorporeal, neither male nor female, and by nature incorruptible.

man.[36] However the tradition which he here follows was formulated, or wherever he may have learned it, he handles this conception of the Heavenly Man as something which has really been given, in no way as something new or unheard-of. In the same way this thought appears in Paul as undoubted and unquestionable. It is not, therefore, too bold to assume that this same tradition was known to both. Of course Paul gives a turn to the thought which is lacking in Philo, viz. in the eschatological direction; that is to say, according to his teaching the Heavenly Man, who was first created (Col. 1:15), will appear first at the end of time, as the last, the second Adam. This combination of the thought of the Heavenly Man with the Messiah-idea, which cannot be traced in Philo, depended upon the fact that Paul conceived of the Messiah as at the same time the 'Son of Man' of the Books of Daniel and Enoch.

(d) *The Incarnation.* After what has been said above (pp. 485f), we cannot be surprised when Paul goes on to assert the 'Incarnation' of the 'Heavenly Man.' Strictly speaking, of course, this expression is lacking in Paul, as is also the Johannine 'becoming flesh' (*incarnatio* John 1:14). In the only passage in which the former could appear (Phil. 2:7), it does not really say, "He became man," but an expression is used which is difficult for us to translate, but which somehow means, "He came in a form which was like that of men," or, "He appeared as man and was found, in bearing, as a man."[37] What does

[36] *Leg. Alleg.* i. 31: There are two types of men; the one is the heavenly man, the other the earthly. The heavenly man, having been made 'after the image of God,' is altogether without part or lot in corruptible and terrestrial existence; but the earthly one was compounded out of the matter scattered here and there which Moses calls 'dust' (χοῦν). For this reason he says that the heavenly man was not 'formed,' but was stamped with the picture (image) of God; while the earthly is a 'moulded' product (πλάσμα) of the artificer, but not his offspring.

[37] Cf. SNT, *ad loc.*: 'Was made like men.' The expression ἐν ὁμοιώματι ἀνθρώπων, 'in the like form of men,' has had to suffer many explanations. A ὁμοίωμα is a likeness, hence a picture. However, we may now judge the portrait according to circumstances; we can emphasize the fact that it is very like, almost an equivalent of the personality, or that it is very like but even so only a picture, in fact, entirely different from the original—so one could by ὁμοίωμα here and also in Rom. 8:3, indicate either the *complete* likeness, as in the translation, "He was made like men," or *only* a likeness, whereby it results that in truth he was no man, but only very like a man. Even so, the second half of the sentence receives meanwhile another emphasis according as it is translated, "He was found in bearing [form, appearance] as a man," i.e. a closer examination shows that he was really a man; or: "He was found as a man," i.e. he was, in his essential being, so like men that one must really believe that he was a man. According to the conception one either finds here the full (earthly) humanity of Christ indicated, or his appearance after the manner of men, by which the reservation is made that in the essence of his being he was not man at all but something more. That this is the real meaning seems to follow from the fact that

Eschatological thrust of the "heavenly man."

this paraphrase, this almost evasive expression, actually mean? It tends to emphasize or to explain what previously has been described by the words, "He renounced the 'form of God,' and took on the 'form of a slave.'" The expression 'form' (μορφή) plainly enough refers to the outer form of the existence or appearance, and it is thus plainly stated that the subject of this metamorphosis (μεταμόρφωσις) still remains the same. Accordingly, those expressions mean: "He appeared in the form of men and was found in fashion and bearing like a man," that he, of course outwardly, manifested himself as a man; but it is of course assumed that he remains, in the depths of his being, what he was previously, and that he carried with him the heavenly pre-existent 'divine form.' This metamorphosis from heavenly to earthly being corresponds exactly to the later passage in Phil. 3:21, where he exchanges once more the body of our humiliation for the body of glory. It cannot be denied that, for Paul, the human body which Christ possessed upon earth means something like a disguise, appropriate to a rôle which he played here; he avoids, even purposely, the more direct and more powerful expression, 'he became man,' because he still does not dare to express the complete humanity of Christ. The reason for this is to be perceived still more plainly in Rom. 8:3. Here the context would really have demanded that Paul should say, "God has sent his Son in the flesh of sin"; but he avoids this by saying, 'in the likeness of sinful flesh' (ἐν ὁμοιώματι σαρκὸς ἁμαρτίας). He does not wish to state that Christ had borne flesh which, like our own, was ruled by sin. It would seem to him like blasphemy. Therefore he uses—we cannot put it differently—an expression of double meaning. The reason for this avoidance lies in the fact that he finds himself under the pressure of an antinomy. On the one hand, namely, the idea expressed in Rom.

ὁμοίωμα, in the literary usage of the Greek Bible, indicates the form in which someone divine, a god or an angel, appears upon earth. Thus it is stated in Ezek. 8:2f, "I beheld, and lo, a likeness as the appearance of a man or the form of a man (*ὁμοίωμα ἀνδρός*). . . . And he put forth the form of a hand (*ὁμοίωμα χειρός*). . . ." Here the Seer is conscious that he did not see the real hand of a real man, but that a heavenly being appeared to him in the form of a man. So it is also stated in Rev. 9:7, "And the appearance (*ὁμοιώματα*) of the locusts was like (*ὅμοιοι*) horses, armed for battle"; i.e. they appeared in the form of horses. Nothing else is meant when it is stated in Dan. 10:16, "And behold, something like a 'Son of man' (Theod.) or something like a hand of man touched my lips" (*ὡς ὁμοίωσις χειρὸς ἀνθρώπου* or *υἱοῦ ἀνθρώπου*); similarly, 10:18. The author means that it was a higher being, an angel in human form. Also, the 'Son of man,' 7:13, is thus described: "One like a son of man" (*ὡς υἱὸς ἀνθρώπου*)—in order to indicate that it only looked like a man. Finally, in Rev. 1:13, the appearance of Christ is described with the expression, 'like a son of man,' in the sense that he assumed human form in order to appear to John.

8:3f implies that sin in the flesh has been put to death by Christ's death on the Cross, and further that sin has dwelt even in the flesh of Christ, for otherwise it could not have received its death-blow at the Cross. But on the other hand it is incomprehensible, for Paul, that he who had had no experience of sin (II Cor. 5:18) should have entered into such a close relationship with sin. He seeks to evade this difficulty—of course, without any convincing result—through the choice of that mediating expression. He permitted himself, in thinking of the Incarnation, to waver more or less in the balance between an actual humanity and a merely external assumption of a human body, as a result of which the inner being of the personality of Christ remains untouched by actual earthly humanity and sinfulness.[38] In this Paul grazes the later heresy of 'Docetism.' The conflict in which we here find Paul involved is in the highest degree significant for his religious outlook. As in so many similar cases, he stands under the compulsion of very different traditions. Through his inherited Judaism, he is dominated by the apocalyptic picture of the heavenly Messiah; on the other hand, the tradition of the primitive community offers him the earthly Jesus. Now it was necessary to harmonize both representations—a fundamentally impossible task. For, according to the Jewish view, the nature of the heavenly spiritual world and that of the world of men of flesh and blood were sharply distinguished;[39] a union of the two is simply unthinkable. One recalls that Paul himself says, "Flesh and blood cannot inherit the Kingdom of God"; it must first be transfigured in heavenly glory. Accordingly, it is even more incomprehensible that a heavenly, spiritual being, who of all beings is closest to God, should assume flesh and blood. The conception is possible only as a result of a compromise, which we plainly perceive in the passages which have been considered.

How Paul conceived the Incarnation of the Pre-existent One in

[38] As Paul distinguishes in men the 'outer' and the 'inner' man (II Cor. 4:16), so he assumes that the inner man, by reason of his sympathy with the Law of God (Rom. 7:22), really has no share in sin; and so also he will have made the distinction in the case of Christ, though these expressions do not actually occur. A reference to this lies in the difficult antithesis 'according to the flesh'—'according to the spirit of holiness' (Rom. 1:3f). The inner being of Christ accordingly is and remains, through the earthly period, fully permeated by the divine Holy Spirit.

[39] One can realize this manner of feeling in the fact that Enoch (ch. 15) blames the fallen angels because they left the high, holy heaven, and that, although they were eternal living spirits (πνεύματα), they mingled with men. Naturally, this occurrence is comparable only to a certain degree; but the antithesis between the heavenly, spiritual beings and the perishable, tainted human nature, appears here very plainly.

relation to his human birth, is still less clear. Strictly taken, the two are mutually exclusive. The Son of Man, living in heaven since primitive ages, can really descend to earth only as a complete personality; that he must nevertheless pass through birth from a woman (Gal. 4:4) can scarcely be harmonized with this. For in birth a new being comes into existence, which previously was not existent; even if we should call to our aid the idea of the pre-existence of the soul, that is still something quite different from the pre-existence of the heavenly Messiah.[40] Here it appears once more that the tradition concerning the life of Jesus, the Son of David, cannot be truly harmonized wth the teaching concerning the pre-existent Son of God.

(e) *Christ's Death and Resurrection.* That the death of Christ first hovers in the mind of Paul as a concrete, once-and-for-all, historical fact,[41] is seen from the often used expressions, 'crucified,' 'the Cross of Christ'—therein lies a recollection of the Roman death-penalty. In this connection there is no deviation; not once is there mentioned any other cause of death. At most, one might recognize some slight uncertainty in the fact that in I Thess. 2:15 the Jews, instead of the Romans, are designated as the murderers of Jesus. But both these views lie elsewhere side by side, and that the Jews were the moral instigators of the death of Christ is primitive tradition. More definite circumstances are not referred to by Paul, except the delivering-up or betrayal 'in the night' (I Cor. 11:23); there is occasional mention of the 'sufferings' (II Cor. 1:5; Phil. 3:10) or the 'woes' (Col. 1:24) of Christ, and the 'picturing of the crucified before the eyes' (Gal. 3:1) could refer very well to a life-like depiction of the crucifixion and its torture. In any case it is psychologically very improbable that Paul would have been satisfied with the knowledge of the bare fact of the crucifixion, without attempting to picture it to himself more closely and more sympathetically. For the death on the Cross had, for him, no mere factual value, but a highly personal one; it was an expression of personality of the first rank, so that he would not only have represented it to himself with the deepest feeling but would also have spoken of it with personal sympathy—however little we should dare attribute to

[40] *Wisdom of Solomon* 8:19ff, "I was a youth of good intention, and a good soul was given to me; rather, because I was good, I have entered into an untainted body."

[41] Once for all opposed to the fantastic notions of those who would make the death of Christ a particular instance of the story of the vegetation-gods who die and come to life again every year. Were there nothing else, it would appear strange that not only the Resurrection but also the death of Christ should be placed in the spring of the year. In the earliest period, we find no indication whatever of a yearly celebration of the death of Christ; rather, it seems that the Lord's Supper was celebrated weekly.

him a blood-and-wound theology and a sentimental 'lyric' of the Cross.

But the modern radical Myth-Hypothesis is, in this respect, entirely right: the death of Christ is for Paul by no means only a 'historical,' human, earthly occurrence. The gnosis of Paul places it in the center of cosmic happenings, indeed considers it as in itself a cosmic event. In order to understand this we must, of course, go back once more to the 'Incarnation.' First, we have not yet explained the enigmatical expression, 'he did not consider it robbery to be equal with God.' Moreover, the negative statement, as such, demands an explanation. Why does not Paul at once say, positively: "He humbled himself and took on the form of a servant?" The negative introduction is understandable only if that which it denies were also possible, if it had lain, so to speak, in the way of Jesus to snatch to himself the 'God-likeness as an act of robbery.' The presupposition is, of course, that he possessed the form of God, but not, or not yet, the like rank with God; following Enoch 61:8, we may say that at that time he had not yet sat upon the throne of glory, although by virtue of his divinity and likeness to God he had a claim upon it. How far then would it have been possible for him to grasp for himself this dominion? Possibly analogous cases streak before the mind of Paul, e.g. that of Adam. He was created after the image of God; that is to say he was, like the angels of God, clothed in glory; but when the devil led him astray and tempted him to become like God, by eating of the fruit, then was he robbed of his glory (cf. *The Life of Adam and Eve,* ch. 20). On the contrary, Christ not only had not aspired to God-likeness, but had even freely yielded up his divine form (his 'glory') and had taken upon himself the form of a human servant—in this, as in every other respect, a contrast to the first Adam.[42] Whether, now, it is this reference or

[42] Other possibilities: according to the *Life of Adam and Eve,* Satan is robbed of his budding glory because he would not worship Adam but 'would exalt his place above the stars and be equal to the Most High' (ch. 15); cf. also Isa. 14:12-15 and Phil. 2:6. Again, according to the suppositions of others (M. Dibelius, *Die Geisterwelt im Glauben des Paulus,* pp. 105f), Paul had in mind another myth which is handed down in the *Ascension of Isaiah,* ch. 10: here the descent of Christ through the heavens is described: when he comes into the firmament, where the prince of this world dwells, it says: "They did not praise him because of this, but they fought each other out of envy, for there the power of evil prevails, and envy concerning the least of things. And I saw as he descended, and he became like the angels of the air, and he was as one of them. And he gave no pass-word, for one robbed and overcame the other." According to Dibelius' conjecture, Paul 'sets the prince of the future aeons over against the spirit-powers of this age, fighting and robbing one another; what they could not gain by robbery he gains by humble obedience.'

some other that is presupposed, the pathos of the statement lies in the fact that Christ willingly, out of his love to Christians, became poor (II Cor. 8:9), had renounced himself. This self-emptying (*kenosis*) accordingly consisted in this, that he laid aside the 'body of glory' (Phil. 3:21), the 'divine form' (Phil 2:6); and this means, positively, that he had assumed, upon his descent into the earthly world, its prevalent body-form (flesh and blood).[43] Paul calls this the 'form of a servant,' because he, though born Lord of all things, became like men, the slave of the 'elements of the world.' This, plainly, is the tacit presupposition of such passages as Col. 2:20, "With Christ, we have died to the elements of the world"—only because Christ himself was subject to them was it possible for him to die to them, and with him the Christians; and Gal. 4:3ff, i.e. men who were enslaved under the elements of the world he could ransom only because he himself, 'born of a woman and placed under the law,' had entered into the sphere of these world-elements and under their rule.[44] All this is merely indicated; doubtless other such

[43] This 'change' is described in detail in the *Ascension of Isaiah,* ch. 10, how in his descent from one lower heaven to another, he occasionally assumes the form (*μορφή? σῶμα?*) of one of the angels living there, so that 'his appearance is like their own.'

[44] The assumption made here, that servitude under the Law is at the same time a servitude to daemonic world-elements, seems strange to us. Paul evidently thinks that the Law was thus the medium by which the spirit-world was bound and chained to the cosmos. Through the Law death really came to men (I Cor. 15:56; cf. Rom. 6:14; 7:13). Servitude to the world-elements (that these daemons are spiritual powers seems clear from such passages as Gal. 4:8ff; Col. 2:20) accordingly extends equally over the Jews and the Gentiles, over the whole of humanity. We read in *Poimandres* (Reitzenstein, p. 331) of a myth which shows how man came into this servitude, and how it happened that he only belonged to half of this world: but the All-father, the highest reason (Νοῦς), who is light and life (cf. the Gospel of John) bore (primitive) man, who was like him; he loved him as his own child; for he was especially beautiful, since indeed he bore the image of his father; for, rightly, God loved his own form (*τῆς ἰδίας μορφῆς*). Now he has entrusted to him (*παρέδωκε*; cf. Matt. 28:18; 11:27?) all his works. . . . and since he possessed, in himself, all power over the world, he broke through the 'circle of the spheres' (*διὰ τῆς ἁρμονίας*) and bowed himself downward (*παρέκυψεν*) hither, and revealed to nature below (earth and water) the beautiful form of God. But when she saw how eternally and wonderfully beautiful he was, and how he had in himself all the power of the world, and the form of God, then she smiled in an eager desire, for she had indeed seen this picture of the splendid form of the 'primitive man' in the water, and her own shadow upon the earth. And when he saw a form like unto his own, reflected in the water, he loved her and wished to dwell there. But nature took him, who was yearning for her, completely into her embrace and they became one, in love. And therefore man is above every other kind of life on the earth, disunited, divided, mortal as to the body, immortal as to the essential man (*διὰ τὸν οὐσιώδη ἄνθρωπον*). Immortal he was, and had power over all things—now he suffers the fate of the mortal, because he is subject to destiny (*τῇ εἱμαρμένῃ*); he was exalted above the circle of the spheres (*τῆς ἁρμονίας*)—now he is exiled in the circle, a slave. . . .

cosmic-mythical speculations lie in the background. For the purpose of redemption it was essential that the Son of God should be able to overcome this thraldom of the cosmos, and free himself from it. In order to show how this took place, let us select a few further references.

In the last analysis, according to I Cor. 2:8, it is not really men who have crucified the 'Lord of glory,' but the 'rulers of this world.' It will be readily acknowledged, today, that by this Caiaphas and Pilate are not meant, but super-earthly spirits and angelic powers. That Satan was guilty of the death of Jesus is indicated even in the later evangelic tradition (Luke 22:3; John 13:2,27); but here, clearly, a more fully developed mythos is assumed; this is suggested by the feature, that they would not have crucified the Lord of glory if they had recognized the Wisdom of God, that is to say if they had been admitted into his counsel.[45] This makes sense only if the counsel of God pointed to the destruction of these very rulers of the world, and if they, unknowingly, had furthered it by the crucifixion. More than this we cannot say. Somewhat more light is to be found in Col. 2:14f; according to this passage a double act is bound up with the crucifixion and the closely related resurrection and exaltation. First, there is the nailing of the Law to the cross, i.e. the complete removal, nullification, and abrogation of the Law; and secondly, it is stated that God has robbed the principalities and powers of their might, and has openly put them to shame, in that he carries them away in triumph in (or with) Christ. In these few words is presented the idea of a battle between God and the spiritual powers, in which they are woefully defeated. God has snatched away from them their seemingly certain booty and has led Christ, thus saved from death, to heaven; and along with him, the principalities and powers, now robbed of their authority, are so to speak chained to his triumphant chariot. How this happens, Paul does not state in detail; he merely points out the fact. But it appears that he somehow has in mind a defeated effort of the spiritual powers. They thought themselves victorious, whereas in fact they had been annihilated. They believed they had killed the divine and immortal one; in truth, their empire and their might were destroyed. Christ

[45] Thus it does not appear there that the ruler of the world had not recognized the Lord of Glory as such, as Dibelius deduces from *Asc. Isa.* 11:16. Nevertheless this writing offers the parallel that 'the god of that world [Satan] will stretch forth his hand against the Son of God, and they will take him and crucify him without knowing who he is.'

seemed to have been put to death; in truth, it is sin in the flesh which has been put to death (Rom. 8:3f); the flesh, through which sin rules, is crucified, but the Son of God is snatched from death and from the rule of the cosmic powers. They stand humiliated before him, they have, indeed, altogether lost their game; their seeming victory was the beginning of their total destruction, which Christ, after his exaltation, will complete (I Cor. 15:24-28). Thus we may attempt more or less to reconstruct this mythological drama which Luther, with sure instinct, has described:—

> Es war ein wunderlicher Krieg,
> Da Tod und Leben rungen;
> Das Leben es behielt den Sieg,
> Es hat den Tod verschlungen.
> Die Schrift hat verkündet das,
> Wie ein Tod den andern frass,
> Ein Spott aus dem Tod ist worden.[46]

Thus the death and resurrection of Christ mean not only an experience of Christ, but are the beginning of the end of the world, the destruction of the ruling powers which are controlling the present age, and the beginning of the 'new creation' (II Cor. 5:17). Christ, the first-fruits of those who had fallen asleep, has become the Beginning (ἀρχή) of a new world and of a new humanity, since he has received again the divine form, the body of glory (Phil. 3:21) which always belonged to him, and the fulness of the divine being again dwells in him and he becomes the first in rank among all beings (Col. 1:18f). Now all beings shall bow before him and all shall acknowledge him as Lord (Phil. 2:10f).

Once again we perceive how, in the Pauline gnosis, an earthly, historical event is combined in thought with a super-earthly, super-historical, mythical world-drama. That the two outlooks do not fully harmonize with one another is clear. The historical Jesus is fitted into a system of ideas which did not have him in view.

[46] The same idea appears in an Easter-sequence from the 12th or 13th century, *Mors et vita duello conflixere mirando; dux vitae mortuus regnat vivos* ("Life and death were engaged in a wonderful duel; the prince of life, being dead, rules the living"). Cf. Luther's *Greater Catechism:* 'so that, risen again, he swallowed up and devoured death.' From an Easter sermon of 1526: "The devil devoured Christ, but the bits stick in his throat and choke him to death" (Brunswick edition of Luther's *Works*, vol. viii, pp. 46f). The stanza quoted above has been used already: see page 101 above, where it is translated.

CHAPTER XVI

The New Relationship to God

MOST of the statements of Paul concerning God are those of one who has been converted, of one who at a definite moment in his life received a revelation from him (Gal. 1:17), and because of this has now entered into a new, into his present true relationship to him. He likewise speaks to converts, to those who at a fixed moment came to know God (Gal. 4:8), and, after casting off their former manner of life, turned to him (I Thess. 1:9). Indeed, he even speaks of God as if the recent events formed an epoch in the life of God himself. God made the decision to save the world through the foolishness of the Cross (I Cor. 1:21), and 'when the time was fulfilled' sent his Son (Gal. 4:4), and revealed his righteousness in an entirely new manner (Rom. 3:21). He is not the unchanging father of the universe releasing his powers by immutable laws from within his celestial retreat, he is rather the conductor of the world drama, who has drastically intervened with this last act of his. And now, since he has revealed himself in an entirely new aspect, he has opened up an entirely new way of Salvation, so that what men now experience through him and toward him is something wholly new, which former generations could neither anticipate nor learn. It is not the universal religion of humanity, which they all might have known 'from nature'—in spite of Rom. 1:19ff—for true knowledge of God and true salvation have been withheld from men by tyrannical powers hostile to God. They had to be released from blindness and servitude in order to know their relationship to God. Even the devout Israelite could not find the way to peace with God, for the Law shut him off from it, held him fast in enmity to God, and removed salvation far from him.

Here we observe the most profound difference between the religious thinking of Paul and that of Jesus. The essential thing in the religion of Jesus is indeed just the naturalness and certainty with which he rests in the consciousness of his kinship to God. God's love and grace are given, as of old, to humanity, as freely as the rain and sunshine. Man need only see and use this ever-present salvation. It is not necessary first to become a child of God through a complicated process of redemption. One is already that whenever he so desires to be. The Law, for Paul, is a wall, erected between God and the soul; for Jesus it is the bridge over which one enters the Kingdom of Heaven. Not Jesus, but Paul, was a 'seeker after God.' Jesus was a friend of God, a son of God 'by nature.' One must keep strictly in view this difference in natures and development. One must not read Paul's ideas of God into those of Jesus. Only when one has first known both in their differing peculiarities can he find that which is common to both.

1. *Reconciliation.* The most common and comprehensive expression for the event which Paul had experienced, and which all Christians must experience, is undoubtedly 'reconciliation'; "God reconciled the world to himself"; "We beg you, for Christ's sake, be reconciled with God"; "We have received the atonement"; "the ministry, the word of reconciliation" (II Cor. 5:18ff; Rom. 5:11). The Greek word (καταλλάσσειν, καταλλαγή) indicates that there takes place between two parties a trade, an exchange, or agreement which has an effect upon both, and not just upon one.[1] The religious concept presupposes a separation, a division which is felt by both; it describes the bringing together, reuniting, peace, between those who have been estranged by objective enmity. But the separation may have various causes, a subjective enmity of one party against the other, or of both against each other. Where God and man oppose each other one may conceive of a sinful enmity of men towards God (this seems to be the case in Rom. 5:10; cf. 5:8; certainly in Rom. 8:7); but there can also be the anger or repugnance of God toward the sinners, whom he cannot bear in his presence, and this may stand in the foreground, so that one may speak of a reconciliation of God as well as of a reconciliation of men.[2] But the emphasis of the word does not lie especially upon the subjective procedure by which the mind of one party is changed, but rather upon the restoration of the disturbed intercourse. Here it is obvious that men yield their wills to God's will, and that God, instead of retaining his anger and portioning out punishment, permits love and grace to rule. But the expression 'reconciliation' gives

[1] That καταλλάσσειν could mean 'to turn around,' cannot be proved. καταλλάκτης means the 'money-changer,' καταλλαγή is the trading, the exchanging in which both parties give and receive something. It means just the act of changing. καταλλαγὰς ποιεῖσθαι πρός τινας means to 'make a comparison with someone.'

[2] In II Macc. mention is frequently made of the reconciliation of God, e.g. of a change from anger to favor, 5:20 (ὀργή—καταλλαγή); cf. 7:33, "And if for rebuke and chastening our living Lord hath been angered a little while, yet shall he again be reconciled with his own servants"; cf. 8:29; 1:5.

no heed at all to these inner occurrences, and so it is possible for Paul to speak (Rom. 5:11) of a 'receiving of the reconciliation,' as if this were something objective like a gift, and also (II Cor. 5:18ff) of a 'reconciliation of the world to God,' although it is not a change of feeling in men that is here emphasized but rather God's non-reckoning of sin.[3] The exhortation, 'let yourselves be reconciled,' has also, here, the meaning that men should be willing to accept God's forgiveness. One perceives therefore that 'reconciliation' or 'atonement' is the comprehensive expression for the whole work of salvation. Further it becomes very plain how exclusively Paul grants the initiative to God. This is very characteristic of his religious thinking. Even though men have become children of God after being 'enemies of God,' (Rom. 5:8ff; 8:7) nevertheless this is God's work, not in any way the work of men.

2. *Justification.* The way in which the reconciliation is consummated is thus the 'non-imputation of sins,' or 'justification'; its result, peace with God, access to him, and the hope of salvation (Rom. 5:1f). Let us now consider in detail these ideas.

'Forgiveness' or 'remission of sins,' the expression which so frequently appears in the Gospels, is found in Paul only once in a secondary passage (Col. 1:14 = Eph. 1:7), and once in the quotation (Rom. 4:7 = Ps. 32:1). He uses instead such negative and positive expressions as 'not reckoning unto them their trespasses' or 'it was reckoned unto him for righteousness' sake' (4:7,6). We meet the former in the important passage II Cor. 5:19, the latter in the equally important Rom. 4:22ff. It is conceived in a genuinely Rabbinical manner, and belongs to the series of ideas clustered about the conception of a heavenly 'book-keeping' in which the doctrine of retribution, which dominates all Pharisaic thinking, finds its purest expression.[4] According to this, not only are all acts and words entered into a book by God, but also a 'reckoning' is carried out;[5] the good and evil deeds, the keeping of the commandments and their transgression, are looked upon as debits and credits. They are reckoned over against each other, and judgment is based on which side of the balance outweighs the other. According to Rabbinical teaching this determination takes place daily, but a final reckoning will follow at the end of life or—in eschatological ideology

[3] In the same way, in Matt. 5:23f, it is demanded of the brother who is not angry that he be reconciled with the other, e.g. resume the old relationship with him.

[4] Cf. Weber, *Jüdische Theologie*, § 60.

[5] השבון from חשב, i.e. Ps. 32:2; Gen. 15:6, to charge someone with a sin or to reckon something as righteousness; Greek λογίζεσθαι.

Lutheran emphasis on justification by faith comes through quite strongly

—at the judgment. He who has kept the commandments or whose good works outweigh his transgressions, will be counted as righteous (Hebrew צדיק, later Heb. זכאי), or his actions will be reckoned unto him as righteousness (לצדקה, לזכות, לזכו, εἰς δικαιοσύνην). This expression does not indeed indicate a description of the real facts of the case. It does not say what a man is in himself, but it states that he is considered, in the eyes of God and according to his judgment, right 'with God,' and God considers him worthy to receive reward or salvation. 'There is, then, no question that the concept of 'righteousness' (זכות) passes over into that of worthiness to receive a blessing; it indicates a claim for a reward as something that has been earned (*meritum*).'[6] But apparently God can also reckon in another way, different from that which one would expect according to strict justice. He can either not consider sins as such, or he can 'reckon as righteousness' something which is not in itself a fulfilment of the Law, e.g. the faith of Abraham (Gen. 15:6; Rom. 4:3; Gal. 3:6; Jas. 2:23). And this is the unheard-of thing, contradicting all Pharisaic assumptions, disrupting all theories of retribution, which Paul—on the ground of his own experience—proclaims, namely that God, in this final period of time, will not keep an account of the sins of humanity, is willing to consider them as non-existent. To emphasize the paradox even more strongly, Paul in one place definitely states (Rom. 4:5) that God 'declares the ungodly just,' that he not only proclaims him to be a righteous person, but wishes to deal with him as though he had fulfilled the commandments.[7] He expresses this in another manner in Rom. 3:24: "We are justified freely (δωρεάν)." One cannot emphasize this incredible thing too strongly. A judge who should judge 'according to truth' (κατὰ ἀλήθειαν Rom. 2:2) and with whom there should be no question of favor or 'gift,' presents to men a verdict of acquittal upon which they have no claim whatever. We cannot reiterate too strongly that Paul all the time feels this procedure of God, not as obvious, but as utterly unforeseen. One would think that once God had revealed himself in this manner it would be clear that, fundamentally, he could not act in any other way at all, since it corresponds to his innermost nature to grant pardon. But Paul, in spite of all his independent thinking, is still too much a Pharisee to cease to be astonished at this paradoxical manner of action on the part

[6] Weber, *Jüdische Theologie,* § 59:2.

[7] The Greek word δικαιοῦν corresponds, in this connection, to the Hebrew הצדיק (זכות). In this is included not only the public proclamation but also the actual treatment of the sinner as a righteous man.

here, and not surprisingly, for Lutheran thought is primarily Pauline.

of God, therefore he expresses the matter in such a way that the concepts employed cancel each other. For a declaration of the innocence of sinners, and a righteousness which is neither punishment nor reward but is given as a gift, is no righteousness, nor is it a true declaration of innocence (p. 428). When he, in spite of this, says that herein the righteousness of God is revealed or proclaimed (Rom. 1:17; 3:21,25f), it is possible only because the concept of the 'righteousness of God,' through Old Testament usage, has received a double meaning. So he can define the nature of judicial impartiality, which 'renders to everyone according to his deeds' (Rom. 2:5f), but he can also change over into the idea of pardoning grace.[8]

Under these circumstances it certainly would have been more to the purpose if Paul had chosen a new mode of expression for this wholly new idea, which no longer fits into the framework of the Pharisaic understanding of justification. But since, especially in the Epistle to the Romans, he bases his exposition upon Jewish thought, he still retains the Pharisaical concepts which are incompatible with the new meaning. Where he speaks very freely, without regard to Jewish modes of thought, he makes use of other forms of expression. Thus he explains in Rom. 3:26 that it is really very difficult to understand how God could still be called 'righteous,' if he actually declares one righteous who cannot produce anything else for himself than his faith in Jesus.[9] So he places side by side in Rom. 3:24 the mutually exclusive concepts 'to be justified,' 'without merit,' 'through his grace.' Thus he drops entirely the idea of justification in such important passages as Rom. 5:20f; 6:14f; 11:5f; Gal. 2:21; 5:4; I Cor. 15:10; II Cor. 6:1, by deriving salvation solely from the grace of God—recognizing clearly that grace would no longer be grace (Rom. 11:6; 4:4) if it were still, in any sense, recompense for the deeds of men. Therefore, the formula 'from faith,' e.g. 'to be justified on the ground of faith' (Rom. 3:30; 5:1; Gal. 2:16), no longer fits the case, for then it would appear as if God had seen in this faith a compelling necessity to declare sinners righteous. By means of the antithesis 'not on the ground of works'

[8] Cf. I John 1:9, "He is faithful and just to forgive us our sins." Ps. 51:16, "Deliver me from bloodguiltiness, O God, Thou God of my salvation; So shall my soul sing aloud of thy righteousness." Ps. 143:11,12, "For Thy name's sake, O Lord, quicken me; in Thy righteousness bring my soul out of trouble. And in thy mercy cut off mine enemies. . . . for I am thy servant." Cf. pp. 431f.

[9] I translate: so that he remain 'righteous,' even if he pronounces him 'righteous' who has (nothing else than) faith in Jesus.

but 'on the ground of faith,' support is constantly given to the idea that faith is, as it were, the one substitute satisfactory to God for the many works that are lacking. This would be completely contrary to Paul's innermost convictions, for with this there would again be postulated a sort of a reward of man, and a kind of pledge on the part of God (Rom. 4:4), and it is just this that should be eliminated once and for all. The Apostle's meaning is most plainly seen—aside from the 'gratuitous' gift (δωρεάν)—from Rom. 3:27, where he says:

> Where then is the glorying? It is excluded!

The 'glorying' (καύχησις) does not mean, in this passage, the bragging of a man before other men, but the sure consciousness of desert which the devout disciple of the old Jewish school believed he should have toward his God, or should strive to possess, the feeling, 'I have done my duty, now let God do his.' Religion is here a contract which binds God as well as man, and gives to the devout not only obligations but also rights. He may make demands of God, he may bring pressure to bear upon his actions. This 'glorying,' says Paul, is now 'excluded.' Herein, perhaps, lies his greatest, his essentially religious discovery. From a relationship of barter and exchange religion develops into a relationship of the most utter dependence of men upon God. Man is always only the receiving agent. He thanks God for everything, for whatever he is and whatever he has. By a detour, Paul thus comes round to the relation of sonship to God, as Jesus lived it and taught it—only with this difference, that the goodness of God is accepted by Jesus in a much more simple manner, as something which could not possibly be otherwise because it corresponds to the innermost being of God. He has to love his human children and desires only to be loved in return. Jesus to be sure also had the consciousness that such kingly love, portioned out to both the good and the evil, might appear to the natural man all too generous and even unjust—the brother of the Prodigal Son is a witness to this (SNT on Luke 15). But with Paul there is always a trace of the feeling of shame in the new peace with God. The light of the divine grace contrasts very sharply with the unworthiness of the pardoned one.[10] The exceeding great 'riches of his goodness and

[10] This feeling, which in I Cor. 15:9, Gal. 1:13, is expressed, one must admit, with moderation and dignity, is strongly exaggerated at the expense of Paul in Eph. 3:8, when he is made responsible for the self-designation, 'less than the least of all saints.' It seems to be needlessly intensified in the Pastoral epistles, where Paul not only appears as a type of the saved and pardoned sinner (I Tim. 1:16), but is also very liberally provided with the titles of the chiefest among sinners, blasphemers,

forbearance and long-suffering' (Rom. 2:4) should indeed make the natural man turn to humility and self-examination. How much more then the Christian, who from his own experience has a heightened realization of the fact that 'it does not depend upon willing or doing, but upon God's compassion' (Rom. 9:16); that his salvation is based alone upon the will of God, entirely unaffected by any human action (9:11f). He even goes so far as to make it appear possible to criticize such election of grace as being arbitrary and unjust (9:14-23)—but who would dare dispute with God; it is his affair! It is to be observed how Paul in this famous passage on predestination holds in check the Jewish, that is to say his own, objections to this concept of righteousness: his religious certainty is here stronger than his interest in the correct understanding of it.

In the famous profession of 'justification on the ground of faith' in Rom. 5:1, we note again the significant 'pre-dating' of what is really an eschatological act of salvation. In itself, dogmatically considered, justification is an occurrence which will take place only on the day of the divine judgment (Rom. 2:12f,16), and incidentally Paul further states that we 'by faith, wait for the hope of righteousness,' Gal. 5:5). But, just as the other decisive moments of salvation, the sending of the Messiah, the beginning of his rule, have already taken place—earlier than expected—so the Christian has also already experienced justification (Rom. 5:1,9; 8:30; I Cor. 6:11;[11] 1:30). Here the question arises, how does the Christian know that he is justified, what are the marks of the divine grace, the proofs? This became, for the later church, a burning practical question. Dogmatics attempted to determine the marks of justification in the individual, and practical religion, especially pietistic religion—even up to our own day—has often striven to reach a personal assurance of salvation and grace. If one be not satisfied (according to Ritschl) with the thought that the gift of justification has been delivered to the Church, and is simply to be claimed by each individual in free faith, then it is very difficult to indicate in one's own life the moment we should dare to be sure of justification. For in our religious development there is usually lacking any clear consciousness of the sharp point of change when we pass from despair to peace with God,

persecutors, injurious ones (I Tim. 1:15,13), which then to be sure is all taken back through the statement that all his actions had been done 'unknowingly in unbelief' (I Tim. 1:13). Here also we find the famous 'I obtained mercy' (I Tim. 1:13,16). The picture of Paul as the type of the converted man, which is often met with in theology and popular religion, derives its main features from these passages.

[11] The word 'justified' in this passage—in virtue of the elasticity of meaning in the Greek word—signifies an actual state of righteousness, the putting-off of sins.

from unhappiness to grace. For, differing from Paul and his Gentile Christians, we do not consciously step over from Judaism or heathenism to Christianity, or from enmity to God to peace with him. We grow up in the Church itself, in which God richly and fully forgives us our sins daily. We live from childhood in the sunshine of God's grace, which, for the Apostle, arose in deep night, like a light-giving star never seen before. We have therefore never had this great experience, which for Paul and his community was something of an additional pledge of justification or a proof of their assured salvation, and which is described in the words: "The love of God hath been shed abroad in our hearts through the Holy Ghost, which was given unto us" (Rom. 5:5).

It need not be proved again that here 'love for God' is not meant, but God's love, which, as something plainly to be felt, as something quite objective, is present in the hearts of the believers through the granting of the Spirit at the moment of the conversion or call. It is felt by those who share in it to be something entirely new and by nature strange to them, a joyfulness (I Thess. 1:6) and strength (I Cor. 2:4f; 4:19f; II Cor. 4:7; 6:7; 12:9; 13:4), or even as an almost palpable miraculous power (Gal. 3:2,5) which one might almost say is viewed as an objective fact. This appears most plainly in those moments when the Spirit drives men into ecstatic confession (I Cor. 12:3) or ejaculations in prayer (*Abba*, Gal. 4:6; Rom. 8:15). Paul is very strongly convinced that these assertions of the new relationship to the Lord Christ are 'involuntary,' i.e. do not proceed from the volition of the converts, but are placed upon the tongue by the now indwelling Spirit, in order that they may be convinced of the grace of God and of their adoption by him. He recognizes thus, in himself, and in the experiences which have occurred to the members of the community, which appear to him as objective proofs, that they have been adopted by God through grace. So compelling do these appear to him that (Gal. 3:2-5) he argues from these experiences against the Galatians, as from incontrovertible facts, "Ye have indeed already in your hands the proof of your justification on the ground of faith; why then do you now need further assurance and proof?" We cannot emphasize too strongly or too plainly that for Paul justification is not merely an inner subjective occurrence, a merely superficial appeasing of the feelings, but a real act of judgment, since God, with the cooperation of his Spirit, has given to believers an absolutely clear pledge of his favor (II Cor. 5:5; 1:22). He does not admit any possibility of self-deception.

That is the reason his confessions have so much joyousness and power, 'We have [mg] peace with God, and access to him' (Rom. 5:1)—everything which has separated us from him, sin and enmity, suspicion and fear, has been removed; 'We have now received the reconciliation' (Rom. 5:11)—therefore, we may also hope to receive the full, present, yet pending salvation—for it is in line with the divine plan of salvation that 'those, whom he has justified, them he also glorified' (Rom. 8:30); 'He has, indeed, not spared his own Son—how could it be conceivable that he with him will not give us all things?' (Rom. 8:32); 'Who can be against us, if God is for us' (8:31); and if perhaps some hostile spirit, either angel or devil, should still accuse us to God, tear us away from his love—he cannot do it, for God has declared us righteous (8:33-39). For this jubilant, victorious feeling Paul has again picked up the word that in Rom. 3:27 he declared to be ruled out for all time. He says, "Let us *glory* [mg] in hope of the glory of God"; "We also rejoice (glory) in God" (Rom. 5:2,11; 15:17). "He that glorieth, let him glory in the Lord" (I Cor. 1:31; II Cor. 10:17; cf. Gal. 6:14; Phil. 3:3; Jas. 1:9). Thus, in some sort, a rebirth has taken place. The basis of this state of mind is not one's own accomplishment, but an act of God. We might describe it as 'exultation, conviction, boldness in God' or something similar. It is the highest expression of what we usually call 'faith.'

3. *Adoption*. The new relationship to God is expressed in still another figure, sonship or adoption. It is again a noteworthy difference that Jesus sees the relationship of sonship to God as something which has been given. The Father in heaven only expects that his children will make use of their privileges, pray to him, trust in him, that they may become like his own actual children. For Paul also, God is simply 'our Father' or 'the Father,'[12] and the formal liturgical use of this name[13] permits the conclusion that he had long been familiar with it, even from his Jewish past; that, indeed, he considered the 'relationship of sonship' as one of the great blessings of Israel (Rom. 9:4). Yet when he describes the nature of the Christian he speaks as if we first became the sons of God by a special act of adoption. In place of a condition of servitude, in which fear must

[12] The seemingly legal mode of expression in Gal. 4:1ff, placed too in a legalistic context, perhaps originates from the Mystery religions. Here initiation is understood not only as re-birth but occasionally also as an adoption of the candidate by the deity, as E. Rohde, in *Psyche* II, pp. 421f, 2d ed., maintains.

[13] Rom. 1:7; I Cor. 1:3; II Cor. 1:2,3; 6:18; Gal. 1:4; Phil. 1:2; 4:20; Col. 1:1,3; 3:11,13; II Thess. 1:1,2; 2:16 — I Cor. 8:6; Gal. 1:1.

rule them, they have entered into a relationship of sonship (Rom. 8:15). They have 'received' adoption (Gal. 4:5) and the sign of this, their mark of identification again, the Spirit of God (Rom. 8:14f; Gal. 4:5f) 'Who has witnessed with our spirit that we are the children of God' (Rom. 8:16). The development of the relationship of sonship is thus wholly parallel to justification—even in its results. If peace with God, access to him, trust and constant hope is the result of justification, then also from the child-relationship there follows a kind of claim to justice, a certainty of inheritance, 'If children, then heirs,' as Paul states in Rom. 8:17 and in Gal. 4:7 in almost the same words. Adoption too, like justification, is considered as really a matter of the future; 'We wait for the adoption' (υἱοθεσίαν ἀπεκδεχόμενοι Rom. 8:23); 'the revelation of the sons of God,' 'the glory of the children of God' (Rom. 8:19,21) is still awaited. From this it follows that Paul's presentation of the matter —differing from the usual view of Jesus—is an eschatological, future one, as in the Beatitude, Matt. 5:9, where it is stated that the peacemakers 'shall be called the children of God,' which runs parallel with the other, that the pure in heart 'shall see God' (5:8). The condition of angels is meant, i.e. the heavenly transfiguration which of necessity precedes complete nearness to God, the seeing of God face to face (I Cor. 13:12), as it is described in I John 3:3—'We shall be like him, for we shall see him as he is.' In this way, also, Rom. 8:29 depicts the destiny of the Christian as 'likeness to the image of his [God's] Son,' 'so that he is only the first-born among many brethren.' Thus the frequent expression, 'the God and Father of our Lord Jesus Christ,' receives an especial significance.[14] The Christians stand as it were with Christ in a row before God as their God and Father from whom they may expect what he as 'the first-born from the dead' (Col. 1:18), as 'the first-fruits of them that are asleep' (I Cor. 15:20), already has received. So 'adoption,' in so far as the Christian already possesses it, is as in the case of justification the anticipation of the glorious condition of the end: "We are now the children of God, and it does not yet appear what we shall be" (I John 3:2).

Justification and adoption form the basis of a strong and joyous

[14] Rom. 15:16; I Cor. 15:24; II Cor. 1:3; 11:31; Col. 1:3. That we may not in the last reference translate, 'God who is also the Father of Jesus Christ,' seems clear, not only on grammatical grounds (the article belongs to both nominatives, and the genitive therefore depends upon both, which by article and genitive are closely bound together), but also from the fact that I Cor. 15:24 makes it fully clear that Christ gives back the dominion to his God and Father; cf. also Eph. 1:17 and John 20:17.

Hope —

hope. They confer a right to perfection and communion with God, and at the same time they bestow even now a blessedness and confidence which make all the sufferings of the present appear of small importance in comparison with the glory which shall be revealed in us (Rom. 8:18). For one of the fundamental experiences of primitive Christianity was that we through much tribulation must enter into the kingdom of God (Acts 14:22), that the way to glory led through suffering (Rom. 8:17). But in these trials and conflicts the Christian has a strong hold upon the certainty of the grace and love of God. The consciousness of the fact that 'God is for us' gives him that heroic confidence which suffering only stimulates and out of which streamed forth the glorious confession of Rom. 8:31-39. We note here a revival of the Stoic thought that all things are subject to the wise man, that he is the true Lord and King of the world,[15] in truth a wonderful re-birth: life and death, things present and things to come, all are yours because you are Christ's, and, therefore, God's, you are hidden in his hand, certain of his care. On this basis, trust in God receives a new note. It is no longer the childlike trust in the goodness of the heavenly Father, who allows his sun to rise upon the evil and upon the good—'what our God has created, he will also maintain.' It has a more profound ethical meaning, and rises to heights of pathos. God adopted us while we were yet sinners, he overcame the resistance caused by our sins and hostility. He did not even spare his own Son. How could it be possible that sufferings and dangers, difficulties or death, angel or devil, could tear us away from the love of God? God must bring his elect to the blessed consummation (Rom. 5:6-11; 8:31ff)! Here the character of Christianity as an ethical religion of redemption is fulfilled. The underlying reason for this is the perception by a sensitive conscience that the greatest danger is sin; the greatest affliction, estrangement from God through sin; with this removed, all else is thereby granted. Moreover, the love of God is not merely kindness and friendliness but includes an active desire to perfect his children. That this purpose will moreover surely reach its sacred goal is the deepest reason for the joyousness which is the fundamental characteristic note of this religion, and must ever remain so.

4. *Election.* But the picture of the Pauline faith would be incomplete if we did not consider the fact that its certainty of salvation and confidence rests also upon the conviction of divine election. Just as the deeply religious consciousness of the people of

[15] Cf. my Commentary on I Cor. 3:21-25.

Israel is rooted in the conviction that God had previously chosen this nation above all others (Rom. 11:2) [16] to bestow his benefits upon it, so also the Christian, who by conversion has experienced the grace of God, may conclude that he belongs to the elect of God. As has been said, this is a conclusion *a posteriori* from what he has already experienced—for what God does is not in any sense accidental. He does not allow himself to be influenced in the least by the acts of men (Rom. 9:11f).[17] He is working out a plan prepared from of old. Behind this there lies a lofty concept of God: it is indeed a profound religious sentiment which can think of God independently of all earthly human events. It is the same religious motive that is the basis for the statement of 'justification by faith, not by works,' in which all 'glorying,' every claim of man is excluded; God's free-will alone is to make the decision. And when Paul now (Rom. 9-11) has to confess with grief that the message of God has been successful only with a few, and above all, not with Israel, then according to his conception, it should not be explained by the accidental nullification by men of the plan of God. It is inconceivable that the purposes of God should be wrecked by the evil wills of men. The reason must be that he had from the beginning only destined a chosen few for salvation and in these he has realized it. In the same way, Jesus concludes from bitter experience that though, indeed, the call had gone to many, only a few had proved themselves 'elected' (Matt. 22:14). When the disciples enter into a house and pronounce their greeting of salvation and peace, it will often happen that the peace will return to them because no 'son of peace' is there, no receiver with whom the transmitted power could

[16] The expression used here, 'He had foreknown,' has its analogy and finds its explanation in Amos 3:2, "You only I have known (ἔγνων) of all the families of the earth." It goes back to an old Semitic mode of expression, which is found among the Babylonians. Thus it is said in the calling of the king Merodachbaladan II, "Marduk . . . . took a liking to the land of Akkad (= Babylonia) . . . . held a review among all peoples, mustered together mankind. From among all nations and all dwelling-places with firm resolve he made choice of Merochbaladan, the king of Babylon. . . . he looked upon him joyfully, and announced by his decree: 'This man shall be your shepherd who shall bring together those who have been scattered etc.'" Or in the prayer of Assurnasirpal to Ishtar: "Thou, O Ishtar, awful ruler among the gods, hast chosen me with the glance of thine eyes (literally, 'known' from *idu* ידע), borne a longing for my dominion, thou hast brought me from the hills and called me to be a shepherd of men etc." (Zimmern, *KAT*[3] pp. 381ff).

[17] Judgment had been passed concerning both sons of Rebekah, even before their birth, even before they had yet done either evil or good, for 'the fore-ordination of God must be free choice, wholly independent of the action of men, depending alone on his calling'—from the will of him alone who is making the election shall the decision come.

come in contact. But where there is a 'son of salvation,' there the salvation, brought by the messengers, will 'rest upon him,' and the circuit is closed (Luke 10:6). By his receptiveness such a one proves himself one of the 'elect.' This is also the view of Paul. Where the Gospel is not only heard but is also received in faith, there the invitation has become the 'call,' which is proof of the preceding divine election, and a pledge of the still incomplete glorification (Rom. 8:29f).[18] 'Those whom he predestined, he also called: and those whom he called, he also justified: and those whom he justified, he also glorified.' With God 'any idea of vacillation is excluded; when he begins a work he carries it through, step by step, to the end. There runs a straight line from the pre-temporal election by grace to the transfiguration forming the end of the story' (SNT *in loc.*). So Paul's certainty of salvation is in the end anchored to his firm trust in God's steadfast desire for man's salvation, 'for the gifts and the calling of God are without repentance' (Rom. 11:29), unshakable his faithfulness (3:3ff). Again and again the confession recurs, 'God is faithful, by whom ye are called' (I Cor. 1:9; 10:13; II Cor. 1:18; I Thess. 5:24; II Thess. 3:3), 'He who has begun the good work, will also complete it' (Phil. 1:6).

5. *Faith, Love, Knowledge; God-Mysticism*. It is hardly necessary perhaps to repeat that this faith, on the basis of which God confers justification, is not conceived by Paul as one's own act, as a 'work' to be substituted for other works. The appearance in mankind of faith is just one step in the process designated as the 'calling,' and is itself the work of God in man. Of course, this is not specifically stated; rather does faith always appear by the necessities of language and logic as a function of man, occasionally as a rendering of man's obedience upon which God only waits in order to show him his grace.[19] It is in truth nothing but a giving up of one's own activity which is in strict logic contrasted with it (Rom. 4:5). This faith is only an action of the will in so far as it is a subjection to grace or its opposite (Rom. 10:3), an obedience of faith (Rom. 1:5; 16:26),

[18] In the 'calling,' therefore, the 'election' is realized; so that loosely speaking the calling itself, e.g. the conversion, the taking into the Church (Rom. 9:24; I Cor. 1:9; 7:15ff,17ff,20ff; Gal. 5:13) can be considered the same as election (I Cor. 1:26-29). Thus the Christian might just as well be given the name of 'the called' (Rom. 1:6f; 8:30; I Cor. 1:2,24) as 'the elect' (Rom. 8:33; 16:13; Col. 3:12; I Pet. 1:1).

[19] By Rom. 12:3, 'according as God hath dealt to each man a measure of faith,' and I Cor. 12:9, where faith appears among the gifts of grace, we understand not so much that fundamental conversion-faith as rather the heroic accomplishments of bold confidence in God among genuine Christians.

the opposite of which is disobedience (Rom. 10:16), just as Paul bluntly designates the unbelief of the Jews as disobedience (Rom. 11:31; 15:31; 10:21). Of course they are responsible for this self-will, but Paul leaves no doubt as to the fact that God did not permit himself to be surprised by this, or his plans to be crossed. He it is, himself, who gave men the spirit of dullness of hearing. 'Ears that do not hear, and eyes that do not see'; he has closed them (Rom. 11:8). Just in the same way the faith of the believer is not something he has earned. Least of all can Paul say that of himself. Had God not chosen him from his mother's womb and revealed his Son to him (Gal. 1:15f), had the Lord not appeared to him who was unworthy, he would always have remained a persecutor of the Church. He knows this very surely: 'By the grace of God, I am what I am' (I Cor. 15:8ff). The initiative of God and the passivity of the believer is more clearly expressed where Paul on occasion describes the relation to God as 'love' or as 'knowledge.'

It is characteristic of the Apostle of Grace that the demand for love to God, which Jesus designates as the greatest commandment, never finds an express echo in him. Only in three passages does he speak of 'loving God.' The first is a quotation ('what God has prepared for those who love him,' I Cor. 2:9), and the second also (Rom. 8:28) seems not to have been first formulated by Paul: 'we know that to them that love God all things work together for good'—here one would expect from the whole context that it would state, 'to them whom God loves,' and it is again characteristic that Paul at once adds, as if to correct the thought, 'even to them who are called according to his purpose.' He means to say, not the love of men to God, but the love of God, is the basis of all salvation! He makes a similar correction in the third passage, I Cor. 8:1ff. Here he places love and knowledge opposite each other, just as in 13:8ff. And, of course, it is knowledge in the sense of the gnostic 'knowledge of God,' the result of which is freedom; and love, in the sense one would at once expect of brotherly love, as immediately afterwards in 8:9ff; but no, the thought is at once transposed in paradoxical fashion:

> Knowledge puffeth up, but love edifieth.
> If any man thinketh that he knoweth anything
> He knoweth not yet as he ought to know.
> But if any man loveth God
> The same is known of him.

We meet here with a double surprise: we expect the antithesis that brotherly love should not be neglected for the sake of knowledge; instead we find true knowledge is not present where self-conceited knowledge prevails, but only where love to God is found. But this thought is again turned about: it is not, 'he who loves God has truly known,' but, 'he has become known of God.' In this, it is now maintained that love to God is not really an act of man's, but only a reflection or working-out of a previous religious experience in which it is God who really has taken the initiative.[20] Here, in any case, love to God is not perhaps a necessary condition of salvation, but rather one of its effects, just as in Gal. 2:20; 'faith in him who loved me' has almost the same meaning as an overflowing response of love and thankfulness.

But still more important is the surprising change from the active 'to know' to the passive 'to be known.' It occurs in Paul in two other places, I Cor. 13:12 and Gal. 4:8f—here with the thought emphasized that it is really more correct to say, 'after ye have been known of God,' instead of 'after ye have known God.' This is then a favorite idea with Paul.

Wherever it may have had its origin it is one of the convictions that lies close to Paul's heart that the new knowledge of God which has so illuminated the souls of the believers (II Cor. 4:6) is in no way the result of any act of man himself of which he might be proud, but a gift of God. Not only has God made himself known to his own[21] but he has first 'known' them. What does this mean? This

[20] Cf. my Commentary on I Cor. 8:1-3. One may entertain some doubt as to whether in vs. 3, *εἴ τις ἀγαπᾷ τὸν θεόν*, the object should not be stricken out (then perhaps in the next clause *ὑπὸ τοῦ θεοῦ*?) since in ℵ 17 Clem. the *ὑπ' αὐτοῦ* after *ἔγνωσται* is omitted. *ἔγνωσται* without *ὑπ' αὐτοῦ* would be just as understandable as *ἐπεγνώσθην* in I Cor. 13:12, and the simple *ἀγαπᾷ* would then correspond to the climax of ch. 13, where the question concerns 'love' without the mention of any object. And when in vv. 4-7 the streaming-forth of brotherly love is the main idea, one might and in fact must ask whether by 'love' is not meant an abundance of overflowing tenderness which is not really directed toward any one object, so that actually the object is not the really important thing, but rather the very feeling itself. Cf. my Commentary on I Cor. 13.

[21] So it is stated in the pseudo-Hermetic Poimandres prayer of thanksgiving (Reitzenstein, p. 338): "Holy is God, who wishes to be known and makes himself known to his own." Comparable to this passage is another found in Tractate 10 (10:15); "For God is not ignorant of man, but both knows him and wishes to be known;" again, the previously quoted passages, p. 465, note 18, in which it is stated: "Thou knowest me, and I thee." On the other hand, the passages quoted by Norden in *Agn. Th.*, 287f, from the Odes of Solomon VII, 12ff, and Manilius IV, 905ff, say only that God presses 'knowledge' of himself upon man in such a way that he cannot escape this knowledge.

mode of expression is only to be understood by a consideration of the Hebrew habit of thought, where 'to know' frequently means a purposeful act of affection, even sexual union (Adam knew his wife, Gen. 4:1; Luke 1:34). It also means to be concerned about someone—Isa. 63:16, "Abraham knoweth us not (οὐκ ἔγνω ἡμᾶς) and Israel doth not acknowledge us (οὐκ ἔγνω ἡμᾶς); But thou, Lord, art our Father"; (Ps. 101:4) "I will know no evil thing"; (Job 9:21) "I despise my life," literally, I do not know my soul (cf. 'to deny oneself,' Mark 8:34). In Amos 3:2 it plainly means election (p. 392, note 1). So it should stand in the three Pauline passages for election or calling, but with an important though slight difference in meaning. This 'knowing' is a yearning towards man, actually an intimate contact with his soul. The paradox of these three passages is the paradox of mysticism. In the flaming-up of the knowledge of God in his soul the mystic knows indeed a contact through God himself, and love for God is then but the radiation from this. We recognize here, in keeping with those previously discussed tendencies to Christ-mysticism, the characteristic notes of a God-mysticism as well, and here again the question arises as to how it was conceived, and to what degree it was really experienced.

According to the beautiful words of Erwin Rohde (*Kleine Schriften,* ii. 331), "Mysticism is a form of religion which, rightly understood, has for its aim the most intimate union of man with deity, presupposing an innate oneness of man's nature with that of God. 'Thou canst only know what thou thyself art,' says Meister Eckhart, 'but thus thou shalt, since thou knowest God, thyself be God.' The man who knows God will himself become God. He was God from the beginning, but in his life as mortal the divine became dulled and dimmed; he must win back to God in his purity. To this end mysticism points the way." The problem is whether the chief mark of the mystical type of thought, the assumption of a likeness of nature between God and man, is present in Paul. He could have made some use of Stoic terminology in this connection. The Stoic perceives in the human soul, in its indwelling logos something of the divine, a direct effluence from God.[22] This gives the right basis for

[22] Zeller, *Die Philosophie der Griechen* III, 1[3], p. 200: "The individual soul is related to the world soul as the part to the whole. The soul of man is not only a part and effluence of the universal life-force in the same way as are all other forces, but because of its rationality it stands in a special relationship to the divine being, a relationship which becomes more apparent the more exclusively we permit the divine that is our reason to rule in us." Cleanthes *Hymn,* line 4, 'For we are thy offspring' (cf. Acts 17:28). The expression 'relationship with God' is found in Posidonius (Cic.,

the mystical view. The divine in man comes into contact with the divine external to him.[23] But Paul feels that this fundamental assumption of something divine in the nature of man is too uncertain for him to base upon it a mystical doctrine or a mystical experience. Of course, he recognizes a sympathy between the 'inward man' or the 'mind' and the law of God (Rom. 7:22f,25). But this ethical conception is not capable of supporting the far-reaching idea of an original relationship to God and the experience of a contact of the inward man with him. The difference is felt as too great, the chasm too wide, between the divine and the human. 'The natural man (ψυχικός) receiveth not the things of the Spirit of God: for they are foolishness unto him' (I Cor. 2:14). We cannot emphasize too strongly that man, of himself, cannot attain to a true 'knowledge of God,' and certainly not to a mystical union with him. This becomes possible only when he 'receives the Spirit of God.' This is the essential difference between the Stoa and Paul. The former thinks of an innate and inborn divine nature; the latter of a divine, supernatural equipment, given at the time of conversion. Of course, he who possesses the Spirit of God can really and truly know God, since this Spirit is nothing else than the self-consciousness of God (I Cor. 2:16). The conclusion, therefore, of I Cor. 2:16 might actually read: 'But we have the Spirit (or the mind, νοῦς, *animus*) of God,' and it is, to a certain degree, a surprising though understandable [24] change when Paul states, in its stead, the 'reason' or 'mind of Christ.'

De Divin. I, 30,64). Epict. I. 14,6, "Our souls are joined together with God as parts and fragments of him." Marcus Aurelius V, 27: "The soul is a part, an outflow, a fragment of God." Seneca, Ep. 41,2: "A holy spirit dwells within us;" 62,12: "Reason is nothing else than a part of the divine spirit sunk in a human body;" 31,11: "The good and upright mind is the great God dwelling in the human body." Philo, *Op. Mundi* § 69: "For after the pattern of a single mind, even the mind of the universe as an archetype, the mind in each of those who successively came into being was moulded. It is, in a fashion, a god to him who carries and enshrines it as an object of devotion; for the human mind evidently occupies a position in men precisely answering to that which the great ruler occupies in all the world"; § 135, "(the soul) for that which he breathed in was nothing else than a divine breath that migrated hither from that blissful and happy existence for the benefit of our race, to the end that, even if it is mortal in respect of its visible part, it may, in respect of the part that is invisible be rendered immortal;" *De Plant.* § 18, "Now while others, by asserting that our human mind is a particle of the ethereal substance, have claimed for man a kinship with the upper air. . . ."

[23] So the Areopagus speech is genuinely Stoic; the expression, "In him we live and have our being," is intimately connected with the idea of a relationship to God which immediately follows in Acts 17:28,29. Cf. Norden, *Agnostos Theos,* pp. 19ff. Reitzenstein (*Neue Jahrbb.* 1913, p. 397) contributes the fine parallel, Sen., Ep. 41,4: "God is near thee, with thee, within thee."

[24] Cf. my Commentary on I Cor. 2:10-16.

The 'spiritual' man knows and judges not only the being of God, but everything else, for the Spirit penetrates everything, even the deep things of God (I Cor. 2:15,10). These are the confessions of a spiritual ('pneumatic') mystic; his feeling of exaltation, his sense of superiority and unassailability are especially asserted in the statement (2:15), 'but he himself is judged of no man.' [25] However, in this there is retained the consciousness that such supernatural endowments and knowledge are a gift of grace, and thus 'wisdom and knowledge' appear under the charismata (I Cor. 12:8)—'And if I have the gift of prophecy and know all mysteries, and all knowledge' (13:2)!

Here also we must raise the question whether or not these mystical formulae correspond to an actual experience or feeling. The formula 'in God' occurs very seldom, and, indeed, we never find 'God in us.' [26] Those devout outpourings which strive to tell of a permanent mystical mood, of a union regularly sought after and experienced, are entirely lacking. Nor do we find here, any more than in the Christ-mysticism, that poetry of mysticism, that lyrical delight in the formulae which depict the sinking of self into God, the full and complete union. Paul certainly was not of a mystical nature, and mystical ecstasy is not his ideal. He undoubtedly had had some great mystical experiences, the 'revelation' at his conversion, the lifting up into the third heaven (II Cor. 12:2ff); but just because these are referred to as special experiences they could not have been frequent or regular happenings.

The thing that has special significance for us in this connection is that this new knowledge of God possessed by Paul and the other converts is an activity and a gracious gift of God, just as are justification and faith. It is a working out of God's purpose of election—and so we have that surprising change from active knowing to passive being known.

[25] Cf. R. Reitzenstein on this passage, *Hellenist. Mysterien-religionen*, p. 164, and my Commentary on I Cor. 2:16.

[26] I and II Thess. 1:1; 2:2.—In I Cor. 14:25 the words, "Truly God is in you," are spoken by a Gentile listener, and one might ask whether it did not mean 'among you.' See my Commentary on this passage. The only passage which might be mentioned in this connection, Col. 3:3, "our life is hid with Christ in God," has quite probably another meaning.

CHAPTER XVII

The New Creation

WE have up to this point represented the 'new life' of the Christian as faith in Christ and as a new relationship to God. However, in the discussion at the end of the previous chapter we spoke of the fact that in the experience of conversion there took place a transformation in the convert himself—through the gift of the Spirit. This change, which meant that 'the old things are passed away; behold, they are become new' (II Cor. 5:17), we now wish to consider.

1. *Redemption*. It is customary to include these subjective changes under the concept of 'redemption,' and to a certain extent this is correct. The word and the idea (ἀπολύτρωσις, λύτρωσις, cf. p. 429) come from the vocabulary of Jewish Messianism and referred originally to the political liberation of the people of Israel from foreign domination. Like many other messianic concepts, this one was stripped of its political and national significance by the Christians, including of course Paul, and was antedated. Just as in Matt. 1:21 the task of the Savior who is Jesus is given a new meaning as the rescue of his people *from their sins*, so in the case of Paul who is here merely the mouthpiece of primitive Hellenistic Christianity, 'redemption' is considered as something already fulfilled through Christ, something that was accomplished in him and with him: he 'was made unto us—redemption' (I Cor. 1:30), 'the redemption that is in Christ Jesus' (Rom. 3:24). The meaning of the word, he assumes, is well known;[1] he does not really explain it. Only this much is plain, that it is in some way associated with justification or propitiation, though its exact shade of meaning in this connection is not quite clear.[2] The concept therefore belongs rather to the range of ideas discussed in the previous chapter. There is however

[1] The actual sense of the words seems to have escaped both the writer to whom is due the present form of Col. 1:14, Eph. 1:7, and his readers. He interprets it—decidedly too narrowly—as 'the forgiveness of sins.'

[2] In I Cor. 1:30 it stands beside righteousness (justification) and sanctification; in Rom. 3:24, justification results from redemption. By this means, it has been made possible for God to grant 'justification apart from works.' Whether the thought is here of a ransom from death (as in Mark 10:45) or of an atonement for sin (Heb. 9:15) or the wholly general idea of the removal of the hindrances to righteousness is not clear to us now.

one place at least in which the word is plainly used in a different sense (Rom. 8:23). Here the elevation to heavenly adoption and glory is identified with the 'redemption of the body,' and the discussion is on the liberation of the individual from those powers of sin, of the flesh, and of corruption which keep him down and distant from the goal of eternal life. This is in accordance with the language of the modern science of religion when it would describe the Pauline scheme of salvation without entering into the question of an imaginary or judicial change in man's status before God but concerns itself only with actual alteration in the man himself. Here the problem is not, "How can I prevail upon God to be gracious?" but "O wretched man that I am! Who shall deliver me out of the body of this death?" (Rom. 7:24).

2. *Freedom from the Power of Sin.* The religion of Paul would be incompletely described if one presented it only as the consciousness of the forgiveness of sins. He is conscious not only of the fact of being freed from the guilt, but also from the power of sin (Rom. 6:18,22; I Cor. 15:17). What this means is to be understood from his moving description of his earlier condition. It is noteworthy that he speaks as seldom of sins in the plural as he does of individual transgressions: [3] he thinks of sin as a uniform, almost personal power (p. 434) which, having once entered into the world, then develops a royal dominion over mankind (Rom. 5:12f,21), or which, like a harsh tyrant, holds man enslaved (Rom. 6:6,20; 7:14), paying men for their service the miserable wage of death (Rom. 6:23); or he pictures it as a demon who first seduces men (7:11), and then takes them fully into his possession, dwelling in them (7:17), forcing on them his will and his law (7:20,24). Deeply moving is the famous description of this servitude (7:14-25): how man's ego is completely swallowed up by that of the demon, how it no longer does what it wishes but what it does not wish, how it is dragged hither and thither between two contending powers, 'laws' Paul calls them.[4]

[3] Rom. 4:7; 7:5; I Cor. 15:3—the common primitive-Christian usage. I Pet. 2:24; 3:18; 4:8; Acts 2:38; 3:19; 5:31; 10:43; 13:30; 22:16; 26:18.

[4] It has been questioned whether Paul here pictures the condition of those 'reborn,' or his own former condition as a devout Pharisee. The first is completely excluded, as 8:2 shows: what purpose could rebirth and redemption have had, if they could not even remove the unhappy condition of inner conflict or servitude? On the other hand, Paul is not describing his own life as a Pharisee: the distinctively Jewish colors are lacking, and more especially the past tenses required in this case are wanting. Perhaps this may be explained as follows: Paul is picturing the universal human condition as it is disclosed to the observation of deeply-sensitive and lofty souls. Just as the fall into sin, described in Rom. 7:7-11, is not that of Paul merely, but the condition of every

From this 'law' of sin and death[5] the Christian is now liberated (Rom. 8:2), and, of course, through the fact that another 'law' has gained control in him, the 'law of the spirit of life in Christ Jesus.' The matter is viewed just as if it were a question of dynamics: the operation of the one power is stopped, shut off, by the entrance of another, which is superior to the former as the 'Spirit' is superior to the flesh, the divine to the human, life to death. And the result is that now the sacred and inviolable demand of God (τὸ δικαίωμα) can be fulfilled, for now those thus liberated can lead their lives 'in the direction,' 'after the norm,' 'under the power' (all this in indicated by the κατά, Rom. 8:4) of the divine Spirit. When Paul calls this new status, even though it is one in which the Christian is really a tool and object of divine power and is actually in a passive condition, 'liberty'[6]—'where the Spirit of the Lord is, there is liberty' (II Cor.

individual, so also, in 7:13-25, the 'I' is universal. Paul places himself in the abstract after the manner of rhetorical writers, in the situation of man (αὐτὸς ἐγώ) before he comes under the influence of the divine Spirit, with such deep feeling that even today his words move one's soul. Especially has he given expression for all time to man's yearning for redemption, which he had himself formerly felt in his own experience (vs. 24). It is significant that the Jew Paul, who was of course also a Hellenist, can speak so feelingly from the standpoint of the soul of a man with Greek sensibilities. In vs. 24 we see the dualistic yearning for redemption of Hellenism, while the combat pictured in vv. 13-23,25 reminds us of Stoic doctrines: Epictetus I,17,14f, "Though it is true that all sin against their will (ἄκοντες), thou hast come to know the truth thoroughly so thou canst not do otherwise than act rightly. 'But, by Zeus, I do not follow the will of nature.'" Epictetus II,26: "Every error implies conflict; for since he who errs does not wish to go wrong but to go right, plainly he is not doing what he wishes. For what does the thief wish to do? What is to his interest. If then, thieving is against his interest, he is not doing what he wishes. But every rational soul by nature dislikes conflict; and so, as long as a man does not understand that he is in conflict, there is nothing to prevent him from doing conflicting acts, but, whenever he understands, strong necessity makes a man abandon the conflict and avoid it, just as bitter necessity makes him renounce a falsehood when he discovers it, though as long as he has not this impression he assents to it as true. He then who can show to each man the conflict which causes his error, and can clearly bring home to him how he fails to do what he desires and does what he does not desire, is powerful in argument and strong to encourage and convict." It is obvious that Paul is here making use of Stoic language. On the other hand, Seneca *De Vita Beata* 8:5ff pictures the condition of the freeman as follows: "In this way there will be born an energy that is united, a power that is at harmony with itself, and that dependable reason which is not divided against itself nor uncertain in its opinions, or its perceptions, or in its convictions; and this reason, when it has been regulated, and has established harmony between all its parts, and, so to speak, is in tune, has reached the highest good . . . . it will do everything under its own authority . . . . for where agreement and unity are. . . ." (there must the virtues be).

[5] The word 'law' does not simply imply the imperative or norm here, but compulsion, as in our 'law of nature.'

[6] That Paul calls this condition where man is able to do the good, 'liberty,' also shows dependence on Stoic literary usage, according to which only the wise man is

3:17)—it is a name for the religious and moral enthusiasm which is the true mark of the vitality of primitive Christianity. Here there are no longer commands and obedience, no longer are there compulsions and servitude, but the soul, seized by the Spirit of God, is joyously attuned to the will of God, and this powerful impetus serves to carry it over divisions and weaknesses; the power of the good and the love for the good is mightily enhanced. The ideal of love is here realized: "It rejoiceth not in unrighteousness, but rejoiceth with the truth" (I Cor. 13:6).

We must call this conviction 'enthusiastic,' for in its bold, far-reaching statement it soars above realities which at other times stand, all too sternly, in the path of inspired utterance. When we read Rom. 8:5-9, we get the impression that Paul altogether denies the possibility of sinning for a Christian; how, indeed, could he still sin: 'spiritual men' (οἱ κατὰ πνεῦμα ὄντες) must, of necessity, follow along the lofty ranges of the Spirit, just as the fleshly must 'mind the things of the flesh' (τὰ τῆς σαρκὸς φρονοῦσιν). Not only thought and sentiment but also all impulses and feeling are completely transformed. Just as 'enmity to God' had been the conscious or unconscious working motive, so now the Christian's entire nature strives for life and peace (or for salvation, blessedness). Very significant is the description of the 'fruits of the Spirit' (Gal. 5:22), which Paul selects in order to depict this, as it were, inevitable growth of the new life from its new germ. According to another description, it is the rule of God which already here below unfolds itself in new power, in peace and joy in the Holy Spirit (Rom. 14:17; I Cor. 4:20). We are dead to sin (Rom. 6:6), it no longer exists for us: that sinful passions 'wrought in our members,' is a completely past condition (7:5)—Paul mentions this not only as a general theory, he also addresses his church: "And such were some of you: but ye were washed, but ye were sanctified, but ye were justified" (I Cor. 6:11).[7]

---

really free, and freedom consists in this, namely that a man has his will under control (ἐξουσία αὐτοπραγίας); cf. Cicero *Parad.*, 34. Especially does the play on the ideas of freedom and slavery in Rom. 6:18,20—free from sin, to have become slaves of righteousness; slaves of sin, free in respect to righteousness—remind us of the Stoic paradox. A full dependence upon Stoic teaching cannot be denied in the post-Pauline sayings in Jas. 1:25; 2:12; John 8:32f. Cf. also J. Weiss, *Die christliche Freiheit nach der Verkündigung des Ap. Paulus* (Christian Liberty according to the teaching of Paul), Göttingen, 1902. Bonhöffer's remarks on this question, *Epictet u. d. N. T.* (Epictetus and the New Testament), pp. 166f, are quite beside the mark.

[7] Here ἐδικαιώθητε is to be understood not only of declaring righteous but of actually becoming righteous.

3. *The Enthusiastic Anticipation of Perfection, Here and Now.* But the last passage also shows that this enthusiastic view of the new life is in truth a bold anticipation which does not correspond to reality. For the preceding sections (I Cor. 5; 6:1-11) show that the church, in many of its members, indeed in its entirety, by no means corresponds as yet to this ideal. In other passages too, it is evident how Paul himself feels that his eager idealism has gone far ahead of reality. After he has said in Rom. 6:5ff, as emphatically as possible, "Our old man was crucified with him, that the body of sin might be done away, so that we no longer should be in bondage to sin," he continues at once (6:11),[8] "Even so, reckon ye also yourselves (literally, you must judge yourselves) to be dead unto sin"—here it is quite clearly stated that what is now actual can be developed to a fuller and more vital reality only if the Christians by their own verdict and intention agree to it. They must willingly accept the new freedom from sin or the new obedience to righteousness and now really offer themselves and their bodies for the service of righteousness (Rom. 6:18f). It is highly significant how the view of redemption as having already taken place, as an event in which Christians are so to speak passive, changes into the imperative. Here the watch-word which rings clearly throughout the whole of primitive Christianity breaks through: "Be what you may become" (cf. I Cor. 5:7; p. 254). But this is by no means to be understood, in forms of modern thought as, "Realize in yourselves that ideal which hovers before you, to which you are inclined"; rather there appears here a wholly miraculous, supernatural view, which we can best make clear to ourselves from a consideration of Rom. 8:2-9 (with which compare 8:12f).

It cannot be stated more emphatically than it has been in Rom. 8:2-9, that sin in the flesh has been put to death, annihilated; that its influence has been cut off, that its law of compulsion has been removed. So much the more surprising then is it when we find it stated in Rom. 8:12, "We are debtors—not to the flesh, to live after the flesh." It had sounded before as if Christians could no longer live after the flesh, since the new power of the Spirit had, as it were, taken them upon its wings and removed them from that sphere. And now suddenly again the talk of 'debt' and 'must' and 'willing!' Even a threat is added: "For if ye live after the flesh, ye must die." Paul suggests a kind of alternation between two opposite points

[8] I consider verses 8 and 9 as an interpolation.

of view when he adds (8:14; Gal. 5:18) the idea, 'led by the Spirit,' where, perhaps, the translation 'permitting oneself to be led by the Spirit' may be allowed, in other words to yield to his power, to submit to him. So too the imperative of Gal. 5:16, "Walk in the Spirit," may be understood as though the will of the believer can actually do something so that the Spirit may operate in him (Gal. 5:25). But this 'psychological' way of looking at the matter is after all only a 'mediation' between two essentially irreconcilable modes of thought. It is and remains an entirely different thing whether one acts as 'led by the Spirit' of God, or whether one asserts his own will. How can Paul harmonize both ideas?

Here we come on a double viewpoint which permeates the whole of primitive Christianity, and with which we must wholly saturate ourselves if we wish to come to an understanding of it. The preaching of Jesus and the faith of the old churches in general consider the Kingdom of God as still future; in any case, it has not as yet succeeded in establishing direct contact with this world. But Jesus has the conviction that God has already taken the decisive step for the founding of his dominion: through his Spirit and Jesus himself, he is pushing the kingdom of evil into the background, and his kingdom is thus already asserting itself powerfully in the world—visible only, of course, to the eye of faith. Moreover, the primitive community, though it must still wait for the return of the Messiah to this world, yet believes that his rule has already begun in heaven, as also has his subjugation of the spirit-world; the decisive beginnings have already taken place. Thus the Seer of Rev. 12 sees the fall of Satan and the beginning of God's rule as already accomplished in heaven—at the very moment that, upon earth, the final battle of Satan with the people of God first begins. This is just what primitive Christian belief was: to be certain of victory in the intensified battle and the increased troubles of the last times; to know that the victory has already been won by God in the world above in the realm of spirits, and that now it has only to be fought through again here below in the lives of individuals.

It is from this point of view chiefly that the peculiar double aspect of redemption in Paul is to be understood. Sin as power has actually already been put to death (Rom. 8:3), because the principalities and powers which stand behind it have been overcome by God; through the death upon the cross and the resurrection of Jesus they have been robbed of their power and have been carried away in triumph (Col. 2:15). By this the power of sin, throughout the whole extent of the cosmos and of the flesh, has been broken.[9] It is now necessary to carry through this victory in the life of each individual and to destroy the last remnant of the power that opposes God. This final struggle is, however, no longer hopeless; it will and must also end in victory here, because the backbone of the enemy has been broken and because the stronger power of the Spirit of God is on our side. And God is faithful: he will not forsake us in this struggle, but will lead us to full communion with his Son; the Lord Christ will strengthen us so that on the day of judgment we can appear before him blameless (I Cor. 1:8f; I Thess. 5:24; II Thess. 3:3; Rom. 8:31-39).

The idea just expressed is essentially of an eschatological nature: a hope for the future; it is, therefore, mythological, gnostic. It is not to be understood apart from those mysterious supernatural events which took place at the crucifixion and resurrection of Christ, nor apart from the dualistic antithesis between God and the cosmic powers, from whose authority the Christian has now been torn away. But how should that which happened to Christ have at the same time such an effect upon the believer? Here that logical mode of thought (p. 433), so strange to us, plays a part: the sphere of the flesh (σάρξ) is a unity; what has happened at one point becomes effective in every single member of this organism.

4. *Death and Resurrection with Christ*. But there is also found here an idea that is genuinely mystical, or wrapped in mystery, one which is most clearly expressed in the statement: "I have been crucified with Christ," "In the cross of Christ the world hath been crucified unto me, and I unto the world" (Gal. 2:19; 6:14; cf. also Rom. 7:4; 8:3), and again in the comprehensive saying concerning baptism (Rom. 6:4; Col. 2:11f), "We were buried therefore with him through baptism unto death . . . . we have become united with him by the likeness of his death." We shall see later, in considering baptism, that the basic idea of those widely-spread sacramental cults (mysteries) of Adonis-Attis-Osiris is here present: that in these rites the believer must experience in his own person what once originally happened to the cult god. Where and how Paul may have become acquainted with this conception, even indeed if it was arrived at independently by him and thus ran parallel to that of the mysteries, in any case his thought is quite clear: that the new life of the Christian will be first of all characterized by this, that he, in a real sense, has experienced in himself the death and resurrec-

[9] On the mode of thought that prevails here see pp. 433f.

tion of Christ. This is, of course, an entirely different concept from that of the disciples of Jesus as the Gospel tradition presents it. It also goes far beyond the call to take up the cross and follow (Mark 8:34), although this also has influenced Paul[10]—the Christian must have had in himself a secret, miraculous experience. Even though the expression 'rebirth,' which occurs in the mysteries, (παλιγγενεσία Tit. 3:5; ἀναγέννησις I Pet. 1:3; ἀναβίωσις, *renatus in aeternum*)[11]

[10] It is usually overlooked that in Rom. 6:3f the first εἰς τὸν θάνατον [into his death] has not yet its full mystical sense, since it stands parallel to βαπτισθῆναι εἰς Χριστόν [to be baptized into Christ] and since here the common primitive Christian meaning of belonging to Christ is intended. So here εἰς θάνατον must mean: for his death, i.e. with the obligation to die his death. Only in vs. 4 (with οὖν) is this εἰς [into] to be taken as it were literally and the idea of being buried in his death brought out. Thus in vs. 3 the thought still prevails of taking up the cross, which, in fact, baptism demands. Here also the thought of following Christ comes in as in I Cor. 11:1; Phil. 2:4,5ff.

[11] A. Dieterich, in *Eine Mithras-Liturgie,* has traced out the figure of rebirth through the primitive and mystery religions. He begins with the important and irrefutable statement: "One must keep clearly in mind that the primitive thinking of man does not know the idea of development but conceives of the natural processes of change (like puberty) as religious transformations, and a 'conversion' of any kind as a definite moment of change in man, and thinks of it all as the coming into existence of a new man. One man dies and the other is born. It is extremely important to understand how late it was that men even among peoples of high culture learned to grasp the concept of development. Among certain strata of our own society it is still even today inconceivable, and one can easily observe how in the popular religious conceptions of particular sects and conventicles, 'conversion' is continually thought of as a more or less magical, miraculous act. Indeed even the official dogmatics of the Christian Church has only with difficulty and incompletely removed from the theory of particular stages in conversion the stamp of the old idea of a single magical rebirth." In addition to the examples which he cites from the life of primitive peoples, Dieterich also refers to Frazer's *Golden Bough* III, 422-446. The fact that the figure of rebirth does not seem to be found among the Jews and Semites generally is proof enough that his Hellenistic environment had its part in suggesting it to Paul. There are several instances in Apuleius *Metam.* XI, ch. 21 (cult of Isis), 'in a manner reborn'; and 24, where the day of dedication is called the sacred birth day. Also in Firmicus Maternus *De Errore Profan. Rel.* ch. 18, 'as in a certain temple a man *about to die* waits to be admitted to the inner recesses,' and Sallust, περὶ θεῶν καὶ κόσμου [On Gods and the world], 4, (Cult of Attis): "Then there follows a felling of trees and fasting since for us too the further course of life is to be cut off, then the feeding with milk since we are newborn." Then we have the formula *renatus in aeternum* [reborn into eternal life] on inscriptions for men who have undergone the taurobolium ceremony, and in Themistios (Stobaeus VI, p. 107 M) the word-play on τελεῖν (initiate) and τελευτᾶν (to die). Compare also Tertullian *De Bapt.* 5: "At the Apollinarian and Eleusinian games they are baptized; and they presume that the effect of their doing that is their regeneration and the remission of the penalties due to their perjuries." Again in the mysteries of Mithra (Dieterich, *op. cit.,* 4,13), 'that I may be reborn in mind,' and 12,3, 'This one today reborn because of thee and out of so many thousands called to immortality,' also 14,31ff, 'Born again I depart, while I increase and grow up, I die, through the birth that produces life, I am dissolved in death.'

But above all on the question of rebirth must reference be made to the tractate which Reitzenstein has edited from the Corpus Hermet. XIV (Poimandres p. 339):

does not appear in Paul, this is to be considered merely as an accidental circumstance. Paul was compelled by the historical circumstances of his Lord's life not to use the general expressions of dying and living-again, but the particular ones, crucifixion and resurrection; logically, however, it is 'rebirth.' But in any case the 'being crucified with him' assumes an intimate, almost literal link with Christ, if his death is not simply to draw after it that of his own followers, but to include it. Thus we understand in what sense Paul says that the Christian has 'died from the world' (Col. 2:20; 3:3), that he has 'put off' the 'body of the flesh' (Col. 3:9; 2:11), that the 'body of sin' is 'done away' (Rom. 6:6), that he is no longer 'in the flesh' (Rom. 7:5; 8:9), that 'I live no longer' (Gal. 2:19), 'the old man is crucified' (Col. 3:9). This is by no means simply a strong expression for the moral revolt of the will from the past; no, it means to state that the Christian no longer lives 'in the world' at all (Col. 2:20); the bond between him and matter, we should say, is severed. Of course, Paul must certainly admit that he still 'lives in the flesh' (Gal. 2:19)—it is not very easy to 'go out of the world' (I Cor. 5:10). To this extent those passages contain a daring, unbelievable paradox which contradicts everyday facts and appearances.[12] But it is on just such paradoxes that the language of mysticism thrives. Its climax is reached at that point where it speaks of the new life which has taken the place of the old. 'Raised with Christ' (Col. 2:12), 'in newness of life' (Rom. 6:4), 'to have put on a new man' (Col. 3:10)—these are the key words of this belief. 'Newness of Spirit' (Rom. 7:6) fills them, they have become 'spiritual men' (Rom. 8:5,9; I Cor. 2:5); they are really no longer men (I Cor. 3:3) but already, here below, 'children of God,' and with Paul this means almost as much as angelic, divine beings. They are brethren of the Risen One, who in this sphere is still only the first-born (Rom. 8:29). They shall not only become conformed to his image at the Parousia (Phil. 3:21), no, they are already such

That no one can be saved before his regeneration. There it is said: "As I saw all at once in myself a monstrous sight which fell to my lot through the mercy of God, then I stepped out of myself into an immortal body, and now I am no longer what I was before but I am new-born in mind. . . . Thou seest me, indeed, my child, with thine eyes, but what I really am, thou canst not perceive if thou viewest me simply in the body with thine eyes; not with these eyes can I now be seen . . . this is the case of him who can attain to birth in God."

[12] Just as paradoxical and daring is the mysticism of Philo, e.g. *Leg. Alleg.*, II, 55: "The soul that loves God, having disrobed itself of the body and the objects dear to the body and fled abroad far away from these, gains a fixed and assured place in the perfect ordinances of virtue."

because of this faith, and shall, here below, become still more like it: 'Christ shall be formed in them,' e.g. he shall rise again, or be reborn (Gal. 4:19) in each individual Christian; every individual shall become an image of Christ. Of course, this 'life' is meanwhile [13] still hidden from the sight of men, 'hidden with Christ in God,' e.g. it is just as invisible as the exalted Christ, but it is none the less just as really present (Col. 3:3).

5. *The New Life in its Physical Aspect.* These paradoxes are the more daring since by this 'life' is not just simply meant a new moral life somewhat after the model or in the spirit of Christ's, no—in this word, just as in the words 'salvation' and 'savior,' spiritual, moral, religious and *physical* ideas are included. As sin was once the constant companion of the flesh, so the new 'life' is not only the overcoming of sin but also of material corruption. Life and incorruption or immortality (ἀφθαρσία and ἀθανασία I Cor. 15:53f), life and 'glory' (δόξα) are, essentially, similar possessions; and 'glory' means that state which is above all that is earthly, corrupt, impure and ungodly, that state in which God, his angels, and the exalted Christ are found.

The mystical paradox now actually goes so far as to maintain with passionate emotion that already in the present, in this earthly, sickly, sin-marred body of the Christian, there is growing and ripening that heavenly, divine life in its glory. This is just the full meaning of Rom. 8:2. The answer to the baffling question: "Who will deliver me from the body of this death?" (Rom. 7:24) is, "The law of the Spirit of life made me free from the law of sin and of death." For the Spirit of God is, indeed, not only an ethical and purifying power (I Cor. 6:11), it is, since the creation (Gen. 1:2), the source of all life upon the earth: 'the life-giving Spirit' (I Cor. 15:45). Therefore where the Spirit is, there is life. And 'if the Spirit of him that raised up Jesus from the dead,' if this wonderful life-creating Spirit thus 'dwelleth in you, he that' (it can be done no other way) 'raised up Christ Jesus from the dead shall quicken also your mortal bodies' (and so not yet dead) 'through his Spirit that dwelleth in you' (Rom. 8:11). The certainty expressed in this statement probably does not refer to the resurrection at the return of the Lord, but to an event completing itself in the present. Through the indwelling of the Spirit our corporeality will be changed from within into immortality. What I Cor. 15:52 describes as a sudden occurrence at the time of the Parousia appears here

[13] Cf. the pseudo-hermetic saying at the end of note 11.

as a gradual process. In similar fashion Paul says that the 'life of Jesus,' i.e. a power or substance indestructible by suffering and death, 'may be manifested in our mortal flesh' (II Cor. 4:10), or that while our outer man is being destroyed by suffering the inner man shall be renewed from day to day (4:16). This mysterious process of the continual regeneration of that which is wearing out, this revivifying of the dead, this transfiguration of the corruptible, is also assumed when it states in Col. 3:4, "When Christ, who is our life, shall be manifested, then shall ye also with him be manifested in glory," i.e. then it will be revealed that you weak, miserable, sinful men already secrete within yourselves a treasure of glory; then the last fleshly shell will fall away and you will appear as the angels of God (cf. also Rom. 8:18, 'the glory which shall be revealed in you'). That is the 'power of Christ's resurrection' which the Christian will experience in his own body, and by which he will be led to meet the real, final 'resurrection of the dead' (Phil. 3:10). This bold expectation is also connected with eschatology, for what happens here to the individual is nothing else than the beginning of that 'new creation' (II Cor. 5:17; Gal. 6:15), which is awaited at the time of the end, when a new heaven and a new earth will appear.[14] Thus we find here also that daring anticipation of the future which was as far as we can see an original primitive Christian conviction. However we believe we make no mistake when we hear in these paradoxes an echo of the language of that Hellenistic-Mystery teaching of rebirth. This becomes especially clear in a peculiar line of thought which only once finds expression in Paul.

In II Cor. 3:18 Paul says, "But we all, with unveiled face beholding as in a mirror the glory of the Lord, are transformed into the same image—from glory to glory even as from the Lord, who is the Spirit." The expression 'to see in a mirror,'[15] means here, as in I Cor. 13:12, the imperfect perception of divine things, as is only possible here below. We do not see the thing itself, but its image: *we* might say, 'with the imagination,' Paul expresses it, 'by faith and not by sight' (II Cor. 5:7). Now however the thought appears that in seeing, or through this seeing, we shall be changed into the same image which we perceive, namely into the glory of the Lord, and of course in a gradual victorious ascent 'from glory to glory.'

[14] Enoch 72:1; Rev. 21:5; Isa. 43:18; 65:17; II Pet. 3:13. It is remarkable that in Matt. 19:28 the consummation of the end is described by the word *palingenesia* which really refers to individual rebirth (Titus 3:5).

[15] This is here the only possible meaning.

The deeper we think ourselves into the image of the exalted one, the more intensively we see 'the things that are unseen' (II Cor. 4:18), so much the more do we ourselves grow into the sphere and nature of the invisible world, into the divine glory. This conception of a gradual transfiguration through the mystic 'seeing' of the deity, which is so strange to us, is quite common in the literature of Hellenistic mysticism.[16] Here again is a point in which the thought of Paul is illuminated by these contemporary parallels. The Christian can even now in the present permit himself to be permeated and transformed by immortal life and heavenly glory, if he will faithfully and unhesitatingly fill his soul with the image of his exalted Lord.

This is a different idea from that previously considered. There it was the divine creative Spirit himself who, linked with the exalted Lord, continuously streams into us; here it is conceived less materially, it is the spiritual connection with the Exalted One through the contemplation of the Gnosis, or through the Gnosis as contemplation through which the transformation is accomplished. But both ideas are by their nature mystical, and that means that here (a conception quite different from Old Testament and primitive Christian religion) life is not awaited as a gift to be received from God, as an act of his world-governance, but as the fruit of an immediate contact with Christ, whether by the out-pouring of the power of God or by faith or by Gnosis.

However, it appears once more in regard to this idea that Paul cannot carry it all the way through. For over against the mystical anticipation of transfiguration, there remains still the statement that not until the Parousia of the Lord shall the survivors be suddenly changed by a miracle of God or of Christ (I Cor. 15:52). This is also again made very clear in Phil. 3:21, according to which the Lord Jesus Christ, whom we await as Savior from heaven, will transform our lowly bodies, so that they will become like unto his transfigured body—by the power of his might which is able to subject all things to himself. At this point the mystical view with its anticipation of the future clashes again with an entirely different line of thought, namely with the eschatological.

[16] Cf. Reitzenstein on 'Knowledge as Sight' in *Mysterienrell.*, pp. 124ff, also the parallels in the Papyrus Mimaut and the *Corpus Hermeticum*, in which the idea is repeated that the Gnostic is himself deified by the vision of God: "Because by the sight of thyself, thou hast deified us while still in our bodies," and Poimandres 1:26, "This is the glorious aim for those who have knowledge: how to be deified (θεωθῆναι)."

CHAPTER XVIII

The Hope

If the mystical experience is the anticipation of future blessedness here and now, then mysticism is in a sense the abrogation or conquest of eschatology. Then in so far as the eschatological hope still prevails in the religion of Paul, to that extent it is not mystical. But this hope is very pronounced with him; therefore there is very little room for mysticism in his religion.

1. *The Longing for Christ*. Union with Christ cannot then have been understood by Paul as complete, or in any case only at certain moments when there was present an earnest desire for Christ, and this of course was not a desire for complete absorption and merging of oneself in him, but simply the longing to see him. The 'waiting' for the Parousia (I Thess. 1:10; I Cor. 1:7; Phil. 3:20) appears to have been the normal prevailing state of mind of the Christians and also of Paul. He longs to depart and be with Christ (Phil. 1:23; I Cor. 1:9; II Cor. 5:8; I Thess. 4:17). The Parousia however means for him, first of all, the revealing of the now hidden Lord (II Thess. 1:7; 1 Cor. 1:7; Col. 3:4). Since the Christians have held so long to the invisible Christ (II Cor. 5:7) and have been loyal to him with the courage of faith in spite of all their suffering and persecution for his sake, since they must often have been asked, "Where then is your Lord?"—surely they should and would have the experience at last of 'seeing him face to face,' and of his appearing in power and glory from heaven to judge unbelievers and be greeted by his saints with awestruck wonder (II Thess. 1:7-10). There lies in this hope a trace of that Jewish mode of thought which is also the basis for the faith in the resurrection (p. 100), namely that it must once more be revealed to the whole world that Jesus is really the Messiah, the Son of God, and that his followers are justified in their belief. Their conviction of the intrinsic truth of their belief, their own spiritual victory and their own personal experience of salvation—all must yet culminate in their living to see the outward triumph of the Son of God, even of God himself.

2. *The Victory of God over the World*. For this is indeed the final thing which Paul expects of the future, namely—according to apocalyptic teaching—the complete and conclusive victory of

God. It is the task of the exalted Christ to destroy all 'principalities, powers and dominions,' i.e. to rob them of their power, to eliminate their influence on the course of the world (I Cor. 15:24).[1] This is replaced in the verses following by the words of a Psalm (110:1), 'till he hath put all his enemies under his (or God's) feet,' so that he, Christ, and thus God, stands forth as victor (vv. 25-28). This is expressed in quite another way in Col. 1:20, according to which the final aim of the divine purpose is that all things or all beings on earth and in heaven shall again be reconciled through Christ, not 'with God' but 'unto him' (δι'αὐτοῦ ἀποκαταλλάξαι τὰ πάντα εἰς αὐτόυ or αὑτόυ). Because of this 'all things,' 'to reconcile' is really not a fitting translation, for the question here is not so much about the removal of a persistently hostile attitude toward God (cf. p. 514)—although this idea also plays a part, in that the spirits ruling in the cosmos are indeed for the most part 'enemies' of God—but rather that the world in some way or other has fallen away from God, released itself from him, removed itself from his influence, and will again return to him, will again be united with him.[2] We do not know the myth[3] of the world's apostasy from God which lies in the background, but whatever it may be it forms the presupposition for this 'cosmic doctrine of reconciliation.' When, then, the world-powers have been brought into subjection under God or to God, or have again been incorporated into the divine being and power, then the condition will be reached when 'God will be all in all' (I Cor. 15:28). This is a more abstract and philosophical expression for what the primitive Church called the 'dominion of God'.[4] Actually it indicates the same thing, only with the differ-

[1] The word καταργεῖν means 'to cause to be inactive,' 'to make ineffective.' Our modern 'eliminate' *(ausschalten)* is a suitable translation for it.

[2] Cf. Dibelius on Col. 1:20 in HBNT where Berakoth 16b (Bab. Talmud 1, 60. Goldschmidt) is quoted: "After his prayer R. Saphra used to say as follows, 'May it be thy will, O Lord our God, to establish peace in thy family above and below.'" In addition Hippolytus, *Philosophumena,* p. 156, 62 (Reitzenstein, *Poimandres* p. 93, § 21): "The name of Attis Papas means the cry of things in heaven and earth and under the earth: παῦε, παῦε τὴν ἀσυμφωνίαν τοῦ κόσμου (Make an end to the disharmony of the world)."

[3] Perhaps there is an allusion to it in Rom. 8:20, 'For the creation was subjected to vanity, not of its own will, but by reason of him who subjected it.' It is not quite clear to me what Paul means in this statement. He can hardly be thinking of Adam; more likely of Satan or of some world spirit who by his insubordination had brought the world to ruin.

[4] In the Mechilta (Friedmann 56a) it is stated: 'Then will God (המקום) [lit. The Place] be alone in the world and his dominion will endure for ever and ever.' In the prayer (עלינו) which originated in Babylon about 240 A.D., utterance is given to the expectation that God through his royal dominion will finally reduce the world to order

ence that God is not here thought of as a personal king, but as that world-force which permeates the universe and decides the fate of all living things. If God is 'all in all,' this means even more than that God has dominion over all. Should not the thought be then that, as all things once came forth 'from God' (Rom. 11:36; I Cor. 8:6) and are destined to return 'unto him' or empty into him, so God, at the end as it were, takes everything back into himself, so that he alone remains?

However Paul may have conceived of this conclusion of world-history or pictured it in detail, this much is clear, that he did not assume an enthronement of Christ by the side of God for all eternity. We recall (p. 474) that Christ, at the end, after the complete subjugation of the rulers and powers, is to deliver up the kingdom to (his) God and Father and subject himself to him; he returns in fact to the rank of creatures; he also is one of the beings in whom God is all in all.

3. *The Dominion of the Saints*. To the traditional ideas taken from apocalyptic and primitive Christianity concerning the end, there belongs also the hope that the 'saints' will reign as kings (Rom. 5:17; I Cor. 4:8) or will share in the Lordship of God (I Thess. 2:12; Gal. 5:21; I Cor. 6:10; Eph. 5:5). This is also expressed in another way, namely they will rule with Christ (II Tim. 2:12), or be glorified with him (Rom. 8:17,30). They will 'judge' the world, especially the fallen angels (I Cor. 6:2f). This idea of the salvation which comes at the time of the end is exactly like that of the prophecy of Daniel which culminates in the conception that the saints of the Most High shall receive royal dominion (over the world).[5] Here it is Israel's world-dominion which is meant. Paul however applied the word 'saints' to the Christians. It cannot be accurately determined how he conceives of this ruling and judging —whether the Christians will merely have seats on the tribunal at

---

(לתכן), so that 'all will bow under the yoke of thy rule.' Another prayer (Seder Kam Amram 1, 9a) reads: 'Our king and God, make thy name the only one (יחד) in thy world, make thy rule the only one in thy world, make thy remembrance the only one in thy world' (Cf. Dalman, *Worte Jesu* 1, 82). Clementine Homilies: 'O thou ruler and lord of all—Thou art the cause, Thou the power—Thou the helper, the physician, the savior, the wall, the life, the hope—In a word, thou art all things to us.' CIL X, 3800: 'Goddess Isis, thou who though one art all things.' Martial V 24: 'Hermes alone is all things and thrice one' [cf. Hermes Trismegistus]. Cleanthes, Hymn, 7ff, 'But thou hast skill to make the crooked straight and to turn disorder into order. Unfriendly things are friendly in thy sight, for so dost thou combine all good and ill that out of all appears one Reason that endures always.'

[5] Dan. 7:18.

the last judgment of God or of Christ, or whether they will have an active part as judges themselves, or whether—after the destruction of the principalities and powers and after the judging of the sinners—there will still be any fit objects over which to rule. One is left with the impression that these representations are traditional material to some extent grown lifeless, with which Paul is with difficulty combining a conception that is clear and vital. In any case, in the principal passage, Rom. 5:17, 'they shall reign in life' (ἐν ζωῇ βασιλεύσουσιν), the emphasis seems to lie much more strongly upon the living than upon the ruling.[6]

4. *Life, Salvation, Glory*. The commonest expression by far, for the future blessedness, is 'life'[7] or 'eternal life.' Next in order is 'deliverance' or 'salvation' (σωτηρία),[8] both having essentially the same meaning. Then just as the word 'salvation,' or 'deliverance' has both a material and a spiritual, religious sense (cf. p. 429), so also the word 'life' has a double meaning. It means of course first of all that the 'saints' or the 'elect' will not die at the Judgment Day (Rom. 8:13), but will remain alive and will have overcome the last traces of corruption and mortality. Death will be swallowed up by life (I Cor. 15:55; II Cor. 5:4). They will thus be 'made alive' (I Cor. 15:22) in the sense of possessing immortality. But just as their 'salvation' means also redemption, peace with God, freedom from sin, communion with God, so also 'life' has the other meaning of true, genuine, divine life, as we find notably in Rom. 7:9,24; 8:2, where it stands in sharp antithesis to 'death' in sin.[9]

[6] The word 'reign' (βασιλεύσουσιν) seems almost to have been introduced here through the influence of the previous 'death reigned' (ἐβασίλευσεν).

[7] Ζωή [life] Rom. 5:17f; 7:10; 8:2,10; II Cor. 2:16; 5:4; Phil. 4:3; Col. 3:3f. Ζωὴ αἰώνιος [eternal life] Rom. 2:7; 5:21; 6:22f. Ζῆν [to live] Rom. 1:17; 8:13; II Cor. 6:9; 13:4; Gal. 3:11f; I Thess. 5:10.

[8] σώζεσθαι [to be saved] Rom. 5:9f; 8:34; 10:9,13; 11:26; I Cor. 1:18,21; 5:5; 15:2; II Cor. 2:15; I Thess. 2:16; II Thess. 2:10. σωτηρία [salvation] Rom. 1:16; 10:1,10f; 13:11; II Cor. 6:2; Phil. 2:12; I Thess. 5:8f; II Thess. 2:13. As regards this idea in Hellenistic religion, cf. p. 233 and Wendland, *Hell.-Röm. Kultur,* pp. 75ff, 82; Reitzenstein, *Hellenist. Mysterien-rel.*, pp. 12, 25, etc. Cf. especially the mystical verse from the mystery of Attis (Osiris?): "Be of good cheer, ye initiates, since the god is saved (σεσωσμένου), for to us will be salvation (σωτηρία) from toils." The double meaning of σώζειν should be noticed, in one place of rescue from death, in the other of rescue from suffering, affliction, sin(?). Cf. Apuleius, *Metam.* XI, 29: 'Hope of salvation *(salutis)* restored to thee.' Also *Corpus Hermet.* XIV, 1: 'That no one can be saved (σωθῆναι) before the regeneration.'

[9] This meaning which is very common in Philo (an echo of Heraclitus' philosophy?) and is prevalent in the Gospel of John, occurs also in Matt. 8:22; Luke 15:22, but is less frequent in Paul than might be expected. The chief passage (Col. 2:13) is under suspicion of having been interpolated from Eph. 2:1,5.

In addition to this there appears the hope of glorification (δόξα, δοξάζεσθαι) [10] or transfiguration, i.e. the change from a state of corruption, vassalage, and sinfulness, into the heavenly condition of 'sons of God,' i.e. into the condition of the angels. It is characteristic of Paul that the hope set up for the individual is more often and more strongly expressed than the expectation of the great world-catastrophe. The thought of the Kingdom of God as something to be realized by all, falls into the background because of his concern for the salvation of the individual. This feeling of the importance of the individual may perhaps be designated as Hellenistic. The Jewish 'messianic' hope is applied first to the people of God, secondly to the victory of God over the world, and only thirdly to the participation of the individual in the Kingdom of God. The devout Hellenist would ask first of all, how do I gain life, how do I overcome death?

Life, salvation, glory are future possessions. This is the prevailing view, and when Paul in Rom. 8:30, boldly anticipating, says that God 'has glorified his elect,' or when he believes that he experiences that transfiguration and life already in the present (II Cor. 3:18; Rom. 8:10f), he himself indicates (Rom. 8:24) that this is a paradoxical exaggeration of the reality: 'by hope we are saved.' [11] Actually the idea of 'life' or of 'glory' cannot be carried to a conclusion in this world for the reason that he assumes as a fundamental principle that 'flesh and blood cannot inherit the Kingdom of God, and corruption can never inherit incorruption' (I Cor. 15:50). Paul is too deeply impressed with the unbridged chasm which exists between the divine and the human, between the heavenly and the earthly, between spirit and flesh, between the glory of the divine nature and the weak, impure, corruptible nature of men. He already had this feeling as a Jew, how much more as an Hellenist! From the viewpoint of later Judaism it is before all else the distance between man and the Most High God; in Hellenism it is

[10] Rom. 3:23; 5:2; 8:18,21; 9:23; I Cor. 2:7; 15:43; II Cor. 3:18; 4:17; Phil. 3:21; Col. 3:4; I Thess. 2:12; II Thess. 2:14.

[11] Τῇ ἐλπίδι ἐσώθημεν—The phrase is moderate and restrained in this place, but in Eph. 2:5 the mode of expression, "By grace ye have been saved" (σεσωσμένοι ἐστέ) is exaggerated as so often in Ephesians, e.g. "God . . . . quickened us together with Christ . . . . and raised us up with him, and made us to sit with him in the heavenly places, in Christ Jesus" (Eph. 4:5,6). The phrase in Tit. 3:5 is more strongly ecclesiastical; there the baptized is saved merely by his baptism. But Paul himself has set the example in this way of speaking when he speaks of 'winning' and 'converting' as 'saving,' using the language of missionary address. Cf. I Cor. 7:16; 9:22.

the stamp of corruption on man which makes impossible any lasting union between God and man as he now is.

The overcoming of death is an absolutely essential feature in Paul's picture of the future. The 'last enemy, death, shall be destroyed' (I Cor. 15:23; cf. Rev. 20:14). Even though we might wish to eliminate this somewhat disjointed sentence from the original text it nevertheless contains Paul's meaning. For indeed it is the final and highest triumph of God, that death shall be 'swallowed up in victory' (I Cor. 15:54), that same death of which it is said in Rom. 5:12 that it came into the world through Adam, according to the *Wisdom of Solomon* (2:24) through the envy of the devil.[12] The destruction of death is evidently the same procedure as the freeing of the creature from the bondage of corruption (φθορά) into the liberty of the glory of the children of God (Rom. 8:21). Paul expects a general world-transfiguration, a new creation (II Cor. 5:17; Gal. 6:15). To the faith of the mystic it is already beginning here below; but it will be fully consummated only in the future.

5. *Resurrection*. This great event Paul, with a phrase borrowed from Judaism, calls the 'Resurrection' (I Cor. 15) or 'the resurrection of the dead.' It belongs to the dogmas of the faith taken over quite obviously from the messianic teaching of the Pharisees by Paul[13] as also by Jesus (Mark 12:25ff). The resurrection of the dead is by no means the really distinctive teaching of Christianity as the author of the Book of Acts considers it. In the religion of the Pharisees it is connected in the closest manner with the messianic hope. If indeed salvation and retribution are to appear only at the time of the end, then the 'righteous' of former generations who died without having experienced a reward for their righteousness would be the losers. God would remain permanently indebted to them if he did not, by the resurrection of the dead, provide an opportunity to repay them that to which they were entitled. To meet this demand the hope was directed in the first place toward the resurrection of the righteous,[14] but there appears also the

[12] We notice here once more, as in the case of 'sin' and 'flesh,' that semi-personification of an abstract idea, as though there were an angel or demon of death.

[13] The phrase has become such a fixed dogma with Paul that he occasionally uses it of Christians of whom he elsewhere takes it for granted that they will live to see the Parousia (I Cor. 6:14; II Cor. 4:14; Phil. 3:11).

[14] *Psalms of Solomon* 3:16 ,"But they that fear the Lord shall rise to life eternal, and their life shall be in the light of the Lord, and shall come to an end no more." 14:2, "The pious of the Lord shall live in him forever;" vs. 4: "But not so are the sinners and transgressors." Vv. 6f: "Their inheritance is Sheôl and darkness and destruction . . . . but the pious of the Lord shall inherit life in gladness."

thought of a universal resurrection for judgment.[15] In the Book of Revelation these two events are arranged one before and the other after the thousand-year reign of the Messiah. The martyrs who are restored to life for the purpose will share in this (Rev. 20:4). At the close of this period the general judgment of the dead who have been raised will take place (Rev. 20:12f). Paul too is firmly convinced that the resurrection of the Christians will come first, I Thess. 4:16: the dead in Christ shall arise first; I Cor. 15:23: those who are Christ's will arise at his coming. Indeed it seems that he thought only of a resurrection of Christians, for when it is stated in I Cor. 15:22: 'as in Adam all die, so in Christ shall all be made alive'—it would seem that membership in Christ is a necessary condition for resurrection. However one may also take the second 'all' in a more general way: as through one man death came into the world (Rom. 5:12), so, the logic of this section seems to demand (p. 434), through Christ death has been eliminated, with the result that through him life is brought to all men, and it is in fact so stated in Rom. 5:18. On the whole it appears to follow from Paul's reasoning that all, both the dead and even the ungodly, will in some way be finally reunited with God and brought under his authority. Thus we should be obliged to postulate for him the doctrine of a general resurrection of the dead even though it were not expressed. Moreover this does really seem to be done. For in I Cor. 15:23f, three groups are differentiated at the resurrection. The first-fruits of those that slept, who come to life again, is Christ; then follow those who belong to him; then—and now comes a word (τέλος) which can perhaps be understood in this sense—then (will be made alive) the rest, i.e. the rest of the dead.[16] In this case we should have the view of a double resurrection in Paul as well as in the Book of Revelation. There may perhaps also be assumed here a longer interval of time between the Parousia of Christ and the transfer of dominion to the Father.

However the case may be with this particular question, at any rate Paul believes firmly in the resurrection of the dead. It is indeed

[15] Daniel 12:2; *Book of Enoch* 51:1f, "In those days shall the earth also give back that which has been entrusted to it, and Sheôl also shall give back that which it has received, and hell shall give back that which it owes . . . . and he (the Elect One) shall choose the righteous and holy from among them" (cf. Schürer III[4], § 29, 10, pp. 638ff.)

[16] Another way of taking it is: 'then (comes) the end;' but this interpretation is less convincing; a new verb would be needed. As the words stand τὸ τέλος goes with ζωοποιηθήσονται. Cf. my Commentary on I Cor. 15:24.

for him an essential constituent part of the messianic hope.[17] Moreover, since the messianic hope has been to a large extent realized in the appearance of Christ, this is also the case with the resurrection. It has begun already with the resurrection of Christ. If he is the first-fruits, or the first-born from the dead (I Cor. 15:20,23; Col. 1:18), it is then certain that the full harvest will follow—this is contained in the picture of the 'first sheaf.' The great drama of the end of the world has already been inaugurated by the resurrection of Christ.

This fact, for him irrefutable, was plainly proved not only by Scripture but also by the experiences of the primitive Church and by his own (I Cor. 15:3-8), and formed for him the firm foundation of all faith and all hope—so much so that he would rather give up the reality of the experience of salvation and the truth of all his preaching of the Gospel than it (I Cor. 15:14,17); "If Christ be not risen then is your faith vain, and ye are still in your sins." His whole life, rich in sacrifice and suffering, would be senseless and without purpose if Christ were not risen. Yes, he even goes so far as to make the deduction, surely not intended seriously: "Let us eat and drink, for tomorrow we die!" He could not have written all these sentences if they had not been wholly unreal to him. He merely plays with the hypothesis, he just grants the thesis of his opponents that there was no resurrection of the dead, then consequently there was no resurrection of Christ (I Cor. 15:12-19). But this latter is indeed a fact. By this one case then that universal negative assertion has been shattered and proved to be untrue. Truly one senses here as it were the taking of a long deep breath, marking the return from that unreal manner of argument to reality: "But now hath Christ been raised from the dead!" (15:20). The miracle of God has brought to shame the enlightenment of the Hellenistic deniers of the resurrection.

But to be sure he is not so far removed from those deniers as he himself supposes. We must examine more closely the deeper reasons for the controversy that is fought out in I Cor. 15. The opponents were Christians. They too had once faithfully accepted the message of the resurrection of Christ (15:11). How then did they come to say, there is no resurrection of the dead?

We do not know their views and arguments in detail, but we

[17] Cf. *Apocalypse of Baruch* 30:1 [II Baruch in Charles, *Apocrypha and Pseudepigrapha,* vol. II], "And it shall come to pass after these things, when the time of the advent of the Messiah is fulfilled, that he shall return in glory. Then all who have fallen asleep in hope of him shall rise again."

shall certainly not be wrong in assuming that they did not wish to deny 'immortality' and 'life'—for otherwise they would not have been Christians. They were combatting the peculiarly Jewish doctrine that the dead would appear from their graves with the same bodies with which they were buried. The imprint of corruption and of the destruction of the body through death is too deeply engrained in Hellenistic sentiment to be able to believe in the reanimation of the material body. Indeed it cannot even appear to it to be desirable, for the Greek belief in immortality, brought to its highest expression in the Orphic religion and in Platonic philosophy, took for granted the idea that the soul is imprisoned in the body and that separation from the body means its liberation.[18] Therefore from this standpoint the Jewish belief in the resurrection must appear not only as rationally unthinkable but also senseless and absurd. It was in the face of such a denial that Paul now most firmly and unconditionally held to the 'resurrection of the dead.' But, as he had already conceived of the resurrection of Christ (pp. 83f) in quite a different sense from that of the popular view, not as a return to the earthly life, but as an exaltation into the heavenly life, as a release from material flesh and an investiture with the transfigured body of glory, so he likewise gave an entirely new meaning to the resurrection of the dead. For him the question was, "How do the dead arise? With what body do they come?"

The putting of these questions was highly significant. He thereby departed from a simple belief in the soul. He could not imagine a disembodied soul, or as he says, a 'naked' existence after death.

[18] Erwin Rohde, *Psyche* II[2] pp. 121ff, 126, "The essential thing is that according to this (Orphic) teaching, life in a body is not the soul's natural destiny but is its opposite." "The wages of sin is in this case that life upon earth which for the soul is death." The body is a grave (*σῶμα σῆμα*, Plato *Cratylus* 400c). "It is beyond calculation what power has been wielded since their first appearance by the Platonic Dialogues in the confirmation, dissemination, and precise definition of the belief in immortality—a power that with all its alteration in the passage of the centuries has maintained itself unbroken into our own times" (p. 265). The soul is 'older than the body.' In the *Phaedrus* this 'fall into birth' appears as the necessary result of an intellectual fall. Though enclosed within the body, it remains a stranger to the body, bound to the body through impulses of a lower kind; not unscathed does it leave behind it, in death, its ill-assorted companion, the body (*τῆς ψυχῆς ἀπὸ τοῦ σώματος ἀπαλλαγή*, *Phaedo* 64c) [release of the soul from the body]. Then it goes into an intermediate region of bodiless existence in which it must do penance for the misdeeds of its life on earth. After that it is driven once more into a body—thus it lives through a series of earthly lives. Its task is plain: it must free itself from its impure companions. If it can succeed in this it will find once more the 'way upwards' which at last leads it into complete immunity from renewed incarnation and brings it home again into the kingdom of everlasting untroubled Being (pp. 265-277). [See W. B. Hillis' translation of *Psyche,* New York, 1925.]

He was only sure that 'we shall not be found naked' (II Cor. 5:3)[19] —even after we have put off this earthly body. The picture of the putting-on or off of a garment[20] can be appreciated only if the conception of the inner and outer man is kept in mind (II Cor. 4:18). The inner man in both stages is unaltered, he merely changes the garment. After the putting-off of the flesh[21] (Col. 2:11), he will put on a new body, of course a heavenly, spiritual one, i.e. not of flesh and blood, but consisting of that fine, imperishable, heavenly fabric which may then be designated as 'conformed to the body of his glory' (Phil. 3:21). This is just what is meant by the phrase 'being glorified with Christ' (Rom. 8:17). This body is, according to a tradition used by Paul, already present in heaven (II Cor. 5:1), one for each separate individual,[22] in the place of the earthly tabernacle 'a building from God'; instead of the perishable body, 'an eternal habitation'; in place of the tangible, corporeal, one 'not made with hands.' How this change or transfiguration (μεταμόρφωσις, μετασχηματισμός, Phil. 3:21) takes place cannot be clearly known. Paul says in I Cor. 15:52f, 'the dead shall be raised incorruptible.' Since

> This corruptible must put on incorruption,
> and this mortal must put on immortality,

[19] The idea of existence without a body is also found in Seneca, *Ep.* 66, 3: "If she (nature) could have produced souls by themselves and naked, she would have done so." Cf. also *Gorgias* 523 EC; Lucian, *Necyomant.* 12. In II Cor. 5:3, *εἴπερ* (BFG) *καὶ ἐκδυσάμενοι* (FG) *οὐ γυμνοὶ εὑρεθησόμεθα* [If indeed we shall be found not naked even when we have been unclothed] should be read. Cf. my Commentary on I Cor. 15:38.

[20] Very frequently in this connection, e.g. Philo *Leg. Alleg.* II, § 80; Seneca, *Ad Marciam* 25: 1; Ascension of Isaiah 4:16; 8:14; Corp. Hermet., VII, 2, 3, "But first you must tear off this garment which you wear, this web of ignorance, this prop of evil, this bond of corruption, this cloke of darkness, this living death (Reitzenstein compares Rom. 7:24: 'from the body of this death'), this conscious corpse, this tomb you carry about with you." There is a striking correspondence between this and the picture of the house in II Cor. 5:1f. The word *σκῆνος* [tent] is quite common in Greek writers, meaning body, without any consciousness of metaphor, e.g. Plato (Clement Al., *Strom.* V, p. 293); *γήϊνον* [of earth] *σκῆνος*; *Wisdom* 9:15, *τὸ γεῶδες* [the earthly] *σκῆνος*; Corp. Herm. XIII = Reitz. XIV, p. 344: *τὸ σκῆνος τοῦτο*; CIG III 609 = Kaibel Ep. Gr. 711: *σκῆνος λιπόσαρκον* [skinny].

[21] Maximus of Tyre, *Diss.*, 16: 2, "The soul stripped of the body wandered in the air like a bird."

[22] In the *Ascension of Isaiah* [London, S.P.C.K., 1918] we read of 'the garments, and the thrones, and the crowns which are laid up for the righteous (8:26); and it is said, "There I saw all the righteous from the time of Adam—stript of the garments of the flesh, and I saw them in their garments of the upper world—standing there in great glory" (9:7ff). Cf. Corp. Hermet. XIII (Reitz. XIV), p. 340, "I passed through myself into an immortal body"; p. 344, "This tent (body) which we have passed through is formed from the circle of animals" [the zodiac].

this change must take place either at the moment of the resurrection, or, more probably, during the rest in the grave. Perhaps it was conceived somewhat in this manner, that in the case of these dead—at first only the Christians who have died are in mind—the Spirit of God which was in them had meanwhile slowly completed the 'quickening' of their mortal bodies (Rom. 8:11; pp. 523f), so that at the moment of the resurrection the final remnant of the mortal body remained behind in the grave as a cast-off garment, and they emerged from the grave now fully transfigured in bodies of glory. By this conception of the resurrection of the dead Paul avoided the offence which this idea gave to Hellenistic sentiment; it had to do of course with the resurrection, but not with the reanimation of the earthly body. Mortality or corruption were still its due; the grave retained that which was mortal, and what proceeded out of it was what the Greeks would call the 'soul,' but which Paul called the 'inner man.' Except that the soul or ego, bodiless as a shadow, did not 'wander like a bird through the air' (Maximus of Tyre, see p. 535, note 21), but possessed a new definite form, a distinct appearance, an instrument of vigorous life, a new body consisting of celestial material—all this lay in the Pauline concept of body (σῶμα), which one might at times almost translate as 'personality.' Paul laid a decided emphasis on this idea. The bodiless woeful existence of the shades in Hades (in the '*Nekuia*' of the Odyssey, or in Isa. 14:9f), or of the souls hovering over the graves, wandering through the realm of the air, or vanishing into outward space, seemed to him an unbearable condition, the opposite of that blessedness or immortality for which he yearned. He who desired to be united with Christ, to dwell near to God, must rise again to full and perfect life. In this conviction he was in agreement with the Jewish doctrine of resurrection, and for this there was needed of course a 'body,' certainly not an earthly, fleshly one, for

> Flesh and blood cannot inherit the Kingdom of God,
> neither doth corruption inherit incorruption

—in this he is again in agreement with Jew and Hellenist.[23] Thus

[23] Josephus, *War,* VII § 344: "For association with what is mortal is unbecoming for what is divine." *Book of Wisdom* 6:19, "Incorruption bringeth near unto God." *Mithras-Liturgie,* Introd.: "Since it is not within the reach of me that have been born a mortal to approach the golden flashings of the immortal lustre." Cf. especially the *Apocalypse of Baruch,* chh. 50, 51: "Then the dead rise just as they were delivered to the earth, for then it will be necessary to show to the living that the dead have come to life again and that they are returned again (ἦλθον; cf. ἔρχονται [do they come] I Cor.

we see that Paul in his doctrine of the resurrection took a middle position between the crude physical belief of popular Judaism and the more spiritual hope common to Hellenistic thought. Here we might also ask, as in the case of the resurrection of Christ, whether he could not have done without the concept of the resurrection altogether. It seems as if he might have developed some such theory as this: that the dead, at the very moment of death, after the stripping-off of their mortal bodies, are at once removed to heaven and transfigured into heavenly glory. We can see at once that this idea is not in itself so remote from his thought (cf. Phil. 1:23)—but it is never clearly developed, nor does it become predominant, because the Jewish Apocalyptic tradition, according to which the dead who are asleep in the grave (Dan. 12:2; I Thess. 4:13f) shall only be awakened at the last day, had had too strong an influence upon him.

6. *The Transformation of those who Survive to the Resurrection*. In I Cor. 15 and I Thess. 4 Paul was occupied with still another problem, namely the fate of those still alive at the Parousia. That the old Christian communities and Paul himself were convinced that the majority of the brethren would live to see the second coming of Christ may be seen especially from the section I Thess. 4:13ff. The excitement of the Thessalonian community over some cases of death in its midst (p. 295) had reached such a height only because it feared that these 'who had died in Christ' would now fail to attain salvation. Paul appeased this anxiety with a word of the Lord, which proved that they who are yet alive will not precede those who are fallen asleep.[24] They will arise first, then we the living, the survivors, will be snatched up into the clouds at the same time with them to meet the Lord in the air. Just how this is to happen is

15:35). And when they have severally recognized (it is for this purpose that they must rise in bodily form) those whom they now know, then judgment shall grow strong—and after that appointed day has gone by, then shall the aspect of those who are condemned be afterwards changed and the glory of those who are justified. For the aspect of those who now act wickedly shall become worse than it is, as they shall suffer torment, also the glory of those who have now been justified in my Law—their radiance (δόξα) will flash out in a different manner—and the appearance of their faces will be changed into its dazzling beauty that they may be able to acquire and receive the world that doth not die—they will be changed into the radiance of angels—and time shall no longer age them, for in the heights of that world shall they dwell and they shall be made like unto the angels (ἰσάγγελοι, Luke 20:36) and be made equal to the stars. And they shall be changed into every form they desire—from beauty into splendor and from light to the radiance of glory" (cf. ἀπὸ δόξης εἰς δόξαν, II Cor. 3:18).

[24] If one wishes to restore the word of the Lord there remains—after removing the additions—only the following: "(we that are alive) that are left (unto the coming of the Lord) shall in no wise precede them that are fallen asleep."

not evident. It is only clear that Paul does not express himself as to what the condition will be of those who are yet alive who are thus united with Christ. But it may be assumed that this 'snatching away' will in some way take place 'in the spirit' (as e.g. Rev. 4:2); that is, they are transplanted into a purely 'pneumatic' state, are changed into the condition of heavenly spiritual existence. Paul clearly expresses himself with this meaning in I Cor. 15:52, and of course this change will take place suddenly in a moment, i.e. miraculously, as if by magic. We have already seen (pp. 524f) that this idea comes into conflict with the mystic concept. According to the latter, this change is to take place now in the present through the transforming, glorifying influence of the life-giving Spirit (Rom. 8:10f; II Cor. 3:18). The contradiction between these two points of view may perhaps be harmonized in this way, that only at that final, sudden transformation shall the last remaining remnant of earthly corporeality fall away and be absorbed by life, so that henceforth the Christians shall be 'manifested in glory' (Col. 3:4). The transfiguration which has already taken place within shall come to light. They 'shall be revealed' as the 'sons of God,' which they already are in their secret souls (Rom. 8:19). Thus the 'quick' will have just the same experience as the dead who are rising again, viz. transfiguration into heavenly bodies. Without this they could have no part in salvation.

But still a further question engaged the Apostle. Paul in general shared the expectation of the churches; he hoped to live to see the Parousia; quite confidently and simply he says, "we that are alive" (I Thess. 4:15,17; I Cor. 15:51f). But that experience in the province of Asia (II Cor. 1:8) where he had to face almost certain death, as well as that martyrdom which threatened him at the time of his imprisonment, seem to have made him familiar with the thought that he might have to die before it took place, and that was quite in accordance with his wish at the time of the Epistle to the Philippians; he had a 'desire to depart.' However when he then continues 'and to be with Christ' (Phil. 1:23) he evidently does not consider his future to be similar to that of those 'who have fallen asleep in Christ.' He does not speak of the peace of the grave or of resurrection, but of an immediate union with the Exalted One at the moment of death. Here the other idea of death and of the exaltation to heaven in power comes into view, one which we noticed earlier (p. 26; Luke 16:22; 23:43,46; 22:69). Just as in our popular view today two conceptions are impartially accepted: the idea that we conceal our dead in the bosom of the earth until the day of the joyful resurrection; and the other, that at the moment of death they are already standing before God and from above are looking down upon us, so too both appear in Paul. Did he feel them at variance with each other, did he seek to reconcile them? This seems to be the case in the obscure section II Cor. 5:1-5, the exegesis of which has up to the present been far from successful.[25] Without going into all the questions which it raises we will just quote from it that sentence which is certainly puzzling enough: "We would not be unclothed (put off the garment of the earthly body) but be clothed upon (with the heavenly body), that what is mortal may be swallowed up of life." Here the hope or the wish seems to be expressed that instead of mournful, dreadful death there might be granted to us that miraculous transformation which is to be the lot of those who will still be living at the time of the Parousia, but before the Parousia, even *now*, if God wills it. And then this process is more fully described: the new body which will be laid like a garment upon the old shall absorb the latter, just as the cloak of Nessus devoured the body of Heracles with fiery torments. However this passage may be interpreted, it is most significant how Paul in this matter too is dependent upon different sets of ideas offered to him by tradition: the Jewish teaching concerning resurrection, and the idea of an immediate ascent to a heavenly existence; the former very closely connected with eschatology, the latter fundamentally quite independent of apocalyptic conceptions of the end. This juxtaposition is a further indication of how Paul stands between two worlds, between the Jewish apocalyptic and that hope of immortality which appears, it is true, in Judaism, but is found also in Hellenism.[26]

[25] Cf. an important discussion in Reitzenstein, *Hellenist.-Mysterienrell.*, p. 175.

[26] Cf. Bousset, *Religion des Judentums,* XIII: 7, 2d ed., 'The Resurrection of the Dead,' pp. 308ff, and XIV, 'The Recompense in the World to Come.' In Judaism, and indeed not only in Judaism that was definitely Hellenistic, was also found the conception of the exaltation of the faithful to God at the moment of death. This is found especially in the Similitudes of Enoch where Enoch sees the dwelling places of the righteous and the elect with the angels beneath the wings of the Lord of Spirits (39:4ff). In just the same way is Lazarus carried directly by the angels into Abraham's bosom (Luke 16:23). Cf. also the views of Posidonius on the continued existence of souls in the realm of the air, 'in the mansions above' (Tert., *De Anima,* 54); 'transferred into the air' (Marcus Aurelius, 4:21) 'the place beneath the moon' (Sextus Empiricus, *Adv. Phys.,* 1:73). Cf. Rohde, *Psyche* II², pp. 320f; Seneca, *Ad Marciam de Consol.,* 25, 1ff: "There is no need, therefore, for you to run to the tomb of your son; what lies there is his basest part, and a part that in life was the source of great trouble; bones and ashes are no more parts of him than were his clothes and the other protec-

7. *The Judgment*. The proclamation of 'the wrath to come' (I Thess. 1:10; Rom. 1:18; 2:5; 3:5; 5:9; Col. 3:6) and of the righteous judgment of God (Rom. 2:5,16; II Thess. 1:5) [27] forms the very basis of the missionary preaching of Paul. That God 'will judge the world' (Rom. 3:6,19; I Cor. 6:2; 11:32) is to him as to all Jews a fixed tenet. What we are to understand by 'world' is shown in I Cor. 4:9, namely angels and men: the judgment will extend even to the angels (I Cor. 6:3,5).[28]

In this judgment, as has been said earlier (p. 528; I Cor. 6:2f), the Christians will also participate.[29] If this idea were thought through to its logical conclusion it would mean that Christians will not be subjected to the judgment at all. And indeed they are really the ones who shall be rescued from the wrath to come (Rom. 5:9; I Thess. 5:9); their 'salvation' consists just in this, that they escape the judgment. This is the result of the apocalyptic conception of the judgment which even from the beginning was intended only for pronouncing a verdict on the heathen world, sinners and powers hostile

tions of the body. He is complete and has fled away, leaving nothing of himself behind and has wholly departed (ἐξεδήμησε? cf. ἐκδημῆσαι, to be absent; II Cor. 5:8). For a little while he tarried above us while he was being purified and was ridding himself of all the blemishes and the stain that still clung to him from his mortal existence, *then he soared aloft and sped away to join the souls of the blessed,* the Scipios and Catos and those who despised life and found freedom by the grace of death. Your father, Marcia, though they are all akin with all, keeps near him his grandson, rejoicing in the new-found light, and teaches him the movements of the neighboring stars and gladly initiates him into nature's secrets, not by guesswork, but by experience, having true knowledge of them all—for it is a pleasure to look back from on high on all that has been left behind and to allow one's gaze to rest on the earth far below—the paths are smooth for all and souls moving freely and unencumbered are pervious to the matter of the stars and in turn are mingled with it." Cf. also Cicero, *Somnium Scipionis.* On the popular beliefs as revealed by inscriptions, cf. Rohde II^2, pp. 384f. Even though only the soul's continued existence is spoken of here, there recurs beside this, on the Hellenistic side, the old Greek belief in the Translation of Souls (Rohde I^2, pp. 68ff). Thus as regards kings and emperors, Arrian (*Anabasis* vii. 27, 3) mentions as the popular belief about Alexander that his birth was from a god and his going would be to the gods. Cf. the standard phrase, 'to transfer from among men to the gods' (Dittenb., *Syll.* 246,16; *Pergam. Inscr.* I, 240,4; I, p. 39a) and of Osiris (Diod. Sic., i. 25. 7), 'departed from among men.'

[27] In the picture of the final scene in I Thess. 4:15ff and I Cor. 12:23-28 there is certainly no place left for this act: Paul is there directing his entire attention to the resurrection so that he neglects to complete the list of events. One may however assume that the judgment must be inserted after the rising of those 'who are left' (I Cor. 15:24).

[28] *Enoch* 90:24f; 91:15; Isa. 24:21.

[29] *Enoch* 95:3, "Fear not the sinners, ye righteous, for again will the Lord deliver them into your hands, that ye may execute judgment upon them according to your desires." 98:12, "Know (ye sinners) that ye shall be delivered into the hands of the righteous and they shall cut off your necks and slay you and have no mercy upon you." 96:1, "Be hopeful, ye righteous, for suddenly shall the sinners perish before you and ye shall have lordship over them according to your desires."

to God, while the sparing of the people of God or the righteous was taken as a matter of course.[30] However along with this there appears in the missionary preaching of Paul the thought taken over from Pharisaism or even from Hellenistic Judaism, of the general and twofold judgment of both the just and unjust whose impartial character he describes in detail in Rom. 2:3-11, not without expressly placing the Jews under this judgment (Rom. 2:10-13,16). Really we might say that in this section Paul discusses the lot of humanity as it would be if a new way of salvation had not been offered to it by the Gospel; and as for the Christians who are standing upon the firm ground of the new salvation, and who have indeed already passed through the judgment, in so far as they have already been declared righteous (Rom. 5:1), all this would no longer be true; and especially would the basic principle that God 'will reward everyone according to his works' disappear, for works as the standard of judgment would henceforth be eliminated (Rom. 3:28 χωρὶς ἔργων) and salvation would be granted to them on the ground of faith alone. In fact the logic of the situation seems to demand that it is not because of the doctrine of justification by grace through faith alone, but it is above all because of the experience of justification and redemption that the Christians can no longer be concerned with the Last Judgment, since they have already received their sentence, grace, forgiveness and adoption. Nevertheless Paul sets not only 'them that are without' (I Cor. 5:13) but Christians also before the seat of the judgment (I Thess. 4:6; I Cor. 4:4f; 11:32; Rom. 14:10; II Cor. 5:10; Col. 3:25, etc.). It is essential for them too on the 'day of the Lord' to stand before Jesus Christ blameless and unreproveable (I Cor. 1:8; I Thess. 3:13; 5:23; Phil. 1:6,10; Col. 1:22). One sees here again that the anticipation of the justifying verdict of God was a bold paradox of faith, quite parallel with those other anticipations—although Christ is already here, nevertheless his coming (παρουσία) is still awaited; although the Christians already have redemption they must nevertheless wait for the full redemption (Rom. 8:23); they already have the adoption and shall

[30] *Enoch* 1:7ff, "And there shall be a judgment upon all men, but with the righteous he will make peace and will protect the elect." 38:1, "When the congregation of the righteous shall appear and sinners shall be punished for their sins and shall be driven from the face of the earth." 100:4f, "In those days will the angels descend into the hiding places and gather together into one place all those who helped to introduce sins; the Most High will arise on that day of judgment to execute great judgment amongst sinners. Over all the righteous and holy, he will appoint guardians from among the holy angels to guard them as the apple of his eye until he makes an end of all wickedness and all sin; even though the righteous sleep a long sleep, yet they have nothing to fear."

nevertheless receive it (Rom. 8:23); they have already been glorified (Rom. 8:30) and nevertheless hope for it (Rom. 8:17); they have life and shall nevertheless receive it. So also justification is theoretically something still in the future (Rom. 2:13; I Cor. 4:4; Gal. 2:17), a hoped-for boon (Gal. 5:5: we await, in virtue of our faith, the hope of righteousness). And it is not merely pedagogical wisdom when Paul admonishes his own to persevere and be faithful, as he points out to them the future ultimate decision. It is really meant seriously. For salvation can always be lost again if Christians do not 'continue in God's goodness' (Rom. 11:22) and 'continue steadfast in the faith' (Col. 1:23). There is certainly no longer any reference to a verdict 'on the ground of faith' (ἐκ πίστεως) in those passages which treat of the judgment of the Christians. Here it is once more plainly to be seen that the 'faith' which plays the deciding rôle in justification in this life is not considered as performance or as 'work.' It is only the simple grasping of the offered salvation, the surrender to God's grace wherein naturally there is included a moral decision for God. However the 'time when we first believed' lies far behind (Rom. 13:11). Henceforth it all depends upon this, whether the Christians have 'proved' themselves (Rom. 5:4; I Cor. 11:19; cf. Jas. 1:12; II Tim. 2:15); whether they have earnestly fought through the battle against the flesh in the power of the Spirit (Rom. 8:13), whether they have really cast off the works of darkness (Rom. 13:12), and put on the Lord Christ (13:14), whether they have mortified their earthly members (Col. 3:5), put away sins (Col. 3:7), whether they have really entirely put off the 'old man' (Col. 3:9). Here all these experiences of redemption return again in the form of imperatives or questions of conscience, and once more we see how in redemption—along with the decisive intervention of an act of God—the will of man must still coöperate. Thus the ethical character of this religion of salvation constantly reappears. The attitude toward the judgment is to the highest degree serious and conscientious, full of a sense of responsibility; for the impartial judge (Col. 3:25) will surely bring before his tribunal even the hidden thoughts and counsels of the heart (Rom. 2:16; I Cor. 4:5). Not only does it depend upon deeds (II Cor. 5:10; Col. 3:25), not only upon external blamelessness and innocence, but upon inner purity, holiness and moral maturity (Col. 1:22,28)—salvation must be gained with fear and trembling (Phil. 2:12). In spite however of this ever-present fear of the judge, we should not fail to notice the joyousness and confidence with which

Paul looks forward to the judgment. The experiences of grace through which he had already passed are too powerful for him to question the certainty of his salvation. We shall be saved (Rom. 5:9f); we rejoice in the hope of the glory of God (5:3); "Who shall lay anything to the charge of God's elect?" (Rom. 8:33); "He which began a good work in you will perfect it" (Phil. 1:6); "It is God which worketh in you both to will and to work" (Phil. 2:13); he is faithful and will also confirm us to the end (I Cor. 1:8). Especially does his confidence rise high within him when he hears the attacks and accusations of his opponents. Calmly and composedly he awaits the heavenly judge (I Cor. 4:4f).

Sometimes God appears as judge (Rom. 2:5; 3:6; I Cor. 5:13), sometimes Christ (I Cor. 4:4f; I Thess. 4:6). It is worthy of note that both in Rom. 14:10 and II Cor. 5:10 it is said in almost the same words that we must appear before the 'judgment seat,' in the former case 'of God,' and in the latter 'of Christ.' Here we note the persistence of the traditional formula which is given in one case a more Jewish, in the other a more Christian tone.[31] Here again we see (cf. p. 474) how the Messiah is fitted into the apocalyptic system, which could very well exist without any mention of a Messiah. Thus in the admonitions that form the basis of the Book of Enoch the judgment is described without the intervention of the Messiah (chh. 92-105), while in the parables, 61:8; 62:2, it is the 'Son of Man' who holds assize upon the throne of his glory. In the evangelical tradition the 'Son of Man' appears in like manner sometimes as judge and sometimes merely as the chief witness for the prosecution or as advocate before the tribunal of God. This latter idea is found also in Paul in Rom. 8:33f, where Christ stands as advocate beside the judging or rather pardoning God to ward off accusations or accusers, just as in the Book of Enoch two of the four angels of the Presence make intercession for men and ward off the satans (40:6f).

8. The further *details of the apocalyptic drama* of the day of judgment are of little interest to us in this connection since they are taken from the apocalyptic tradition as more or less conventional decorative features and are to be considered more as evidence for the latter than for the religion of Paul; as for example the sound

[31] Rom. 14:10 and II Cor. 5:10. Cf. also the word παριστάναι ['stand before' in Rom. 14:10] in I Cor. 8:8 [commend]; II Cor. 4:14; 11:2; Col. 1:22,28; Eph. 5:27 [present]. In Rom. 2:16 we find a statement which combines the two mentioned above: 'In the day when God shall judge the secrets of men according to my gospel, by Jesus Christ.' It is assumed that 'by Jesus Christ' is not to be taken with 'gospel.'

of the last trumpet, the call of the archangel, the flaming fire at the Parousia (I Cor. 15:52; I Thess. 4:16; I Cor. 3:13; II Thess. 1:8). Noteworthy also in this connection is the unsystematic, variable and arbitrary manner in which the particular features are more or less casually chosen. This only means that the Pauline churches possessed fuller information on all these things so that he only needs to touch upon the details (notice the article: *the* last trumpet) in order to be understood at once. Many details are hard for us to understand. For example how are we to think of the catching up of the Christians into the clouds to meet the Lord in the air (I Thess. 4:17)? Is this only meant to be a sort of reception of Christ as he descends to the earth? Or will Christ then take them back with him into heaven? Or will the kingdom of Christ be established in the realm of the air (cf. p. 539, n. 26), between heaven and earth? Moreover it is not clear just what the length of the reign of Christ will be. It has already begun with the exaltation (Col. 1:13; Rom. 1:5). But when will the destruction of the dominions and powers (I Cor. 15:24-28) take place? Was not their overthrow begun at the time of the resurrection and continued into the present; or will it really only begin after the Parousia? We have no answer to these questions.

The question of the time of the Parousia is of importance only in connection with Paul's religious position and outlook. It appears from I Thess. 4:13ff that Paul's announcement had aroused in the churches the expectation that the Parousia would soon take place. The excitement in the church, the appearance of restless, idle visionaries, shows that the tension had risen to the highest point (II Thess. 3:6-15; I Thess. 4:11f). Paul may have been the cause of this: his statement, 'The time is shortened' (I Cor. 7:29), of course means that the end is expected sooner than one might think from general calculations and expectations. He seems to have reckoned upon a very brief period of time when he says (Rom. 13:11), 'Now is salvation nearer to us than when we first believed.' Here surely even a couple of years make a difference, and the rousing cry, 'Now it is high time for you to awake out of sleep,' seems very urgent. On the whole he is of the opinion, and so too apparently are the churches, that the day of the Lord may come quite unexpectedly like a thief in the night (I Thess. 5:2, 'yourselves know perfectly!'). Thus they should always be sober and vigilant (5:6f). Yet over against this Paul still counts upon a considerably protracted continuance of present conditions. Not only that he in spite of his yearning for death must wait still longer (Phil. 1:24f), not only that he personally still has great plans (Spain: Rom. 15:24)—he firmly believes that the end cannot come before 'the fulness of the Gentiles' will have received salvation (Rom. 11:25; cf. Mark 13:10). This of course means the performance of a great work which cannot be accomplished in a short time. We do not know what spheres he had in view, what lands and peoples he had in mind for future labors—but this territory could not have been small in extent. And then too still another miracle is to take place, the final conversion of Israel (Rom. 11:25-32). Great things are thus impending and we cannot think that all this could happen so very soon. Thus we observe also in Paul the juxtaposition of that tense feeling on the one hand which expects the end at any moment, and on the other the conviction based upon tradition and revelation that a series of preordained events must still take place before the Lord can come again. Therefore we cannot consider as un-Pauline the little apocalypse of the Second Epistle to the Thessalonians in which he expects the appearance of Anti-Christ in Jerusalem, and his proclamation of himself as Son of God in the temple; this was to precede 'the falling away,' that is the seduction of the Jewish people and the removal of that power which he calls, using a secret apocalyptic name, 'that which restraineth' or the 'one which restraineth' (ὁ κατέχων, τὸ κατέχον, II Thess. 2:3-12). One perceives plainly that he is here following an apocalyptic tradition which to him is just as fixed in all its details as is, on the other hand, the certainty that the day of the Lord is coming finally, yet suddenly and at a time none can calculate. In this he does in fact show himself to be dependent upon the apocalyptic tradition, but he himself is not an apocalyptist. He does not fix the time of the end, for he knows it even less exactly than those prophets. His only concern is, with the aid of these apocalyptic ideas, to set in motion ethical and religious forces, to suppress morbid unrest, to waken dull indifference, to spur on missionary zeal, to keep alive the hope of the conversion of the whole of mankind. He is well aware of the greatness of the task and the shortness of time for its accomplishment. Therefore he continues to press on. Therefore, it is his sacred desire that the Word 'may run' (II Thess. 3:1), that the Gospel be 'fully preached' everywhere (Rom. 15:19).

CHAPTER XIX

The Pauline Ethic

We shall attempt now to show briefly how the Apostle's ethical viewpoint was formed and developed under the influence of the primitive Christian tradition and of his conversion, as well as by the influence of religious zeal and the community life and its needs. At the same time, of course, we shall see that attitudes which he derived from Judaism and Hellenism were not eliminated but were differently organized and received different emphases, and underwent a process of amalgamation with new ones. Here also we shall be prepared to find little of a carefully constructed system as one might expect to find in a fully established theory developed in every respect. Among his statements which have been accidentally preserved to us many things will be said only to meet a given situation and for a distinct reason; many things will be rooted in his mind more deeply and more systematically than we can know. As many different moods pass through the Apostle's mind, so he judges many things, now in one way, now in another. He speaks differently when he sets up universal and far-reaching ideal demands based on the highest possible point of view, than when, on the other hand, he deals with concrete individual cases, soberly, practically and elastically. Nothing could be more wrong than to expect unity and consistency everywhere. We must let this rich variety of his have its effect upon us, and yet we must also ask what were the norms and motives operative in the fundamental judgments and demands of this ethic.

1. *Its Norms.* If we inquire concerning the norms or sources of the Apostle's ethical viewpoint we meet first of all with the problem of his

(a) *Relation to the Law.* Can there be anything that Paul has expressed more clearly than his concept of the Christian's freedom from the Law? As surely as the Jew must remain under the Law, and at the judgment be judged according to his performance of its demands (Rom. 2:12f), just so certainly, the Christian is no longer under the Law (Rom. 6:14f; 7:1-6; Gal. 3:25; 4:5); he has died to the Law (Gal. 2:19); the Law has been laid aside, both as a document accusing of sin (Col. 2:14) and as one making demands; Christ has become the end of the Law for the believer (Rom. 10:4). This is Paul's conclusion because he has found salvation in another way, and from this point of view the Law appears to him as something to be viewed wholly in retrospect and not as something permanent and eternally binding. Psychologically considered, it plays the part of the awakener of sin; it has first made man acquainted with sin, has seduced him into sin, and for the first time has actually made sin to be sin (Rom. 7:7-13). The tragedy which he sketches here in very general terms, namely that of man ruled by the flesh and by sin, to whom the holy commandment of God becomes not life but death, and instead of a blessing a curse—this he has personally experienced in the highest degree, since merely for the sake of the Law, out of faithfulness to it, he became a persecutor of Christ (Gal. 1:13f). The law had led him so deeply into sin that he pictures his former condition under the Law as being the same as being ruled by sin (Rom. 7:5).

Here he goes so far that he actually fears that his words may be quoted as implying that the Law is sin (7:7). But any such view based on passages like Rom. 6:14; 7:5 he could never have agreed with—God forbid! However there is no doubt that he does form a kind of philosophical theory out of universal human experience as well as his own personal experience, according to which the Law had only a temporary mission and was but a means instituted for the purpose of preparing for the new salvation, and was added only for the sake of transgressions, as Gal. 3:19 says all too briefly. What is evidently meant is that the effect of the Law was to change sin from being an action which man committed more or less unconsciously and therefore without complete responsibility, to an action which was a conscious breaking of the Law (Rom. 4:15); its effect was further to increase sins (Rom. 5:20) and to enmesh men so deeply in sin that they, like captives, could no longer help themselves (Gal. 3:22f), but must trustfully stretch forth their hands to the redeeming Christ. After it had fulfilled this purpose it became superfluous: after faith as a new power for salvation has come we are no longer under the school-master.[1] The purely temporary significance of the Law becomes especially clear in Paul's argument

[1] This is perhaps the sense of these exceedingly compact sentences. What the figure of the steward in Gal. 3:24 means is not clear; the *tertium comparationis* is certainly the harsh, loveless character of the Law, which, in the end, left man no other choice than to surrender to the mercy or displeasure of Christ. But the idea here is not entirely obvious.

that, in fact, the prophecy in respect to the actual principle of salvation cannot be overthrown by the Law which came 430 years later (Gal. 3:17). This mode of thought, so very strange to us, to which we have already alluded, has its roots in the fundamental view which appears also in Mark 10:6ff, that the oldest revelation stands closest to the innermost nature of God and reproduces his actual intent. The later pronouncement can be only a concession (Mark 10:5) or an elaboration (Gal. 3:19) which for some reason or some purpose appears necessary, yet only in a distinctly conditional sense.

A similar idea appears in Rom. 5:12-19 where the entire history of the world revolves about the two poles of Adam and Christ, while Moses is not mentioned at all. First it is said in 5:20 that the Law has not only 'slipped in' (cf. 5:12, the 'penetration' of sin), but 'has slipped in along with' something in some illegitimate manner (as did the false brethren, Gal. 2:4) through a side-door. One could not emphasize more strongly either the secondary, transitory character of the Law or its eternally valid and binding nature. Indeed Paul expresses himself in just this way in Gal. 3:19 (following Jewish tradition),[2] i.e. as if the Law in fact had not really been given directly to Moses by God, but 'through the mediation of angels' who are, after all, subordinate to God. Here one may assume that it is at most only semi-divine, and in fact possesses a demoniacal character. And this seems to be the Apostle's actual meaning when in Gal. 4:3,9 he designates both the bondage of the Jews under the Law and that of the heathen under their so-called 'gods' (which are really demons, I Cor. 10:20) as one and the same condition, namely servitude to the 'elements of the world.' It has not yet been made clear how Paul can harmonize Judaism and heathenism from this point of view (cf. p. 493, note 44, and ch. 20). However, this much is plain: that he wishes in this way to place the Law, as belonging to this world, on the same level as matter, closely bound up with the flesh. For indeed redemption through the death of Christ is at the same time a redemption from the world, from the flesh and the Law, just as Christ was at the same time born of a woman and also placed under the law (Gal. 4:4). Here Paul nearly makes a mistake that later would be called gnostic; he seems inclined to separate completely the Mosaic Law and the nature of the highest God. Indeed he almost seems to place it in opposition to God.

This almost passionate struggle against the Law in the Epistle to

[2] Acts 7:38,53; Heb. 2:2; Josephus, *Ant.* xv. 5, 3; cf. Dibelius, *Die Geisterwelt im Glauben des Paulus* (The Spiritual World in Paul's Faith), pp. 27f.

the Galatians is explained, in part at least, by the emotion and personal bitterness which the attacks of the Judaizers in Galatia had aroused in him. Yet the theory is more than a mere passing expression of emotion. It is so closely connected with other views that one is compelled to take it seriously. The difficulty lies only in this: that Paul not only does not repeat these sharpest antinomian statements in the Epistle to the Romans, but in fact substitutes for them a considerably more positive estimate of the Law. One cannot conclude from this that there has been a *development* in his way of thinking, for we still encounter in the Epistle to the Colossians (2:13f,16,20f) the same view of the Law as a magnificent power closely bound up with the 'world-elements,' and from bondage to these the Christian is set free through the death of Christ. Again, in the Epistle to the Romans (6:14; 7:5) Paul approaches the blasphemous statement that the Law is sin; so closely in fact that one cannot assume that he had rejected the antinomian ideas of the Epistle to the Galatians. So much the more puzzling is the fact that he not only restrained himself from these extreme views in the Epistle to the Romans, but also in closest proximity to them presents other daring assertions—in fact an entirely different treatment of the Law.

In their context these positive assertions create the impression of an amendment. After Paul had deeply aroused the feelings of the Jews—as well as his own feelings—indeed, had injured them, he seems to have been compelled to consider the subject from another angle (7:7; quite similarly, 3:1). He shifts the blame for the wretched state of affairs in the past, which he had seemed to attribute to the Law (7:4-7), from the Law to the flesh. The Law was only the *cause* of sin, it could not be of any help because of the weakness of the flesh, yet in itself the Law is sacred, the commandment holy, just and good (7:12). In contrast with the flesh it appears as originating 'from the spirit' (πνευματικός, 7:14). It is here expressly stated to be 'the Law of God' (7:22). To whatever degree one may be able to explain these assertions and the rebuttal of accusations against his Gospel by reference to the practical purpose of winning over the Jews, it cannot be denied that the statements of Paul appear here to be somewhat contradictory. In our rather microscopic consideration of the problem it seems inconceivable that Paul should not have felt this inconsistency. But for him both views appear to be equally true and irrefutable and according to the particular necessity he prefers the one or the other. The two trains of thought are comprehensible only as deposits of two different epochs of his life. The antinomian originates in the period of the great crisis when he learned to consider as loss everything which he had formerly thought of as gain. It had been strengthened at the time when he was obliged to protect the Gentile Christians against the attempt to enmesh them again under the yoke of the Law. On the other hand the positive series of ideas originated in his Hellenistic-Jewish past, when he was confident that he could become 'a leader of the blind, a light for those in darkness,' because he believed that in the Law he possessed the 'embodiment of knowledge and truth' (Rom. 2:20) and thus was confident that he possessed a wisdom superior to that of all Hellenism. The Hellenistic origin of this train of thought appears especially in the fact that for him the 'Law of God' is identical with that 'of nature' inscribed in the heart (Rom. 2:14f), with the law of reason (Rom. 7:23), in which the 'inner man' has an accepting joy (7:22). There can be no doubt that here Paul establishes a synthesis between the written Law of Moses and the unwritten law of reason, the *Nomos agraphos* of the Stoics.[3] Certainly this does not substantially change the concept of the Law. For it is clear that by this 'law of reason' Paul could not have had in mind the concrete totality of the Mosaic ceremonial Law. Otherwise the fact that the Law is written in the heart of man and that there are heathen who do these things 'by nature,' would have been wholly excluded. It cannot be denied that Paul, even though he never consciously develops this distinction, nevertheless understands the law of God as being primarily a concept of moral demands which are of a general human kind[4] and thus could be comprehended and fulfilled by non-Jews. (This is most certainly the point of view of the Hellenistic-Judaistic propaganda.[5]) But yet again there is the Mosaic Law with its innumerable prescriptions, the exact fulfilment of which he had attempted, as a Pharisaic disciple; so that it lies in the very nature of things that he should alternate between these ways of thinking, always in accordance with the position which he assumes. If the question is the protection of his Gentile Chris-

[3] Cf. R. Hirzel, 'Νόμος ἄγραφος', *Abh. d. Sächs. Ges. d. Wiss.*, xx, 1900.

[4] It is significant that where he speaks in quite general terms of the effect of the Law upon man, as in Rom. 7:7, he selects only one of the numberless statements of the Law: "Thou shalt not covet."

[5] It is characteristic that he conceives the idea of 'truth' as a knowledge of God accessible to all men, and at the same time as an epitome of moral obligations; therefore, he places it formally in antithesis to 'unrighteousness' (ἀδικία): Rom. 1:18; 2:8; 3:4f,7; I Cor. 13:6; II Thess. 2:10.

tians from the obligations of the Law, he naturally has in mind, just as his opponents, the genuine Mosaic Law. But when he propounds the question, "What in the future, for the Christians, shall be the norm of all actions?", he is convinced that the will of God contained in the Law naturally remains binding upon them also. Thus in Rom. 8:4 he can point out that as a result of redemption the redeemed who possess the Spirit of God can henceforth fulfil the 'just demands' of the Law, a thing which was impossible for the pre-Christian because of the weakness of the flesh. These 'demands of the Law' (δικαιώματα) remain in force in spite of everything, and are meant to be fulfilled, except that the Christian, by the power of the Spirit, can perform them and does so, not by slavish obedience, but because the Spirit drives him through the pressure of a heart filled with God.

The theory of the 'fulfilling of the Law,' stated both in Gal. 5:13f and Rom. 13:8ff, is also to be understood from this point of view as representing a certain *via media* between rejection and acceptance of the binding force of the Law.

The similarity of the wording in both passages shows that for the moment Paul had not, in fact, visualized the idea, but reaches back to a Jewish theory which would also have been accepted in the main by the Judaizers. In the Epistle to the Galatians, at least, his argument seems to be calculated upon it. When Paul says, "Serve one another in love," and follows with the reason, "For the whole Law is fulfilled in the one word, You shall love your neighbor as yourself," he apparently seeks to show, as against the Judaizers, that in the mighty establishment and practice of the commandment of love everything which they maintain as an indispensable demand upon the Christians is sufficiently carried out. In the Christian community which is free from the Law there is no lack of understanding, and the sincere will fulfil the commandment of God.[6] The statement is comprehensible only if one construes 'in one word' as a shortened sentence, as is frequently done. The whole Law is fulfilled if the one word is fulfilled. If you love one another you have thereby fulfilled the Law, or as Rom. 8:4 says: thereby you have fulfilled God's de-

[6] The readings in these verses are very difficult. Zahn has: *διὰ τῆς ἀγάπῆς δουλεύετε ἀλλήλοις. ὁ γὰρ πᾶς νόμος ἐν ἐνὶ λόγῳ πεπλήρωται, ἐν τῷ ἀγαπήσεις τὸν πλῆσιον σου ὡς σεαυτόν* "Through love ye serve one another; for all the law is fulfilled in one word, namely, thou shalt love thy neighbor as thyself." In Marcion's text it reads: *τῇ ἀγάπῃ τοῦ πνεύματος δουλ. ἀλλ. ὁ γὰρ πὰς νόμος ἐν ὑμῖν πεπλήρωται. ἀγαπήσεισ* etc. "By love of the Spirit serve ye one another. For the whole law is fulfilled in you: thou shalt love," etc. It seems to me that the last phrase, especially, makes no sense. It must read: *ἐὰν ἀγαπήσητε* or something similar.

mand contained in the Law. The Jewish theory lying in the background is of course only hinted at here and is not developed further. One cannot see here just how far love is the fulfilment of the Law. This becomes somewhat clearer in the conclusion drawn in Rom. 13:8ff, which however is certainly mutilated. Here it is said, using the same perfect tense, that he who loves another *has* fulfilled the law. This thesis can be proved as follows. First of all it is said that all the separate commandments are 'summed up' in the term 'brotherly love.'[7] At the same time this is only an assertion. It is clarified in a measure by the following statement: 'Love does no evil to one's neighbor.' In this is implied the so-called 'golden rule' of Judaism; as Hillel has it, "What is hateful to you, do not do to your neighbor; this is the whole Law, and all else is exposition."[8] In the various commandments (not to commit adultery or murder, not to steal or covet!) the principle of 'do no evil to your neighbor' is developed, since love consists in the fact that one does no evil to his neighbor, and 'love is therefore the fulfilling of the law.' This fundamental negative concept of love is certainly not Paul's own; it is Jewish. One thus perceives clearly that the whole argument is developed on a Jewish basis. Paul is arguing here from Jewish-Hellenistic hypotheses. The leading thought is the simplification and concentration of the divine commands. Although he appropriates this, he can also assert as a Christian that where the basic Christian demand of love has become life and reality, there the innermost nature of the Law has been fully satisfied, there the Law is fulfilled.[9] In this sense therefore Paul upholds the basic demands of the Law as also binding for Christians. Thus in other respects as well he has no misgivings in supporting its moral demands and its legal prescriptions by Scriptural proofs.[10]

The later development (e.g. in the Epistle to the Hebrews and First Clement) in the use of the Old Testament to its widest extent

[7] The word ἀνακεφαλαιοῦν alludes to the fact that the detailed contents may be comprised briefly in a form, such as a chapter superscription, from which the contents can be recognized.

[8] *Sabbath* f. 31a; cf. Tobit 4:15; Philo in Eusebius, *Praeparatio,* viii. 7. 6; Test. Naphtali (Heb.) 1 (Kautzsch, ii, 489); Aristeas, § 207; Didache 1:2; Acts 15:20d; Bousset, *Religion des Judentums,* 2d ed., p. 159.

[9] The same view is found also in Matt. 7:12; 22:40. It is significant that it is just this Jewish Christian writer who, by means of this theory, upholds the ideal content of the Law for Christians. Can Matt. 5:17 be taken in the same way? (Cf. SNT *ad loc.*).

[10] E.g. Rom. 12:16 = Prov. 3:7; Rom. 12:17 = Prov. 3:4; Rom. 12:19 = Deut. 32:35; Rom. 12:20 = Prov. 25:21f; I Cor. 9:9 = Deut. 25:4; II Cor. 8:15 = Ex. 16:18; II Cor. 9:7 = Prov. 22:8; II Cor. 9:9 = Psalm 112:9, etc.

as a Christian collection of sayings exists already in principle in Paul, and surely he must have made more frequent use of it than we can learn from the Epistles. That in this respect the ethical parts of the Old Testament are prior to the ceremonial follows quite naturally. But Paul does not perhaps discriminate in principle between these two sides of the Law. He does not take pains—at least in the extant Epistles—to demonstrate that the ceremonial law is antiquated and ineffectual, as the Epistle to the Hebrews does so thoroughly, and as was done by Jews and Christians in their customary informative propaganda.[11] It is only in regard to circumcision that such lines of thought are found (e.g. Rom. 4:9ff), but only because it was the practical point of contention. In particular the antinomian assertions of Paul stand, throughout, under the banner of battle with Judaism and should be considered as battle-cries. Because Judaism set up the keeping of the Law as the requirement of salvation, Paul, to whom salvation had disclosed itself in another manner, was compelled in order to protect his Gentile Christians from fresh servitude and from an aimless way of salvation, to combat the binding force of the Law and its indispensability for salvation. But for the Christian who has already found salvation in this new way—apart from the Law—it is self-evident that it can no longer be a condition of salvation. A new bondage, a new enmeshing in sin by the Law, is for him out of the question. The Law can no longer and must no longer be an obstacle for him on the way to redemption, since in truth he already possesses salvation in the Spirit of God, and by his power he can perform an action [12] which corresponds to the demands of the 'law of God,' that is, to its great moral and basic demands. He does this not because it is written in the Law, but rather because he, under the impulse of the Spirit, cannot do otherwise; his action is born of the same Spirit from which the revelation of the will of God also originates. He is no longer 'under the Law,' yet he is not

[11] Echoes of this appear in isolated cases: the circumcision of the heart, not of the flesh (Rom. 2:28); the New Covenant, not of the letter, but of the spirit (II Cor. 3:6); the Law consisting of maxims (Col. 2:14), 'commandments and teachings of men' (Col. 2:22; Isa. 29:13; Mark 7:7). At this point the Epistle to the Ephesians goes far beyond Paul, when it speaks of the 'so-called uncircumcision and circumcision' (Eph. 2:11); these were far too powerful realities for Paul to express himself thus. The writer of Ephesians, moreover, builds upon the work begun by Paul. For the church of his time these differences already lay far behind, in the shadows of the past.

[12] It is very characteristic that Paul, when he speaks of the deeds of a Christian, usually no longer speaks of 'works,' in the plural, but of 'work,' as a uniform, organically determined, life-work born of one Spirit: I Cor. 3:13ff; Gal. 6:4; Phil. 1:6; I Thess. 1:3; one must certainly add πᾶν ἔργον ἀγαθόν, II Cor. 9:8; Col. 1:10.

'one without law toward God' (ἄνομος θεοῦ, I Cor. 9:20f), but the 'will of God' (Rom. 12:2; Col. 1:9; 4:12; I Thess. 4:3; 5:18) is for him the highest court. It is self-evident that all this can be expressed only in a series of detailed requirements (cf. I Thess. 4:3ff; Rom. 12); so that the imperatives must move along parallel to that enthusiastic mode of thought according to which the new life is a fruit of the Spirit. Occasionally the expression 'the law of Christ' also appears (Gal. 6:2; cf. also I Cor. 9:21: 'bound by the law of Christ'). Here appears the old pre-Pauline mode of thought, according to which the life of the Christian is a life after the words and commandments of the Lord. With this we come to a second norm of the Pauline ethic:

(b) *The Words and Example of the Lord.* It is due to the primitive Christian foundation of Paul's doctrine that Christ appears not only as Redeemer, not only as mystical head of the Community, but also as teacher whose words are determinative for his disciples. Of course the word 'disciples,' referring to Christians, appears just as infrequently as the words 'teacher' and 'teaching' of Christ—for good reasons. In this very circumstance is reflected the wholly changed character of his religion as opposed to that of the oldest primitive Christianity. The relationship of Paul to his exalted Lord is a purely religious one, and the members of his communities were never in a preponderant majority in the relationship of disciples of Jesus. Again it is exactly they who have learned to know him only as the heavenly divine Lord. His will of course is unconditionally determinative for them, but he is present to them not so much through the memory of former words of Jesus the teacher as through direct manifestations of the Spirit; Christ himself guides their lives from above. It is so much the more noteworthy not merely that Paul occasionally refers back to words of Jesus as the final incontestable authority, but that the communities also, as we surely may assume, have considered the words of Jesus as being to a still greater degree the norm for the conduct of their members. Certainly in the religion of Paul from the beginning the veneration of the exalted Lord is linked with the Jewish-Christian tradition. But we have earlier seen that the sayings of the Lord appear just where the question arises concerning the beginning of legislation in the Church, where it concerns general obligatory regulations. Here it is felt as a defect that there is no statement of the Lord on the subject—it would be better if all quarrels could be settled in this way (I Cor. 7:25). On the other hand there is lacking any reference to such statements where the problem concerns the fashioning of the new moral life of the individual. It is wanting when Paul, out of the fulness of the Spirit, acts from the viewpoint of immediate communion with Christ and sets up practical requirements. The accord with the Lord's sayings, which cannot be mistaken,[13] proves of course an acquaintance with the Gospel tradition, but beyond this it also shows an inner adaptation of its ideas as a legal conception of 'commandments.'[14] Paul the 'pneumatic' is far from setting up a new law in place of the old. Of course in principle this would not prevent him from also occasionally quoting sayings of the Lord—as a matter of fact in Gal. 6:2 he also refers to the law of Christ—but it is characteristic of him that anything of this sort rarely occurs in his epistles.

On the other hand, reference to Christ's example appears frequently, e.g. in II Cor. 8:9 and Phil. 2:5ff. It is of course not the details of Jesus' life of poverty which he holds up before the Corinthians, but the great act of self-revelation in the Incarnation. The particular idea of the 'grace of our Lord Jesus Christ' appears almost formally in Phil. 2:4f and in I Cor. 10:24,33; 11:1—"Look not every man to his own advantage, let no man seek his own, but every man another's."[15] In this act of self-denial the life work of Christ is summed up for Paul. It shines forth as the great model for Christians;[16] in such giving of self everything is included that can be demanded of them. We may at once assume that Paul, where he does not expressly say it (as in I Cor. 13), also connects this basic demand of love with the personality of Christ. Love, grace, devotion to others is certainly the fundamental feature of his being as he

[13] Cf. Titius, *Der Paulinismus,* pp. 12ff. Among the passages which he enumerates, the following support this contention: Rom. 12:14,17; I Cor. 4:12; 6:7 and Luke 6:27f; I Cor. 9:19 and Mark 10:44f; II Cor. 11:7 and Matt. 23:11f; Rom. 2:1; 14:13 and Matt. 7:1f; Rom. 16:19 and Matt. 6:25.

[14] The word 'commandments' (*ἐντολαί*) is never used by Paul of the sayings of Jesus.

[15] I Cor. 10:24, *μηδεὶς τὸ ἑαυτοῦ ζητείτω, ἀλλὰ τὸ τοῦ ἑτέρου,* "Let no man seek his own, but each his neighbor's good"; 10:32, *μὴ ζητῶν τὸ ἐμαυτοῦ σύμφορον, ἀλλὰ τὸ τῶν πολλῶν,* "Not seeking mine own profit, but the profit of the many"; Phil 2:4, *μὴ τὰ ἑαυτῶν ἕκαστοι σκοποῦντες, ἀλλὰ τὰ τῶν ἑτέρων ἕκαστοι,* "Not looking each of you to his own things, but each of you also to the things of others"; Rom. 15:3, *καὶ γὰρ ὁ Χριστὸς οὐχ ἑαυτῷ ἤρεσεν,* "For Christ also pleased not himself."

[16] The expression *μιμητὴς Χριστοῦ,* 'imitator of Christ,' I Cor. 11:1; I Thess. 1:6, is extraordinarily instructive for Paul's conception of the follower of Christ. If he can say *μιμηταί μου γίνεσθε καθὼς κἀγὼ Χριστοῦ* (I Cor. 4:16), "Be ye imitators of me, as I am of Christ," if he also places his own prototype parallel with that of Christ, then Christ would appear here much less as *κύριος* than as teacher. Of course the question, in both cases, concerns neither an outward imitation nor, perhaps, simply the impression of teachings, but has to do with the joining of the personality to that of the teacher, in respect to one's view of life, convictions, and conduct (cf. Phil. 3:17). On this point see the Greek parallels in my Commentary on I Cor. 4:6.

apprehends it (Gal. 2:20). He who lives 'in Christ,' he who has 'the mind of the Lord,' can do nothing else, since the love experienced by him is again radiated—after the manner of the Lord (κατὰ κύριον), as he incidentally says (Rom. 15:5; II Cor. 11:17; Col. 2:8).[17]

(c) But on the whole it is characteristic of the Apostle's way of thinking that a norm lying outside his personality tends to disappear, since what he thinks, does and demands, he conceives of as a working of *the Spirit*. This is especially plain in I Cor. 7, where his own statements appear over against the legal statements of the Lord ('but to the rest I say, not the Lord,' 7:12). Yet this is certainly not the opinion of a chance individual (7:25,40),[18] but that of a man who possesses the Spirit of God, of one who is vouchsafed by the Lord in his compassion 'that he may be considered worthy of belief.'[19] The 'Spirit' is here the source or principle of the knowledge of the will of God (I Cor. 2:12-16); therefore the 'right knowledge of the will of God' is present only where there is 'wisdom and spiritual understanding' (Col. 2:9, ἐν πάσῃ σοφίᾳ καὶ συνέσει πνευματικῇ). It is especially important that according to Rom. 12:2 'transformation by the renewing of the mind' (ἀνακαινώδει τοῦ νοός), which naturally takes place through the Spirit (7:6), should manifest itself chiefly in the fact that Christians have 'the sure feeling for that which is the will of God.' 'The good, acceptable, perfect' is not given unconditionally in a written law or in the words of the Lord, for all persons or for every case. Moral judgment (this is the meaning included in δοκιμάζειν; cf. also Phil. 1:10) must decide in every individual case what the will of God is. And this is possible only when the moral reason or mind (ὁ νοῦς) which until now was submerged in the bondage of the flesh and was embittered, is entirely renewed[20] and transformed so that the inner norm and power is no longer the flesh, but the divine Spirit (Rom. 8:5). Thinking and seeking (τὸ φρόνημα, φρονεῖν, ζητεῖν, σκοπεῖν), as the deepest life-interest of the Christian, has become something different, therefore he has not only the power and the eagerness to overcome the flesh

[17] Parallel with this turn of expression is the κατὰ θεόν, II Cor. 7:9ff, and the κατὰ πνεῦμα, Rom. 8:4f; and such a κατὰ κύριον must everywhere be considered as an antithesis, where κατὰ σάρκα, κατὰ ἄνθρωπον is used (Rom. 3:5; 8:4,12f; I Cor. 1:26; 3:3; 9:8; II Cor. 1:17; 5:16; 10:2f; 11:18; Gal. 1:11; 3:15; 4:23,29; Col. 2:8,22).

[18] The word ἰδιώτης may have stood here, as in I Cor. 14:24.

[19] Cf. my Commentary on I Cor. 7:25.

[20] This is the deepest concept of repentance in Paul; Stoic and Posidonian expressions and ideas come into play here, and on this point cf. p. 252, n. 53.

(Rom. 8:4; Gal. 5:16) but also the right judgment, the moral tact (Phil. 1:9f) which especially manifests itself in a new evaluation of the possessions of this world (Phil. 3:7). Now for the first time we understand fully what Paul means by the 'liberty' for which Christ has freed us (Gal. 5:1,13). It is not merely something negative, not merely detachment from the Law, but the ability to do what we really wish (Gal. 5:17; Rom. 7:15ff),[21] and yet also the gift 'to desire that which is pleasing to God' (Phil. 2:13). It is God himself who begins the good work in us and completes it (Phil. 1:6). So the new life is not the copy of a model and not the dead fulfilment of a law, but an original product of the Spirit ever welling up anew, springing from fellowship with God and Christ; a new creation of religious inwardness which draws its laws from its own being. One receives an impression of the power of this moral productivity when one reads the ethical portions of the epistles. In Rom. 12:13 we read how the Paraclesis flows along in a fiery stream, enthusiastically, in wonderful harmony, without formalistic pedantry; it is no mere catalogue of the provisions of the Law but a joyful hymn, full of fervor and love! Or again when Paul corrects the Corinthians in the difficult matters of the new morality we note how surely he decided every matter according to the highest standards, almost always from the heart, quite clearly and without any hesitation, since the answer could not possibly be a different one. It is amazing to what a degree the former Pharisee has freed himself from the support of a written or traditional law, so much the more amazing in fact since certain phenomena in his churches could well have brought the thought to mind that it would yet be better once more to put a check on these Hellenes who were all too much inclined to libertinism, as the Judaizers advised him, perhaps not without reason. But he withstood the temptation. Naturally the purpose of liberty is not the furtherance of the flesh (Gal. 5:13)! But he who would spy out our liberty, to bring us into new bonds, is a false brother (Gal. 2:4)!

(d) And yet Paul could not avoid placing *limits* on the all too subjective urge for liberty. In the many kinds of temptations and

[21] This is also one side of the Stoic conception of liberty; Cicero, *Parad.* 34: *Quid est libertas? Potestas vivendi, ut velis;* "What is liberty? The power of living as you wish." But the other is also present, for if only the wise man is truly free, it is because his knowledge enables him to wish for only the right. Compare with this religious concept of liberty Philo, *Quis omnis probus liber* § 3, M. 448, Τῷ γὰρ ὄντι μόνος ἐλεύθερος ὁ μόνῳ θεῷ χρώμενος ἡγεμόνι, "In fact the only free man is the one who regards the only God as master"; cf. p. 516, n. 6.

conflicts which were confronting the new Gentile Christianity he sees himself time and again compelled to go back to the 'traditions' (I Cor. 11:2) which they had received at their conversion, to the 'commandments' which 'we gave you by the Lord Jesus' (I Thess. 4:2), to the great fundamental demands of penitence which they 'know,' reminding them that gross sinners will not inherit the Kingdom of God (I Cor. 6:9f; Gal. 5:21), in a word, to the catechetical baptismal instructions (pp. 254ff) of the earliest period. We do not know them in their entire extent. In the *Teaching of the Twelve Apostles* we have for the first time a compilation of the 'teaching' which should be imparted to catechumens before baptism (chh. 1-6), a combination of Jewish requirements—the basis is a Jewish proselyte catechism—and of the sayings of Jesus. But there can be no doubt that already in the earliest times there were in existence similar, though richer, collections of commandments which served in a measure as the basic law of the community. Paul, as has been said, refers back to these demands in case of need, where it is a question of a menace to the fundamentals.

Yet one plainly feels that in these passages there is the conviction that a downward step has been taken which in fact should be superseded (cf. I Cor. 6:11; Gal. 5:23f). Fundamentally there should be no need at all of such a law for the 'saints' who have experienced purification in baptism and who with Christ have crucified their flesh with its passions and desires. They should be beyond the Law. It can be seen here how the realities of the community clash with the concept of the ideal of the saints. But at the same time we also observe that the idea of complete freedom from the Law is not sufficient to regulate the life of the community. There is need here of fixed rules of conduct which are binding upon all, and which set limits on individual expression. At the same time of course the ethical character of these demands changes. They become legal rules, and a fundamental law for the community comes into existence. This transition from the uncontrolled morality of spiritual men to obedience toward statutes can already be observed in its inception, in Paul.

But Paul has not only to deal with those who because of generally immature morality or viciousness remain far behind the ideal of the spiritual ethic, but also with those who exceed this idea, fanatically, or in a libertine manner. From the beginning there was a tendency in the churches which so interpreted the liberty of the spiritual man that the consequences of this liberty did not differ greatly from the opposite pole. Its key-word is 'gnosis' (I Cor. 8:1) or 'liberty' (ἐξουσία, I Cor. 8:9; 6:12; 10:23). We shall later learn to recognize the fundamental purpose of this tendency. Here it is important for us to see that Paul with the utmost firmness opposed its watch-word, 'Everything is permitted,' with the basic law, 'Let no one seek his own, but that of others,' and that he presents 'love' as the higher, the absolute demand as against the unrestrained use of 'knowledge' (I Cor. 8:13). Thus a barrier is erected against careless living according to one's own convictions; a high regulative principle is given for all conflicts of duties. We return here to the idea of fulfilling the Law through love; it is the concentrated expression of the will of God to whom everything is to be subordinated. By the setting up of this highest and final norm a check is placed on unrestrained spiritual morality.

2. *The Motifs of the Pauline Ethic.* We must now inquire concerning the real basis of ethical requirements and thus first of all we meet with (a) *the eschatological motif*, which of course is present in Paul just as strongly as in the whole extent of primitive Christianity. He who wishes to share in the Kingdom of God must have broken with the gross sins of heathenism (I Cor. 6:10; Gal. 5:21; Eph. 5:5), for on their account the wrath of God comes (Col. 3:6; Rom. 1:18; 2:8f). To be rescued from this 'coming wrath' (I Thess. 1:10) is and remains the real basic hope of Christians. But it is self-evident that a relapse into conditions prevailing before baptism would mean a mockery of this hope (I Cor. 6:10; Gal. 5:21). The description of the 'day of wrath' and 'the revelation of the just judgment of God' who 'will reward every man according to his work': upon those whose very nature is vileness[22] and who will not bow to the truth but yield to unrighteousness, 'anger and rage.' This description is certainly not aimed at Christians but at mankind in general, which is still far from the Gospel. The cloud of the divine judgment of wrath is hovering over it (Rom. 1:18; I Thess. 1:10). It is taken for granted that death rules over pre-Christian humanity, death as the wages which sin pays to its followers (Rom. 6:23). Like a brazen world-law—like the fate (εἱμαρμένη) of the heathen—

[22] In SNT, Rom. 2:8, τοῖς ἐξ ἐριθείας is translated: 'whose nature is contentious.' It seems to me that the above translation is a more satisfactory attempt. ἐριθεία is not connected with ἔρις, 'contention,' but with ἔριθος, 'day-laborer.' Naturally also, strife, hatred, mob-gatherings, could be considered as of the nature of contention, but this would be too far-fetched here. The word has an aristocratic feeling. The one who uses it looks down upon the proletarian character of the people, so to speak, upon their low, undistinguished nature, as being averse to nobility or incapable of it.

the retribution of evil weighs heavily over all mankind insofar as it has not drawn near to the Gospel. And it is one of the blessed effects of redemption that Christians are or will be saved (I Thess. 1:10; Rom. 5:10); they are 'saved from retribution.'[23] It is so much the more noteworthy that Paul not only threatens 'lapsed' Christians who have fallen behind the ideal condition of the baptized with the judgment of wrath (Col. 3:5f; I Thess. 4:6), but that he places in prospect for all Christians in general, destruction, death and the divine judgment of wrath, if they still 'live after the flesh' (Rom. 8:13). 'He who sows for the flesh shall of the flesh reap corruption' (Gal. 6:8); he who does wrong will bear the brunt of his misdeeds, and 'there is no partiality' (Col. 3:25). "All Christians must appear before the judgment-seat of Christ; that each may receive the thing done in the body, according to what he hath done, whether it be good or evil" (II Cor. 5:10). We are disposed to think of this as a lapse into the Jewish legalistic mode of thought, as a loss of the enthusiastic point of view of one who has been redeemed from retribution. Christians should of course under all circumstances be able to look forward trustfully to the world-judgment, for indeed it has already been pronounced upon them, since they are already justified (Rom. 5:1). "Who shall lay anything to the charge of God's elect?" (Rom. 8:33); "There is therefore no condemnation to them who are in Christ Jesus" (Rom. 8:1). On the other hand it sounds almost like a contradiction when Col. 3:25 gives the assurance (similar to the rejoinder to the Jews in Rom. 2:11) that 'there is no partiality,' a seeming warning against all too-sure confidence in the privileged position of Christians; or when one reads, "Do not err, God is not mocked" (Gal. 6:7); "He who thinks he stands, let him take heed lest he fall" (I Cor. 10:12). There are hortatory passages in the epistles which impress us as almost being sermons to a Jewish diaspora community, which should distinguish itself from the surrounding heathen world by its earnestness and expectation of the retributive judgment. As the Jew should not boast of the possession

[23] So also Gillis Pederson Wetter, *Der Vergeltungsgedanke bei Paulus* (The Retribution Idea in Paul). Though not so expressed, this is the fundamentally basic idea in Paul. The same investigator has observed very acutely that in the sayings of Paul under consideration (e.g. Rom. 1:18,32; 2:2,8f,12f), the personal activity of God in retribution and anger is in the background, while ὀργή, κρίμα, etc., as conceptions, semi-detached from God, as it were, appear as hypostases. But he seems to me to use modern modes of thought when he says that Paul considers retribution as a somewhat mechanical law of nature. The manner of speech is simply the Jewish habit which, if possible, avoids placing God personally in action. In spite of everything, as Wetter says, the mode of expression operates formally, juristically, mechanically.

of the Law and circumcision, but by deeds should obtain divine recognition (Rom. 2:12-29), so also Christians should not be too sure of their possession of salvation; it might happen quite otherwise to them, as it did to the generation in the wilderness (I Cor. 10:1-13). Truly, signs of the divine wrath are not lacking even in the Corinthian community, viz. sickness and cases of death. It is unusually valuable and instructive for the historian to observe how Paul sees himself compelled to go back to the pedagogical methods of Jewish synagogue life in order to keep his community of 'saints' and the redeemed at the highest level.

In view of this, the idea of wages is especially surprising. It really does not fit into the system of Christian thought, in which everything is based on divine grace and election, as Rom. 6:23 clearly teaches. Here the parallelism of members shows a peculiar evasion. After the phrase 'the wages which sin pays is death' there follows 'but the gift of God is eternal life through Jesus Christ our Lord.' According to the context (6:21f) one would expect the 'eternal life' to be the necessary consequence (τέλος); corresponding to the parallelism one would expect to see it designated as the divine wages. When Paul instead chooses the surprising expression 'gift.' (χάρισμα), he does it consciously: he wishes to say that here at least the concept of wages does not apply; he means to exclude every thought of human merit and to emphasize God's grace as the only basis.[24] In the same way it is also very seldom that one finds future salvation considered as wages. For 'wages' has its place where 'performance of work' (ἐργάζεσθαι) is the watch-word (Rom. 4:4), and it is just this Pharisaic standpoint of reckoning with God (pp. 385ff) which is completely relinquished where simple dependence upon God is felt as keenly as it is in Paul's doctrine of grace. Again the concept of 'wages' (μισθός) occurs in several passages where Paul does not of course actually refer to the salvation of man in general, but individually, of one's particular labor in the service of his Lord (I Cor. 3:8,13ff; 9:17). Thus in the first passage Paul expects for himself and for his fellow laborers not only 'praise' (I Cor. 4:5) but always a graduated 'wage' according to work done, as well. Whether this is only a figure of speech which flowed involuntarily from his pen, a figure which might in fact have been a

[24] The expression would be especially significant if Tertullian, *De Carn. Res.* 47, has rendered it correctly by using *donativum* (the imperial gift of clemency). Then the special gift of clemency, which is freely bestowed, would be contrasted with the regular wage *(stipendia)* to which the soldier has a claim (G. P. Wetter).

familiar one to him as a workman,[25] or whether he really meant it, there can be no doubt that in Paul there is also operative the idea that particular actions receive particular acknowledgment. Not only where he reveals the universal human law of retribution (Rom. 2:7-10) does he predict 'fame and honor to everyone who does good,' but also where he places the Christian before the judgment-seat of Christ (II Cor. 5:10) he states that 'everyone may receive the things done in the body, according to that which he hath done, whether it be good or evil.' There is a series of statements in which he expresses this earnest burning desire, almost as if he were covetous of honor. Not only does he wish to be well-pleasing to the Lord (II Cor. 5:9, φιλοτιμούμεθα . . . . εὐάρεστοι αὐτῷ εἶναί), but sometimes he wishes to be able to stand proudly before his face and point to the results of his labors. Here in fact the actual 'Pharisaic' expression, 'boasting,' appears once more; he even speaks once of 'boasting face to face with God.'[26] He is especially fond of pointing to his communities as the object of his pride or his boasting on the day of the Lord (I Thess. 2:19; II Cor. 1:14).

But all of these statements are but striking assertions of the fundamental desire 'to appear blameless at the day of our Lord Jesus Christ' (I Cor. 1:8; Phil. 1:10; I Thess. 3:13; 5:23; Col. 1:22, 28); 'to contend for the heavenly wreath' (I Cor. 9:25); 'to walk worthy of God who has called you to his kingdom—and to his glory' (I Thess. 2:12). This is the watch-word though it is but seldom expressed—it is indeed one of the chief motifs of the Pauline ethic. It appears as a distinct deviation where the question concerns one's inner attitude toward the possessions of this world, as in I Cor. 7:29-35; in view of the shortened period of time it is necessary to become inwardly free and released from attachment to earthly blessings, earthly occupations, earthly interests, in particular from the strong bond with which marriage binds man to this world. The aim is 'to please the Lord.' What degree of importance the eschatological motif has for Paul in his attitude toward the world we shall explain

[25] As Deissmann assumes with great exaggeration, *Licht vom Osten* (Light from the Ancient East), p. 227. Cf. Wetter, *op. cit.*, pp. 122ff.

[26] Rom. 15:17, *ἔχω οὖν τὴν καύχησιν ἐν Χριστῷ Ἰησοῦ τὰ πρὸς τὸν θεόν*, "I have, therefore, whereof I may glory through Jesus Christ in those things which pertain to God"; I Cor. 15:31, *νὴ τὴν ὑμετέραν καύχησιν, ἣν ἔχω ἐν Χριστῷ Ἰησοῦ κυρίῳ ἡμῶν*, "By your rejoicing which I have in Christ Jesus our Lord"; II Cor. 11:10; in I Cor. 9:16 the correspondence between 'glorying' (boasting) and 'wages' appears plainly: *ἐὰν γὰρ εὐαγγελίζωμαι, οὐκ ἔστιν μοι καύχημα . . . . εἰ γὰρ ἑκὼν τοῦτο πράσσω, μισθὸν ἔχω*, "For though I preach the gospel, I have nothing to glory of . . . . for if I do this I have a reward."

later in more detail. In any case it is neither in the marriage chapter (I Cor. 7) nor generally the only motif in the Pauline ethic.

Of at least equal importance is (b) *the religious or holiness motif.* Already in the first mentioned passage, I Cor. 7:32-35, the eschatological motif appears, primarily for the reason that it echoes vv. 29 ff. Another passage reinforces it strongly. The Christian belongs to his Lord, he was bought for a great price (7:23); is he married? If so, 'he is of a divided mind' (vs. 33), and it will be difficult for him 'to develop the sincere surrender to the Lord'[27] which he demands. The idea needs no eschatological emphasis; the heavenly Kyrios, even in the present, claims the mind and will of the Christian to such an extent that a full, naïve surrender to the possessions of this world is no longer possible (τὰ ἐπίγεια φρονεῖν, Phil. 3:19). Since his true 'home is in heaven' (Phil. 3:20), he belongs there, while here he is essentially a stranger; there his interests are rooted, thither his longings turn, there his duties lie. Nor does this idea have only an eschatological note (I Cor. 7:29ff). Certainly the Apostle thinks of the return of the Lord in this connection, but the attitude indicated here would be present even with this prospect lacking. The temporal consideration (of this and the future age) passes very easily into that of the supersensuous (the earthly and the heavenly worlds). What is really essential in both is the negative tone of emphasis: no longer to be at home in the things of this world. Tarrying in the body means for Paul a sojourning in a foreign land because it is absence from the Lord (II Cor. 5:6,8). The conviction prevails 'that we no longer belong to ourselves' (I Cor. 6:19), but are, body and soul, the property of Christ (I Cor. 3:23), in whose service the aim is to bring forth fruit unto God (Rom. 7:4). Thus the center of gravity of existence is moved outside the ego, 'no longer to live to self, but to Christ' (II Cor. 5:15); no longer to have one's own egoistic aims of life (Phil. 2:4); no longer pursuing one's own glory (Phil. 1:18) or profit (I Cor. 10:33).

But this feeling of obligation toward Christ which flows from praise, love, trust and obedience is only one note of the concord which we wish to suggest here. Beside this more personal motif another operates here, and one which perhaps responds still more to the spirit of ancient religion, namely the real holiness motif. By baptism and the bestowal of the Spirit the Christian is bound in a twofold manner. Baptism is of course not only a real and valid

[27] Thus I understand that the words τὸ εὐπάρεδρον τῷ κυρίῳ ἀπερισπάστως should be translated.

purification and washing away of former sins (I Cor. 6:11), but also includes the pledge to maintain this condition of purity—ye are clean, therefore remain clean! (I Cor. 5:7)—and the bestowal of the Spirit means an inner connection with God and the Spirit which may not be profaned (I Cor. 1:30; 6:11). This religious nobility is thus an obligation. "The will of God is your sanctification" (I Thess. 4:3; Rom. 6:19,22); "God has called you to sanctification" (I Thess. 4:7). This is especially intended to refer to the body: "Know ye not that your bodies are members of Christ?" How can ye profane them by lewdness! "Your body is the temple of the Holy Ghost—therefore glorify God in your body" (I Cor. 6:15,20). So powerful is the element of holiness in the person of a Christian that it also draws within its reach, like a contagion, the heathen husband (I Cor. 7:14),[28] and it shall permeate the whole community by means of Christian marriage (I Thess. 4:4). From this follows the duty of separation from heathenism forcefully expressed in II Cor. 6:14-18 and in general terms in I Cor. 10:1-13, with an earnest warning against sacrifice to idols and lewdness. "Let nothing of the manner of this world exist in you" (Rom. 12:2); "Put away from among yourselves that wicked person" (I Cor. 5:13); do not degrade your nobility as 'saints' by living as the heathen (I Cor. 6:1-11; 5:1ff).

We cannot emphasize too strongly the importance of these ideas in practice. Here also the pedagogic motif arising from the diaspora synagogue persists: along with all the broad-minded sympathy with Greek culture the requirement of separation is still felt strongly, the consciousness of having received as the people of God a special honor and special duties. Among Christians this now takes a sharper form; the feeling of having something divine in their midst, in fact in their souls and bodies, which must be held sacred, stands out very prominently. The self-designation of the Christians as 'saints' is anything but a seat on which to loll in arrogant ease; it contains an ever-active impulse to self-discipline and preservation.

(c) *The fellowship motif.* The ethic of the Apostle is in no way merely an individual ethic though it is certain that for him also 'religious individualism remains the essential idea.'[29] In the first

[28] Cf. my Commentary on I Cor. 7:14.

[29] E. Troeltsch, *Soziallehren* (The Social Teaching of the Churches), p. 59; "The very general idea of individuality and the very free and wavering idea of fellowship which characterized the Gospel have been intensified and appreciably narrowed. In the Pneuma-Christ, pervading all things and identical with the Spirit of God, the sociological idea receives an incalculably efficient presentation for worship of its point of reference as well as a closer dogmatic organic connection among the social

place of course it is a question of the rescue or salvation (σωτηρία) of the individual, of his intimate relationship with Christ and his complete permeation by the Spirit of God. But in Paul's mind individuals do not stand isolated before God and Christ. They are most closely allied with one another, because it is one and the same Spirit, one and the same Christ (I Cor. 12:4-14; Rom. 12:3f); they have duties toward the community as such and toward the individual brethren; to shame them means despising the Church (I Cor. 11:22). Above all, in this motif there is a restriction against living out one's life solely in the state of religious possession. Spiritual enthusiasm carries along with it the immediate temptation for the spiritual man not only to consider himself specially favored, but also to permit himself to be led by religious impulses alone in the enjoyment and practice of his gift, without regard to the community. Paul seeks to check this phenomenon which appeared at Corinth with the principle, "Let all things be done unto edifying" (I Cor. 14:26). In this one observes antithetical modes of thought which are genuinely spiritual. The spiritual man is inclined to place the urge of the Spirit as an irresistible divine impulse above all other considerations: What is higher or more important than to feel vividly a communion with God and the Spirit, and to permit this feeling to flow out as the Spirit wills? Upon such a man the Apostle imposes service to the brotherhood. He sees the divine purpose of the gift in the edification and fostering of the community—the members must serve the body, must serve one another (Rom. 12:5; I Cor. 12:21,27)—and thus purely religious activity receives an ethical form. And if the Gnostic believes that he not only has the right (ἐξουσία) but also the duty to give practical proof of his knowledge by putting aside

relations themselves. The infinite worth of the individual is now related not merely to the process of self-sanctification in obedience to the fatherly will of God, but to Christ, in whom the believer lives and moves. Christ imparts his own life, mystically, to those who trust him: it is he who works through Baptism and the Lord's Supper, forming the true higher life in the believer; Christ indeed in his exalted pneumatic Being is none other than the redeeming Spirit of God Himself, who overcomes the demons, the Law and sin. Filial relationship with God, which was the inclusive content of the absolute religious individualism of the Gospel, becomes the state of being 'in Christ'; along the same lines the fellowship of the children of God in brotherly love becomes brotherhood not in God but in Christ; in the general union of all believers through life in the actual mystical life-substance of Christ, they become members of the body of Christ. Further, the universalism which revealed love as the divine attitude toward the world, and which was aroused by this revelation, remains the same within the Church; it is expressed in missionary effort for the conversion of souls; the aim of this missionary work is to draw the whole world, which is lost without Christ, into redeeming participation in the death and resurrection of the Pneuma-Christ."

concern for the 'weak' (I Cor. 8; Rom. 14), Paul appeals to his conscience to have regard for those whom he endangers morally by his freedom. He demands renunciation of self-expression; "You are called to liberty," and he adds, "but by love ye shall serve one another" (Gal. 5:13). He sets the example himself not only by renouncing the right of sole oversight of the church, but also the right to enforce his own convictions without restraint. To the Jews he becomes a Jew, to those under the Law, as of the Law (I Cor. 9:19-23), in order to 'win' them. He modifies the principle of the free Gnostic: "All things are lawful unto me," by the addition, "but all things are not expedient, all do not edify" (I Cor. 6:12; 10:23). Here we can do no more than suggest the significance which brotherly love has in the ethic of Paul.[30] The strongest expression of the superiority of love is found in I Cor. 13:1ff where the idea is expressed that the strongest proofs of religious enthusiasm are nothing without love.

(d) *The personality motif*. Under this head we group a series of motives which have in common the fact that they set up the ideal of a perfect personality (Rom. 12:2; Col. 1:28; 4:12), self-contained, purified from all excess of passion. Here especially belongs the modification, expressed figuratively, which he gives to the Gnostic principle, "All things are lawful unto me; but all things are not expedient, all things do not edify"—but I will not permit myself to be forced by anything (I Cor. 6:12; 10:23).[31] Against unrestrained use of liberty which only too easily changes bondage into desire, against the 'strength' (Rom. 15:1) of the emancipated spiritual man, which only too easily besmirches the nobility and dignity of personality (I Cor. 6:18), he sets up also the ideal of glorifying God with, or in, the body (Rom. 6:20). When he calls lust (I Thess. 4:4; Gal. 5:24; Rom. 1:26; Col. 3:5) *dishonorable* and demands the preservation of human *honor*, and especially

[30] I Thess. 4:9; Rom. 12:9f; 13:8f; 14:15; Gal. 5:13f,22; I Cor. 8:2; 13:4ff; 14:1, 17; II Cor. 6:6; Phil. 2:1f; Col. 1:4; 2:2; 3:14; I Thess. 1:3; 3:12; 5:8,13; II Thess. 1:3.

[31] While the concept of *οἰκοδομεῖν* has not yet been classified as to its source (cf. my Commentary on I Cor. 8:1), *συμφέρει* goes back beyond the Stoic school to Socrates (cf. H. Maier, *Sokrates*, pp. 312ff; Plato, *Protagoras*, 333d, *ἆρ' οὖν ταῦτ' ἔστιν ἀγαθά, ἅ ἐστιν ὠφέλιμα τοῖς ἀνθρώποις*, "Thus, therefore, those things are good which are useful to men"; *Kleitophon* 409b,c); however, the idea of *οὐκ ἐγὼ ἐξουσιασθήσομαι ὑπό τινός*, "I will not be brought under the power of any," is completely Stoic; cf. Seneca, *Ep*. 92f: *corporis . . . . non amator, sed procurator . . . . nec se illi, cui impositus est, subicit. Nemo liber est, qui corpori servit*, "It [the soul] regards the body . . . . not as a thing to love, but as a thing to oversee . . . . nor is it subservient to that over which it is set in mastery. For no man is free who is a slave to his body."

that of woman (I Thess. 4:4; I Pet. 3:7),[32] this idea corresponds to the nobler kind of Greek morality which sees in too excessive sensuality a degrading *pathos*, an abominable condition.[33] Although the Greek *sophrosyne* is never mentioned it is nevertheless undeniable that Paul conceives this as ideal. As against the over-excited self-evaluation of the spiritual man, not only does he exhort to prudence (Rom. 12:3), but it shines through the ideal personality as he describes it in Gal. 5:22, 'Love, joy, peace, long-suffering, goodness, generosity, faithfulness, gentleness, self-control.' In general his attitude toward asceticism shows a healthy Hellenistic proportion between over-excited abstinence and joyousness of indulgence.[34] Also Greek, that is to say Stoic, is the abhorrence of what is 'contrary to nature' (Rom. 1:26f), and the occasional appeal to that which 'nature teaches' (I Cor. 11:14; cf. also Rom. 2:14). Just so, Rom. 1:28 corresponds to the Stoic expression 'the fitting thing,' that is to say that which is really adapted to man:[35] reasonable action. One must observe in the following catalogue of sins how Paul enumerates transgressions against the elementary moral statutes of mankind, especially in the conclusion: 'without respect toward parents, without understanding, without

[32] The antithesis between ἐν τιμῇ and ἐν πάθει ἐπιθυμίας is decisive here; cf. πάθη ἀτιμίας and τοῦ ἀτιμάζεσθαι τὰ σώματα ἐν αὐτοῖς, 'that their bodies should be dishonored among themselves'; Rom. 1:24,26.

[33] It is Stoic in thought when Paul says: "It is already a *fault* among you (ἥττημα) that ye go to law one with another" (I Cor. 6:7). It is unworthy of the nobility of Christian personality to be ensnared in the common quarrels of the day.

[34] The almost untranslatable words in Rom. 13:14: καὶ τῆς σαρκὸς πρόνοιαν μὴ ποιεῖσθε εἰς ἐπιθυμίας can only be understood as one of those abrupt transitions to a new theme, frequently found in Paul. They contain, in a most compact form, on the one hand a concession, and on the other a warning, the latter in retrospect to Rom. 13:11ff, the former in prospect to chapter 14. Luther's translation is still the most pertinent: "Attend to the body, yet also see that it does not become voluptuous." Parallels: Plutarch, *Mor.* 142a, ὥσπερ οὖν σώματος ἔστι κήδεσθαι μὴ δουλεύοντα ταῖς ἡδοναῖς αὐτοῦ καὶ ταῖς ἐπιθυμίαις, "Thus it is proper to care for the body, not being in slavery to its pleasures and lusts"; Dio Chrysostom, *Or.* 40:2, οἶμαι καὶ τοῦ σώματος δέον ποιήσασθαι τινα πρόνοιαν, "I suppose that one ought to take some forethought for the body"; Cicero, *Offic.* 1:30, *Itaque victus cultusque corporis ad valetudinem referatur et ad vires, non ad voluptatem,* "Thus control and development of the body is for the purpose of health, and for strength, not for voluptuousness"; Seneca, *Ep.* 92, *corporis . . . . non amator sed procurator,* "not to love the body, but to oversee it."

[35] τὰ (μὴ) καθήκοντα; the expression must have been coined by Zeno. It signifies that which can be justified by reference to the reason: ὃ πραχθὲν εὔλογον ἴσχει ἀπολογισμόν, οἷον τὸ ἀκόλουθον ἐν τῇ ζωῇ, 'that which having been done gives a good account of itself; such as is agreeable with life' (Diog. Laert. vii. 107f). According to Chrysippus καθήκοντα are ὅσα λόγος αἱρεῖ ποιεῖν, ὡς ἔχει γονεῖς τιμᾶν, ἀδελφούς, πατρίδα, συμπεριφέρεσθαι φίλοις, 'such things as reason chooses to do, such as tend toward honoring parents, brothers, and one's native land, association with friends.'

character, without heart, without pity'—sins which according to the Stoic point of view are also just the contrary of what is fitting for humanity. The description of the good which is to be found in the heathen world is also Greek: "Unweariedly doing good, striving after glory, honor and immortality" (Rom. 2:7)—one thinks of Heracles, the hero of the Cynics, who abiding in good works (ὑπομονὴ ἔργου ἀγαθοῦ) won for himself immortality. The comprehension of the ideal (Rom. 12:2) in the three words, 'the good, the beautiful and the perfect,' is also more Greek than Jewish;[36] the second expression, which really means 'the well-pleasing,' is especially characteristic. Thus an aesthetic motif enters the ethic, and even this is Greek. Wholly Greek also is the series of exhortations: "Finally, brethren, whatsoever things are true, whatsoever things are honourable (σεμνά), whatsoever things are just, whatsoever things are pure (ἁγνά), lovely (προσφιλή), of good report (εὔφημα); if there be any virtue (ἀρετή), and if there be any praise (ἔπαινος), think on these things" (Phil. 4:8). It is the ideal of the noblest Greeks which Paul describes here. The Greek sense is also felt in the saying, "Let your speech be always with grace, seasoned with salt, that ye may know how ye ought to answer every man" (Col. 4:6). Christians should also be outward examples of exalted and good breeding; the new life which certainly often enough shows itself in a rough exterior and purposely neglects the customary forms of intercourse of this world, should present itself in a winning manner. The ideal of the *euschemosyne* of a decent, dignified manner is often emphasized (I Thess. 4:12; I Cor. 7:35; Rom. 13:13; I Cor. 14:40), and it is the antithesis of *aschemosyne* (Rom. 1:27; I Cor. 7:36; 13:5). Here one may also mention briefly the motif of order which finds expression in I Cor. 14:40, "Everything should be done decently and in order." Furthermore in the exhortations of the Epistles to the Thessalonians (II Thess. 3:7,12; I Thess. 4:11f), instead of pious slothfulness there must be no disorderly way of living, but quietness and diligence, that no one be a burden to anyone. These requirements formulated with a view to propaganda and to the opinion of the surrounding world (I Cor. 10:32) are deeply rooted in the personality of Paul. His deep aversion to boundless, unbridled, unorganized existence infers a certain aristocratic rearing (see pp. 182f). His urging of discipline and order bespeaks the practical organizer. In all

[36] It is to be especially noted how frequently in Paul 'the Good' appears as a concept which is self-explanatory and known to everyone: Rom. 2:10; 5:7; 12:9,21; 13:3; 16:19; Gal. 6:10; I Thess. 5:15; thus also τὸ καλόν, 'the noble': Rom. 7:18,21; II Cor. 13:7; Gal. 6:9.

this one can see the expression of a higher personal culture than had yet been present in the religious movement of primitive Christianity. Here certainly something Greek and Roman begins to find its way into the churches.

3. One must now inquire concerning the form taken by individual applications of the ethical ideal.

(a) We have previously noted that *love*,[37] which not only is the highest and most important quality (Gal. 5:22), but which in reality includes everything else, is the 'bond of perfection' (Col. 3:14). The really practical proof of Christianity is 'faith working through love' (Gal. 5:6); he who has received love in faith (Gal. 2:20), into whose heart the love of God has been poured (Rom. 5:5), who is firmly anchored in the love of God and of Christ,[38] cannot fail to possess love. For Christians it is no longer a command but something that is a matter of course. They 'have been taught by God to love one another' (I Thess. 4:9). Human love is only a reflection or radiation of the divine (I Cor. 8:3; p. 394). Therefore the center of gravity of the word and the concept of love rests more upon the feeling of the lover than upon the good which is done to the beloved. Because of its origin an exalted tone of joyous feeling is attached to the Greek word; it speaks from a full, happy heart which radiates this pure emotion (Gal. 5:22, love, joy, peace).[39]

There is difference of opinion as to whether, in I Cor. 13, love toward God (cf. p. 394) or love toward men is meant, and it can be easily shown in vv. 4-7 that the reference is in every respect to human love. But nothing is thereby said as to the first three verses. Here it would be an attempt at too great precision to seek to determine the object of love exclusively in one direction or the other.[40] The essential thing here is not the emphasis upon one or the other subject but upon the feeling itself. One may possess all gifts and have a cold heart; indeed in an excessive

[37] Rom. 8:35,39; II Cor. 5:14; 13:11,13; Col. 3:12; I Thess. 1:4; II Thess. 2:13,16; 3:5.

[38] We still lack a really comprehensive investigation of the word ἀγάπη along the lines of linguistics and the history of religion and morals, and of the ideals contained in the word; and such an investigation is urgently needed.

[39] According to Passow-Crönert's Lexicon, the etymology of ἀγάπη, ἀγαπᾶν is still doubtful. Formerly the word was joined with ἀγά(αο)μαι 'admire.' The older meaning is 'to be pleased,' 'to be satisfied with,' 'to welcome lovingly,' 'cherish,' 'caress,' 'esteem highly,' 'prefer'; also 'to desire,' 'long for.' On the whole, the emphasis lies more upon the mood of the lover than upon the favor done the beloved.

[40] One also naturally thinks here of brotherly love in this connection, because one reads chapter 13 in closest connection with chapter 12, and especially with chapter 14. But this connection is actually very doubtful. Intrinsically, the chapter belongs with chapter 8. Cf. p. 510, note 20, and my Commentary on I Cor. 13.

ebullition of heroism one can even give all his goods to the poor and still be destitute of love—a deep psychological observation on the part of the Apostle. It does not depend upon the activity or power of the Spirit but upon an inner apprehension of the love of God, the jubilant joyousness which cannot do enough in bearing witness to its experiences. Naturally this will manifest itself in human love (as it is so incomparably described in vv. 4-7). It seems to me that this description is especially aimed at the puffed-up unreflecting Gnostics of chapter 8.[41] At the head stand long-suffering and goodness, virtues in which such people are simply not interested (cf. Gal. 5:22). Love does not possess that envy which would seek to annihilate opposing opinions; it vaunts not itself, is not snobbish and is not puffed-up in the consciousness of spiritual superiority. It does not violate propriety and good manners, for example by incessant accentuation of liberties which one thinks may be permitted. It is again characteristic of Paul the Greek that he also expects from love an aesthetic, well-pleasing outward behavior. Very important is the statement: "It rejoices not in wrong, but has a heart-felt pleasure in the truth." [42] Here the ethical character of love appears; it is the divine disposition which desires the good and has a sincere pleasure in it. It is rich in knowledge and fine moral tact (Phil. 1:9). It is optimistic: "It believes all things, it hopes all things"—even where there seems to be but little prospect of winning the other person—it does not permit itself to be 'embittered' by opposition; it 'suffers all things, endures all things.' Above all else it 'seeks not its own,' but that which is the benefit of others (I Cor. 10:24; Phil. 2:4); in this it is the true imitation of Christ (I Cor. 10:33; 11:1). True 'liberty' is tested in the 'service of love' (Gal. 5:13). Here is echoed the saying of Jesus that the true good subsists in service (Luke 22:26f). "Love edifies"; it seeks to promote the interests of the other person to the highest degree; it feels itself responsible for him (I Cor. 8:1,11ff), and helps to restore the one who has fallen (Gal. 6:1). It knows how to renounce and to sacrifice, as Paul shows by his example (I Cor. 9:18-23; I Thess. 2:9). It rejoices with the happy and weeps with those who weep (Rom. 12:15); it bears the burden of the other person (Gal. 6:2); it shares its own with others in mercy and doing good (Rom. 12:8,13). In the same connection he often mentions

[41] Cf. my Commentary; especially do 'being puffed-up' (8:1), 'boasting,' refer to them.

[42] On the contrast between ἀλήθεια and αδικία, compare, besides Rom. 1:18; 2:8; 3:5,7, also III Ezra 4:37 (Kautzsch, i, 9), as well as Böhlig, *Geisteskultur von Tarsos*, p. 106.

gentleness (πραΰτης, I Cor. 4:21; Gal. 5:23; 6:1; Col. 3:12) and goodness (χρηστότης II Cor. 6:6; Gal. 5:22; Col. 3:12), noblemindedness (ἀγαθωσύνη, Rom. 15:14; Gal. 5:22; II Thess. 1:11). In the catalogue of evils, quarrels, strife, factions and division occupy much space, and the existence of jealousy and strife (I Cor. 3:2) is the sure sign that the Corinthians are not yet mature Christians. But 'peace' is the real proper distinguishing mark of a community in which the 'God of peace' reigns (Rom. 15:33; Phil. 4:9; I Thess. 5:23). God is not a God of unrest, but of peace (I Cor. 14:33) or 'love and peace' (II Cor. 13:11); "God has called us unto peace" (I Cor. 7:15).[43]

But in his letters Paul has erected a monument of his love which far transcends this description. What fervor, tenderness, patience and magnanimity he maintains as he writes! In the First Epistle to the Thessalonians he expresses his longing and loyalty almost excessively. He has given his entire self to the Christians of Thessalonica, has shown them a father's and a mother's love; he feels himself orphaned by the separation: "We can thank God for all the joy we have in you; day and night we pray most earnestly to see your face." How ardently he struggles for the churches which are slipping out of his hand: "Have I become your enemy because I tell you the truth?" "My children for whom I travail again"; "I desire to be with you now and to vary my pleading in every possible way, for I stand in doubt of you" (Gal. 4:16,19f). "O dear Corinthians, our mouth is open unto you, our heart is enlarged. Ye are not straitened in us, but ye are straitened in your own affections. Now for a recompense in like kind (I speak as unto my children), be ye also enlarged." "Open your hearts to us: we wronged no man. I say it not to condemn you: for I have said before that ye are in our hearts to die together and live together. Great is my boldness

[43] Cf. further, εἰρηνεύειν, Rom. 12:18; II Cor. 13:11; I Thess. 5:13; εἰρήνη, Rom. 14:17,19; 15:13. It is not unimportant that the humanitarian idea never is the leading motive of love. Words and concepts drawn from human nature are, on the whole, wanting in the N. T. This is rather the basis of Stoic love of humanity: Seneca, *Ep.* 95,52, "We are members of a great Body. Nature has created us as kinsmen, in that she has caused us to originate from the same material and for the same purpose. She has implanted in us a mutual love and made us social beings *(sociabiles)*. She has founded equity and justice. Her ordinance is that to do wrong (*nocere,* ἀδικεῖν) is worse than to suffer wrong (*laedi,* ἀδικεῖσθαι; cf. my Commentary on I Cor. 6:7; Plato, *Gorg.* p. 509c; *Crito,* 496b; Musonius, ed. Hense, pp. 11,7; Epictetus, iv. 5,10; Plutarch, *Apophth.* p. 190a, *Inst. Lacon.* p. 239a). At her command, the hands are ready to help." The Christian duty of love is not established on natural grounds in Paul's writings; as we have said, it is a result of the love of God which has been experienced. For the idea of the Body of Christ and its relation to the Stoic idea of human nature, see chapter 21.

of speech toward you, great is my glorying on your behalf; I am filled with comfort, I overflow with joy in all my affliction" (II Cor. 6:11f; 7:2-4). The Epistle to the Philippians is an example of tender loveliness; how heartily he shows his thankfulness! What comprehension he has of what the rich gift means to the poor community! But why recount the details? This man glows with love which is for him a powerful emotion, and each word that he writes is inspired; he is full of devotion, sacrifice and inspiration with respect to the cause he serves. The people for whom he labors lie upon his soul; he is responsible for them; he feels responsible to God. So he does what he can and he leaves the remainder to the mercy of God with sincere intercession.

The love which is here the subject of discussion is primarily brotherly love (I Thess. 4:9); it embraces first of all 'all the saints' (Col. 1:4), is grounded in the Spirit which all Christians have (Col. 1:8; Rom. 15:30, love of the Spirit) and in the Lord whose servants all Christians are. All this goes without saying. If, however, we observe Paul himself, we see that his love is limited to the congregation and indeed still more narrowly to those brethren who willingly cooperate with him. And it cannot be denied that he gives little love, makes little attempt to understand, has slight tenderness toward his opponents in Galatia, in Corinth or in Philippi. Here the unbridled passion of oriental hate breaks out without restraint (especially in Gal. 5:12; II Cor. 11:13ff; Phil. 3:2ff). Let it not be said that this is holy zeal—'love envies not'; let us not excuse him by maintaining that he was extremely provoked—'love is not provoked'—we must accept this feature in the picture of the Apostle for what it is. He does not need our apology. But who can deny that this is the reverse side of his enormous energy? To state it paradoxically, hate is the antithesis of his great love. And he would have been the first to condemn himself on this very point if he could have recognized the relative rights of his opponents as we are able to do. In any case he also knows and acknowledges as binding for himself the duty of loving one's enemies. Rom. 12:14 and I Cor. 4:12 plainly echo the sayings of the Lord in the Sermon on the Mount. He firmly accepts the proposition already acknowledged in Greek ethics: "Better suffer wrong than do wrong." He has uttered glorious words concerning the renunciation of vengeance as the winning of the adversary: "Be not overcome of evil, but overcome evil with good" (Rom. 12:19ff). His disposition on this point is indubitable and he surely lived more closely in accordance with it than we can know. He practised forgiveness in one case when it was very difficult indeed for him to do so (II Cor. 2:5-11). He felt deeply the foolishness, fickleness and disloyalty of the Gnostics in Corinth and the insulting credulity of the Galatians, but still he bore with them. Who of us can judge him because of the other things? The measure of the love which he showed is so great that they are outweighed by it. His loyalty toward his fellow countrymen who had cast him out is especially touching. Not only is this shown by the section in Rom. 9-11 but also by his unwearied solicitation for Israel. For this the words in I Cor. 9:20 may serve the motto. But it is characteristic of him that he understands how to justify himself more sincerely to the Jews and to the heathen than to those whom he is compelled to call 'false brethren.' His intolerance is a sign of how highly he esteems truthfulness.

(b) '*Truth*' is a key-word which he frequently uses in a variety of senses. We are acquainted with it (Rom. 2:8; I Cor. 13:6; II Thess. 2:10,12; also I Cor. 5:8) in the ethical sense of the antithesis of 'wrong' as a summary of all good. It also appears as a shortened expression for the objective revelation or knowledge of God (Rom. 1:18,25) and of his will (2:20), especially of the self-manifestation of God made known in the Gospel (II Cor. 4:2; 6:7; Gal. 5:7; Col. 1:5; II Thess. 2:10,12), sometimes more precisely of the undistorted correct conception of the Gospel, 'the truth of the Gospel' (Gal. 2:5,14). Just because the truth, the valid revelation of God, incapable of revision, appears in the Gospel as Paul understands it, there is no other gospel. Thus no man nor even any angel (Gal. 1:8f) dare preach another gospel beyond it or contrary to it. It is for the Apostle a sacred duty to guard the purity and inviolability of this message and teaching with all his might and to resist unto death every 'distortion' or lie. The conviction of its truth is so deeply rooted in him and appears so clear and free from objection that he can see only evil will or satanic insinuation where another Jesus or another gospel is preached. His passion in this regard expresses his feeling that he is permeated by this truth which alone brings blessedness. His conviction has a religious basis but also a strong intellectual character. The thought-system of his Gospel seems to him so flawlessly fitted together that he considers it a moral deficiency[44] if one will not bow to the truth (II Thess. 2:12) but 'gives credence to a lie.'

[44] *Truth* is so luminously true that the human *conscience* must immediately adhere to it: τῇ φανερώσει τῆς ἀληθείας συνιστάνοντες ἑαυτοὺς πρὸς πᾶσαν συνείδησιν ἀνθρώπων ἐνώπιον τοῦ θεοῦ 'by the manifestation of the truth commending ourselves to every man's conscience in the sight of God,' II Cor. 4:2.

Of course ordinary subjective truthfulness (Rom. 9:1; II Cor. 11:10; 12:6) is also a sacred duty to Paul (Phil. 4:8). He can do nothing against truth (II Cor. 13:8) even if it should be to his own disadvantage. He insists particularly upon the inner truth of the conscience.[45] Nothing is more serious or destructive than the insincere lukewarmness of one 'weak' in the faith who with a bad conscience scandalizes himself by taking liberties not equal to his convictions (Rom. 14:20; I Cor. 8:9f). "All things which are not of faith," i.e. do not come of full and clear conviction, "are sin" (Rom. 14:23). Indeed, an ambiguity of action, like that of Peter and Barnabas in Antioch (Gal. 2:13) appears to him like hypocrisy; the state of the community which wishes to keep Easter before having purged gross sin from its midst is completely hypocritical (I Cor. 5:8, purity and truth in contrast with malice and wickedness). Purity, which he likes to specify as purity 'before God' (II Cor. 2:17), he contrasts with 'fleshly wisdom,' i.e. craftiness which pursues selfish interests (II Cor. 1:12). Hence he mentions also that simplicity (ἁπλότης) which has no ulterior motive: simple loyalty (II Cor. 11:3). The word [46] is especially used to refer to cheerful giving (Rom. 12:8; II Cor. 8:2; 9:11,13).

To truthfulness also belongs the proper (c) *self-examination of the Christian.* Nothing is more remote from the Apostle's purpose than the fostering of confession of sins. The great confession of human sinfulness in Rom. 7:14-25 is not that of a Christian; here is a condition of things which have been conquered (p. 515). Surely the remembrance of his great former sin still pursued him and caused him great pain (I Cor. 15:9; Gal. 1:13), but he speaks of it with

[45] The conscience (συνείδησις) mentioned in Rom. 2:15 as a universal human faculty naturally remains for the Christian the regulator of moral life, as well as an ever-present consciousness, accusing or acquitting, as the case may be (Rom. 9:1; II Cor. 1:12; I Cor. 4:4); it is also a so-called 'law-giving' faculty. The expression 'weak conscience' (I Cor. 8:7,10,12) is also important: it means that the moral consciousness of many believers is so sensitive that it reacts against, censures, and is irritated by actions which others can permit themselves without the slightest scruple, e.g. the eating of meats offered to idols. Some have a robust conscience; they can put into practice their conviction of the harmlessness of such foods, without being inwardly troubled thereby; others have won that knowledge with difficulty, but after they have acted in accordance with it, they become conscience-stricken, and so their conscience is 'defiled' or 'wounded.' Among Seneca's statements which are of interest here is especially the expression *salva conscientia,* 'without injuring the conscience' (*Ep.* 117:1). That which is named 'conscience' in I Cor. 8, Paul calls 'belief' in Rom. 14:23; in Rom. 14:2, one 'believes' he can eat all things. The word here perhaps has the force of our 'conviction,' 'to be convinced'; cf. 14:23, 'that which is not done out of deepest conviction' (but half-heartedly, and with a bad conscience) 'is sin.'

[46] There is needed an investigation, along historico-linguistic lines, of the word-group ἁπλοῦς, ἁπλότης, ἀφελότης.

simplicity and moderation rather than with the superlative expressions used in the deutero-Pauline letters. The period is completely past when 'we were still in the flesh, when the passions of sin worked in our members' (Rom. 7:5). He emphasizes this particularly in writing to the church of Colossae, whose certainty of salvation and joyousness had been made doubtful by false teachers: You are made alive, your sins are forgiven, the indictment of guilt has been wiped out, you have died to the elements of the world (Col. 2:12ff,20)—therefore be ye thankful, thankful, thankful (1:12; 2:7; 3:15ff; 4:2)! And this joyousness and confidence are the keynote of the Christian life. It has been said that the Christian no longer sins, a statement which is somewhat too extreme. Certainly, according to Paul's conception the true spiritual Christian in whom the Spirit is everything and the flesh is non-existent, cannot sin. But it is quite significant how in Rom. 6:11f this confession takes the form of the imperative, "Reckon yourselves dead unto sin." Paul often varies the idea so as to apply it to Christian pride: God has given you a high position, therefore take possession of it with conviction, do not esteem yourselves too lowly, as if you were still sunk deep in sin: make the freely given liberation from sin a matter of the will.

The theme has still other variations. For reality often appears in different forms and Paul sees himself compelled to utter a solemn warning against too great confidence (Gal. 6:1). Indeed even a serious fall into gross heathen sins is often more imminent than many think (I Cor. 10:12). It is important to reckon with temptation (I Thess. 3:5). The earnest Christian knows the attacks of Satan only too well—he lies in wait to seize anyone who is too conceited and bring him into his power (II Cor. 2:10f). In addition to extreme asceticism there is the threat of relapse into the grossest sensuality (I Cor. 7:5), and alongside the puffed-up 'super-spirituality' of the Corinthians appears the peculiar case of the incestuous man (I Cor. 5:2). The over-confidence in victory, as though they had already reached the goal of perfection (I Cor. 4:8), touches the Apostle most painfully. Therefore he seeks to check the over-weening estimation of self in the spiritual man with ironical (I Cor. 4:7f) or warning words (Rom. 12:3). He who must needs boast, 'let him boast'—if this expression is suitable here (p. 504)—'in the Lord' (I Cor. 1:31; II Cor. 10:17). If he wishes to know what he really is, let him not look upon those who seem to be less advanced than he, 'let him examine his own deeds'; if the test is successful then he may have self-confidence—but only in private, since he should suppress it in the presence of others (Gal. 6:3f).

However even self-examination is no infallible judge: "For I know nothing against myself, yet am I not hereby justified: but he that judgeth me is the Lord" (I Cor. 4:4). Thus the earnest Christian will never—or at any rate only when he is compelled to do so by slander—look backward; his face is toward the future. The preponderant feeling is certainly this: "Not that I have already obtained or am already made perfect: but I follow after that which lies before, I pursue the distant goal, the prize of the heavenly calling." How far distant it still is! The sign [47] of 'perfection' is just this conviction of imperfection and of the will to advance. Only he is really 'perfect' in whom the Spirit of God is not only present but has permeated his entire existence; this is the completely spiritual man. According to this concept, this should be the condition of every baptized person, but in reality the battle with the flesh remains the continual problem (Rom. 8:13). It must still be said of the Christian, as well as of others, that "the flesh lusts against the Spirit . . . . so that ye cannot do what ye will." Thus the watchful word is, "Be driven by the Spirit" (Gal. 5:16ff; pp. 401f): watch and be sober (I Thess. 5:6), awake from sleep, put off the works of darkness, put on the Lord Jesus Christ (Rom. 13:11-14). All these ethical interpretations which we have been taught to regard as presuppositions in the redemption to a new life return here as imperatives (pp. 401f) and are of course directed most strongly against all inordinate desire for pleasure and against self-confident repose in the possession of the Spirit. Paul has indeed done his part in warning his communities against false security and indolence.

(d) *Education and training*. A notable difference between Paul and the Stoic moralists, such as Epictetus, consists in the fact that the pedagogical and psychological note, especially the idea of training and practical guidance as to what should be done if one would become more and more the master of one's own mind, so strongly in evidence in the Stoics, is almost wholly wanting in Paul. From the practical ecclesiastical viewpoint this is a defect. Many preachers and educators have lamented the fact that the New Testament offers so little in this regard, and it is quite justifiable when a practical Christian such as Carl Hilty continually introduces the Stoic ethical teachers as a complement to the Bible. The deepest reason for this deficiency is clear: even as an ethical teacher Paul is primarily a

[47] This sarcastic use of 'perfect' (τέλειος) has an analogy in the literary usage of Epictetus. In *Ench.* 51:1f he says that he who has determined to progress (προκόπτειν) is with bold anticipation already called 'perfect'; *Diss.* iii. 7, 17, "If you also wish to be a philosopher as he must be, if otherwise you would be 'perfect,' you must follow the teaching." Cf. my Commentary on I Cor. 3:4, pp. 74f.

Spirit-filled man; he expects the new life to shape itself out of the religious impulse, and where this does not suffice he applies prophetical, threatening, conscience-arousing imperatives like Jesus and the aphoristic poets of his people. In the technical sense he was no educator. The idea of guiding Christian education by technical and psychological methods into correct paths for the coming centuries is far from his mind. His ethic, inasmuch as it moves in the imperative, is the alarm-cry of the last hour: still one more mighty, final exertion of strength—then comes the end!

However the training idea is not entirely lacking. In I Cor. 9:24-27 he uses the figure of the prize-fighter who hardens himself by his abstemiousness and training. The concept of 'experience' or ability comes into play here (ἀδόκιμος—δόκιμος—δοκιμή); it also occurs in the famous chain: 'tribulation worketh patience; and patience, experience; and experience, hope' (Rom. 5:4). The idea is treated here psychologically: the school of tribulation produces the ability to endure.[48] Thus a man becomes 'expert' and able, i.e. a character is formed which trusts itself to give proof of strength upon which we can depend.[49] Tribulation and experience are concepts which are in particular correspondence (II Cor. 8:2). Here the virile character of the Pauline ethic appears: there must be struggle, that the qualified man may be revealed (I Cor. 11:19).

Thus the exhortation to (e) *courage and loyalty* also plays an important rôle. "Therefore, my beloved brethren, be steadfast and unmovable"; "Watch ye, stand fast in the faith, quit you like men, be strong" (I Cor. 15:58; 16:13; cf. also Col. 1:23). "Paul has a militant nature, he is familiar with pictures of the soldier's life"; he feels himself to be a field soldier of his Lord (Philem. 2; Phil. 2:25) possessing the weapons of righteousness, for both defence and offence (II Cor. 6:7). His life is a 'struggle' (ἀγών, I Thess. 2:2; Phil. 1:30; Col. 1:29; 2:1; 4:12); his work is a campaign in the service of God (II Cor. 10:3ff). All Christians should be thus armed (I Thess. 5:8) and should be prepared at all times to prove their loyalty; unafraid before adversaries they must be conscious of the fact that it is a privilege to be permitted to suffer for Christ (Phil. 1:27ff).

Therewith Paul utters one of the most important key-sayings of his letters; the tribulations, afflictions, distresses of this final world-period will seem heavy indeed if one does not look upon them in

[48] Cf. also the important expression ὑπομονὴ ἔργου ἀγαθοῦ, 'persevering in doing good.'

[49] Rom. 14:18; 16:10; I Cor. 11:19; II Cor. 10:18; 13:7; II Cor. 2:9; 8:2; 9:13; 13:3; Phil. 2:22.

the light of the glory which is to come.[50] Occasionally the impression is given (Rom. 5:3; 8:18) that the churches considered it strange that the elect of Christ must suffer and that Paul took pains to refute possible doubts concerning salvation which might arise from this cause. Tribulations are no counter-evidence against salvation. They are something which Christians must endure; they are truly the sufferings of Christ which deluge the community (II Cor. 1:5); the measure of his sufferings is not yet full; what is still lacking is the task of the Christians to furnish (Col. 1:24). He who would be 'co-heir with Christ' and share in his glory must also share 'in the sufferings.' This is considered as self-evident (Rom. 8:17). One must not merely endure these sufferings [51] but endure joyfully; this is presupposed when he says that 'we glory in tribulations also' (Rom. 5:3), i.e. despite the sufferings we maintain a happy confidence in the hope of the glory of God (5:2); we do not permit ourselves to be bowed down and discouraged.[52]

One can feel what is implied in such a brave and enduring attitude in the face of unsought-for suffering by considering that heroic series of paradoxes which we have previously learned to recognize as characteristic of Paul's rhetoric. Here their feeling and actual content are to be considered. In II Cor. 4:8f he speaks of how often Christians are led into suffering up to the extreme limit of endurance and yet finally experience the saving help of God; II Cor. 6:8f shows how the sufferer keeps courage despite every distress, because his soul is not thereby affected. Though he be reproached as a seducer he knows that the truth is on his side; [53] though he be misjudged he knows that God understands him (I Cor. 13:12); though he be doomed to death, he is triumphant: 'behold we live.' Though he be punished, no one can 'kill' him; though pain and suffering strike

[50] Rom. 8:18. θλῖψις and θλίψεις, Rom. 5:3; 8:35; 12:12; I Cor. 7:28; II Cor. 1:4, 8; 4:17; 6:4; 8:2; Col. 1:24; I Thess. 1:6,3; 3:7; II Thess. 1:4,6. παθήματα, Rom. 8:18; II Cor. 1:5ff; Col. 1:24. πάσχειν, Phil. 1:29; II Thess. 1:5. συμπάσχειν, Rom. 8:17.

[51] Rom. 12:12, 'patient in tribulation,' θλίψει ὑπομένοντες; 5:3; 8:25; II Cor. 6:4 (ἐν ὑπομονῇ πολλῇ, ἐν θλίψεσιν); 12:12; Col. 1:11; II Thess. 1:4, 'because of your perseverance and your faithfulness, or keeping of the faith (πίστεως) in all the persecutions and necessities in which ye are involved.'

[52] Luther's translation, 'we boast of our tribulations,' is not justified linguistically. 'We boast ourselves' is still connected with the object in vs. 2; ἐν θλίψεσιν, because of the change of the preposition to ἐν instead of ἐπί, is plainly not the object, but a different kind of construction. As for the meaning: this somewhat exaggerated martyr tone fits neither with the context, nor particularly with the thought of Paul.

[53] Here we seem to discern a reminiscence of a saying of Antisthenes: βασιλικὸν μὲν εὖ πράττειν, κακῶς δὲ ἀκούειν, "It is characteristic of royalty to do well but to listen badly."

him, in his soul there is joy; though he be in abject poverty, he controls a treasure out of which he can make many rich. How closely these paradoxes approximate Stoicism in matter as well as form will be appreciated by anyone who has read Epictetus. However it is also beyond doubt that the glowing enthusiasm exhibited here is, above all, religious; it draws its power out of the certainty that 'God is for us.' One may differ as to which form of victory over the world is to be esteemed the higher: the one, entirely dependent upon the virile power and virtue of the Stoic who, knowing the worthlessness of human possessions, reaches true resignation, and by disciplining his will attains self-control; [54] or the other method, viz. the inspired readiness to suffer possessed by the warrior of Christ whose unconquerable courage springs from his conviction of his Lord's victory, from the fact that he feels himself supported by his power and relies upon his mighty protection. Though both types contend with one another in a bitter struggle for existence, and though in the future history may presumably have need of both, as it has used them both in the past—yet in warmth and centrifugal power the Stoic type can scarcely be compared with the Christian. There are other unmistakable differences. The arrogant saying that the wise man can neither be insulted nor wronged [55] is still something quite different from Paul's statement, 'being reviled, we bless;

[54] Seneca, *Dial.* ii. 9, 5, "The wise man belongs to the race of those who, through long and faithful *practice,* have won the power of suffering all that enmity can wreak on them, and rendering it feeble *(lassandi)."*

[55] Seneca, *Dial.* ii, *nullum sapientem nec injuriam accipere nec contumeliam posse* (2:1); *injuria ad sapientem non pervenit* (5:3); *non potest laedi sapiens* (7:2); *sapiens a nullo contemnitur. Magnitudinem suam novit et omnis has . . . . molestias . . . . non vincit, sed ne sentit quidem. Alia sunt quae sapientem feriunt, etiamsi non pervertunt* (cf. καταβαλλόμενοι ἀλλ' οὐκ ἀπολλύμενοι, παιδευόμενοι καὶ μὴ θανατούμενοι), *ut dolor corporis et debilitas aut amicorum liberorumque amissio et patriae bello flagrantis calamitas. Haec non nego sentire sapientem . . . . quosdam ictus recipit, sed receptos evincit et sanat et conprimit. Haec vero minora ne sentit quidem nec adversus ea solita illa virtute utitur dura tolerandi, sed aut non adnotat aut digna risu putat.* ('For no wise man can receive either injury or insult' (2:1). 'Injury does not reach the wise man' (5:3). It is impossible for the wise man to be injured' (7:2). 'But no one can slight him, for he knows his own greatness . . . . and as for all these annoyances, he does not have to overcome them, nay, he does not even have them. Quite different are the things that do buffet the wise man, even though they do not overthrow him, such as bodily pain and infirmity, or the loss of friends and children, and the ruin that befalls his country amid the flames of war. I do not deny that the wise man feels these things . . . . the wise man does receive some wounds, but those that he receives he binds up, arrests and heals; these lesser things he does not even feel, nor does he employ against them his accustomed virtue of bearing hardship, but he either fails to notice them or counts them worthy of a smile.') 'The wise man should regard one who insults him as we look upon children, or as the physician regards his patients, whose revilings in a fever, or in insanity, cannot insult him' (12:13).

being persecuted, we restrain ourselves' (suffer it); 'being defamed, we entreat' (or perhaps 'we console'; I Cor. 4:12f). To call this 'slave-ethics' is of course only to display a very superficial understanding of the principle. The ideal which is here presented cannot be realized by a bound and servile soul, but only by someone who not only has supreme control over himself and is able to consider wrong and abuse as trifling evils, but who also has, above and beyond this, enough warmth and humanity to be well-disposed toward the enemy. Of course it is only in exceptional cases that an entirely genuine and practical proof of this ideal is afforded; often enough hypocrisy and hatred interfere: but the Stoic attitude will just as often be hollow and theatrical. However if one asks which ideal can more deeply ennoble the sufferer and render aid to his neighbors, the answer will be unquestionable.

(f) *The attitude of the Christian toward the possessions and problems of this world.* The problem of *the sex-life* plays an extraordinary part in the ethic of Paul. There are apparently no personal reasons for this. For if I understand I Cor. 7:7 rightly, Paul possessed the gift of continence, or in other words, he did not suffer under the pressure of the sex impulse, he was not as sensitive in this respect as the majority of people. The tendency today is to consider this as being nothing more nor less than a defect of his constitution. It is difficult to express an opinion. Yet it is also evident that there have been men in history who were called to greatness, but who nevertheless, or perhaps for that very reason, were in this respect differently constituted than others. In any case Paul sees in this defect a mercy of God; this is characteristic of him. For there can be no doubt that like many of his contemporaries he saw in sexual lust the actual original sin of humanity. The commandment, "Thou shalt not covet" (Rom. 7:7f), could of course include all egotistic desire.[56] But since in vs. 11 sin appears in the seductive rôle of the serpent, and since in II Cor. 11:3 the seduction of Eve by Satan is evidently of a sexual nature, the narrower significance is probably meant. And if, according to Pauline teaching, all sins, even spiritual ones (Gal. 5:19ff) are rooted in the flesh, if sins of unchastity are foremost among the 'works of the flesh,' the idea easily arises that the close connection between flesh and sin is indissoluble precisely because the flesh is the seat of this 'lust.'[57]

[56] Adam's sin, which is here dimly recollected, is perhaps thought of as πλεονεξία. The word surely means more than avarice; it approaches the idea of egotism. See my Commentary on I Cor. 5:11.

[57] According to Philo, *Op. Mundi,* § 152, the πόθος (of the sexes) *τὴν τῶν σωμάτων ἡδονὴν ἐγέννησεν, ἥτις ἐστὶν ἀδικημάτων καὶ παρανομημάτων ἀρχή, δι' ἣν ὑπαλλάττονται*

The view prevailing here and running through all of Paul's thinking approaches closely to Hellenistic dualism, according to which the flesh as such, being matter, is sinful and inimical to God because it is hostile to the Spirit.[58] In any case Paul stands in close relation to a contemporary attitude which one can interpret as a phenomenon of fatigue or degeneration, viz. a disgust evoked by over-indulgence, a weakening of the naïve and healthy material nature leading to the pessimistic view that in the sexual life the root of all evil is to be sought. Therefore in the catalogue of evils as in the missionary preaching of repentance (pp. 254f), sexual sins stand out as the most important and in their numerous variations occupy a large space. It is from this quarter that the 'saints' are threatened by the gravest dangers (I Thess. 4:3), as the First Epistle to the Corinthians shows. It is natural that seldom even gross sins of lewdness had to be attacked. It is more surprising that the Apostle is obliged to take a strong line, not with the heathen, but with certain Christians, concerning a general apology for unchastity (I Cor. 6:12-20). Their view was that 'everything is permitted' to the free, since sexual intercourse, like reception of food and excretion, is something purely corporeal by which the soul is not touched.[59] To this view Paul opposes another conception of corporeality. The 'body' as he understands it is not merely the material body, the house of the soul, which is destined to destruction, but it is the imperishable mould of the personality. This is violated by immorality: the body belongs to the Lord, but he is lewdly dishonored if he must share this possession of the personality with a harlot. It is true that the obvious objection, viz. that the same point of view must also lead to the abrogation of sexual intercourse in marriage, does not find expression; but a like tone dominates the ascetic tendency in Corinth, which Paul opposes (I Cor. 7:1-7; cf. p. 331). He personally takes a position similar to theirs: that the 'intimate surrender to the Lord' is actually incompatible with married life (I Cor. 7:32-35) and that in general it is much better for a man not to touch a woman (I Cor. 7:1,7ff,37,40). This attitude of his toward marriage has frequently been explained by reference to the eschatological motive (p. 559), and in fact it is expressly said (I Cor. 7:28, 32) that married people will suffer greater affliction than others in the

---

τὸν θνητὸν καὶ κακοδαίμονα βίον ἀντ' ἀθανάτου καὶ ευδαίμονος, "The desire of the sexes begat likewise bodily pleasure, which is the beginning of wrongs and violation of law, the pleasure for the sake of which men bring on themselves the life of mortality and wretchedness in lieu of that of immortality and bliss."

[58] Cf. chapter 20.

[59] Cf. my Commentary on I Cor. 6:12ff.

distress of the final age: but this is plainly only a secondary and incidental argument, and it does not suffice to explain Paul's attitude. The principal motive is religious: the Lord claims the whole man as his property (I Cor. 7:32-35). A still more general motive lies at the basis of it; if married people, after agreement, should abstain from intercourse at the prayer seasons,[60] the decisive factor is the general feeling of antiquity that sexual intercourse and religious activity are incompatible.[61] Although Paul does not emphasize the idea of uncleanness as causing separation from God, yet the idea that by abstaining one will gain in surrender to God is unmistakable; so much so in fact that Paul actually considers sexual intercourse as something which draws man from God and is degrading to him: "It is good for a man not to touch a woman" (I Cor. 7:1). This is his ideal. Since this cannot be carried out in practice, everyone may have his own wife—'because of immorality,' i.e. monogamous marriage is always better than unrestrained sexual intercourse. There is not a word said which would suggest a higher appreciation of the moral aspects of marriage: of the happiness of mutual love, of mutual responsibility, of the blessing upon fruitfulness spoken by God at the Creation, of the education of children 'in the Lord'—not a word of this is uttered here. One can supplement this, however, by I Thess. 4:4 (p. 255). When the demand is made that instead of the 'lust of concupiscence as among the Gentiles,' 'honor and sanctification' should rule marital living, a way is opened to a more civilized and noble view of the relationship. And when in the table of duties to one's neighbor (Col. 3:18-21) one reads the simple command: "Ye men, love your wives," there can be no doubt that love in the highest Christian sense is intended. For the rest, one cannot feel that it presupposes a very high level of thought when the Apostle demands of wives that they be in submission, and of husbands that they 'be not bitter against them,' of children that they be obedient, and of fathers only the requirement, 'provoke not your children lest they be discouraged.' Infinitely much is missing from the ideal of a Christian household, as it was to be realized in the course of centuries and under different kinds of influence, with the result that we can only lament this lack of interest in church instruction. Not once is the ancient situation of family life reflected

[60] Cf. my Commentary on 7:5, p. 174, note 4, where examples of a corresponding Jewish custom are collected; e.g. Test. Naphtali 8, "There is a time for coming together with one's wife and a time for abstention for the sake of prayer."

[61] Cf. E. Fehrle, *Kultische Keuschheit im Altertum* (Ceremonial Chastity in Antiquity), pp. 25ff. Ex. 19:15, "Be ready against the third day: come not near a woman"; Lev. 15:18; Josephus, *Contra Apionem,* ii. 203.

in these meagre words. Above all, the fact is not taken into account that in natural conjugal and parental love there are already a great number of moral forces which, under natural conditions, apart from specially religious or ethical motives, make themselves felt. There is missing the real hearty joy ever present in this glorious bloom of human morality; there is missing the ideal transfiguration of the marital relationship which would be possible only through the spirit of Christian love.

The deepest reason why we miss so much here is reflected in the words, 'that those who have wives be as though they had none' (I Cor. 7:29).[62] This classical passage may well serve as the program of a genuine evangelical immunity from domination by the world. But the question is whether the note which is struck here is precisely the same as that which is perceptible in Luther's similar statements. One must ask, can the customary task which man and wife have in common, the service of self-denial, of intimate understanding, forbearing and helping, and above all, the fervent feeling of love which we experience as the most precious earthly possession and as a glorious gift of God—can these things be combined with this inner uncertainty, with this 'having as if we had not?' The sincere Christian who knows himself, who lives under self-discipline, will indeed be able to discern when the limit would be overstepped beyond which there is too great an indulgence, beyond which one loses oneself in sensuality and stupifying pleasure in family life; such a man will surely extract the kernel of truth from Paul's statements. But after all, our emphasis is somewhat different, and the pure joy in wife and child which is the natural foundation of a Christian family life must be abiding, and we can hardly allow it to be subjected to the principle of 'having as if we had not.' Here however Paul certainly has a different viewpoint than we: he must be thought of as an

[62] This precept, standing at the head of a series of similar ones (vv. 29ff) doubtless has an eschatological motive. This 'parenthesis' begins with the words, 'the time is shortened; the form of this age passes away.' This eschatological argument differentiates the saying from similar Stoic assertions, as e.g. Epictetus, iv. 1. 159. "Take, for example, Socrates, look at him, how he had a wife and children, but as a strange possession. . . ." iii. 24, 59f, "Perhaps Socrates did not love his children? Certainly, but as a free man, ever mindful that it was above all necessary to be beloved of God." 'Freedom from the world,' as it is here attributed to Socrates, was really an ideal of the historical Socrates (cf. H. Maier, *Sokrates,* pp. 322ff) which was vigorously adopted by the Cynics (e.g. Antisthenes). In *form* the Pauline phrases are reminiscent of certain sentences of Aristippus, e.g. Stob. xvii. 18 (Meinecke, i. 280. 18), κρατεῖ ἡδονῆς οὐχ ὁ ἀπεχόμενος, ἀλλ' ὁ χρώμενος μέν, μὴ παρεκφερόμενος δέ, "He who conquers pleasure is not the one who abstains, but the one who makes use of goods, yet is not carried away by them"; cf. also the Aristippian saying, ἔχω καὶ οὐκ ἔχομαι, "I possess, yet I am not possessed," with I Cor. 6:12b.

eschatologically-minded Christian, as a man of the ancient world, as an oriental, as an ascetic anchorite who himself had not experienced family joy and blessedness, and perhaps had for them no taste whatever.

There is all the more reason why we should not forget that the Apostle, in a time of highly wrought emotions and of extremely high ideals, gave warning soberly and practically against hyper-ascetic experiments, and that *against* his own inclinations. With earnest and humane words and with sober and practical counsels he attempted to nullify the current demand that mixed marriages be dissolved for fear of Gentile infection (I Cor. 7:12–16); he combatted the idea that sexual intercourse should not take place in Christian marriage (7:3-6) and the dangerous custom of 'spiritual betrothals,'[63] or virginal marriages (7:25-28,32-38).[64] Above all he reiterates with determination the Lord's inhibition of divorce of Christian couples (7:10f) and thus indirectly witnesses to the indissolubility of the divine institution.

He sets himself counter to the idea of emancipation for women and slaves which was in the air, due largely to the preaching of the Gospel, although—or just because—the idea could have gained support from many of his own statements (Gal. 3:28; Col. 3:11). In regard to marriage particularly, Paul revives the patriarchal principle, valid in Jerusalem, i.e. the superiority of man over woman (Col. 3:18), partly by arguments which seem to us to lie below the level of his usual viewpoint. That woman was created for the sake of man, and not man for woman's sake, that she came out of man, and not the reverse (I Cor. 11:8f), is altogether a Jewish, rabbinical idea which can scarcely be reconciled with the religious equality of both sexes and still less with an ideal conception of marriage. The oriental low estimate of woman here breaks through again, as also in the ugly expression 'vessel' (I Thess. 4:4).[65] Jewish also is the aversion toward women praying with uncovered heads at divine service; perhaps the somewhat free attitude of Greek women may have given sufficient cause for this. Here the motive of order (p. 568) also plays a part. But it is always noteworthy that the Apostle

[63] [*Translator's Note.* Samuel Belkin, "The Religious Background of Paul," *Journal of Biblical Literature,* liv (1935), pp. 41-60, thinks that in I Cor. 7:36-39 'his virgin' refers to a virgin betrothed to a Christian, not to the virgin daughter of a Christian father. However, Belkin gives strong reasons for thinking that 'spiritual marriages' did not exist. The question simply is, should a betrothed man, who has become a Christian, break off the engagement or should he marry the girl?]

[64] Cf. my Commentary on I Cor. 7.

[65] In I Cor. 11:11f this view seems to be half retracted; cf. my Commentary, *ad loc.*

does not object to female prophetical speakers and leaders in prayer (I Cor. 11:5) as such, and the contrary statements in 14:34 f cannot possibly be his.[66] The idea of a complete dissolution of marriage by unrestrained freedom of the sexes is of course wholly outside his field of vision. We have seen how, despite personal ascetic inclinations, a healthy and strong respect for marriage predominates in Paul.

The other social problems of primitive Christianity were more difficult. The Christian churches were like the religious associations of Graeco-Roman civilization in that they granted the same admission, the same privileges, the same spiritual blessings to all stations in life and to free and slave alike. At the Lord's Supper, slaves and masters, men and women, meet together at the same table; at divine service the words of the inspired unlearned man were often of deeper meaning than those of a scholar; here subordination (which again prevailed when the normal life of the household was resumed) was suspended. The ideas of *equality* which sprang up under these conditions concealed within them the germ of serious conflicts; indeed they contained within themselves a certain spark of revolution. What decision was the new ethic to make, in face of these newly appearing problems?

From the very beginning this particular type of the idea of equality contained a protection against social equalization and efforts for emancipation. The equality of the 'brethren' is not based upon the idea of the equality of all mankind, as Stoicism expressed it,[67] but upon the common religious experience: [68] '*in Christ* there

[66] Cf. my Commentary on both passages.

[67] Seneca, *Ep.* 47:1ff, "I am glad to learn, through those who come from you, that you live on friendly terms with your slaves. This befits a sensible and well-educated man like yourself. 'They are slaves,' people declare. Nay, rather, they are men. Slaves! No, comrades. Slaves! They are unpretentious friends. Slaves! No, they are fellow-slaves, if one reflects that Fortune has equal rights over slaves and free men alike. That is why I smile at those who think it degrading for a man to dine with his slave. Why? It is only because pure proud etiquette surrounds a householder at his dinner with a mob of standing slaves (who must keep silence at mealtime but, if and when it should become necessary, lay down their lives for their master (§§ 2-4)." § 5, "I shall pass over other cruel and inhuman conduct toward them, for we never treat them as if they were men but as if they were beasts of burden." Still another picture of indignity in §§ 5-8, "With slaves like these the master cannot bear to dine; he would think it beneath his dignity to associate with his slave at the same table." § 10, "Remember that he whom you call your slave came from the same stock, is smiled upon by the same skies, and on equal terms with yourself breathes, lives and dies. It is just as possible for you to see in him a free-born man, as for him to see in you a slave." § 11, "Treat your inferiors as you would be treated by your betters, and as often as you reflect how much power you have over a slave, remember that your Master has

is neither slave nor free, neither male nor female.'[69] Therefore as a matter of course it is only a question of the equality of Christian brethren, and a general human equality is not included in the prospect; or if it is, it is only in this sense: insofar as all men have need of the same salvation as Christians possess, hence this salvation should be offered to all.[70] It is less likely that a revolutionary struggle for equal social conditions would develop out of this purely religious idea than that differences of social position would become neutralized by these same basic religious ideas existing in the

just as much power over you." § 13, "Associate with your slave on kindly, even affable terms, let him talk with you, plan with you, live with you." § 17, "He is a slave, his soul, however, may be that of a free man. He is a slave, but shall that stand in his way? Show me a man who is not a slave. One is a slave to lust, another to greed, another to ambition, all are slaves to fear"—*Ep.* 95. 52f; cf. p. 571, note 43.

[68] Rather more comparable is the passage in Seneca, *Ep.* 31:11, "What else could you call such a soul but a god dwelling as a guest in a human body? A soul like this may descend into a Roman knight, or a freedman's son, or a slave. They are mere titles born of ambition or of wrong. One may leap to heaven from the very slums. Only rise and mould thyself to kinship with thy God." The only difference consists in this, that according to the Stoic view, the divine in man, though not general, is yet given by nature, or is something to be attained by personal striving; according to the Christian view it is a grace of God.

[69] Troeltsch, *Soziallehren (The Social Teachings of the Christian Churches)*, p. 61, "Since Christian individualism is only found and completed in God, and since Christian universalism as based solely on the all-embracing love of God which leads to the love of one's neighbor, so this idea of equality is definitely limited to the religious sphere. It is an equality which exists purely in the presence of God, and in him, based solely on the religious relation to God as the center of the whole. At first sight, it is true, this equality is in no way an equality of mankind in its claims on God, but it is an equality in which all men feel that they 'have sinned and come short of the glory of God,' a negative equality over against the infinite holiness of God. . . . This 'negative' equality is, however, only the basis for the surrender to that salvation through grace, which is given in Christ, the Church, and its sacraments, which mediate absolute salvation to all believers. . . . It is not based on a common claim or right of nature, but on the impartation of the divine love through grace which (wherever it gives itself at all) can only give itself as a whole, and which of itself alone, apart from all external, social institutions, imparts equality, in spite of all human differences in rank, talent, or ethical achievement. . . ." P. 64, "In spite of the equality of all in their sinful unworthiness and in their possession of grace, however, the real equality in itself, the equal claim of all to an equal share in the highest life-value (through the equal working out of vocation and destiny) is invalidated . . . . there does not exist an unlimited equal claim on salvation . . . . one must be satisfied with the equality of distance from God, and equality of love to God, wherever the latter has taken root. All the rest must be left to God."

[70] In the three passages where Paul speaks of equality (Gal. 3:28; 6:15; Col. 3:11) twice the 'new creation,' the 'new man' is the keyword whereby the close chain of reasoning is completed; in one case (Gal. 3:28) on account of polemic against Judaism the idea 'neither Jew nor Greek' is emphasized (cf. also Gal. 6:15). The statement itself already bears an older impress. It may originate from the Jewish diaspora (cf. also I Cor. 7:19 and my Commentary on it), and may have had originally a more Stoic, rationalistic sense than it has in Paul.

church. For ideally, the position of the individual is entirely changed by his vocation: the slave has become a 'freeman of the Lord,' the master 'a slave of Christ' (I Cor. 7:22), the former is ennobled, the latter pledged to a new kind of self-esteem. For one who accepts this new religious attitude seriously, any difference of station can, in actuality, no longer exist.[71] Thus the predisposition to strive for freedom ceases (7:21) because the motive no longer exists: slavery is no longer felt to be degrading, because the new religious nobility furnishes an adequate counterpoise. This shows that earliest Christianity had not contemplated the general abolition of slavery.[72] Here the eschatological motive also comes in. There is no point in desiring great social reforms when the dissolution of the world and the complete overthrow of all things will shortly make 'all things new' in the Kingdom of God. But the chief reason remains, viz. that slavery is not considered generally to be an unendurable evil. Besides it would be entirely unhistorical to presume or demand that ancient peoples should have our modern feeling toward slavery. Paul, like most of his contemporaries, including Jesus himself (cf. Luke 17:7-10), looked upon slavery as

[71] This paradoxical judgment upon social differences is Stoic in thought. The slave remains a slave, but he no longer feels himself to be such—certainly not because by his own knowledge he could have come to another judgment of his worth, but because he had had a deep religious experience. Here we should remember Epictetus i. 19. 9, where the philosopher says to the tyrant, "Zeus has set me free; do you think that he would suffer his own son to be enslaved? You are master of my dead body; take it." The only corresponding note is in I Cor. 7:22, the idea of the religious purchase of freedom, which Deissmann, in *Licht vom Osten* (Light from the Ancient East), 2d ed., pp. 240ff, places in the front rank of importance as an explanation, since the emancipation documents in the Apollo temple at Delphi and others show that the purchase of a slave was a frequent form of emancipation. "The former master of the slave comes to the temple with the slave, sells him there to the god, and receives the purchase-price from the temple treasury (which the slave had previously paid in from his savings). Thus the slave became the property of the god, but not a slave of the temple, merely its protégé. In respect to men and especially to his former master, he is an entirely free man." In form, the idea in Paul is certainly similar. Even the expressions in the inscriptions (e.g. *ἐπρίατο ὁ 'Απόλλων . . . . ἐπ' ἐλευθερίᾳ . . . . τιμᾶς*) remind us, in fact, of Pauline passages (I Cor. 6:20; 7:23, *τιμῆς ἠγοράσθητε*; Gal. 5:1, *τῇ ἐλευθερίᾳ ἡμᾶς Χριστὸς ἠλευθέρωσεν*); the idea that the slave, by the redemption purchase, has become the property and freedman of Christ, is also parallel. But the difference, viz. that the Christian slave is and must remain a slave, is still a very great one. And the new judgment of his condition as one of ideal 'liberty' is something quite different from the actual, legal liberty of the man liberated by Apollo.

[72] Overbeck, *Studien zur Geschichte der Alten Kirche* (Studies in the History of the Ancient Church), "For the period before Constantine, the common theory of the original purpose of Christianity, as being directed toward the abolition of slavery, has to explain the uncomfortable fact that the Church of the first three centuries, in the face of these reforms which she plainly saw completed, apparently never passes beyond a complete indifference to them" (pp. 168-172).

respectable. In the table of duties to one's neighbor in the Epistle to the Colossians, the lot of slaves often appears lamentable; indeed, even in I Peter 2:18ff, special attention is called to the sufferings of slaves, but this is almost the exceptional situation: to be in subjection to a 'good and gentle' master is certainly not difficult; but one should submit also to the one who is capricious. However slavery, as such, is not deplored as an unbearable condition. Reference is made to the free Christian's letter-patent of nobility, not in order to comfort the slave, but to restrain him from striving after freedom.[73] Thus it did not enter the mind of the Apostle to attack the institution as such. Not once is the idea of the equality of Christian brethren carried to the point of declaring it unseemly to hold Christian brethren in slavery. The demand upon Philemon to liberate Onesimus (Philem. 15f) is advanced somewhat timidly, in any case without the firmness of a definite demand.[74] On the whole we cannot determine how Paul would have the relation of Christian masters to Christian slaves governed; for although the table of duties to one's neighbor in the Epistle to the Colossians refers to Christian slaves (3:22-25) and to Christian masters (4:1), yet it does not say that both masters and slaves are Christians. At any rate there were also still slaves in Christian households such as that of Stephanus (I Cor. 16:15); in fact it appears that occasionally (Acts 16:15,34) at the conversion of the mistress or the master the conversion of the whole family, including the slaves, was expected to follow. But nowhere is it told as a shining example of brotherly love or human love that a Christian has liberated all his slaves. Generally the principle prevails, "Let everyone remain in the station in which the call has come to him" (I Cor. 7:17,20,24). Thus one encounters at first only the negative point of view that the call to God's Kingdom and his glory did not necessitate the changing of one's earthly station in any way. However, the positive opinion is also announced, somewhat in agreement with the Stoic formulation, viz. that the very 'vocation' which comes to one who is in this or that station includes also the 'call' to show oneself worthy in that

[73] In regard to Paul, it would indeed be saying too much to declare 'that the conservative attitude rests not upon love and esteem for the institution, but upon a mingling of disdain, surrender and relative acknowledgment' (Troeltsch, *Soziallehren*, p. 72).

[74] [*Translator's Note.* But see John Knox, *Philemon among the Letters of Paul*, 1935, pp. 4-11. Others, notably E. J. Goodspeed, think that Paul, despite his courtesy, made a demand in the strongest terms.]

same station in life.[75] Thus the degrading element in one's social condition is removed and the situation receives a certain ethical content. It is from this point of view that one is to understand the admonitions in the 'duties to one's neighbor' (Col. 3:22—24:1): slaves are admonished to obey—not because it is necessary to guard against an inclination to lawlessness, or too great an urge for independence (cf. I Tim. 6:1ff); on the contrary, the warning is against servile eye-service and men-pleasing, which would perform the obvious outward duty merely for the sake of one's own advantage and without interest in the duty itself and without any inner participation. Slaves should fulfil their 'service' 'from the heart,' with 'simple hearts,' i.e. without secondary purposes. This means that they should have devotion to duty conscientiously and in an orderly manner; but certainly should also regard their work as a service rendered to Christ, in fear of the heavenly Lord to whom they are responsible and from whom they will receive reward. 'Earthly masters'—literally 'masters only according to the flesh'—seem almost to be eliminated by this principle; no inward disposition nor self-respect, nor even respect for slaves is demanded. Nor is there a word said to the effect that the slave should also include his Gentile master in his love. Fundamentally the condition of slavery represents for the Christian the manner, in no way significant in itself, in which he has to fulfil his duty toward Christ. Naturally there may thus result a formally correct and good behavior, yet under the circumstances it will be a rather unhappy situation for the master. Certainly in practice Christian slaves must have gone beyond this minimum and must have shown loyalty, attachment, willingness to sacrifice; but just as often they may have been indifferent to the true interests of the household,

[75] Cf. my Commentary on I Cor. 7:20, "Let every man abide in the same 'calling' wherein he was 'called.'" "Essentially, everything is clear: Paul wishes that one should remain in the (civil or, in general, external) condition in which he was when called to the community. But it is not clear how this condition in which one found himself at the 'calling,' in a Christian sense, can be designated 'calling' (κλῆσις)." "The obscurity in question is explained by the fact that here the Christian literary usage 'called,' 'calling,' conflicts with one taken from the Stoic popular philosophy." "In Epictetus, i. 29, 33-49, the keyword 'called' recurs frequently. The wise man steps upon the stage of life, like a witness called of God (§ 46); he is vouchsafed the honor of witnessing for God (§ 47); if he now recoils and laments over his condition (§ 48), is this bearing witness?—No, it is really disgracing the call with which God has called him, since he had held you deserving of this honor and worthy to be brought upon the stage for such testimony. . . . 'Calling' (κλῆσις) is thus here, quite properly, the *vocatio*, the mission to fulfil, in a particular condition of life (κληθεὶς εἴς τινα κατάστασιν) a particular task. . . . This linguistic usage approximates our 'call.'"

in which case they were a dumb and continual reproach to the master, an uncongenial element in the *ménage*. What is lacking in Paul's admonition is full acknowledgment that the welfare of the master and of the household is a moral task set for the slaves by God; the relationship of slavery is not made completely ethical. And if nothing more is demanded of the masters than that, thinking of their heavenly Master, they should grant to their slaves what is right and fair; this general humanitarian requirement falls far short of the good deeds which a Christian master might do for his slaves. Nothing is said, moreover, about leading them to Christ or showing them love. The idea that the new ethic, even aside from fraternal fellowship, should permeate all relationships of life, does not, at any rate, receive expression, although in reality often enough it may have unconsciously governed action. However, a certain coolness toward the 'world' prevails; the idea that one can serve it only by devoting oneself to it in love is not expressed: "They who associate with the world should not give themselves over to it."[76]

The same attitude, that of a cool indifference, is shown toward *the state*. In Rom. 13:1-7 one sees no evidence of a warm disposition toward the state, nor any enthusiasm for the ordinances of authority. Instead, Paul's precepts tend to show that there prevailed in the Pauline churches an inclination to despise the political order. Doubtless there was something of the same revolutionary tone which existed in certain Jewish or Jewish-Christian circles, which declared the paying of taxes was degrading to the 'saints,' called as they were to the kingdom of God, an attitude which had also penetrated into the Gentile communities. And although Jesus (Mark 12:17; cf. *SNT, ad loc.*) declined to sanction this attitude as of divine right, and although Matt. 17:24-27, while assuming in principle the right of tax exemption, nevertheless recommends submission 'in order not to offend them,' (cf. *SNT, ad loc.*)—so Paul also says, taking exactly the same view as Jesus, 'give to everyone what you owe him,' 'owe no one anything'—as though these duties were a matter of course and belonged to the natural human ethic from which the Christian cannot claim exemption. He is, however, not motivated by actual Christian opinion, but speaks as perhaps a preacher of the Jewish diaspora would have spoken; he speaks as to people who are after all still citizens of this world. Here the motive of order (pp. 568f) appears again, a motive which is not secondary in the personality of

[76] Thus I seek to translate I Cor. 7:31, οἱ χρώμενοι τὸν κόσμον ὡς μὴ καταχρώμενοι; cf. my Commentary, *ad loc.*

the Apostle. It appears on a higher level when he declares that authority is of God and is the servant of God for good. Probably there underlies this a religious idea taken from the Wisdom of Solomon;[77] but the fact that Paul could possibly entertain the idea that in the political order of the time, in the administration of the officials of his period, a divine principle operated, could come about only because fundamentally he was not a Rome-hating Jewish fanatic, but a Hellenist and a Roman citizen. Up to a certain degree he shares the thankful feeling of the provinces which saw in the empire the refuge of peace, the principle of cosmos as against chaos, and the guarantee of law.[78] One need only compare with this the attitude of the Revelation of John, which sees in the empire an instrument of Satan, in order to estimate the difference. Nor can we forget that Paul had learned (e.g. from Gallio)—and would still further learn—that Roman officialdom, despite all its defects, was still a more reliable protection for his activity than were those who should have been his primary protectors, viz. the leaders of his own people. But beyond these personal experiences he must have had also a deep aversion to the zealotism of Palestine;[79] a natural agreement with the forces of law and order was ingrained in him. The state is the principle which 'checks' the full development of evil (II Thess. 2:6f).

To be sure, his recognition of the state does not go so far that he can comfortably contemplate Christians who seek justice before Gentile tribunals (I Cor. 6:1ff). In this he sees a degradation of the 'saints' who are called to the highest life possible; by so doing they are forgetful of the proud distinction conferred upon them; how can they have anything to do with the 'godless?' These words are to be interpreted by reference to a particular historical situation; as the communities of the Jewish diaspora had the privilege of deciding disputes of their members before their own forum, so Paul also demands this for the Christian community as well. It must remain conscious of the separatist position which it must occupy in the midst of its Gentile environment; the motive of fellowship is here operative and

[77] *Wisdom of Solomon,* 6:1ff, "Hear now, ye kings . . . . your power is given you of the Lord, and your dominion of the Most High; he will prove your doings . . . . for although ye were ministers of his kingly power, ye have not judged aright."

[78] In this connection the significant note about Paul, as related in the Acts of the Apostles, will be explained by the fact that he was on terms of friendship with certain Asiarchs, that is, probably, members of the Asia Minor diet. These men favored the imperial cult and were, so to speak, warm patriots, on account of their positions.

[79] Does it correspond somewhat to the 'mystery of iniquity which doth already work' (II Thess. 2:7)?

the organization as such is emphasized. If the Gentile judges are summarily dismissed as godless or 'unjust,' this fact does not militate against the idea developed in Rom. 13. In the first place it is here a question of the small local, civil court and not the great institution of the Roman world-empire. He does not indeed say that these judges must necessarily give wrong verdicts; he merely points to the paradox that the 'saints' seek justice before people whom they otherwise despise as 'unjust.' And certainly no demand is made to seek the Gentile court; it is only that a warning is given against great insubordination (Rom. 13:2).

He gives a further basis for his warning by pointing out that the good have no reason for fearing or hating authority since it only punishes the evil and desires to foster the good. Here great confidence is expressed in the state's administration of justice, but at the same time the feeling is also present that the Christian is under obligation, moreover, to keep in harmony with the civil law, 'for conscience's sake.' Again, the idea prevails here that in human justice something of the 'righteousness of God' (Rom. 1:32) has been revealed and that Christians who do the will of God cannot be in conflict with it. This confident view of the parallel between political law and the basic demands of Christian ethics certainly shows that the state had hitherto made no move to persecute the Christians as such, or to suppress the preaching of the Gospel.[80] This same idea appears in a somewhat different form in the demand 'that ye walk honestly toward them that are without' (I Thess. 4:12; I Cor. 10:32), which also is repeated in I Pet. 2:12 (cf. also Rom. 2:24).

This motive, a particular form of the order-motif, operates especially in the admonition to quiet, orderly *labor* in one's civil vocation (II Thess. 3:6-15; I Thess. 4:10ff). Pious leisure and speculation on the subject of brotherly love he dreads. Just as he maintained himself, independently of others, by great personal sacrifice and by the work of his own hands, and freed the Gospel from every monetary charge (I Cor. 9:18), just so every one in the community ought to earn his bread by his own labor and become a burden to no one. Here is also missing the idea of serving of God by ordinary labor, a familiar note to us since the Reformation. The Apostle contents himself with honest independence for which he gives the wholly popular reason: "If any will not work, neither let him eat" (II Thess. 3:10; cf. Luke 16:3). For him labor is not a gratification of

[80] This also proves that a section such as Rom. 13 must have been written at least before the Neronian persecution.

the mind but simply an ever present necessity—and he wastes no fine words on it. This conception of life which in the last analysis is sound, hardly stands in close connection with the highest religious and ethical motives. Here the enthusiastic Christian does not speak; it is instead the able civic-minded individual who thinks something of himself and would be ashamed to receive benefits from others. It is well that this is to be found in the Bible, and not unimportant results follow from such words. Yet we still miss here, as in the preaching of Jesus, express statements and attractive instruction for the ethical idealization of common labor so necessary for our own day, and to be found in Luther. Still the fact remains that this highly-tensioned religious idealism has as its consequence a sort of alienation from the world, or rather an indifference to the interests of everyday civil life. Creative and elaborately planned enterprises, e.g. those of modern industry or wholesale business with its keen desire to open up new countries, could not thrive on this soil where the impulse of gain is tied down by the demand that 'those who buy act as though they possessed not' (I Cor. 7:30). The problem of whether a merchant can be saved is not thereby solved. The difficult question as to how labor, conjoined with delight in a worldly (especially a gainful) calling, can be combined with concentrated 'devotion to the Lord' (I Cor. 7:35), is considered neither from its psychological side nor from the other. There is no discussion as to whether there are any worldly aims at all to which a Christian may devote himself with burning zeal, or whether the earning of money as a selfish purpose can possibly be permissible for him. These questions lie outside his field of vision. However, he would not have attacked the seller of purple, nor Aquila and Priscilla, nor the city chamberlain Erastus on the ground of their professions, since they had made such good use of their property. Nor is one to assume that scruples arose here: the giving away of one's entire possessions is referred to in I Cor. 13:3 as a rare exception; there is no mention of a general requirement of this sort. Besides, rich people and those carrying on a large trade were certainly exceptional among the members of the church, and if they—as it happened—placed their homes and goods at the service of the church, a necessary recompense was made. No communistic ideals or demands are uttered by Paul. He violently denounces it as sin against the spirit of the Lord's Supper when those who have food eat their own supper first, and put to shame those who have none (I Cor. 11:22). He demands of those who have received possessions that they be able to share with others, that they do it 'with simplicity,' that is without secondary aims, and do it from the heart (Rom. 12:8), thus distributing to the necessity of the saints. Hospitality (12:13) belongs to the self-evident duties of the well-to-do as well as of the poor. A final echo of the 'communism of love' of the primitive community is found in the provision for the 'saints' in Jerusalem. Paul uses all his energy in furthering this good work, and it is amazing how he understands how to argue on behalf of this duty and to inculcate its importance (Rom. 15:27; II Cor. 8:9). With tender understanding he knows what this sacrifice means to the poor communities of Macedonia and Achaia. Thus he also knows how to estimate fully the charity of the Philippians (Phil. 4:10-20) as being simply a gift of love: he regards it as a sacrifice, not as an obligation. To illustrate the feeling of the Apostle toward money, one may cite, moreover, the following statements, reminiscent of Stoic parallels: "I have learned in whatsoever state I am, therein to be content. I know how to be abased (ταπεινοῦσθαι); and I also know how to abound (αὐτάρκης εἶναι): in everything and in all things have I learned the secret both to be filled and to be hungry, both to abound and to be in want. I can do all things in him that strengthened me" (Phil. 4:12f). He wanders through the land like a roving Cynic preacher, under a thousand privations, poverty-stricken and despised, in rags and without a roof over his head (I Cor. 4:11f); he is above all necessities, detached from every comfort and luxury. But just for this reason he also lacks a feeling for that which adorns and transfigures life. He seems to have had no eye for art, and if he had had it, it would now belong to the things which he had thrown away as dirt, for the sake of his Lord Christ (Phil. 3:7f). He had become a stranger in this world; his home was in heaven (Phil. 3:20). Therefore we can expect from him no ethic which could show us how, living in the midst of the world, working close to it and with it, surrounded by the practical problems of civilization and the magic of its art and its enjoyments, we may at the same time satisfy the world's demands and the demands of God without becoming unfaithful to one or the other. This problem lies beyond his ken, for the simple reason that he believes the world to be hastening toward destruction and the judgment (I Cor. 7:31; 11:32). Cultural values which would carry their justification within themselves he does not know; that there is something divine in the state and in art, trade and commerce, in industry and in science, that here also are problems which God has given to his humanity—all this is foreign to the Apostle Paul.

CHAPTER XX

The World-View of Paul

In the earlier chapters of this book, passing from the center to the periphery, so to speak, of Paul's devotion, we were simply compelled to postulate many kinds of representations and concepts of the nature of the world and of man. Now the attempt will be made to present this background of world-view, at least in its essential points. Of course it will only be incomplete, since the comparatively few statements of Paul will permit no more. Moreover, the full harmonization of the ancient ideas of the world, both Jewish and Hellenistic, into which these details can be fitted, we must withhold for the first volume of our work. However, it is characteristic of Paul that, in spite of his cosmic Christology and in spite also of his doctrine of redemption from the cosmos, he fails to develop a complete cosmology. In this his gospel differs from the Gnostic systems. It is not an explanation of the world, it is not philosophy, but a proclamation of salvation directed to the individual. The cosmological ideas are only the frame-work of the whole upon which he touches only occasionally and when absolutely necessary.

1. *The Universe and its Several Parts.* We begin with the word 'world,' 'cosmos,' which like so many others, because of its previous Greek history, has many meanings. We find its most common meaning where mention is made of the work of creation (Rom. 1:20), for which also 'the creature' (κτίσις, Rom. 8:19ff; Col. 1:15) can be used, or of the 'elements of the world' (Gal. 4:3; Col. 2:8,20). Here the Greek use of language appears, just as we see it, for example, in Posidonius' spiritual writing 'Of the World.'[1] But closely connected with this there also appears a use attested by the Stoics, according to which the 'world' embraces the totality of all (spiritual) beings.[2] Just as the cosmos is here called the 'system which is composed of gods and men,' so Paul in I Cor. 4:9 changes the concept into 'angels

[1] Text and commentary in Wilamowitz, *Griechische Lesebuch* II; cf. also Capelle, *Das Buch von der Welt,* ch. 2: 'Cosmos' is the system which consists of heaven and earth and the beings (φύσεις) contained therein. In another relation 'cosmos' is also called the order and division (τάξις καὶ διακόσμησις) which is maintained by God and in the mind of God (διὰ θεόν).

[2] Cf. Epictetus I. 9. 7; *Diogenes Laert.* VII. 138. Chrysippus in v. Arnim, *Frag. Stoic. Vet.*, No. 527.

and men.' Still other paraphrases for it are 'heavenly, earthly, under-earthly' (Phil. 2:10); 'all beings in heaven and on earth, visible and invisible' (Col. 1:16). But then, also, the word simply denotes humanity, or the human family from the time of Adam (Rom. 5:12; 3:6,19; I Cor. 14:10; II Cor. 1:12),[3] so especially in the Jewish phrase, 'to go out of the world' (I Cor. 5:10).[4] It appears also somewhat in the sense of world-culture (Rom. 1:8; 10:18; Col. 1:6). It is used with a sharpened application of non-Christians and Gentiles (Rom. 11:12,15; I Cor. 1:21; 6:2; 11:32; II Cor. 5:19). Naturally it thus receives a peculiar emphasis, in that there is bound up in it a certain depreciation: the community is sharply contrasted with the non-Christian world. In the midst of a world destined for judgment (I Cor. 11:32), it knows itself to be an island of safety (I Cor. 1:18), even though it consists preponderantly of such elements as are despised by the world (I Cor. 1:27f; 4:13). 'Cosmos' is, finally, the epitome of all goods and values which have lost their charm for the Christians (I Cor. 7:31,33f), and with whose affairs they will have nothing more to do (I Cor. 2:12; II Cor. 7:10; cf. Rom. 12:2). They have been once and for all removed from the order of natural existence, the 'cosmos,' by the death of Christ (Gal. 1:4; 6:14; Col. 2:20). Thus there was already developed in Paul the manner of speech which later came so sharply into prominence, especially in John. There is an unbridgeable chasm between the 'world' and the community.

We know but little concerning the details of Paul's cosmological views. We can only say this much, namely, that the tripartite division, as Phil. 2:10 gives it ('heaven, earth, nether-world'), concurs with the bipartite division 'heaven and earth' (I Cor. 8:5; Col. 1:16, 20), the latter being the old Biblical concept (Gen. 1:1) which goes back to the oriental, presumably Babylonian, manner of thought.[5] It corresponds so much the more closely to the religious thinking of the Apostle as in this distinctive manner he can express the great antithesis by which he is completely dominated.

Concerning Paul's idea of the nether-world we know nothing. He conceives of it as the abode of the dead (Rom. 10:7),[6] but also,

[3] In *Wisdom of Solomon* 10:1, Adam is called 'the father of the world.'

[4] אזל מן עלמא Targ. Koh. 1:8; John 16:28; also אתא בעלמא 'come into the world,' Targ. Koh. 3:14; John 18:37; here also must belong II Cor. 1:12.

[5] Jensen, *Die Kosmologie der Babylonier* (Cosmology of the Babylonians), 1890.

[6] The expression 'Hades' does not appear; in I Cor. 15:55, where Hosea offers it, Paul seems to have avoided the expression. Instead of this Paul says 'abyss' (Rom. 10:7). Cf. also Baba Mezia f. 94r. (Bab.): "When you ascend to heaven or descend to the abyss"—these are the same proverbial expressions, so that cosmological conclusions

perhaps, inhabited by other beings (Phil. 2:10). Whether he has assumed a special angel or spirit of the dead, as we might conclude from I Cor. 15:25, is not certain (p. 531, n. 12), since with him it is often difficult to distinguish between an abstract, merely rhetorically personified concept and real personality (cf. Rom. 8:38, 'death or life,' with 'angels and principalities'). In any case it is not to be assumed that death and Satan are at once identical for him.[7] Heaven or 'the heavens,' as Paul alternately says, seems to be divided into several stories placed one above the other (II Cor. 12:2). Whether the third heaven, mentioned here, is the highest, or only the third of the seven heavens frequently assumed in Judaism, cannot be determined with complete certainty. But it is surely more important that Paul's experience of being carried off to the third heaven brought him actually to the innermost and highest sanctuary and not merely to its porch or entrance. Moreover, 'Paradise' is considered to be situated in this third heaven. For when in II Cor. 12:2 and 4 he speaks of his being carried off into the third heaven, and then into Paradise, these are, perhaps, not simply different degrees of exaltation, but the speaker actually has drawn nearer, step by step, to the secret, and has expressed this fact by a solemn, double, rhetorical turn.

2. *Conflicting Estimates.* Paul's view is not consistent. We find in him that admiration of the cosmos which is found almost parallel in both Judaism and Hellenism; in its works the 'invisible nature of God,' 'his eternal power and Godhead' is expressed (Rom. 1:20), so that humanity, had it chosen to apply its 'wisdom,' could have recognized God's 'wisdom' by it (I Cor. 1:21); for indeed, the creation is nothing less than the 'image of the invisible God' (Col. 1:15). And if one reflects that Paul not only knew the inspired proofs of Deutero-Isaiah and the Psalms, inherited from Judaism and used in the divine services of his communities, respecting the greatness and glory, the order and wisdom of nature, but that he must have made them in full measure his own, we must believe that this line of thinking was actually expressed much more strongly than is indicated by the few utterances which have been preserved. On the other hand there is certainly also a wholly different manner of consideration, of a pessimistic, dualistic kind, which could not pos-

are not to be built upon them. Cf. Bertholet, *Jüdische Religion* (Jewish Religion), p. 397.

[7] That Satan has power over the dead (Heb. 2:14) is also clear in Paul (1 Cor. 5:5). But for this reason he need not have thought of it in I Cor. 15:25,54ff (against this cf. Dibelius, *D. Geisterwelt im Glauben des Paulus*, pp. 114ff).

sibly have come from Old Testament sources, but is of syncretistic, perhaps Gnostic, origin. But of course there is in addition, blended with this, a real characteristic Jewish criticism: the conception of the nature of the creation is no longer the original one,

> God made not death,
> And delighteth not when the living perish:
> For he created all things that they might have being,
> And all the races of creatures in the world are filled with life,
> And there is no poison of destruction in them,
> Nor hath Hades royal dominion upon earth,
> For righteousness is immortal.
> But ungodly men by their hands and their words called death unto them;
> Deeming him a friend they consumed away with love of him,
> And they made a covenant with him,
> Because they are worthy to be of his portion.
>
> For God created man for incorruption,
> And made him an image of his own proper being;
> But by the envy of the devil death entered into the world,
> And they that are of his portion make trial thereof.

Thus speaks the *Wisdom of Solomon* (1:13-16; 2:23f). And this is also Paul's meaning. In IV Ezra 7:11 we read: "When Adam broke my commandments the creation was condemned." This is also the background for the teaching in Rom. 8:20, according to which 'the creation was subjected to corruption not willingly, but after the will of him who subjected it.'[8] As since the sin of Adam death has ruled over men (Rom. 5:12-21), so corruption has since then ruled over

[8] Beresh. rabba f. 2:3. Although all things were created perfect, they have nevertheless since the sin of the first man become evil, and will not return to their standard until the Messiah comes; IV Ezra 5:6ff; Gen. 3:17: *ἐπικατάρατος ἡ γῆ ἐν τοῖς ἔργοις σου* (so also LXX for בעבודך ; Theod., *ἐν τῇ παραβάσει σου*; Symm., *ἐν τῇ ἐργασίᾳ σου*; Aq., *ἕνεκέν σου*)—no translation has *διὰ σέ*; for this reason it is very doubtful whether *διὰ τὸν ὑποτάξαντα* refers to Adam. But it is also difficult to think of God: one should expect *ὑπὸ τοῦ ὑποτάξαντος*. Above all, the use of *οὐχ ἑκοῦσα* is not clear: it should, indeed, say that the creation was guiltless. Yet in the antithesis *οὐχ—ἀλλά*, which in this connection seems unmotivated, appears like Phil. 2:6 to imply a reference to someone else who has subjected himself, of his own free will, to corruption—in order, perhaps, to gain something higher. Does this mean Adam? Then the *ὑποτάξας* will be a third being, perhaps the devil, into whose care God had given the creation, so that he dared to subject it thus. He had perhaps promised him that the world must be subject to corruption 'in respect of him.' One need not consider further the self-evident expressions, 'bondage of corruption' and 'liberty of glory' (8:22). The impression is left that the world has been at the same time placed in the charge of other powers. Evidently mythical views which we can no longer reconstruct are fundamental here.

the entire creation. But even here the personification of creation and corruption, which predominate, point at the same time to another type of thought, which in a real sense is neither Jewish nor Stoic. This is especially true of the touching words of the yearning of the creation for redemption, the sign of which will be the revealing of the Sons of God (Rom. 8:19ff).

Since redemption through the death of Christ means, at the same time, the redemption of the cosmos (Col. 2:20), and since the work of Christ is likewise a bringing back of all things to union with God (Col. 1:20), so it follows that the world has been punished with corruption. A kind of falling-away or estrangement from God is, therefore, assumed. This is naturally only possible because the world is ruled and watched over by a multitude of personal, spiritual beings, which obviously do not stand in a right relationship to God and have alienated the cosmos from him. We come now, therefore, to Paul's views concerning the spirit-world.[9]

3. *Angels and Satan.* The world of angels plays a great rôle in the thought of the Apostle. Here also we cannot recognize details or anything in the way of a clear-cut system. The enumeration in Col. 1:16, 'thrones, principalities, dominions, and powers,' only teaches us that Paul was familiar with a division of angels into classes or groups. But how the distinctions or gradations were actually conceived, we cannot know in our present state of knowledge. The Jewish belief that the angels participate with lively interest in the life of men (I Cor. 4:9; 11:10; cf. Enoch 9:1ff) is frequently assumed in the thinking of the Apostle. That they will form the train of the Messiah at the Parousia (II Thess. 1:7; I Thess. 3:13); that, in particular, an 'archangel,' with a great shout, accompanied by the sound of trumpets (I Cor. 15:52), will proclaim the arrival of the Lord (I Thess. 4:16); that the angels' songs of praise are a kind of lingual speech (I Cor. 13:1), only occasionally illuminates the background of his perceptions. It is more important that he once makes use of the coöperation of the angels in the giving of the Law (Gal. 3:19)—as opposed to their original character, which signifies a glorification of the Law—in order to indicate the inferiority of the Law. He could not do this if the angels were nothing more to him than congenial tools of the will of God. The whole connection demands that he place them in another sphere not directly dominated by God.

[9] Cf. here the instructive book by M. Dibelius, *Die Geisterwelt im Glauben des Paulus* (The Spirit-world in the Belief of Paul), 1909; and also the older book by Everling, *Die paulinische Angelologie und Dämonologie* (The Pauline Angelology and Demonology), 1888.

God, in a certain sense, has entrusted the world-period of law to the angels, so that the Jews were actually, during this time, more under their rule than under the direct guidance of God. They signify here, to a certain degree, a note of estrangement from God. In like manner, in Rom. 8:38, there appear among the powers of the cosmos those who would and could separate the Christians from the love of God, beside life and death, beside the present and the future, beside the astrological magnitudes, 'height' and 'depth,' and beside that which appears under the collective concept, 'nor any other creature,' also angels and principalities. They appear here throughout as on the side of creation, and are very far from being the helpers of God in the work of redemption. Yes, they seem here to carry on the old business of Satan, accusing men and placing them under suspicion before God (Rom. 8:33). These angels are, in truth, 'Satans' (Enoch 40:7). Thus the word 'angel' has here an almost 'demonological' meaning. In this connection it is to be noted that good angels hardly ever appear in Paul. Almost everywhere they are presented as powers hostile to God and his elect and stand as opposed to both, and only very seldom do they appear as devoted followers of God or of the Messiah. With Paul, the leading-back of all things to God (Col. 1:20) is a reunion of both earthly and heavenly beings. The victory of Christ in his death and resurrection means a triumph over the 'principalities and powers' (Col. 2:15), and the task of Christ in his position as ruler is the destruction or removal of 'principalities and powers' hostile to God (I Cor. 15:24ff; cf. I Cor. 2:8). According to I Cor. 6:2, a judgment of the angels will take place at the end. Above all, it is significant that the angels not only appear as servants of God, but also as independent ruling powers. However the particular expressions, 'thrones, principalities, powers, and dominions,' may be explained, they signify, collectively and individually, ruling powers; and of course with this Paul has in mind not only the dominion over the nations taught in Judaism, but also dominion over the cosmos.[10] Essentially, they are to be compared with the 'rulers of this world' (I Cor. 2:8; cf. Col. 2:15 and pp. 493f), and thus, to some degree, with the 'elements of the world' (Gal. 4:3; Col. 2:20), to which pre-Christian humanity was in bondage. Perhaps it is not too bold a thing to think that by 'powers' (δυνάμεις) are especially meant the 'powers of heaven' (Mark 13:25), that is to say

[10] Deut. 32:8, LXX: when the Most High divided the nations, he placed limits to them according to the number of the angels; Dan. 10:13,20f: here they are called the princes of the nations, ἄρχοντες and στρατηγοί; Enoch 89:59ff; Jub. 17:17.

the stars, which Paul also conceived of as personal beings (I Cor. 15:40f). This same explanation touches upon that of the 'thrones' (Col. 1:16); and likewise in the 'elements (στοιχεῖα) of the world' the idea of the constellations lies close at hand. In any case the whole manner of consideration, according to which pre-Christian humanity must be redeemed from the cosmos, borders very closely upon the astrological belief of the surrounding world. Just as man is there the slave of fate because he has entered into the circle of nature, as there the 'entire life is guided by the stars,'[11] so, according to Paul, man, because he was born into this world (Gal. 4:4), entered into a state of bondage to those beings which he calls the 'elements of the world' (Gal. 4:3,9; Col. 2:20), and these are the spirits or demons that rule over all parts of the cosmos.[12] These representations have an especial pathos for Paul, owing to this, namely, that from his standpoint of redemption, all these things lie behind him. For him, who has had an experience of the highest, the one true God, these are simply and only 'paltry and weak elements' (Gal. 4:9).[13] But, above all, they were those which separated him from God,

[11] For example, Vett. Valens IV, ii, p. 172:33f, etc.; Stobaeus i. 5. 20.

[12] An interesting example of this literary usage is found in Fr. Pfister, *Philologus* 69, pp. 411 ff, taken from the Alexander-Romance, where, for example, it is said: τὰ γὰρ κοσμικά στοιχεῖα λογῳ πάντα αὐτῷ ὑπετάσσετο; according to another passage this whole concept of κοσμικὰ στοιχεῖα is included in τὰ ἀέρια πνεύματα καὶ οἱ καταχθόνιοι δαίμονες. Pfister refers to a number of Papyrus passages in which the demons are invoked according to the following classification: πᾶς δαίμων οὐράνιος καὶ αἰθέριος καὶ ἐπίγειος καὶ ὑπόγειος καὶ χερσαῖος καὶ ἔνυδρος (Pap. Lond. 46:165ff; p. 70 ed. Kenyon). The whole expanse of the cosmos is circumscribed, as for example also in the *Book of Jubilees* 2:2: there is the angel of the fire-spirit, and of the wind-spirit, an angel of the clouds and one of the darkness, one of snow, hail, frost, thunder and lightning, cold and heat, winter, spring, harvest and summer; cf. also Enoch 60. M. Dibelius, *Die Geisterwelt*, p. 80, says, "One cannot over-value the extent of this circle of thought. Babylonian, Persian and Greek thought may have met here. Rudiments of a long-since overcome heathenism seem to have been revived—everything is united with the conception that nothing on earth, ordained by heaven, down to the flower in the field, is without its angel."

[13] I am obliged to refer here to some words of Reitzenstein: "Now there rules as θεὸς τοῦ αἰῶνος τούτου as ἄρχων τῆς ἐξουσίας τοῦ ἀέρος (i.e. between heaven and earth) the prince of those ἄρχοντες, the evil one (a second doctrine, originally independent of astrology, concerning the enemy of God and his worshippers, has exercised some influence at this point), and the creation itself sighs and yearns for liberty. However, even without hope of that new world-period in which the ἄρχοντες are to be overthrown and the κτίσις renewed, the Christian possesses in contrast to the comfortless emptiness of a fatalistic religion, which would dissolve the relation between man and God, the blessed consciousness of an indestructible love, of a reunion with God: those dark powers rule only outward events and his earthly part, and he knows this to be certain (Rom. 8:38). This wonderful message can only be grasped by the fact of one's own innermost experience, for which Paul himself had yearned under the pressure of a fatalistic religion."

because they controlled the whole man on the side of the flesh, forced him to enmity toward God, and thereby condemned him to death (Rom. 8:6f). Thanks be to God, that we have died to them (Col. 2:20) and have nothing more to do with the flesh and the whole cosmos (Gal. 6:14; 7:5; 8:2; etc.)!

That the angels are not only good and beneficent servants of God appears in this, that Satan also has control over them (II Cor. 12:7), and through them can do bodily harm to man. Satan appears chiefly, in Paul as in the whole of primitive Christianity, at least quite as much the bearer of evil as of sin. The evil-doer is turned over to him for the destruction of the body (I Cor. 5:5), and this means that at the moment when, by the power of the name of Jesus Christ, he has been cast out from the community, and from the protection of the Spirit of Christ, he falls into the hands of Satan who will destroy him. For the latter, in fact, is only lying in wait for this purpose, namely, that the servants of Christ, whom Christ had snatched from him, may fall once more into his hands (II Cor. 2:11; cf. I Pet. 5:8). He stands, so to speak, ready to spring, violent, crafty, waiting to turn the community away from its Lord (II Cor. 11:3). So also the angels and powers, who, according to Rom. 8:38 might make the attempt, though in vain, to tear away the Christians from the love of God, may be angels of Satan, who, perhaps, through his instruments, might thus once again try to carry on the old business of accusation (Rev. 12:10); but in so doing he would, as once was the case with Michael (Rev. 12:10; cf. Enoch 40:7),[14] now meet the invincible Advocate, Christ himself (Rom. 8:33f). So he seeks at least to hinder, to imperil, to weaken the work of God wherever he can (I Thess. 2:18; II Thess. 3:3; Rom. 16:20). He dazzles the minds of the unbelievers so that no beam of the Gospel light strikes them (II Cor. 4:4); he is the tempter to sin, to apostasy (I Cor. 7:5; I Thess. 3:5; II Cor. 11:3). Especially will he finally bring his opposition to a head (II Cor. 6:15) by arming the 'men of sin' at his 'parousia' with power and signs and wonders (II Thess. 2:9f)—but even in this he will not succeed, for the Lord Jesus will slay his adversaries 'with the breath of his mouth.'

The most significant designation of Satan is 'the god of this world'

[14] Cf. *Test. Dan.* 6: "And now fear God, my children, and beware of Satan and his spirits. Draw near unto God and unto the angel who intercedeth for you, since he is a mediator between God and man and for the peace of Israel. He shall stand up against the kingdom of the enemy. Therefore is the enemy eager to destroy all that call upon the Lord. Since he knoweth that upon the day on which Israel shall repent, the kingdom of the enemy shall be brought to an end."

(II Cor. 4:4). This word cannot simply be taken in a figurative sense (according to Phil. 3:19), as if men had devoted themselves to him to such a degree that they had apparently chosen him as their God; no, just as the 'rulers of the world' (I Cor. 2:8) have this world really in their power, so the expression means that Satan really exerts divine power and rule over the present age. This is, indeed, a far-reaching dualism, which has an analogy only in the Persian belief in an eternal antithesis between Ahura Mazda and Angra Mainyu, and has probably been influenced by it. The question here is merely to what extent Paul has taken seriously the view inherent in these words, and how they are related to the rest of his thought-world. Above all he agrees with optimistic Parseeism in this, namely, that the final victory of God and his sole rule are taken for granted. Because of this idea his monotheism perhaps becomes theoretically but not actually endangered, in any case not at the period when it becomes known to us from his letters. He may have previously, as a Jew, considered the rule of Satan over this world with deep pessimism, but now that is overcome, since the decisive blow has already been delivered; the 'principalities and powers' have already been partially defeated by God (Col. 2:15), they will surely be destroyed by Christ, be 'eliminated' (I Cor. 2:8; 15:24), and Satan also will be completely overcome. Paul is thoroughly convinced of this, although it is nowhere expressly stated. But now he (Satan) still has power enough; his 'unlimited sphere of rule is heathendom' (II Cor. 6:15), and he is constantly seeking to widen it again. But the divinity and rule of Satan is at once designated as limited by the expression, 'the god of this age,' as in I Cor. 2:8 'the rulers of this age' are likewise described.

4. *The Two Aeons.* With this we come to a fundamental conception of Paul's, which, unfortunately, we cannot understand or trace, as we should wish, from the view-point of the history of religion.[15]

[15] A comprehensive examination of the concepts *κόσμος* and *αἰών*, based upon historical literary usage and its corresponding Semitic equivalents, is still lacking. Above all, moreover, this is true of any history of the idea of world-periods, which is naturally connected with astrological thought. Especially, it has not been explained how Judaism came to assume only two aeons, and how this belief is to be harmonized with the antithesis between God and Satan. It has not been fully enough explained how the Hellenistic concept of 'aeon' originated. Meanwhile, see M. Dibelius, *Die Geisterwelt* etc., pp. 193f: "The belief that the course of the world is accomplished in a series of periods rests, fundamentally, upon astrological observations: after a fixed time there return again the same or similar cosmic relationships, and then one period is completed. This fundamental idea is found among many peoples; the expression depends upon what circle of time one is reckoning. From the astral character there results at once a connection with the spirit-world: the particular period is reckoned from the

'This world' (I Cor. 3:19; 5:10; 7:31) or 'this age' (Rom. 12:2; I Cor. 1:20; 2:6,8; 3:18; II Cor. 4:4; Gal. 1:4; Eph. 1:21)—the words include an antithesis to 'that' or to 'the coming age,' an expression which, perhaps accidentally, does not occur in Paul (except in Eph. 1:21). The fundamental conception that this present world will be replaced by a new world, a 'new creation' (II Cor. 5:17; Gal. 6:15),[16] while the former itself 'passes away' (I Cor. 7:31), is the basic apocalyptic pattern of all of Paul's thinking. In the expression 'aeon' there is still retained a reminder that the question is, first of all, only of two successive world-periods; but since he freely varies its use with that of 'cosmos,' one perceives that this temporal conception is not the only prevailing one. Plainly it appears still in I Cor. 10:11, according to which the 'points' or 'ends' of (both) ages just meet in the present generation; [16a] it is the dividing-line of the ages. However, generally with Paul 'aeon' has wholly the meaning of 'world,' and the antithesis between both ages or worlds is no longer simply considered temporally, but above all else quantitatively: 'this world' is that of the earth, the world of creation, of corruption, of sin; 'that' world is the one pertaining to heaven, the world of everlasting life, of glory. But the 'new creation', which according to the sketch in the Apocalypse is really yet to be, in some sense, has not only begun in time, it is in truth always present in heaven, and projects into the life of Christians through the reign of Christ, through the Spirit, and through the beginning of their transfiguration. They have already experienced the powers of the world to come within themselves (Heb. 6:4). This antithesis becomes essentially a religious world-judgment, and all the dark shadows fall upon this present world. It is thoroughly wicked (Gal. 1:4). In what sense this is

course of the stars. The particular star-spirit rules the world during this period. Thus the aeon-theory and the belief in the 'world-ruler' are closely combined. The view of the periodic return of fixed cosmic conditions corresponds to the eschatological thought that the time of the end and primitive time will be similar. If the eschatological expectation becomes especially acute, the end of a period is felt to be near. Thus the earlier world-ages that have already been lose interest, and one only feels now the antithesis of two magnitudes, the present and the future. Thus it occurs in Jewish thought in the antithesis between חעולם הזה and העולם חבא (*αἰὼν οὗτος* and *αἰὼν μέλλων*), this present world and the world to come."

[16] Especially strongly expressed in IV Ezra, namely in 4:26ff: The aeon hastens to its end. For it cannot fulfil the predictions which have been given to the pious concerning the future; since this aeon is full of sorrow and distress. For the evil has been sown, and its harvest has not yet appeared. Therefore, since that which has been sown has not yet been harvested and the place of the evil seed has not yet disappeared, the ground where the good is sown cannot appear.

[16a] With the usage of *καταντᾶν* in the sense of 'proceed forth', 'run a course', cf. Psalm 18(19):7 LXX.

meant, whether in a purely ethical one or in that of evil—in any case, this also is connected with sin—it is obvious that the critical judgment of this world is thoroughly pessimistic, with which the estimate that it was 'very good,' once formed of it by its creator, has scarcely anything to do. Here Paul has withdrawn farthest from the Old Testament or Jewish basis of his thinking. This conception of the cosmos, and of redemption as an overcoming of the cosmos, has at once a decided 'gnostic' characteristic, and it cannot be denied that here the Apostle is under the influence of the same spiritual current which later was developed, in the classical period of Gnosticism, into a very real danger to the church.[17]

5. *Anthropology.* The 'Gnostic' suggestion also becomes very plain in Paul's anthropology. Here of course the Old Testament, Jewish basis is obvious. When he places in antithesis the exalted God and man in his impotency, weakness (Rom. 9:20; I Cor. 1:25; 2:9; 3:3f,21; 7:23; II Cor. 5:11; Gal. 1:1,10ff; Col. 2:8; I Thess. 2:4,6,13; 4:8), he conceives it in the actual Old Testament, we might also say the strictly human, manner. When he designates the nature of man as of 'flesh and blood' (I Cor. 15:50; Gal. 1:16), this is in no way a type of dualism traceable to Gnosticism. When he speaks of the weakness of the flesh (Rom. 6:19) as due simply to corporeality (Rom. 9:3,5,8; 13:14; I Cor. 7:28; 15:39; II Cor. 7:1,5; 12:7; Gal. 4:13f; Col. 1:24; 2:5), and when he means by the expression 'all flesh' the creatureliness of mankind (Gal. 2:16;

[17] In this regard I must agree fully with the judgment of Bousset, who in his book *Kyrios Christos,* pp. 233f, says: "At first glance it appears as if the Gnostics could not refer to Paul for support in their opinion concerning the denial of the visible natural world, and for their prejudice against the creating-gods; to the Paul, who in good orthodox Stoic fashion (I add, also in good orthodox Old Testament fashion) bases his objections to the hardened heathenism upon the fundamental hypothesis that God has revealed himself to his creation by proclamations (Rom. 1:18ff; cf. I Cor. 8:22f). However, on the other hand, the thoroughly pessimistic teaching regarding the σάρξ—which is certainly chiefly conceived of in an essentially anthropological manner, forces its extension here and there (cf. Rom. 8:22f) to the whole earthly, sensible creation. . . . comes to Paul from the way of the Gnosis." P. 235: "We have referred to this above, namely, that there comes clearly to expression the especial peculiarity of Gnostic dualism, in its demonizing of the star-powers, which in a later Hellenistic piety of educated men, were considered as actual gods, and for whom redemption was conceived as liberation from destiny, which was ruled by the star-powers. In this basic view Paul's doctrine of angels finds now a striking parallel." P. 236: "And there is not entirely lacking in Paul also that special Gnostic conception of redemption as liberation from fate, although there certainly are only slight indications of this to be found in him. At least echoes of this are clearly found in his representation of the bondage of pre-Christian humanity under the rule of the στοιχεῖα. . . . Nowhere does it appear more plainly than here, how closely the thought-world of Paul and that of the Gnosis are related."

I Cor. 1:29), he is simply reiterating the Old Testament, Jewish usage.

The problem begins with the question concerning the relationship of the flesh to sin. According to the already-mentioned literary usage, characterized as a semi-animistic personification, Paul conceives this condition as a kind of present possession. Sin dwells in the flesh and obstructs the free self-determination of the ego: "But now I no longer act, but the sin which dwells in me, that is, is in my flesh" (Rom. 7:17f,20). But this primitive manner of expression may really obscure the problem. Far more indicative are the expressions in which the flesh itself appears as willing, acting, striving, as in Rom. 8:6f,12: 'The thinking and striving of the flesh ends in death,' 'is enmity against God,' 'the works of the flesh or of the body,' 'the desire of the flesh' (Gal. 5:16f,24). Here it appears as an independent power in opposition to God, controlled by no one, paralyzing everything good (Rom. 8:8), and, from its very nature, evil; it cannot subject itself to the law of God, because by its nature it for ever lusts against the Spirit (Gal. 5:17). Here there is almost never any thought of the corporeality of the individual, but the flesh appears as a uniform, cohesive being in which the individual, in a certain measure, shares, somewhat like the members of the body. Here not only does the 'realism of universal concepts' operate (p. 434), but also a metaphysical, almost mythological manner of thought. The flesh is a part of the cosmos which has fallen away from God, and is inimical to him. By the flesh the individual is actually connected with this cosmos; the putting-off of the flesh signifies, at the same time, redemption from the world elements (Col. 2:11,13 and 20). But how is it conceivable by a former Jew that corporeality originating from the hand of God has fallen into such a dependence upon the powers of the cosmos, and into such enmity against God? According to Jewish theory, the Fall of Adam plays a part here. The Fourth Book of Ezra answers the question as follows: Adam, because of the will of his evil heart, fell into sin and guilt (3:21); because a little kernel of evil seed was sown in his heart (4:30), his descendants have continued to sin, for God did not remove from them this evil heart (3:20). But the theorist does not explain how this evil heart came into Adam, nor how it agrees with the conception of his creation by God (3:5ff). Nor does Paul either put or answer the question. He is satisfied with this, namely, that 'by one man sin came into the world' (Rom. 5:12), i.e. by the act of Adam. Thus it is that sin exists in humanity. Again, he does not answer the question how it passed from Adam to other men[18]—it suffices him that all men have sinned (Rom. 5:12), and must, like Adam, forego the divine glory which Adam possessed in the beginning (Rom. 3:23).[19] Again, according to Rom. 7:7-12, the Fall and its consequences seem to repeat themselves in every human life. One would think that this explanation must be the only and prevailing one for Paul, as a Jew. By man's free act he has delivered himself into the bondage of sin, and now he is in its power. But still, ever and again, those above mentioned statements create the impression that he must sin because he, once upon a time, was fettered to the cosmos, and thus came into the control of the world-elements. Moreover, taken strictly, the fact of the redemption of the flesh from the world really presupposes the thought that man was innocent at the time of his arrest on the charge of sin, because it was really connected with his natural endowment. Here a decidedly dualistic manner of consideration—taken from the Hellenistic Gnosis—stands out in Paul's Jewish thinking, which is especially plain in the statement of Gal. 5:17: "For the flesh lusts against the Spirit, and the Spirit against the flesh; and these are contrary to one another, so that ye cannot do the things that ye would." This is meant, first of all, individually; in each one of us flesh and

[18] That Rom. 5:12ff offers no teaching concerning original sin is generally acknowledged. Paul assumes the universal spread of sin, but does not explain it. On the other hand, the passage gives the theory of the inheritance of death, conceived as a punishment suspended over Adam, and one which, like fate, rules over his descendants. This statement Paul proves especially in respect to the generations reaching to the time of Moses, which, indeed, had no law, and therefore, strictly speaking, could not be made responsible as breakers of the Law, and were yet destined to death (Rom. 5:13f). They must all die because of the sin of Adam; *Apoc. Baruch* 23:4: "Because when Adam sinned and death was decreed against those who should be born. . ." However, as the *Apoc. Baruch* 54:15 again says: "For though Adam first sinned and brought untimely death upon all, yet of all those who were born from him each one of them has prepared for his own soul torment to come. . ." And so Paul also adds (5:12) "because they all have sinned," so that still each individual is guilty of his own death (cf. also Rom. 7:7-12). But, strictly taken, this passage does not fit in with the trend of thought in 5:12-21. For by it Paul at once tries to show that the righteousness of Christ also serves for salvation to many who have not earned it, just as the sin of Adam destined many to death. The emphasis in the whole treatment is laid upon the 'free gift.' Thus if 5:12b is genuine, then another series of thought has forced itself into the mind of the Apostle (death as the wages of sin, Rom. 6:23) which has just as much truth in itself as the other—one of his many antinomies.

[19] So indeed it appears that ὑστεροῦνται τῆς δόξης τοῦ θεοῦ can best be explained. In the *Life of Adam and Eve,* ch. 20 (Kautzsch, II, 522), Eve says: "At the same hour mine eyes were opened and I knew that I had been stripped of the righteousness with which I had been clothed. Then I wept and said, 'Why have you done this to me that I should be separated from my glory with which I had been clothed?'" In *Beresh. rabba* 12 it states: "Adam had lost, through sin, this glory (זיו = δόξα)." Cf. R. H. Charles, ed., *Old Testament Apocrypha and Pseudepigrapha.*

divine Spirit are combatting one another. But the universality of the formulation permits a greater generalization of the conclusion, in respect to the thought which lies in the background. Flesh and Spirit are two world-powers, which, in accordance with their very nature, must oppose each other. Here we have a dualism of a particular type which we are forced to consider in still another connection. One might expect in Paul an anthropological dualism, after the manner of that Poimandres passage (p. 600, n. 11), which reads: "Because man is subjected to Fate, entangled in the sphere of the cosmos, therefore he is a being to be twice slaughtered, mortal as to the body, immortal as to the real man." According to this one could claim that Paul meant: "According to the flesh, to sink into death, into sin, in respect to the Spirit, descended from God, desiring God, endeavoring to fulfil the will of God." Do we actually find this manner of thinking in him?

As a matter of fact, tendencies in this direction are not lacking. We do meet with the wholly popular antithesis: 'according to the body, according to the Spirit' (I Cor. 5:3). Above all, we have the highly significant contrast between the 'inner' and the 'outer' man (Rom. 7:22; II Cor. 4:16), and of course, in a very different manner, once, that of the pre-Christian man, who 'in respect to the inner man,' i.e. with the reason (7:23,25), faces the law of God sympathetically and willingly, yet cannot carry out this will owing to the opposition of the flesh. Then again there is the Christian whose 'outer man' is destroyed by suffering, while the 'inner,' renewed day by day, grows toward the heavenly transfiguration. But these antitheses are isolated. On the whole, we miss throughout any vivid, comparative evaluation of body and soul, flesh and spirit, in the individual sense. Paul certainly knows the spirit of man, his soul, his reason,[20] his heart, as his highest part [21]—but he does not make use of this knowledge in a way which one might expect from one living in the sphere of Hellenism, from a contemporary of Philo.[22] In particular, the

[20] Philo, *Leg. alleg.*, I, § 39: "As the face is the dominant element, in the body, so is the mind the dominant element of the soul."

[21] Cf. Rom. 1:9; I Cor. 5:3; Rom. 2:9; 13:1; 16:4; I Cor. 1:23; Phil. 2:30; etc., for the distinction between 'spirit' and 'soul.'

[22] Bousset, *Kyrios Christos,* p. 136: "In the whole scope of genuine Greek philosophy the idea is unheard of that the best and highest as the purpose of all human living is not innate in the human soul, yes, is foreign to it, strives against it through a natural tendency. Foreign to it also is the assumption of a redemption from without and from above. The fundamental conviction of the Greek wise-man, so far as he has an idealistic aim, lies in the thought that he holds and bears his life and his fate firmly in his own hands, that he should find the foundation of his whole life, should he

soul is aligned so closely with the creature-like, sub-divine nature of man, that the term 'soul-man' (ἄνθρωπος ψυχικός) does not designate one in whom the soul (instead of the body) predominates, as an element wholly permeating him, elevating him to the true spiritual life, but just the reverse, as the one who, wholly untouched by the divine spirit, and without understanding, is opposed to the

---

reflect upon it, in the depths of his own being." Bousset shows, further, that Philo had already turned away from fundamental Hellenic ideas: "He knows no greater and no more dangerous opponent of true piety than the spirit of Greek philosophical aristocracy." "The devout one who wishes to find his God must leave behind the whole world of his self-conscious ego. He must not only reject the help of his lowly, bodily, sensible existence, he must also give up his *λόγος* and his *νοῦς* if he wishes to reach God." For example he says, *Quis rer. div. haer.* § 66: *ἀσώματοι φύσεις νοητῶν πραγμάτων εἰσὶ κληρονόμοι.* 68f: *τίς οὖν γενήσεται κληρονόμος; οὐχ ὁ μένων ἐν τῇ τοῦ σώματος εἱρκτῇ λογισμὸς καθ' ἑκούσιον γνώμην, ἀλλ' ὁ λυθεὶς τῶν δεσμῶν καὶ ἐλευθερωθεὶς καὶ ἔξω τειχῶν προεληλυθὼς καὶ καταλελοιπὼς, εἰ οἷόν τὲ τοῦτο εἰπεῖν, αὐτὸς ἑαυτόν. "ὃς γὰρ ἐξελεύσεται ἐκ σοῦ," φησίν, "οὗτος κληρονομήσει σε"* (Gen. 15:4). *πόθος οὖν εἴ τις εἰσερχεταί σε, ψυχή, τῶν θείων ἀγαθῶν κληρονομῆσαι, μὴ μόνον "γῆν," τὸ σῶμα, καὶ "συγγένειαν," (τὴν) αἴσθησιν, καὶ "οἶκον πὰτρὸς." τὸν λόγον, κᾶταλίπῃς, ἀλλὰ καὶ σαυτὴν ἀπόδραθι καὶ ἔκστηθι σεαυτῆς, ὥσπερ οἱ κατεχόμενοι καὶ κορυβαντιῶντες βακχευθεῖσα καὶ θεοφορηθεῖσα κατά τινα προφητικὸν ἐπιθειασμόν.* ("For it is incorporeal natures that inherit intellectual things." 68ff: "Who then shall be the heir? Not that way of thinking which abides in the prison of the body of its own free will, but that which released from its fetters into liberty, has come forth outside the prison walls, and, if we may so say, left behind its own self. For 'he who shall come out of thee,' it says, 'shall be thy heir' (Gen. 15:4). Therefore, my soul, if thou feelest any yearning to inherit the good things of God, leave not only thy land, that is the body, thy relations, that is the senses, thy father's house, that is speech, but be a fugitive from thyself also and issue forth from thyself. Like persons possessed and Corybants, be filled with inspired frenzy, even as the prophets are inspired").

This all-inclusive view is only occasional in Philo; as a general rule he simply states that man in ecstasy must leave body and sensibility and even the *νοῦς* behind. In general there prevails in Philo that literary usage according to which the soul appears to be that which in man is related to God, and alone fosters a higher *Gnosis;* the antithesis *σῶμα—ψυχή* represents an essentially religious difference. Cf. Reitzenstein, p. 148: "The concept of the *ψυχή*, as the spiritual and divine in man, became so dominant that it could assume this terminology." In spite of agreement in subject, one can scarcely imagine a greater antithesis than that between the passage from *Qu. deus sit imm.* § 55: *οἱ μὲν ψυχῆς, οἱ δὲ σώματος γεγόνασι φίλοι. οἱ μὲν οὖν ψυχῆς ἑταῖροι νοηταῖς καὶ ἀσωμάταις φύσεσιν ἐνομιλεῖν δυνάμενοι. . . .* ("The comrades of the soul have indeed become friends of the body. The comrades of the soul, therefore, can hold converse with intelligible, incorporeal natures". . . .) and I Cor. 2:14: *ψυχικὸς δὲ ἄνθρωπος οὐ δέχεται τὰ τοῦ πνεύματος τοῦ θεοῦ* ("The 'natural' man does not receive the things of the spirit of God").

Formally divergent is also the literary usage of the Hermetical literature, as Bousset, pp. 139f, pictures it, where the *nous* assumes exactly the same position as the divine *pneuma* in Paul. "There are two wholly differing classes of men, the possessors of the *nous* (1:21 *ὁ ἔννους ἄνθρωπος*), the few, who stand over against a whole world, and who, misunderstood, oppressed, and persecuted, yet with the deep feeling of divinely pardoned men, oppose the dull and slothful mass, which does not possess the *nous.*"

divine (I Cor. 2:14).[23] The soul belongs so definitely to the body that earthly, fleshly bodies could at once be called 'soul-like bodies' (σώματα ψυχικά, I Cor. 15:44). This literary usage, which would be entirely incomprehensible to a Plato or a Philo, which in fact has only been made bearable to the Bible reader of today by the veiled translation, 'natural bodies,' the 'natural man,' demands an explanation. One might first think of the Old Testament manner of speech, according to which 'each flesh' and 'each soul' are about equally evaluated, because the *nephesh* is really the natural, animal life through which the body first becomes a living soul (Acts 20:10). A 'psychic man' would, therefore, be one who is above all nothing else than a corporeal being, animated by the breath of life, one who has in no way yet lifted himself above the original creature-likeness (I Cor. 15:45=Gen. 2:7). However, this does not explain the polished, formal expression. It is only to be understood upon the view that the divine Spirit alone was intended to rule in man. There is concealed in it a sharp antithesis between this divine Spirit and the human soul. This low estimate of the creature-like human being, and the opinion that man with his innate spiritual forces is still remote from and foreign to the divine, must have its origin in a wholly transcendental, mystical view of the world. Its ideal is the spiritual man, the Spirit-drenched mystic, completely lifted out of himself by the divine afflatus. It is highly probable that Paul found this method of thought and the corresponding literary usage, which contradicts both the Old Testament and the Hellenistic, already expressed in a particular circle of Hellenistic religion and literature, which we, however, cannot more definitely determine.[23a] It is the same point of view which we later come upon again in the churchly Gnosis, where we find the spiritual man and the psychic man

[23] Philo, *Leg. Alleg.* I, 38: πῶς ἂν ἐνόησεν ἡ ψυχὴ θεὸν, εἰ μὴ ἐνέπνευσε καὶ ἥψατο αὐτῆς κατὰ δύναμιν. . . . εἰ μὴ αὐτὸς ὁ θεὸς ἀνέσπασεν αὐτὸν πρὸς ἑαυτόν, ὡς ἐνῆν ἀνθρώπινον νοῦν ἀνασπασθῆναι. . . . ("For how could the soul have conceived of God had he not breathed into it and powerfully laid hold of it, had not God himself drawn it up to himself so far as it was possible that the 'nous' of man should be drawn up. . . .").

[23a] Cf. Reitzenstein, *Hell. Mysterienrell.*, pp. 44, 108ff, 136ff, and my Commentary on I Cor. 15:43. Reitzenstein refers chiefly to the introduction in the so-called 'Mithras Liturgy' (Deiterich, p. 4, ll. 23-29). Here the neophyte, called to rebirth and the vision of God, prays as a mortal (θνητὸν γεγῶτα) for whom it is 'impossible to rise to the heights with the golden exhalations of flame of the imperishable lights'; 'but today I shall behold, with deathless eyes—I born a mortal of a mortal mother—the immortal Aeon . . . . consecrated through holy dedications . . . . and let mortal human nature cease, for the moment.' The ψυχικὴ δύναμις is human nature, which must be left behind in the deifying vision. Cf. Bousset, *Kyrios Christos,* pp. 140ff, 237ff.

opposed to each other; [24] and it comes from the same root both in Paul and in Gnosticism, so that we may, therefore, call it 'Gnostic,' since in both cases an ideal of knowledge of God is striven for which is denied to the natural abilities of man, and can only be attained by a special revelation or self-communication of God, by a special outfitting of man with divine powers. Let it be repeated yet once again: what Paul calls the new 'spiritual' life of the Christian appears to him in no way as an enhancing or heightening of the natural life, but as something entirely opposed to it and in a manner foreign to it, a 'new creation.' Thus we perceive how wonderfully new and powerful was the effect of the words, 'Let there be light,' how new and divine was the light of the knowledge which has flashed up in the hearts of Christians (II Cor. 4:6). Yes, still more must be said: if man really desires to come into communion with Christ, with God, he must himself be 'deified.' Naturally this expression is lacking in Paul—he could not have uttered it—but the thought lies in the background. In this wholly pessimistic consideration of the nature of the 'natural' man, there seems to be forgotten the fact that man comes from the hand of God, above all, that his soul has really descended from the breath of God. Forgotten also is the view held by Jesus and prevailing also in Judaism, that man, just as he is, is a child of God, is summoned to communion with him. Yet this manner of consideration must also, indeed, be present in Paul, as when in the imperatives of his penitential preaching he makes such strong demands upon the wills of men, as when he summons them to faith, i.e. to trustful self-surrender, as when he also expects much from natural gifts and virtues, from the love of the wife and the tenderness of the husband, from discipline and from carefree goodness. Even over against the supernatural, gnostic doctrine of redemption and its hypotheses, there still remains effective a good part of the Old Testament, Jewish, and primitive Christian tradition of the preaching of Jesus and of the first group of disciples.

6. *Human Nature.* Paul judges mankind in general in the same manner as he judges the individual.[25] The verdict of universal

[24] Although the antithesis is softened by the juxtaposition of the 'earthly men,' cf. Bousset, *Kyrios Christos,* pp. 240f. Interesting also is the passage in Irenaeus concerning the Valentinian eschatology (I:7:1; cf. *Ex Theodoto* 64). "The Marcosians speak in their prayers of the Gnostic wandering into his home, having broken his bonds." Other Gnostic passages concerning the antithesis πνεῦμα—ψυχή appear in the same place. Cf. pp. 241f.

[25] Let it be remembered that there is in the New Testament no word for 'humanity.' Not once does the expression, 'the human race,' occur, though it is frequently found

damnation (Rom. 3:9-20), that the whole world has fallen under the judgment of God, that all are under the domination of sin, that there is nothing good in the whole sphere of the flesh, still permits considerable exceptions. Not only is the good-will of the reason acknowledged (Rom. 7:23,25), not only is it granted that individual heathen by nature fulfil the demands of the Law (Rom. 2:14f,27)—there are even people who, 'unwearied in doing good, are striving for glory, honor and incorruptibility,' who 'do good' (Rom. 2:7,10), and who, as the expression shows, are not confined to the Jews but are found also among the Greeks. And the great general guilt of humanity, that it has not glorified God in spite of his revelation in nature, and has not thanked him (Rom. 1:21; I Cor. 1:21), is really a lamentable condition of which it is innocent, because its majority lacked God's word of revelation (Rom. 3:2), 'the embodiment of knowledge and the truth in the Law' (Rom. 2:20). Therefore men served ther false so-called 'gods' in ignorance, because they had not yet experienced God, had not yet received a revelation (Gal. 4:8f; I Cor. 8:5). If occasionally the harsh, haughty Jewish condemnation of the heathen as 'sinners' breaks through (Gal. 2:15; I Cor. 6:1,4), he had certainly, already as a Jew of the diaspora, looked upon the heathen as not simply a *massa perditionis*. To the convictions brought over from Hellenism there really belongs also a statement similar to that in I Cor. 7:19, "Circumcision is nothing and uncircumcision is nothing, but only the

---

in Hellenistic inscriptions. (Only in Acts 17:26 we have 'the whole race of men'). We have, merely, 'all men' (Rom. 5:12,18; 12:17f; II Cor. 3:2; I Thess. 2:15), and only in the first two passages in a universal sense. Much more frequently we find in its place 'the world' (ὁ κόσμος), as in Rom. 5:12; II Cor. 5:19. As a rule it appears in Paul as divided, and of course in different ways according to the particular manner of consideration. Most frequently we have, in this connection, the antithesis 'Jew and Greek' (Rom. 1:16; 2:9f; 3:9f,12; I Cor. 1:22f; 10:32; 12:13; Gal. 3:28; Col. 3:11) because it is thought of not only as national, but also with regard to its earlier religious history and divisions. For him both of these represent great mission-fields. Cf. also the antithesis between uncircumcision and circumcision, e.g. in Gal. 2:7; etc. There is a difference in the antithesis Greeks and Barbarians, learned and unlearned (Rom. 1:14), or Greeks, Jews, Barbarians, Scythians (Col. 3:11); here there is present something like a circumscription of humanity, but the circle of vision is narrowed by literary convention. The Scythians are most remote of Barbarians, and there is no mention of the tribes of Africa or of India. The geographical purview also seems to be a very narrow one here: the expression, 'these regions' (κλίματα), in Rom. 15:23 appears to embrace the original Greek half of the Latin world—naturally with no emphasis upon differences of language. He also considers Rome and Spain as belonging to the Hellenistic world. Did he know anything of Gaul, Germany or Africa south of the Empire? Did he conceive them to be within the scope of his mission-task? We do not know.

keeping of the commandments"[26] (cf. Rom. 2:25-29). If by the keeping of the commandments, the difference between Judaism and heathenism can thus be bridged over, yes, wiped out, the double task is nigh at hand, namely that of becoming 'a light for those who sit in darkness' (Rom. 2:19). Thus Paul was already, as a result of his Hellenistic past, the born missionary to the heathen. Of course the full conviction of the religious equality of the heathen will first have been realized when, in battling for the liberty of the Gentile Christians, he recognized still more clearly that God only expects from man the trustful acceptance of his grace, which is something the heathen can do quite as well, yes, and perhaps sooner than the Jew. Thus there grows out of this new religious background a neutralization of national differences, developed not so much from the Stoic-rational, nor from any particular humanitarian ideas, as from the thought of the all-embracing father-love of God and the rich grace of Christ: there is no difference between Jew and Greek, one and the same Lord is over all, who manifests his richness to all who call upon him (Rom. 10:12). Moreover, this new concept of divinity and humanity agrees with the Jewish-Hellenistic: God is not only the God of the Jews, but also of the heathen (Rom. 3:29).

It is a fact accounted for by the development of Paul, that he criticized Judaism much more sharply than heathenism. Of course he finds himself frequently compelled to acknowledge how favored, how richly endowed, his own people are (Rom. 3:1f; 9:4f). He can share the pride which the Jews, the Israelites, the sons of Abraham feel (II Cor. 11:22; Phil. 3:5), and in spite of all he is convinced that the grace of God and his calling are unforfeitable (Rom. 11:29). He does not give up the hope that Israel will once more be converted and saved, a hope founded upon a revelation through which this has been assured him (Rom. 11:23-32), and in burning love and yearning he would sacrifice his own salvation for this glorious goal (Rom. 9:3). But as for the moment his countrymen have placed themselves outside it, he can only feel for them great sorrow and continual pain (Rom. 9:2). They are on the wrong road because they wish to win salvation by their own actions, instead of by yielding themselves to the righteousness of God and the preaching of the faith (Rom. 9:31—10:13), which they have heard (Rom. 10:14-21), so that they cannot excuse

[26] On this saying, which comes from an apocryphal work dealing with Moses, see my Commentary *ad loc.*

themselves. He can only attribute their unbelief to a divine hardening of their hearts. God wished at once to create room for the influx of the Gentiles and also, in this way, to inspire the Jews to zeal once more (Rom. 11:1-12). It is clear that Paul conceives the reasons for this process as follows: if the Jews had accepted the Gospel in great numbers, it might have happened that the Gentiles would have remained without, and salvation would have been limited to the people of God. But in that God laid upon them the 'spirit of dulness of hearing,' he has for the time being kept them at a distance, in order to be able to open the door to the heathen (Rom. 11:8,11,25,30f). Therefore this hardening is only temporary. Of course, until salvation draws near, dreadful things must yet come upon Israel: the great apostasy among the people, the spread of godlessness, the appearance of the 'man of sin' (II Thess. 2:3f). Even now Paul thinks that he can observe the 'secret of godlessness' (vs. 7) which creeps in darkness—is he perhaps thinking of the zealot party, the activities of robbers and assassins?—and therefore, as the Jews oppose him in all his ways, as enemies of the Gospel who would grudge salvation to other people, they seem to him on the way to fill up the measure of their sins (I Thess. 2:15f). We are not surprised therefore that the hope of Israel does not dominate all of the Apostle's thinking—over against this is the thought, scarcely to be reconciled with Rom. 11:25-32, that only a selected portion of the people of God has been determined for salvation, yes, that the prediction concerned only a part of the descendants of Abraham (Rom. 9:6-13; 11:2-6), the true Israel, 'the Israel of God' (Gal. 6:16; I Cor. 10:18). These contradictory judgments are all to be understood as different opinions; but there can be no doubt that finally hope won the victory. In any case, Paul, in spite of his separation from his people, in spite of all the opposition he had to endure from them, remained loyal to them. His ever-renewed labor in the mission witnesses to this (I Cor. 9:20), but above all the Epistle to the Romans, in which he presents his Gospel in such a way that it cannot give offence to the Jews (cf. pp. 364ff).

Instructive from the view-point of religious history is the triple division which he outlines in I Cor. 10:32, when he places the Hellenes, the Jews, and the community of God side by side. Thus he gives a division of mankind according to religions, and the *tertium genus hominum*[27] of the Christians he separates sharply from both of the older groups.

[27] The expression appears first in Aristides (ch. 2) = *τρία γένη ἀνθρώπων ἐν τῷδε τῷ κόσμῳ*.

CHAPTER XXI

The Church

In acquainting ourselves, in this chapter, with Paul's views concerning the Church, its possessions, its functions and its tasks, we prepare the way for the following book in which the fundamental features of the life of the missionary communities and the beginnings of the Church will be presented. In the nature of the case it is impossible that the ideals and claims of the Apostle be understood without considering existing conditions; this chapter therefore will anticipate much that would naturally fall within the scope of the following book.

1. *The Church of God:* thus Paul designates the whole fellowship of Christians (I Cor. 10:32; 11:22?; 15:9; Gal. 1:13), and also the single community (I Cor. 1:2; 11:22?; II Cor. 1:1), a failure to make distinctions which is best explained by the fact that he also speaks of the 'churches of God' in the plural (I Cor. 11:16; I Thess. 2:14; II Thess. 1:4); once also of the 'Churches of Christ' (Rom. 16:16); [1] occasionally of 'Churches in (God the Father and the Lord) Christ Jesus' (II Thess. 1:1; I Thess. 1:1; 2:14; Gal. 1:22). Similarly the word 'Church' alone in the singular and also in the plural, occurs in reference to the single community; [2] but there are also many passages where 'ecclesia' is used as representing the totality of all Christians, as in I Cor. 12:28; Phil. 3:6; Col. 1:18,24. In this double usage there lies a problem which, despite a lively discussion, is not yet fully solved. The dispute is whether, in the thought of primitive Christianity, the idea of the Church as the totality of all Christians forms the starting point of the considera-

[1] This singular expression appears in an especially difficult passage; how can Paul say: "All the churches of Christ greet you"? This is somewhat different from the hyperbolic expression that all the Gentile churches thank Aquila and Priscilla (16:4); since it is assumed that 'all the churches' were in Paul's neighborhood, which of course is impossible. One might think that the deputation making the collection was regarded as consisting of representatives of 'all' Pauline churches, but even so the expression remains an almost impossible hyperbole.

[2] Singular: Rom. 16:1; I Cor. 6:4; 11:18; 14:4f,12,19,28,35; Phil. 4:15; Col. 4:16; I Thess 1:1; II Thess. 1:1. It is especially worthy of notice that he also occasionally speaks of 'the whole Church': Rom. 16:23; I Cor. 14:23. Plural: Rom. 16:4; I Cor. 16:1,19; II Cor. 8:1,19,23f; 11:8; Gal. 1:2,22; I Thess. 2:14; II Thess. 1:4. A group of passages which speak of 'all churches' (I Cor. 4:17; 7:17; 11:16; 14:33f; II Cor. 8:18; 11:28; 12:13) will be given special treatment later.

tion: and thus whether the single community is fundamentally only the 'appearance of the whole in the part'; or whether the consideration proceeds first from the single community and develops from this point to the formulation of the idea of the unified body of Christ —the Church. The question, as in most similar cases, can be answered only by looking into the previous history of the concept.

That the brotherhood of the 'saints' is designated by a word which in Greek means a 'gathering of the people,' emphasizing not the gathered *people*, but of course the action of *gathering*,[3] is in no way conclusive, but is nevertheless a very striking phenomenon; many other Greek expressions were available, as for example *thiasos, syllogos, eranos, synodos, koinon,* etc.[4] The choice is explained by the fact that the expression was taken from the Septuagint, but therein lies a high declaration of rights and an incisive value-judgment. As Christians call themselves 'saints' and thus lay claim to all the predictions (e.g. in the book of Daniel the 'saints of the Most High') that are accorded to the Jews, so their self-designation as the ecclesia of God asserts that they feel themselves to be the heirs of all the ideal rights of Israel, as being the 'Israel of God' (Gal. 6:16). A judgment rejecting the 'Israel after the flesh' (I Cor. 10:18) is implied, a judgment of the sharpest degree imaginable.[5] But this is fully expressed only where the entire phrase, 'Church of God,' is used. Here the Old Testament title 'community of Yahweh' is taken over with complete awareness of its implications. One may also attribute the fact that the expression 'synagogue,' which in any

[3] This is proved especially by the formula frequently found in inscriptions, ἔδοξεν τῷ δήμῳ ἐν ἐκκλησίᾳ, 'The people voted in assembly'; cf. *Gorg*. 456b, ἐν ἐκκλησίᾳ ἢ ἐν ἄλλῳ τινὶ σμλλόγῳ, 'in assembly or in a similar meeting.' This linguistic usage influences Paul also, when he designates the state of being in meeting with ἐν ἐκκλησίᾳ (I Cor. 11:18; 14:19,28,35); the opposite is 'at home,' I Cor. 11:34; 14:35; (παρ') ἑαυτῷ 14:28; 16:2 (Acts 19:39). Cf. B. Keil in *Einleitung in die Klass. Altertumswissenschaft* (Introduction to the Study of Classical Antiquity), iii, 338ff, 344ff.

[4] According to Schürer, the following designations are found for the communities of the Jewish Diaspora: οἱ Ἰουδαῖοι; πολίτευμα, κατοικία, λαός, ἔθνος, σύνοδος, συναγωγή. "Originally συναγωγή, like σύνοδος, is a meeting for a festival celebration, and also appears in this sense among Greek cult brotherhoods' (4th ed., ii, pp. 505f). From the meaning 'coming together,' 'congregation,' developed, as in σύνοδος, the meaning of 'church.' Thus the LXX also uses it frequently for עדה, an expression meaning the whole congregation of Israel. But in later times συναγωγή is the ruling body of the local community." Cf. Acts 6:9; 9:2, etc. According to the assumption of most critics, συναγωγή stands in Jas. 2:2, in place of ἐκκλησία; but in Jas. 5:14 ἐκκλησία appears. In general, the Fathers understood by συναγωγή the Jewish community and by ἐκκλησία the Christian; cf. Harnack's note on Hermas, Mand. 11:9.

[5] In Rev. 2:9; 3:9 it is expressed with the greatest force, "those who call themselves 'Jews' but are not."

case was available in the Septuagint, is wholly omitted in the oldest sources, to a desire of Christians to differentiate themselves from the Jews. Or could it be that *ecclesia* was really conceived of as the higher, more religious expression as opposed to *synagogue*, which perhaps designated rather the empirical community?[6]

In any case the expression, 'Church of God,' exalts the community of Christians far above the small associations of heathen groups and cult societies. It comprises a claim to being a great, organized community with a glorious past, and a no less splendid future. If further proof were needed that the new religion did not start as a group of conventicle cult-communities with a non-historical worship of a spiritualized vegetation god, save the fact that it consciously traced its descent back to a great world religion, the historical cult of the Jewish people, it would be found in just this self-designation.[7] Indeed so energetically is this connection asserted that by emphasizing the relationship to the one true God, the specifically Christian connection with the Lord Christ to a great degree recedes into the background. The expression, 'Church of the Lord,' is never found, and it would seem as if the most important things in the community were the avowal of monotheism and of the historical communion with the God of Israel, and not the relationship of servi-

[6] Schürer, 4th ed., ii, 504, note 1, "In the Christian sphere ἐκκλησία has certainly from the first, even from the time of St. Paul, maintained the supremacy. This contrast between the Jewish and Christian usage of language is at first sight strange, since no actual distinction is made in the Old Testament between συναγωγή and ἐκκλησία. The LXX put συναγωγή for עדה , and as a rule ἐκκλησία for קהל ; as the Targums do כנישתא for עדה, and generally קהלא for קהל . The former is used chiefly in the books of Exodus, Leviticus, Numbers and Joshua, the latter in Deuteronomy, First and Second Chronicles, Ezra and Nehemiah, both very frequently without real difference to designate the 'congregation' of Israel. Later Judaism, however, seems already to have made a distinction in the use of the two terms, and such a one that συναγωγή designated the congregation more on the side of its empirical reality, ἐκκλησία more on that of its ideal signification, συναγωγή being the 'associated' congregation, as constituted in some one place; ἐκκλησία on the other hand, the assembly of those called by God to salvation, especially like קהל , the ideal church of Israel (on קהל cf. in the Mishna, *Yebamoth* viii, 2; *Kiddushin* iv, 3; *Horayoth* 1, 4-5; *Yadayim* iv. 4). . . . Συναγωγή only expresses the empiric matter of fact, ἐκκλησία contains as well a dogmatic judgment of value. From this distinction between the terms which, as it seems, soon became a prevailing one even in Judaism, it is easily understood that Christian usage took possession almost exclusively of the latter expression."

[7] Harnack, *Mission* (1st ed.), p. 177: "This conviction that they were a people—i.e. the transference of all the prerogatives of the Jewish people to the new community viewed as a new creation which exhibited and put into force whatever was old and original in religion—this at once furnished adherents of the new faith with a political and historical self-consciousness."

tude to the Kyrios Christ. It is significant that this relationship is always denoted by the particular expression 'servants of Christ,' while on the other hand, where reference is made to the organized body, nearly always (except Rom. 16:16; p. 482, n. 1; I Thess. 1:1; 2:14; II Thess. 1:1 and Gal. 1:22) God is preferred as the unifying point. So strongly does the consciousness of the inheritance of Israel operate! [8] And yet, too great emphasis should not be placed upon 'people,' [9] nor should the interpretation 'the gathering of the people' be too strongly pressed: the word actually has an essentially cultic significance from the Old Testament. Because later Israel was in fact a national community and at the same time a cult-community, or because here nationality and the honoring of God fully coincided, so the designation 'ecclesia' has something of the meaning of our word *congregation* or even *church.* So much the less may this word be disregarded when, in later Judaism, especially in the diaspora, a phenomenon appears [10] which can be characterized most accurately by the word 'church.' The separation of religion from the life of the Jewish national state, begun in the time of the Exile, accelerated at the period of the Herodian and Roman rule, greatly expedited by the diaspora and completed by the destruction of the Temple in Jerusalem, finally produced a structure which in many respects was the model for the Christian Church which was in process of formation. Many devout ones scattered over the whole world, numerous local communities held together by like religious duties and possessions, by common recollections and hopes, gathered around an ideal center, formerly the Temple in Jerusalem, now the heavenly Zion. They still constituted a nation—though that nation of course was extended beyond its natural constituency by the addition of the proselytes, but it was no longer a political entity. If it continued to call itself the 'community of Yahweh,' the word ecclesia had lost the last touch of political significance; and if the Christians took over the concept they could do so because it had already been stamped with a religious character, and also because it really desig-

[8] This fact is an important corrective of Bousset's view (pp. 105,107): "The correlative to the κύριος Χριστός is in all expressions of primitive Christian worship which we have enumerated, not the individual but the church, the ἐκκλησία, the σῶμα τοῦ Χριστοῦ and, of course, above all, the individual church organized for divine service." Several question marks could be placed after this. Cf. also (pp. 455ff) what is said concerning the meaning of the Kyrios-name.

[9] The expression 'people of God' appears only in Paul in quotations: Rom. 9:25; II Cor. 6:16; otherwise only in Tit. 2:14; I Pet. 2:9f (quotation); Rev. 21:3 and Heb. 4:9, also as an addition to a quotation.

[10] Bousset, *Religion des Judentums,* 2d ed., pp. 60ff.

nated the thing which it was meant to designate, viz. a religious fellowship independent of racial ties.

In accordance with this idea then, the expression doubtless designates first the totality of all Christians. This is comprehensible also from the viewpoint of historical development. Originally, the Church of God in Palestine was gathered together in limited space (I Cor. 15:9); then it spread out and sent out colonies which, however, were still closely connected with itself for the most part. There is some justification therefore in declaring the universal concept of 'ecclesia' to be the primary significance, and the single organizations to be reflections of the one ecclesia of God. When the phrase appears (as e.g. in I Cor. 1:2) 'the Church of God which is in Corinth,' one is indeed tempted to understand first 'the great total community in so far as it appears in Corinth.' But such an import would not seem compatible with Paul's use of language. If he had so understood the expression he would not have formed the plural: 'Churches of God.' It represents of course an entirely different literary usage and an entirely different view which stands counter to that ideal and universal one. One might imagine that the separate cities had set the example of calling separate communities 'ecclesiai'; however there are other and better analogies. Indeed in Judaism we observe a parallel procedure by which the separate local community is also designated by the same expression [11] as the whole community, namely as a synagogue.[12] On the whole this example suffices to explain the Christian literary usage. There may have been another motive for the preference of the word 'ecclesia' over 'synagogue' in addition to those reasons previously presented (p. 616)—viz. that Greek associations here and there also called themselves 'ecclesiai,' [13] and that in the Septuagint 'ecclesiai' also occasionally occurs in the sense

[11] It is very instructive in this connection that the Jewish military colony on the Island of Elephantine, of which the so-called *Assuan Papyri* make mention, is called עדה (cf. Ed. Meyer, *Der Papyrusfund von Elephantine*, p. 31) and of course the word is used here in a special military sense; but because the Jews living there have a temple, they also form a cult-community (Ed. Meyer, *op. cit.*, p. 37).

[12] Thus in an inscription from Phocaea: ἡ συναγωγὴ ἐτείμησεν τῶν Ἰουδαίων; especially in Roman epitaphs (Schürer, 4th ed., iii, 82): a συναγωγὴ Αὐγουστησίων, a σ. Ἀγριππησίων, Βολουμνησίων, Καμπησίων, Σιβουρησίων, Ἑβραίων, Βερνακλησίων or Βερνακλώρων *(vernaculorum)*, Ἐλαίας (of the olive tree), Καλκαρησίων (lime burners). These are all independent, organized communities, each with its own synagogue, government and community officials. "There is no trace of a unified organization of the whole of Roman Jewry under *one* γερουσία."

[13] Cf. Liebenam, *Römisches Vereinswesen*, pp. 272f.

of separate meetings.[14] Furthermore one may observe more prosaically that in 'ecclesia' there is implied (as in 'synagogue') the idea of a 'meeting in one place.' One might, by doing violence to the expression, insist upon the ideal sense of the word by saying that Christians of all places, at all times, were gathered, so to speak, before the face of God to worship—but this somewhat ingenious fiction had to yield before the daily evidence that only the local brotherhood appeared definitely thus assembled.

Ecclesia therefore finally becomes a particular designation for the organized local church. Often there is a feeling for ideal, religious meaning, as is shown by the insertion of the genitive, 'of God,' or the mystical, 'in God and Christ Jesus' (I Thess. 1:1; 2:14; Gal. 1:22); but just as often this is far in the background when Paul regards the actual church with all its faults, imperfect as it is, which he often defines yet more closely by geographical additions ('of Galatia,' 'of Asia'). This usage of terminology operates most strikingly when mention is made of 'house churches' (I Cor. 16:19; Rom. 16:5; Col. 4:15; ἡ κατ' οἶκον αὐτῶν [αὐτῆς] ἐκκλησία). Here where small circles are under consideration, the word 'ecclesia' would be unsuitable if it necessarily retained the full meaning of 'national community' or 'national meeting.' Here it appears in the full sense of a local cult-gathering, with an almost conventional flavor. When, in contrast to this, mention is made of future gatherings of the 'whole Church' (Rom. 16:23; I Cor. 14:23)—although even here only the local community is meant, especially when the Apostle speaks of 'all the churches' (Rom. 16:16; I Cor. 4:17; 7:17; 14:33; II Cor. 8:18; 12:13), instead, for example, of the 'Church' as a whole—it is also plain that the universal meaning of the expression strongly recedes into the background in favor of the local. It appears again in the letter to the Colossians and especially in that to the Ephesians, but here the concept has become the subject of speculation. Such a

[14] Ps. 25 (26): 4f: *οὐκ ἐκάθισα μετὰ συνεδρίου ματαιότητος*
καὶ μετὰ παρονομούντων οὐ μὴ εἰσέλθω,
ἐμίσησα ἐκκλησίαν πονηρευομένων
καὶ μετὰ ἀσεβῶν οὐ μὴ καθίσω.
"I have not sat with men of falsehood;
Neither will I go in with dissemblers.
I hate the assembly of evil-doers,
And will not sit with the wicked."

The parallelism between *συνέδριον* and *ἐκκλησία* gives the concept a connotation pertaining to conventicles. In vs. 12 we read: *ἐν ἐκκλησίαις εὐλογήσω σε Κύριε*, 'In congregations I will bless thee, Lord,' as if the word thus, without any addition, could designate nothing but the lawful Jewish gathering for divine service, and of course the temporary and individual one, not merely the local gathering.

speculation would certainly not be possible if the ideal were entirely forgotten. However this is not the case.

It is clear that the possessors of the Spirit whom God 'has installed in the Church' (I Cor. 12:28) are considered as organs of the whole community; that the contrast of the community of God with the Jews and Greeks (I Cor. 10:32) does not refer only to the Corinthian community, and that the persecution of the Church of God (Gal. 1:13; I Cor. 15:9) is not to be thought of as simply being geographically limited: the question of course is that of a struggle against a principle. Above all the idea of the 'Body of Christ' is conceived and developed in universal terms (Rom. 12:4; I Cor. 12:12-27; Col. 1:18,24; 3:15). The Epistle to the Colossians is not the first to contain teaching of a speculative character; it is to be found also in the First Epistle to the Corinthians.

There is employed here an exceedingly frequent rhetorical commonplace found in Graeco-Roman literature, especially in the Stoic diatribe.[15] It is instructive, however, to note how the figure takes a different form in Paul's hands. Instead of naturally existing unity (whether in the state or in the human-divine community) there comes into existence here a new organism, in a supernatural 'mystical' way, because Christ, by the outpouring of the Spirit (and this means at the same time the effluence of his own being) has united his own people with himself and with one another into one being (Gal. 3:28; cf. pp. 463f): "Filled with one Spirit, we were baptized into one Body" (I Cor. 12:13)—one Body is the result. One must never press too far the significance of such metaphors in Paul; but obviously one should enlarge upon this figure somewhat: as the same blood passes through all the arteries of the body and thus establishes

[15] Cf. my Commentary on I Cor. 12:12ff. Especially important for us here is the comparison of a state government with the body in Josephus, *B.J.*, iv. 7. 2, §§ 406f or with human *societas,* Cicero *De. Off.* iii, 5; Seneca, *De Ira,* ii, 31; of the greatest importance are the cases where the image is applied to the great unity between gods and men, e.g. Seneca, *Ep.* 95:52: *omne hoc, quod vides, quo divina et humana inclusa sunt, unum est: membra sumus corporis magni. Natura nos cognatos redidit, cum ex isdem et in eadem gigneret. Haec nobis amorem indidit mutuum et sociabiles fecit.* ("All that you see, that which comprises both god and man, is one, we are the parts of one great body. Nature produced us related to one another, since also she created us from the same source and to the same end. She engendered in us mutual affection, and made us prone to friendships.") Cf. also Marcus Aurelius, 2:1; 7:13, *οἷόν ἐστιν ἐν ἡνωμένοις τὰ μέλη τοῦ σώματοσ*, "Such as are the members of the body in unified beings," so among separate beings are *τὰ λογικά* related one to another, *πρὸς μίαν τινὰ συνεργίαν κατεσκευασμένα* . . . . *μέλος εἰμὶ τοῦ ἐκ λογικῶν συστήματος*. . . , "Prepared for some one work in common . . . . I am a part of the complex whole of intellects . . ." Sextus, *Adv. Math.*, ix, 78f (cf. my Commentary on I Cor., p. 307).

the unity of the organic life, so this Body is thus a complete unity, so that the same Spirit unites all members with one another and with Christ. The figure is then developed in two different directions: according to I Cor. 12:12,27, Christ himself is the body, as also in Gal. 3:28: "Ye are all one in Christ," i.e. since ye are in Christ, a new being has come into existence. In the Epistle to the Colossians, on the other hand (and in Ephesians), Christ appears as the head of the Body. By the head (according to a naïve conception) the whole body is not only held together but also supplied with the nourishment of life (Col. 2:19).[16] But Paul is never satisfied with the mystical figure and turns at once to the ethical, especially in Rom. 12:4, and also in the Epistle to the Colossians, while the author of the Epistle to the Ephesians develops the speculation further.

2. *The Community and the Spirit.* From this representation of the community as a unitary organism, based upon supersensual operations, there follow various decisions and commands of the Apostle which are important not only for his religious view-point, but also for the practice of his communities. First it appears from I Cor. 12:13 that membership in the community does not depend so much upon the mere wish to join, nor upon external measures such as the paying of a contribution or an entrance fee, as upon the wholly supersensual experience of the conferring of the Spirit in baptism. In this experience the 'calling' is completed and the 'election' (I Cor. 1:26ff) receives visible expression. The implication of this mode of thought is that baptism is less an act of the individual[17] than an experience in which he is entirely receptive and almost passive. According to this idea it would be impossible for anyone to be baptized who does not belong to the elect. There is never a thought of a possible situation in which the baptism of many Christians is only an empty ceremony undertaken perhaps in the hope of gaining unworthy aims. This indicates not only the unexampled obscurity of the enthusiastic period of the beginnings of the Church, but this

[16] Seneca, De Clem., ii, 2, 1: *a capite bona valitudo in omnes (exit: omnia) vegeta sunt atque erecta aut languore demissa, prout animus eorum vivit aut marcet.* ("It is from the head that comes the health of the body; it is through it that all the parts are lively and alert or languid and drooping according as their animating spirit has life or withers.")

[17] The Jewish expression, 'to baptize oneself,' (cf. p. 631, note 27) appears only once, I Cor. 10:2 *ἐβαπτίσαντο*; otherwise it is always passive, or in any case as in I Cor. 6:11, middle, *ἀπελούσασθε*: 'you have washed yourselves' or 'permitted yourselves to be washed.'

conception, seemingly all too idealistic, seems to have had its basis and support in a rather realistic rule of which traces are still present.

One must thus ask oneself the question: upon what is the assumption that the conferring of the Spirit was regularly connected with baptism actually based? Was it merely a sanguine, optimistic assumption, a faith without sight, as in the case of baptism today, that with the pouring of water or laying on of hands the baptized absorbs the Spirit of God? Or are there distinct proofs or signs of this? In whatever way this question is put, the other question at once thrusts itself to the fore: which is primary in the relationship, baptism or the reception of the Spirit (I Cor. 6:11; 12:13)? Is it perhaps the descent of the Spirit, as in the case of Cornelius (Acts 10:44,47), or the baptism itself, as in Jerusalem (Acts 2:38) and in Samaria (Acts 8:12,15)? Here is presented a problem which has not been sufficiently studied. The three passages in the Acts of the Apostles reflect the development of the idea most instructively. The oldest entirely enthusiastic and supernatural conception is as follows: By sending down the Spirit upon men God shows that he has chosen them (cf. Rom. 5:5; Gal. 4:6; 3:2); here baptism must follow this heavenly indication and carry out in an earthly manner that which God has already determined. The second step is found in Acts 2:38; it is firmly hoped that he who has been baptized will also receive the Spirit. But it is very striking that in a following verse (2:41), although it is recorded that three thousand souls were baptized and that they 'were added,' no further mention is made of the reception of the Spirit. This takes place however in a most striking manner in Acts 19:5f, after it is said, to be sure, that Paul laid his hands upon the baptized: "The Holy Spirit came upon them, and they spoke with tongues." This is the transition to the third step (Acts 8:12,15ff), according to which baptism which is performed by one of the Seven does not of itself mediate the reception of the Spirit, which is accomplished only by prayer and the laying on of the hands of *the Apostles*. Therefore baptism by another Christian does not suffice; it is an Apostle who, by laying on his hands, works the miracle. Which stage in this development does Paul represent? It is indeed significant that he often speaks of the conferring of the Spirit as a proof of the love and grace of God, as a seal of God's adoption (Rom. 5:5; Gal. 4:6; II Cor. 1:21ff), without reference to baptism: the sign of membership in Christ is the Spirit (Rom. 8:9); that is to say essentially he stands for the oldest, supernatural, charismatic form of the idea.[18] This is especially indicated by a phenomenon which has not yet received sufficient attention.

In I Cor. 14:23 the hearers of the discourses delivered at divine service are referred to as 'laymen' and 'unbelievers.' These are not the same, but are obviously different groups. The 'laymen' (ἰδιῶται) are especially mentioned (I Cor. 14:16) as regular participants in the meetings, where they apparently have regularly marked-off places and join in saying the *Amen*, while the 'unbelievers' are not mentioned. Who are these 'laymen,' *idiotai?* According to fixed Greek literary usage a layman is one who does not hold a definite rank or office in connection with a particular specialty, be it an art or an activity; in contrast with the artist or scholar he is a layman; as opposed to the soldier, the citizen, the official or ruler, he is a private person. In connection with I Cor. 14, the layman can only be the one who does not possess the above-mentioned gift of speaking in tongues. All other members of the community could of course be styled laymen. But since the laymen, like the unbelievers, appear to be guests of the church (I Cor. 14:23), they remain one degree removed from the church beyond the other Christians, and also a degree nearer than the 'unbelievers.' They form a middle group between the unbelievers and the community, a kind of proselyte or catechumen group, if we may use this latter expression here. The non-possession of the Spirit, a distinguishing mark, is hinted at rather than stated, for the very reason that they do not fully belong to the church.[19] If this be correct we arrive at the

[18] He himself, of course, doubtless, had become conscious of his pardon and of his calling *before* he had undergone baptism. "In the case of Paul himself, the baptism was, in any case, not the decisive thing, but the Christophany on the road to Damascus" (Deissmann, *Paulus*, p. 89).

[19] The word appears in a religious sense: Inscription, in Foucart, No. 2: ἐὰν δέ τις θύῃ τῶν ὀργεώνων οἶς μέτεστιν τοῦ ἱεροῦ, ἀτελεῖς αὐτοὺς θύειν ἂν δὲ ἰδιώτης (i.e. one who is not a companion of the cult society) θύῃ τῷ θεῷ διδόναι τῇ ἱερέᾳ. . . . "If any one of the priests who have a claim to the temple shall sacrifice, it shall be free of charge, but if a layman . . ." Inscription from Andania (Michel, No. 694, p. 597 = Ditt., *Syll.*, 635) 16ff. οἱ τελούμενοι τὰ μυστήρια . . . . καὶ αἱ μὲν ἰδιώτιες ἐχόντω χιτῶνα . . . . παῖδες . . . . δοῦλοι . . . . αἱ δὲ ἱεραῖ. "Those who are perfect in the mysteries . . . . and the laymen shall have a chiton . . . . servants . . . . slaves . . . . but the priestesses." Theodoret explains ἰδιῶται through the use of ἀμύητοι; Severian *(Catena)* through τὸν μὴ βαπτισθέντα. The Valentinians (Ptolemaeus) despise the members of the great churches, who detest their sexual mysteries, ὡς ἰδιωτῶν καὶ μηδὲν ἐπισταμένων, ἑαυτοὺς δὲ ὑπερυψοῦσι, τελείους ἀποκαλοῦντες καὶ σπέρματα ἐκλογῆς 'as being utterly contemptible and ignorant persons, while they highly exalt themselves and claim to be perfect and the elect seed' (Irenaeus, i. 6. 4); here there appears the antithesis of ἰδιῶται and τέλειοι which, in a certain measure, is also presumed by Paul when he places the τέλειοι (I Cor. 2:6) on equal footing with the true 'pneumatikoi' (I Cor. 3:1). Cf. Origen, *Contra Celsum*, 1:12, οἱ μὲν Αἰγυπτίων σοφοὶ

following picture: a person eager for salvation comes to church as a guest-hearer, in general sympathy with the message of salvation, and is allowed to attend the meetings regularly and is assigned a regular though perhaps somewhat secluded place. But in the meanwhile he is not baptized. For what is he waiting? For the signs of the Spirit which have not yet appeared in him.

This of course implies confidence in the ability to recognize by outward perceptible signs whether or not anyone possessed the Spirit. Here appears the older, enthusiastic view, viz. that the workings of the Spirit are revealed in special performances and powers: in inspired ebullitions, outpourings of speech, ecstasies, miraculous perceptions, heroic acts and amazing impressions upon others, e.g. in unmasking or driving out demons, in healing sicknesses and the like. It further follows that the conferring of the Spirit was not at first necessarily connected with the sacramental act of baptism: it proceeds in its own characteristic manner. To be sure, it may often have coincided with it, e.g. when, after an enthusiastic, inspiring speech by the Apostle (I Thess. 1:5f) the workings of the Spirit at once manifested themselves, and at that moment baptism was demanded and performed. There may have been mass conversions in which whole families, households, all retainers of influential men, whole masses of those who had heard the preaching, carried away by impressive occurrences, were baptized and inspired so that it was almost impossible to discern whether the Spirit had demanded the baptism or the baptism had brought the Spirit. But just as often there must have been quieter and therefore not so strikingly obvious cases when, although there was a willing disposition, one first waited for the spiritual development to take place and postponed baptism. Here there lies concealed a practical problem concerning the solution of which we know only this: that the development finally ended in a victory for baptism; it became more and more the actually decisive step, and one trusted that it included the Spirit. In proportion as enthusiasm ebbed, in proportion as the view of Paul prevailed, viz. that the Spirit is above all the force of a moral regeneration, a mighty, irresistible power of course, but nevertheless one which worked primarily in silence and invisibility—in that same

κατὰ τὰ πάτρια γράμματα πολλὰ φιλοσοφοῦσι περὶ τῶν παρ' αὐτοῖς νενομισμένων θείων, οἱ δὲ ἰδιῶται μύθους τινὰς ἀκούοντες, ὧν τοὺς λόγους ἐπίστανται, μέγα ἐπ' αὐτοῖς φρονοῦσιν, "The Egyptian savants, learned in their country's literature, are greatly given to philosophizing about those things which are regarded among them as divine, while the vulgar, hearing certain myths, the reason of which they do not understand, are greatly elated because of their fancied knowledge."

proportion baptism would have been granted only upon the resolution and solemn vow of those who participated in it, who had given evidence of their faith in the preaching of the Gospel and of their will to lead a new life. We cannot observe this procedure in detail; we can only infer here *a clash between the principles of enthusiastic, supernatural religion and that of organized, pedagogical religion.* In the long run it certainly proved impractical to wait for an extraordinary sign of the Spirit in the case of each proselyte; it was finally necessary to accept all kinds of people if one did not wish to give up propaganda and expansion in the hope that the Spirit would do his work after the baptized person had been received into the organism of the Church.

Another problem is closely related to this. "He who has not the Spirit of Christ is none of his," the Apostle says in Rom. 8:9. That all Christians have received the Spirit is the hypothesis of the whole doctrine of redemption (cf. e.g. Rom. 5:5; 8:29,11-16,23; I Cor. 12:13; Gal. 3:2-5; 5:18,25; I Thess. 1:6; 4:8). But in addition to this we come upon still another literary usage, according to which only individuals provided with particular gifts of grace, especially those who speak in tongues (I Cor. 14:37), are called 'spiritual persons.' Thus alongside the one Spirit which permeates all Christians there are the separate 'spirits of the prophets' (I Cor. 14:14, 32). The latter is an age-old animistic view, according to which a spirit sent from God enters the prophet (a *ruach,* 'breath'; cf. I Kings 22:21f). This conception however is also a remnant of an ancient idea which Paul has essentially overcome: [20] if the Spirit of God is perceptible only in particular performances of power on the part of individuals, the picture here is that of a stormy, fitful influence of supernatural forces which seize a person from time to time and use him as an instrument. But we also observe at the same time how this older view begins to change. This operation is not necessarily restricted to definite individual persons, and it is entirely natural if, for example, now this man and now that man receives revelations involuntarily and intermittently (I Cor. 14:30). When Paul, in his enumeration of the charismata, mentions not only the abstract gifts such as 'powers, gifts of healing, speaking with tongues,' but also persons such as 'Apostles, prophets and teachers' (I Cor. 12:28), it indicates that particular gifts are attached permanently to particular individuals so that the idea of a

[20] Cf. H. Gunkel, *Die Wirkungen des heiligen Geistes* (The Operations of the Holy Spirit).

temporary seizure by supernatural powers changes to that of a permanent 'gift.'[21] The concept is completely changed when mention is made of the 'indwelling' of the Spirit (Rom. 8:9,11), of the lifelong control of the Spirit (Rom. 8:4f). But the older, enthusiastic conception still occasionally recurs: 'to be driven by the Spirit' (Rom. 8:14; Gal. 5:18), ecstatic crying in the Spirit (Rom. 8:15; Gal. 4:6); moreover the Spirit of God is mentioned alongside the spirit of man (Rom. 8:16), as if a double spirit dwelt in him. But on the whole we see Paul on the way toward considering the entire inner life of the Christian in all its expressions, as permeated by the Spirit, so that the human spirit seems to be absorbed by the divine. At the judicial action (I Cor. 5:4)[22] against the man accused of incestuous fornication, when the statement is made that besides the power of the Lord Jesus Christ the spirit of the Apostle ('my spirit') is present and operative, there is no notion that it is only the memory of Paul and not the natural human spirit of the Apostle which abides among them. It is much more: the Apostle's will, completely filled with the Spirit, furnished with divine power, will be with them, coöperating with the power of Christ. And if the condition of the Christian life is called a 'newness of the spirit' (Rom. 7:6), if the Christian henceforth consists of 'spirit and flesh,' if he 'lives in the Spirit,' 'after the Spirit,' the picture is the same: the divine Spirit has completely merged himself with his inner being. It is all the more evident that, according to this idea, every Christian is a *pneumatikos* (Gal. 6:1), and not only particular individuals.

There is however still another point of view (I Cor. 2:6-16; 3:1ff). The 'spiritual man' appears in these passages as the lonely gnostic, understood by no one, responsible to no one; but most of the people of the church cannot yet be considered spiritual (although they *should* be spiritual)—they are still fleshly: "Ye are still 'men' and walk 'after the manner of men' "; ye who unreceptively and ignorantly oppose that which comes from the Spirit of God are still 'psychical' (pp. 608f); only a minority belong to the spiritual ones, 'the perfect,' to whom spiritual gifts can be imparted. Whatever this expression may mean, or whencesoever it comes,[23] it

[21] This process becomes complete in the development of the theory in the Pastoral Epistles, where the charismata appear not only as enduring gifts (I Tim. 4:14), but seem to be so fused with the spiritual uniqueness of the bearer that one can speak of 'stirring up' the charisma (II Tim. 1:6) as if it were a personal trait. In such cases Paul would urge that one should pray for a charisma (I Cor. 14:13).

[22] Cf. my Commentary, *ad loc.*

[23] The problem is not yet fully solved; cf. my Commentary on I Cor., p. xviii, note, and on 3:3, pp. 73ff. While W. Bauer understands the τέλειος as a mature,

is at any rate an idea and a literary usage which does not exactly fit in with that conception of the spiritual *church* (I Cor. 3:16), and has its origin in an entirely different environment in which the gnostic or spiritual man is the *individual*, endowed with grace as contrasted with the mass of men. This conception, transplanted into Paul's field of thought, leads to a contradiction which cannot be wholly resolved. It appears in the beginning of I Cor. 3. The reproach contained in verse 3, "ye are still carnal, ye walk as men, are still nothing more than men," can be understood thus: "In actuality you should all be spiritual, and you must endeavor gradually to become so; you should also become 'perfect.' " While he confronts them with the 'perfect,' he speaks as if the ideal could be attained by growing into the sphere of the Spirit, as if the possibility of spiritual growth depended upon the will of man. Here the Gnostic ideal of the spiritual man becomes democratized, but at the same time transposed into a totally different key. A condition in which, according to this viewpoint, all Christians should share, naturally can no longer be purely miraculous or supernatural to the same degree. We have previously observed that alongside the purely supernatural conception, that of 'being driven by the Spirit,' there appears another and more ethical view, viz. that the Christian, by *giving* himself to the Spirit, shall *permit* himself to be driven by him. This interposition of a more psychological or volitional way of thinking permits us to recognize fully that the statements to the effect that all Christians possessed the Spirit, all were spiritual, was an idealistic view, soaring beyond reality, which must often have contradicted the hard realities of life. Here two entirely different series of facts and modes of thought clash with one another. On the one hand there

grown-up person, others (as Reitzenstein, *Mysterienreligionen,* pp. 165ff) perceive echoes of the Mysteries. I myself, on the other hand, have decided on the influence of a Stoic literary usage (cf. p. 576, note). But even then the question is not fully answered. It does seem that Paul had found the concept τέλειος = πνευματικός in some sort of connection with the Mystery religions, but that he had changed it, under the influence of a Stoic literary usage, so that it had a more ethical connotation. Irenaeus, speaking of the Valentinians, says: "For this reason, they tell us that it is necessary for us whom they call animal (ψύχικοὺς) men, and describe as being of the world, to practise continence and good works, that by this means we may attain at length to the intermediate habitation, but to them who are called 'the spiritual and perfect' (πνευματικός τε καὶ τελείοις) such a course of conduct is not at all necessary. For it is not conduct of any kind which leads into the Pleroma, but the seed sent forth thence in a feeble, immature state, and here brought to perfection (τελειούμενον)." Cf. also i. 6. 1; 13. 6. In the latter passage the τέλειοι are the ones who have the highest degree of knowledge. This last consideration differs from Paul, in that with him, τελειότης appears as a *condition* for receiving the highest knowledge, but it nevertheless is present *in* the very receiving of this knowledge.

are extraordinary prophetic personalities in the Church, like Paul, who are leaders, and who, in contrast with the whole group, regard themselves as lonely yet especially favored (I Cor. 2:14f). On the other hand these leaders insist upon judging the community according to their own qualities, and either presume in good faith that the masses undergo the same experiences as themselves, or heroically demand of them the same standards, standards which they are actually unable to put into practice. From this situation result two very different views of the Church itself: on the one hand Christianity considers itself to be something supernatural, laid hold on by God, redeemed, united into a community, blessed with all the powers of the Spirit. On the other hand there is still present the empirical fact, viz. that the community came into existence by the voluntary coalition of a great number of people possessed of ethical qualities and religious fervor in quite different degrees. The lofty ideal concept of the 'Church of the saints' concurs with the fact of a very earthly, variegated community which, though held together by high ideals and hopes, as well as by common experiences, nevertheless still shows in detail very different gradations of holiness and 'spirituality'—and this is an eternal conflict which has persisted through the whole history of the Church and has called forth many upheavals, reforms and divisions.

The conflict of modes of thought and the differences of gradation within the Church are still purely imaginary in Paul's time, and we must resist energetically the temptation to conceive the 'perfect' (I Cor. 2:6) as perhaps being an actually separate group of mature Christian churchmen, the elite among the 'pneumatics,' so to speak, in contrast with the mass of 'psychics' who would possibly be placed on the same level as the 'laity' (I Cor. 14:16). Although the latter group is divided distinctly from the former as a kind of group of proselytes separate from baptized Christians, yet it is also true that there is lacking any clear-cut and especial proof of a real distinction between two kinds of Christians within the Church. This does not exclude the fact that Paul occasionally held meetings with the 'perfect' (I Cor. 2:6) in contrast with meetings of the 'whole Church' (I Cor. 14:23). But the distinction between the two groups is, like all the ideas of this sort, a fluctuating one, less organizational than idealistic.

3. *The Sacraments.* That Paul knows of two sacred rites in the Church, and *only* two, is seen from the remarkable fact that in I Cor. 10:1-5 he traces them back typologically to the story of the

wanderings in the wilderness. The parallelism of members which is carried out here (baptism in the cloud, and in the sea; divine food and drink) shows that the two together form in his mind a unity in some sense, a unity which includes especially high favors which were vouchsafed then, as now, to the people of God. Thus they occupy a unique place alongside previous charismata as being extraordinary arrangements, supernatural in a special sense.

(a) *Baptism*, which Paul regarded as something divinely given—he himself was baptized—he took over from the Hellenistic Church (p. 177). Even the interpretation of this act, which he also occasionally expounds, he considers as universally known and acknowledged, even in the Roman community with which he was unacquainted (Rom. 6:3ff). We may not therefore consider these ideas (pp. 520f) as being original with him; he deals with them as he does with other universally Christian ideas.

Among the various interpretations of the traditional rite, that which is uppermost is the view of baptism as an act of *purification*, a washing-away of sins (I Cor. 6:11: you have been washed, or have permitted yourselves to be washed). Although one used to attribute the modern Protestant, symbolical conception of the act to Paul, it is strongly emphasized today that he regarded this washing as being completely real. In fact, according to ancient ideas, 'water can really do very great things.'[24] Since sin in the ancient oriental and Old Testament view[25] involves an uncleanness

[24] Cf. Konstantin Hartte, *Zum semitischen Wasser-Kultus* (The Semitic Water Cult), Tübingen dissertation, 1912, especially pp. 59-87; Wilhelm Brandt, *Die jüdischen Baptismen* (Jewish Baptisms), pp. 1-8 and elsewhere, e.g. p. 88.

[25] 'Sin' is here used only as a convenient abbreviation. In fact the lustrations are for many different things, e.g. infection by the 'holy.' "The holiness of higher beings infects by their touch, and even by their near presence, and infects men as well as things. . . . Outside the sphere of these divine beings their holiness would, however, certainly inflict damage and would indeed act in a destructive manner: therefore it is necessary on stepping out of their reach . . . . that one rid oneself of holiness." "Another phenomenon is . . . . that it was believed that in certain bodily conditions, e.g. sickness or sexual states, one was receptive more than ever to the influence of spirits, or to gods and their dangerous holiness. At such a time one protects oneself before taking up again the daily associations with the world of men; he protects both them and himself by purifications." In proportion as faith in the unique holiness of Yahweh penetrates, "the other gods and spirits of the dead are considered unclean, and he who has entered into relationship with them has 'defiled' himself and needs purification if he wishes to draw again into communion with Yahweh. . . . From this it would appear that the words קדש, טהר, טמא, which we may translate from the Hebrew as 'holy,' 'clean,' and 'unclean,' and which in certain other Semitic languages mean 'bright,' 'polished,' 'clean,' and 'contaminated,' 'dirty,' seem to indicate that holiness, among the Semites and consequently among the Israelites also, was conceived very early as being an external condition, a material something which adhered to the

attached to the body, there is need of bodily cleansing before a person can again approach the Deity. Intercourse with heathenism is considered especially polluting, according to the Jewish conception;[26] thus when a proselyte became a Jew he was compelled to undergo immersion.[27] This proselyte baptism which followed upon circumcision was very likely the prototype which was actually determinative for the Christian churches of Jewish-Hellenistic origin when they undertook to baptize those who came over from heathenism, circumcision being omitted. The only question is how it came about that former Jews, e.g. Paul, were baptized. It is difficult to assume that this was a reactionary generalization of proselyte baptism. In that case we would have to assume a permanent influence of the baptism of John. This, however, had a somewhat different meaning than did proselyte baptism, for it was administered to Jews living under the Law and could not thus be taken in the strict sense as being a purification after demoniacal defilement. Nor could it be compared with the customary ablutions after defilement, since it is plainly regarded as an act performed once and for all.[28] Its *messianic* character is clear: he who is baptized may hope to escape the wrath to come (Matt. 3:7; Luke 3:7). Since repentance (μετάνοια) is mentioned (Matt. 3:8; Luke 3:8; Mark 1:15) as being an indispensable condition of this salvation; since, furthermore, baptism is called a 'baptism of repentance' (Mark 1:4; Luke 3:3; Acts 13:24; 19:4), or 'for' repentance (Matt. 3:11), it was in any case considered by Christian tradition—quite correctly—as a *sign* of moral and religious reformation. Though the idea of a sacramental purification from sins may have been included; though even the mystical interpretation of striving and being born again may have been injected into it (pp. 172f), there was also contained in

body. Bathing and washing for the removal of a condition of tabu correspond to this theory especially, and must naturally lead to its gradual dominance if such washing takes the most prominent place among rites" (W. Brandt).

[26] Ez. 36:25, "I will sprinkle clean water upon you, and ye shall be clean (καθαρισθήσεσθε); from all your uncleanness and from all your idols I will cleanse you."

[27] W. Brandt, pp. 57-62, "A man is circumcised, and after the wound has healed is led to baptism. While he stands in the water, the rabbis, who stand by as witnesses, declare to him once more some of the greater and lesser commandments. Then the candidate immerses himself completely in the water and rises out of it a complete Israelite" (according to Bab. Talmud, *Yebamoth,* fol. 45-47). [Cf. F. Gavin, *Jewish Antecedents of the Christian Sacraments.*]

[28] According to Josephus also (*Ant.* xviii. 5. 2, § 117), Baptism did not take place for the 'putting away of individual misdemeanors'—was not, therefore, to be placed on the same level as the Jewish washings for purification—but assumes a soul 'previously purified through righteousness.'

it in every case a moral note: a resolution or vow of repentance. One must not give a one-sided interpretation: in such a rite, especially when it is not newly created but depends on old forms, manifold motives, moods, interpretations and new meanings play a part. Thus from the beginning, at least among Christians, the sacramental and the ethical will both have operated; however, where the ethical interpretation predominates, the act of baptism will be only too readily dissolved in symbolism. If, with this in view, one evaluates the chief passage which is relevant, I Cor. 6:11, one sees that the idea is present beyond doubt, that Christians have had their sins washed away, i.e. it is a sacramental idea of purification; but at the same time the ethical motive is present: "Ye were once" sinners; you should have nothing more to do with those things which lie in the past; he thus makes an appeal to the pride and the moral wills of the baptized. In the same sentence occur the words, "Ye have indeed been justified." Whether one refers this to the forgiveness of sins or to justification, or rather to an actual process of becoming righteous,[29] in any case the Apostle thinks of an effect in connection with baptism which is not included in the simple conception of sacramental purification.[30] For Paul certainly does not consider that the forgiveness of sins (or the failure to reckon them) as well as the actual inner change of the will and of the moral faculty, as he elsewhere describes it, is accomplished by the immersion or washing, but by quite other factors. Justification is granted because of the faith which is expressed by this transaction; the new righteousness is the effect of the Holy Spirit imparted (but see pp. 622f) at baptism. The two experiences are more often referred to than not without any reference to baptism, as if this were not at all necessary. Generally speaking, baptism recedes almost so completely into the background in the great confessions of faith and characteristic phrases of the Pauline religion of redemption that it has indeed been said that the religion of Paul could be just as well conceived without the sacramental basis in baptism. However, this would again be wrong. Most

[29] Cf. my Commentary, *ad loc.*

[30] W. Brandt, p. 86, "The forgiveness of sins is something quite different from the purification of the people of Israel, from all acts of guilt (עונות) which the God Yahweh proclaims in Ez. 36:16-25,36. For there transgressions are still conceived of as uncleanness. . . . Forgiveness, pardon . . . . of sins is out of the question in Ezekiel's conception; it belongs to a different series of ideas. . . . If misdemeanors cleave to man as spots of dirt, when these spots have been washed away, the anger of God will be without cause and die out. If they are considered as actual deeds, then the deity who wishes to spare the sinner must lay aside his anger, let him go, and have mercy, etc."

certainly the deepest and most original religious ideas of Paul which are especially contained in the doctrine of justification orient the new conception of God in a direction which is far remote from all sacramental character. Nevertheless, Paul is historically connected by strong roots with the ancient soil out of which the sacramental ideas grow, and entire fields of his religious thinking cannot be separated from sacramental considerations.

In I Cor. 6:11, along with 'washing' and 'justification,' 'sanctification' is mentioned, yet it is not inherently necessary to think of this as being directly connected with baptism. For Christians become 'sanctified,' i.e. are drawn into the sphere of the divine nature and are made the property of God, by the impartation of the Spirit,[31] and as we have seen (pp. 624f), this need not necessarily coincide with baptism. But in the classical passage I Cor. 6:11, baptism is, however, also thought of in connection with sanctification. Indeed, through its connection with the 'washing away,' the word 'sanctified' takes on a tone which is more cultic and ritualistic than spiritual and religious. One cannot help thinking of a single act of dedicatory nature with an outward and visible sign, since not only the 'Spirit of our God' but also 'the Name of the Lord Jesus Christ' is mentioned as being the power actually operative. Here we plainly enter into the sphere of sacramental and miraculous activity. We have previously pointed out (p. 177) what is the significance of the naming, crying out, or invocation of the name of Christ in baptism. However little we may know of the liturgical form of the old celebrations of baptism, yet it is clear that it involved uttering the name of Christ in a vigorous, expressive manner; probably by the baptizer, possibly also by the baptized person.[32] We do not know in what manner or at what moment of the ceremony this happened.[33] Above all we do not know whether in the earliest period there were added to the name closer definitions or facts drawn from the life of Christ, as we shall observe to be the case later.[34] But we can scarcely doubt

[31] II Thess. 2:13, ἐν ἁγιασμῷ πνεύματος, 'in sanctification of the Spirit'; Rom. 15:16: ἡγιασμένη ἐν πνεύματι ἁγίῳ, 'sanctified in the Holy Spirit.' Although Christians are often called 'saints' (in the genuine letters about twenty-six times) yet, as a general rule, sanctification appears just as often as an object or task to be striven for, as if it were an event based on salvation: I Thess. 5:23; Rom. 6:19,22; I Thess. 4:3f,7—I Cor. 1:30; II Thess. 2:13; I Cor. 1:2.

[32] W. Heitmüller, *Im Namen Jesu*, pp. 88-93.

[33] Later the baptismal water was consecrated by the invocation of the name of Christ; cf. the passages in Heitmüller, pp. 245f.

[34] Cf. Heitmüller, pp. 251ff. As they are presented in the Babylonian magic literature in incantation fragments or whole collections of myths (Jastrow i. 361ff), so

that "the solemn mention of the name of Jesus at baptism was not merely a figurative form used perhaps for the sake of example in making confession of the Messianic nature of Jesus, but it was considered in connection with real, mystical, mysterious actions . . . . real possession by the power which is designated by the name of Jesus, sealing inward connection with the bearer of this name, a driving-away of all hostile powers, consecration, and inspiration."[35] In the popular mind of the churches the element of magic and sorcery in this series of interpretations has prevailed. Baptism is conceived of wholly as a medium of exorcism, of liberation from spirits, and the appropriation of the exalted Christ's ownership; the question arises only as to how strongly Paul had felt the magical and supernatural side of the act, or whether he views it as merely a form or vesture in which an inner experience is clothed. This question is difficult to answer. In any case there are lacking throughout any indications of a 'spiritualizing' or 'symbolizing' tendency. Paul gives no indication that he felt the use of the name Christ to be only a form—quite the contrary. An assembly of the Corinthians 'in the name of Christ' (I Cor. 5:4) had additional weight, and the power of Christ present among them is evidently all the nearer by virtue of the fact that at their gathering this name is on all lips. The phrase in Col. 3:17, "Everything that ye do, in word and deed, do ye all in the name of the Lord Jesus," is also important. These words can only mean that the Christians, though they may not actually pronounce the Name, should have it in mind.[36] We learn what the actual practice was from the fact that Paul, in especially important exhortations, uses the name of Christ as a form of adjuration:[37] at the moment the sacred name is uttered or called to

separate features in exorcisms, which also recur in the baptismal symbol, especially the crucifixion under Pontius Pilate, are brought into prominence, as also in the exorcism of I Tim. 6:13.

[35] This judgment of Heitmüller (p. 268) rests especially upon a comprehensive treatment of an ancient belief in names (pp. 132-217), and the use of the name of Jesus, especially in early Christianity, e.g. for the purpose of exorcism (pp. 218-257).

[36] The ἐν is not so strongly instrumental as to suggest an accompanying phenomenon; I prefer to translate it by 'with.'

[37] Not only is II Thess. 3:6 to be mentioned here: παραγγέλλομεν ὑμῖν . . . . ἐν ὀνόματι τοῦ κυρίου ἡμ. 'Ι. Χρ., 'We command you, brethren, in the name of our Lord Jesus Christ,' but also I Thess. 4:1, παρακαλοῦμεν ἐν κυρίῳ 'Ιησοῦ, 'We exhort you in the Lord Jesus,' and vs. 2, παραγγελίας ἐδώκαμεν διὰ τοῦ κυρίου 'Ιησοῦ, 'What charges we gave you through the Lord Jesus'; I Cor. 1:10, παρακαλῶ . . . . διὰ τοῦ ὀνόματος τοῦ κυρ. ἡμ. 'Ι. Χρ., 'I beseech you . . . . through the name of our Lord Jesus Christ'; cf. also II Cor. 10:1, παρακαλῶ . . . . διὰ τῆς πραΰτητος καὶ ἐπιεικείας τοῦ Χριστοῦ, 'I entreat you by the meekness and gentleness of Christ.' The meaning of these formulae

remembrance, all resistance, all indolence and every evil will must yield. Of course this is only an attenuated, spiritualized echo of exorcistic formulae. Yet the fundamental feeling persists that the sacred name is a power to which one must yield. If, now, the name is uttered at baptism, an occurrence which is felt to be somehow miraculous, Paul must also have had the feeling that it is not merely an empty ceremony, but that it has a real effect on men's spirits. If Satan still continues to besiege baptized Christians in order to get them into his power again (II Cor. 2:11), if he is only too eager to gain control again over those who have been exorcised (I Cor. 5:5), and if he still retains control of the corporeal part of the Apostle (II Cor. 12:7)—how much the more will he and the demons watch with liveliest interest the baptismal procedure by which their former servants are to be snatched from them! They will hear the sound of the words when the Name of Christ is uttered and feel the power contained in it.

On the other hand it may be truly said that Paul did not consider the act of baptism to be entirely magical or possessing an irresistible force. 'To be baptized in the name of Christ' certainly means that the baptized are thus brought into the state of belonging to Christ.[38] By the act of baptism, by the utterance of the Name of Christ they become his bondsmen, his servants: the mention of the Name over a person or a thing is a real act of possession.[39] But when Paul (I Cor. 1:13) plays with the idea that Christians might also be baptized in the name of Paul, it may be recognized that Paul can also consider this possession or relation of ownership as something non-miraculous and non-magical, but rather dependent upon the will. In short it must be acknowledged that Paul has a certain hesitation between the sacramental and the symbolical modes of thought. When he refers, in I Cor. 15:29, to 'baptism for the dead,'[40] the

is not weakened in the parallels Rom. 12:1: *παρακαλῶ . . . . διὰ τῶν οἰκτιρμῶν τοῦ θεοῦ*, 'I beseech . . . . by the mercies of God,' or Rom. 15:30: *παρακαλῶ . . . . διὰ τ. κυρ. ἡμ.* 'I. *Χρ. καὶ διὰ τῆς ἀγάπης τοῦ πνεύματος*, 'I beseech . . . . by our Lord Jesus Christ, and by the love of the Spirit.' Everywhere there is present the basic feeling that the explicit recalling of names and things which are holy to Christians must break down all resistance or indifference.

[38] Heitmüller, p. 116; W. Brandt, *Elchasai*, pp. 87ff.

[39] Deut. 28:20, *καὶ ὄψονταί σε πάντα τὰ ἔθνη τῆς γῆς, ὅτι τὸ ὄνομα τ. κυρίου ἐπικέκληταί σοι*, 'And all the peoples of the earth shall see that thou art called by the name of the Lord'; Isa. 63:19, *ἐγενόμεθα ὡς τὸ ἀπ' ἀρχῆς, ὅτε οὐκ ἦρξας ἡμῶν οὐδὲ ἐκλήθη τὸ ὄνομά σου ἐφ' ἡμᾶς*, 'We are become as they over whom thou never barest rule; as they that were not called by thy name'; Jer. 14:9, *τὸ ὄνομά σου ἐπικέκληται ἐφ' ἡμᾶς. μὴ ἐπιλάθη ἡμῶν*, 'We are called by thy name; leave us not'; Jas. 2:7, *τὸ καλὸν ὄνομα τὸ ἐπικληθὲν ἐφ' ὑμᾶς*, 'The good name by which ye were called.'

[40] Cf. my Commentary, *ad. loc.*

passage shows only that the Corinthians attributed very far-reaching sacramental effects to baptism. How Paul himself regarded that custom we cannot know with certainty. So far as his own dealings with it were concerned he had no occasion to find fault; he is merely arguing here from the standpoint of the Corinthians. However, one may properly conclude from the words of I Cor. 1:16f that the specifically sacramental conception was not altogether natural to him: Christ has not sent him to baptize but to preach the Gospel; he had only baptized in exceptional cases. We can only understand the words to mean that Paul, in addition to the gift of revival preaching which was peculiar to him, did not possess in the same degree the gift which manifested itself at baptism. One is furthermore to assume from this that a baptizer's duty was not simply to perform an outward function to be accomplished without further ado, but that the ceremony also possessed a richer liturgical setting. In particular, we may consider that the invocation of the Name of Jesus demanded in the tone and method of the exorcist a certain attempt to produce an ecstatic or suggestible condition in order to secure corresponding effects in the participants, and that Paul's peculiar gifts and inclinations were not adapted to this. This deficiency of his nature he considered to be a limitation of his task; to us it is a sign that the state of exorcism related to the baptismal act does not at all appeal to him.

Nevertheless Paul has in another way attributed a special importance to baptism in that he conceives the event to be a dying and rising again with Christ (Rom. 6:4ff; Col. 2:12), and from this he directly deduces the mystical union with Christ (Gal. 3:27). These important statements demand a detailed discussion (cf. pp. 532ff).

First, as regards the expression, 'to be baptized in Christ' (εἰς Χριστόν), it seems to me that it is straining the interpretation if the preposition is taken in the strictly local sense: 'into Christ.' For it is clear that in the protases of Rom. 6:3 and Gal. 3:27 Paul takes it in the general Christian sense and not in his own particular sense, and it is only in the apodoses (Gal. 3:27) that he gives it a mystical meaning. But in the general Christian formula it surely means nothing else than an expression of belonging to Christ.[41] This follows from the fact that Paul can also fashion the formula, 'to be

[41] It corresponds somewhat to a Hebrew ל ; cf. the change from *Χριστοῦ εἶναι*, 'to be of Christ,' to *Χριστὸς ἐν ὑμῖν*, 'Christ in you,' Rom. 8:9f, and to the expression in Rom. 16:5, *ἀπαρχὴ τῆς Ἀσίας εἰς Χριστόν*, 'the firstfruits of Asia unto Christ'; *εἰς τ. ὄνομα τ. Χριστοῦ*, 'in the name of Christ' has no different meaning, as I Cor. 1:13 (cf. vs. 12) indicates.

baptized into Moses' (I Cor. 10:1), by which a mystical conception is excluded; but the meaning of 'belonging to,' still better, 'under obligation to' Moses is demanded. But this latter nuance is certainly also included in the phrase 'in Christ.' For 'belonging to' means at the same time an obligation to obedience and 'following,' and it is in this sense that we must in any case understand the phrase, 'to be baptized into his death' (Rom. 6:3). They are allied with Christ for death or life, they assume the obligation to die as he died. It is only in what follows later that Paul expounds this in a mystical sense. Nor is it permissible to translate I Cor. 12:13 as 'were baptized into one body,' but only 'to one body,' i.e. one body is the result of the baptism by the Spirit. But there is no doubt that now Paul is thinking of a mystical union with Christ as a result of baptism. He expresses it thus: by the likeness of his death 'we have grown together with him' (Rom. 6:5, σύμφυτοι γεγόναμεν τῷ ὁμοιώματι τοῦ θανάτου). This sublime expression[42] that he has chosen means, in effect, that by the fulfilment of baptism the mythical union is brought about because this is in 'the likeness of his death.' This turn of expression can only be understood from the language of the mysteries (pp. 520f), and a contemporary reader could comprehend it only by reference to familiar analogies between the mysteries and baptism. Independently of all other ideas it is incomprehensible that a 'copy' of the death and resurrection of Christ, made by the immersion and emergence from the water, could at the same time bring about a mystical union with the divine personality; it would be sufficient to find only the idea of imitation here. But in the mystery religions the idea is self-evident. When the original destiny of the mystery god—that of dying and rising again—is accomplished

[42] It is used in its original sense by physicians (*ὀστέον διακοπὲν οὐ συμφύεται*, 'a bone which has been cut in two does not grow together,' Hippocrates, 1257a,c) and agriculturists (*συμφυήσεται τὰ νέα κλήματα*, 'new shoots grow together,' *Geoponica*, iv. 12. 9); of the centaur (Xenophon, *Cyr.*, iv. 3. 18); of soul and body (*Phaedr.*, p. 246d; Marcus Aurelius, 12:3); of the desire of the sexes (*ἐπιθυμοῦντες συμφῦναι*, 'desiring to be together,' *Symposium*, 191a); humorously of Heracles and his shadow, *ἐκτὸς εἰ μὴ ὥσπερ Ἱπποκένταυρός τις ἦτε εἰς ἓν συμπεφυκότες ἄνθρωπος καὶ θεός*, 'unless you two, god and man, be grown together into one being like a centaur' (Lucian, *Dial. Mort.*, 16:4); with a religious significance in the parallel to the speech on the Areopagus in Dio Chrysostom, 12:28 (von Arnim, i, p. 162), *ἅτε οὐ μακρὰν οὐδ' ἔξω τοῦ θείου διῳκισμένοι καθ' ἑαυτούς, ἀλλ' ἐν αὐτῷ μέσῳ πεφυκότες, μᾶλλον δὲ συμπεφυκότες ἐκείνῳ καὶ προσεχόμενοι πάντα τρόπον*, 'Since they are not far from nor outside the divine in living by themselves, but are grown up in the very midst of it, or rather are grown up with it and are attached to it in every way.' Cf. I Cor. 6:17, *ὁ δὲ κολλώμενος τῷ κυρίῳ ἓν πνεῦμά ἐστιν*, 'But he that is joined unto the Lord is one Spirit.'

in the worshipper, he does not merely experience this in his life, but actually becomes identical with the deity.[43] The view appears in a weakened form in Paul: the full identification with Christ, the idea of deification, is of course wanting. But the mystery concept appears here to be wrought into the structure: union with the deity is accomplished by imitating his experiences;[44] no reader of antiquity could understand the words of the Apostle in any other sense. Again, the question is only whether in these interpretations which were not created for the first time, but taken over by Paul, his own view is fully expressed. Of course in addition to this there is another idea, viz. that already in the crucifixion of Christ the flesh especially is crucified with him, so that baptism is only the subsequent realization or only the representation in detail of a universal occurrence. Furthermore there is a series of statements regarding crucifixion with Christ (Gal. 2:19; 6:14; Rom. 7:4), in which baptism not only is not referred to, but is on the whole completely outside the circle of vision. The decisive event is rather the giving of the Spirit which, as previously stated (pp. 622f), can also take place apart from baptism.

All things considered, it cannot be denied that the mystical-sacra-

[43] Cf. Bousset, *Kyrios Christos,* p. 149: "This Greek mystery-piety does not emphasize life in the Deity, with the Deity, so much as the mystical union of identity with the Deity. When, at the height of the Isis-mysteries which Apuleius has pictured for us, the mystic, clothed in a costly mantle reaching to the ankles, and ornamented with figures, which the initiated call 'the Olympic stola,' is hidden at first and later, with the brightly burning torch in his hand, and bearing a crown of palm leaves upon his head, 'decked like the sun,' is presented suddenly to the worshippers statue-like, by a quick drawing aside of curtains—this simply means that at this moment the initiated one is considered as the incarnate mystery deity. When, at the height of the Attis celebration, the mystic, after the example of his cult-hero, has performed upon himself the frightful act of emasculation, he has himself thereby become Attis, and experiences with him his death and his return from death. For this theory, which is deduced from interpretation of the celebration itself, we have a further witness, viz. the report of Damascius concerning the entrance into the cave of Hierapolis (*Vita Isidori,* in Photius, *cod.* 242, p. 354a, ed. Becker): *ἐδόκουν ὄναρ ὁ Ἄττης γενέσθαι καί μοι ἐπιτελεῖσθαι παρὰ τῆς Μητρὸς τὴν τῶν Ἱλαρίων καλουμένων ἑορτήν—ὅπερ ἐδήλου τὴν ἐξ ᾅδου γεγονυῖαν ἡμῶν σωτηρίαν*, 'I thought that in a vision I had become Attis and that before me had been accomplished by the Mother's deed the festival which is called that of the Hilarii—and as I have shown, she came from Hades to be our salvation.' "

[44] 'Osiris, Attis and Adonis were *men,* who died and rose again as *gods.* If we unite ourselves with them, take them up into ourselves, or clothe ourselves with them, we have the certainty firm as a rock, of our own immortality, and indeed *deity.*' These words of Reitzenstein, somewhat too strongly tinged by Christian terminology, stress the general meaning of both the Mystery faith and the Christian baptismal belief which Paul in Rom. 6:5 assumes, and in Col. 2:12 explicitly states. One can only doubt whether the order should be reversed, viz. the union with deity follows just this imitation of the divine destiny.

mental interpretation is present in Paul—he finds it ready to hand—however, it does not play the decisive rôle in the mysticism of redemption as is frequently assumed, to say nothing of other spheres of his religious thinking, e.g. the doctrine of atonement. One perceives plainly how a tendency of Hellenistic piety thrusts its way into his own religion without thereby becoming fundamental. Two observations will make this clear. According to Gal. 3:27 the mystical 'putting on' of the Lord Christ is accomplished in and with baptism; but since alongside this appears the imperative 'put ye on the Lord Jesus' (Rom. 13:14), the idea of sacramental union could not have been entertained in complete earnest and regarded as paramount; at least the idea that the mystical union could be accomplished *only* by the sacrament is excluded. Fundamentally, however, the hypothesis in the case of a real sacrament is that it offers something which cannot be attained in another way. It has often been said, furthermore, that the Christian's crucifixion with Christ and awakening to a new life are by no means surely and indubitably given with baptism, which must be the case in a genuine sacrament; they are gifts which must ever again be gained anew, perhaps not by a repetition of baptism, but by the exertion of the will (cf. the change in treatment between Rom. 6:4-7 and vs. 11). From the beginning, before Paul, indeed even as early as the preaching of Jesus, the ethical requirement of repentance and the baptism of redemption with its magical, sacramental operation were in competition one with the other; just as, on the other hand, the free working of God's will to grant grace, long since firmly established in 'election,' was entirely independent of any sacred rite. One would think from this that the sacrament would have shown itself to be superfluous and would have died out. But the contrary is the case; the mystery ideas ever more powerfully sweeping in from heathenism have, in fact, intrenched baptism, with all its non-essential magical assertions, most firmly as a sacrament in the Church.

(b) *The Eucharist* (cf. pp. 56-66). Paul found the 'Lord's Supper,' as he calls it[45] (I Cor. 11:20), already observed in the

[45] In the use of the adjective κυριακός (in the New Testament only in Rev. 1:10) one perceives how deeply rooted in the church is the reverence for the Kyrios. The word is taken from Hellenistic speech; it is used especially in the terminology of the Emperor cult ('imperial finances,' κυριακαὶ ψῆφοι; the 'imperial treasury,' κυριακὸς λόγος; Deissmann, *Licht vom Osten,* pp. 268ff). It does not follow from this that the Christians would consciously have taken it up as an antithesis to emperor-worship. Nevertheless, there still remains a striking analogy to the official language, in that the same exclusive obviousness with which official documents speak of 'the Lord'—as if

community. In no sense does he appear as the founder of the custom, and never specifically as its reformer. The two passages from the travel document in the Book of Acts (20:7; 27:35) in which Paul takes part in the common Christian observance, are important here, for the expression, 'the Lord's Supper,' is not used, but instead the older term, 'the breaking of bread.' This also appears in I Cor. 10:16; close beside it of course is 'the table of the Lord' (10:21), an expression which immediately calls to mind the heathen cult-meal at which the cult-god is thought to be present.[46] Different views are reflected in these two designations: the older view, originating in the Church, according to which the repast is an act of fellowship of the disciples who thereby thank God for their common religious possessions (cf. the prayers in the Didache) and break the bread as Jesus had broken it (pp. 56-66); and the newer Hellenistic view, according to which the Lord himself is not only the center but also in some way the object of the celebration. The two views appear somewhat confusedly in Paul and indeed in I Cor. 10:16f. It is the older view which is more in evidence, while in 11:20-34 it is rather the newer conception. In the first passage the sequence of cup and bread is very striking, since it is also found in the Didache (pp. 63f) and in the original Lucan text (pp. 60f). This sequence points back to a time when the cup had not yet been related to the blood of Christ, and the repast as a whole was not yet an actual celebration of the death of Christ in the narrower sense. For the expression of this narrower concept the sequence *body and blood=bread and wine* (I Cor. 11; also Mark, Matt., Luke in the present text) is determinative and indispensable. I Cor. 10:17 also contains a reminiscence of the time when the celebration as a whole was called 'the breaking of bread,' and this act of breaking was the essential thing (pp. 57f); for in his conclusion he speaks only of the bread—he could easily have referred to the cup also—"Because one bread (is present) we, the many, are one body; for we all have part in the one bread."[47] 'One body' merely implies an organic unity;

---

there were only one—also prevails in Christian usage. The adjective κυριακός could not have been used in this way unless ὁ κύριος had for a long time been used in the fully exclusive manner.

[46] Not only is the parallelism with the 'table of the demons,' e.g. the heathen gods (10:21) important here, but especially also the parallel expressions in papyri and inscriptions (cf. Lietzmann, *Handbuch zum Neuen Testament*, on I Cor. 10:21), e.g. the famous *p. Oxy*. i, 110: "Chaeremon invites you to eat at the table (literally εἰς κλίνην, 'on a couch') of the Lord Serapis in the Serapeum, tomorrow the 15th, at nine o'clock." In an inscription from Cos (Dittenberger, *Syll.* ii, 734,99) mention is made of the τράπεζα τοῦ θεοῦ 'table of the god.'

[47] On the difficulties of the text, see my Commentary, *ad loc.*

this is simply the general idea of antiquity that companions at any meal, and not merely a cult-meal, are joined together in a most intimate communion by partaking the same food.[48] Paul however certainly interjected the idea that the eating of the bread in common represents and confirms the unity of the body of Christ (I Cor. 12:12f), although naturally it does not produce it in the first place. Here there is certainly an echo of Jesus' saying (Luke 22:19a), according to which the bread, broken (and distributed) by Jesus, is his body, so that they who eat of it are in a mystical way united with him and with one another.

However, the words as they stand represent on the whole still another stage of the development of the idea. To the breaking of the bread he adds the blessing of the cup, and the double act—despite the old sequence which still lies in the background—somehow contains in Paul's view a 'representation' (if we may thus express it) of the body and blood of Christ. Fundamentally of course the whole procedure is experienced as a unity which is merely included in the form of a synthetic parallelism;[49] the communion meal as a whole, which is expressed in the two solemn acts, thus represents and effects a communion with Christ. The 'communion' is not yet thought of as a physical union with Christ through the eating of the flesh of Christ; the idea is that of table-communion. Paul means to say: "When we bless the cup and break the bread, is not Christ there with

[48] Robertson Smith, *The Religion of the Semites,* p. 263, "In rejoicing before his God a man rejoiced with and for the welfare of his kindred, his neighbor and his country, and, in renewing, by a solemn act of worship, the bond that united him to his god, he also renewed the bonds of family, social and national obligations." P. 269, "Those who sit at meat together are united for all social effects; those who do not eat together are aliens to one another, without fellowship in religion, and without reciprocal social duties. . . . Among the Arabs every stranger whom one meets in the desert is a natural enemy. . . . But if I have eaten the smallest morsel of food with a man, I have nothing further to fear from him. . . . The Old Testament records many cases where a covenant was sealed by the parties eating and drinking together. In most of these, indeed, the meal is sacrificial. . . . The value of the Arabic evidence is that it supplies proof that the bond of food is valid in and of itself, that religion may be called in to confirm and strengthen it, but that the essence of the thing lies in the physical act of eating together." P. 271, "The table companionship can be thought of in an entirely real sense, as one established by kinship and self-founded." P. 313, "In later times we find the conception current that any food which two men partake of together, so that the same substance enters into their flesh and blood, is enough to establish some sacred unity of life between them; but in ancient times this significance seems to be always attached to participation in the flesh of a sacrosanct victim, and the solemn mystery of its death is justified by the consideration that only in this way can the sacred cement be procured which creates or keeps alive a living bond of union between the worshippers and their god."

[49] As it also lies before us in Rom. 4:25.

us at the table?"[50] But certainly the division of the meal into the two actions would not have been emphasized in such rhetorical manner if Paul had not, for a long time, been convinced that each of the two actions had its particular meaning. While this passage shows earlier and later conceptions side by side, I Cor. 11:20-34 reveals the actual viewpoint of Paul in a purer form.

The dominical sayings which Paul hands down are essentially parallel with those in Mark and Matthew. At any rate the deviations are unimportant in contrast with the extraordinary agreements, viz. the sequence of bread and cup, and the express connection made between the celebration and the death of Christ and with the atoning death in particular.[51] There is a complete correspondence with

[50] This interpretation of the words (cf. my Commentary, *ad loc.*) seems apparent to me: (1) because the *κοινωνία* must be explained by *κοινωνοὶ τῶν δαιμονίων*, vs. 20; accordingly Paul could also say here *κοινωνοὶ τοῦ κυρίου*; (2) because he would probably have said of the partaking of the Body and Blood *μετέχειν, μετοχή*. Cf. also Aristides, *In Serapidem* = *Or.* 8, pp. 93f. Dind. (*Or.* 45, 27 Keil) *καὶ θυσιῶν μόνῳ τούτῳ θεῷ διαφερόντως κοινωνοῦσιν ἄνθρωποι τὴν ἀκριβῆ κοινωνίαν, καλοῦντές τε ἐφ' ἑστίαν καὶ προϊστάμενοι δαιτύμονα αὐτὸν καὶ ἑστιάτορα*, "And men enjoy real communion differently from elsewhere in the sacrifice to this god alone, inviting him to the hearth and standing before him who is both invited guest and host"; "Serapis himself is . . . . the giver of the feast, his 'table companions' become partakers of the feast" (Leitzmann).

[51] I illustrate the relationship among the three texts as follows: that which is common to Paul and to Mark or all three is underlined; that which differs is printed in spaced letters; while material which Mark and Matthew have in common is indicated by ordinary type. Differences in word order are not taken into consideration.

Mark.	Matthew.
καὶ ἐσθίοντων αὐτῶν	ἐσθιόντων δὲ αὐτῶν
λαβὼν ἄρτον εὐλογήσας	λαβὼν ὁ Ἰησοῦς ἄρτον καὶ εὐλογήσας
ἔκλασεν καὶ ἔδωκεν αὐτοῖς	ἔκλασεν καὶ δοὺς τοῖς μαθηταῖς
καὶ εἶπεν· λαβετε·	εἶπεν· λάβετε φάγετε·
τοῦτό ἐστιν τὸ σῶμά μου.	τοῦτό ἐστιν τὸ σῶμά μου.
καὶ λαβὼν ποτήριον	καὶ λαβὼν ποτήριον
εὐχαριστήσας ἔδωκεν αὐτοῖς	εὐχαριστήσας ἔδωκεν αὐτοῖς
καὶ ἔπιον ἐξ αὐτοῦ πάντες	λέγων: πίετε ἐξ αὐτοῦ πάντες.
καὶ εἶπεν αὐτοῖς·	
τοῦτό ἐστιν τὸ αἷμα μου τῆς διαθήκης	τοῦτο γάρ ἐστιν τὸ αἷμά μου τῆς διαθήκης
τὸ ἐκχυννόμενον ὑπὲρ πολλῶν	τὸ περὶ πολλῶν ἐκχυννόμενον
	εἰς ἄφεσιν ἁμαρτιῶν.

Paul.

ἔλαβεν ἄρτον καὶ εὐχαριστήσας ἔκλασεν καὶ εἶπεν·
τοῦτό μού ἐστιν τὸ σῶμα τὸ ὑπὲρ ὑμῶν·
τοῦτο ποιεῖτε εἰς τὴν ἐμὴν ἀνάμνησιν.
ὡσαύτως καὶ τὸ ποτήριον μετὰ τὸ δειπνῆσαι λέγων·
τοῦτο τὸ ποτήριον ἡ καινὴ διαθήκη ἐστιν ἐν τῷ ἐμῷ αἵματι·
τοῦτο ποιεῖτε, ὁσάκις ἐὰν πίνητε, εἰς τὴν ἐμὴν ἀνάμνησιν.

The variations: (1) The changes in Matthew from the Marcan text are all easily understood and to be considered secondary: *δέ* instead of *καί*, the addition of ὁ Ἰησοῦς,

Pauline thought in the statement that the body of Christ is 'for you,' i.e. is sacrificed for you (cf. Gal. 2:20; Rom. 8:32), and the fact that Jesus himself says this corresponds exactly with the Apostle's view that Christ had with full consciousness given himself over to death for the Christians (Gal. 1:4; 2:20). We presume that it is not Pauline in the special sense when it is said that the blood of Christ

---

of *καί, δούς* instead of *ἔδωκεν . . . . καί*, and the addition of *φάγετε*; the transposition of narrative into a saying of the Lord (cf. Matt. 26:2 and Mark 14:1), also the dropping out of the words *καὶ εἶπεν αὐτοῖς*; *περί* instead of *ὑπέρ* and the addition of *εἰς ἄφεσιν ἁμαρτιῶν*. Matthew is related to Mark perhaps as the Targums were to the original Hebrew text. (2) The variations between Paul and the Synoptic type are for the most part quite unimportant and rather stylistic: *εὐχαριστήσας* in the first member instead of *εὐλογήσας* (however cf. Luke); *μου τὸ σῶμα* instead of *τὸ σῶμά μου*; the connection with the use of the cup by *ὡσαύτως*. Here Paul has abbreviated; perhaps also in leaving out *ἔδωκεν αὐτοῖς, ἔπιον ἐξ αὐτοῦ πάντες* (?). More important is the statement *μετὰ τὸ δειπνῆσαι*; here one may ask whether these words already belonged to the type of story which he had before him, as did the words *ἐν τῇ νυκτὶ ᾗ παρεδίδετο*, or whether they were added by him because at the Lord's Supper it was customary to serve the cup after the meal. We assume the latter, since they are wanting in Mark and Matthew and do not fit into the old Lucan text. Although the addition may indeed have been made before Paul's time, it must, in any case, have originated in the time in which the sequence of bread and cup was already firmly established. The addition *τὸ ὑπὲρ ὑμῶν* is later than that preserved by Mark, and also later than the text to which Luke bears witness, besides; an omission by Mark would be incomprehensible; also the applicative *ὑμῶν* in place of a phrase corresponding to Mark, vs. 24 *ὑπὲρ πολλῶν* (cf. also Mark 10:45 and pp. 113ff) argues for the Pauline origin of the word (cf. Gal. 2:20, *ὑπὲρ ἐμοῦ*; Rom. 8:32, *ὑπὲρ ἡμῶν πάντων*); the bare *τὸ ὑπὲρ ὑμῶν* certainly leads one to conclude that the words were already a sort of formula for him before the writing of First Corinthians. The most important addition of Paul, *τοῦτο ποιεῖτε εἰς τὴν ἐμὴν ἀνάμνησιν*, is certainly later than the shorter text in Mark. Naturally Mark is based also on the point of view that one 'should do this in remembrance of Jesus,' and at his time it had long been done so; but the carrying back of this usage to an expression of the Lord, as at baptism (Matt. 28:19; Mark 16:16) is a later development. As for the words pronounced at the giving of the cup, one may hesitate; the Pauline text is harder, that of Mark is unharmonious in itself, an expansion of *τὸ αἷμά μου* and *τὸ αἷμα τῆς διαθήκης* and therefore scarcely to be considered as original; and of course, the words *τῆς διαθήκης* might be thought of as original rather than the *μου*, which is under suspicion of being conformed to *τὸ σῶμά μου*. The omission of *καινῆς* in Mark seems earlier than Paul's addition, the reference to the blood immediately after *τοῦτό ἐστιν* more harmonious than the Pauline text.

Since it is beyond all doubt that neither is Mark dependent upon Paul, nor Paul upon Mark, it must be agreed that Mark and Paul present two parallel versions which, in the last analysis, go back to a primitive form. It must have read somewhat as follows: λαβὼν ἄρτον εὐχαριστήσας (Luke) ἔκλασεν (καὶ ἔδωκεν αὐτοῖς) καὶ εἶπεν· λάβετέ· *τοῦτό ἐστιν τὸ σῶμά μου. καὶ λαβὼν ποτήριον εὐχαριστήσας ἔδωκεν αὐτοῖς (καὶ ἔπιον ἐξ αὐτοῦ πάντες) καὶ εἶπεν (αὐτοῖς)· τοῦτό ἐστιν ἡ διαθήκη ἐν τῷ ἐμῷ αἵματι.*

"Taking the bread he gave thanks (Luke) and broke it (and gave it to them)
And said, 'Take this; this is my Body.'
And taking the cup he gave thanks and gave it to them
(And they all drank of it) and he said (to them),
'This is the new covenant in my blood.'"

If one compares this with the shorter Lucan text, he is struck by the great correspondence in the first member with the second member in Luke (vs. 19a):

is the basis and sacrifice of the New Covenant (after the analogy of the offering on Sinai, Ex. 12:14). The idea of the New Covenant does not appear elsewhere in Paul, and the conception that the old is succeeded by something new is rather more indigenous to the Epistle to the Hebrews, or rather to the whole Jewish-Christian-Hellenistic sphere of ideas; while Paul conceives the opposition of the new to the old in a much more clear-cut fashion. This interpretation of the death of Christ was already known in Antioch and, as it would seem, in Rome also; perhaps it received its formulation among circles of Hellenistic-Jewish Christians. The peculiarly Pauline idea of the shedding of blood as an atoning sacrifice is found elsewhere only in Mark, and there also only in connection with the covenant sacrifice; but it is not so in I Cor. 11. We cannot therefore make Paul responsible for the formulation of the words of the Lord's Supper in

---

15. *ἐπιθυμίᾳ ἐπεθύμησα τοῦτο τὸ πάσχα φαγεῖν μεθ' ὑμῶν πρὸ τοῦ με παθεῖν·*

16. *λέγω γὰρ ὑμῖν, ὅτι οὐ μὴ φάγω αὐτό, ἕως ὅτου πληρωθῇ ἐν τῇ βασιλείᾳ τοῦ θεοῦ.*

17. *καὶ δεξάμενος ποτήριον εὐχαριστήσας εἶπεν· λάβετε τοῦτο καὶ διαμερίσατέ εἰς ἑαυτούς.*

18. *λέγω γὰρ ὑμῖν, ὅτι οὐ μὴ πίω ἀπὸ τοῦ νῦν ἀπὸ τοῦ γενήματος τῆς ἀμπέλου, ἕως ὅτου ἡ βασιλεία τοῦ θεοῦ ἔλθῃ.*

19a. *καὶ λαβὼν ἄρτον εὐχαριστήσας ἔκλασεν καὶ ἔδωκεν αὐτοῖς λέγων· τοῦτό ἐστιν τὸ σῶμά μου·*

21. *πλὴν ἰδοὺ ἡ χεὶρ τοῦ παραδιδόντος με μετ' ἐμοῦ ἐπὶ τῆς τραπέζης, ὅτι ὁ υἱὸς μὲν τοῦ ἀνθρώπου κατὰ τὸ ὡρισμένον πορεύεται, πλὴν οὐαὶ τῷ ἀνθρώπῳ ἐκείνῳ, δι' οὗ παραδίδοται.*

That this text could not have originated with Mark, and yet that it is in some way related to Mark, is significant. It must, with the Marcan and Pauline texts, go back to the same source. If I call this source Q, I do wish to assert with certainty that it is the Saying Source, commonly called 'Q.' The genealogy of witnesses which I present here includes still other middle terms, the tradition and usage of the Antiochene and Roman Churches. Between Q and Mark-Luke I insert still another middle member, Q_1 or Q_2, for reasons which I cannot elucidate here.

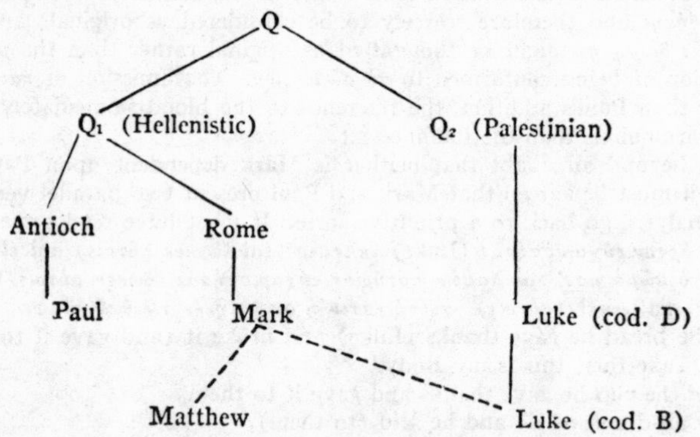

[Compare the conclusions of Lietzmann, *Messe und Herrenmahl*, 1926, e.g. chh. xiii, xv, xvi.]

I Cor. 11. In the main Paul must have found them already in use. Hence it is not an innovation on the part of Paul that after the breaking of the bread, the cup is brought into prominence in a wholly parallel manner and is placed in relationship to the blood-shedding of Jesus. Thus the whole procedure becomes a celebration of the death of Jesus. This of course strongly opposes the general trend of Pauline thought, but it is older than Paul, older at least than the First Epistle to the Corinthians. The celebration of the Lord's Supper as a memorial of Jesus[52] need not in any event be an addition from the hand of Paul, but probably corresponds to the usage already practised before his time in the churches. This surely also represents the opinion of those for whom the text of Mark was authoritative, although the words under consideration are not found in it. The particular point in Paul's conception is that he wishes to have the Lord's Supper thought of not merely as a memorial meal in general, but also as a celebration of thanksgiving for the salvation which Christ has brought to the Church; not merely as a celebration of communion with him and therefore a simple cult-meal, but, as he says with great emphasis, the Supper must be or is *a proclamation of the death of Christ,* as indeed the form of the Lord's words suggests. It may be questioned whether Paul *demands* (as an imperative) that at the Supper, 'as often as ye eat this bread and drink this cup,' the death of Christ must be vividly visualized—in its concrete historical details or in its significance for salvation or in relation to the experience and will of Jesus himself—whether through express words, perhaps in the form of a narrative or confession of faith, or in hymns

[52] Like the 'feast for the dead, which was held in honor of the deceased by his family, his slaves, or his friends, regularly every year on the day of his death or oftener.' Also 'a philosophical school could be founded through a bequest to a religious guild; and in memory of its founder such a school held regular festival gatherings' (Lietzmann, *Handbuch zum Neuen Testament,* on I Cor. 11:22). Cf. the inscriptions given by Lietzmann in the appendix (pp. 162f), which contain such expressions as these: *ob merita Claudiae Hedones et memoriam Ti. Claudi Himeri fili eius cultoris Herculis universi . . . . uti quodannis in perpetuum . . . . natale Ti. Claudi Himeri colerent vescerenturque in templo Herculis,* 'Because of the good deeds of Claudia Hedone and in memory of Tiberius Claudius Himerus her son, worshipper of universal Hercules . . . . that annually forever . . . . on the birthday of Tiberius Claudius Himerus shall pay him honor and feast in the temple of Hercules' (Dessau, *Inscr. Lat. Sel.,* 7215). In one testament, the erection of a *cella memoriae* is ordered, in which the memorial feast is to be held. Testament of Epicurus (Diog. Laert., 10:18; Usener, *Epicurea,* pp. 165f), . . . *ὥσπερ καὶ εἰς τὴν γινομένην σύνοδον ἑκάστου μηνὸς ταῖς εἰκάσι τῶν συμφιλοσοφούντων ἡμῖν εἰς τὴν ἡμῶν τε καὶ Μητροδώρου μνήμην,* '. . . . and so it is for the feast which consequently will take place each month on the twentieth, held by those who have followed the pursuit of philosophy with us *in our memory* and that of Metrodorus.'

or instruction, with full Old Testament coloring, or with use of gospel themes. Various things favor this view.[53] But the other interpretation is possible, viz. that Christians, as often as they are met together for the Lord's Supper, by the very fact that they do break the bread (and fill the cup, or administer it) actually 'proclaim' the death of Christ (indicative), and by this action or actions bring him to mind and to a certain degree 'represent' him in symbolic form. There would then be here an analogy to the mystery cults in which, by a symbolic action, impressive features from the myth of the mystery deity were represented.[54] Today the latter interpretation of the words is frequently preferred, and perhaps rightly. In any case it corresponds with the import of the rite as a whole to this extent, viz. that whether by words or actions, or both, the death of Christ is not only to be brought to remembrance, but—according to Paul's conception—is to be brought to mind in the most emphatic manner so that the participants shall, as it were, experience it anew. Not

[53] In my Commentary on I Cor. 11:26 I entirely rejected it, because taking καταγγέλλετε as an imperative is made impossible by the introductory γάρ of the sentence; one should expect instead an οὖν. But this argument seems not to be very compelling. One may also take the γάρ as an introduction to an exegetical explanation, so to speak; one needs only to place the expression taken from the words of the Lord in quotation marks, and all will be clear. Naturally, we must make a pause after vs. 25, and continue with vs. 26 in an entirely different tone, perhaps in the tone of the Scripture words paraphrased by the interpreter in the synagogue preaching: 'ὁσάκις' γὰρ 'ἐὰν ἐσθίητε' τὸν ἄρτον τοῦτον 'καὶ' τὸ ποτήριον 'πίνητε'. . . . "For 'as often as ye eat' this bread 'and drink' this cup," etc. In that case καταγγέλλετε can really be taken as an imperative. Against the second theory which I presented, viz. that καταγγέλλειν is here a pregnant expression and is not meant in its natural sense, in other words, that it is a proclamation not in words but in deeds, that here a δρώμενον, in the sense of the ancient mystery cults, is present, one may say that there arises the circumstance that the text does not state: 'So often as ye break this bread' and perhaps 'pour out the cup'; instead it is a question of eating and drinking; yet this can only with difficulty be understood as a presentation of the death of Christ. It is an especially misleading circumstance that the act of using of the cup is not as obvious or as suitable a vehicle for dramatic action as the breaking of the bread. The latter action is carried out by the one who presides at the meal, visibly and expressively; on the other hand, the action with the cup is wholly symbolical, and is of course performed by a servant; in any case, it precedes the moment when the one who presides takes the cup in hand and passes it around. One again sees that the parallelism of the cup and bread is not original.

[54] Cf. Anrich, *Das antike Mysterienwesen,* p. 307, "As the third part, there follows the *epopsia* . . . . a dramatic presentation of the sacred cult-myth, a religious pantomime . . . . But this is restricted to the representation of several leading scenes; the rest of the drama was indicated by exhibiting the all-holy symbol appropriate to the god, the meaning of which was understood by everyone. The two methods of representation are designated by the stereotyped expression: τὰ δεικνύμενα καὶ δρώμενα ἐν τοῖς μυστηρίοις ('the things shown and done in the mysteries')"; also Rohde, *Psyche,* i, 295. Cf. my Commentary on First Corinthians, p. 289, note 1.

that the idea of the ever-repeated sacrifice was already existent, although one cannot fail to recognize a germ of the Roman Catholic interpretation of the sacred action since doubtless the bread and wine are no longer considered to be common food, but in some way already symbolically represent the Body and Blood and in fact embody them. At the sacred repast one receives not only bodily but 'spiritual,' i.e. supernatural divine food and drink (I Cor. 10:3f); and it is sacrilege for one not to 'discern the body' (I Cor. 11:29),[55] e.g. for one not to 'distinguish' this bread from common bread, i.e. not to acknowledge its higher significance.[56] He who devours the bread and wine voraciously only to appease hunger and thirst (I Cor. 11:34), eats and drinks 'unworthily' of the bread and cup, and commits sin, violates the 'body and blood of the Lord' (I Cor. 11:27f). It doubtless becomes clear from these assertions that the elements of the sacred act are already conceived of as sacred objects; they *are* in some wondrous way the Body and Blood of Christ, and in them Christ himself is present at the table (I Cor. 10:16). We cannot know whether they are changed by the formula of blessing and by the action of the breaking of the bread into this miraculous state, but the Apostle's conception of their sacredness is so thorough that he regards sicknesses and deaths (I Cor. 11:30) in the church as disciplinary punishments for such profane eating. Here we meet with an ancient, almost primitive feature which is in any case sub-Christian: the sacred objects react against profane handling by damaging the bodies of guilty persons. It cannot be denied that here the foundation is laid for a solidly sacramental, magical and miraculous interpretation of the Lord's Supper. This interpretation, however, only serves to exhibit the reality of Paul's religious interpretation of the Supper.

We should very much like to know what Paul thinks of the effect of the Supper, partaken in faith and reverence. Unfortunately it is not clearly stated; we can only venture a conjecture. But it seems reasonable to assume that Paul sees in the imitation or experience of the death of Christ a confirmation of that union with the Cross of Christ which should really form the keynote of Christian piety. The person who enters by means of bread and wine into communion with the Body and Blood of Christ, who thereby is drawn anew into that condition of dying with him which he experienced in baptism, feels again

[55] Here also the Body only is referred to, not the Blood; the bread is primary, the cup was added afterward.

[56] Cf. my Commentary on I Cor. 11:29.

the 'he has been crucified with Christ.' On the other hand in these brief words there is lacking anything which might point to a theory of the Supper as a 'medicine of immortality.' Paul may indeed have had some such feeling, but in these passages he says nothing on the point. Furthermore the mystical connection with the Lord is not only experienced through the Supper but is also strengthened, yet there is still missing here the peculiarly sacramental formula of the eating and drinking of the Body and Blood of Christ which John 6:52-59 presents in such strong terms: in particular the expression 'eating Christ' does not occur. One may grant that in Paul everything points in the direction of this very ancient sacramental idea of eating the deity; but one must also say that at least he has not carried it out to its logical consequence. By falling just short of this in his formulation he has of course failed to be clear-cut and direct and has presented us with a riddle. Yet he permits us to know that this finality and clarity is not congenial to him. He may have felt an aversion to it which we ought to acknowledge instead of forcing him, by too realistic an interpretation, to fit into the general pattern of thought which the history of religions teaches us was current.

So much the more one must not fail to recognize that in the words, 'until he come,' there remains a touch of the eschatological tone which found expression in the ancient prayers (pp. 63f), that yearning for the Parousia. This is a sign that the full tendency toward a mystery religion has not yet come to development, with its strong joy in the bodily presence of Christ, or the nearly materialistic feeling of bodily union by which the Parousia would be anticipated. The 'proclamation of the death of Christ until he come' remains, so to speak, as a help in time of need, just as the charismata are to be a comfort during the time of waiting which is imposed upon all Christians (I Cor. 1:7).

Perhaps, however, the peculiar significance of the rite does not find full expression, because Paul in both passages employs his interpretation of the Supper only as a means to other ends: in I Cor. 10, to warn against meats offered to idols; in I Cor. 11, to censure the unfraternal conduct of various members of the church. The full development of ideas in I Cor. 11:20-34, considered in relation to its context, is dominated by two different tendencies; vv. 20-22 by the social, and vv. 23-34 by the sacramental, so that the critic seeking for interpolations might hit upon the idea of rejecting the latter group of verses (23-32). And in fact it is not entirely manifest how far the appeal to the Lord's sayings and the exposition of the significance of the celebration are to serve the purpose of combatting Corinthian immorality. It is here that the peculiar problem of the passage lies. We could solve it more satisfactorily if we possessed a somewhat clearer idea of the external conditions of the Supper. Nevertheless one may still make such an attempt. The error which Paul censures is 'that each eats his own supper first' and that people do not 'wait one for another' (vv. 21,23); this is blameworthy not only for the reason that the poorer, who are expected to share in partaking the gifts of the rich, receive nothing and are 'put to shame' (vs. 22), but especially because it is impossible to hold a real 'Lord's Supper' in this way (vs. 20). These words can only so be understood—especially in connection with verse 20—as meaning that a Lord's Supper can take place only when the meal *is begun* in common. This makes sense only if it is the beginning of the Supper which is the decisive moment. We understand from this that the breaking of the bread should take place at the beginning, but was frequently enough omitted altogether or was lost in the general disorder; it was the same with the blessing of the cup 'after supper.' Therefore the rite as a whole should be constructed around these two actions.[57] If the Corinthians sat together in the same room, and, without waiting for the full number of the brethren to be gathered together, separated into groups, ate their meal, occasionally in a mood of levity, so that instances of drunkenness even occurred, 'they despised the Church of God' itself, i.e. they did not treat the repast as a solemn religious action but as an ordinary meal, at which eating and drinking is the essential thing. Thus Paul says, "What? have ye not houses to eat and to drink in?" One can now easily recognize the connection between the two groups of ideas. The unsocial conduct of the Corinthians is a sign that they do not take into account the religious character of the repast. If they would celebrate the festival in its true sense they would not act in such an unbrotherly manner.

In this chapter we have discussed Paul's theory of the Church in a few of its principal features. We recognize quite plainly, however,

[57] Here one perceives that the Agapê or love feast and the Eucharist are not yet completely separate. Cf. the reference of Josephus to the common meal of the Essenes, in *B.J.*, ii. 8. 5, § 131: "The priest offers a prayer before the beginning of the meal (προκατεύχεται . . . . τῆς τροφῆς), and it is forbidden to partake of anything before the prayer. At the end of the morning meal he prays (ἐπεύχεται) again. At the beginning as well as at the end, he praises God as the giver of life." It is not entirely clear to me whether in προκατεύχεσθαι with the genitive and ἐπεύχεσθαι there is present, along with the temporal significance, also the idea of offering prayer 'over' the food before and after the meal. I am strongly inclined to assume that there is such an idea present.

that on the one hand the Apostle's treatment of it is based on actual conditions, and yet comes into conflict with them. These considerations lead us to the subject of the next book.

Summary

The study of Paul, presented in the foregoing chapters, has resulted in a picture of extraordinary variety. We have seen for ourselves that all the spiritual currents of the time have met in him: Old Testament prophetic piety and rabbinical Judaism; Hellenistic-Jewish enlightenment and Stoic ethics; syncretistic Hellenistic mysticism and dualistic, ascetical Gnosticism. In addition the strong imperatives of the ethical preaching of Jesus are present, the vivid, eschatological emphasis on the end of the age which is found in the Baptist, in Jesus and in the primitive Church, and above all the victorious conviction that the salvation of the final age has already come. All this is held in unity by the personal, thankful, humble consciousness of having himself experienced the grace of God and of having been won forever by the love of Christ. It is in this that the man's variegated world-view and mode of thought, full of contradictions as they are, have their unifying principle. In this personal religious experience which he concisely calls his *faith,* he possessed the power to accomplish his task and to place his mind at the service of his actions. For the primacy of the will over the imagination was dominant in Paul if it ever has been in any man—he is the antithesis of a thinker without hypotheses, and ideas are for him means for the attainment of his great ethical and religious purposes, and he groups and gives them emphasis just as he needs them. It is therefore impossible to outline a 'system' of his theology; but it is equally impossible to overlook the fact that his theology was one of his chief weapons and instruments.

And it was just this theology—not only that which we learn to know from his Epistles, but also that which he used in his preaching and teaching, that was also the means by which his influence has persisted in history. It seems in fact as if the stream of Paulinism, from a time soon after its origin, flowed in subterranean concealment until first rediscovered, chiefly through the work of Marcion the heretic. But this observation, as we shall show, is only partially correct. In any case Paul, as his Epistles became the reading matter of the Church, brought to Graeco-Roman Christianity and thereby to Christianity as a world-religion the water of life from the religion of the Old Testament, from the Gospel preaching of Jesus and of the primitive Church, and thus protected Christianity from becoming wholly Hellenized; just as on the other hand he was certainly the first in whom we can observe the fusion of the oldest primitive Christianity with Greek thought and with certain forms of Greek religion. His theology became one of the principal sources of Catholic dogma, but also of many heresies; but his personal grasp of religion has ever again proved to be a perennially fresh fountain of the true religion of Jesus. His *disclosure* of faith as the soul of religion, his heroic *experience* of this faith—"If God be with us, who can be against us!"—and his glowing exaltation of love as the necessary radiance from the faith of a child of God—this is the imperishable heritage which he, as an Apostle of Jesus Christ, has left to the Church.

BOOK IV

THE MISSIONARY CONGREGATIONS AND THE BEGINNINGS OF THE CHURCH

Translated by Sherman Elbridge Johnson

Prefatory Note

THE great place which the person and teaching of St. Paul occupy in our story is due to the nature of our sources. We have abundant information about him, concerning his personality and his viewpoints, as well as the story of his life. We can survey the chief features of his missionary work, and can trace the course of his life nearly to the end. We need not, however, permit ourselves the illusion that in so doing we have surveyed the entire primitive Christian mission, and that the religion of Paul is primitive Christianity. It is a rather difficult historical problem which lies before us when we try to portray this unfolding picture of the mission and expansion of Christianity, of the life and viewpoints of the churches founded by St. Paul and others, as these things actually were, and not merely as the great Apostle conceived that they had been and should be. Unfortunately the sources for this are not nearly so concrete or so plentiful as they are for Paul himself, and our treatment must here follow an entirely different course. A narrative is no longer possible; we must be content if we can succeed in getting a general view and sketching a few lines of development. The great historical problem of how the organization and teaching of the Catholic Church arose out of primitive Christian beginnings, lies of course completely beyond the scope of our problem. This development actually was consummated during the second century of Christianity (130-230), but its beginnings fall directly in the period of time which we have considered. The older view, viz. that the emerging Catholicism was a great force which departed completely from 'New Testament' Christianity (if we may use this term at all) can no longer be maintained. The result of our portrayal will be to show that the 'beginnings of the Church' are much earlier than was previously supposed, that the development toward a Church was accomplished more rapidly, that the New Testament literature—the genuine letters of St. Paul, the travel-document of Acts, the sources and earliest strata of the evangelic writings—all these point to the later period rather than to the earlier. Indeed this is the case chronologically. Before the year 70 —and we may mark this point as the end of the 'apostolic' age properly speaking, i.e. the first generation after Jesus—before 70, the Gospel of Mark at least had arisen, and also at any rate the Proto-

Apocalypse of John (existence of which may be assumed from study of the Apocalypse) including the letters to the seven churches of Asia Minor, while the writing as a whole belongs to the end of the century. To the later age, to the nineties, belong also the Acts of the Apostles and perhaps the Epistle to the Hebrews; somewhat earlier, the Gospel of Luke and perhaps at about the same time the Gospel of Matthew had their origin, both of them thus in the same period as the extra-canonical epistle of First Clement. In the years 70 to 90, probably, fall the First Epistle of Peter and possibly Hebrews; in the period from 100 to 125 may be placed the Gospel and Epistles of John, as well as the Pastoral Epistles, i.e. quite near the time in which the Epistle of Barnabas, the letters of Ignatius, and the Epistle of Polycarp arose. This is stating it cautiously. In face of the tremendous difficulty of the chronological problems which surround our studies here, it is more important to emphasize the fact that the later New Testament writings prove themselves more akin to the 'post-apostolic' literature than was previously supposed. These preliminary remarks may serve to offer reasons for the validity of our attempt to draw a picture of 'the primitive missionary congregations and the beginnings of the Church.'

CHAPTER XXII

The Expansion of Christianity During its First Hundred Years (A. D. 30-130)

1. *The Mission Field.* The missionary work of St. Paul, geographically considered, was quite limited: it included, except for the communities founded by him in company with Barnabas, only the provinces of Asia, Macedonia, and Achaia.[1] Prior to this in time came the propagation of the gospel in Judaea (I Thess. 2:14: churches in Judaea—Lydda, Joppa, the Plain of Sharon, Caesarea—Acts 9 and 10), Samaria and Galilee (Acts 8; 9:31; 15:3), Damascus (9:19); in the rest of the province of Syria, including the 'Phoenician' cities, Antioch (11:20ff), Tyre (21:17), Sidon (27:3), Ptolemais (21:7), in Cyprus (11:20; 13:4-13) and Cilicia (Gal. 1:21; Acts 9:30; 11:25). We have previously (p. 204) considered the possibility that the gospel may already have had success as far away as Cyrene (cf. Acts 6:9; 11:20), as in point of fact in some form or other it had come to Alexandria (Acts 18:24f). In any case, it is quite extraordinary that St. Paul never once mentions Africa as lying outside his mission field (Rom. 15:20f,23). Finally Italy (Puteoli, Acts 28:13), and of course Rome, must be mentioned. St. Paul was not the first to bring the gospel hither. This is, roughly, the state of affairs toward the end of Paul's life.

If now we take our stand at the end of the period of time which we have to consider, the picture of expansion has not really been altered. Only in Asia Minor has Christianity considerably expanded its compass: the salutation of First Peter includes, beyond the previous limits of Galatia and Asia, Pontus, Cappadocia, and Bithynia, as being spheres of the Christian diaspora, and the Letter of Pliny (*Ep. ad Traj.* 96 [97]), written in the year 112, corroborates this with respect to Bithynia-Pontus. We do not know how the gospel penetrated into these regions. The fact that First Peter is addressed to them does not indicate that perhaps St. Peter had done missionary work there, for the same epistle is addressed also to the undeniable missionary fields of Paul, Galatia and Asia. The fact that the letter is written from 'Babylon' must not lead us to conclude that we have

[1] For Illyricum see p. 358.

to do with a Christian church in the regions of the Euphrates, for 'Babylon' means Rome. It seems likely, on quite other grounds, that the new religion had quite soon arrived in this eastern locality, whether from Jerusalem or from Damascus or Antioch. The huge Jewish community which had been established there (Schürer, 4th ed., iii, pp. 6ff; Engl. tr., 2d div., ii, pp. 223ff), had many points of contact, and a much-traveled road led from Antioch to Edessa, the later central point of the Syriac national church. When Tatian brought his harmony of the gospels to his native church (about 172), Christianity was already present, and there is nothing to prevent us from supposing that its first beginnings there are to be placed toward the end of our period (130), since indeed its firmer organization, it is strongly to be supposed, took place before 150.[2] On the other hand, the mission from Jerusalem and Damascus had already penetrated quite early into Transjordania and into the immediate neighborhood of Palestine, the Nabataean kingdom of 'Arabia' (cf. Gal. 1:17; p. 197).

We learn nothing new about Egypt and North Africa in this period.[3] But even here we may hope that some day we may learn something about the earliest age of Christianity, through new discoveries. Previous discoveries of papyrus fragments of the New Testament do not reach back beyond the third century; [4] the various fragments of 'sayings of Jesus,' however, are to be placed close to the end of the period which we are studying, especially if some of them belong to the Gospel of the Egyptians, the origin of which is at least likely to be in the first third of the second century.[5] The Epistle of Barnabas, composed quite soon after 117, is considered by many to be of Egyptian origin, and its supposed older prototype, the Epistle to the Hebrews, was written by a Christian educated in Alexandria. Likewise the origin of the 'Missionary Preaching of Peter' may

[2] Cf. F. C. Burkitt, *Early Eastern Christianity*, p. 10.

[3] "The most unfortunate gap in our knowledge of earliest Church history is our nearly complete ignorance of Christianity in Alexandria and Egypt before the year 180" (Harnack, *Mission*, ii. 132; 2d Engl. ed., ii. 158f).

[4] [*Translator's Note.* Dr. Hans Gerstinger and Prof. Ulrich Wilcken date the Chester Beatty and Michigan MSS. of Paul in the second century; cf. E. J. Goodspeed, *Journal of Biblical Literature*, liv, p. 126.]

[5] Cf. Hennecke, *Neutestamentliche Apokryphen*, p. 22; "Die apokryphen Herrenworte" in Preuschen, *Antilegomena* (2d ed.), pp. 22ff; E. Klostermann, *Apokrypha*, ii. 11f; iii (2d ed.), 26. On the Gospel of the Egyptians, cf. M. R. James, *The Apocryphal New Testament*, pp. 10ff; on the agrapha, pp. 25-34. [*Translator's Note.* Attention must here be called to the latest discovery of this sort, published by H. Idris Bell and T. C. Skeat, *Fragments of an Unknown Gospel and Other Early Christian Papyri* (Oxford, 1935). The new gospel fragment has remarkable contacts with the Fourth Gospel.]

without unlikelihood be placed in Egypt in the first third of the second century.[6] The Teaching of the Apostles perhaps also ought to be considered a product of the Egyptian church. Whether, in the complete form in which we now have it, it is older than 130, is debatable.[7] To the old original Greek mission fields of St. Paul, the pseudo-Pauline literature adds Crete (Tit. 1:5), Dalmatia (II Tim. 4:10), and Nicopolis in Epirus (Tit. 3:12). We remain in the dark as to whether Paul was able to realize his plan to go to Spain. Thus the mission field at the end of our period is not substantially greater than it was at the death of St. Paul.

The concretely defined picture of the mission field which we have just sketched stands completely in opposition to the numerous hyperbolical statements in which St. Paul[8] and others say that the gospel

[6] Cf. Hennecke, *Neutestamentliche Apokryphen,* p. 169; M. R. James, *op. cit.,* pp. 16-19.

[7] Cf. Hennecke, *op. cit.,* p. 187.

[8] One must here discriminate: St. Paul himself says, I Thess. 1:8, that the faith of the Thessalonians has, not only in Macedonia and Achaia, but 'in every place,' become known. But this passage offers unusual exegetical difficulties (cf. von Dobschütz, *ad loc.*), and it has not yet been settled whether it is interpolated. 1:7 means that the Thessalonians have become the pattern for the faithful in Macedonia and Achaia. Vs. 8: ἀφ' ὑμῶν γὰρ ἐξήχηται ὁ λόγος τοῦ κυρίου [οὐ μόνον] ἐν τῇ Μακεδονίᾳ καὶ Ἀχαίᾳ [ἀλλ' ἐν παντὶ τόπῳ ἡ πίστις ὑμῶν ἡ πρὸς τὸν θεὸν ἐξελήλυθεν] ὥστε μὴ χρείαν ἔχειν ἡμᾶς λαλεῖν τι. . . . "For from you sounded forth the word of the Lord, [not only] in Macedonia and Achaia, [but in every place your faith to God-ward is gone forth;] so that we need not to speak anything." It would be helpful if we could strike out the bracketed words, for as the text reads, it contains in the antecedent and in the conclusion two separate thoughts; it is furthermore quite difficult to say where one is to find the place to which faith of the Thessalonians has been made known. As to the hypothesis of Zahn (cf. p. 296, note 25): it seems quite likely to me that there is interpolation in the two places in Colossians. 1:6, τοῦ εὐαγγελίου τοῦ παρόντος εἰς ἡμᾶς, [καθὼς καὶ ἐν παντὶ τῷ κόσμῳ ἐστὶν καρποφορούμενον καὶ αὐξανόμενον καθὼς καὶ ἐν ὑμῖν], ἀφ' ἧς ἡμέρας ἠκούσατε. . . , "The gospel, which is come unto us; [even as it is also in all the world bearing fruit and increasing, as it doth in you also,] since the day ye heard . . ." The double καθώς, which links the comparison with the thing compared, is so artistic and unnatural that I cannot think St. Paul capable of writing it. Notice also the middle καρποφορούμενον beside the active καρποφοροῦντες, vs. 10, and the whole phraseological turn, viz. that the gospel 'bears fruit and increases.' Col. 1:23, τοῦ εὐαγγελίου οὗ ἠκούσατε, τοῦ κηρυχθέντος ἐν πάσῃ τῇ κτίσει τῇ ὑπὸ τὸν οὐρανόν, οὗ ἐγενόμην ἐγὼ Παῦλος διάκονος, 'of the gospel which ye heard, which was preached in all creation under heaven; whereof I Paul was made a minister.' This passage betrays, in the double οὗ, in the heavily-laden, close definition of the gospel, another hand than St. Paul's. I see in these additions the Catholic redactor of the letter collection. As certainly Pauline there remains only Rom. 1:8, ὅτι ἡ πίστις ὑμῶν καταγγέλλεται ἐν ὅλῳ τῷ κόσμῳ, 'that your faith is proclaimed throughout the whole world.' Here, however, the spread of the gospel to the whole world is indicated; but yet only indirectly and rather rhetorically and hyperbolically. In all cases, such hyperboles go far beyond the actual conviction of the Apostle, who had still so much work before him (Rom. 15:23) and who speaks concretely and geographically about the fields in which he worked (Asia, Macedonia, Achaia).

has been 'spread throughout the whole world.' But this exaggerated expression is purely rhetorical and is apparently an imitation of an older Jewish turn of speech which affirmed somewhat boastfully the extent of the Jewish dispersion throughout the world.[9] It is hardly a tolerable hyperbole for Paul, who lived in full consciousness of his still unfulfilled missionary task (Rom. 15:23); the man who had wandered through no more than half the world cannot properly say that the whole world is already won. The 'fulness of the Gentiles' (Rom. 11:25) is still far from having 'come in.' The actual feelings of a man who works with 'things as they are' in the missionary field is shown to us in such a passage as Mark 13:10, 'the gospel must first be published among all nations' (cf. Matt. 24:14). And this signifies a span of time which is not brief; for the evangelist is about to show, in his eschatological discourse, that the end is *not to come soon.* It is also more rhetorical than in correspondence with reality when Colossians (1:6,23) says that the gospel has already been proclaimed to all creation under heaven, and when St. Paul in Romans 10:18 applies the passage in the Psalm to the preacher of the gospel: 'Their sound went out into all the earth, and their words unto the ends of the world.' Such rhetoric is particularly comprehensible in the writers of the post-apostolic age, who generalize and idealize the work of the Apostle, e.g. I Clem. 5:7, 'Paul, who taught righteousness to all the world.' At bottom, it is only the reflection of the missionary task, as the first missionary generation had formulated it, stated in expansive form.

2. *Judaism and the Gentiles.* 'All peoples' or 'all Gentiles'—such was the missionary program, as (already foreshown in Old Testament passages; cf. Rom. 15:11; Gal. 3:8) it was comprehended by St. Paul. To be sure, only occasionally does he speak explicitly of 'all' Gentiles (Rom. 1:5); much more often it is merely 'Gentiles,' for he senses always the contrast with Judaism. He himself has a feeling for the difference between Greeks and Barbarians, but he

[9] *Or. Sib.*, iii. 271: *Πᾶσα δὲ γαῖα σέθεν πλήρης καὶ πᾶσα θάλασσα,* "Every land and every sea are full of thee"; Strabo in Josephus, *Ant.* xiv. 7. 2, § 115, *εἰς ηᾶσαν πόλιν ἤδη παρελελύθει, καὶ τόπον οὐκ ἔστι ῥᾳδίως εὑρεῖν τῆς οἰκουμένης, ὃς οὐ παραδέδεκται τοῦτο τὸ φῦλον, μηδ' ἐπικρατεῖται ὑπ' αὐτοῦ,* "They [the Jews] have now gotten into every city, and it is not easy to find any place in the civilized world which has not admitted this race, yet no place is ruled by it;" *B. J.* vii. 3. 3, § 43, *τὸ γὰρ 'Ιουδαίων γένος πολὺ μὲν κατὰ πᾶσαν τὴν οἰκουμένην παρέσπαρταὶ τοῖς ἐπιχωρίοις,* "For the Jewish race is dispersed widely among the natives throughout all the civilized world;" Philo, *in Flacc.*, ch. 7 (M. ii. 524; tr. C. D. Yonge, London, 1855, iv. 61-99); *Leg. ad Caium,* ch. 36 (M. ii. 587; Engl. tr., iv. 99-180).

always remains bound by his obligation to Judaism (I Cor. 9:20), and his behavior in missionary work is in keeping with this. For him, in fact, the resistance of the Jews is only a temporary matter, and he still hopes for the final conversion of all Israel (Rom. 11:25f). His colleagues, like Apollos (Acts 18:26,28) and Aquila and Priscilla (18:20), have also beyond doubt kept themselves consecrated to the Jewish mission.

But the post-Pauline missionary church saw its task as being exclusively concerned with the Gentile mission. The development of this consciousness is reflected instructively in the development from Mark to Matthew. According to Mark 6:7-13, the Twelve were at all events sent to the Jewish people, while Jesus himself in the section 7:24—8:9 is shown as working in Gentile territory in the neighborhood of Tyre and in the Decapolis, and the 'gospel' which was to be proclaimed to the 'whole world' (14:10) is destined for 'all nations' (13:10). Now in Matthew, the holy obligation upon the Twelve (10:5f) is limited to Israel, but finally they are sent to all nations (28:19). It is similar in the spurious ending of Mark, 'Go out into all the world and preach the gospel to all creatures' (16:15), and in Luke 24:47, except that here the original destination of the Twelve to Israel is completely forgotten. This stands out most surprisingly in Acts 1:8, where the Twelve are sent out 'to the ends of the earth,' while in the book itself not one of the Twelve goes outside Palestine, nor has the single representative of the Gentile mission, St. Paul, heard of this commission. This development becomes complete in Justin Martyr, *Apol.* 1:39, 'From Jerusalem, men, twelve in number, went out into the world; and although unlearned and without talents of speech, they have, through the power of God, made the whole race of men to understand that they have been sent out by Christ to teach the word of God to all.' Here not only is the original task of the Twelve forgotten, but St. Paul is forgotten also —so strong is the conviction that from the first the saving good news has been intended for all mankind. For the view that the Church from of old had existed solely for the Gentiles had become more and more dominant. St. Paul still had the idea that a Jewish minority was existent in the community, a chosen group from Israel, a remnant (Rom. 9:27ff; 11:5; Isa. 10:22f; 1:9; I Kings 19:10,18; cf. also Gal. 4:27; Isa. 54:1 and II Clem. 2). The Apocalypse of John also speaks of the innumerable multitude from all nations, tribes, peoples, and tongues (7:9) as contrasted with the carefully reckoned number of the 144,000 sealed from the twelve tribes of Israel

(7:3-8).[10] The Epistle to the Ephesians retains the harmonizing, idealistic view that Christ had made a *unity* out of the two peoples, Jews and Gentiles (2:14f). But, generally speaking, the view predominates that the Jews are on the whole outside the Church of God, and that the third race, which has come in alongside Gentiles and Jews,[11] has taken over the place of the Jews in sacred history.

The saying in Hosea about 'No-People' and 'People' (Hos. 2:25) which St. Paul had already applied to the Gentile Christians, is reflected triumphantly in I Peter 2:10, 'which in time past were no people, but are now the people of God.' What Paul intends to say by his contrast of the 'Israel of God' (Gal. 6:16) and 'Israel according to the flesh' (I Cor. 10:32), is expressed brilliantly and forcefully in I Peter 2:9, "Ye are an 'elect race,' a 'royal priesthood,' a 'holy nation,' a 'people for God's own possession.'" We simply have here the honorific titles of Israel taken over and applied to Christians; moreover, the feeling has become widespread that the 'new people' (Barn. 5:7; 7:5) are the 'holy people' (Justin, *Dial.* 119).[12] Justin says concisely and clearly, 'The true, spiritual Israelite people, the people of Judah and Jacob and Isaac and Abraham, who in the beginning received a witness of their faith in God by circumcision, and who were blessed and called the father of many people, *are ourselves,* who through this crucified Christ were brought to God' (*Dial.* 11).[13] This proud consciousness expressed itself in the fact that the Old Testament as a whole came to be Christian property. From the beginning it was written with an eye to the Christians (I Cor. 10:11; Rom. 15:4); to *them* was spoken the 'today' of the Psalm (Heb. 3:7—4:11). Everywhere it pointed to Christ and the new religion (Rom. 1:2; 3:21; Luke 24:27,44; John 5:39); Christ himself appeared in it (I Cor. 10:4); he himself, through his Spirit, which was in the prophets, had prophesied in the Old Testament (I Pet. 1:11). Still more, in fact: the Old Testament history is the early history of Christianity: Abraham, the pattern of faith, is our father (Rom.

[10] This is the original meaning of the antithesis in the Proto-Apocalypse of John (cf. *SNT,* on Rev. 7:4-8), while for the editor the 144,000 were those who were saved from the final peril.

[11] Cf. Harnack, *Mission,* i. 208ff (2d Engl. ed., i. 240-278).

[12] That the Christians actually called themselves the 'people of the twelve tribes' cannot be proved from the address of the Epistle of James; the words ταῖς δώδεκα φυλαῖς ταῖς ἐν τῇ διασπορᾷ, 'to the twelve tribes of the dispersion,' are, like the whole salutation, an addition from the hand of the redactor who attributed the epistle to the Apostle of the Circumcision; they refer to the Jews. Nor can Rev. 7:3-8 refer to the totality of Christians (cf. note 1); τὸ δωδεκάφυλον (Acts 26:7) = the Jews.

[13] Knopf, *Das nachapostolische Zeitalter,* p. 347.

4:11f; Gal. 3:7; I Clem. 31:2); the Jews of the generation in the wilderness are 'our fathers' (I Cor. 10:1); the Christian women are daughters of Sarah (I Pet. 3:6). In proportion as the allegorical method of interpretation of the Old Testament made possible each Christian significance found in it, the realization that the books of the Old Covenant were historically the property of the Jewish people decreased more and more. The 'holy scriptures' belonged simply to the Christians; they were 'our scriptures.'[14]

Although St. Paul of course blamed the Jews for their great sin (Rom. 9:32; 10:3,16,21: 'All the day long, did I spread out my hands into a disobedient and gainsaying people,' Isa. 65:2), yet he explained their lack of faith partly from imperfect understanding (Rom. 10:2), partly from stubbornness (11:8,25). On this account, despite their enmity against God's commandments and the gospel (I Thess. 2:15f), he cannot believe that they will be utterly repudiated (Rom. 11:1f). Indeed, sometimes he so paints the picture as if to indicate that only a few of them are without belief (3:2f). Yet he always comes to the conclusion that Israel had trifled away his salvation through his own sin and that in no way whatsoever is it to be regained.

In the Gospel of Mark, particularly, we also meet the idea of stubbornness (4:11f). It was impossible to comprehend how the Jews, in spite of the preaching of Jesus, in spite of his deeds, in spite of his undeniable sonship to God, remained unbelieving. Above all, it was unthinkable that God's plan of salvation should be vitiated by the perversity of the Jews. Thus it was assumed that this very unbelief had been the work of God: they *were not intended* to attain knowledge of God; this, or the secret of the Kingdom of God, was to remain veiled to them. In this connection the idea of the messianic secret becomes clear for the first time:[15] Jesus did not wish them to know him as Messiah; therefore he forbade the demons to make him known (1:25,34; 3:12), therefore his miracles were to be concealed (1:44; 5:43); while the man healed on heathen territory was to bear witness of all that the Lord had done for him (5:19); therefore to this generation the sign which they demand is completely refused

[14] Thus Justin says (*Dial.* 29) to the Jews, 'In your Scriptures, or rather, not yours but ours;' Tatian, *ad Graec.*, *οἱ καθ' ἡμᾶς προφῆται*, 'the prophets among us;' *Acta Scillit. Mart.*, p. 6, *αἱ καθ' ἡμᾶς βίβλοι*, 'our books;' in which certainly Old Testament books were included. Tertullian, *Test. Anim.* 1, nostrae literae, 'our literature;' 5, divinae scripturae, quae penes nos vel Judaeos sunt, 'the divine Scriptures, which are in our possession rather than the Jews'.'

[15] Cf. Wrede, *Das Messias-Geheimnis,* and J. Weiss, *Das Aelteste Evangelium.*

(8:12); therefore again and again Jesus withdrew from public view (1:35,45; 3:7; 4:35; 6:31; 7:24; 8:27; 9:30). But this theory of veiling and of stubbornness, of course, cannot be supported throughout, in the face of the material at hand, since the individual narratives protest continually against the conception. And so, alongside it, another idea was advanced, viz. that of the sin of the Jews, especially the leaders of the people. Their heart was hardened or numbed (3:5), they were burdened with the unforgivable sin of blasphemy against the Spirit (3:28ff); they were the 'hypocrites' whom long ago Isaiah had condemned. Their heart was far from God (7:6f); the Sanhedrin had 'rejected' Jesus (8:31), he was taken prisoner by means of an ambush (14:43), condemned to death (14:64), the people were incited against him (15:11), and because of 'envy' they forced Pilate to change his mind (15:10,15). In the later gospels the tendency to unburden Pilate of the guilt and lay it upon the Jews goes still further; even a writer as early as St. Paul, in I Thess. 2:15, assigns all the crime to them. In Luke, the effort is quite obvious. Here it is said pointblank that Pilate found no guilt in Jesus (23:4, 14,22), nor did Herod (23:15); he *wanted* to release Jesus (23:20; Acts 3:13), and only because the Jews put pressure on him did he grant them their desire (23:23,25). In the crucifixion even the share of the Roman soldiers seems to be eliminated (23:33); they appear only as mockers (23:36). The irresolution of Pilate is, of course, painted still more strongly in the Gospel of John. Here also he is completely convinced of the innocence of Jesus (18:38; 19:4,6), and wishes to release him (19:12). The high point of this development is exemplified in the apocryphal Gospel of Peter, where not Pilate but 'King Herod' appears as judge; he and the other Jews are unwilling to wash their hands[16] (1:1; 11:46). And when it has the Jews going home from the crucifixion in full consciousness of the villainy which they have done, with the words, 'Woe upon our sins; judgment and the end of Jerusalem are near at hand' (7:25), we hear in it the same note, the same idea which is expressed in the Gospel of Matthew when Pilate washes his hands 'in innocency' and the people cry, 'His blood be on us and on our children!' (27:24f). It

[16] Cf. Hennecke, *Neutestamentl. Apokryphen;* Preuschen, *Antilegomena,* (2d ed.), pp. 16-20; E. Klostermann, *Apokrypha* (2d ed.), i. 4; M. R. James, *The Apocryphal N. T.,* pp. 13f, 90-94. That which is found in complete form in the Gospel of Peter is perhaps intimated already in the present text of Mark (3:6; 8:15; 12:13 and Matt. 22:16), for here, along with the Pharisees, Herod or the Herodians appear as enemies of Jesus. In this connection one cannot suppress the suspicion that behind this, as behind the Gospel of Peter, rests a confusion with the father of Herod: father and son are blended in the grim personality of the tyrant.

is especially in the Gospel of Matthew that the connection between guilt and the rejection of Israel is pointed out with unusual impressiveness. The whole gospel is meant to be read with the idea that ever since that time, the awful judgment has been brought against the people: 'the sons of the Kingdom are cast out' (8:12), the 'Kingdom has been taken from them and given to another people' (21:43). Since they have not accepted the invitation to the Son's marriage feast, the King has destroyed their city (22:7). The transformation of the idea of stubbornness in Matt. 13:13 is also noteworthy: *since* seeing they cannot see, the secrets of the Kingdom of Heaven are made known to them only in parables: they were quite incapable of understanding them.[17]

The idea that salvation has departed from the Jews and come to the Gentiles receives powerful expression in Mark and Matthew but especially in the two-volume work of Luke. The fact which had become clear in the synagogue of Nazareth (Luke 4:16-30), that Jesus found no acceptance in his father's city, and that there he had withheld his wonderful deeds, is brought to complete development in the picture given by the Book of Acts. The Jews, through their persecution of the disciples but especially by the murder of Stephen, have hastened the spread of the good news beyond the borders of Judaea—they themselves have been the cause of bringing the gospel to the Gentiles (chh. 8-11); in the diaspora they have again and again (13:45ff; 18:6; 19:9; 28:25-28) 'thrust the word of God from them and judged themselves unworthy of eternal life' (13:46). Finally, through their persecution of Paul they have assisted in bringing the gospel even to Rome. Even in Mark, the Canaanitish woman and the centurion at the foot of the Cross stand as shining contrasts to the unbelief of the Jews, and to this Matthew and Luke add the centurion of Capernaum, while in Luke there are the Samaritans (10:30ff; 17:16), and in Acts, Sergius Paulus, the jailor of Philippi, the just and impartial governor who denied that there was any crime on the part of St. Paul; in short, noble Gentiles who serve as a good foil to the black thanklessness and unbelief of the Jews. Thus in the Gospel of John the Greeks come to Jesus at the instant when he prepares to go to death (12:20ff); indeed this event is the signal of death for the one who precisely *through* his death was to bring together the children of God from the whole world (11:52). In this connection, then, the mission of the Twelve to the Gentiles (Matt. 28:19; Luke 24:47) gains an especially pathetic tone.

[17] [*Translator's Note.* Cf. D. W. Riddle, *Jesus and the Pharisees.*]

Anti-judaism, which appeared to be substantially mitigated in Paul because of his deep sympathy with his people (Rom. 9:1-5; 10:1ff; 11:1) and his hope for them (11:25), becomes sharper and sharper in the later literature. How harsh sounds the curt judgment on their rejection of Christianity in I Pet. 2:8, 'For they stumble at the word, being disobedient, *whereunto also they are appointed*'; how vehemently is it repeated, 'Them which say they are Jews, and they are not, but are a synagogue of Satan' (Rev. 2:9; 3:9); how cold and unloving is the short epithet 'hypocrites' in the Didache (8:1f)! The height of this development is to be found in the Gospel of John: its judgment upon the 'Jews' is as severe and devoid of hope as possible: they are sons of the devil (8:44), they are in every respect the typical representatives of the unbelieving and God-opposing world. They are in no wise capable of hearing the word of Jesus and coming to a state of belief (8:43ff; 5:44; 12:39), for they are not of the truth, but of the lie (8:44; 18:37); moreover, the idea of rejection appears again in John (12:40).

One must conclude from an observation of these points of view that the mission to the Jews has been abandoned as completely hopeless. And, in fact, the impression gained from the Book of Acts is chiefly that the attempt of Paul to win over his people was never again repeated. The Gentile Christian missionary church was adapted completely to the mission to the Gentiles, and since our sources derive nearly completely from this church, we hear nothing more explicitly from the mission to the Jews.

And yet the propaganda within Judaism was not completely given up. That is, of course, true for the primitive Church. So long as it was settled in Jerusalem and Judaea, it did not desist from attempting to convert the people. The first Apostles, especially Cephas and James, had not forgotten their commission (Gal. 2:9) but felt that they should continue to be Apostles to the circumcision. The Palestinian community after the year 70 still retained a certain attractive force which made converts (cf. ch. 23, below). But even the Jewish diaspora had not been given up as hopeless. The fact of the Apostles' decree (cf. pp. 311ff) speaks on behalf of this. The decree was indeed proclaimed expressly with an eye to the Jews of the diaspora (Acts 15:21); it was therefore hoped that they might be won. St. Paul reports to the other Apostles, the brothers of the Lord and Cephas, regarding his missionary journeys (I Cor. 9:5); there is no reason to assume offhand that by degrees they had confined their missionary work exclusively to Gentiles; they had sought, as had

Paul, to work from the synagogue as their base. And even the Jewish missionaries who, in Galatia, Corinth (and Colossae), had forced their way into the churches founded by St. Paul, surely must have occupied themselves in the first instance with the mission to the Jews; their endeavor was, in fact, to transform the Gentile Christian communities into Jewish ones. And, just as in the Pauline churches there was always a Jewish minority,[18] so it is possible that throughout the very provinces in which St. Paul worked, Jewish missions were carried on by men from the older churches. It is not even impossible that in the same city, alongside the Gentile Christian communities of the Pauline missionary circuit, Jewish Christian groups arose also. Were not the 'brethren' who made trouble for Paul in Rome (Phil. 1:15; cf. p. 386) Jewish missionaries who enviously and even bitterly opposed him (διὰ φθόνον καὶ ἔριν, 'because of envy and strife')?

Above all, we do not forget that the pre-Pauline church of Damascus, as well as that of Antioch, and certainly still other Syrian churches, was chiefly Jewish Christian in origin and nature, although they all had a Hellenistic coloring and some Gentile Christian mixture. The whole sphere of missionary activity from which Paul dissociated himself (pp. 275f) was after all not so decidedly Gentile Christian as were the churches founded by St. Paul himself. It was here, in fact, that the Apostles' decree had its chief importance; here the mission to the Jews continued to be carried on. And when later the decree was applied to other fields (e.g. in Asia, Rev. 2:14,20,25), the same situation obtained in those communities. Even the extremely harsh anti-Judaic author of the apocalyptic letters expected the conversion of the unfriendly Jews of Philadelphia (3:9); and the number 144,000, reckoned so systematically, shows that after all he did not estimate the multitude of Jewish Christians—whether present or future—as being few in number. But above all, the raging hatred with which the Jews persecuted not only St. Paul himself, but the whole Christian mission (I Thess. 2:15f; Acts 13:50; 14:2, 19; 17:5,13; 18:12; Rev. 2:9f; 3:9; John 16:1; Luke 6:22; Mart. of Polycarp 12:2; 13:1; 17:2; 18:1; Mart. Pion. 3:6; 4:8; 13:1; Tertullian, *Apol.* 7), proves that the Synagogue had experienced the competition of Christian propaganda in its midst, and it is not necessary to suppose that this means merely that they failed to draw

[18] In the commendatory letter for Phoebe (Rom. 16), besides Aquila and Prisca, four Jewish Christians are named: Mary, Andronicus and Junias, and Herodion; in the salutation of 16:21, three, Lucius, Jason and Sosipater; and in Col. 4:10f, three, Marcus, Aristarchus and Jesus Justus.

hearers from the surrounding Gentiles; the apostasy of many Jews to Christianity played a part here as well. Since our sources are one-sidedly Gentile Christian, we see very little of the results of the mission to the Jews. But a single report, such as that in Eusebius (*H. E.* iii. 35), that up to the time of Trajan innumerable Jews, including the later Bishop of Jerusalem, Justus, had gone over to Christianity, lights up the darkness. Evidences are not lacking that there was also a Jewish Christianity in the diaspora.[19] One may mention here especially the Epistle of James. Against the prevailing notion (e.g. SNT, *ad loc.*), we must maintain that the situation of 2:2f is best explained by supposing that the rich man who is so flattered is not a Christian but a Jew who reviles the honorable name given the Christians (2:7) and drags them before the court (2:6). Such a man is not to be sought for in the Christian congregation; thus the 'synagogue' in which the Christians encounter him is the *Jewish* synagogue, which the Christians still attended. This points to a Jewish Christianity which was not yet fully detached from the Synagogue. Unfortunately we know absolutely nothing about the circumstances of the separation of the Jewish Christian communities from their compatriots; but Luke 6:22 and John 16:1f presume that one could, although a Christian, still belong to the Jewish community, and this condition may have continued very much longer in some circles of the diaspora than in others. An early dating of the Epistle of James (e.g. before Paul) is not thereby demanded.

But above all the Gospel of Matthew is only to be understood as a work intended for Jewish Christian readers, of course for the Jewish Christians of the diaspora. The zeal with which the author adduces proof of the Messiahship of Jesus (his family tree, his descent from David and Abraham, and the scriptural evidence), his studied disproof of the Jewish calumnies relative to the birth and resurrection of Jesus, the method by which he removes the obstacle in the fact that Jesus had come from Nazareth in Galilee (2:23; 4:12-16), calls attention to the mission of Jesus to Israel (10:5f; 15:24) although he must finally direct the Twelve to go out among the Gentiles (28:19), indeed the great interest which the author has in the rejection of Israel and its reasons (21:43)—all these things reveal him as a man enlisted for the Christian mission who has the viewpoint and interests of Judaism. Above all, this is indicated by the

[19] [On the whole question of Jewish Christians, cf. D. W. Riddle, "The So-Called Jewish Christians," *Anglican Theological Review,* xii (1929), 15-33.]

fact that he contends for the unbroken maintenance of the Law (5:18) and against those who say that Jesus had annulled it (5:17, 19), against the advocates of antinomianism (7:23; 13:41). Indeed he would not even neglect the ceremonial commandments: 'These ought ye to have done, and not to leave the others undone' (23:23). He retains in his account a saying from which one must infer that the Sabbath continued to be kept by the early Jewish Christians (24:20). He interceded in favor of the teachings of the scribes themselves, though he must admit that they do not live according to them (23:3). With these viewpoints, which are thoroughly Jewish Christian and true to the Law, he stands apart from the circle of the great Gentile church, and it has not yet been proved that he did not have in mind—if not Paul himself, at least the school of the Apostle —when he wrote of the 'teachers' who annul the commandments (5:19) or the enemy who sowed the weeds in the field (13:25). In any case his theory of the sending of the Twelve to the Gentiles shows that for him the age of Paul and the work of the great man were not so obviously important in his eyes as they are in ours: it is indeed thinkable that he viewed him somewhat critically.

Finally we must mention here the fact that recently the accounts of the so-called Nazarenes have come into clearer light. This Jewish Christian community in Beroea of Coele-Syria, at unity with the universal Church in all essentials, acknowledged the Apostle Paul completely and differed only in two particulars, viz. that they kept the Law and practised circumcision, without however desiring to impose them on the Gentile Christians, and that they made use of an Aramaic version of the Gospel of Matthew.[20]

[20] Thus the picture of this completely local group appears in Schmidtke, "*Neue Fragmente und Untersuchungen zu den judenchristlichen Evangelien,*" 1911 (*Texte und Untersuchungen*, xxxvii, part 1 = third series, vol. vii, part 1). Schmidtke sums up the result of his penetrating investigations as follows: "Among the Jewish Christians of Beroea in Coele-Syria, who had grown up in the primitive Catholic Church, and who as a separate community under the earliest name of the Christians (Nazarenes) existed as late as the second half of the third century, there arose after 150 a targumistic translation of the Gospel of Matthew in the Aramaic (Syriac) language and in Hebrew characters, the Gospel of the Nazarenes (NE). This re-worked gospel was to have the fortune of being considered the original, in place of the Greek text. . . . Certain textual peculiarities of this Syriac Gospel of Matthew were utilized by Hegesippus. From that time on, however, the NE remained for a century and a half completely concealed from the view of ecclesiastical writers, until in one exemplar it came into the hands of Eusebius of Caesarea and by him was immediately received and used as the original Hebrew Matthew of tradition, long believed lost. The example of Eusebius was followed by Apollinaris of Laodicea, who in Beroea made for himself a copy of the NE, cited it abundantly as the original writing of Matthew, and in addition described its tradition, and in his exposition of the prophet Isaiah imparted to the world a number of

But apart from these documents, a line of early Christian writings (Romans, Hebrews, Barnabas; Mark, Luke, Acts, John; Justin's *Dialogue with Trypho the Jew*) contain very vigorous polemic against the Jews. This points toward the fact that the Synagogue was a force which was for the Church in no wise a thing of the past, but was at the very least an exceedingly serious spiritual opponent. One can conceive of this theological struggle with Judaism, which continued until late in the following century, in various ways. On the one hand, it may be thought of as a purely literary debate, which was actually addressed to a Gentile or Gentile Christian public. Since the Christian and Jewish propaganda sued for the Gentiles side by side, it was maintained—in order to demonstrate before this forum that Christianity was superior to Judaism in every respect—that the Jewish scriptures were the Christians' own, that in these very scriptures one could read how the Old Covenant, now obsolete and conquered by the New, passed over into the New: in this sense, at any rate, the Epistle to the Hebrews is to be understood, as a letter that had for its purpose not the conversion of the Jews, and not even for a moment the strengthening of the Jewish Christians, but instead the edification of Gentile Christians in the faith (cf. 3:12; 6:1f). On the other hand, it is possible to find in these writings the literary outcome of controversies with the Jews which actually took place, and thus a demonstration that the debates, like those which St. Paul had occasioned in the synagogues, continued until much later.[21] And this would afford proof that the Gentile

Nazarene interpretations. From the commentary on Matthew of the Laodicean writer, the 'Z' recension of the gospel, which appears in the marginal apparatus of the Matthaean text, has been compiled. The pertinent accounts of Epiphanius furthermore rest upon the reports which Apollinaris published, regarding the NE and its readers. But even Jerome has borrowed nearly all his examples of the NE and the Nazarene interpretations of Isaiah from Apollinaris, from whose commentary on Matthew, finally, we have a large NE fragment interpolated into the old Latin translation of the *Tomoi in Matthaeum* of Origen." Just as Schmidtke asserts that this NE is sharply to be distinguished from the 'Gospel of the Hebrews,' so the local community of these Nazarenes is to be distinguished from the Jewish Christian sect of Ebionites, with whom we have to deal later. [*Translator's Note*. Cf. M. R. James, *The Apocryphal N. T.*, pp. 1-8. James identifies the Gospel of the Nazarenes with the Gospel of the Hebrews.]

[21] A picture such as the author of Acts paints in 28:17-28, of St. Paul and the Roman Jews, must suit the writer's own age as truly as that of Paul. The literary *genre* of the controversies between Jews and Christians, of which an example is contained in Justin's *Dialogue with Trypho the Jew,* proves after all that similar disputations had taken place. An often mentioned dialogue (Origen, *Contra Celsum,* iv. 51f; Jerome, *Comm. in Gal.* 3:13; *Quaest. Hebr. in lib. Gen.*, p. 3, Lagarde) of Aristo of Pella between Jason and Papiscus, is lost to us; it is, however, often used by later writers (Harnack, *Geschichte d. altchr. Lit.*, i. 94f). And Origen (*Contra Celsum,* i. 43, 55) mentions the fact that he had taken part in such a disputation before umpires.

Christian Church did not abandon its mission to the Jews, though it was mostly in the form of apologetic and polemic. Both viewpoints have something to be said for them, and it is not admitted that the first alternative is the only correct one, which would disavow the propaganda among the Jews, especially in the post-Pauline age. It must be insisted that the Gentile Christian Church, despite its missionary program for 'all the Gentiles,' did not give up Judaism completely, and that in the diaspora, and not only in Palestine and the east, there were Jewish Christian communities, just as in the Gentile Christian churches Jewish Christian minorities were never lacking.

Attempts to judaize the Gentile Christian communities by imposing the obligation of circumcision upon them failed completely. On this point, St. Paul obtained an *enduring* victory at the conference in Jerusalem. We have seen that even the dispensation in the Apostles' decree (pp. 311ff) merely confirmed in essence the point that there should be no more debate about the circumcision of Gentile Christians, and that its precepts in actuality meant more a restraint of the Jewish Christians, who under its express stipulations no longer had an occasion for refusing table fellowship to their Gentile brethren. Although St. Paul was forced to carry on the struggle in the Epistle to the Galatians, in Romans the circumcision *of Christians* is no longer discussed, and even in the Corinthian Epistles is so incidentally and lightly touched (I Cor. 7:18) that one would say it was no longer a question of principle. In Colossians, it is touched upon once in passing (2:11), but in such a completely different tone—circumcision appears here as one of the means of practising asceticism—that one judges that it was not demanded by the gnostics in Colossae in the sense that Gentiles must become Jews in order to have a part in the messianic salvation, but rather as a means of perfection or of detachment from matter.[22] The older gospels provide no word of Jesus on the futility of circumcision. The Epistle to the Ephesians speaks of the 'so-called' circumcision (2:12) as a peculiarity which, from the point of view of the mixed Church made up of Gentiles and Jews, lies far in the past. The Epistle to the Hebrews does not mention it at all. In the Epistle of Barnabas (ch. 9) the physical circumcision of the Jews is portrayed as a stupid misunderstanding of the will of God: a wicked angel had led them astray; God had asked for the circum-

[22] [*Translator's Note.* It is strange that Weiss does not refer here to Phil. 3:2—4:1, in which the question of circumcision comes to the front; cf. pp. 387f, above, in which he tends to attribute the section to St. Paul, though he does not think that it belongs with the present Epistle to the Philippians.]

cision of the heart. Not once does the author admit that it is of value as a 'seal' of the people's covenant: even the Syrians and Arabs and idolatrous priests circumcise themselves. He explains the circumcision of the 318 servants of Abraham by allegorical interpretation as referring to the cross of Jesus. Since Justin, *Dial.* 47, says that Jewish Christians who keep the Law can also be saved, if only they do not attempt to persuade Gentile Christians to be circumcised likewise, one may gather that he knows of Jewish Christians who persist in these demands, but they obviously do not have the least power to impose them on the Gentile Church. On the contrary, there is, even in Justin, a tendency in the Church which would in general refuse fellowship to those Jewish Christians who are true to the Law. However, he does not wish to condemn those who have submitted themselves to the demands of the Jewish Christians; *perhaps* they also can be saved. Apparently it is meant here that the Jewish Christians who keep the Law are considered as a mere tolerated minority, which is completely without influence. After all, there was still this minority in and alongside the Gentile Christian missionary Church.

The victory of Gentile Christianity and the repression of Jewish Christianity have their literary reflection in the Book of Acts, where there is portrayed the victorious march of the gospel from Jerusalem to Rome, overcoming all obstacles and guided by God. Historically it appears in the midst of a mighty shift of focus of Christianity which Harnack[23] has described as follows: "About the year 50, Christianity is a great ellipse which has its foci at Jerusalem and Antioch; fifty years later these foci are located directly at Ephesus and Rome. In the light of this fact, the greatness of the work of St. Paul and of the first Christian missionaries stands out in the boldest relief." We have seen this state of affairs appearing already on the horizon. St. Paul at the time when he wrote the Epistle to the Romans cherished the plan, since he had 'no more any place in these regions' (15:23), of organizing, with Rome as a base of operations, a mission to the Latin west. For the author of the Book of Acts, Rome appears only as the end-point of a line of development; but in fact it was the mid-point of the pagan world; the results of Paul's work there amounted practically to a symbol of conquest of the world. And indeed the author of First Clement felt himself standing at the center of the world, since he says of St. Paul that he had been a herald in the east and the west, that he had taught

[23] *Mission,* 2d ed., i. 72; 2d Engl. ed., i. 83.

righteousness to the whole world, and that he had gone as far as the uttermost bounds of the west, i.e. to the pillars of Hercules.

3. *The Leaders in the Mission: the Apostles.* The view of apostleship previously discussed (p. 661) has governed the ecclesiastical viewpoint since the end of the first century. Justin gave it the following form: 'From Jerusalem, men—twelve in number—went out . . . . and they have made the whole race of men understand that they have been sent out by Christ to teach the word of God to all.'[24] This is based on statements in the gospels, viz. such passages as Matt. 28:19; Luke 24:47; Acts 1:8; (Mark 16:20).

Luke is especially important here, since in his account he speaks not only of 'the Apostles' (9:10; 17:5; 24:10) or 'the twelve Apostles' (Acts 1:2,26), but also deals with the relation of the Twelve to the great body of 'disciples' (Luke 6:17; 19:37). This specifically involves the idea that Jesus 'chose out' the Twelve from them and 'called them Apostles.' He has thus preserved not merely the recollection that Jesus had many more disciples than the twelve Apostles, but also a recollection that there were many more missionaries than the Twelve; for the juxtaposition of the mission of the seventy disciples (Luke 10:1) with that of the Twelve (9:10) is nothing less than an admission of this fact. But this picture, which has been adapted to actuality, is lacking in Mark and Matthew. For them (Mark 6:30; Matt. 10:2[25]), 'the Twelve' and 'the Apostles' are in all respects identical. In Matthew, neither the existence of a greater circle of disciples nor the possibility of other Apostles is envisaged.

This theory, however, has no support in the facts of the earliest age. In particular, the identification of 'the Twelve' and 'the Apostles' which appears everywhere in the basic material militates against it. We here face the question of whether actually in the lifetime of Jesus and shortly after his death there was a tightly-closed circle of twelve disciples (cf. p. 33; SNT on Matt. 3:16ff).

[24] Cf. also Luke 1:2, 'as they [of the second generation] delivered them unto us, which from the beginning were eyewitnesses and ministers of the word;' Heb. 2:3; I Clem. 42:1, 3, "The Apostles received the gospel (*εὐηγγελίσθησαν*) from God . . . . having therefore received their commands, and being fully assured by the resurrection of our Lord Jesus Christ . . . . they went forth preaching the good news that the Kingdom of God is coming;" Barn. 5:9, *ὅτε δὲ τοὺς ἰδίους ἀποστόλους τοὺς μέλλοντας κηρύσσειν τὸ εὐαγγέλιον αὐτοῦ ἐξελέξατο*, 'but when he chose out his own Apostles, who were to preach his gospel;' 8:3, *οἱ εὐαγγελισάμενοι ἡμῖν τὴν ἄφεσιν τῶν ἁμαρτιῶν* . . . . *δεκαδύο*, 'they who preached to us the forgiveness of sins . . . . twelve.'

[25] The reading of the Sinaitic Syriac, which has 'disciples' instead of 'Apostles,' cannot change the result, since evidently the text has been conformed to 10:1.

But there can be no doubt that our oldest witness, St. Paul, understands by 'the Apostles' another circle wider than that of the Twelve. In fact he probably does not mention the Twelve at all, for the reading of the single passage I Cor. 15:5 is doubtful (pp. 24,45). And if the Twelve are actually mentioned here, it is all the more evident that they are distinguished from 'all the Apostles' (I Cor. 15:7). He includes among the Apostles, e.g. Barnabas (I Cor. 9:5f; Gal. 2:9), James the brother of the Lord (Gal. 1:19), Silvanus and Timothy (I Thess. 2:7; cf. II Cor. 1:19) and Andronicus and Junias (Rom. 16:7). "Indeed, the term nowhere permits a strictly closed group; for as God has 'placed in the Church' prophets and teachers, so he has also placed in it Apostles as the first rank (I Cor. 12:28f). This charismatically-called order is not numerically limited, for its membership follows of necessity as God makes it known." These words of Harnack (*Mission*,[26] 2d ed., i. 269; 2d English ed., i. 321f) are not incontrovertible in themselves. In any case they explain and give further foundation to the fact that St. Paul could never consider the apostolate as limited to the Twelve; otherwise he would not have been able to consider himself an Apostle. 'The Apostles' are for him not a college of incontestable authority, incapable of expansion, founded by Jesus' previous appointment, but one with a sharply defined yet wider limit. A dispute may arise as to whether or not someone belongs to the Apostles—he himself had experienced such a difficulty.

[26] In I Cor. 9:5f, the brothers of the Lord are enumerated beside the 'other Apostles,' but so also is Cephas. Obviously, then, they are brought into especial prominence, since the opponents of St. Paul had laid great weight on these individuals as standing especially close to Jesus. The words ἐπίσημοι ἐν τοῖς ἀποστόλοις, οἳ καὶ πρὸ ἐμοῦ γέγοναν ἐν Χριστῷ (Rom. 16:7, 'of note among the Apostles, who also have been in Christ before me'), remain debatable. The question is whether Andronicus and Junias are included among the apostles because of the ἐν τοῖς ἀποστόλοις, or whether ἐν merely means 'according to the judgment of the apostles.' The latter explanation is not very convincing. In this case, 'the judgment of the Apostles' means little more than 'the judgment of all Christians' (cf. vv. 2, 4), and ἐπίσημοι would stand completely without connection, if the ἐν ἀποστόλοις did not designate the circle within which the men are included. That in other respects we know nothing of their missionary deeds is no reason for rejecting this interpretation; only once more we learn how limited is our knowledge of the earliest mission. In any case, the reference is to two Jewish Christians whose Christianity is older than that of St. Paul. Why he called especial attention to the two is difficult to understand. The first group of those greeted (Prisca and Aquila, Epaenetus, Mary, Andronicus and Junias) stands out as people who are somehow more prominent than the rest of the group; it is as though St. Paul wished to strengthen their authority over the church. If he says only of Andronicus and Junias that they were in Christ before himself, it has meaning only if addressed to a circle of readers for whom Paul otherwise is the highest authority, i.e. not Rome, but perhaps Ephesus.

He could not speak of 'the signs of an Apostle' (II Cor. 12:12) or of 'false Apostles' (11:13) if these words applied to a group the number of which was once for all defined. On the other hand, Paul sometimes speaks as if the number were limited and fixed (I Cor. 15:7, 'all the Apostles'; 15:9, 'the Apostles'; cf. Rom. 16:7; I Cor. 4:9; 9:5; Gal. 1:19), and there can be no doubt that he looks upon '*the* Apostles' as a Palestinian, Jerusalemite group: Gal. 1:19; I Cor. 15:7; 9:5. At any rate, this circle coincides with the circle which led Jesus' disciples in Jerusalem, except that he includes James the brother of the Lord, Barnabas, and still others, in it. On the other hand, a passage such as I Cor. 12:28f does not permit us in the slightest to suppose that all the Apostles must be derived from the earliest community. Still less does the Didache (ch. 11) imply this when it speaks of 'apostles.' An inexact usage of speech lies behind this phenomenon, and this perhaps makes an explanation possible.

The word 'Apostle' in itself has an entirely neutral—one might almost say 'secular'—character. Without laying stress on its use in ordinary Greek speech[27] (we have evidence for this use in St. Paul: the Apostles of the churches in II Cor. 8:23 and Epaphroditus in Phil. 2:25 are bearers of gifts and aid), this use of the word calls to mind the ambassadors of the Jewish patriarch, for whom we have good evidence after the year 70, whose duty it was to arrange collections of money in the Jewish communities of the diaspora.[28] 'Apostles' means, according to Eusebius (in Jes. 18:1f), the ambas-

[27] Hdt. i. 21; v. 38, 'an ambassador;' Hesychius, *ἀπόστολος· στρατηγὸς κατὰ πλοῦν πεμπόμενος* ('a general sent on board ship'); cf. Harnack, i. 274, note 1; 2d Engl. ed., i. 327, note 2. Josephus, *Ant.* xvii. 11. 1, § 300, *ἀφίκετο εἰς τὴν Ῥώμην πρεσβεία Ἰουδαίων Οὐάρου τὸν ἀπόστολον αὐτῶν τῷ ἔθνει ἐπικεχωρηκότος ὑπὲρ αἰτήσεως αὐτονομίας*, "An embassy of the Jews reached Rome, Varus having granted the nation [the right to send] the expedition on behalf of their request for autonomy." Here the word signifies not 'the head of the embassy' as Harnack would have it, but 'the embassy,' 'expedition' = *ἀποστολή*.

[28] Epiph., *Haer.* 30:4, *εἰσὶ δὲ οὗτοι μετὰ τὸν πατριάρχην ἀπόστολοι καλούμενοι, προσεδρεύουσι δὲ τῷ πατριάρχῃ καὶ σὺν αὐτῷ πολλάκις καὶ ἐν νυκτὶ καὶ ἐν ἡμέρᾳ συνεχῶς διάγουσι, διὰ τὸ συμβουλεύειν καὶ ἀναφέρειν αὐτῷ τὰ κατὰ τὸν νόμον* . . . , "Those who are next after the patriarch are called apostles; they sit beside the patriarch and with him often both night and day spend the time with him continually counselling with him and consulting him about matters of the Law;" chapter 11, on the Jewish 'Apostle' Joseph: *ἀποστέλλεται εἰς τὴν Κιλικίαν γῆν· ὃς ἀνελθὼν ἐκεῖσε ἀπὸ ἑκάστης πόλεως τῆς Κιλικίας τὰ ἐπιδέκατα καὶ τὰς ἀπαρχὰς παρὰ τῶν ἐν τῇ ἐπαρχίᾳ Ἰουδαίων εἰσέπραττεν* . . . , "He is sent into Cilicia; he returned thither from each of the cities of Cilicia, after collecting tithes and first-fruits from the Jews in the province of Cilicia." [*Translator's Note.* Cf. F. Gavin, *The Jewish Antecedents of the Christian Sacraments* (London, 1928), pp. 103-111; F. Gavin, 'Shaliach and Apostolos,' *Anglican Theological Review,* ix (1927), 250-259, especially the bibliography given there.]

sadors of the Sanhedrin, who were sent into the diaspora with letters to warn people against the Christian preaching before they heard it. Such an 'apostle' St. Paul may have been, since he traveled to Damascus with letters against the Christians from the Sanhedrin (Acts 22:5).[29] The essential point in this idea is that those who had this business to do traveled as confidential agents regularly commissioned, often equipped with letters of commendation (II Cor. 3:1), and were chosen by the congregation.[30] Barnabas and Paul on the first missionary journey (Acts 13:2f; 14:27) were such Apostles of a congregation, and St. Paul says (Rom. 15:24) that he wishes to be sent on to his Spanish mission *by the Roman Church*. Thus it was quite within the realm of possibility for one to be an apostle 'from men' (ἀπ' ἀνθρώπων, Gal. 1:1). If, despite this, St. Paul denies so vehemently that this is his situation, a narrower idea of apostleship now comes into play. He insists on being counted as one of the circle of '*the* Apostles,' as the 'least of the Apostles' (I Cor. 15:9), to be sure, as one called late to the office (Gal. 1:17), perhaps even as the one called *last*, by means of whom the circle of '*the* Apostles' in the narrow sense is completed and closed (I Cor. 15:8). The characteristic mark of such an Apostle is that he has been called *personally* by Jesus: Cephas and the others either during his lifetime *or* during the appearances of the risen Lord (I Cor. 15:5ff). Paul of course had received his call only after the resurrection (15:8; 9:1). It appears, however, that it was already felt that the relation to the earthly Jesus had to reach its consummation in the resurrection appearances; [31] otherwise St. Paul would not have had to proclaim his own vocation so earnestly. The concept of apostleship in this narrower sense, in any case, must have developed somehow out of the disciple relation. The word 'disciple,' however, does not occur in St. Paul; the decisive thing is the vocation to the apostleship, i.e. to the preaching of Jesus. So there was after all, it appears, an objective mark by which one may recognize an apostle, and we do not hear that the apostleship of Cephas and the others

[29] Cf. Harnack, *Mission,* 2d ed., i. 274ff; 2d Engl. ed., i. 330, note 1.

[30] II Cor. 8:19, *χειροτονηθεὶς ὑπὸ τῶν ἐκκλησιῶν*, 'appointed by the churches;' Justin, *Dial.* 108, *ἄνδρας χειροτονήσαντες ἐκλεκτοὺς εἰς πᾶσαν τήν οἰκουμένην ἐπέμψατε*, "Appointing chosen men you have sent them into all the world;" he speaks of the Jewish apostles, who were to hunt out Christianity.

[31] It is very interesting that in Acts 1:25 conditions for filling the place of Judas in the apostolate are given as follows: (1) that the one concerned must be a witness of the resurrection; (2) that during the whole time, when Jesus 'went in and went out among us, beginning from the baptism of John, unto the day that he was received up from us,' he must have been a companion of the Apostles.

was ever challenged. So much the more, that of Paul *was* challenged, for he could not prove his relation to the living Jesus, or prove that he belonged to the circle of the original Apostles.

For this reason it was important to discover other marks by which one could recognize an Apostle, an Apostle of Jesus Christ, and could distinguish him from pseudo-apostles. This was necessary, not only for St. Paul's sake, but increasingly so on account of the missionaries who went out from the Gentile Christian churches. The question concerning Paul came to a crisis at the Apostolic Council in Jerusalem, and indeed (Gal. 2:7ff) it was the evidence presented by the experimenting Apostle himself that turned the scale: 'They saw the grace which was given to me; they saw that the gospel of the uncircumcision was committed unto me, as the gospel of the circumcision was to Peter; for he that wrought effectually in Peter to the apostleship of the circumcision, the same was mighty in me toward the Gentiles.' The proofs, the letters of commendation to the Apostles, are his *work*, the *churches* founded by him (I Cor. 9:1f; II Cor. 3:2). If others dispute his apostleship, still the Corinthians must know that he is an Apostle (I Cor. 9:2). The fact that he succeeded in his preaching at Corinth gives him self-consciousness as an Apostle (II Cor. 10:15); he is a tried and true Apostle, whom the Lord commends (II Cor. 10:18): for it is not he himself, but Christ, who accomplishes all things through him, who has led him from Jerusalem even as far as Illyricum (Rom. 15:18f). Furthermore, if II Cor. 12:12—a passage not without difficulties[32]—enumerates especial 'signs' of an Apostle, signs and wonders and deeds of power (Rom. 15:18), it is only an especial unfolding of the 'Spirit' and of the 'power of God,' by which the Apostle must be ordained, and by which he is recognized as an Apostle and his word as God's word (I Cor. 12:8,28; I Thess. 1:5; 2:13; I Cor. 2:4; Rom. 15:19). The apostolate is the first and most important charisma, it is a 'gift of God's grace' (Rom. 1:5; 15:15; I Cor. 3:10; 15:10; Gal. 2:9). Herewith another path of thought is opened up, which is indeed less objective than the previous one which derived from the primitive Church, but which was for the consciousness of St. Paul not less convincing and indisputable. He himself is a *spiritual* Apostle, completely filled with his life's work, supported by the highest self-confidence (καύχησις) of his calling (Gal. 1:15f). We know, however, that this did not suffice

[32] The absence of a γάρ after μέν, and the double sense in which σημεῖα is used—in one place as 'mark,' in the other as 'wonder'—are extraordinary.

for the other party, which had denied his right to be an Apostle. At this point the two concepts of apostleship clash, and St. Paul was in a difficult position. But the power of facts won justice for him. Not only were such strange occurrences as that which happened in Antioch, when new men were called by a prophetic voice to the apostleship (Acts 13:2f), insurmountable hindrances to the claims of the Jerusalemite primitive Apostles, but especially also the results of the Gentile Christian missionaries whose God-given character could not be denied. A new, altogether universal concept of 'Apostle' developed more and more: that of *the travelling missionary*. For this fact the Didache is a startling documentary witness (11:3-6). Naturally such men would not have dared to lay claim to this title, if they had not been able to point to weighty proofs; there must have been inspired, eloquent preachers with the especial charisma of *revival preaching*. Did. 11:5 compares with the 'Apostle' the 'false prophet'—a sign that the categories of Apostles and Prophets distinguished by St. Paul in I Cor. 12:28 were in fact often combined, as in the case of Paul, who was both. Peter, in the account of Pentecost, appears also as a prophetic preacher (Acts 2:14), and in the Matthaean story of the Mission of the Apostles (10:41; cf. 5:12) the Apostles are practically equated with Prophets. Especial gifts and effects thus belong to apostleship; and it was very difficult to pretend to the title, particularly since it also demanded the *sacrifice of all personal possessions*.

It was, to be sure, not necessary for other Apostles to go as far as St. Paul, who earned his bread by his own toil. That was his especial 'glory' and pride (II Cor. 11:9f). He had his own reasons for it, viz. to shun any appearance of having a selfish secondary purpose (I Thess. 2:5, οὔτε ἐν προφάσει πλεονεξίας, 'nor a cloke of covetousness'), for he asserted as dogmatically as possible his *right* to support from the congregation (I Cor. 9:4-14), even if he had not availed himself of it. For the other Apostles the principle had no decisive importance other than as it affected their support; they must lay claim to this meagre livelihood in order to maintain their efficiency, for in other respects they were without home or possessions. In this connection the missionary discourses of the gospels are unusually instructive; both the ideal and the practical necessities and experiences of missionary practice are reflected in the variation of their texts. The oldest form of the directions,[33]

[33] From Q; contained in the purest form in Luke 10:2-12, 16; and in Matt. 10:5-16, 40, but with several characteristic variations.

intended for the messengers of the Kingdom who wandered through Palestine (p. 136), demands that they *take with them* no money-purse (Luke 10:4; Matt. 10:9, 'no money'), no haversack, no sandals for the journey; rather they are to accept quarters and food as they are tendered to them (Luke 10:7). Along with this they are enjoined against changing their lodging place (Luke 10:7a; Mark 6:10=Luke 9:4=Matt. 10:11b). This is added, in case someone invites them in order to entice them away. The foundation of these principles is expressed in Luke 10:7b, in a clear and businesslike way, 'for the laborer is worthy of his hire'; i.e. in return for preaching the good news to the people, it is right for him to lay claim to their support as his reward. St. Paul presents this principle in the following form (I Cor. 9:14): 'The Lord hath ordained that they which preach the gospel should live by the gospel.' The same argument is repeated in Matt. 10:10b, and at that after the negative commandment: "Provide [earn, κτήσησθε] neither gold, nor silver, nor brass in your money belts . . . . for the workman is worthy of his meat"—this form is illogical only if the emphasis lies, first, on the fact that their preaching is not to be *paid for* with money, and secondly, on the fact that they have a right only to their *keep*. One sees clearly that the principle of Luke 10:7, I Cor. 9:14, was not in practice always understood thus, but that rather it was taken in the sense of a payment for the preaching. The idealism of missionary work would not, however, permit this perversion of the old word of the Lord! Anxiety on this very point meets us in Did. 11:6. The Apostle travelling abroad is to receive only bread when leaving a place, and only enough to enable him to reach his next (Christian) night's lodging: [34] 'But if he ask for money, he is a false prophet.' As for lodging, the earliest form of the discourse (Luke 10:5ff) furnishes a supernatural test for a suitable house: if the salutation of peace 'rests upon' the occupant, i.e. if receptiveness and congenial understanding are found there, it is a sign that the 'son of peace,' chosen by God, is there; *in that house* the Apostle is to stay! (cf. SNT, *ad loc.*). This direction, which proceeds from the ancient enthusiasm of the primitive Church, already by the time of Matthew is no longer perceived or understood (10:11); its place is taken by the cool, rational regulation, 'And into whatsoever city or town ye shall enter, inquire who in it is *worthy;* and *there* abide till ye go thence!' This saying presupposes

[34] This statement not only assumes a certain density of colonization, but also a great expansion of Christianity in villages and towns. This would be the case in Egypt earlier than elsewhere; perhaps in the delta or the Fayûm.

unfortunate experiences with the precept regarding quarters; it enjoins caution. But the soul is gone out of the old sayings, especially when they are expressed thus: 'And if the house be worthy, let your peace come upon it: but if it be not worthy, let your peace return to you' (Matt. 10:13).[35] The Didache, in this connection, takes such a completely different point of view that it considers a longer stay for the Apostle in a given community to be especially improper: he must stay no longer than one or two days at the most, otherwise he is a false prophet who is trying to make himself comfortable at the expense of his missionary task (11:5f). This document is intended for existing churches which themselves no longer carried on missions, or at any rate in which this kind of work had subsided. The missionary discourses of the gospels, on the contrary, had in view cities and villages which were still completely untouched. In both cases the Apostle is a missionary and only that, not the leader of a church. He dare not rest, the field is still a broad one, and the laborers are few (Luke 10:2= Matt. 9:37f).

This understanding of the office and significance of the Apostles now changes in the course of time. If in the second and third centuries the anti-heretical Fathers based themselves—as against the false Gnosis—on the *apostolic* tradition as the pillar and ground of the truth, if they replied to those who proffered 'lying scriptures' with the *apostolic* scriptures as the sole sources of truth, the fact remains that this high esteem of and emphasis upon the apostolic religion as the only true Christianity has continued down to our own epoch. The beginnings of a belief in an authoritative 'teaching of the Apostles,' an 'apostolic canon of scripture,' and an 'organization of the Church reaching back to apostolic arrangement' are to be observed right here.[36]

[35] One notices how the future in Luke 10:6 is replaced by the imperative, which completely attenuates the saying! The idea of predestination is no longer understood.

[36] These 'three apostolic norms' are those which, according to Harnack, *History of Dogma,* 4th ed., i. 353f, 2d Engl. ed. (1896), ii. 18-93, are characteristic of the consolidated Catholic Church in its struggle with Gnosticism. "The second century of the existence of the Gentile Christian churches received its special character through the glorious struggle with Gnosticism and the Marcionite church, through the gradual development of an ecclesiastical and learned doctrine, through the restraint of the primitive Christian enthusiasm, above all through the establishment of a great ecclesiastical union, which was at the same time a political community, school, and cultural association, which rested upon the strong foundation of an 'apostolic' rule of faith, an 'apostolic' collection of writings, and—finally also—an 'apostolic' organization—the *Catholic Church*" (p. 337; Engl. ed., ii, p. 1). The beginnings of this development lie, however, directly in our period.

In the letters of St. Paul the following generation saw not so much the picture of a missionary and revival preacher, but rather that of a father who rears up churches which already exist to be his own children (I Cor. 4:14f), of a teacher who had transmitted truth to them as he had received it from the Lord (I Cor. 11:23; 15:3ff), and who devoted his great powers to the task of keeping them steadfast in this truth (e.g. I Cor. 15; Gal. 3:1ff; 5:7; Col. 2:6ff), of an organizer who regulated the government and life of the Church by his mighty word. Though St. Paul had indeed written to only a few churches, it was after all not difficult to apply his exhortations and advice to others as well. In the present text of First Corinthians a number of passages are to be found [37] in which it is expressly emphasized that what Paul writes here is in force, or should be, for all churches. It is not in itself unlikely that St. Paul thought and wrote so—though it will not harmonize well with his customary way of limiting himself to *his own* churches or with his directness in devoting himself in each letter to a single church—but since each of these passages offers considerable linguistic and stylistic difficulties, the assumption is all too obvious that these turns of expression are traces of a catholicizing redaction, proceeding according to the axiom (expressed in Tertullian and later) that the Apostle speaks to *all* when he speaks to single churches (*Adv. Marc.* 5:17). This catholicizing viewpoint makes its weight felt also in the words of salutation in First Corinthians, which is addressed, not merely to the church in Corinth, but also to 'all that in every place call upon the name of Jesus Christ our Lord, among them as among us' (1:2).[38] These words, which are very difficult to justify stylistically in this context, produce the impression of being an interpolation by means of which universal validity for all Christians was to be imparted to the letter. They were all the more appropriate since First Corinthians formed the beginning in the earliest collection of the Pauline epistles.[39]

[37] 4:17; 7:17; 11:16; 14:33,36. On this point see J. Weiss's Commentary.

[38] Cf. my Commentary, *ad loc.*

[39] Muratorian fragment; cf. Th. Zahn, *Gesch. des Kanons,* ii, 344ff. [*Translator's Note.* On the whole question of the Pauline letter collection, and especially the place of Ephesians in it, see E. J. Goodspeed, *New Solutions of New Testament Problems;* and *The Meaning of Ephesians;* also "The Place of Ephesians in the First Pauline Collection," *Anglican Theological Review,* xii (1930), 189-212; C. R. Bowen, "The Place of Ephesians among the Letters of Paul," *Anglican Theological Review,* xv (1933), 279-299. It has been suggested by John Knox (*Philemon among the Letters of Paul,* ch. iv, Chicago, 1935) that Marcion's list represents the earliest list of Pauline letters, except that Marcion has changed the places of Galatians and Ephesians (the introductory,

However one may criticize these passages, the important fact is that someone made a collection of the letters of Paul which was intended for the whole Church, and this evidently shows that the Apostle was not regarded as one of many missionaries in the period of the Church's beginnings, not simply as the founder of several important communities, but as a father and teacher of the Church, whose word could not be followed carefully enough, either intensively or extensively. There is some dispute over the time when the first Pauline collection was arranged, and we can say nothing certain about it. However, Ignatius, and apparently also the author of the First Epistle of Clement, have apparently made use of such a collection, certainly not our own,[40] in any case one which already contains the Epistle to the Ephesians. It may have arisen before the end of the first century. But this very *Epistle to the Ephesians* is an excellent document for the point of view which we are considering. It is, above all, an undoubtedly 'Catholic' document, and the author has in mind the whole Church, even when in the address he names a single community or has written a salutation 'in blank' to be filled out variously. He writes the epistle as a sort of testament of St. Paul, in which he expresses himself on the subject of his life's work. The specific contents of his gospel, viz. that the Gentiles should be co-heirs and comrades in 'the body' and participators in the promise (3:6), has by this time been realized in the Church: the 'so-called' circumcision and the 'so-called' uncircumcision are united in one people (2:11-22). The Apostle appears as possessor of a secret revealed to him (3:3,9), as a martyr who suffers on behalf of the Gentiles (3:1),[41] who always makes intercession (3:14-19) for the Church. Above all, the later Catholic interpretation of the Apostle makes a clear appearance when the author, in a significant departure from I Cor. 3:11 (in which Christ is the

---

encyclical epistle) because of his desire to call especial attention to the former. The letters were originally arranged in order of length, with the exception of Ephesians, which served as an introduction. Mr. Knox argues that I and II Cor. were counted together and so head the list; the important thing is that St. Paul wrote to *seven* churches.]

[40] At the present time we possess in all Greek MSS the same order, in which the letters were disposed according to length, at least the ten. [But see the Beatty papyri.]

[41] This view appears also in Col. 1:24, *νῦν χαίρω ἐν τοῖς παθήμασιν ὑπὲρ ὑμῶν*, "Now I rejoice in my sufferings for your sake;" 2:1f, *θέλω γὰρ ὑμᾶς εἰδέναι ἡλίκον ἀγῶνα ἔχω ὑπὲρ ὑμῶν καὶ τῶν ἐν Λαοδικίᾳ [καὶ ὅσοι οὐχ ἑόρακαν τὸ πρόσωπόν μου ἐν σαρκὶ], ἵνα παρακληθῶσιν αἱ καρδίαι ὑμῶν* [text: *αὐτῶν*], "For I would have you know how greatly I strive for you, and for them at Laodicea, [and for as many as have not seen my face in the flesh;] that your [text: 'their'] hearts may be comforted." The bracketed words are an interpolation, analogous to that in I Cor. 1:2; cf. also in Col. 1:6, the words from the first *καθώς* to *καθὼς καὶ ἐν ὑμῖν*.

foundation), says that the Church is built upon the foundation of the Apostles and (Christian) Prophets, Christ Jesus being the cornerstone (2:20). Here speaks the later, post-apostolic generation which looks back with admiration upon 'the Apostles' as the first, classical generation, and the protection and support of the truth, and by now calls them 'holy' Apostles (3:5). The attitude of the author is completely clear when he imitates St. Paul's passage on the three groups of Spirit-filled persons (I Cor. 12:28), with a significant modification (4:11)—

I Cor. 12:28	*Eph. 4:11*
. . . God hath set . . .	He gave some to be
first Apostles	Apostles;
secondly Prophets	and some, Prophets;
	and some, Evangelists;
	and some, Pastors
thirdly Teachers.	and Teachers.

The interpolation of evangelists into the third place teaches us that Apostles and Prophets, in the author's view, belong together as the onetime founders of the Church; therefore, for the missionaries of his own age he no longer uses the expression 'Apostles'—which remains reserved for that first generation—instead he chooses the word 'evangelists.'[42] The Epistle to the Ephesians is one of the first examples of pseudo-apostolic writing, and in any case one of

[42] Here it is clear that the retention of the title of Apostle for the missionaries in the Didache is a characteristic of the greatest antiquity; measured by the Epistle to the Ephesians, it is an anachronism. Although the former may be a later literary production than Ephesians, in its contents it here seems to have preserved something from earlier times. In any event it does not represent the view which obtained authority in the Church. This view reserves the title of Apostle for the earliest Apostles, and adopts instead the title of Evangelist. That is, e.g., evident from the Acts of the Apostles. Whether Philip (ch. 8) was one of the Twelve or not (cf. p. 121)—in any case the author wishes to distinguish him from them; since, however, he was beyond doubt a missionary, he calls him an evangelist (21:8). The Timothy of the Pastoral Epistles is in the first rank of church leaders, not a missionary; but this fact must not be lacking in the picture, so he is admonished to do the work of an evangelist (II Tim. 4:5). This usage is met with in classical ecclesiastical form in Eusebius (iii. 37. 1, 2), who says of the *disciples* of the Apostles, that they, building further on the foundations laid by the Apostles, accomplished the work of evangelists, since their glory lay in the fact that to them was committed the task of *preaching* to those who had not yet received the word of faith, and to them were given the divine gospels. Here a second, still narrower usage is intermingled, by which the authors of written gospels are designated. But this is a relatively late viewpoint and mode of expresson. This second motive is still lacking in v. 10. 2: there were, that is, even at that time, numerous evangelists of the word whose concern it was to contribute zeal inspired by God, after the manner of the Apostles, to the vigilant edification of the people with the word of God—one of them was Pantaenus.

the most important and instructive. Above all, one cannot say it strongly enough: the fact that someone caused a departed Apostle to speak on issues of the day proves the existence of the later Catholic view of an Apostle as a teacher and leader of the Church commissioned by Christ; it is the same view which led to the formation of an ecclesiastical collection of all the genuine Pauline letters which were obtainable. And it has not yet been settled, whether the author of the Epistle to the Ephesians is not the same person as the collector of the Pauline corpus. Certainly his spirit, perhaps also his hand, makes itself perceptible not only in the editing of Colossians, but also in the editorial closing doxology of the Epistle to the Romans (16:25ff).[43] Such a collection and edition of apostolic writings, augmented by original composition in the spirit of the Apostle, has a parallel in the manner in which the editor of the Apocalypse of John[44] deals with the older prophecies which he has utilized and reworked, especially the book of the prophet John of Asia Minor written for the seven churches. The words spoken directly from the mouth of Jesus in the form of a letter from heaven to the several churches—Jesus says 'I' and addresses the churches as 'thou'—is important from the point of view of the author, who takes occasion, in the seven letters, to speak especially of '*the* churches.' And according to his view it is no longer Jesus himself who speaks directly here, but 'the Spirit' (2:7,11, etc.), i.e. the spirit of prophecy (19:10) in which John and other prophets have spoken (1:4; 4:2; 21:10). While the editor makes his redaction with the highest respect for this prophecy (1:3; 22:7,10,18f), nevertheless he feels himself also called to prophesy (10:11), and does this while at the same time he explains, makes use of, gives new interpretations to, expands and amplifies the older prophecy—in short, he proceeds as perhaps the author of Ephesians did in working with the material before him, the Epistle to the Colossians or Laodiceans. The analogy is, of course, not complete. For example, the apocalyptist differentiates himself in that he does not proclaim his authority as that of an 'Apostle' but of a 'Prophet.' Even so, his work is another illustration of Eph. 2:20; 3:5, where alongside the holy Apostles the Christian Prophets appear as the foundation of the

[43] In the oldest collection (Muratorian canon) Romans stood at the end; the editorial concluding doxology would be very appropriate here. We may have, thus, in the additions in Cor. 1:2 and Rom. 15:25ff, traces of the earliest collection before us. [*Translator's Note.* If Marcion's order is actually the oldest, on this supposition, the concluding doxology is still later.]

[44] Cf. J. Weiss, *Die Offenbarung des Johannes.*

Church. They are, in short, the first generation of witnesses, who have received revelation from Christ himself.

We have in the First Epistle of Peter, in my opinion, still another example of pseudo-apostolic writing which perhaps goes back to the year 70, and in the Pastoral Epistles a still later one which is probably to be dated after 100. The latter are indeed the classic and earliest examples of an 'apostolic church order.' Here material is added to strengthen the strictly Catholic ideas of First Clement, viz. that the Apostles appointed in country and city their 'first-fruits' (ἀπαρχάς) as Bishops and Deacons (42:4). The Apostle Paul took pains to regulate the method of government of the church and ecclesiastical discipline, but he especially gave directions for maintaining the purity of the faith and the rejection of false teaching. Significantly enough, it is impressed upon the readers that Paul's followers shall hold fast to the teaching handed down to them from the Apostle and shall pass it on (II Tim. 1:13; I Tim. 4:6; 6:14, 20; Tit. 2:1): the *reminder* of the apostolic doctrine (II Tim. 2:8), the anxiety for sure propagation of the apostolic tradition (II Tim. 2:2) are the chief objects of interest of the writer. It is due to the power of Paul himself that his letters were made, by means of their collection, the common property of the Church, and have served as patterns for new productions. The sound basis for this view lies in the fact that only the documents which he himself wrote exhibit his spirit. However, the huge importance of the great personality continued to operate, a personality which in spite of misunderstanding and distrust, against which he had to contend, succeeded in its task. But it is worthy of note that another, who undoubtedly belonged to the Pauline missionary and doctrinal circle, caused St. Peter to speak to posterity, and at that to the churches of the Pauline missionary field. He would not have been able to do this if he had not been convinced that Peter and Paul were in all essentials of precisely the same mind (this is surely the meaning of I Pet. 5:12), and that both wished to serve the one Church. St. Peter, moreover, appears in this epistle as being not so much a missionary as an exhorting, comforting, teaching Prophet. Just so he appears in Acts 2:14-40 as a Prophet, and St. Paul appears in the speech at Miletus (20:20ff,27) at least as much in the rôle of church leader and teacher as in that of missionary.

The Book of Acts, throughout, is a document which is characteristic in exhibiting the concept of 'apostolic' which we are here considering. It is significant that the author of the two-volume work, after the words and deeds of Jesus, adds those of the Apostles, patterns their wonders and sufferings after those of Jesus: they are the continuers of Jesus' work. The speeches of the Apostles are couched in the modes of thought and style of the author's age, especially the speeches of Paul, for there is no doubt in the author's mind that the Apostles proclaimed the very same teaching which was of such value for the Church of the later day. Naturally they are in this respect united one to another; serious opposition cannot have arisen between them, and the Apostolic Council reveals this complete concord. The council's Decree, which is the flower of this union, is a work of the Holy Ghost (15:28) and therefore unconditionally binding upon the Church. The fundamental unity between Peter and Paul is especially illustrated by the parallelism between the two which is carried through so carefully. Just as St. Peter stands over against St. Paul, so First Peter stands alongside Ephesians and the Pastoral Epistles. So in I Clem. 5, Peter and Paul are counterparts, both of them noble martyr-Apostles. This state of affairs has its sufficient reason in the fact that a richer and more edifying tradition came into being *only* because of both of the men. So much the more noteworthy is the contrast: the author of the Book of Acts places the Twelve at the very fountain-head of the missionary work, and it is the Twelve who have been sent by Jesus to the ends of the earth (1:8), while in the book itself he knows little or nothing to relate about the eleven Apostles. Here we see how the theory of the Twelve collides, on the one hand, with these facts; on the other hand, with the very early developing honor paid to Peter and Paul, which is especially manifest in Rome. In the Gospel of Matthew it is St. Peter who dominates; in the Gospel of John it is—by Peter's own recognition—the Beloved Disciple who is coördinate with him and even tentatively ranked above him (20:3-10; 21:15-23). It is worthy of remark that, more and more, apostolic legend finds its way into Christian literature; the apocryphal Peter passages of Matthew (14:28-31; 16:17ff; 17:24-27) and Luke (5:1-9) and the passage regarding the Beloved Disciple (especially John 21, but also 19:26f, 35; 20:3-10), the Thomas legend (20:24-29) and the single sayings of disciples scattered here and there in the Fourth Gospel (11:16; 14:5,8,22) show how fancy had begun to engage itself with the various figures. The canonical Acts already adorn Peter and Paul with miracles, the apocryphal Acts of Apostles carry the development much further; in the latter, still other legendary tales predominate. 'The Apostles' come to be honored more and more as saints and martyrs, and their picture is enhanced still more with the divine.

The view that 'the Apostles' [45] are the founders of church *organization* comes to expression in the Book of Acts as in the Pastoral Epistles, e.g. in the fact that the Apostles *and they alone* can transmit the Spirit through the laying on of hands (8:16f; 19:6)—an idea which was unheard of in the earliest period (cf. pp. 40ff). So Timothy has also received his charisma through the laying on of hands of the Apostle (II Tim. 1:6), but—on the contrary—according to I Tim. 4:14, through the laying on of hands of the presbytery. This contradiction is resolved by I Clement (chh. 42-44), according to which the Bishops (who are in fact the same as the Presbyters) and Deacons are appointed by the Apostles, as the Book of Acts (14:23) has already related it. This is particularly told of the Deacons—for the Seven are for the author the pattern of the later Deacons (6:2-6); and here special attention is called to the laying on of hands by the Apostles. This view of the 'Apostles,' finally, receives its classical expression in the 'apostolic church orders.' We must mention, finally, the distinctive title of the Didache: 'The Teaching of the Lord *through* the Twelve Apostles'; the so-called 'Apostolic Church Order' goes still further; in it the Twelve one by one receive the commission to preach concerning the dogmas and ordinances of the Church.

4. *The Earliest Gospel: Mark.*[46] The word 'gospel,' it is true, meets us in the Gospel of Mark in several sayings of Jesus (13:10; 14:9; 8:35; 10:29; 1:14f), but it is not thereby demonstrated that Jesus actually made use of it; important considerations militate against it.[47] It may be, however, that the saying 'to the poor the glad tidings are preached' (Matt. 11:5; Luke 7:22, in conjunction with Isa. 61:1), which was already to be found in Q, goes back to Jesus. This question is not so important for us as the recognition that the word, as it appears in Mark, does not refer yet to the written gospel, but to that which was proclaimed by the missionaries 'in all the world' and 'to all peoples' (14:9; 13:10). It refers not only to the content but also occasionally to the preaching

[45] [*Translator's Note.* On the question of the primitive ministry, cf. B. H. Streeter, *The Primitive Church.*]

[46] On this matter, cf. J. Weiss, *Das Aelteste Evangelium,* especially pp. 29-42, and Th. Zahn, *Einleitung in das N. T.* § 48, 'Das ungeschriebene Evangelium,' (Engl. ed., *Introduction to the N. T.*, ii. 367-386).

[47] Cf. pp. 29ff, *Das Aelteste Evangelium.* On the meaning of the word, cf. *Handbuch zum N. T.*, in Mark 1:1.

itself (8:35; 10:29); in short, it is an expression for missionary preaching. So we find it also in St. Paul,[48] sometimes in the sense of the occupation of preaching,[49] sometimes in the sense of the content of the preaching.[50] 'The word'[51] and 'the preaching'[52] are completely parallel terms—a sign that the written 'gospel' cannot be in the writer's mind, a thing which is readily conceivable in the earliest period. If, then, the word 'gospel' appears in the superscription of the Gospel of Mark[53]—and indeed it is obviously appropriate for the beginning of the *book* ('the beginning of the Gospel of Jesus Christ [the son of God]')—we have no reason to deviate from the strongly established interpretation gained from its use in missionary work. The book is not in itself 'a gospel'; rather the gospel is contained in this book. In it is written down the content of the good tidings which previously has been proclaimed by word of mouth. This is important in two respects: first, for the criticism of the work and its form. One can understand it rightly only if it is considered neither as memoirs of an eyewitness nor as biography; it must be read as a piece of missionary literature. Thus we establish premises regarding the mode and content of the missionary preaching, which are especially important for the question of what rôle 'the historical Jesus' played in it.

When Justin Martyr wishes to explain the character of the gospels

[48] In the Acts it appears only twice (15:7, τὸν λόγον τοῦ εὐαγγελίου, 'the word of the gospel;' 20:24, τὸ εὐαγγέλιον τῆς χάριτος τοῦ θεοῦ, 'the gospel of the grace of God'). Much more often the verb is used, followed by an object denoting the people to whom the gospel is preached (κώμας, 'villages'; πόλεις, 'cities,' 8:25,40; 13:32; 14:21), or the contents (Ἰησοῦν, 'Jesus;' τὸν λόγον, 'the word;' τὰ περὶ τῆς βασιλείας, 'the things pertaining to the kingdom;' εἰρήνην, 'peace;' τὸν Κύριον, 'the Lord;' τὴν ἐπαγγελίαν, 'the promise'; ἀνάστασιν, 'resurrection'; 5:42; 8:4,12; 10:36; 11:20; 13:32; 17:18, etc.).

[49] Rom. 1:1; 15:16,19; I Cor. 4:15; 9:12,14b,18; II Cor. 2:12; 8:18; Gal. 2:7; Phil. 1:5; 2:22; 4:3,15; I Thess. 1:5; 3:2.

[50] Rom. 1:9,16; 2:16; 10:16; 11:28; 16:25; I Cor. 9:14a,23; 15:1; II Cor. 4:3f; 9:13; 10:14; 11:4,7; Gal. 1:6f,11; 2:2,5,14; Phil. 1:7,12,17,27; Col. 1:5,23; I Thess. 2:2,4,8f; II Thess. 1:8; 2:14. The distinction cannot always be made clearly; many passages can be placed in both categories and some can be shifted from one to the other.

[51] Of the Cross (I Cor. 1:18), of reconciliation (II Cor. 5:19), of God (I Cor. 14:36; II Cor. 2:17; 4:2; Phil. 1:14; Col. 1:25; I Thess. 2:13), of the Lord (I Thess. 1:8; II Thess. 3:1); of truth (II Cor. 6:7; Col. 1:5), of life (Phil. 2:16); simply 'the word' (Gal. 6:6; Col. 4:3). The word itself often becomes a refinement of technical terminology in the missionary literature properly so-called, the gospels and Acts, e.g. Mark 2:2; 4:14-20,33; (16:20); Luke 1:2; Acts 10:44; 14:25; 16:32(?); 17:11; much more often ὁ λόγος τοῦ θεοῦ or Κυρίου.

[52] I Cor. 1:21; 2:4; 15:14; Rom. 16:25.

[53] There is no trace of it in Matthew and Luke.

to the cultivated public which he has in mind when he writes his apology, he calls them 'reminiscences' or 'memoirs' of the Apostles; [54] he ranks them with that *genre* of literature the most eminent model of which was Xenophon's *Memorabilia of Socrates*.[55] This characterization is hardly suitable for the Gospel of Mark, which lacks the actual characteristics of such literature. The author of *apomnemoneumata* guarantees the truth of the matters which he relates either because he has lived in the midst of them or has learned of them from reliable authorities. Therefore he must exhibit his own personality, not only at the beginning of his work, but elsewhere as well; he must declare how he came upon this piece of information or that. In Mark, on the contrary, one is struck by the completely impersonal character of the work. Not only does the author fail to give his name, but he never turns to speak personally to his readers, as do Luke in his preface and John at the conclusion (20:30). Never does he say that he has been present at any of the events which he relates, and if his presence is suggested in the group of fleeing disciples (14:51f), no uninitiated reader could detect the reference. He never calls upon his authorities (Peter was perhaps one of them) or renders an account of his sources. All this is understandable only if the credibility of the narrated facts is not questioned either by him or by his readers; it is in no respect the theme of his work. Criticism and reflection are foreign to the author; he feels himself borne along completely in the stream of the tradition, and he passes on that which has come to him. The tone in which he writes is that of one who is enthusiastic and filled with his subject, he speaks of it like a preacher who does not expect any contradiction. For this reason his book cannot be considered as missionary literature in the sense that the unconverted or Christians who are still wavering are intended to be won over by it. In that case there ought not to be lacking objective 'proofs,' e.g. an allusion to the fact that specific persons who were healed, or witnesses, like the

[54] *τὰ ἀπομνημονεύματα τῶν ἀποστόλων*, 1:67; *τὰ γενόμενα ὑπ' αὐτῶν ἀπομνημονεύματα, ἃ καλεῖται εὐαγγέλια*, 'the memoirs which came from them, which are called gospels,' 1:66; *ὡς οἱ ἀπομημονεύσαντες πάντα τὰ περὶ τοῦ σωτῆρος ἡμῶν* 'Ιησοῦ Χριστοῦ *ἐδίδαξαν*, 'as those who, having recalled to mind everything about our saviour Jesus Christ, taught us,' 1:33. 'Memorabilia' is not the proper translation, but 'reminiscences.' Cf. Th. Zahn. *Geschichte des Kanons,* i. 471, and E. Köpfe, 'Über die Gattung der *ἀπομνημονεύματα* in der griechischen Literatur' (On the Literary Species of *ἀπομνημονεύματα* in Greek Literature), 1857 (*Progr. d. Ritterakademie Brandenburg*).

[55] [*Translator's Note.* Cf. F. C. Grant, *The Growth of the Gospels*, pp. 36-52; C. W. Votaw in *American Journal of Theology,* xix (1915), pp. 45ff, 217ff; H. J. Cadbury, *The Making of Luke-Acts,* ch. 10.]

centurion, were still alive and could be questioned, or that the empty grave was to be seen at the present time. The only feature of this kind is to be found in the names given of the sons of Simon of Cyrene, Alexander and Rufus (15:21), but this shows only the so-called 'intimate,' i.e. non-public, character of the book; it is intended for a circle in which these men are well known, perhaps the Roman church (Rom. 16:13). The readers whom the writer has in mind are at least acquainted with the outlines of the life of Jesus already: the Baptist (1:4), Pilate (15:1), and above all Jesus himself (1:9) are introduced as well-known and important persons. The readers appear to have an especially great interest in Simon Peter (1:16; 3:16); to an extraordinary degree he is central in the work. The author does not explain the scene of action and he makes no statement about the time when the action takes place —as Luke (1:5; 2:1; 3:1f) and Matthew (2:1; 3:1) do. And if the superscription is from his own hand, as we have no reason to doubt, both the double name Jesus Christ (instead of, e.g., Jesus of Nazareth) and the technical word 'gospel' prove that he writes for readers who live already in the midst of Christian ideas, nay more, in the Christian faith. Therefore his work is intended either for missionaries as a compendium of the salient facts for preaching purposes, or as an introduction to these matters for Christian catechumens or proselytes, or perhaps as an introductory reading book for the mission churches composed of one-time pagans. Even this last-named use, which indeed was certainly usual in later times, as Justin (1:67) testifies, was perhaps at the very first included in the writer's purpose. This would especially be the case if the old tradition (from the time of Papias) be correct, according to which Mark received the words and deeds of the Lord as he was able to remember them from the accounts of St. Peter—a substitute, as it were, for Peter's oral teaching. As Peter, of necessity, had illustrated and given authority to his instruction by imparting words of the Lord, so also Mark's writing is to be looked upon as a teaching document, which depends not so much upon exact, chronological order or upon completeness, as upon truth and accuracy in details.[56]

[56] Peter *πρὸς τὰς χρείας ἐποιεῖτο τὰς διδασκαλίας, ἀλλ' οὐχ ὥσπερ σύνταξιν τῶν κυριακῶν ποιούμενος λογίων, ὥστε οὐδὲν ἥμαρτεν Μάρκος οὕτως ἔνια γράψας ὡς ἀπεμνημόνευσεν· ἑνὸς γὰρ ἐποιήσατο πρόνοιαν, τοῦ μηδὲν ὧν ἤκουσεν παραλιπεῖν ἢ ψεύσασθαί τι ἐν αὐτοῖς*, Peter "used to teach as need dictated, not as though he were making an orderly arrangement of the Lord's oracles as Matthew did; the *τάξις* is lacking in Mark, so that Mark made no mistake in writing down some things as he recalled them; for he had one concern, not to leave out any of the things which he had heard, or to say anything false about them" (Eusebius, *H. E.*, iii. 39. 15).

Peter had not given either a biography of Jesus or a systematic exposition of his teaching, nor are these two things to be looked for in Mark. Nor does he give a connected statement of the *teaching* of Jesus, although he often introduces him as teaching and says much about his teaching.[57] But *what* he teaches is on the whole assumed as being well known; only at the beginning does he give (1:14f) a brief, compressed formulation of his preaching of the Kingdom of God. The matter with which Mark has to deal goes much further than the preaching of repentance and detailed ethical precepts. *One* reason for this, at least, lies in the fact that the readers long ago have known and had possession of the Lord's words. So long as there was missionary preaching the commandments of the Lord had been inculcated (cf. pp. 77ff); indeed it is quite likely that Mark and his readers already possessed the collection of Jesus' sayings which we reconstruct from Matthew and Luke (Q) or a similar compilation. *Another* reason is the naïve, unhistorical assumption that Jesus of course had taught nothing but that which the preaching of the missionaries and teachers contained in the way of teaching and ethical demands. But the *chief* reason is the *shift of interests,* which we observe most plainly in John, and which nevertheless lies before us in Mark. As in the Fourth Gospel the preaching of the Kingdom of God is completely supplanted by Jesus' own testimony as to his person and significance for salvation, just so Mark's writing contains not an account of the teaching of Jesus, but the proclamation of the *person* of Jesus Christ, *the Son of God.* This shift corresponds completely to the vast epochal change in the history of primitive Christianity: from being the preaching of the prophet Jesus of Nazareth it has become the gospel *about* Jesus Christ. Thus out of the preaching of the Baptist there was selected not his call to repentance (1:4) but his witness to a 'mightier one' (1:7f), just as in the Gospel of John his significance is exhausted by his mission to 'witness' to Jesus. Thus the story of Jesus is introduced by his proclamation as 'Son of God' at the baptism (1:11) and ends with the recognition by the centurion that this was a son of God (15:39). The central and highest point is constituted by the confession of Peter (8:29) and the celestial approval in the Transfiguration (9:7). One of the chief interests of the author is to show how it came about that the Son of God, as he undoubtedly was, was not recognized as such by the Jews: he *did not wish* to be recognized, the people must continue in delusion and stubbornness

[57] 1:21f; 2:13; 4:1f; 6:2,6,34; 12:14,35; 14:49; 11:18; 12:38.

(4:11f), hence the many prohibitions against making known the miracles of Jesus and the secret of his person. Only the demons knew him (1:24,34; 3:11; 5:7)—by the power of their supernatural capacity—and only the disciples (who were chosen by Jesus) believed in him (8:29); to them was revealed the secret of the Kingdom of God (4:11) and to them also was the splendor of Jesus revealed (9:3,7). Whatever meaning this scene may originally have had (cf. SNT, *ad loc.*), it was meant by Mark to be interpreted somewhat in the sense formulated in John 1:14—for once they *saw* his glory, which generally was hidden, shining out. For Christian readers this glory was now manifest, especially in the miracles: if Jesus not merely forgave sins but made the paralytics to walk as well, *then he had the power* of the Son of Man (2:10); by the same plenary power he dispensed himself from the Sabbath regulations (2:28). If he healed leprosy, blindness, and all diseases, if he gave commands to the demons, the storm, and even to death itself, he was, as the demons said, the 'holy one of God,' the 'son of the Most High.' Thus for Mark it went without saying that he had foreknowledge of everything relating to himself, his suffering, death, and resurrection. In this respect the picture of Jesus is not different from that of John. The only difference is that for the latter the miracles were valued more as 'signs,' as pieces of evidence in the great trial of the question whether Jesus was really Son of God. In Mark, the apologetic effort still remains fairly well in the background; he is concerned less with the persuasion of opponents than with the building up of the churches. In the miracles he simply lets the divinity of Jesus—in which he and they believed—shine forth. And from this the reader is to derive certainty: the things which Jesus had done in those days can be done even today and always by the Exalted Christ and his name, for those who believe in him. Indeed, it is a question whether that symbolic, allegorical interpretation of the miracle stories, which lies before us in John, had not at least appeared as a faint suggestion—without prejudice to the actuality and concreteness of those things which had happened. Just as John recounts the healing of the man born blind as such a circumstantial story, and yet intends to portray Jesus in it as the 'light of the world,' so also the healings of the deaf-mute and the blind man in Mark are meant, to be sure, as actual happenings in the past, but alongside this a symbolic, allegorical significance also shines through (cf. SNT on Mark 8:26). In the stories of the feeding the question also arises whether or not in Mark they are already intended as mystical portrayals of Jesus' surrender of his life (cf. SNT on Mark 6:40f; 8:1-9), as prophecies of his death, as reflections of the Eucharist; at any rate the proportionate emphasis on the miraculous satisfaction of hunger is very weak. The expulsions of demons were surely for the earliest readers proofs of the power of the Son of God over the pagan gods; the physical healings were also symbols of spiritual 'salvation' (pp. 166f).

The immense weight laid in Mark upon the *passion, death, and resurrection of Christ* is significant as showing the practical, edifying nature of this 'gospel.'[58] The passion narrative is the most detailed, clearest, and most thrilling section in the work. At the very beginning of the book Jesus' death is intimated (2:20), and especially the whole section from the confession of Peter to the entry into Jerusalem (8:27—10:45) is filled with thoughts on the necessity of the death of Jesus. In it is disclosed the basic idea of the whole work; the true purpose and meaning of Jesus' coming to earth are found in his death for the many (10:45); the evangelist does not seek to justify it as a stumbling-block which cannot be evaded—no, it is the characteristic mystery of the new religion; one cannot understand Jesus without it; the interpretation of him in the sense that he 'had come' to fulfil the hopes of Israel, as 'king of Israel,' is nothing but the Jewish misconception which even the Twelve could not avoid: certainly, he is the Messiah, but not *in spite of* his Passion (the point of view of the earliest Church) but precisely *through* his Passion. The misunderstanding of the Twelve is a foil for the blessed recognition which the evangelist preaches to his readers: the Cross is the real significance of his life. The evangelist here shows himself to be a follower of the Pauline gospel,[59] and with a certain disdain he looks back upon the Twelve, who failed so completely to find this true meaning of the Gospel because their thoughts were purely human, not divine.[60] How did this come about? Because of their earthly, ambitious disposition of mind which was made evident in their dispute over precedence (9:33f), in the pride of the sons of Zebedee (10:35-41), in St. Peter's question about reward (10:28-31), in the blessing of the children (10:14). The

[58] [*Translator's Note.* On the whole question of the part played by the Passion Narrative in Mark, cf. F. C. Grant, *The Growth of the Gospels,* pp. 96-150; B. W. Bacon, *Jesus the Son of God* (1930); A. E. J. Rawlinson, *The Gospel according to St. Mark,* which is now the standard commentary in English.]

[59] [*Translator's Note.* Cf. M. Werner, *Einfluss paulinistischen Theologie im Markusevangelium* (The Influence of Pauline Theology on the Gospel of Mark; Giessen, 1923).]

[60] 8:17f,21,32f; 9:32; 10:32.

secret of the Cross can be understood only by the one who has prepared himself for service, humility, renunciation, suffering and martyrdom. Thus in this passage the gospel of the Passion becomes interwoven with the exhortation to humility (9:35ff), respect for the lowly (9:41f; 10:13-16), renunciation of worldly goods (10:17-31), serving in imitation of him who had given over his life on behalf of many (10:42-45). It is especially characteristic of our evangelist that he connects the prediction of passion and martyrdom of the disciples (8:34-38) with the first passion prediction (8:31ff). Just here we come to the really central point of the gospel, its actual peak; here we feel that the author is writing in an age of suffering and martyrdom: to be a Christian, to be a disciple of Jesus, means for Mark to bear Jesus' Cross, suffer and die as he did. This is also a Pauline note. It appears, however, to be especially accentuated in our author—because of the experiences which the Church had undergone not long since and which still reverberated in the minds of the people: the Neronian persecution, the death of Peter in which the saying of 14:31 had been fulfilled and by which the shame of his denial of Christ had been mitigated, perhaps also the death of the sons of Zebedee, who by now had also drunk the cup of suffering (10:39; cf. pp. 309f). But behind the sufferings glimmered the hope. As Jesus himself had risen on the third day—for which Mark offered the empty tomb as proof (16:1-8)—just so he would accept his own followers if they had confessed him (8:38); they would win back the life which they had tossed away (8:35).

The *return of the Lord* is the subject of a second great group of sayings (ch. 13). In this chapter it is not the single sayings which are noteworthy—they are nearly all traditional material—but rather the assiduity with which the author warns against *too early* an expectation of the end. Before this is to take place, the work of the mission to the Gentiles must be *complete* (13:10)—and this means a long period of toil. It is further significant that the writer has Jesus answer the question of the disciples as to the time of the destruction of the Temple (13:1-4) with a speech in which, on the contrary, the signs of his return are given. This proves that for the author the two things are to occur simultaneously. And from this it follows that the destruction of the Temple cannot yet have taken place. On the contrary, the desecration of the Temple (13:14), which is likewise still in the future, is only a sign of the end. Thus the period of writing of the gospel is firmly established as being before the year 70. As St. Paul in II Thess. 2 expected the appearance of Antichrist in the Temple before the end, so does Mark; as Paul expected the end to be *not immediately* near, so also Mark. The reason is in both cases the same: the still undischarged missionary task is still too great for one to be able to count it as being fulfilled in a short time.

That our author is filled with practical *interest in missionary work* one also recognizes from a third group of sayings of the Lord, the parable chapter. From the abundance of parables he selected those which dealt with the destiny of the seed which had been sown, i.e. which had to do with the 'word,' and his interpretation of the 'sower' shows clearly how he connects it all with the experience of the missionaries (cf. SNT, *ad loc.*). To instil in them hope and courage is the aim of all three parables in the evangelist's composition; the sayings which are inserted (4:21-25) serve the same purpose. At the same time the chapter clearly answers the question, why had Jesus spoken in parables? The answer was, on account of the people of Israel, for whom the secret of the Kingdom of God must remain unrevealed. Thus a further, constantly-recurring motive, which plays an important rôle in Mark, is indicated to us: *the break with Judaism.*

Not that the Marcan gospel was intended to convert Jews: it is intended to furnish to missionaries, and also to the churches, a method, ready at hand, by which they can define their teaching as opposed to that of Judaism, a weapon against Jewish calumny, and a sure consciousness—as against the claims of Judaism—that they were the sole true heirs of salvation. First of all, the work is an indictment against Judaism; its leaders had *delivered over* Jesus, the 'Son of Man,' the 'Messiah,' the 'king of Israel' *to the heathen* (10:33), and because of envy at that (15:10), while Pilate, knowing well that he had done no crime (15:14), was ready to release him (15:9); the Jews were thus responsible for the death of Jesus. They had condemned him to death—why? Hardly because he had threatened to destroy the Temple. This false accusation fell to the ground because they were not able to bring in corroborating witnesses who could agree. No: because he had revealed that he was Messiah, the Son of God! They considered this to be blasphemy although it was the clear truth! Then they had abused him (14:65) and mocked him (15:29-32)! This statement shows the attitude of the Gentile Christian missionary churches to Judaism. The anger of this accusation is mitigated by the idea that the Jews were, in fact, only the organ by which God's will had worked: *he* had given over the Son of Man into their hands (9:31; 10:32) in order that the Scripture might be fulfilled (14:49). They could not, nay, they *must* not recognize him, for a divine judgment for their stubbornness rested upon them (4:11f). This is the same idea which St. Paul expresses in Rom. 11:8ff. While Paul still hopes for the final conversion of Israel, this evangelist has abandoned the Jews; he speaks only of the mission to the Gentiles (13:10); the task of going to the Jews, which was the task of the Twelve (6:7-13), lies far in the past. Even Jesus himself had strongly in mind the fact of the reprobation of Israel (12:9; 11:14), and had been the first to go beyond the boundaries into heathen territory (5:20; 7:24—8:9): the saying, '*First* the children, then the dogs' (7:27), corresponds to the missionary principle of Acts 13:46 (Rom. 1:16, if the 'first' is genuine here).

The *teaching and controversial sayings* minister to this idealizing of the break with Judaism; these discourses obviously have a completely practical significance for Mark.[61] It is worthy of note that no sayings of Jesus about circumcision and the food laws are included; apparently the evangelist possessed none; he did not, however, have the necessity of bringing forward the authoritative opinions of Jesus on these points, since for the Gentile Christian churches these questions might be regarded, on the whole, as settled. On the other hand, the question of the Sabbath remained a live one. This best-known and most striking phenomenon of the religious life of the Jews demanded the taking of a definite position, especially since there were Jewish Christian circles which kept the Sabbath (Matt. 24:28). From the two Sabbath pericopes of Mark (2:23-28; 3:1-5) one can see to what absurd consequences the strict observance of the Sabbath might lead. The practice of fasting is, in principle, something which the Christian has transcended; at the most it is suitable for the day of the Lord's death, i.e. Friday (2:20). The Jewish precepts regarding ceremonial cleanliness are antiquated by a new, ethical, inner concept of purity (7:1-23). The attitude toward the Law in general is determined according to the regulative principle of the two commandments of love (12:28-34)—which is of far more value than all sacrifices. The faith in the resurrection (12:18-27) is sharply defined in opposition to the powerful Jewish notion; the

[61] [*Translator's Note.* On the controversies, cf. F. C. Grant, *op. cit.,* ch. 5; B. S. Easton, "A Primitive Tradition in Mark" in *Studies in Early Christianity,* ed. S. J. Case, 1928, pp. 85ff; J. Weiss, *Das Aelteste Evangelium,* pp. 153f, 365-368.]

tribute money (12:13-17) erects a wall between the Church and the revolutionary Jewish zealotism.

The significance of the oldest gospel for church history, however, lies above all in the fact that it created, once for all, a picture of Jesus which was clear in its details and determinative for all later ages, which ever since that time has been printed indelibly in the imagination of the Church. From this one can understand what significance the 'historical Jesus' had for the mission. We have already (pp. 225f) seen that the missionary preaching could not do without a certain amount of information about the life of Jesus. St. Paul himself could not completely forego it. For the faith in the heavenly Kyrios still included the belief that he was the same person who as Jesus of Nazareth had lived on earth and had been crucified. The Gospel of Mark now teaches us that the need for a living, concrete picture of him was very much greater than one has been accustomed to suppose. The newly converted wished to know something certain about Jesus, who was—so they had been told—the Son of God. The churches needed, for the sake of worship and individual piety, a living realization of the one who had died for their sakes. Alongside this, naturally, something of an historical interest was already making itself felt; especially as one by one the eyewitnesses of the life of Jesus died, it became clear that the things which they had committed to tradition must be securely kept. The first gospel is the literary deposit of the oral preaching; also, however, it is undoubtedly a pre-literary written account of the first generation of missionaries.[62] In this way only is it to be understood and criticized properly: one must read it, *on the one hand*, as an expression of the viewpoints and convictions of the evangelist; *on the other hand*, as a collection of older traditions which partly proceed from completely different viewpoints. Expressed in terms of the history of doctrine: it is dominated by and permeated with the Christology of the Pauline and post-Pauline generation, but it also contains material in which the earliest Church's understanding of Jesus is expressed. The Jesus of Mark is the Son of God, who is endowed with divine power and divine knowledge, but he is also the one-time Jewish teacher and prophet with human feeling and limited understanding and power; godhead and manhood interpenetrate one another in an indissoluble unity.

[62] Cf. J. Weiss, *Das Aelteste Evangelium,* and E. Wendling, *Die Entstehung des Markus-Evangeliums* (The Origin of the Gospel of Mark); also J. Weiss's review in *Theologische Rundschau,* 1913.

In this way Mark has for all time set the tone for the popular view and for the theological conception of the earthly Jesus.

For Mark, Jesus was the Son of God (1:1), as he himself says (14:62), as the demons knew (5:7), as the voice from heaven proclaims him at the Baptism and the Transfiguration (1:11; 9:7). In what sense does the evangelist use this name? Surely no longer in the adoptionist sense, viz. that he *became* Son of God only at his exaltation; nor indeed does he understand the voice from heaven in the old sense of the original reading of Luke 3:22 (Codex D), i.e. that at that instant he was 'begotten' as Son of God; on the other hand, a symbolic or theocratic-political conception is far removed from Mark's viewpoint: Son of God is more than Messiah. He certainly understands the name not otherwise than did the centurion at the foot of the Cross (15:39), in the completely popular sense of a person who has been metamorphosed into a god. It is a completely 'popular' note also that he indulges in no reflections as to how it came about that his godhead made its appearance in human form. Whether he thinks of him as having complete consciousness of a divine preëxistence, of a descent from heaven, of an incarnation or a divine birth, is not to be known, and this impossibility of knowing is precisely the thing which is significant; the evangelist had no need of knowledge in this direction (2:10,28).[63] It completely sufficed for him (e.g. 8:31; 10:45) that he was able to display the practical proofs of divine power and knowledge, as well as the manifold opinions about him: he *was* the Son of God; he *was also* 'Son of Man,' for he gave decrees by virtue of the plenary power which only the 'Son of Man' could have (2:10,28). Therefore (e.g. 8:31; 10:45) this name has now become, for Mark, Jesus' sufficient designation for himself, and the words which are spoken before the high priest regarding the appearance of the Son of Man on the clouds (14:62) are by him—in contrast with Luke—considered as additional justification for the evangelist's claims: one will know now that he is the Son of God, the 'Son of Man.' It is the author's purpose that the whole gospel be read from this Christological standpoint. Thus he does not have St. Paul's point of view, viz. that he who became man renounced divine power and glory (*kenosis*); he stands much nearer to John, according to whose view the divine *Doxa* shone out

[63] Whether he actually saw in the Baptism, in the 'complete union of the Spirit with Jesus' (by analogy with I Cor. 3:17), the definite moment when he was sent out by God (Bousset, *Kyrios Christos*, p. 325), is to me quite debatable. The voice from heaven spoke to him merely that the others might recognize his divine sonship as a fact.

in the life of Jesus (1:14; 2:12)—but of course not for all, only for those whose eyes were opened, i.e. the disciples. They were (like John) already the believing Church.

If, now, Mark provides also a great number of human details in his narrative material, we are able thereby to study this material and determine which details of Jesus' life were of especial importance to him and to the church of his age, and to this extent the first gospel is an excellent mirror of the faith in Jesus of the Gentile missionary church.

Above all, the absence of the interest which we call 'biographical' is significant. The very thing which we should desire so keenly, a portrayal of his personality in its outward appearance, his face and form, his way of speaking and his gestures, his appearance and glance, further information about his youth and his growth as a boy, youth, and man, the influence of his environment, his parents and teachers—or at least about his ethical and spiritual development—all this is completely lacking, and the scanty traces here and there, the things which involuntarily reveal something of this, merely show how indifferent the evangelist was to all these matters; they are not in any respect, from his point of view, the subject of his portrait.

For this there are various reasons: the tradition which already lay before him had paid no attention to it; [64] the decisive factor, however, is the fact that the evangelist had not undertaken the consideration of personalities; humanity as such did not interest him, since it was after all only the rather secondary form in which the deeds and words of the Son of God must be expressed. The personal and outward appearance is indeed only the transitory, henceforth completely indifferent drapery, which he once had to wear. That he had received something essential from his human environment is outside the realm of possibility; what he was and what he possessed is simply his divine inheritance. The idea of a spiritual development, therefore, was not at hand for the author's use. Through his words and deeds he vouchsafes us a glimpse into the reasons for Jesus' actions or perhaps into the depths of his self-consciousness—but involuntarily at best.[65] It is completely impossible for us to

[64] Cf. J. Weiss's article, 'Literaturgeschichte des Neuen Testaments' in *Religion in Geschichte und Gegenwart*, iii, 1183-1190.

[65] Jesus' emotions are indeed often called attention to by Mark, e.g. in Gethsemane (14:34) and at the Cross (15:34), but not often where we should expect them, e.g. when Judas kissed him (14:45) or when he is mocked (14:65). An especial position is occupied by those passages in which Mark alone (not Matthew or Luke) portrays strong

obtain from him a view of the inward ways of thinking of Jesus, for Jesus as a matter of course knows sufficiently who he is and what lies before him. He offers neither a development of messianic consciousness nor a dramatic-tragic story of how he arrived at his attitude to this problem; the catastrophe unfolds itself of necessity, having been determined by Jesus' will and the divine plan of salvation. The most necessary thing for a representation of the drama of Jesus' life is lacking, a chronological framework: in effect, everything takes place on a flat plane. All historical or psychological pragmatism is lacking; [66] the whole thing is composed of completely separate fragments which are grouped partly according to practical didactic viewpoints, partly almost according to chance, so that they can be changed in order without serious damage.

We should expect at least one thing from our present-day point of view: a sort of character portrayal in the interest of apologetic, a proof of innocence or a glorification of the ethico-religious nature of Jesus. But we do not meet this either, or at least not in a completely definite manner. For such a 'characterization' the author, who above all does not move within a circle with a high degree of culture, lacks the finer and subtler modes of expression, as well as the necessary literary categories, as they were worked out in Graeco-Roman biography.[67] There is in the whole work no single characteristic word or decorative epithet which the writer uses in describing Jesus. Much more often he makes use of the means of indirect characterization: he shows how Jesus dealt with his environ-

---

emotions of Jesus or especially expressive acts or gestures, e.g. 1:35 (Jesus' prayer); 1:43; 3:5; 4:13; 7:34; 8:12,33; 10:14,16,21. It is also Mark alone who tells something similar about other persons, e.g. 10:13,50; 14:5. It is thus a lame explanation to say that the parallel writers left out these touches because they found no corresponding ones in respect to Jesus. They belong to a large group of highly colored, intensified, touches of restless movement, which only Mark gives, and which did not belong to the original text of the first gospel; on this point, cf. J. Weiss, *Das Aelteste Evangelium,* pp. 17ff.

[66] On this point, cf. J. Weiss, *Das Aelteste Evangelium;* his statement in SNT, his article in *Religion in Geschichte und Gegenwart,* cited above, and his essay in *Archiv für Rel.-Wissensch.,* 1913, pp. 506ff.

[67] F. Leo, *Die griechisch-römische Biographie nach ihrer literarischen Form,* p. 187: "Suetonius and Diogenes Laertius *described,* in short, the ἦθος of their heroes; Plutarch recounted their πράξεις and from these let their ἦθος make itself evident. For Suetonius, the πράξεις were only the framework on which he built his characterization; for Plutarch the character portrayal is contained directly in the story of their deeds and experiences. Suetonius gives a historically arranged survey of the character of the man who has first been placed in his historical setting; Plutarch forms the narrative of the life upon the whole picture of the personality." Mark obviously belongs rather on the side of Plutarch than on that of Suetonius.

ment.[68] To this category belong the famous judgments—about his teaching with authority and not as the scribes, 1:22; the astonishment at his miracles, e.g. 2:12; the Beelzebub calumny spoken by the scribes, 3:22; the surprise of the Nazareth people at his wisdom, 6:2; the faith of the Syro-Phoenician woman, 7:28f; the judgment of the Pharisees on his impartiality, 12:13; the popular judgment regarding him, 8:28 (6:15f), as well as the portrayal of the mighty power of attraction which he exercised over the multitude, and over those who were suffering and desirous of healing; and not least the hatred and helplessness of his enemies (3:6; 11:18; 14:2), as well as the unavailing character of the attempt to investigate him (14:55-61). All of this produces the impression of the unique, partly foreign, partly human, but completely enigmatical greatness of his personality, by which the certainty of Christian readers that he was Son of God could only be strengthened. On the other hand, we feel the absence of a thorough proof of his innocence as well as of an enthusiastic glorification. The sinlessness of Jesus, which in St. Paul or in First Peter is dogmatically presupposed rather than demonstrated, is so well established for our author that he writes without any idea that Jesus had undergone the baptism of repentance for the remission of sins (1:9), that he ventures to place in his mouth the saying, 'No one is good' (10:18)—without feeling that thereby he places him in a false light. Not once does he say that Jesus was victorious over Satan in his temptations (1:13); for him that is understood. It would have been possible for him also to have told how Jesus victoriously repulsed temptations, e.g. to sensuality, ambition, and selfishness. It is quite significant that no one has dared to transmit a tradition of this sort about Jesus. The idea that he had to undergo the temptation to sins universal to mankind is as foreign to the writer as the other idea, viz. that of setting him up as a moral pattern for his disciples: the Son of God can be no pattern for mankind.

The accusations against which he made a defence are largely of a contemporary historical and political nature. In the saying regarding the tribute money it is pointed out that Jesus had nothing in common with the revolutionary moods of Judaism. His position on

[68] To this belong especially the strongly exaggerated portrayals of the pressure of the crowds, e.g. 1:33,45b; 2:2,13; 3:9,20; 4:36; 6:31; 7:24; 9:15 and other touches which are in Mark alone (Matthew and Luke do not have them) e.g. 3:21; 5:20b; 10:17,32b,50. But others are attested by the parallel writers and surely belong to the oldest gospel, e.g. 1:22,27f,45a; 2:12; 3:10ff,22; 4:41; 6:2,15f,55f; 7:37; 10:1; 11:18; 12:12,17,34.

the question of Messiahship (at Caesarea, 8:29ff; at the entry to Jerusalem, 11:2ff; before the high priest, 14:62) shows that he was no political usurper. The sole positive accusation relative to his attempt on the Temple fell to the ground as slanderous [69]—not even on this point could his enemies agree (14:55-60)—they found no real ground of accusation whatever. His silence before his judges is probably not—in Mark's mind—to be thought of so much as a sign of his patience and confidence in the heavenly judge (I Pet. 2:23), as it is to be regarded as an expression of the majesty of Jesus in the face of such charges—the portrait here has something of the Stoic in its features.

The less the evangelist attempts to strengthen the influence of the person of Jesus on the souls of his readers by an ethically ideal picture, the more important it is that in the material which he communicates there be contained manifold touches which must operate directly upon the consciences of Christians of his day. We must be on our guard against interpreting these touches in accordance with our modern feelings. The relation of Jesus to tax-collectors and sinners—the sick, not those who are well, need the physician (2:17)—this touch spoke a language which immediately struck a responsive chord in the churches, which were in great part composed of the poor and despised and of people who for the most part had had little joy in their past lives: the new religion had given them courage to live, had given them a feeling of worth, and had promised them a glorious future. That all this was fully part of the Lord's purpose, stood out clearly from such stories and sayings. The grace of Christ, of which St. Paul speaks, his willingness to forgive the penitent (2:5) was impressively demonstrated by Jesus' word and deed. The one who read such accounts could not picture the heavenly Lord as being otherwise than the earthly Jesus was—mild, loving, ready to aid. His ever-ready willingness to help and save expresses itself in the healing narratives as obviously as does his power to help. Above all, the Jesus who himself was hated and derided, who emptied the bitter cup of suffering, was an encouraging and comforting leader for those to whom persecution and martyrdom might come any day. In this direction lies the edifying power of the Passion Narrative; of especially strong effect was the last word of Jesus (15:34)—of course it was neither meant by Mark nor understood

[69] The present text of Mark has, however, dulled the point of the saying with a spiritual interpretation (χειροποίητον—ἀχειροποίητον); on the other hand, Matthew has not.

by the first hearers as a word of doubt or as a sign of inward loss of God's presence, but as a word of lament because God had abandoned him to his enemies, because he had led him into this depth of suffering. And when immediately after the death of Jesus the veil of the Temple was rent, this was a sign of what this death had won for the Christians: access to the Father (Heb. 9). The significance of the Gethsemane story for the narrator is not, as for us, to be found in the human note of shuddering in the face of death, but in the fact that Jesus had won his struggle to submit himself to the will of the Father: he was obedient 'even to the death of the Cross' (Phil. 2:8).[70]

This is, in some of its principal features, the meaning and significance of the Gospel of Mark, considered for once not as a historical source *for us*, but as missionary literature or an introductory handbook for the mission churches. That which the evangelist offers in his gospel is completed, strengthened, demonstrated by the manifold traditions which circulated in the churches, especially by the treasure of sayings of the Lord, which indeed involuntarily enriched, in many details, above all in its insight into Jesus' mind, the picture of Jesus which came down from Mark to later generations.

How the first gospel took on another character in the later evangelic writings, by means of its combination with the Sayings Source and other traditions, was enriched by new motifs and reworked for other purposes, will be shown later in its proper place.

[70] On this point, cf. *Archiv für Rel.-Wiss.*, 1913, pp. 505-514.

BOOK V

THE SEPARATE AREAS

Translated by Sherman Elbridge Johnson

CHAPTER XXIII

Judaea

1. *Persecutions.* We left the early Church behind at the time when St. Paul, toward the end of the fifties, turned over the collection from his churches, and was taken into custody. According to the We-Document (Acts 21:18), James and all the elders were included in Paul's salutation. The report does not include a reference to 'the Twelve,' nor to 'the Apostles,' nor to individuals such as Peter. Peter, in any case, was no longer in Jerusalem. Where he had gone (Acts 12:17) is quite obscure. We shall consider this question again in connection with the Roman church. Unquestionably, James the brother of the Lord was at the head of the community. This fact implies, moreover, that the more strictly Judaistic tendency—before which even St. Peter yielded—had, for the most part (Gal. 1:19), gained the upper hand in Jerusalem. Without wishing to accuse the church in any way of unfraternal or false conduct, we may yet well imagine that it would have been relieved had it no longer needed to take responsibility for St. Paul, when it no longer needed to protect him against the hostility of the Jews. It had enough to do to maintain itself in the good will of public opinion through adherence to the Law. One can imagine the danger, should Paul's preaching of freedom from the Law have been set down to its account. So much the more reason is there to take cognizance of the fact that St. James met him cordially; so much the less reason to discredit his proposal as one of cowardice or dissimulation. It is striking, indeed, that the fury which prevailed against Paul, according to the account of the Book of Acts, had not yet reached James's community. It is apparent, therefore, that it was actually held in good esteem among influential classes of people and that the ruling party in the Sanhedrin could find nothing against it. However, one should not over-estimate the good will of the ruling circles. We must remember that, as the case of St. Paul and also that of Jesus indicate, a persecution or oppression of Christians had to be quelled immediately by the Roman procurator, who could not tolerate any unruly or illegal goings-on. What was the genuine attitude in the land we recognize in certain sayings of the Lord, such as Luke 6:22 and Matt. 10:17-39, which would not have been set down if they

had not corresponded to experiences of the early Church. In its own body it must have experienced the fact that Jesus had not brought peace but the sword. How often must division have asserted itself in families, as it is described in Matt. 10:35f; Luke 12:52f. How often, in the cities of Israel, must the messengers have experienced repulsion (Matt. 10:14) and persecution (Matt. 10:23). The passage, Matt. 10:32, "Ye shall be hated of all men for my name's sake," negatives the legend of deep peace which should have existed between Jesus' disciples and the people. 'For my name's sake' or 'for the Son of Man's sake' (Luke 6:22)—in this is declared the cause of division, the basis of the hostility. If they do not cease confessing him (Matt. 10:32) they will be 'separated' (Luke 6:22), i.e. they will be cut off from association with family, kindred, and synagogue communities; they will be insulted and in ill-repute. What Justin says (*Dial.* 16), viz. that the Jews reject (ἀθετεῖτε) the Christians and, so far as lies in their power, revile them, while in their meetings they curse believers in the Messiah, can have become so general only at a later time.[1] The 'benediction' against heretics, moreover, which constitutes the eighteenth petition in the daily prayer,[2] must have first come into use at a later date (after 70). The attitude and practice, however, were certainly existent earlier. Indeed, as the dominical sayings show, even an authorized persecution had not been lacking; the followers of Jesus were brought before the local Jewish tribunals (συνέδρια) and were tormented in synagogue assemblies; they were brought before the Roman procurators and Jewish kings (Agrippa I and II), they were cast into prison (Luke 21:12), often upon the denunciation of their nearest kin (Matt. 10:21). Here they have the experience of the fact that the Spirit of God supplies them appropriate words of defence when they do not know what they ought to say (Matt. 10:19f), that is to say

[1] Cf. also Epiphanius, *Haer.*, 29:2, . . . *τρὶς τῆς ἡμέρας, ὅτε εὐχὰς ἐπιτελοῦσιν ἑαυτοῖς ἐν ταῖς συναγωγαῖς, ἐπαρῶνται αὐτοῖς καὶ ἀναθεματίζουσιν τρὶς τῆς ἡμέρας φάσκοντες, ὅτι ἐπικαταράσαι ὁ θεὸς τοὺς Ναζωραίους*, "Thrice a day, when they offer prayers for themselves in the synagogues, they will rise up and anathematize [the Christians] thrice a day, pretending that God will curse the Nazoraeans," Jerome, *in Isa.* 52:5 (Vall., iv. p. 604).

[2] Dalman, *Worte Jesu,* i, 299f. O. Holtzmann, *Die Mischna,* i, 1, 'Berakot', p. 16, "May there be no hope for the persecutors, may the kingdom of insolence be speedily uprooted in our days, and may the Nazarenes and heretics (מינים) suddenly disappear; may they be blotted out of the book of the living, and may they not be written among the righteous." [*Translator's Note.* Cf. R. T. Herford, *Christianity in Talmud and Midrash,* pp. 125ff. The whole section, pp. 97-397, deals with *Minim* and *Minuth.*]

that they frequently escape all dangers triumphantly. In the midst of all the predictions of troublous persecutions, the saying, full of confidence, remains: 'He that endureth to the end, the same shall be saved' (Matt. 10:22)! This section, too, would not have been written down, had it not been so generally the actual situation that hostile people murderously planned to defame their own kinsmen (10:19) before the tribunal of the magistrate and the inflexible judgment of the Roman procurator. One cannot imagine the butcheries and massacres of which the source does not speak. This violent hate had only in a few cases, as Luke 21:16 reservedly says, led to deaths, and indeed, probably more often to assassinations or acts of mob violence than to more regular condemnations. These passages are not filled with fear of wholesale slaughter but breathe a triumphant joyousness. To be sure, each disciple should always be prepared to bear the cross of his Lord and to lay down his life (Matt. 10:38f), but it is not said that it will happen so universally: the disciples are surely held fast in God's hand and they fear his justice more than the judgment of an opponent who can kill merely the body (Matt. 10:28). At all events, they are convinced that the matter must terminate in victory: whereas now they can hold their meetings only in secret, the time is coming when the word which had to be spoken in the ear will be proclaimed from the housetops (Luke 12:3).

2. *The Death of James.* That bloody persecutions were the special lot of the outstanding figures, and that mass executions did not occur, is indicated by the happening in the year 62, when the high priest Ananos, son of that Annas who had conducted the trial of Jesus, took advantage[3] of the time between the death of Festus and the arrival of the procurator Albinus to set up a tribunal and accuse James and certain others as transgressors of the Law and to deliver them over to be stoned.[4] Included among the 'certain others' may

[3] Νομίσας ἔχειν καιρὸν ἐπιτήδειον, "Considering that he had a suitable opportunity," says Josephus, *Ant.* xx. 9. 1, § 200.

[4] Jos., *Ant.* xx. 9. 1, § 200, καθίζων συνέδριον κριτῶν καὶ παραγαγὼν εἰς αὐτὸ τὸν ἀδελφὸν Ἰησοῦ τοῦ λεγομένου Χριστοῦ, Ἰάκωβος ὄνομα αὐτῷ, καί τινας ἑτέρους, ὡς παρανομησάντων κατηγορίαν ποιησάμενος παρέδωκε λευσθησομένους, "He called into session a sanhedrin of judges, and bringing before it the brother of Jesus, called Messiah, James by name, and certain others, accused them as transgressors of the Law and delivered them over to be stoned." The doubts regarding the genuineness of this passage, which are expressed by Th. Zahn, *Forschungen zur Geschichte des neut. Kanons* (Researches into the History of the New Testament Canon), vi. 301-305, among others, but which in actuality are absolutely groundless, have not the slightest support in the text of Josephus itself (cf. also E. Schwartz, *ZNTW,* 1903, pp. 59f). In particular, there is lacking here the passage which is suspected of being of Christian origin, which Origen, *Contra Celsum,* 1:47; 2:13; *In Matth.* tom. 10:17, and Eusebius, ii. 23. 20,

also have been John the son of Zebedee who now would have followed his brother in martyrdom so that the word of the Lord concerning the drinking of the cup (Mark 10:39) was now fulfilled by both. That he was 'put to death by Jews' we are told in a scattered fragment of Papias of Hierapolis.[5] Of course it would also be possible that he may have perished on an earlier occasion—whether through assassination or at the hands of a mob—but if the citation from Papias pertains to a formal execution, it would not be so easy to seek out another suitable occasion on which it might have happened. However the case may be with this question, in any event one perceives from the statement of Josephus that it was not easy for the Sanhedrin to take measures against the Christians. Ananus had to take advantage of an interregnum, during which there was no procurator present; and immediately he, a Sadducee, was denounced to the new procurator because of this illegal procedure, by his opponents, the Pharisees. No sooner had Ananus received a threatening

claim to have read in Josephus, to the effect that the destruction of Jerusalem was a punishment for the murder of James. The alleged words of Josephus read, according to Origen and Eusebius, as follows: *ταῦτα συμβέβηκεν (τοῖς) Ἰουδαίοις κατ' ἐκδίκησιν Ἰακώβου τοῦ δικαίου, ὃς ἦν ἀδελφὸς Ἰησοῦ τοῦ λεγομένου Χριστοῦ, ἐπειδήπερ δικαιότατον αὐτὸν ὄντα οἱ Ἰουδαῖοι ἀπέκτειναν·*, "These things happened to (the) Jews as an avenging of James the Just, who was a brother of Jesus, called Messiah, since the Jews had slain him who was the most just;" (perhaps still further, *καὶ ὁ λαὸς ταῦτα ἐνόμιζε διὰ τὸν Ἰάκωβον πεπονθέναι*, "And the people believed they had suffered these things on account of James"); cf. Th. Zahn, *op. cit.*, vi. p. 303, note. They are not found in our present Josephus text and in fact have no place in it; they are rendered impossible by the previously mentioned words of the present-day text, in which it is explicitly said that the procedure of the (Sadducee) Ananus was condemned by that portion of the people which was faithful to the Law (*ὅσοι . . . . περὶ τοὺς νόμους ἀκριβεῖς*), i.e. by the Pharisees; thus the whole people cannot be made responsible for the deed, as was the case in the interpolation (in Origen, Eusebius).

[5] Cf. *Texte und Untersuchungen*, v. 2 (1888), p. 170. If in the festal calendar of the later Church of Jerusalem, James and John were honored as martyrs on the same day (December 26; cf. Bousset, *Theol. Rundschau*, viii, p. 229; E. Schwartz, *Nachr. d. Gött. Ges. d. Wiss.*, 1907, p. 267), the basis is probably a confusion of James the son of Zebedee with the brother of the Lord. The opinion which I entertained and defended, long before Wellhausen and Ed. Schwartz, viz. that Mark 10:39 is proved to be a *vaticinium ex eventu* by the newly discovered notice of Papias, meets a difficulty in Eus. iii. 5. 2. Here Eusebius enumerates all the apostolic martyrs in Judaea: Stephen, James the son of Zebedee, 'the brother of John,' and James, who first occupied the throne of the episcopate after the ascension of the Saviour. If he knew Papias—and it is generally accepted that he had before him the complete works of the Bishop of Hierapolis—he must have known also of the murder of John by the Jews. He also says in this passage, to be sure, that against the 'other apostles, innumerable plots were made, and that they were driven out of Judaea,' but he appears to have known nothing of the murder of John in Jerusalem. Thus another possibility remains, that John the son of Zebedee was slain elsewhere by the Jews, which indeed is very probable. For Papias says nothing, after all, of a slaying of James and John *at the same time*. [*Translator's Note.* Cf. A. H. McNeile, *Introduction to the New Testament*, pp. 271-275.]

letter from Albinus than he was deposed by King Agrippa—after only three months of rule (Josephus, *Ant.* xx. 9. 1, §§201f). One need not conclude from this action on the part of the Pharisees that they especially favored the Christians or James—a much more sufficient explanation of this step is to be found in the party antagonism between them and Ananus, as well as the difference in regard to a severer or milder exercise of jurisdiction, to which Josephus calls particular attention more than once. And in conclusion, the fact must be considered that the Pharisees always favored the placing of administration and jurisdiction in Roman hands rather than under the Herodian dynasty or a native party group, since they were better able to further their religious endeavors under Roman government than under a native rule which, being lax in reference to religion, would be in opposition to their tendencies.

The tradition that St. James was held in high esteem by the people because of his piety, that he had borne the name 'the Just,' does not originate with Josephus; it does not come out of Jewish tradition, but out of Christian, and goes back, at the latest, to the Gospel of the Hebrews (Jerome, *De Vir. Ill.* 2), in which Hegesippus [6] would have read it about 180. He had assembled, at that time, sundry accounts from Palestinian tradition dealing with the ancient Church in Palestine—among these were included traditions concerning the character and death of James. These bear the mark of Jewish-Christian legend and as such are of the highest value in the consideration of the later Jewish-Christian community. They are not, however, in complete agreement with the account of Josephus, which is completely unobjectionable, historically speaking. It is a matter of choice whether to give preference in this study to the obscure and improbable statements of Hegesippus or to those of Josephus, yet it is certainly impossible to harmonize the two. The later account permits a conclusion *a posteriori* in regard to the character of St. James only insofar as the complete Judaization of his character in Hegesippus corresponds to the original James himself: he must have felt himself a Jew through and through, and must himself have observed the Law to the highest degree. When Hegesippus tells how he prayed so continuously in the temple for forgiveness for his people that his knee-cap became calloused like that of a camel, even this would suit the actual attitude of a man who was chief leader in the endeavor to

[6] For Hegesippus, cf. Th. Zahn, *Forschungen*, vi., 118-181.

gain and convert Israel. But this statement cannot be given much credence as an historical account.[7]

3. *The Flight of the Christians beyond the Jordan.* The death of James was, at all events, a severe blow to the early Church. The greater the recognition among the people of the authority of its leader, the more precarious became its position thenceforth. It was becoming more and more defenceless; public opinion was more and more stirred up, party relationships more divided; and the more violent became the political struggles by which the people were breeding the revolt from Rome and the fall of the city. Since the time of the taxation it had been brewing and now the outbreak became more and more imminent. In so avowedly a messianic movement as was that of the early Church, which daily prayed for the coming of the Kingdom, and in the midst of which arose the infancy narrative of Luke, filled as it was with messianic hope, it must have been a temptation to become attached to fanatical adventurers who

[7] The account of Hegesippus, which Eusebius transcribes verbatim in *H. E.*, ii. 23. 4-18, of course merits a more exact consideration since it is of the highest value as a document exhibiting *Jewish Christian modes of thought.* As it appears, Hegesippus drew upon a written *Hebrew or Aramaic* source. This is indicated by the impossible form of the question which was put to James (8. 12), *τίς ἡ θύρα τοῦ* 'Ιησοῦ, "Which is the door of Jesus?" This must be an incorrect reproduction of "What is the teaching (תורה) of Jesus?" or of "Which is the door to salvation (ישועה)?" As a matter of fact the former possibility is more likely, for only on condition that the opponents assume that the teaching of Jesus is fundamentally that of the Law, can they invite James to bear witness to it, in order to restrain the people from faith in his messiahship (§ 2). And if the answer of James is (§ 8) *τοῦτον εἶναι τὸν σωτῆρα*, 'that he is Saviour,' the supposition that the 'door of Jesus' is the gate of salvation cannot be the content of the question. The Greek expression *θύρα τοῦ* 'Ιησοῦ is probably an echo of John 10:7, 9, since everywhere in the narrative the gospels are echoed: John 12:42, *ἐκ τῶν ἀρχόντων πολλοὶ ἐπίστευσαν εἰς αὐτόν*, 'of the rulers many believed on him;' cf. § 10, *πολλῶν οὖν καὶ τῶν ἀρχόντων πιστευόντων*, 'since therefore many of the rulers believed'—Luke 20:21, *οἴδαμεν ὅτι ὀρθῶς λέγεις καὶ διδάσκεις καὶ οὐ λαμβάνεις πρόσωπον*, "We know that thou sayest and teachest rightly, and acceptest not the person of any;" cf. § 10, *δίκαιος εἶ καὶ πρόσωπον οὐ λαμβάνεις*, "Thou art just and dost not respect persons." The frequent expression *γραμματεῖς καὶ Φαρισαῖοι*, 'scribes and Pharisees,' is Matthaean; from the temptation narrative comes the *πτερύγιον τοῦ ἱεροῦ*, 'wing of the temple'—Matt. 26:64; cf. § 13, *καὶ αὐτὸς κάθηται ἐν τῷ οὐρανῷ ἐκ δεξιῶν τῆς μεγάλης δυνάμεως, καὶ μέλλει ἔρχεσθαι ἐπὶ τῶν νεφελῶν τοῦ οὐρανοῦ*, "And he sits in heaven on the right hand of the great Power, and he shall come with the clouds of heaven"—Matt. 21:9; cf. § 14, *ὡσαννὰ τῷ υἱῷ Δαβίδ*, 'hosanna to the son of David'—Acts 13:27; cf. § 15, *ἐπλήρωσαν τὴν γραφήν*, "They fulfilled the scripture"—Acts 7:60, *Θεὶς δὲ τὰ γόνατα*, 'and he kneeled down;' cf. § 16, *ἔθηκε τὰ γόνατα*, "He knelt."—Luke 23:34; cf. § 16, *κύριε θεὲ πάτερ, ἄφες αὐτοῖς· οὐ γὰρ οἴδασιν τί ποιοῦσιν*, "Lord God, Father, forgive them, for they know not what they do." The comparison of James with Jesus is carried to such a degree that even the prophets are said to have prophesied of him, § 7. 15. The formula, *κινδυνεύει πᾶς ὁ λαὸς* 'Ιησοῦν *τὸν Χριστὸν προσδοκᾶν*, "All the people ventured to expect that Jesus would appear as Messiah," is genuinely Jewish

strove to bring about the Kingdom of God by violence, and with this end in view, attempted the overthrow of Roman rule. Among Jesus' closest adherents, according to Luke 6:15, is found a man, Simon, who either had belonged to the Zealots previously or who later went over to them. We know no other particulars regarding him, but the instance points out how natural it might be for many of the disciples of Jesus to attach themselves to the 'violent, who would seize the Kingdom of God by force' (Matt. 11:12). That the church as a whole had not let itself be swept away was due to the continued indwelling of the spirit of Jesus, who had known well this sort of 'violent one' but who certainly had not sanctioned procedure of that sort. His answer to the question of the tribute money, by which they wished either to make him unpopular with the people as a partisan of Rome, or to cause him to be suspected as an insurgent by the authorities (cf. SNT on Mark 12:13-17), indicates without question that he supported neither course. Nevertheless he

---

Christian. It is especially characteristic that James is not only called the Just—a name which was given by the Christians as by the Jews, even by the scribes and Pharisees (§§ 4, 7, 10, 12, 15, 17, 18)—but also *ὠβλίας*, i.e. a bulwark of the people and of righteousness: the idea is that James was a protection for the people against corruption; hence immediately after his death misfortune arose, § 18. Indeed he is not only the people's intercessor, but he is actually a priest; one might almost say, the people's high priest. This is made clear by the circumstance that he alone (of all non-priests) was allowed to enter the Holy Place and to pray there. This historically impossible tale shows as plainly as possible the tendency to represent James as the ideal Jew, in fact as being actually the saint of Israel, a sort of saviour of the people, whom they had rejected to their own shame. With this is connected, in a way that is not completely clear, the idea that he was a Nazirite from his mother's womb—like John the Baptist—and that for this reason one of the Rechabite priests (Jer. 35) also interceded for him. But not only did he not drink wine, but abstained from meat as well; this points to a Jewish Christianity such as meets us in Rom. 14 and Col. 2, probably of an Essene complexion; it meets us again only in the 'Gospel of the Ebionites.' This account is as instructive for the ideal of later Jewish Christianity as it is impossible to utilize as an historical narrative. In particular, the minute details of James's death are told in a way which is quite divergent from Josephus' story: there is no judgment by the Sanhedrin, no mention of Ananus, but only a crafty murder: he was cast down from the front of the temple. Of course the stoning is mentioned in Hegesippus, but it is merely added as a secondary cause of death, which was without success, until a fuller slew him as he was praying for his enemies. This last detail may, on account of its popular character, rest upon reminiscence. The Pharisees, who in Josephus are opposed to Ananus' judgment, are the murderers in Hegesippus. The position of the members of the 'sects' in Hegesippus is quite obscure. Cf. especially on the indefiniteness of the narrative, E. Schwartz, *ZNTW*, iv. (1903), pp. 48ff. That Eusebius made use of an already interpolated account of Hegesippus is not so likely as that Hegesippus himself made still more confused a narrative in his possession which perhaps had been muddled already by abbreviations and additions. [*Translator's Note.* A very interesting but erratic treatment of this Hegesippus material is to be found in R. Eisler, *The Messiah Jesus,* pp. 514-527.]

defined the province of religion as distinct from that of politics. He had safeguarded his followers from desiring to realize their hopes by participating in political conspiracy. They were proof against the seduction of those who might thereafter say, "I am he" (Mark 13:6). And when the day came when they longed to see even one of the days of the Son of Man (Luke 17:22), they were in a position not to follow when it was said, 'Look! here comes the Kingdom of God' (Luke 17:21; cf. also Mark 13:21), for they knew well enough that the rule of God is not initiated in such a way that one can observe it from outward signs. All at once it will be among them as a flash out of heaven, overpowering them, taking them unaware (Luke 17:24-37). Not with horrible riotings, secret conspiracies, plundering and assassination will it come. Above all, a sign was given to them, whether by Jesus, by predictions of Daniel, or by a prophecy founded on Daniel, whereby they could know when the time was actually come: not war nor rumors of war; not earthquake, not famine; but the appearance of the 'abomination in a holy place.' What it would be no one knew more definitely—the evangelist Mark himself had not known. In any case, however, it was something horrible that would show itself in the temple in Jerusalem. We may understand from II Thess. 2:3-11 that it would be a representation of Satan, the Man of Sin, the Son of Corruption; in the gospel, it is only intimated indefinitely (cf. SNT on Mark 13:14). When the 'abomination' comes, then the faithful are not, at any time, to interfere and to let themselves be misled along with the majority; instead, they are not to remain at all in the environs of the 'abomination': "Let them that are in Judaea flee unto the mountains"—i.e. to the Judaean wilderness or to the more distant highlands of Transjordania—for Jerusalem itself is situated in the mountains.

And it was thus that it did come about, as a matter of fact. Eusebius (iii. 5. 3) tells us that the church in Jerusalem, on the basis of an oracle which had been given to its leaders (τοῖς αὐτόθι δοκίμοις), left the city and went over to Pella in Transjordania. The opinion is tenable that either in the words of Mark 13:14-20 or of Matt. 24:15-22 this oracle may be recovered; and in fact, this command is contained in those passages.

In addition, the setting of the Lucan parallels certainly harmonize with this situation. Here the 'abomination of desolation' will have gained possession after Jerusalem is surrounded by armies—that is, not at the fall of Jerusalem, but at the beginning of the siege. Then those who are in the city are to leave and those who are in the country are not to enter—'exactly the contrary, therefore, of what the Jews did, who streamed into the city, seeking protection behind its walls,' since they could not bring themselves to believe a conquest or overthrow of Jerusalem possible. But that which is contained in Luke 21:22f,28, was experienced, for the most part, by the very soul of the Jewish Christian church:

> Then are the days of vengeance,
> When whatever has been written will be fulfilled.
> There will be great misery in the land
> And anger will come upon this people.
> When this begins, look up;
> Lift high your heads,
> For your deliverance is near.

The disaster which has befallen Jerusalem is its punishment for what it had done to the Christians, e.g. in the murder of James. It is the day when God will avenge his chosen (Luke 18:8). It is the beginning of the 'freeing' of the Church from the oppression of its enemy. Therefore, the Christians are to leave the city which has incurred judgment. It is not the Gentile Christian author of the gospel who gives this explanation, but an old source of Jewish Christian origin, in which the hostility between the Church and Judaism receives penetrating expression.[8] But of course this opinion in regard to the fall of Jerusalem, as a judgment against it because of the rejection of Jesus and the persecution of the Apostles, had gained a foothold among all Christians. In the form in which we now read the Parousia Discourse in Luke, it meant to early readers that the siege and overthrow of Jerusalem were a judgment of wrath upon 'this people' (Luke 21:13). In the moving passage which depicts Jesus weeping over Jerusalem (Luke 19:41-44), which may well be either genuine or invented *ex eventu,* is also reflected the vivid

[8] The relation of sources in this section cannot be solved by recourse to the simple Marcan hypothesis. Certainly Matthew is dependent upon Mark and is often secondary in comparison with Mark, e.g. in the reference to Daniel (v. 15) and in the explanation 'in a holy place' instead of the mysterious expression in Mark. But in *one* detail at least Matthew has preserved the older form, 'that the flight be not on the Sabbath.' Whence he borrowed this expression, whether from an older text of Mark or from a parallel document, cannot be made out. Similarly, Luke is partly secondary and has received its form *ex eventu,* e.g. in v. 24, and also shows traces of the Marcan text, e.g. in v. 21a, which is hardly tolerable between vv. 20 and 21 b (Spitta); but he has also undoubted features which cannot be explained from a reworking of Mark or as *ex eventu,* e.g. vv. 21b, 22, 28. It is hardly to be believed that the words ὁ ἀναγινώσκων νοείτω are always to be translated, 'let the reader take notice,' when they mean something completely different, 'let the reader *understand*' the secret!

impression made upon Christians by the overthrow of Jerusalem. The same thing is reflected in the arrangement of Matt. 21:41,43; 22:7.[9] This pragmatic and edifying view had thus become operative rapidly in Christianity. So Hegesippus connects the beginning of the campaign of Vespasian (or the siege of Jerusalem) directly with the assassination of James (Eus. ii. 23. 18). In similar fashion the interpolation in Josephus lying behind Origen's statement (*Contra Celsum,* 1:97) describes the destruction of Jerusalem as punishment for the murder of James (Eusebius, ii. 23. 20).

The Jerusalem church had taken refuge in Pella (Eus. iii. 5. 3), a city founded in the period of the diadochi, which, after a short period of subjection to Jewish rule (from Alexander Jannaeus to Pompey), had again become a free Hellenistic city belonging to the Decapolis.[10] Lying on one of the trade routes of Transjordania, it was, in fact, well adapted to maintain intercourse with the diaspora church and the rest of the world as well. That the church here subsisted not merely as an intimidated flock in hiding, but continued its communal living and its propaganda, is undoubtedly probable. A Christian writer of the second century, Aristo of Pella (on him, cf. Eusebius, iv. 6. 3) gives evidence of this. Further support for this comes from accounts in Epiphanius, which are, of course, rather confused, according to which the sects of the Nazarenes and Ebionites had their origin in Peraea, particularly in the Decapolis in the region of Pella, and in Basanitis in the so-called Kokaba (Kochaba; cf. *Haer.* 29:7; 30:18; 40:1). Thus one is quite able to gather from these narratives that Jewish Christianity, rejected later by the Church as a whole, spread abroad widely in the Trans-Jordan region and there developed its own peculiar characteristics.

4. *The Brethren of the Lord.* So much the more decisively does the ecclesiastical tradition maintain that the Jewish Christianity which it considers the legitimate development of the primitive Church, after the Jewish war and down to the time of Hadrian, again had its seat and focus in Jerusalem.[11] One must concede without

[9] The words of I Thess. 2:16, ἔφθασεν δὲ ἐπ' αὐτοὺς ἡ ὀργὴ εἰς τέλος, "The wrath is come upon them to the uttermost," are also to be understood most readily as being a gloss of the collector, written because of impressions gained from the events of the year 70.

[10] The site of the city has been fixed at the ruins of Khirbet Fahil, 'on a terrace overlooking the Jordan, diagonally opposite Scythopolis;' cf. Schumacher, *Pella* (London, 1888); Schürer, ii. (4th ed.), pp. 173-176, Engl. ed., 1st div., ii. p. 230; Josephus, *Ant.*, xiii. 15. 4, § 397; xiv. 4. 4, § 75; *B. J.*, i. 7. 7, § 147.

[11] According to Eusebius, *Demonstr. Ev.*, iii. 5. 108, there had been a very great Christian Church there in the period before Hadrian.

further ado that it is possible that Jerusalem had not been completely destroyed and depopulated.[12] It would be of the greatest interest to us if we could furnish any more accurate information regarding this *second period of the primitive Church.* But the ecclesiastical accounts concerning it (in Eusebius and Epiphanius) are difficult to criticize. In the main they probably go back to *Hegesippus.* This writer, very likely of Jewish origin (Eus. iv. 22. 8), who wrote his 'reminiscences' (memoirs, *hypomnemata*) in the time of the Roman bishop Eleutherus (174-189), surely was able personally to recall events in the time of Hadrian (117-138; cf. Eus. iv. 8. 2), perhaps even in that of Trajan (98-117). Since he most probably came from Palestine, since furthermore he calls the church in Jerusalem simply 'the Ekklesia' (Eus. ii. 23. 4; iv. 22. 4), as if he had personally belonged to the church, since furthermore, according to Eusebius (iv. 22. 8), he was able to impart all sorts of 'unwritten Jewish tradition,' we may regard him as a trustworthy authority for several accounts which in themselves are unobjectionable. To these belongs especially the report (Eus. iv. 22. 4) that after the death of James, Simeon, the son of Clopas, the uncle of James (and Jesus) 'was installed as bishop,' that all had 'preferred him, since he was a cousin of the Lord.'[13] Eusebius (iii. 11. 1) had learned the same thing from still another tradition.[14] Various things are important in this brief notice. The election of a relative of Jesus, and indeed, since there were no direct descendants of Jesus and James, the choice of a cousin of both—as Eusebius says, by the consent of several other kinsmen of Jesus—is to be regarded in the first place as a phenomenon of oriental family feeling. The 'sons of the house,' as the kinsmen of Jesus are called,[15] are those who were connected with the

[12] Knopf, *Nachapost. Zeitalter* (The Post-Apostolic Age), p. 12: "Jerusalem was always, in the period from the destruction by Titus down to its restoration by Hadrian, an inhabited city, even if it preserved only a shadow of its earlier greatness. There was no prohibition against living there, and the garrison, a whole legion with its train, must necessarily have drawn a great number of civilian residents into the city. Various definite traditions also point explicitly to the fact that Jerusalem, after the destruction, had not become a completely desolate city at all. We have for our consideration various passages from the Rabbinic tradition, and also passages from church fathers, e.g. Eusebius, *Demonstr. Ev.*, vi. 18. 10 (half of the city was ruined under Titus, the other half was banished under Hadrian); Epiphanius, *De Mens. et Pond.*, 14 (in Jerusalem there were only seven miserable synagogues, like huts, and a little church, when Hadrian visited the city)."

[13] On the interpretation of this, cf. Th. Zahn, *Forschungen*, vi, 236f.

[14] λόγος κατέχει, "His word prevailed;" he attributes to Hegesippus only the note that Clopas had been a brother of Joseph; cf. Th. Zahn, *Forschungen*, vi, p. 238.

[15] This is probably the best translation of δεσπόσυνοι, which Julius Africanus (Eus.,

family of Jesus by blood relationship; relationship with the 'Lord' Jesus is not emphasized so much as is the fact of belonging to the illustrious messianic family of Davidic descendants.[16] This estimate of a relationship reminds us of the struggle for the caliphate of Islam, in which blood relationship with Mohammed, especially descent from Ali, the cousin of Mohammed, and his wife Fatima, Mohammed's daughter, played the principal rôle. One would hardly dare say therefore that the idea had prevailed that in the family of Jesus the tradition of the teaching or of the life of Jesus had been more truly kept than it had elsewhere. Disciples like Cephas and perhaps his immediate pupils would probably have been able to furnish greater warrant for their testimony than would others. Here, however, the messianic expectation appears to have turned the scale; the kinsmen of Jesus are nearest to the throne of the coming Messiah (such attitudes in the primitive Church are attested by the discourse involving the sons of Zebedee, in Mark 10:35ff); thus the installation of Simeon is a symptom of a sort of dynastic honor.[17] The retirement of Jesus' own disciples before the relatives signifies a displacement of relationships which in other circles appear to have been accepted without question. If in Mark 10:35ff the aspiration of the sons of Zebedee to places of honor next to the throne of Messiah—which, indeed, rested perhaps upon blood relationship with Jesus[18]—

---

i. 7. 14) gives as a designation of the relatives of Jesus; cf. Passow, *ad vocem;* for this he cites the passages of Anaxandrides in *Athen.*, 4, p. 131c (here δεσπόσυνοι ἡμέτεροι, i.e. the native house, δόμος ἡμέτερος, is contrasted with a foreign one), and Appian, Civ., 4:44 (the whole passage is dominated by the opposition of slaves and freedmen to their δεσπότης; he says, ἕτερος δὲ ἀπελεύθερος τάφον δεσπότου φυλάσσων τὸν δεσπόσυνον [*herilem filium*] προγραφέντα ἐφύλαξεν ἐν τῷ τάφῳ μετὰ τοῦ πατρός, "Another freedman, guarding the tomb of his lord, guarded the aforesaid heir in the tomb along with his father"). The expression really corresponds to the description ἀπὸ γένους τοῦ κυρίου, 'of the race of the Lord' in Hegesippus and Eusebius (iii. 20. 8). On the other hand, it appears to me that the translation, "belonging to the 'Lord,'" as though it were to be derived from the designation of Christ as Lord (mâr=kyrios), like κυριακός, does not correspond to the meaning of the word.

[16] In this period may have arisen both of the genealogies of Jesus (pp. 123ff) which endeavor to prove the descent of Jesus from David. According to Julius Africanus in Eusebius, i. 7. 11, the relatives of Jesus, whether as a boast or simply as a matter of explanation, had at any rate given out rather openly the tradition that Herod had burned the public Jewish genealogical register, but that some who possessed private catalogues either in their memories or as transcripts, had given themselves airs on the fact that the remembrance of their noble birth had been preserved. These registers had now come into the hands of the desposunoi (ὧν ἐτύγχανον) and they explained the Lucan genealogy, as best they could, from the 'journal.'

[17] Cf. Th. Zahn, *Forschungen*, vi, pp. 298ff.

[18] If Salome, the mother of the sons of Zebedee (Mark 15:40; Matt. 27:56), is identical with the sister of Jesus' mother (John 19:25), John and James were cousins of Jesus.

is accompanied by a decided disapproval on the part of the other disciples (10:41), if the discourses on discipleship in Mark 9:33-37; 10:42-45 oppose ambition so forcibly, this is perhaps an echo of attitudes in Petrine or Pauline circles. But in particular the sayings regarding Peter as the rock of the Church and possessor of the keys of the Kingdom of Heaven (Matt. 16:17ff) are hardly understandable otherwise than as a rebuttal of the extraordinary favoritism (John 21:15ff) shown another Apostle, and thus also of another conception of the Church and its head. This cannot have been directed against St. Paul, for we can recognize no trace of the notion that he had laid claim for himself to such a position of headship over his own followers; and to assume that in this passage are mirrored the claims of the Roman church to leadership over other churches is to assume a situation which at the end of the first century is quite premature. It is superfluous to state that here are emphasized resolutely the rights of the disciples of Jesus, the missionary Apostles, as over against those of St. James, who only later became prominent in the movement, or, better yet, those of Simeon, who appears to have had no right whatever, as a disciple, to the oversight of the Church. Where this tradition of Peter's headship arose, whether in Antioch, Asia Minor, or Rome, we do not venture to say. It is very significant, however, that Matt. 16:18 considers St. Peter the sovereign authority for the whole Church. In this is reflected again the viewpoint opposite to that which maintains that the head of the church in Jerusalem stands at the head of the whole Church—that the congregation there represents the Church in general. We see in Matt. 16:18, on the other hand, the self-consciousness of the missionary church making itself felt. While here the whole Church is bound together under the leadership of Peter, it has freed itself from the authority of Jerusalem and has emphasized that the strength of the Church lies in the mission field. Along with this we see here the origin of the later Catholic view that the true Church is wherever there is an Apostle who was sent out as a missionary by Jesus, and that the tradition handed down by such a one affords more of a guarantee of legitimacy than does blood kinship with Jesus.

5. *The Monarchical Episcopate.* Although thus, in the selection of Simon, there appears to lie a claim to theoretical sovereignty over all Christendom, this fact operated together with the beginnings of the *monarchical episcopate in the local church*, and there can hardly be any doubt that from Jerusalem this idea of organization was carried

to Antioch and to Asia Minor.[19] To be sure, it is a reading-back of later conditions into earlier times, when Eusebius and Clement of Alexandria, probably depending upon Hegesippus,[20] designate James as already a bishop, for in the first place James was probably not elected at all, but rather had been able to create his position for himself by virtue of the great importance of his personality; besides, he had still other disciples, such as Cephas and John, at his side (Gal. 2:9), and in the New Testament evidence not only is the expression 'bishop' not applied to James, but he appears, despite his overwhelming importance, in a group with the other 'elders' (Acts 21:18). And Hegesippus himself says (Eus. ii. 23. 4) that he had, *together with* the Apostles,[21] taken over the church (from the Lord). But there can be no doubt that James, especially after St. Peter went on his travels, advanced into the position of a monarchical leader of the church. Indeed the departure of Peter may be connected with the fact that alongside James there was no place for him. Thus one may also doubt whether Simeon already bore a title which would correspond to the Greek *episkopos*. Hegesippus calls him bishop; at the same time he uses, in referring to other kinsmen of Jesus (Eus. iii. 32. 6) the less definite expression, 'standing at the head' (προηγοῦνται), although their position in their churches may have corresponded to that of Simeon in Jerusalem. In fact, the monarchical episcopate is probably already present here; it thus existed not only in Jerusalem, but also in other churches of the Holy Land. This is suggested by the expression which is used regarding the descendants of Judas the Lord's brother, who after their return from the trial before Domitian (Eus. iii. 30. 1-6; 32. 6) stood 'at the head of every church.' 'Every church' would mean whatever church they resided in.[22] Of course the expression (προηγοῦνται πάσης ἐκκλησίας) is not completely clear, and it might be taken to mean that 'in every church in whose midst they stayed at any time, as martyrs and kins-

[19] Cf. also Th. Zahn, *Forschungen*, vi, p. 299.

[20] Of course Hegesippus, in his extant fragments, does not directly call James a bishop, but he says of Simeon in Eus., iv. 22. 4, πάλιν . . . . καθίσταται ἐπίσκοπος, "Again . . . . a bishop is appointed," from which one may argue that James was one. Clement of Alexandria is clearer in Eus., ii 1. 3. Eusebius himself, with his predilections, uses the expression 'throne of the episcopate of James' (ii. 1. 2; 23. 1; iii. 5. 1; 11:1; 35; vii. 14. 29), elsewhere only of Corinth (iii. 23. 1) and Rome (vi. 29. 4)—according to E. Schwartz's table.

[21] So also the variant reading of Rufinus, while the Syriac reads 'of the Apostles.'

[22] Eusebius rewrites the words of Hegesippus in iii. 20. 6 as follows: τοὺς δὲ ἀπολυθέντας ἡγήσασθαι τῶν ἐκκλησίων, ὡσὰν δὴ μάρτυρας ὁμοῦ καὶ ἀπὸ γένους ὄντας τοῦ κυρίου [this last is his explanation of δεσπόσυνοι], "And they, having been released, ruled the churches, since of course they were at the same time martyrs and of the race of the Lord."

men of the Lord, they immediately gained esteem and influence.'[23] Whatever may be the case with these other descendants of the royal family, the presence of other local bishops outside Jerusalem is *probably* attested by the first part of the episcopal list which Eusebius (in the *Chronicle* and in the *H. E.* iv. 5. 3) and Epiphanius (*Haer.* 66:20) transmit, as Eusebius says, 'according to Christian tradition.' They refer of course, as Eusebius expressly emphasizes, to the *city* of Jerusalem (iv. 5. 4). This is, however, unlikely for the following reason. In the list, down to the siege (πολιορκία) of Jerusalem by Hadrian (132-135; cf. p. 722 below), no fewer than fifteen bishops are enumerated.[24] Now since the second in the list, Simeon, must have suffered a martyr's death under Trajan (98-117), there thus remain thirteen bishops for the years from 100 to 132. Thus they must either, as Eusebius says, have been very short lived, or there are included in the list bishops who reigned, not in Jerusalem, but somewhere else in the land of Judaea; thus perhaps the Zacchaeus named in the fourth place is the one who is designated as Bishop of Caesarea in the *Clementine Homilies* (3:63-72). This whole question is not settled and is difficult to decide with certainty. There is always something dangerous in thus breaking episcopal lists which are expressly connected with Jerusalem; on the other hand, it is remarkable that Eusebius, after telling of Simeon's entrance into office, explicitly indicates (iii. 35) only that of the third on the list, Justus (Epiphanius calls him Judas), while he is not able to give either the duration of the other bishops' terms of office or any details of their reigns whatever. Whatever may be the situation with regard to the bishops outside Jerusalem, there is sufficient testimony for a monarchical episcopate in Jerusalem, on the 'throne' of James, which was regarded by the early Jewish Christian Church as the

[23] Thus Th. Zahn, *Forschungen,* vi, p. 300. But προηγοῦνται is probably all too concrete an expression for this. Besides, I cannot suppress a certain doubt as to the correctness of Hegesippus' text. Although Eusebius rewrites πάσης ἐκκλησίας into τῶν ἐκκλησιῶν, I still might question whether πάσης ἐκκλησίας in both passages (p. 268, 22 and 23f) must not mean 'the whole church,' whether one must actually introduce the article or assume an incorrect mode of expression. In this case, the two descendants of David would not have held the episcopate, but actually only—as Zahn has it—have had a highly respected and leading position. In any case, in the episcopal lists of Eusebius, the names of the two descendants of Judas, Zoker and James, are missing (cf. p. 726, note 34). Eusebius (i. 7. 14) does not say that they had lived long in Nazareth and Kokaba.

[24] The names are nearly all Jewish: James, Simeon, Justus (or Judas, in Epiphanius), Zacchaeus (or Zacharius, Epiph.), Tobias, Benjamin, John, Matthias, Philip, Senecas, Justus, Levi, Ephres, Joseph (Joses, Epiph.), Judas; all 'from the circumcision,' as Eusebius says.

continuation and the provisional equivalent of the throne of David, which was to be occupied by Jesus.

Thus Simeon, the cousin of Jesus, the son of Clopas,[25] held the control from the death of James (or better, following the restoration of the church in Jerusalem after 70) down to the age of Trajan. For his martyrdom we have the information of Hegesippus (Eus. iii. 32. 3,6) that at the age of 120 years [26] he was denounced by certain Jewish 'heretics'[27] to the proconsul Atticus[28] as a descendant of David and a Christian, that during the course of several days he was put to torture, which he endured wonderfully, to the astonishment of the judge himself, and afterwards was crucified. His follower was Justus (Epiphanius: Judas).

6. *Bar-Kochba.* The fate of the Jerusalem church underwent a decided change under Hadrian (117-138). In the great uprising of the Jews under the Messiah-prophet Bar-Kokhba (132-135), Jerusalem fell into the hands of the rebels;[29] and even during the

[25] Clopas is not, as has been many times proposed, to be identified with Alphaeus, חלפי, but is a Greek name, = Κλεοπᾶς = Κλεόπατρος. It is quite noteworthy that an uncle of Jesus should bear this Greek name. He is mentioned also in Luke 24:18 as an adherent of Jesus.

[26] This account is one which evokes but little confidence. Of course he must, if he belonged approximately to the same generation as Jesus and lived to the time of Trajan, have been more than one hundred years old. This is not beyond the realm of possibility.

[27] So say Eusebius, iii. 32. 2, and Hegesippus, 32. 3; in another passage the latter says, iii. 32. 6, συκοφαντηθεὶς ὑπὸ τῶν αἱρέσεων, 'having been accused falsely by the heresies' (cf. also the remarkable expression in ii. 23. 8, τινὲς οὖν τῶν ἑπτὰ αἱρέσεων, 'certain ones, therefore, of the seven heresies;' 9, αἱ δὲ αἱρέσεις οὐκ ἐπίστευον, 'but the heresies did not believe'). Schlatter conjectures ingeniously in "Die Kirche Jerusalems vom Jahre 70-130" (*Beitr. z. Förd. chr. Theol.*, ii. 3), p. 27, that Hegesippus here is "speaking in Jewish manner: the *Minim* = αἱρέσεις, did it, except that this is the name he gives the Jews. In contrast to the αἱρέσεις stands 'the people,' ὁ λαός, i.e. the believing Christian Israel." "The 'seven parties' . . . . are the whole περιτομή." "A parallel to this is afforded by the use of ὑποκριταί (חנפים) in the Didache." But is this interpretation correct? In any case, in the James-fragment of Hegesippus (ii. 23), πᾶς ὁ λαός is not the Christian people, but Israel.

[28] "While Judaea before the war was under governors of equestrian rank (procurators), it now received governors of the senatorial class. The earlier dependence upon governors of Syria was at the same time abandoned" (Schürer, i, 3rd and 4th eds., pp. 642f; Engl. ed., 1st div., ii, 257). Atticus' period of office has not been established (cf. Schürer, i, 3rd and 4th eds., p. 645; Engl. ed., 1st div., ii, 260; Th. Zahn, *Forschungen*, vi, 242). In the Chronicle (in Jerome) the year 107 is given, but this statement is arbitrary (cf. E. Schwartz, *Eusebius' Kirchengeschichte*, iii., p. ccxl); Eusebius provided no dates. In any case, Atticus must have held office in Judaea before the end of Trajan's reign (117).

[29] Cf. Schürer, i, 3rd and 4th eds., p. 685; Engl. ed., 1st div., ii, 301. Especially valuable for proof of this are the coins struck in honor of the 'delivery of Jerusalem' and the accounts which say that Hadrian again had to 'besiege' it and conquer it (Eus.,

Bar-Kokhba revolt the Christians had much to suffer at their hands;[30] it may thus be assumed without further ado that the Jerusalem church would have been destroyed by them, although we have no accounts of the matter. But it is attested sufficiently enough that after the second conquest of the city by Hadrian and the foundation of the *Colonia Aelia Capitolina* on the site of ancient Jerusalem, no Jew was allowed to live in the city; at the same time also the last remnant which probably remained of the Jewish Christian church would have been driven out. The Christian church which thenceforth existed in Aelia was purely Gentile Christian;[31] its first bishop in Eusebius' list, Mark, inaugurates a line bearing Latin and Greek names.[32]

7. *The Later Christians in Palestine.* As to the Christians in the *country* of Judaea, Samaria, and Galilee, in our period, we learn extraordinarily little. Eusebius says that in the time of the Jewish war under Vespasian, not only Jerusalem, but the whole land, had been made destitute of 'holy men' (iii. 5. 3); he does not, however, say that all Christians, including these from the country, had fled to Pella. We may, nevertheless, assume that the beginning of the revolt and the war had brought the Christians, in many ways, into very difficult internal and external situations, so that the rhetorical statement of Eusebius is perhaps not so completely wrong. Many may have fled, whole churches may have disbanded: whether all had gone to Transjordania, or whether many had wandered to the Syrian cities, Damascus for example, we do not know. But it is certain that the Jewish war did not destroy all churches, and did not destroy the

iv. 4. 2, πολιορκία; thus *Demonstratio,* vi. 18. 10); Appian, *Syria,* 50, speaks of destruction (κατέσκαψε); cf. also Schürer, i, 3rd and 4th eds., p. 692, note 126; Engl. ed., 1st div., ii, 273f.

[30] Justin, *Apol.,* 1:31, Καὶ γὰρ ἐν τῷ νῦν γεγενημένῳ Ἰουδαϊκῷ πολέμῳ βαρχωχέβας, ὁ τῆς Ἰουδαίων ἀποστάσεως ἀρχηγέτης, Χριστιανοὺς μόνους εἰς τιμωρίας δεινάς, εἰ μὴ ἀρνοῖντο Ἰησοῦν τὸν Χριστὸν καὶ βλασφημοῖεν, ἐκέλευεν ἀπάγεσθαι, "And indeed in the recent Jewish war, Bar-Kokhba, the leader of the uprising of the Jews, condemned the Christians alone to be led away to dreadful torture if they would not deny Jesus was Christ and blaspheme him;" Eusebius, *Chron.* (ed. Schoene, ii, 168ff), on the year of Abraham 2149 (ed. Karst, p. 220): Qui dux rebellionis Iudaeorum erat Chochebas, multos e Christianis diversis suppliciis affecit, quia nolebant procedere cum illo ad pugnam contra Romanos, "Kokhba, who was leader of the rebellion of the Jews, inflicted various penalties on many of the Christians, since they would not go out to battle with him against the Romans;" Orosius, 7:13.

[31] Eusebius, iv. 6. 4, Καὶ δὴ τῆς αὐτόθι ἐκκλησίας ἐξ ἐθνῶν συγκροτηθείσης, πρῶτος μετὰ τοὺς ἐκ περιτομῆς ἐπισκόπους τὴν τῶν ἐκεῖσε λειτουργίαν ἐγχειρίζεται Μάρκος, "And when the church there was gathered together from the Gentiles, the first man after the bishops of the circumcision who took up the ministry among the people there was Mark."

[32] Cassianus, Publius, Maximus, Julianus, Gaius, etc. The list contains a great preponderance of Latin names.

Church permanently. From the period between Titus and Hadrian we have some meagre but not completely worthless notices of it.

We have already seen earlier (p. 722) that Hegesippus *probably* mentions several churches which had the monarchical episcopate (Eus. iii. 32. 6). But even if this passage were to be interpreted otherwise, still the assumption would lie ready to hand that the churches in the province had patterned their organization after the model of Jerusalem. We learn nothing in detail about these churches; here also we are left to make for ourselves a picture of their life from the sayings of the Lord, and from the old evangelic tradition, as, e.g., it appears in the special source of Luke, to form an idea of their care in treasuring up memories of Jesus. Perhaps we may also think that the source in the first part of the Book of Acts, with its partly legendary, partly quite concrete, reminiscences of the glorious beginnings of the primitive Church, arose in this period and in these circles. Thus in particular the story of the centurion Cornelius in Caesarea could have had its origin here, as well as perhaps the story of the death of Herod Agrippa. At any rate the chapters 9:31—11:18 have a somewhat local coloring (Lydda, Sharon, Joppa) and furnish certain local reminiscences (Aeneas, Tabitha, Simon the tanner, the Italian cohort). In Jerusalem these stories would scarcely have been collected, since the personality of Peter here completely occupies the central position and James was acknowledged as having his own significance (12:17; 15:13ff), but hardly ever appears otherwise.[33] If the Cornelius story lived on in these circles, they were not narrow-mindedly Jewish Christian: in the population of the Jewish cities, strongly mixed with Gentiles, especially on the coast, a strict separation was not at all unlikely, and in the neighborhood of Gentile Christian churches (e.g. in Tyre and Sidon) the idea of reception of Gentiles into the churches would easily occur (cf. also Luke 4:26f).

[33] The way in which 'the people' is referred to (10:2) is quite Jewish Christian in manner, just as is the attention paid 'good works, alms and prayers' as marks of piety (9:36; 10:2), and the reference to the Jewish attitude of prayer (on the roof) and hours of prayer (10:9; cf. 3:1), and just as is the tacit supposition that among 'all' beasts there must necessarily be some unclean ones (10:12,14; cf. also the technical cult expressions *καθαρίζειν* and *κοινοῦν*); Peter must be brought, by some special divine revelation to *κολλᾶσθαι ἢ προσέρχεσθαι ἀλλοφύλῳ*, 'to join himself or come unto one of another nation' and to call no man *κοινὸν ἢ ἀκάθαρτον* 'common or unclean' (10:28). The expression in 12:1,5, *ἡ ἐκκλησία*, used of the Jerusalem church, as if it alone bore this title, is interesting also. From this one can draw the conclusion that the 'saints' (9:32) dwelling in Lydda and elsewhere did not consider themselves to be 'the Church,' or at least they felt themselves only diaspora in covenant with Jerusalem. The narrator is also at home in Jerusalem (12:10,12). On this source see further, pp. 7f.and 143f.

The interest in the Samaritans is likewise worthy of notice; this appears in Acts 8 and in various passages of the Lucan source (9:52ff; 10:30ff; 17:11-19). Thus the fundamental character of these traditions is, after all, Jewish Christian. Here one must mention especially the Infancy Narrative, already referred to above, with its lively messianic hopes and its good acquaintance with the locality of Jerusalem, Jewish temple usages (1:8ff), and domestic customs (1:58ff). Its continuing interest in the Baptist, the story of whose infancy it has formed out of narratives which circulated in the highlands of Judah (1:65), is worthy of mention. The psalms contained in it may give us a picture of Jewish Christian piety, in which one may be permitted, e.g., to connect the verses (1:51ff) regarding the fall of the mighty and the exaltation of the lowly, with the judgment which has been visited upon the Jewish autocrats, and the exaltation of the family of Jesus to the 'throne' of David (1:69). That the church was able to live unmolested in Jerusalem and the Holy Land, one might well call a 'salvation from our enemies, and from the hand of all that hate us' (1:71). In any case, these songs first attained their actual vitality when one read them from the point of view of those who had lived to see such great things as did the Christians after the year 70. The tender, kindly tone of this tradition has often been observed, the striking way in which women stand out, and the strong interest in the feminine emotional life which it displays (e.g. Luke 1:39ff; 2:19,35,48; 7:36-50; 8:1ff; 10:38-42; 11:27f; 23:27f, etc.). One may perhaps conclude from this that there was a somewhat stronger emphasis on the feminine element, or at any rate a considerable refinement of feeling, in these circles. Even if most of this material is derived from old, genuine tradition, yet it is significant that the *collector* chose just this material. Furthermore, it is an important emphasis which Luke's special source places on the love of Jesus for the poor and needy and for the sinners, while the 'teachers of the Law' and Pharisees appear as the haughty ones who are an abomination in the eyes of God (Luke 16:15; 18:9-14), but at the same time as the propertied classes (16:14), against whom Jesus had called down woes (6:24f). In this circle the 'poor' and the 'elect of God' coincide, as conversely do the 'rich' and those 'rejected of God,' a fact which stands out especially in the parable of Lazarus. That special attention is not called to Lazarus' piety and Dives' godlessness is significant in itself; for this was self-evident in this circle of believers. The disdain with which the dishonest steward is mentioned (16:3) has a counterpart in Hegesippus' story of the two grandsons of Judas the brother of Jesus (Eus. iii. 20. 1-4, 5-8), who despite their kinship with the Lord, now exalted to glory, possessed in common only a miserable plot of ground—39 plethra—worth 9,000 denarii [$2400 in the present United States currency], which they cultivated with their own labor (αὐτουργία; they held no slaves)—as their rough outward appearances and the callouses of their workingmen's hands showed. Significant also is their declaration that they did not consider the 'kingdom of the Messiah' to be an earthly one, but, as Eusebius expresses it, a 'celestial and angelic one' which would not come until the 'end of the ages' at the Parousia.[34] The Lucan source names in 24:18 still another kinsman of Jesus, viz. Clopas, who must be identical with the father of Bishop Simeon, the cousin of Jesus. Luke mentions him (just as does John 19:25) as a well-known personage, and so does Hegesippus. He must thus have lived for a relatively long time as a respected member of the church either in Jerusalem or in the surrounding country. We should look for the peasant descendants of Judas in the country, perhaps in Galilee. On the other hand, Clopas appears to be no longer living, since under Domitian the accusation was made against the two descendants of Judas.[35] Ostensibly Domitian (81-96) had ordered that the family of David be exterminated. The heretics already mentioned (p. 722, note) had informed against them on account of their Davidic lineage, and they were deported to Rome under military guard and brought before the imperial tribunal. On account of their complete inoffensiveness they were set free; Domitian by an edict suspended the persecution of the Church which he had ordered, and deep peace prevailed in the Church until Trajan. It is a striking thing that in this account there is nothing about legal proceedings against Simeon at this time, but that he lived until the time of Trajan. He might well have been accused, not merely as a Christian, but also as a descendant of David (iii. 32. 3).

The Christians in the Holy Land were disturbed by the Jews more severely than by the Roman government, or at least the intellectual struggle with them was continued under aggravated conditions, since

[34] Their names Zoker and James were found in Hegesippus by Philip of Side (*Texte und Untersuchungen,* v. 2, p. 169); cf. also Th. Zahn, *Forschungen,* vi, p. 240.

[35] Eus., iii. 19; 20. 1-4, 5-8. Only 1-4 is a verbatim quotation from Hegesippus; the Latin loan words, ἐδηλατόρευσαν and ἠουοκᾶτος are quite remarkable; that they were transported to *Rome* is not explicitly said, but it may reasonably be assumed (the text merely says ἤγαγε πρὸς Δομετιανὸν Καίσαρα, "He led them to Domitian Caesar"). This deportation and the anxiety of the emperor about a parousia of the Messiah are rather remarkable, of course. By the words ὡς καὶ Ἡρώδης, 'like Herod also,' the historian perhaps reveals that the story is patterned after Matt. 2.

after the fall of Jerusalem the scribes had obtained a new center for their activity in Jamnia and had 'pursued their work in the Law with greater zeal than ever' (cf. Schürer, ed. 3 and 4, i, pp. 656ff; Engl. tr., 1st div., ii, 273f). Several anecdotes preserved in the Talmud bear witness to the strongly felt antipathy[36] to the Minim, the 'people of Capernaum.' The sentence in Tosefta, Chullin 2:20 (Zuckermandel, 503, 9ff), is significant 'What the Minim slay is a sacrifice to idols; their bread is bread of the Kuthi [Samaritans], their wine is wine of an idolatrous sacrifice, from their fruits the taxes are first paid; their books are soothsayers' books and their sons are illegitimate. One should sell them nothing and buy nothing from them; one should not marry their daughters nor should anyone give a daughter to them in marriage; one should not teach a trade to their sons or receive any help from them, either money or medical help.'[37] As an example of this absolute separation the following story is told: "It happened to R. Eleazar b. Dama, that a snake bit him, and Jacob, the man of Kaphar Sama, came to heal him in the name of Jesus, the son of the Panther, and R. Ishmael did not permit him. He said to him, you are not permitted, Ben Dama! He said to him, I will furnish you proof that he can heal me. But he had not finished bringing proof before he died. R. Ishmael said, Happy are you, Ben Dama, for you have departed in peace and not torn down the fence of the wise men. For to those who tear down the fence of the wise men punishment will come at last, as it is written: 'He who tears down a fence will be bitten by the snake.'"[38] The story illustrates not merely the sharp repulsion of Christians by the rabbis, but also the inclination toward use of the 'name of Jesus' and confidence, on the part of some at least, in that use of the name (cf. Mark 9:38). We are also told of various conversions: 'Khananya, the nephew of Rabbi Joshua, went to Capernaum, and the heretics did something to him [i.e. they baptized him] and brought him in, riding on an ass on the Sabbath [they thus did not keep the Sabbath, and since Khananya permitted this, he also broke the Sabbath]. He went to his friend Joshua, who anointed him with oil and he was healed [cf. Jas. 5:14; Mark 6:13; here, however, the healing is a sort of exorcism on account of apostasy]. He said to him: since the wine of that impious one has dwelt in you [i.e. because he had drunk of the chalice], you cannot dwell in the land of Israel. He went thence to

[36] Cf. Schlatter, "Die Kirche Jerusalems vom Jahre 70-130" (*Beitr. z. Förd. chr. Theol.*, ii. 3), pp. 1ff.

[37] [Cf. R. T. Herford, *Christianity in Talmud and Midrash*, p. 177.]

[38] German translation by Schlatter, *op. cit.*, p. 8; [cf. Herford, *op. cit.*, p. 103].

Babylon and died there in peace' (Koh. 1:8; quoted in Schlatter, p. 10).[39] "Rabbi Eliezer was seized on account of Christianity [for heresy] and they brought him before the seat of judgment, but he was freed. He was much grieved by the suspicion that had fallen on him; then R. Akiba sought him out and said to him, Perhaps one of the Minim said a heretical word to you and you were pleased by it? He said, By heaven! You have reminded me. Once I went on the road to Sepphoris; I met Jacob, the man of Kaphar Sicanim, and he said a word of heresy in the name of Jesus, the son of the Panther, and it pleased me, and I was affected by heresy because I transgressed the word of the Torah, 'Put far from her [the harlot] thy way and come not near to the door of her house, for she has brought many who are dead to their fall' " (Tos. Chullin 2:24).[40] One recognizes again from this the holy dread of having satisfaction even from a word of the hated Jesus. The abusive name 'harlot,' used for the Church, is obvious enough.[41] To take, in conclusion, another case: in Lydda a scribe came into suspicion of having an inclination to Christianity, and before he had come out openly with his confession, he was spied out and stoned (Schlatter, p. 19). These thumbnail sketches light up clearly the tense situation existing between synagogue and church in the Holy Land. The abusive name 'Son of the Panther,' given to Jesus, which refers to a birth out of wedlock, will concern us later (cf. W. Bauer, *Das Leben Jesu im Zeitalter der Neutestamentlichen Apokryphen*, The Life of Jesus in the Period of the New Testament Apocrypha, p. 459). Eusebius, however, explicitly tells us that the Church gained many adherents in the time of Trajan (iii. 35). Among others, the third bishop of Jerusalem, Judas, was at that time converted from Judaism.

On the whole we may think of the churches in the Holy Land during this second period as a circle of 'the quiet in the land,' completely occupied with the expectation of the coming of Jesus as Messiah, with full pride because they had the 'sons of the household' in their midst, not without certain hopes that on account of this they would have a share in the dominion over Israel and the Gentiles; obedient to the words of the Lord, which they preserved as a holy tradition, but certainly not unfruitful in bringing forth new sayings and stories of Jesus for the decision of important questions of controversy and life. How widely they remained true to the law of their

[39] [Cf. Herford, *op. cit.*, pp. 211f.]
[40] [Cf. Herford, *op. cit.*, pp. 137f.]
[41] [Cf. Herford, *op. cit.*, pp. 138ff.]

race we cannot learn: alongside traces of freedom from the Sabbath commandment stand other signs of faithfulness to the Law, such as the saying in Matt. 24:20. Oppressed by Roman persecution in the time of Domitian, at least in the person of their leaders, and again under Trajan, engaged in continual struggle with the Jews, especially the scribes, a saying such as Luke 18:7 was applicable to them: 'And shall not God avenge his elect, which cry to him day and night?' It would be a cry from the very soul for them to say: 'If two of you shall agree on earth as touching anything that they shall ask, it shall be done for them of my Father which is in heaven. For where two or three are gathered together in my name, there am I in the midst of them' (Matt. 18:19f). The common faith in the exalted Jesus, the consciousness of his helpful presence, the experience of his power in the use of his name, the prospect of his promise, 'Fear not, little flock; for it is your Father's good pleasure to give you the kingdom' (Luke 12:30)—all these would have given them power to endure to the end, to confess themselves bravely and truly before the Son of Man, and to take his cross upon themselves.

8. *The Heretical Jewish Christianity*. The brief notice of Justin (*Dial*. 47) that there were Jewish Christians who tried to compel the Gentile Christians to live according to the Law of Moses, and who otherwise refused them fellowship, can hardly refer to Jewish Christians of the diaspora, but it can hardly refer either to the Jerusalem church, which in Justin's time was no longer Jewish Christian. He must have had in mind the Jewish Christian movement which was considered by still later fathers (Irenaeus, Origen, Hippolytus, Eusebius, Epiphanius, Jerome) to be a heretical schism from the universal Church. We cannot here undertake an exhaustive treatment of their partly contradictory reports, especially the confused account of Epiphanius,[42] although such a treatment is urgently needed.[43] But we do not require it, at this point, inasmuch as the phenomena considered by them lie, in general, beyond the epoch which we are portraying here. However, the beginnings of the movement and its connection with the older and, so to speak, legitimate or ecclesiastical Jewish Christianity are so important to us that we cannot forego some discussion.

[42] Irenaeus, i. 26. 2; iii. 15. 1; 21. 1; iv. 33. 4; v. 1. 3. Origen, *Contra Celsum,* 2:1; 5:61, 65; *De Principiis,* 4:22; Hippolytus, *Philosophoumena,* 7:34; 10:22; Eusebius, iii. 27; Epiphanius, *Haer.*, 29, 30; Jerome, *Ep.*, 89, 112, 113.

[43] [*Translator's Note.* Cf. D. W. Riddle, "The So-Called Jewish Christians," *Anglican Theological Review,* xii (1929), 15-33.]

This connection is shown, first of all, by the name which they gave themselves and by which they were called by others. The designation as Nazarenes or Nazoraeans which appears in Epiphanius and Jerome[44] is to be understood as a contemptuous nickname taken over and accepted, a name which the Jews had given the worshippers of Jesus of Nazareth who lived among them (Acts 24:5). In this fact is exhibited not only powerful boldness in the face of hatred and persecution, which would be the basis for the adoption of such an abusive word as a title of honor, but at the same time there is also shown an energetic profession of the name of that despised Jesus of Nazareth. In the Nathanael story of the Gospel of John (1:47) and in Matthew's proof from prophecy (2:23) there is manifest the full consciousness of what this name signified for the Christians. That the Jews used it also against the Christians outside Judaea in the empire, we learn from the wording of the 'benediction' against heretics (p. 708, note 1).[45] That, on the other hand, the Christians of the great Church abandoned it, is understandable enough; the name 'Christiani' displaced it. It is thus perhaps only a symptom of the fact that the larger or smaller group of Jewish Christians, which called themselves and were called by others Nazarenes, stood far away from that stream of development; the 'Christ' name, being a specifically Graeco-Roman one, had not reached them. Thus perhaps in the Nazarene name is expressed merely the fact that these Jewish Christians were the successors of the old Palestinian primitive Church. Without any special pathos, without any deeper signification, the name simply clung to them, until one day it was regarded by themselves and by the men of the great Church as a sort of curiosity, a fossilized relic, and was thenceforth emphasized as such. The name Ebionaeans or *Ebionites*, which Irenaeus (i. 62. 2), Hippolytus (7:34; 10:22), Tertullian (*De Praescr.*, 33), Origen (*Contra Celsum*, 5:61; *De Principiis*, 4:22, etc.), Eusebius (iii. 27), Epiphanius (*Haer.* 30), connected with a heretical Jewish Chris-

[44] Whether this actually became the general name for heretical Jewish Christians, which was used interchangeably with that of Ebionite (so Jerome), has been made quite doubtful by the investigation of Schmidtke; he connects it with a purely local group in Beroea of Coele-Syria.

[45] Cf. also Tertullian, *Adv. Marc.*, 4:8, Nazaraeus vocari habebat secundum prophetiam Christus creatoris, unde et ipso nomine nos Iudaei Nazarenos appellant per eum. Nam et sumus de quibus scriptum est: Nazaraei exalbati sunt super nivem (Lam. 4:7), "It was considered that Christ was called a Nazaraean according to prophecy of the Creator, thus they call those of us who are Jews by the same name, Nazarenes, on account of him. For we are those of whom it is written: The Nazaraeans are whiter than snow" (Lam. 4:7).

tianity, was, to be sure, partly referred by them (*not* by Irenaeus) to a supposed founder Ebion; there can, however, be no doubt that this figure was freely invented by them and that the name is nothing but a Hellenized form of *ebionim*, 'the poor.' Beyond doubt it goes back to a self-designation of this group, rather than to the two Pauline passages in which the Apostle chances to speak of the 'poor' in the primitive Church (Gal. 2:10; Rom. 15:26). Nor is it to be understood as a representation of the actual state of their fortunes, but as a religious confession: 'Despite our poverty, nay on account of our very poverty, God has chosen us.' They connect the beatitudes of the Sermon on the Plain (Luke 6:20f) with themselves, consider themselves the brothers of poor Lazarus, above all they appropriate the numerous passages of the Old Testament in which 'the poor' is a designation either of the people of Israel as a whole or of the true Israel, the pious among the people, and consider it their right to designate themselves thus as being the truly righteous and beloved of God, as the elect who are certain of a glorious future.[46] It is clear that at the same time a fundamental conviction or attitude of the primitive Church was maintained (pp. 73ff). Thus there is present here, as in the name Nazarene, a relic of the earlier period, which was not washed away by the development in the empire. How perplexed the men of the great Church were made by this name is shown by their attempt at its explanation. Besides relating it to the mythical Ebion, they speak of the 'poor' mode of thought of these people, especially the poor Christology; but they no longer understand its original meaning. So much the more evident is the connection of heretical Christianity with the primitive Church on this point.

But this connection is shown also in one of the chief points of their heretical teaching: in the Christology. If the reproach against them, that they considered Jesus a 'man from men,' the offspring of Joseph and Mary, was constantly repeated from the time of Justin and Irenaeus[47] on, this view may have had still another ground unknown

[46] Count von Baudissin, "Die alttestamentliche Religion und die Armen" (The Old Testament Religion and the Poor), *Preussische Jahrbücher*, 149, pp. 193f, 1912, who says, for example, "In this custom of considering the poor as a social class of elect people who have received promises not given to others, a turn of expression seems to make its appearance from the exile on (perhaps in some of its details still earlier), in which the designation 'the poor' becomes a title of honor for the people of Israel, or 'the poor' among the people are distinguished from the people as a whole as the true Israel which is well pleasing to God" (pp. 209f).

[47] Justin, *Dial.*, 48, *εἰσί τινες ἀπὸ τοῦ ὑμετέρου* (if one is to read it thus) *γένους ὁμολογοῦντες αὐτὸν Χριστὸν εἶναι, ἄνθρωπον δὲ ἐξ ἀνθρώπων γενόμενον ἀποφαινόμενοι,*

to us, or a dogmatic purpose; *one* reason for it, however, was surely the nationalistic conviction that Jesus was born of the seed of David. This principle of Jewish messianic faith we have already recognized in St. Paul (Rom. 1:3) as a piece of tradition from the primitive Church (pp. 124f); from this conviction and from the nearly dynastic reverence which was paid the family of Jesus after the death of James, is to be explained the origin of the family trees of Jesus (p. 718). And it is these which bore emphatic witness to the Jewish Christian opinion that Jesus had been son of Joseph; only thus could he be regarded as a scion of David. If one now sees how, in our present text of the gospels, the connecting link of both genealogies has been broken (Luke 3:23; Matt. 1:16; cf. pp. 124f), one recognizes perfectly that they did not have their origin in the circle of the Greek evangelists. The Jewish Christian author of the first gospel himself advocated with absolute conviction the virgin birth of Jesus by the Spirit;[48] he thus cannot in any case have belonged to

---

"There are some of our ['your'? So E. J. Goodspeed, *Die Aeltesten Apologeten, ad loc.*] race who acknowledge him to be Messiah, but declare him to be a man born of men," to which Trypho answers, *ἐμοὶ μὲν δοκοῦσιν . . . . οἱ λέγοντες ἄνθρωπον γεγονέναι αὐτὸν καὶ κατ' ἐκλογὴν κεχρῖσθαι καὶ Χριστὸν γεγονέναι πιθανώτερον ὑμῶν λέγειν . . . . καὶ γὰρ πάντες ἡμεῖς τὸν Χριστὸν ἄνθρωπον ἐξ ἀνθρώπων προσδοκῶμεν γενήσεσθαι καὶ τὸν Ἡλίαν χρῖσαι αὐτὸν ἐλθόντα*, "It seems to me . . . . that those who say he was born a man and *anointed by choice and made Messiah* speak more persuasively than do you . . . . for indeed all of us expect the Messiah to be born a man from men and that Elijah will come to anoint him." Irenaeus says of the Ebionites that they tell the same fables of Christ as do Cerinthus and Carpocrates (i. 26. 2), namely (according to i. 25), that Jesum autem subjecit (*ὑπέθετο*) non ex virgine natum, fuisse autem eum Joseph et Mariae filium (cf. also Iren., iii. 21. 1; iv. 33. 4; v. 1. 3), similiter ut reliqui omnes homines, et plus potuisse justitia et prudentia et sapientia ab omnibus, "He suggested that Jesus was not born of a virgin, but that he was son of Joseph and Mary, just like all other men, and that he had been more powerful than all in righteousness and intelligence and wisdom." Origen knows at least a group of Ebionites, who *ἐκ Μαρίας καὶ τοῦ Ἰωσὴφ οἴονται αὐτὸν εἶναι*, 'suppose that he was from Mary and Joseph' (*In Matt.* tom. 17:12); likewise Eusebius, iii. 27, *λιτὸν μὲν γὰρ αὐτὸν καὶ κοινὸν ἡγοῦντο κατὰ προκοπὴν ἤθους αὐτὸ μόνον ἄνθρωπον δεδικαιωμένον, ἐξ ἀνδρός τε κοινωνίας καὶ τῆς Μαρίας γεγενημένον*, "They believe that he was a plain and common man who alone was justified, because of the advancement of his ways, born of the intercourse of Mary and a man" (vi. 17, *αἵρεσις δέ ἐστιν ἡ τῶν Ἐβιωναίων οὕτω καλουμένη τῶν τε τὸν Χριστὸν ἐξ Ἰωσὴφ καὶ Μαρίας γεγονέναι φασκόντων ψιλόν τε ἄνθρωπον ὑπειληφότων αὐτόν*, "It is a heresy, so called from the Ebionites, who allege that the Christ was born of Joseph and Mary and suppose that he was a mere man"). Epiphanius, 30:2, *τὰ πρῶτα δὲ ἐκ παρατριβῆς καὶ σπέρματος ἀνδρὸς, τουτέστι τοῦ Ἰωσήφ, τὸν Χριστὸν γεγενῆσθαι ἔλεγεν*, "He [Ebion] said, first of all that Christ was born of intercourse and of the seed of a man, i.e. Joseph;" so 30:3, 14, 16, 18, 20, 34.

[48] It is an almost incomprehensible blunder when, as von Soden does, one introduces the reading of the Syriac version into the text of Matthew.

the Ebionite Jewish Christians. But that such family trees were to be found at all, points to a Christology which knew as little about the super-human *birth* of Jesus as did St. Paul (Gal. 4:4). This was for the Jewish Christians, above all, nothing more than the oldest view of the primitive Church, to which they adhered; that later, when another doctrine penetrated into the great Church, they held to it firmly, is only too comprehensible. Thus it is hardly to be taken as an accident that in the Syriac church in the region of the Euphrates, the original conclusion which once was a part of the genealogy, was still preserved, in the words 'Jacob begat Joseph, Joseph, to whom Mary the virgin was betrothed, begat Jesus who was called Christ.' The one who wrote thus must still have known the genealogy in its original form, quite probably detached from the Gospel of Matthew. Of course the original reading is no longer retained here in its present form: for, since Mary is not designated as the actual wife, but as the *fiancée* of Joseph, the birth narrative of Matthew still influences the form (1:18f). The family tree given in Luke exhibits more purely the original form, since it reads: 'He was the son (as was supposed) of Joseph, the son of Eli . . .' And the old idea that Joseph was father of Jesus still peeps through in the Infancy Narrative of Luke, most obviously in 2:4, where Mary was originally called the wife of Joseph (cf. SNT on Luke 2). Thus in this respect also Ebionite Christianity is the continuation, in a direct line, of the older primitive Church, considered legitimate by the Fathers. So the idea that Jesus 'by reason of divine election was anointed and thus became Messiah' which Justin displays to the Jew Trypho as being ostensibly the Jewish concept, but which is probably also the Jewish Christian one, is nothing less than the preservation of the pre-evangelic idea of the events at the Baptism. Here the baptism of Jesus signifies the beginning of his Messiahship, and hence decisive importance is also to be assigned to the *anointing* of Jesus with the Spirit in Acts 10:38 (4:27). We have earlier (p. 123) pointed out that this is a reading backward of the very earliest idea of Messiahship. According to the view of the oldest Christian circles the Messiahship began with the exaltation to divine glory (cf. Acts 2:36 and Rom. 1:4). If, now, the signs of messianic royalty were exhibited as existing already in the life of Jesus, this is perhaps connected with the conspicuous reverence paid the royal family of Jesus in the later primitive Church. And it is furthermore comprehensible that the Ebionites emphasized, as a doctrine differentiating them from the great Church, what was originally only an idea preserved from antiquity.[49] With this is further connected the fact that although they emphasized the humanity of Jesus, yet various sorts of honorific titles were applied to him: it was said that he was a prophet, that he had been selected from among men because of his virtue, or his righteousness, or the fact that he fulfilled the Law.[50] But one may well explain this as an echo of an older Jewish Christian interpretation: one may consider the predicates 'the righteous' (Luke 23:47; Matt. 27:19 [24]; Acts 3:14; 7:52) and 'the prophet' (Luke 7:16,39; 9:8,19; 13:33f; 24:19; Acts 3:22). Something still different comes into play here. For example, in the words of Hippolytus (7:34; see the note) stands the statement that Jesus had been made righteous or 'justified' because he had kept the Law, in internal connection with the sentence to the effect that the Ebionites 'live according to Jewish customs, for they say that one becomes righteous by reason of the Law!' And so Irenaeus calls attention to the fact that they submit to circumcision and persist in the usages of the Law.[51] And in this respect also we may consider them as successors of the primitive Church. That they practised the circumcision of their sons should not surprise us at all; this is certainly a practice which is comprehensible in itself, in the primitive Church, and a practice not attacked by St. Paul. The question is, however, a critical one,

[49] Another branch from the same root is the gnostic doctrine that in the baptism a higher being, either the Christ or Sophia or some other divine power, came upon Jesus and united itself with him; cf. Bousset, *Kyrios Christos,* pp. 257ff.

[50] Eusebius, iii. 27, *κατὰ προκοπὴν ἤθους αὐτὸ μόνον ἄνθρωπον δεδικαιωμένον*, "Because of the advancement of his ways he was the only man justified;" Epiph., *Haer.,* 30:18, *προφήτην τῆς ἀληθείας καὶ Χριστὸν υἱὸν Θεοῦ κατὰ προκοπὴν καὶ κατὰ συνάφειαν ἀναγωγῆς τῆς ἄνωθεν πρὸς αὐτὸν γεγενημένης. αὐτὸν δὲ μόνον θέλουσιν εἶναι προφήτην καὶ ἄνθρωπον καὶ υἱὸν θεοῦ καὶ Χριστὸν καὶ ψιλὸν ἄνθρωπον . . . . διὰ δὲ ἀρετὴν βίου ἥκοντα εἰς τὸ καλεῖσθαι υἱὸν θεοῦ*, "That he was a prophet of truth, and Christ, Son of God by his progress and his conjunction with an influence which came down upon him from above. They will have it that he alone is prophet and man and Son of God and Christ and mere man . . . . because of the virtue of his life he attained the designation, Son of God;" Hippolytus, 7:34, *καὶ τὸν Ἰησοῦν λέγοντες δεδικαιῶσθαι ποιήσαντα τὸν νόμον· διὸ καὶ Χριστὸν [αὐτὸν] τοῦ Θεοῦ ὠνομάσθαι καὶ Ἰησοῦν, ἐπεὶ μηδεὶς τῶν ἄλλων* [or *πρὸ αὐτῶν* for *ἄλλων*] *ἐτέλεσε τὸν νόμον· εἰ γὰρ καὶ ἕτερός τις πεποιήκει τὰ ἐν νόμῳ προστεταγμένα, ἦν ἂν ἐκεῖνος ὁ Χριστός*, "And they say that Jesus was justified because he kept the Law; wherefore they call him the Messiah of God and Jesus, since none of the others [or, no one before them] had fulfilled the Law; for if any other had done the things prescribed in the Law, that one would have been the Messiah."

[51] According to Epiphanius, *Haer.,* 30:32, they laid the greatest emphasis on keeping the Sabbath and on circumcision, besides the daily ablutions.

whether they demanded circumcision of such Gentiles as joined their churches, and whether they denied recognition and fellowship to the great Gentile Christian Church because it had renounced the demand of circumcision. By reason of Justin's assertion, already noticed above (p. 723 n. 30), we must answer the latter question in the affirmative. On this point they are the successors of Paul's opponents, followers of the right wing of Judaists from Jerusalem. The great Apostle had repulsed their assault upon the developing Gentile Christianity; we know that after the Apostolic Council in Jerusalem they had agitated still more (pp. 299ff, 311ff, 337ff); what they had not been able—despite some results in Galatia, Corinth, and Colossae—to *carry through* to a conclusion, they now attempted, at least in their own circle, to maintain strictly. But just as their sulky repudiation of the Gentile Christian church remained without practical influence and could be a matter of relative indifference to that church, so also the demand of circumcision actually had very little significance in the real propaganda efforts of these Jewish Christians. If a Gentile had no inclination to submit to this demand, there were Gentile Christian churches aplenty in the neighborhood which would receive him without this; if, however, he submitted to it, he was obviously already so much Judaized that he was no loss to the great Church. In this very demand one recognizes clearly the insignificance of Jewish Christianity, which stood apart as it did from the main course of development.

The rejection of St. Paul as an apostate from the Law, to which Irenaeus and Epiphanius bear witness, of course remained practically without consequences, in any case; nevertheless this attitude had, as it appears, not merely a local and purely heretical significance. In the Gospel of Matthew, product of the great Church, the repudiation of teachers who say that Jesus wished to suspend the Law (5:17,19) is to be detected most clearly, and even if it is not said in so many words that the 'least of all' (5:19) or the 'enemy' who sows the weeds in the field (13:25) is Paul (it is more likely the 'devil' of 13:39), yet this interpretation lies in the direction of the attitude of the Gospel of Matthew. The Mission of the Twelve [Eleven] at the conclusion of the work, with its complete disregard of St. Paul, is only comprehensible if the great Apostle of the Gentiles—to say the very least—was not included among those who were objects of the author's veneration. The denunciations of Paul, of which Epiphanius tells us,[52] lie beyond our epoch; in our sources no trace of them is to be found. Moreover, the rejection (Irenaeus: *recusant*) of the Apostles, which Eusebius (iii. 27. 4) connects directly with his letters, first became actual after these letters were recognized as Scripture to be read in the Church, and Paul thereby was exalted to the rank of a bearer of revelation which was binding upon the Church. Just so the statement that they had used only the Gospel of Matthew[53] makes sense only in the time when there was a Gospel of Matthew, i.e. after the end of the first century. Even the information that they chose the Gospel of Matthew *alone* for themselves from a great number of gospels, is difficult to accept. In any case Irenaeus means to say that of the four gospels they used only the *one*. Of course the facts which lie behind this statement are still not fully clarified.[54] The probable assumption recently made, that the Nazarenes in Coele-Syrian Beroea made use of a Matthew translated into Hebrew, that on the other hand the Transjordanian Ebionites used the so-called Gospel of the Hebrews, a reworking of Matthew (with Lucan interpolations), depends upon the state of affairs in the second century. It would be more important for us to know whether in the period from 70 to 100 they possessed sayings of the Lord and the narratives of the Lord's life in a written account. On this point we know nothing definite. It seems, however, reasonable to conjecture that accounts which arose in Palestine and which lie at the basis of our gospels, such as the Sayings Source (Q) and the Lucan Special Source (LQ), were accessible to them, and thus were models which were authoritative for them before the so-called Gospel of the Hebrews arose.

If we still possessed the gospel of the Ebionite Jewish Christians, we would be able to provide for ourselves a more exact picture of them; however we must content ourselves with a few fragments, which are quite interesting indeed.[55] It is significant for the Chris-

[52] Epiph., *Haer.*, 30:16: Paul was of Greek descent, and in Jerusalem he fell in love with the daughter of a Jewish priest; since, however, he could not obtain the girl, he followed the impulse of his anger and wrote against circumcision, the Sabbath, and the Law. In particular, an identification of Simon Magus with Paul still lies completely outside the field of vision of the New Testament writers, especially the author of Acts.

[53] Irenaeus, i. 26. 2; iii. 11. 7; Epiphanius, *Haer.*, 30:3.

[54] Schmidtke's investigations (cf. above, p. 730, note 44), are most convincing to me.

[55] Cf. Hennecke, *Neutestamentliche Apokryphen*, pp. 19-21; Preuschen, *Antilegomena* (2d ed.), pp. 4-9; E. Klostermann, *Apocrypha*, ii (Kleine Texte, Heft 8). The newest collection, in Schmidtke, pp. 32ff, includes also the fragments of the 'Gospel of the Ebionites' which has been hitherto distinguished from the Gospel of the Hebrews, since

tology of these Jewish Christians that the 'Gospel of the Ebionites' lacked not only a genealogy [56] but an infancy narrative as well. It began with the appearance of the Baptist and introduced Jesus with the words, 'There appeared a man (ἀνήρ τις) named Jesus, who was about thirty years old.' If the true humanity of Jesus was emphasized in this way, the story of the baptism of Jesus amounted to a pointblank protest against the doctrine of the Virgin Birth; for here is to be found alongside the voice from heaven, as it is given in Mark, the divergent form derived from Psalm 2:7, which Codex D and the Itala attest for Luke 3:22, and which is also contained in Justin. According to this, the begetting of Jesus to be Son of God took place not at the birth but at the baptism, and it is thus connected, not with a wonderful birth, but with election—in the full sense of the Ebionite Christology. If this concept can be considered a very old one which goes back to the primitive Church,[57] it is yet intended here in the Gospel of the Ebionites to be a sharp dogmatic contrast to the views of the Gentile Christian church.

One asks, however, how this baptism story tallies with the other, which Jerome attributes to the 'Gospel of the Nazarenes,' according

---

he considers both identical. An examination of this hypothesis is withheld for the present, but attention is called to the difficulty in the text, which arouses scruples against this identification. [*Translator's Note.* Cf. M. R. James, *The Apocryphal New Testament*, pp. 8ff.]

[56] When Epiphanius, *Haer.*, 30:14, calls attention to the fact that the genealogies were excised (παρακόψαντες τὰς παρὰ τῷ Ματθαίῳ γενεαλογίας, 'cutting off the genealogies in Matthew'), he says too little; the genealogies were, indeed, relatively favorable to the idea of Jesus' human origin.

[57] Bousset has recently (*Kyrios Christos*, pp. 57, 66ff, 69, 88) expressed the conjecture that the whole baptism narrative, especially the name 'Son of God,' is not derived at all from the tradition of the primitive Church, but that this is all fundamentally Pauline theology which the evangelist Mark has introduced into the portrayal of the life of Jesus. He has thus raised a problem, the investigation of which is quite necessary. In particular, Bousset holds that the form of the heavenly voice in Luke 3:22 which we have before us in D it Justin, is not older than that of Mark, where he is disposed to assume that the oldest reading is the text σὺ εἶ ὁ παῖς μου ὁ ἀγαπητός, ἐν σοὶ ηὐδόκησα (p. 69, note 2). The messianic interpretation of Ps. 2, which is quite unusual in Judaism, would according to this be purely Christian. In reserving a closer test of this important view, I might here raise only the question: how could the begetting as Son of God at the baptism find its way into the gospel *after* the Virgin Birth was already well established? The idea could only arise *before* the infancy narratives were included in the gospel. If one wishes, however, to assume that the form of Luke 3:22 in D is of Ebionite *origin*, and *arose as a protest* against the Virgin Birth, I would raise the question: How did this text find its way into Justin and the tradition of codex D? The question of Justin's special gospel comes into prominence again here, and still demands a solution.

to which "The source of all holy Spirit descended, rested upon him and said to him, 'My son, in all the prophets I expected thee, that thou mightest come and that I might rest in thee. For thou art my rest, thou art my first-born Son, who reignest in eternity.'" It is, after all, very difficult to assign both these narratives to *one* gospel,[58] especially since in the Gospel of the Ebionites the words from heaven are nowhere described as words of the Holy Spirit as such. Now since here and in the other words, 'Then my mother, the Holy Ghost, seized me by one of my hairs and carried me off to the high mount of Tabor,' the Holy Spirit is designated as the *mother* of Jesus, then nothing is thereby said as to the Virgin Birth of Jesus by the Spirit; but probably this saying does not harmonize very well with the premeditated emphasis upon the purely human birth of Jesus from a human married couple, which the Ebionites otherwise must have taught. One cannot close one's mind to the impression that in both these sayings something of the 'gnostic' character of later Jewish Christianity is already to be detected. If the 'mother' of Jesus had sought her 'first-born Son' for a long time, in order to 'find her rest' in him, the word 'mother' is no longer, in any sense, used in connection with birth. The Holy Spirit appears here as an aeon which aspires to incarnation; it has sought it 'in all the prophets,' but in vain; now he—or she—has found for the first time one with whom she can be united permanently.[59] In these words the Gospel of the Hebrews seems, after all, to be far removed from original Judaism.

It appears to be completely in the spirit of the later primitive Church when in a fragment (Jerome, *De Vir. Illust.*, 2), the appearance of the Lord to James is told in detail (cf. I Cor. 15:7); the brother of the Lord is here placed alongside the earliest circle of disciples. Likewise the words of the risen Christ to him, 'My brother, eat this bread, for the Son of Man is risen from them that sleep,' have a contact, in the title 'Son of Man,' with the faith of the primitive Church; at the same time they are in contact with the James story of Hegesippus (p. 711). The words of the 'Ebionite gospel' on John the Baptist and his vegetarian habits show themselves to be also akin to the saying; according to this narrative 'His

[58] Bousset also, *op. cit.*, p. 325, note 2, casts doubt upon this hypothesis of Schmidtke.

[59] This is very reminiscent of *Clem. Hom.* 3:20, where it is said of the true prophet that he 'who from the beginning of the world, changing his form at the same time as his name, wandered through the world until he came to his own age, anointed, on account of his striving for God's mercy, will forever find his rest,' even if the idea is somewhat modified.

food was wild honey, the taste of which was that of manna, like *cakes in oil'*; the same observation can be made regarding the story of the Eucharist, where Jesus says, 'Have I perhaps desired to eat this Passover *meat* with you?' Vegetarianism, which Hegesippus attributed to James, and which recurs in these apocryphal fragments, is a feature which had a place neither in the canonical tradition nor in the primitive Church. We see before us here the beginnings of a new development which lies beyond our epoch, just as does the form of Jewish Christianity which we meet in the pseudo-Clementine literature after its contact with the Elkesaites.

CHAPTER XXIV
Syria

1. *The Churches.* Under this head we are not to consider the beginnings of the later Syriac national church of Edessa; by this title we mean, instead, the Roman province of Syria. The name of course does not cover all that we wish to discuss in this section. The matter in hand pertains to a circle of churches on Hellenistic soil, whose beginnings go back to the age after the persecution of Stephen, and which occupy a peculiar position inasmuch as they belong neither to the Palestinian Jewish Christian communities [1] nor to the later independent mission field of St. Paul. In part they existed before Paul's time—one may name Samaria, Damascus, and Antioch—in part, they were the work of St. Paul himself (Syria and Cilicia, Gal. 1:21), except that they are not exactly to be designated as Pauline foundations. In any case, St. Paul did not reckon them as being in his jurisdiction, properly speaking; he had received money here for his collection, and indeed according to the tradition (Acts 18:22) he had had occasion to return there (pp. 306f) but only in passing; never in his letters does he mention 'the churches of Syria and Cilicia' as his children or foster-children. On the other hand, we observe e.g. the Church of Antioch, but also those of Syria and Cilicia (Acts 15:23) in close connection with Jerusalem, nearly, in fact, in a position of dependence. The visits of Barnabas (Acts 11:22) and Peter to Antioch (Gal. 2:11ff), the influence of James which reached thither (2:12), the dispatch of the Apostolic Decree to the churches of Syria and Cilicia (Acts 15:23), the personal connections back and forth (Judas, Silas), all illustrate this. From the very beginning Antioch was regarded as a sort of colony of Jerusalem, and the mother church held a sort of control over it, a control which for a long time seemed intolerable to St. Paul. After his departure this province was to lie completely in the sphere of influence of Jerusalem. We have here a sort of middle term between the Palestinian Jewish Christianity and the Pauline missionary church, and by this token an object for our observation which is most important and instructive histori-

[1] The 'Church of the Hebrews,' as it is called in the Clementine Homilies, in the first epistle of Clement to James.

cally.[2] Certainly there were other similar spheres of work, as for example Egypt or the church in Rome before the Epistle to the Romans—but unfortunately we know little more of them than we do about this province, of which we can obtain only small and scattered bits of information. We have already said earlier that the honor paid Christ as the heavenly 'Lord' received here the full and powerful form which it was to bear (pp. 175ff),[3] that here also the

[2] Heitmüller in his article "Zum Problem Paulus und Jesus" (On the Problem of Paul and Jesus) in the *Zeitschrift für neutestamentliche Wissenschaft,* 1912, pp. 320ff, has called attention to the importance of this middle ground of 'the Jewish Christianity of the diaspora,' in which I agree with him completely. However I find no basis for the way in which he severs every connection between St. Paul and the primitive Church.

[3] This idea appears in Bousset, *Kyrios Christos,* pp. 92-125, with a one-sidedness which imperils its accuracy. It is to be granted fully that the title Kyrios was taken over from Hellenistic surroundings, as Bousset shows in pp. 108-119; and likewise it is to be granted that the name Kyrios is the correlative of a *cultus.* But this does not settle the question: how did the churches come to apply the name Kyrios to Jesus, of whom they were substantially ignorant; how did they arrive at the idea of dedicating their worship to him? The adoption of the Kyrios title presupposes a cultus—certainly; but the cultus presupposes a religious reverence as already existing in some sense. Whence did this arise? If one severs all connection with the primitive Church and supposes that this religious veneration, this cultus of Kyrios, arose altogether spontaneously in Antioch, as Bousset does on p. 119 and with such emphatic language, one plays directly into the hands of the theory of B. W. Smith and A. Drews, viz. that the Jesus-worship had long since been present in these areas as an actual divine worship, and the personality of a historical Jesus had no influence upon it. The problem is not merely the emergence of a cultus, but rather of the cultus connected with a human who shortly after his death was exalted to divinity, and at that by men who had had no personal relation to him whatever. This remains an insoluble problem if one cuts off the only possibility of explanation, viz. the assumption that the religious veneration of Jesus was already present in essence in the earliest church, but that it developed from the human honor paid the Christ, as I have attempted to show on pp. 26ff, explaining this process of transformation by its motives. Naturally this shift from the disciple relation to religious worship was accomplished very gradually, and among different people in very different ways, and it must not be denied that the process of its completion took place first in the Hellenistic *milieu.* Alongside this chief question, whether the rise of the *religious* reverence first occurred there or reaches back in its beginnings to the earliest church, there is a relatively subordinate question, whether the title Kyrios was *carried over* to Jesus because the early church had already called Jesus 'Lord' or 'our Lord' (Marân), an appellation which was chiefly an expression of the reverence felt toward a teacher and gradually came to be a religious term more and more. I must, in spite of Bousset's conclusions, hold to this point: that in the ὁ κύριος ἡμῶν, frequent as it is, the Aramaic Marân reëchoes, that the Marân atha, which St. Paul hurled against the Palestinian intruders, was taken over by the early church. The meeting of this Marân with the Hellenistic Kyrios is one of the numerous convergences which we observe in this province. If Bousset lays so much weight on the fact that the title Kyrios does not appear in the gospel tradition, I would ask him in turn, how could it occur there? In the *sayings* of Jesus it must of course be lacking. In the *narrative* it must be lacking in the oldest stratum, just as 'Son of Man,' 'Son of God,' and 'Christ' must also. After all, it is worthy of note that in the later strata in Luke and John the name Kyrios occasionally comes to the surface; cf. also the fragment of the Gospel of the Hebrews on James, and the frequent Marân in the old Syriac version. Among

first and decisive contact with the Hellenistic mystery religions took place. One must estimate these contacts and influences very highly, and certainly they were quite extraordinary, although the founders of these churches already had brought with them the presuppositions which made possible their taking over of these things, viz. faith in the significance of the person of Jesus for salvation, and a veneration of his person which must be considered as being already religious. The circumstance that the Judaism of these provinces was different from that of Palestine itself (because of its many connections with its environment it was to a certain degree hellenized) appears rather more important from the standpoint of the history of religion and culture. The Jew Paul is the typical example of this and he may teach us that in this province all sorts of presuppositions existed, while on the other hand restraints to development were lacking, restraints which in Palestine operated as leaden weights. It is no wonder that the rise of the first mixed communities took place in Antioch so easily—of course!—and that the questions of circumcision of the Gentiles and table fellowship were quite naïvely ignored by them, until people from Jerusalem disturbed the feeling that these easy ways were inoffensive. It is, however, conceivable also that the struggles were ended with one or two victories for the more liberal

---

honorific titles, ὁ κύριος was the only one which in the linguistic feeling of the ancient Christians could be connected not only with the heavenly Lord but with the earthly also. In this connection it should be remembered that the earthly Jesus was called 'Lord,' although in a different sense.

[*Translator's Note.* E. Lohmeyer, *Kyrios Jesus: eine Untersuchung zu Phil. 2:5-11* (Heidelberg, 1928; Sitzungsberichte der Heidelberger Akademie der Wissenschaften, Philosophisch-historische Klasse, 1927-8), has more recently carried this argument of Weiss's one step further. He begins by pointing out that Phil. 2:5-11 is originally a Christian psalm which St. Paul has used (cf. J. Weiss, "Beiträge zur paulinischen Rhetorik" in *Theol. Studien für Bernh. Weiss,* pp. 190ff; A. Deissmann, *Paulus* (2d ed.), p. 149; H. Lietzmann, *Messe und Herrenmahl,* p. 178), and goes on to argue that because of its use of the aorist participle which is 'possible only in Semitic speech' (p. 9), although it was originally written in Greek, its author was one whose mother-tongue was Semitic. He argues that the Kyrios faith of the psalm need not depend upon Hellenistic ideas. In the later Hebrew religion, the contrast between the all-transcendent God and the world in need of redemption became so strong that the problem of mediation between God and the world led to such concepts. "To state it briefly: the final demonstration of the Mind of the world and of history, which is God himself, is carried further. Thus this Mind can be realized only in a divine being, since the world stands against God and God is beyond doubt enthroned in his own Kingdom. But this Mind of the world and of history is also the coincidence of the divine and the human, of faith and history, of grace and suffering. Thus it may be not only a transcendent Being, but it must also—to use the words of the Philippian psalm—be a 'human figure'" (p. 87). "Thus the points of connection of its Christological view are provided directly within Judaism, and one need not resort to the question of whether it is conditioned by foreign influences" (p. 88).]

party; for the apostolic decree essentially signifies a recognition of table fellowship with the one-time Gentiles—though indeed under certain conditions. On the other hand one may assume that the permanent influence of Jerusalem and the retirement of St. Paul maintained permanently a certain influence of Jewish Christianity, though of a more liberally adjusted sort. We must especially assume that in this province very diverse cultures stood side by side, churches which were purely Jewish Christian, purely Gentile Christian, and mixed churches, the last-named of course most numerous. But one must also consider that in this true motherland of syncretism, very curious mixed cultures arose; and one might be in doubt about the fundamental character of these, whether they were Jewish, Christian, or pagan. If only we possessed sources from this region which were in some degree guaranteed! But we are only very poorly furnished with such sources. In the following sections I make an attempt at assigning certain documents to this place and time; whether or not there are sufficient grounds to establish this, the critics may decide.

2. *The Epistle of James.* In considering the *Epistle of James* here, I seek to approximate the solution of a problem which has been in the most unsatisfactory condition possible. I must confess that I cannot connect the epistle with any James, nor can I consider it a letter. The first preliminary condition for understanding this highly significant piece of writing appears to me to be that one shall perceive clearly that the epistolary address, which in any connection is an impossibility, is an ornamentation imposed by a collector who wishes thereby to assign it a place in a collection of primitive apostolic writings.[4] The writing itself is the opposite of a 'catholic epistle'; it is addressed to a locally restricted circle in closely established

[4] The letter contains an unlikely *quid pro quo* in the address: 'To the twelve tribes of the dispersion.' The interpretation still current (most recently adopted by Windisch, *Handbuch zum N. T.*, in James 1:1), viz. that it refers to all Christendom as the true Israel, is entirely unsupportable. The parallels adduced to support it, Rev. 7:4; 14:1, indicate nothing; for the 144,000 from the twelve tribes, which are *named one by one*, can be only the 'remnant' of Israel, according to the earliest draft; in the present text they are given a new interpretation, viz. the *élite* of Christians. This secondary meaning is however a strained one and can be understood only by reference to the peculiar condition of the text. In Hermas, Sim. ix. 17. 1f, however, the interpretation is quite ingeniously changed to refer to the twelve Gentile peoples. Otherwise there is no other place in which Christendom is designated as the 'twelve tribes.' How can this be possible? One can of course say: *we* are the chosen people, the Israel of God—but how can one who wishes to assign to Christianity the number twelve, which belonged to the tribes, establish his point? Above all, there is not in the address of the Epistle of James the slightest suggestion that this name is to be understood as applied in a

social and religious relationships. The 'hearken' (2:5), and especially the strongly oratorical form of the whole writing, causes us to think of a sermon rather than of a letter, an admonitory speech to a very definite group of people with definite faults and temptations. More important than the question of the literary *genre* to which it belongs is the other, viz. how we are to think of the church for which it is intended. That it is written to *Christians* is beyond doubt, not because of the mention of the name of Christ in 2:1,[5] for this can be dismissed all too easily as an interpolation, but on account of the fundamental viewpoint which is manifested, especially in 1:9 and 2:5. To what extent may the humble boast of their miseries? Why may the poor consider themselves the chosen and heirs of the Kingdom? The paradox of these sentences lies quite close to the level of the Beatitudes in Matthew. Just as there the poor are proclaimed blessed, since it is precisely they (above all) to whom the Kingdom of God is given, so also here, it appears, the poor *as poor* are praised as being the especial friends of God. If it depended solely on this, the author and readers might be Jews like Jesus himself; in fact they do not need to have experienced Christ at all.[6] But a more deeply-rooted difference lies at the base. In

---

paradoxical sense. Those who are addressed are not characterized as Christians by even the merest suggestion. Any impartial reader must connect the words with *Jews,* and indeed, since down to the fall of Jerusalem only the ten tribes were regarded as existing in the diaspora, one must connect them with a Judaism which after 70 was scattered through the whole world, without an earthly centre. It is consequently thought—as Spitta claims on account of the salutation—that the letter must have been written (by a Jew) to Jews. But this hypothesis cannot be upheld logically; it is wrecked by the fact that, as we shall show, *Christian* readers are presupposed in the composition itself. The only possible conclusion is therefore that the superscription did not originally belong to the composition. How did it arise and become attached to it? It can be explained from the Catholic ecclesiastical viewpoint, viz. that James, the apostle of the circumcision, whose authorship of the epistle one sought to vindicate—on no matter what grounds—could most naturally have written only to Jews. A trace of this viewpoint shows itself in the assertion of the apostolic lists: "Under the names Hippolytus and Dorotheus, it is said of James the son of Zebedee that he preached the gospel to the twelve tribes of Israel in the dispersion;" to which corresponds the subscription in the old Latin version (Wordsworth, *Stud. Bibl. Oxon.,* i, 113-123): explicit epistola Iacobi filii Zebedaei, "Here endeth the epistle of James the son of Zebedee;" cf. Th. Zahn, *Einleitung,* § 5, 3 (Engl. ed., *Introduction to the N. T.,* i. 106ff).

[5] It would be a stylistic improvement if in 2:1, *τὴν πίστιν τοῦ κυρίου [ἡμῶν Ἰησοῦ Χριστοῦ] τῆς δόξης*, one could strike out the bracketed words; cf. Spitta, *Zur Geschichte und Literatur des Urchristentums,* (On the History and Literature of Primitive Christianity), ii. 4ff.

[6] Spitta, *loc. cit.,* is of the opinion that passages such as Jer. 9:23f; Sir. 10:21; 11:1, lie back of it. These passages say that the poor man especially may boast of knowledge or fear of God. But these passages, insofar as they are comparable, have a point which is completely different from the idea of James. For in them, things are enumerated, of

Matthew the Beatitudes have the character of a promise which the poor may appropriate for themselves; only the future will prove who belongs to these blessed poor. Here, however, the peculiar fact of the case is that the poor already know that they are the ones with whom this promise is connected. It is the same situation as in the Beatitudes of Luke, in which, however, the disciples of Jesus are simply regarded as equivalent to the blessed poor. The poor of the Epistle of James must have experienced something by which they would conclude that they were heirs of the Kingdom, viz. their election—not their predestination by the will of God, but their election *realized* in their calling (cf. I Cor. 1:26; I Pet. 1:1), by which they —although not rich in worldly goods—became rich in faith, the 'new birth from God,' through which they became 'a kind of first fruits of his creatures' (1:18). The 'noble name which is called upon them' (2:7) is of course the name of Christ which has been spoken over them in baptism.[7] If it is blasphemed by the rich oppressors and persecutors, these latter cannot be Christians: the honorable name cannot have been named over those who are now the 'blasphemers.' If the readers are thus Christians, the 'rich' must be non-Christians. Are they pagans or Jews? The answer is given in the scene 2:1-4. If the Christian readers meet the rich in the same congregational meeting (synagogue), it cannot be the Christian meeting.

---

which the poor man can boast although he is poor. In James however it is a question of the high rank of which he may boast, since in fact he belongs to the poor who have been chosen by God.

[7] Spitta (p. 65) adduces a number of Old Testament passages, in which the phrase *τὸ ὄνομα (τοῦ θεοῦ) ἐπικέκληται ἐπί* is used of the Jewish people, and it is not impossible that Jews are also thought of here. But when in 2:7 the question is, what it is that the poor Jews suffer at the hands of their compatriots and co-religionists, there is (1) no occasion to make use of this solemn title. But this is certainly quite inconclusive; for (2) the *ἐφ' ὑμᾶς*, 'upon you,' instead of something like *ἐπ' αὐτούς*, 'upon them,' or *ἐφ' ἡμᾶς*, 'upon us,' shows that the rich *do not belong* to those upon whom this name is named; they thus cannot be Jews if the *ὑμᾶς* are Jews, not Christians; but those who are addressed may be Christians. One is disposed to take the last alternative because of the fact that, without a moment's hesitation—almost without realizing it—one compensates for the 'blasphemies' with the concept 'to make an affront,' 'to provoke,' 'to be the cause for the blasphemy of the Name.' These two things are, however, difficult to keep separate, as is the case in Rom. 2:23f: *τὸν θεὸν ἀτιμάζεις· τὸ γὰρ ὄνομα θεοῦ δι' ὑμᾶς βλασφημεῖται ἐν τοῖς ἔθνεσιν*, "Thou dishonourest God; for the name of God is blasphemed among the Gentiles because of you." The blasphemers in James 2:7 are what they are, not because of their deeds but because of their words; cf. also Polycarp to the Philippians 10:2f, ut . . . . et dominus in vobis non blasphemetur. Vae autem, per quem nomen domini blasphematur, "And that the Lord be not blasphemed in you. 'But woe to him through whom the name of the Lord is blasphemed.'" Ignatius, Trall. 8:2, *οὐαὶ γάρ, δι' οὗ ἐπὶ ματαιότητι τὸ ὄνομά μου ἐπί τινων βλασφημεῖται*, "For 'woe unto him through whom my name is vainly blasphemed among any.'"

For such impassioned opponents as are portrayed in 2:7 could not appear among Christians as invited hearers (I Cor. 14:26). But a situation is quite conceivable in which Jews who have become Christians still attend the synagogue of their compatriots. Such a situation is, e.g. still presupposed in the persecutions pictured in Luke 6:22 and John 16:2; in Ephesus, at least for the first three months, such a situation obtained (Acts 19:9; cf. p. 318). That in Pauline churches, especially in the Gentile Christian ones, this juxtaposition was impossible for a long period of time, is self-evident. It is not, however, understandable why Jewish Christians could not maintain this connection with their national community. One might say that this is unthinkable, since we have seen for ourselves the severe tension between church and synagogue in the Holy Land. But those days and our own are on a different footing. That which must appear as an unheard-of sacrilege in the environment of the now doubly zealous rabbinism, may easily appear in the freer air of the Hellenistic diaspora communities as something which is, to be sure, objectionable, but not after all a mortally sinful heresy. In Palestine the faith in Jesus as Messiah was permeated with very powerful dynastic tendencies and a strong animosity against the murderers of Jesus; in the diaspora, as our epistle itself shows, the Messianic notes appear to be definitely toned down—Jesus here is not regarded as 'the Messiah,' but in good Hellenistic manner as 'the Lord' (of glory). Certainly faith in him was the mark of difference between Jewish Christians and their fellow-countrymen; but one does not obtain from this piece of literature the impression that much emphasis is laid upon this difference. The nearness of the Parousia and the judgment is indeed quite strongly to be seen and is utilized in practice (5:7ff), but it is not emphasized that the expected 'Lord' is Jesus of Nazareth. So much are the person of Jesus and the recollection of his life in the background that the Christian provenance of the writing has been disputed.[8] These Jewish Christians have without doubt laid much stress on the things which they have in common with their compatriots; in practice they seem to be differentiated from them only by their more present expectation of the Parousia, their feeling of the importance of belonging to the

[8] [*Translator's Note.* One of the most striking pieces of work on the Epistle of James since Weiss's time is that of Arnold Meyer, *Das Rätsel des Jacobusbriefes* (Giessen, 1930; Beiheft 10 to the *ZNTW*). Meyer takes a position entirely different from that of Weiss. An older Jewish allegory of Jacob and the twelve tribes, strongly influenced by the Test. XII Patr., lies behind the epistle, and has been reworked by a Christian. Meyer believes that he can detect passages referring to the various patriarchs.]

elect, and the great earnestness of their way of life. If, in spite of this, they did not remain unassailed, no purely religious persecution had taken place. The surprise over their heresy was given vent to by blasphemies of the 'honorable Name'—the name itself was possibly kept secret purposely[9]—at least the 'trials' (1:2,12ff) which they had to suffer consisted in social oppression. The rich, who have the ascendency over the unbelieving Jews, cause their disapproval or contempt to be felt in the economic sphere. The legal actions to which they are exposed (2:6) are throughout depicted as not involving religious accusations. The reference is to severe civil actions of rich men against poor, as also in 5:4 the crime of keeping back the hire of laborers is in question. Apparently such cases in which the 'just' were condemned, even killed (5:6), could arise easily. Whether this is to be understood as allegorical, perhaps as a reminiscence of Jesus or James, or as real, cannot be decided. The author never exhorts his readers to steadfastness in the faith, as if there were an express denial of it, but he pleads for a decision between God and the world (4:4-7), for resoluteness and certainty of conviction (1:6f), for upright self-consciousness in opposition to wealth (1:9; 2:1,5,9), and for patience (5:7-11). The apostrophe to sinners (4:8) and rich men (4:13—5:6) is of course to be understood as purely rhetorical. It is intended for Christian readers; in the close parallel of the Christian poor and the unbelieving rich, the orator needs have no hesitation in speaking to the latter as if they were present (cf. the speech against the Pharisees, Matt. 23, which according to 23:1 is addressed to the people and the disciples). At least we have to do with a church of humble people, in which the sins of petty animosity (3:14) and quarreling (3:16; 4:1), of envy (4:2), slander (4:11), toadying (2:1-13), and hardheartedness against neighbors (2:5,13) are rife. Such conditions are possible in any church, even a Gentile Christian one; however, that a Jewish Christian circle lies before us is shown by the position of the author and his readers with respect to *the Law.*

In his exhortations the author is dependent for both substance and form upon the wisdom literature,[10] on the one hand, and upon

[9] It was originally lacking in 2:1 also; one could indeed plead that these Jewish Christians spoke of Jesus only by a circumlocution; especially since they took over the Old Testament expression Kyrios to apply to *their* 'Lord.'

[10] The parallels to Jesus Sirach are quite numerous, but the Wisdom of Solomon is drawn upon still oftener; one feels oneself reminded occasionally even of Philo's language. The echo of Jewish and Jewish-Hellenistic literature is, on the whole, astonishingly strong. Spitta has done a great service by his numerous citations. There can be no doubt about the Judaism of the author.

the words of Jesus, on the other; [11] but nowhere is there an express quotation. The contents of this material have come to him by word of mouth. On the contrary, in 2:9-12; 3:11f, *the Law* is pointed to as unconditionally binding, as a norm which righteousness is to follow, as—in fact—the 'law of liberty,' the 'perfect law' (2:12; 1:25). These details indicate that the author thinks of the Mosaic Law, neither in its complete extent, nor in its literal sense. He thinks of 'perfect' in the sense in which Matthew, perhaps, understood the saying about 'fulfilling' the Law (5:17; cf. SNT, *ad loc.*): Jesus has completed Moses' lawgiving, has brought it to its logical conclusion. At any rate, in the expression a point is made against those who revere and keep the Law in incomplete form or in an imperfect way, i.e. against popular Judaism. As in the Gospel of Matthew we feel as though we were on the territory of a rather liberal Jewish Christianity which does not intend to break entirely with the Law, but is conscious at the same time of being more free than are the Jews, and yet of more perfectly fulfilling it than do the Jews themselves. The 'law of liberty' is, however, an expression which is not without Jewish parallels,[12] but is also taken over from the language of Stoicism.[13] The author intends to prove that the Law is no longer felt as a restraint; since, received according to its own purpose, it is fulfilled in freedom.[14] These ideas, of course, are encountered also on Gentile Christian soil, but they are as conceivable and perhaps more so, on the territory of a more liberal Jewish Christianity of the diaspora. It must further be regarded as completely certain that the author was a Hellenist, not without a certain contact with popular philosophical literature and

[11] Especially Matt. 5:34ff appears to be echoed in 5:12; also Matt. 6:24 in 4:4; Matt. 7:7 in 1:5; 4:3; Matt. 23:12 in 4:10. Whether the author was already acquainted with the Gospel of Matthew is debatable; in 5:12 the saying about oaths is given in a variant form of apparent primitiveness; cf. SNT in Matt. 5:34ff.

[12] Pirqe Aboth 6:2, "Read, not 'chārut' (engraved) but 'chērut' (freedom), since thou findest none who are free save those who are engaged in study of the Torah" (Fiebig).

[13] Cicero, *Parad.* 34: Quid est libertas? potestas vivendi, ut velis . . . . qui legibus quidem non propter metum paret sed eas sequitur atque colit, quia id salutare maxime esse judicat. "What is liberty? The power to live as you choose . . . . he [is free] who indeed submits to the laws not because of fear, but follows and cherishes them, since he judges that this is the most wholesome way;" Philo, *Q. omnis probus,* book 7, *ὥσπερ τῶν πόλεων αἱ μὲν . . . . δουλείαν ὑπομένουσι . . . . αἱ δὲ νόμοις ἐπιμεληταῖς χρώμενοι καὶ προστάταις εἰσὶν ἐλεύθεροι, οὕτω καὶ τῶν ἀνθρώπων . . . . ὅσοι μετὰ νόμου ζῶσιν, ἐλεύθεροι,* "Just as some of the cities . . . . endure bondage . . . . and others, making use of laws and overseers and leaders, are free, so among men . . . . those who live by law are free."

[14] Cf. Barn. 2:6, *ὁ καινὸς νόμος τοῦ κυρίου ἡμῶν* Ἰησοῦ Χριστοῦ, *ἄνευ ζυγοῦ ἀνάγκης ὤν,* 'the new law of our Lord Jesus Christ, which is without the yoke of necessity.'

with complete mastery of the Greek language. I would lay less weight on the quoted—or involuntary and fortuitous—hexameter of 1:17, than upon rhyming words such as ἀνεμιζομένῳ καὶ ῥιπιζομένῳ; ἐξελκόμενος καὶ δελεαζόμενος; φλογίζουσα τὸν τροχὸν τῆς γενέσεως καὶ φλογιζομένη ὑπὸ τῆς γεέννης; θηρίων τε καὶ πετεινῶν, ἑρπετῶν τε καὶ ἐναλίων; δαμάζεται καὶ δεδάμασται (1:6, 'driven by the wind and tossed'; 1:14, 'drawn away and enticed'; 3:6, 'setteth on fire the wheel of nature, and is set on fire by hell'; 3:7, 'of beasts and birds, of creeping things and things in the sea'; 3:7, 'is tamed, and hath been tamed'); the play of words, ἀδιάκριτος ἀνυπόκριτος (3:17, 'without variance, without hypocrisy'). Wendland refers to the tendency to make chains of words in 1:3f,14f, which has parallels not only in Paul (Rom. 5:3ff; 10:13ff) but especially also in the Wisdom of Solomon, 6:17-20; 7:22ff. The numerous connections with the diatribe in form and content are especially noteworthy; cf. Geffcken, *Kynika und Verwandtes*, who has, for example, established that the passage 3:1-11 is patterned after a Hellenistic diatribe (pp. 45-53). Characteristic of the diatribe style are the clauses which are midway between interrogatory sentences and protases of conditional sentences, in 3:13; 5:13f (cf. my Commentary on I Cor. 7:18, 21, 27), as well as the ἀλλ' ἐρεῖ τις in 2:18, which of course is not necessarily borrowed from St. Paul (cf. also Wendland, *Literaturformen*, pp. 370f, and my article "Literaturgeschichte des Neuen Testaments" in *Religion in Geschichte und Gegenwart*, iii. 2211).

The fact that we do not find ourselves in the great Pauline or post-Pauline missionary Church—paganism, conversion, and missionary work are never subjects of discussion—shows, finally, that we have to consider a polemic against a doctrine of which St. Paul must be regarded as being the historical representative (2:14-26). The author writes not merely subsequently to Paul in time—he certainly had read St. Paul's letters, at least the Epistle to the Romans [15] —but also he desires to engage in polemic against his teaching. This is as clear as is the fact that the actual meaning of the historical Paul cannot be found by recourse to his controversial remarks, for

[15] The numerous reminiscences of St. Paul which have been found in James must be sifted out carefully. If 1:3 is compared with Rom. 5:3-5, it must be observed that the climax also gives the impression of a quotation from Paul; the contrast 'hearers' and 'doers' in 1:22 and Rom. 2:13 had certainly become current coin in Judaism, as well as the principle of conduct of 2:10 and Gal. 3:10; 5:3. On the other hand, 4:1, *ἡδονῶν ὑμῶν τῶν στρατευομένων ἐν τοῖς μέλεσιν ὑμῶν*, 'of your pleasures that war in your members,' reminds one strongly of Rom. 7:23; 4:12, and besides is reminiscent of Matt. 7:1 and Rom. 2:1; 14:4. The passage 4:17 may be borrowed from Rom. 14:23. On 3:16, cf. I Cor. 3:3.

his discussions far transcend these matters. If one can seriously defend—and with arguments which are not to be despised—the hypothesis that James did not attack Paul, but Paul attacked James instead, this is to be explained only by the fact that the polemic of the author is only very superficially concerned with St. Paul, that it touches upon an already existing dispute not depending upon St. Paul (cf. pp. 230f), in which the words 'faith' and 'works' already played a formula-making rôle (IV Ezra 7:24; 6:58; 9:7f; 13:23); the example of Abraham's faith had also previously (I Macc. 2:52) been recognized. Still it has not yet been proved that anyone before Paul had stressed so one-sidedly the solely decisive significance of faith as did St. Paul himself. Therefore it is undoubtedly possible that the author wished to attack *St. Paul's* fundamental thesis, which seemed to him to be so completely repugnant to common sense, and which in 2:24 seems most obviously to be reproduced from Rom. 3:28.[16] He takes for granted, however, that every one of his readers will agree with him when he says, 'Faith, after all, cannot save you!' From this it follows that in the circle for which he writes, the letters of Paul can have had no authority. Thus it is regarded as *well-known* and self-evident that Abraham 'was justified by works' (2:21), as though St. Paul had never adduced Abraham as the example of justifying faith. In the Gentile Christian church of the second century, in which the letters of Paul were at the very least a force which was not to be despised, one would not have dared to write thus—but such writing was possible in a circle in which Paul was known, but which was foreign to him and indeed looked upon him as something of a dangerous innovator who fortunately had sought another field in which to put his theories into practice, than the field in which he had grown up. The orator did not understand what it was that St. Paul called 'faith'; he understands it in the sense of the Jewish faith in God's teaching, which even the demons possessed (2:19). Obviously word had come to him that a dangerous piety of word and appearance had been produced in the missionary church by the one-sided emphasis on faith. How senseless, how purposeless, if one *says* that he has faith—and yet has no 'works!' It would, in fact, be as if one were to try to feed a poor

[16] Rom. 3:28, *δικαιοῦσθαι πίστει ἄνθρωπον χωρὶς ἔργων νόμου.*
Jas. 2:24, *ἐξ ἔργων δικαιοῦται ἄνθρωπος καὶ οὐκ ἐκ πίστεως μόνον.*
Jas. 2:20, *ἡ πίστις χωρὶς τῶν ἔργων ἀργή ἐστιν.*
(Rom. 3:28, "A man is justified by faith apart from the works of the law."
Jas. 2:24, "By works a man is justified, and not only by faith."
Jas. 2:20, "Faith apart from works is barren.")

beggar with words (2:14ff)! Both must operate together; faith completes itself only in works, without them it is dead (2:22,26)! These are sound, earnest sayings, completely parallel to those respecting the hearing and doing of the Law (1:22-25), true service of God (2:26f), and true wisdom (3:13-18)—but St. Paul's doctrine is not affected by them.

For the date of composition of the writing we have a *terminus post quem* in 5:12, in which the oath by Jerusalem is left out of account, since it no longer remained standing as 'city of the great king.' We can perhaps find a *terminus ante quem* in the fact that in 5:14 the 'elders of the church' are alone regarded as being the pastoral authorities, i.e. not *the* bishop, mention of whom would be expected in the second century. If we assume a time between 70 and 100, and think of a small urban community in Syria as being its place of origin, we will probably not be far from the truth.

An especially characteristic trait is the warning against a too eager rushing into the *office of teacher;* the author, who takes this opportunity to make himself known as a *didaskalos* (3:1), knows how great the responsibility of that office is. He looks with anxiety upon people who give themselves out to be wise and understanding (3:13) but who represent an 'earthly, sensual, demonic wisdom'—instead of the wisdom 'from above' (3:15,17) [17]—because of which they lie against the 'truth' (3:14) and produce confusion and other evil results (3:16). The moral conduct of these 'teachers' is blemished (3:13f,16f), and the deviation from the 'truth' occurs simultaneously with their fall into sin (5:19f). Thus in the circle of vision of the author there appear to be teachers and learners who are dangerous for the religious and moral stability of the Church; perhaps hyper-Pauline antinomians, against whom the section 2:14-26 is directed; perhaps, however, still others whose wisdom appeared to him to be 'demonic.'

3. *The Gospel of Matthew.* One may consider us daring in placing the *Gospel of Matthew* here, and in fact it is an escape from a dilemma if in our lack of a definite, useful account of its origin, we can attempt to find a place for it in this section.[18] As to its date,

[17] These passages also would seem to indicate acquaintance with I Cor. 3, if both these passages did not appear to be dependent upon the same group of Hellenistic ideas. Especially the representation of a σοφία ψυχική appears to have been current already in the time of Paul.

[18] The ancient ecclesiastical tradition in actuality says nothing definite about *where* the Gospel of Matthew arose; for Irenaeus, *Adv. Haer.*, iii. 1. 1 (= Eusebius, *H. E.*, v. 8. 2) says after all only something about the language and environment: M. ἐν τοῖς

we can say only that in 22:7 it alludes to the destruction of Jerusalem, and that it must be older than the Gospel of John and the Ignatian letters, in which it is already utilized. Thus we come to a period between 70 and 100. There are lacking any traces of the monarchical episcopate (18:15ff), indeed one could conclude from such a passage as 23:8ff that there is resistance against such attempted courses of action. On the other hand we come upon the extraordinarily strong attention paid to Peter. The special Petrine narratives of the gospel (14:28-32; 17:24-37; 18:21; 16:17ff) point not only to an especial interest in St. Peter; apparently Peter is represented as the *first* of the twelve Apostles (10:2, πρῶτος), he is more frequently the spokesman of the others than even in Mark (15:15; 17:24,26; 18:21); he is especially designated as the rock on which Christ has founded his Church (16:18),[19] and the power of binding and loosing, which belongs to all the disciples in 18:18, is especially conveyed to him in 16:19. This extraordinary exaltation of Peter over the other Apostles must have had some special reason. It is only conceivable in a church in which St. Peter is valued as *the* Apostle, for which he represents the correct tradition in opposition to others. This attention to Peter is unthinkable in Jerusalem in the lifetime of James or after the installation of Simeon (pp. 558ff). But neither does it necessarily point to Rome; in this period, rather, the word of Peter *and Paul* was predominant there (cf. I Clem. 5 and the Book of Acts). On the other hand, much is to be said for Syria, especially Antioch.[20] One may easily comprehend that someone here in the missionary territory did not approve of the

---

Ἑβραίοις τῇ ἰδίᾳ διαλέκτῳ αὐτῶν καὶ γραφὴν ἐξήνεγκεν εὐαγγελίου ("Matthew produced also a writing of the gospel among the Hebrews in their own language"); but from the context: τοῦ Πέτρου καὶ τοῦ Παύλου ἐν Ῥώμῃ εὐαγγελιζομένων καὶ θεμελιούντων τὴν ἐκκλησίαν ('while Peter and Paul were in Rome preaching the gospel and founding the church') one can conclude that ἐν Ἑβραίοις is also meant geographically, i.e. 'in Palestine.' This tradition, however, because of the assertion as to the language, does not suit our present Gospel of Matthew. For the latter is not a work written originally in Hebrew or Aramaic, which is present only in translation (in spite of the arguments of Zahn, *Einleitung,* § 56; Engl. ed., ii, 570-601, who believes that he has proved it); instead it is a composition which was written in Greek at the very start, which of course is partly fashioned from sources which were originally Aramaic. Above all the Gospel of Matthew is not conceivable in the *milieu* of the primitive Jerusalemite church dominated by James, but only in that of a broad-minded church of the diaspora Jewish Christianity which was devoted to world missionary work.

[19] On this passage, cf. the article of Dell, *ZNTW,* 1914, pp. 1ff, who argues that Matt. 16:17-19 originally and properly belongs to the Gospel of Matthew.

[20] [*Translator's Note.* Cf. especially the work of B. H. Streeter, *The Four Gospels,* ch. 9; B. W. Bacon, *Studies in Matthew* (New York, 1930); F. C. Grant, *The Growth of the Gospels,* ch. 7, especially the bibliography on p. 176. Streeter (pp. 500-523) argues strongly for Antioch.]

privileges given the Jesus-dynasty, and placed the missionary Apostle (who in Jesus' life had stood closest to him and was treated by him with distinction in so many ways) in opposition to the relatives of Jesus, who could not rival him in these respects (pp. 718f). Especially, since in Antioch the impression made by St. Peter must have been not merely transitory, but much more enduring—a fact to which the Antiochene episcopal lists seem to allude. On the other hand one cannot fail to recognize a certain rejection of Paul, as would be comprehensible in Antioch, since the work of the Apostle to the Gentiles ended in defeat there (Gal. 2:11,14) and in his separation from the mother church (Acts 15:36-41; cf. pp. 206f). If, in 28:19 the Twelve were sent to all nations, this complete ignoring of St. Paul is quite conceivable as soon as the gospel had arisen in its own peculiar missionary district; and the threat against teachers who wish to annul the Law (5:17,19) is best understood as a tacit opposition to the works and teachings of Paul—even if the word 'least' is not an allusion to the Apostle's designation of himself in I Cor. 15:9. Upon the whole, it is no longer the Apostle who is combatted in person, but there are 'false prophets,' against whom the evangelist warns (7:15-23); their way of life has given them the lie (vv. 16-20), their confession of Christ, their miracles, cannot protect them from condemnation in the judgment, since they are doers of *lawlessness*. This party cry (ἀνομία) is repeated in 13:41 in connection with the nearly technical expression *skandala* (18:7), which in Rev. 2:14 is specially applied to meats from idolatrous sacrifices, and to unchastity. The increase of lawlessness is in 24:12 one of the signs of the last age; its consequence is that love grows cold (cf. Rev. 2:4), and indeed it is a symptom of the propagation of proud Gnostic ideas, which in turn are incidental phenomena of libertinism. The vigorous warning against false Messiahs and false prophets, who seek to lead astray the elect with signs and wonders (24:24), is easily understood in the face of the Samaritan Gnosis spread by 'magi' such as Simon and Menander. Similarly, as in the Epistle of James, the 'perfect Law' is the inviolable validity of the law which was brought to perfection on the Mount by Jesus, the second Moses, and affirmed with all vigor; on the other hand, as in the 'royal law' of James (Jas. 2:8), the entire content of law and prophets goes back to the golden rule (7:12) and the double commandment of love (22:34-46). If, moreover, the saying, 'I love mercy rather than sacrifice,' is twice quoted (9:13; 12:7), and is certainly not spoken against sacrificial worship at all, but rather on behalf of intercourse with tax-collectors and sinners and in justification of Jesus' work on the Sabbath, then this *new interpretation* proves (1) that for the author the actual sacrificial worship no longer existed in Jerusalem; (2) that he perhaps set up a sort of principle of distinction between ethical and ceremonial commandments. Since 'mercy' (ἔλεος) meant for him nearly the same thing as 'love,' since furthermore he made Jesus' lawgiving reach its climax at the end of chapter 5, as well as in 7:12, in the praise of love, since, finally, in 23:23 he made justice, compassion, and faithfulness to be regarded as the weightiest matters in the Law, he appears actually to aim—on the whole—at expounding only the ethical content of the Law as binding. But such a statement would not be completely accurate, for in 5:18 he expresses himself on the permanent validity of the very written characters; according to 24:20 he considers the Sabbath to be of unconditional obligation; and in 23:23 *he* (not Luke or Q) adds to the saying on the tithing of mint, dill, and cummin, 'These ye ought to have done, and not to have left the other undone.' Indeed, despite all his sharp attacks on the 'scribes and Pharisees,'[21] the author explains, 'All things therefore whatsoever they bid you, these do and observe: but do not ye after their works; for they say, and do not' (23:3). These words, which are lacking in Luke (and thus also in Q), show evidently that the author intends to remain, in principle, fixed to the viewpoint of the scribes; he is indeed, as all his work shows, a searcher of the Scriptures (though in another way) like the opponents of Jesus. This characteristic fluctuation in the critical judgment of the Law is highly significant. The author is unmistakably a natural-born Jew who can detach himself from the Law of his fathers only with very great difficulty; on the other hand he is, after all, too strongly touched by the spirit of the Judaism of the diaspora and by the development of Hellenistic Christianity to be able still to plead in narrow-minded and minute manner for the complete literal validity of the Law. The saying that the Law is not annulled but 'fulfilled' (5:17), in its very ambiguity—it is to be understood partly of the 'fulfilment' of prophecy, partly of the 'completion' of the Law (cf. SNT, *ad loc.*)—is quite characteristic of him. He denies passionately that he holds any revolutionary

[21] This unlikely and unhistorical juxtaposition of a designation of occupation and a party name, which coincide partly but not completely (there are also scribes of the Sadduceean party; cf. Mark 2:16), proves in itself that the author was no Palestinian Jew, who knew conditions before 70 by personal observation.

antinomian theories; however, he is persuaded with equal conviction that for the disciples only the commandments of Jesus can be binding, and these mean for him the Law taught by Jesus in its completeness, not the word which was once said by those of old time, in all its literal sense and externality, and with all its ceremonial detail. 'Law and prophets' are for him a unity (5:17): as the prophets contained commandments (7:12; 22:46), so the Law contains prophecy also, and is 'fulfilled' by the lawgiving of Jesus. This fulfilment, to be observed in many specific details, is of course a chief interest of the 'scribe who hath been made a disciple to the kingdom of heaven' who 'bringeth forth out of his treasure things new and old' (13:52).

Finally, it is uncertain also whether his position with regard to the Jewish people is any different from his attitude to the Law. Although in the infancy narrative, as in the resurrection narrative, he must come out clearly against malicious Jewish calumnies (p. 222), in many respects he still has the feelings of a Jew. Thus in the genealogy he represents Jesus as son of David and Abraham; at times he simply calls him 'the Messiah' (1:17f; 11:2),[22] in whom all the prophecies are fulfilled. With considerable emphasis he calls attention to the mission of Jesus to the lost sheep of the house of Israel (15:24); accordingly he stresses also the fact that the Twelve had first of all been sent to the Jews (10:5f). But, to be sure, he still holds the view that the 'sons of the Kingdom,' as he calls them (8:12), must be cast out, and that the Kingdom will be given to another people (21:43). However, he does not accept this conclusion with a light heart as something natural, but seeks to understand it and offer reasons for it. How did it come about? The material which he took over from Mark, and the Sayings of Jesus, it is true, already gave plenty of answers to these questions; but by a variety of little inserted or altered touches Matthew makes it understood still more clearly (e.g. 12:45b; 21:35; 22:3,6); the Passion Narrative expresses it most clearly of all: may his blood be upon us and our children (27:26)! The rejection of Jesus, the unbelief (21:28-32), the fact that they *would not* accept the invitation, the old disposition to kill prophets (21:35; 23:37), this it is which has brought damnation upon the Chosen People—the consequence of it is the sending of the Apostles to the Gentiles (28:19f). In the contradiction between this latter missionary commission and

[22] These passages are the more significant, since otherwise he has taken over from Mark the double name Jesus Christ (1:1).

the earlier one in 10:5f is reflected the tragic development of which the evangelist was fully aware, and in his own way had brought to expression. Thus he stands on completely the same ground as did the great mission to the Gentiles, but not without some misgivings. For among those wedding guests brought together from the highway of the Cross there are both bad and good ones (22:10); both good and worthless fish are caught in the net of missionary enterprise (13:47f), in the field of the Church weeds flourish along with the wheat, along with the sons of the Kingdom there are sons of the Evil one (13:38)—these are the consequences of the great mission which has opened its doors wide and without conditions. What is to be done about it? The evangelist is no fanatic who might wish to exterminate the unworthy with fire and sword; he warns against judgments which are human and all too facile (13:29) and trusts in the final judgment. When the King shall come to inspect his guests he will cast into the outer darkness those who have no wedding garments (22:13; cf. 13:30,41f,50; 7:23). One enters here into the soul of a man who, to be sure, recognizes this development of conditions as necessary but yet must regard with sorrow and anxiety such a motley company gathered together in the great Church; the prospect of a winnowing judgment is for him a solace and a protection against fanatical inclinations.

If we ask what the things were which caused unfortunate impressions, what the 'scandals' were, what the 'lawlessness' was which made its appearance in the author's environment, we cannot give a sufficient answer from the book itself. Perhaps, however, if we have placed the Gospel of Matthew in its correct setting, it is to be understood by reference to the phenomena which we include under the following section headings.

4. *The Samaritan Gnosis.* Syria and its neighborhood, especially Samaria, is regarded by the church fathers as the peculiar spawning ground of Gnostic heresy, and in fact one may regard these regions as a storm center of syncretistic cultures, which had assimilated a more or less Christian character. For the period which we are studying we have to consider the traditions reported to us about the Samaritans, Dositheus, Simon Magus and Menander (the last-named is said to have worked in Antioch also), and Saturninus, the Antiochene.[23] Their activity falls in the period before Hadrian.

[23] On Dositheus, cf. Hilgenfeld, *Ketzergeschichte des Urchristentums* (The History of Heresies in Primitive Christianity), pp. 155-161. According to Justin, *Apol.* 1:26, Simon came from the Samaritan village of Gitta, Menander from the village of Caparathaia

They form not merely a geographical group, but also are a group as regards the content of their teaching, inasmuch as they stand in the period before the appearance of the important Valentinians and Marcion, but especially because strong influences of Christianity, especially that of St. Paul, cannot be proved to have touched them. They are all the more important and instructive as parallel phenomena, since they teach us that the features which they possess in common with (e.g.) Paul have arisen from the source of a common world-view and attitude.[24]

But it cannot be our task to portray completely and systematically these groups which stood outside the Church, and their doctrines; and the derivation of their nature from pre-Christian ideas and attitudes, which naturally is very difficult, cannot be dealt with in these contexts. Here we wish, as in the case of heretical Jewish Christianity, to throw into relief those of its traits which exhibit its relations to neighboring Christianity, as well as the divergences which caused it to be rejected by the men of the emerging Church as a dangerous adulteration.

Dositheus, Simon, and in his way Menander also, exhibit types of *pseudo-Messiahs*. Thus Dositheus, apparently without any antipathy to Christianity, declared himself to be the 'prophet-Messiah' foretold by Deut. 18:15,18.[25] This contact with the Mosaic prophecy is a parallel to the ideas of the primitive Church (Acts 3:22; 7:37; cf. p. 86), and throws light on the popular expectation in the time of Jesus (cf. John 1:21; 6:14): the Messiah need not come forward as king, he may be a *prophet* instead. In Menander likewise, according to the traditions, there is lacking any express antithesis against the belief in Jesus as Messiah, since he purported to be the *Soter* from above, sent out from the invisible world [26] for the salvation of mankind. The parallel found in this idea to the Pauline-Johannine Christology is worthy of note: the descent of a *Soter* from

---

(according to E. Schwartz misread for *καπαραπαία*, כפר אפיא). Saturninus was, according to Eusebius, *H. E.* iv. 7. 3, Ἀντιοχεὺς τὸ γένος, 'Antiochene by race;' in any case he worked in Antioch.

[24] Yet one cannot say of these phenomena what Bousset (*Kyrios Christos,* pp. 232f) concludes as to later gnosticism: "When we face the question of how it comes about that this great gnostic movement, which in its beginnings and basis had nothing to do with Christianity, came to lie in such close proximity to it and bound itself up so intimately with it that with few exceptions we know it only as a movement rivaling Christianity, we must answer that it was the form which Paul gave to Christianity which, magnet-like, drew the gnostic circle close to itself."

[25] Origen, *Contra Celsum,* 1:57; *In Joannem tom.* 13:27.

[26] Irenaeus, *Adv. Haer.* i. 23. 5; for the invisible aeons, cf. Eusebius, *H. E.* iii. 26.

celestial heights. The same mode of thought is found also in Simon or among his adherents.[27] As early as the end of the first century the author of the Book of Acts places him, *on the one hand*, with the succession of other false Messiahs whom he mentions; [28] *on the other hand,* he typifies a sort of incarnation-doctrine, under the influence of which people are made to say of him, "This man is that power of God which is called Great." [29] At this point the teaching of Simon's disciples comes into close relationship with the Christology of the churches, and indeed, properly speaking, not the exaltation Christology of the primitive Church, which still lacked any Gnostic influence, nor the Kyrios faith of the Hellenistic communities, but rather the Pauline and Johannine. The teaching of Simon's disciples regarding descent calls to mind certain ideas which though not expressed in St. Paul nevertheless lie in the background or within the purview of his thought. If it is said that he transformed himself and made himself equal to authorities and powers (μεταμορφούμενον καὶ ἐξομοιούμενον), in order to deceive them (Tertullian, *De An.*, 34 [30]), one thinks involuntarily of the Pauline idea of the adoption of another form (μορφή) and likeness (Phil. 2:7, ἐν ὁμοιώματι ἀνθρώπων, 'in the likeness of men'; Tertullian, *configuratus aeque hominibus*) or the idea of I Cor. 2:8, viz: if the world-rulers had recognized the Wisdom of God, they would not have crucified the Lord of glory.[31] This parallel with St. Paul is especially instructive because an idea such as that of incarnation is joined almost of necessity with Gnostic ideas of this sort; it is by nature mythological, and St. Paul must have known a form of the descent myth similar to that of the Simonians, which he supplied with the figure of a Christ,

[27] On Simon, cf. the article "Simon der Magier" by Waitz in Herzog, *Realenzyklopädie,* 3rd ed., xviii, 351ff. Waitz regards Acts 8:10, 14-19, as a redactional addition to the source.

[28] The mode of expression of 8:9, 'giving out that himself was some great one' (*λέγων εἶναί τινα ἑαυτὸν μέγαν*) is as significantly mysterious as that used in connection with Theudas in 5:36, *λέγων εἶναί τινα ἑαυτόν*, 'giving himself out to be somebody,' as if the author shrank from saying that he had claimed to be the Messiah; similarly in Luke 21:8, *ἐγώ εἰμι καὶ· ὁ καιρὸς ἤγγικεν*, "'I am' and 'the time is at hand.'"

[29] A. Klostermann (*Probleme in Aposteltext,* pp. 15ff) has of course interpreted this remarkable expression as a misunderstanding of a Samaritan word מגלא or מגלי, i.e. 'the revealer' or 'revealing oneself.'

[30] Epiphanius, *Haer.* xxi. 2. 4, *ἐν ἑκάστῳ δὲ οὐρανῷ μετεμορφούμην, φησίν, κατὰ τὴν μορφὴν τῶν ἐν ἑκάστῳ οὐρανῷ, ἵνα λάθω τὰς ἀγγελικάς μου δυνάμεις καὶ κατέλθω*, "'In each heaven I transformed myself,' he said, 'into the form of those in each heaven, that I might escape the notice of my angelic powers, and descend.'"

[31] On this point, cf. Dibelius, *Geisterwelt* (The World of Spirits), pp. 93, 106; and my commentary on I Cor. 2:8.

while the Samaritans used that of Simon.[32] But that which, because of a certain bias, is painted vividly by the Gnostics, remains unexpressed in Paul and in the background: the Apostle lays all the weight upon the ethical power of the idea—self-renunciation, humility, resignation—and curbs his fancy for the sake of its practical application; it was precisely the imagination of the believers which the Simonians wished to reach, hence they assigned great importance to the vivid details.

As distinguished from Dositheus and Menander, however, an explicit opposition to Christianity is found among the Simonians. The Simon religion was itself to be regarded as a serious competitor to the Jesus-faith in these areas. Not without reason does Justin, the compatriot of Simon (*Apol.* 1:26), take pains to dissociate Simon from the cause which he himself was pleading.[33] How great his influence was one can learn from Justin's words, which carry weight despite their rhetorical exaggeration: 'Nearly all the Samaritans, and also a few in other nations, confess him and honor him as the supreme god' (*Apol.* 1:26), 'exalted above all lordship and authority (*Dial.* 120). Irenaeus says the same (i. 23. 1), 'This man is honored by many as God . . . . as being the highest power (*sublimissimam virtutem*, τὴν ὑπὲρ πάντα δύναμιν, Hippolytus, 7:19), the father exalted over all' (Iren.; Tert. *De An.*, 34). Above all, we have here a parallel to the Kyrios cult of Christianity: the combination of a historical personality with the worship of a celestial divinity. But Simonianism signifies still more: among the Gnostic sects

[32] The same pattern is found in the Naassene hymn (Hippolytus, 5:10) which of course is not pre-Christian (as it has of late been boldly asserted to be), but can well go back to the same pattern of the descent-myth:

σφραγῖδας ἔχων καταβήσομαι,
αἰῶνας ὅλους διοδεύσω,
μυστήρια πάντα διανοίξω,
μορφὰς δὲ θεῶν ἐπιδείξω·
καὶ τὰ κεκρυμμένα τῆς ἁγίας ὁδοῦ
γνῶσιν καλέσας παραδώσω.

"With the seals I shall descend, I shall travel through entire aeons, I shall unlock all mysteries and make known the forms of gods; and summoning knowledge I will impart the hidden things of the sacred way."

[33] Cf. also the probably spurious passage, *Apol.* 2:15, *καὶ τοῦ ἐν τῷ ἐμῷ ἔθνει ἀσεβοῦς καὶ πλάνου Σιμωνιανοῦ διδάγματος κατεφρόνησα*, "And I disdained the impious and erroneous Simonian teaching [current] in my own nation;" the assertions in *Dialogue with Trypho*, 120, *οὐδὲ γὰρ τοῦ γένος τοῦ ἐμοῦ, λέγω δὲ τῶν Σαμαρέων, τινὸς φροντίδα ποιούμενος ἐγγράφως Καίσαρι προσομιλῶν εἶπον πλανᾶσθαι αὐτοὺς πειθομένους τῷ ἐν τῷ γένει αὐτῶν μάγῳ Σίμωνι, ὃν θεὸν ὑπεράνω πάσης ἀρχῆς καὶ ἐξουσίας λέγουσι*, "For in addressing Caesar in writing—since I felt no partiality for my own race, I mean, that of the Samaritans—I said that they were in error in believing in Simon, that magician of their race whom they call a god far above all lordship and authority."

it is unique in that it *identifies* Simon with Jesus. If it is said that Simon had—before he manifested himself in Samaria as Father—*appeared to the Jews as Son*,[34] then certainly the assertion of his identity with Jesus is implied.[35] In view of such doctrines, sayings such as Mark 13:21ff=Matt. 24:23ff; Matt. 24:5 and parallels, become for the first time quite understandable.[36] In connection with this, the old account in the Book of Acts, to the effect that Simon received baptism (8:13), requires examination. It takes us into an age in which the identification of Simon with Jesus *cannot yet* have been maintained, and if it is worthy of credence, as one need not doubt, it teaches us that Simon himself had as yet made no messianic claims for himself; otherwise he would not have submitted to baptism in the name of Jesus. On the other hand, it shows that Simon and the movement which included him had first of all sought a merger with Christianity; afterwards, to be sure, the memory was preserved only in the later form, according to which it was maintained that the peculiarly Simonian religion was of the higher rank, for in Samaria Simon had appeared as *Father*. In this is seen the characteristic self-consciousness of the sect, as opposed to Christianity. The assertion is noteworthy: 'He submitted himself, letting himself be called by humans by whatever name they wished.'[37] This apparently points to a half-syncretistic, half-monotheistic point of view: it is still the same supreme God who is invoked in various religions under various names; it is still the highest power, Simon, who has revealed himself in various forms. The connection of this syncretistic, liberal judgment on other religions with a worship addressed quite narrowly to a historical person is important for the study of the history of

[34] Iren., i. 23. 1; Tert., *De An.* 34. Irenaeus adds that he appeared to other peoples as the Holy Ghost.

[35] Here belongs also the statement of Hippolytus, 6:20, that Simon had asserted that he would rise from the dead on the third day.

[36] Mark 3:21f, *καὶ τότε ἐάν τις ὑμῖν εἴπῃ· ἴδε ὧδε ὁ Χριστός, ἴδε ἐκεῖ, μὴ πιστεύετε. ἐγερθήσονται γὰρ ψευδόχριστοι καὶ ψευδαπροφῆται καὶ ποιήσουσιν σημεῖα καὶ τέρατα πρὸς τὸ ἀποπλανᾶν, εἰ δυνατόν, τοὺς ἐκλεκτούς*, "And then if any man shall say unto you, Lo, here is the Christ; or, Lo, there; believe it not: for there shall arise false Christs and false prophets, and shall shew signs and wonders, that they may lead astray, if possible, the elect." This is, to be sure, older than the Simonian movement. One may consider however what a feeling of reality Matthew would find in these words, as he took them over and wrote them down: *ἰδοὺ προείρηκα ὑμῖν*! "Behold, I have told you all things beforehand!" Or when he renewed the old warning: *βλέπετε μή τις ὑμᾶς πλανήσῃ. πολλοὶ γὰρ ἐλεύσονται ἐπὶ τῷ ὀνόματί μου λέγοντες. ἐγώ εἰμι ὁ Χριστός, καὶ πολλοὺς πλανήσουσιν* (24:4f, "Take heed that no man lead you astray. For many shall come in my name, saying, I am the Christ; and shall lead many astray.")

[37] Irenaeus, i. 23. 1, *sustinare vocari se quodcumque eum vocant homines;* Hippolytus, 5:19, *ὑπομένειν δὲ αὐτὸν καλεῖσθαι οἵῳ ἂν ὀνόματι καλεῖν βούλωνται οἱ ἄνθρωποι.*

religions—a connection which exhibits a certain parallel with the Christian Kyrios cult, particularly with the Johannine logos Christology, in which the relation to a man Jesus is combined with the idea of an absolute and unique source of revelation.

The Antiochene, Saturninus (Satornilos), who is supposed to be dependent upon Menander, stands one step nearer to Christianity. Eusebius, it is true, places him as late as the time of Hadrian (117-138); nothing prevents us, however, from supposing that he flourished earlier, under Trajan (98-117).[38] He is no pseudo-Messiah. He regards it as an established fact that the *Soter* had once before appeared in history, and in some way or other he identifies him with Jesus, whom he credits with the overthrow of the god of the Jews as his chief accomplishment (Iren. i. 24. 1; Hippol. 7:28). *Docetism,* which was already present in Simonianism, comes into the open in Saturninus. If Jesus was the one supreme *dynamis,* which revealed itself in changing forms, there could be only an apparent incarnation;[39] in particular, as Son, he could not actually have been human; above all, he could only *apparently* have suffered.[40] According to Saturninus' doctrine the *Soter* was 'unborn, without body, without form, and merely appeared to be man.'[41] Again we remind ourselves of how closely St. Paul approached such docetism in his doctrine of the incarnation (pp. 488ff);[42] every Christology which starts from the preëxistent, heavenly Christ, runs the risk of this heresy. That a heavenly being had appeared as a man among men, could indeed be maintained, without the need of entering into further reflections on the matter. But if one must declare, as well, that this being who

[38] Cf. Th. Zahn, *Ignatius von Antiochien,* p. 307.

[39] For precisely this reason, Simeon could not have held this doctrine; it arose in his church.

[40] Hippol. 6:19, *ἄνθρωπον φαίνεσθαι αὐτὸν μὴ ὄντα ἄνθρωπον, καὶ παθεῖν δὲ ἐν* Ἰουδαίᾳ *δεδοκηκέναι μὴ πεπονθότα, ἀλλὰ φανέντα* Ἰουδαίοις *μὲν ὡς υἱόν, ἐν δὲ* Σαμαρείᾳ *ὡς πατέρα,* 'that he appeared as a man though he was not a man, and was thought to have suffered in Judaea though he did not, but appeared to the Jews as Son, and in Samaria as Father.'

[41] Hippol. 7:28 (= Iren. i. 24. 2), *τὸν δὲ σωτῆρα ἀγέννητον ὑπέθετο καὶ ἀσώματον καὶ ἀνείδιον, δοκήσει δὲ ἐπιπεφηνέναι ἄνθρωπον.* Here we meet for the first time the expression 'epiphany' which was to obtain as great a significance on gnostic soil as on that of the Church; cf. e.g. I Tim. 6:14; II Tim. 1:10; 4:1,8; Tit. 2:11,13; 3:4.

[42] It again becomes clear here that the tradition of the historical, crucified Jesus was for him so strong that it preserved him from these consequences; it is clear also how loose and external remained the connections of these gnostics with the historical beginnings of Christianity. In particular there appear to be lacking allusions to it in the written gospels; only the general idea, that Jesus appeared in Judaea and suffered, meets us, while on the other hand not a single trace of gnostic changes of interpretation is to be found in the various gospel stories, as, e.g. in the story of the baptism.

humbled himself and became man, had suffered, had died, the question must arise: how can this be predicted of one who was originally of a heavenly and divine nature? And it was paradoxical to assert both these things of Christ, a paradox which St. Paul did not feel as such, but which in John—and especially in Ignatius—was maintained in entire consciousness of its paradoxical nature, and with a certain note of defiance. From the point of view of an incarnation Christology, this position of the Church's writers is inconsistent; the consistency all lies in the direction of docetism.[43] It is therefore no wonder that 'the theological atmosphere, especially in Syria and Palestine, in this age, was laden with Gnosticism' (Lightfoot). The significance and danger of this tendency becomes especially clear in the Ignatian letters, the author of which carries on the struggle to the utmost of his ability.[44]

A pessimistic judgment upon creation is common to the various forms of Samaritan Gnosticism: the world was created by angels and powers and is administered badly by them (Iren. i. 23. 3f; i. 24. 1—Simon, Menander, Saturninus); thus redemption is a question of liberation from the power of angelic forces.[45] Here we are again reminded of St. Paul, in whom we have observed a close approximation to this dualistic and pessimistic Gnosticism (pp. 513ff). Since a reciprocal influence appears to be excluded, we have here before

[43] Cf. Lightfoot, *The Apostolic Fathers,* part 2, i, 378f.

[44] Epistles to Trall. 9 and 10; Smyrn. 1-3; Magn. 11, etc.—Docetism is stamped deeply in the teaching of *Basilides,* who was regarded by Irenaeus as a colleague of Saturninus (i. 24. 1; Epiphanius, *Haer.* 23 calls him *συσχολαστής*, schoolfellow'): the Christ who is identical with the Nous, the first offspring of the Father, did not suffer, but Simon of Cyrene was crucified in his place; he had however changed his appearance to that of Simon and stood nearby, laughing his enemies to scorn. For he was an incorporeal Dynamis and the Nous of the unbegotten Father, and metamorphosed himself at will; thus he ascended to him who had sent him, and laughed at his enemies, since he could not be taken captive and was invisible to all (Iren. i. 24. 4).

[45] Iren. i. 23. 3, *Qua propter . . . . liberari eos, qui sunt ejus, ab imperio eorum, qui mundum fecerunt, repromisit* (Simon), "Hence he promised in turn that those who were his would be freed from the power of those who had made the world;" Tert., *De An.,* 34, exinde ad hominum respexerit salutem quasi per vindictam liberandorum ex illis potestatibus (Simon), "Next he was mindful of men's salvation, as though it were by the liberation of those who are to be freed from those powers." Menander: (Iren. i. 23. 4; Eus. iii. 26), *Διδάσκων δὲ μὴ ἄλλως δύνασθαί τινα καὶ αὐτῶν τῶν κοσμοποιῶν ἀγγέλων περιγενέσθαι, μὴ πρότερον διὰ τῆς μαγικῆς ἐμπειρίας ἀχθέντα*, 'teaching also that one could not overcome those world-creating angels otherwise than by being guided through the magical knowledge.' Saturninus (Iren. i. 24. 1; Hippol. 7:28), *καὶ διὰ τὸ βούλεσθαι τὸν Πατέρα καταλῦσαι πάντας τοὺς ἄρχοντας, παραγενέσθαι τὸν Χριστὸν ἐπὶ καταλύσει τοῦ τῶν Ἰουδαίων Θεοῦ καὶ ἐπὶ σωτηρίᾳ τῶν πειθομένων αὐτῷ*, "Because the Father wished to destroy all the rulers, Christ overcame them with a view to the destruction of the god of the Jews [who is one of the seven world-creating angels] and the salvation of those who believe in him."

us similar branches stemming from the same pre-Christian syncretistic gnosis. As against the Gnostic conception which rested its doctrine of redemption on these hypotheses, Paul possessed a strong counterbalance in the Old Testament idea of God and creation, as well as the Stoic cosmological argument for God's existence; but in the Gnostic system such a counterbalance appears to be completely lacking.

One might conceive of at least an external influence from St. Paul in the anti-Judaic and antinomian features of this teaching. If Saturninus explains the god of the Jews as a world-creating angel at whose destruction (κατάλυσις) the Father and the Christ aim (cf. note 45, above), if Simon describes the prophets as inspired by the world-creating angels and tells his own people 'not to trouble themselves with them but, as free men, to do what they wish; for one is saved because of (his) grace' (not by reason of righteous deeds; Hippol. 6:19; Iren. i. 23. 3)—favorite Pauline words seem to be echoed. But this supposition is not necessary, since Paul in Gal. 5:13 has already been forced to guard against a similar misuse of freedom. But one understands such passages as I Pet. 2:16, Jude 12-16, and especially the anti-Pauline discourse of the Epistle of James doubly well, if such doctrines were present in the writers' surroundings.[46]

The Helena myth of the Simonians or rather the doctrine which is interwoven with it, that the divine idea (*Ennoia*) begot the world-creating angels (Iren. i. 23. 1; cf. also for Menander i. 23. 4), is important for us. The Jewish doctrine of the Wisdom who was entrusted with the creation of the world is reflected here. And we can understand how, after the time of Paul, and completely after the time of John, it would be insisted, that as far as Christians were concerned, such polytheizing and mythologizing ideas must be confined to the commission given the Logos-Christ to create the world.

Yet many other syncretistic doctrines and states of mind in this territory and period may have aroused minds and offended the churches. One learns from the polemic of the Ignatian letters how curious were the mixtures and shapes that were present; they were directed against a teaching which appears sometimes as Judaism and sometimes as docetism.[47] Above all, one can hardly grasp how Judaism and docetism

[46] The identification of Simon with St. Paul lies beyond our period.

[47] At least it is assumed today—and rightly too—that the author does not mean two different teachings, but *one;* cf. e.g. Lightfoot, *The Apostolic Fathers,* part 2, i. 373-82; Knopf, pp. 311ff. Since the heretics appeared also in the churches of Asia Minor,

could have coalesced at all. If this 'Judaism' affirmed the permanent validity of the Law, in any case it cannot have been the teaching of the Samaritans, according to which the Law belonged, together with the cosmos, to the angelic world which was subordinate to God and inimical to him; these ideas, however, are again the hypotheses of docetism: for a *Soter,* sent by the highest, super-cosmic God must, so to speak, go untouched through the cosmos. In any event, it is not Saturninus against whom Ignatius contends; the former was harshly anti-Judaic, since he maintained that the *Soter* had come to overthrow the god of the Jews. If therefore one is not satisfied to accept a purely accidental and disorganized aggregation of various hypotheses regarding these 'Judaistic docetists,' one must attempt to solve the problem from another approach.

It is especially clear that these Judaizers did not demand the circumcision of Gentile Christians, as did those of the age of St. Paul; but in other respects as well, they do not appear to have maintained the permanent validity of the Law; indeed it is not once said in Magn. 9 that they required observance of the Sabbath.[48] In what, then, consists the 'life according to the way of Judaism' which is forbidden by Ignatius as incompatible with the possession of grace?[49] To think of it as a question of practical observances is to succumb to an illusion; according to the manner of thought and expression of Ignatius, 'Jewish life' means nothing other than sharing in the ideas of those who were not persuaded of the true nature of Christ either 'by the prophecies or by the Law of Moses or the Gospel or the martyrdoms.'[50] 'To Judaize' means substantially to 'live

---

Ignatius is acquainted with them so completely that one must assume that 'the struggle with the docetists is not something that has recently and accidentally obtruded itself on him; it is, as his language shows, the struggle of his life' (Reitzenstein, *Gött. gel. Anz.*, 1911, p. 541).

[48] The *μηκέτι σαββατίζοντες ἀλλὰ κατὰ κυριακὴν ζῶντες*, 'no longer keeping the Sabbath but living in observance of the Lord's day,' as a characteristic mark, is spoken only of the converted Jews; cf. Did. 8:1.

[49] Magn. 8, *εἰ γὰρ μέχρι νῦν κατὰ ἰουδαϊσμὸν ζῶμεν, ὁμολογοῦμεν χάριν μὴ εἰληφέναι· οἱ γὰρ θειότατοι προφῆται κατὰ Χριστὸν Ἰησοῦν ἔζησαν*, "For if we are living until now according to Judaism, we confess that we have not received grace. For the divine prophets lived according to Christ Jesus;" 10, *ἄτοπόν ἐστιν Ἰησοῦν Χριστὸν λαλεῖν καὶ ἰουδαΐζειν*, "It is inconsistent to talk of Jesus Christ and to practise Judaism." To be sure, we have before us an imitation of Paul in Gal. 5:2,4; but one may not on this account interpret *ἰουδαΐζειν* according to Gal. 2:14.

[50] Smyrn. 5, *ὅν τινες ἀγνοοῦντες ἀρνοῦνται* (cf. Magn. 9) . . . . *οὓς οὐκ ἔπεισαν αἱ προφητεῖαι οὐδὲ ὁ νόμος Μωΰσεως, ἀλλ' οὐδὲ μέχρι νῦν τὸ εὐαγγέλιον οὐδὲ τὰ ἡμέτερα τῶν κατ' ἄνδρα παθήματα*, "There are some who ignorantly deny him (cf. Magn. 9) . . . . whom neither the prophecies nor the law of Moses persuaded, nor the gospel even until now, nor our own individual sufferings;" on this point, cf. Magn. 8, *διὰ*

without Christ' (Magn. 9), to deny him (*ibid.*), or to be denied by him (Smyrn. 5),[51] i.e. not to be convinced by the birth and passion and resurrection (Magn. 11). To this corresponds the fact that Judaism is designated not as a way of life (perhaps a πολίτευμα or a θρησκεία), but as 'heterodoxies' and 'useless old myths' (Magn. 8); one must not listen to one who 'expounds Judaism' (Philad. 6), i.e. who pleads for Jewish ideas by reference to Scriptural texts. And when Ignatius, in the famous controversy over the 'records' (ἀρχεῖα) in which the Judaizers insist upon Scriptural proof of the teaching of the Gospel, and call in question the Church's evidence, curtly declines this method of procedure, while he declares that the 'records' are Jesus Christ himself, his Cross, his death, his resurrection, and the faith awakened by him, because of which he hopes to be justified, one understands that the opposition sought to make good, by a method to which Ignatius was not equal, its 'Jewish'—and this means 'docetic'—interpretation, or at least to deny the Church's arguments from Scripture.[52] To this whole picture belongs also the detail, that the 'Judaizers' were apparently not born Jews but Gentiles.[53] From all this it is proved that their 'judaizing' is of another sort than that attacked by Paul. Ignatius gives their doctrine this name because they sought to support their docetic ideas by 'old fables,' i.e. by cosmological myths, which they verified from the Scriptures. They are thus Gnostics of non-Jewish origin, but with a Jewish secret wisdom—just as, for example, Saturninus developed his doctrine of man from Gen. 1:25. More than this we unfortunately cannot say; we recognize, however, that these docetists need not

---

τοῦτο [οἱ προφῆται] καὶ ἐδιώχθησαν, ἐμπνεόμενοι ὑπὸ τῆς χάριτος εἰς τὸ πληροφορηθῆναι τοὺς ἀπειθοῦντας, ὅτι εἷς θεός ἐστιν ὁ φανερώσας ἑαυτὸν διὰ Ἰησοῦ Χριστοῦ τοῦ υἱοῦ αὐτοῦ, "Therefore they were also persecuted, being inspired by his grace, to convince the disobedient that there is one God, who manifested himself through Jesus Christ his son."

[51] Reminiscence of Gal. 4:8.

[52] The much debated passage in Philad. 8 reads, "I have heard some men saying 'If I find it not in the records, I do not believe it [when it is written] in the Gospel'" (or, "I do not believe in the Gospel") "And when I said to them that it is in the Scripture, they answered me, 'That is exactly the question.' But to me the records are Jesus Christ, the inviolable records are his cross and death, and resurrection, and the faith which is through him; in these I desire to be justified by your prayers." [*Translator's Note.* Cf. K. Lake, *The Apostolic Fathers,* i, 247, for a note on the Greek of the passage.]

[53] Philad. 6, "But if anyone interpret Judaism to you do not listen to him; for it is better to hear Christianity from the circumcised than Judaism from the uncircumcised. But both of them, unless they speak of Jesus Christ, are to me tombstones and sepulchres of the dead, on whom only the names of men are written" (i.e. not the name of Christ; they are not 'Christophoroi').

be so far removed from Samaritan Gnosticism as appeared at first glance. In any event, they belong also to the pattern of syncretistic, Gnostic movements, with which the young Church of Syria was surrounded.

5. *The Church of Antioch,* which has been significant in every respect for primitive church history as the first mixed church of Jews and Gentiles, as a point of departure for the first mission to the Gentiles, as a base of operations for men like Barnabas and Paul, as a center of the oldest Hellenistic Kyrios faith—in our period lies, unfortunately, in nearly total darkness. We have lost it from view since the controversy between St. Paul and the Jewish Christian leaders of the Church (pp. 273-276) over table fellowship with the Gentile Christians, in which St. Peter appeared in such an ambiguous position. From the fact that Paul had left Antioch and henceforth had separated from Barnabas in his missionary work, we have concluded that at that time he was essentially defeated, and that the stricter or more scrupulous party remained master of the field. Furthermore we have seen that the Apostolic Decree issued from Jerusalem without the assistance of St. Paul, was calculated precisely for Antioch (pp. 311-315); here it was first of all put into effect. In this fact is reflected the enduring influence of Jerusalem upon Antioch; the other side of the picture is that St. Paul continued to withhold his activity from this region. It is reflected also in the later ecclesiastical tradition[54] that Peter had been the first bishop of Antioch. There may well be concealed in this a recollection that the sojourn of St. Peter there was not a temporary one, and that in the place of St. Paul he had labored there for a much longer time (cf. pp. 273ff). But we know nothing certain. Euodius is considered to be second bishop,[55] but of him we have no more exact information. On the other hand it is an important tradition and one to which no objection can be raised, that only *one* bishop is named. From the seven letters of Ignatius, who is designated as the successor of Euodius, we learn that the monarchical episcopate had been adopted in this region. The enormous stress which he lays on it is not to be interpreted by the supposition that he takes pains to establish an entirely different order of things; at the most, he seeks to place its significance—not completely appreciated in the churches of Asia—in the right light; but the fact that *one* bishop stands over the

[54] Eusebius, *Chron.*, on the year of Abraham 2055; *H. E.* iii. 36. 2; Origen, *Works,* ed. Delarue, iii, 938a; Jerome, *De Viris Illustr.* 16.

[55] Eusebius, *Chron.*, year of Abr. 2058; *H. E.* iii. 22.

presbyters at the head of each separate church,[56] appears to *him* to be something which is completely obvious. So early and unmistakable an appearance of the monarchical episcopate—and in Syria—is, on the other hand, a demonstration of the permanent influence of Jerusalem, which we have found attested historically still earlier (pp. 719f). Just so, the presence of the institution of the presbyterate, which goes back to the very earliest period (Acts 14:23; 20:17; 21:18), is to be regarded as taken over from Jerusalem into Syria and Asia Minor. One question is whether St. Ignatius occupied the position of chief bishop of a province, as one might conclude from Rom. 2 (τὸν ἐπίσκοπον Συρίας, 'the bishop of Syria'). On linguistic grounds no certain answer can be given to this; on factual grounds the analogy of Asia Minor (John, Polycarp) tends to give an answer in the affirmative.

6. *Ignatius of Antioch.* The seven letters of Ignatius whose genuineness is undeniable and which belong in the time of Trajan,[57] give us, to be sure, little information otherwise about the Antiochene church—apart from the fact that in Antioch a persecution took place in the time of Trajan (or Hadrian)—nor do they throw light upon the church of Asia Minor to which they were addressed. They exhibit to us a man in the high tension of a mystical ecstasy of martyrdom, concerned for the unity and stability of the Church, concerned also for true Christianity, as he understands it. The personality of the man is not in this place the subject of our consideration, nor are the details of his literary ideals and teaching, but rather we are to consider his *whole interpretation of Christianity*, in regard to which we must raise the question, to what extent is this typical of his time and place?

In the first place, it must be said that Ignatius is not to be regarded as being in any way typical of that mediating Christianity, standing between Judaism and Hellenism, which we must assume existed in Antioch and its environs in the earliest period (pp. 170ff). One cannot, in any sense, speak of Jewish Christianity in relation to him. The vehement repudiation of Judaism (p. 763)—though

[56] Of various churches neighboring on Antioch, Philad. 10 says, *ὡς καὶ αἱ ἔγγιστα ἐκκλησίαι ἔπεμψαν ἐπισκόπους*, 'even as the neighboring churches have sent bishops;' and others—*αἱ δὲ πρεσβυτέρους καὶ διακόνους*, 'presbyters and deacons.' In this region then presbyters and bishops are certainly no longer identical, and the plural *ἐπισκόπους* is conditioned by that of *ἐκκλησίαι*, and thus of course is no argument against the monarchical episcopate.

[57] If they were not genuine, they would not be less interesting and instructive. The author in that case would have been taking care to delineate the ideal type of a martyr bishop, which would throw a bright light on the age and its attitudes.

perhaps it is not a very Jewish religion!—with such very deliberate and disdainful expressions,[58] shows that not even the slightest religious bond connects him with Jewish Christianity (of Jerusalem or the Syrian cities). Indeed, one may perhaps say that he loses too completely the consciousness of a historical connection with the religion of Israel. 'Judaism has passed over into faith in Christianity, to which every tongue which believes in God has united itself': [59] humanity—so far as it is faithful—has definitely embraced Christianity; Judaism is completely antiquated. The pattern of prophecy and fulfilment, in which the present always appears as a continuation and completion of a far-away past, a way of thinking which is always historical, is hardly to be detected at all in him;[60] Christianity is indeed read back, by means of a decided paradox, into antiquity, and thereby in some sense is transformed into something super-historical: the prophets, although they were also expecting him, were already disciples of Christ, they lived in the spirit of Christ Jesus (κατὰ Χρ. 'Ι.), they preached with the Gospel in view; they were, in brief, Christians, they are in the fellowship of Jesus Christ, saved by faith (Magn. 8 and 9; Philad. 5 and 9). They were inspired by his grace to convince the unbelieving (in the present age this includes also the false teachers) that God is one, that he has revealed himself through Jesus Christ, his Son, who is his 'Word' . . . . The writings of the prophets and the Law of Moses are nothing more nor less than instruments of missionary work and conversion—just as are the Gospel and the martyrdoms of Christians (Smyrn. 5). They thus do not operate by means of prophetic proof, which may be adduced from them, but quite immediately as the Christian revelation itself. To be sure, the Gospel has priority over them, since it contains the actual epiphany of Christ, his sufferings,

[58] In Magn. 8 he speaks of the 'useless old myths' (*μυθεύμασι τοῖς παλαιοῖς ἀνωφελέσιν οὖσιν*); similarly in Magn. 9 of those who lived according to 'old,' i.e. in his view completely obsolete, 'ways' (*ἐν παλαιοῖς πράγμασιν*) and now have obtained a new hope—he thereby means Jewish Christians like Peter (Magn. 9). For Christians however this old way of life is so completely abolished that Ignatius makes use of the expression 'yeast which has become old and turned sour.' That this expression, *παλαιωθεῖσαν καὶ ἐνοξίσασαν* (Magn. 10) exactly reproduces the idea of the writer, the context shows: "Turn ye to the new leaven, which is Jesus Christ, be salted in him, that none among you be corrupted (*διαφθαρῇ*), since by your savour you shall be tested."

[59] Magn. 10, *ᾧ πᾶσα γλῶσσα πιστεύσασα εἰς θεὸν συνήχθη*; I accept Lightfoot's reading *ᾧ* in place of *ὡς* (G), but not his interpretation. I connect *ᾧ* with *συνήχθη*, and *πιστεύσασα*, not with *ᾧ* but with *εἰς*. [*Translator's Note.* K. Lake, (*op. cit.*, i, 206) adopts this reading as well as Weiss's translation.]

[60] The frequent calling of attention to the descent of Jesus from David comes about solely because of anti-docetic interest (Eph. 20; Trall. 9; Smyrn. 1), not because of attempts to prove fulfilment of prophecies.

and his resurrection—it is the perfection of immortality (Philad. 9). Therefore St. Ignatius makes very little use of the Old Testament; the argument from prophecy is completely lacking. And when the argument from prophecy becomes burdensome or doubtful in controversy with the 'Judaists,' he simply puts the 'old records' aside and limits himself completely to the 'factual records' given in the Cross and resurrection of Christ (Philad. 8). Just as he is foreign to the peculiarly Scriptural Jewish Christianity, so Ignatius is far also from enlightened Hellenistic Judaism, and one cannot designate his religion as a 'kind of diaspora Judaism plus the Cross.'[61] It is, above all, not strongly oriented toward eschatology. Though there are not lacking certain conventional assertions regarding this,[62] yet we feel that the thoroughly eschatological attitude is missing: in particular we do not find the idea that the appearance of the Messiah means at the same time the end of the world and that redemption involves the destruction of the old world; instead he substitutes a *displacement* which is quite remarkable. For the 'old kingdom' which began to be destroyed when the star appeared at the birth of Christ is designated also as the sphere of Satan's authority, not precisely in the sense of Matt. 12:28, but rather in an eschatological sense: 'All magic was annulled and every bond of wickedness vanished away, ignorance was removed, for God was manifested as man for the newness of eternal life, and that which had been prepared by God gained a beginning. Hence all things were disturbed, because the abolition of death was being planned' (Eph. 19). The old kingdom was that of death, that of the enslavement of creation, up to now opposed only by the insufficient means of magic, but now conquered by the appearance of the true life. This reminds us quite strongly of St. Paul in some ways;[63] it is however merely the Hellenistic, cosmic side of his doctrine of redemption which is here echoed; the ethical doctrine

[61] As that of I Clement is described by Bousset, *Kyrios Christos,* pp. 356ff.

[62] Eph. 11, *ἔσχατοι καιροὶ . . . . τὴν μέλλουσαν ὀργήν*, 'the last times . . . . the wrath to come;' Magn. 5, *τέλος τὰ πράγματα ἔχει καὶ πρόκειται τὰ δύο ὁμοῦ, ὅ τε θάνατος καὶ ἡ ζωή, καὶ ἕκαστος εἰς τὸν ἴδιον τόπον μέλλει χωρεῖν*, "There is an end to all, and the choice is between two things, death and life, and each is to go to his own place;" Eph. 16, *βασιλείαν τοῦ Θεοῦ οὐ κληρονομήσουσιν*, "They shall not inherit the Kingdom of God." [*Translator's Note.* Cf. D. W. Riddle, "From Apocalypse to Martyrology", *Anglican Theological Review,* ix, (1926) 260-280; also "A Literary Allusion in the Martyrdom of Polycarp", *Anglican Theological Review,* viii (1925), 136-142; and *The Martyrs* (Chicago, 1931). Riddle believes that the problem of social control attacked at first, and in Jewish circles, by apocalypses, came to be solved by the martyrology. Ignatius would therefore stand at one of the points of change.]

[63] The abrogation of death in I Cor. 15:26; the freedom from bondage to the elements of the world in Col. 2:20; the ruler of this aeon, II Cor. 4:4.

of justification, on the other hand, is only present to a much lesser degree.[64] And this very thing is quite significant. Since Ignatius counts less upon the resurrection of the dead at the Parousia than upon immediate union with God and Christ at the instant of death,[65] salvation in Christ is to him 'life,' and above all else the Eucharist is a 'medicine of immortality' (Eph. 20).[66] This catastrophic Hellenistic turn given the doctrine of redemption is maintained quite in the style of the mystery religions, and not by accident does he call the virgin birth and death of Christ 'mysteries' which God prepared in silence and henceforth proclaims clearly.[67] *Here* we actually have for once the type of a religion which is completely detached from its Israelitish motherland, a Christian mystery religion almost detached from history, which has often been discovered quite falsely in St. Paul or, still more falsely, has been regarded as being in general the same as Christianity. One can only say that in Ignatius this Hellenistic element has been detached from its close linkage with the Israelitish-Jewish element with which it is found in St. Paul. Here we observe also—in a more or less pure state—the type of a Kyrios faith which is fairly well detached from messianism and eschatology, which has repeatedly been taken for granted, onesidedly and prematurely, as being normal to the *earliest* age of Antiochene Christianity. We have here, in fact, the individual reverence and the communal worship of the Jesus Christ or Christ Jesus who is exalted above all history since he is immortal, in which the frequent 'our Lord' still echoes, however, the old *Marân.* The fact that this phrase can mean at the same time 'our God,' corresponds absolutely to the state of affairs: for this Kyrios worship is in the fullest sense divine honor; hymns and glorification (ᾄδειν, δοξάζειν, λιτανεύειν) are addressed directly to him (Eph. 4; Rom. 4), as they are

[64] Only once 'intellectually' reproduced in Ign. Rom. 5:1, from I Cor. 4:4.

[65] Rom. 4, *θεοῦ ἐπιτυχεῖν*, 'to attain to God;' 5, *Ἰησοῦ Χριστοῦ ἐπιτυχεῖν*, 'to attain to Jesus Christ;' 6, *ἐκεῖνον ζητῶ . . . . ἐκεῖνον θέλω*, "I seek him . . . . I desire him;" along with this, of course, goes the passage, *ἀπελεύθερος Ἰησοῦ Χριστοῦ καὶ ἀναστήσομαι ἐν αὐτῷ ἐλεύθερος*, "Jesus Christ's freedman [i.e. through sufferings] and in him I shall rise free," Rom. 4. This freedom is connected with the moment of death. Death is his birth, his true life, the acceptance of new light, true incarnation, 'resurrection' (Trall. 9).

[66] Cf. von der Goltz, "Ignatius von Antiochien" (*Texte und Untersuchungen,* xii, 3), pp. 40f. "The individualistic element in the eschatology of the Bishop is what is effective. Hardly any traces are to be found of the biblical and Jewish idea of a future Kingdom of God and an eschatological drama." "The value of salvation as new *life* is essentially eschatological: a guaranteed hope of life."

[67] *μυστήρια κραυγῆς, ἅτινα ἐν ἡσυχίᾳ θεοῦ ἐπράχθη*, 'mysteries of a cry, which were wrought in the stillness of God,' Eph. 19; cf. also the expression *Παύλου συμμύσται*, 'fellow-initiates with Paul,' Eph. 12.

addressed to God through his mediation (Rom. 2). That which we may call the unhistorical, ever-present character of this Kyrios does not change greatly the circumstance that—in the catechism-like formulae—the characteristics of the historical Jesus, his birth from Mary and from David's race, his actual crucifixion and bodily resurrection, were, because of anti-docetic interests, called so strongly before the attention. In this way, certainly, his historical humanity is placed on a firm basis; in particular, by the chronological formula 'under Pontius Pilate and Herod the tetrarch' (Magn. 11; Trall. 9; Smyrn. 1). The fact was that this was imparted by tradition, and in this respect there is a permanent difference between Ignatius' Christianity and the timeless mystery cults of an Adonis or an Osiris. But this 'historical' motive does not have nearly the same significance as it had for the earliest primitive Christianity and for Paul, who considered themselves as contemporaries, so to speak, and witnesses of the last world period which had been inaugurated by them. For Ignatius they are not so much facts of the immediate past, the effect of which Christendom still felt directly, but something so completely *in the present* that their temporal, unique actuality does not matter greatly. It is thus also important to be convinced, by means of the understanding, of the factual truth of these events[68]—the true criterion of a Christian is, after all, that he *lives* in lively experience and consciousness of these facts which are *represented* to him in the cultus, particularly in the Eucharist: 'as if nailed to the Cross of the Lord Jesus Christ, both in flesh and spirit, and confirmed in love by the blood of Christ, in sincere persuasion joined to our Lord' (πεπληροφορημένους εἰς τὸν κύριον ἡμῶυ, Smyrn. 1); 'rejoicing in the passion of our Lord without doubting, and is fully assured in all mercy in his resurrection' (Philad., inscr.); to be a 'bearer of Christ' (Eph. 9), 'being kindled by the blood of God' (Eph. 1), "to have a part in the 'Passion' " (Philad. 3), "united and chosen through true 'suffering' " (Eph., inscr.), to 'do all things as though he were dwelling in us, that we may be his temples and that he may be our God in us' (Eph. 15)—these are some of the ardent formulae in which this piety expresses itself. One recognizes throughout the consequence of Pauline modes of expression; this mysticism is a continuation

[68] Magn. 11, *μὴ ἐμπεσεῖν εἰs τὰ ἄγκιστρα τῆs κενοδοξίαs, ἀλλὰ πεπληροφόρησθε ἐν τῇ γεννήσει καὶ τῷ πάθει καὶ τῇ ἀναστάσει τῇ γενομένῃ ἐν καιρῷ τῆs ἡγεμονίαs Ποντίου Πιλάτου. πραχθέντα ἀληθῶs καὶ βεβαίωs ὑπὸ Ἰησοῦ Χριστοῦ*, 'not to fall into the snare of vain doctrine, but to be convinced of the birth and passion and resurrection which took place at the time of the procuratorship of Pontius Pilate; for these things were truly and assuredly done by Jesus Christ.'

and strong intensification of the Pauline. But that which was in St. Paul only *one* phase of his religion among others (pp. 462ff) is in Ignatius the whole thing.

The relation to Paul is especially significant for the man and the age. For the first time we have before us an exceedingly intensive influence of the Pauline letters,[69] which is sharply contrasted with the quite external and superficial borrowing in James or First Clement. Ignatius not only knew the Pauline letters, he lived in them completely; his modes of thought and expression are *saturated* with contacts with them.[70] And indeed he must have known a *collection* which included in any case the Epistle to the Ephesians, but certainly not the Pastoral Epistles. The presence of such a collection about 100-110, which he may have come upon in Asia Minor or—more probably—in Antioch, is quite important. This fact witnesses to the often-denied permanent influence of Paul a high reverence for the Apostle to the Gentiles, at least in purely Gentile Christian circles, and indeed not only an awe-inspired honor paid a man who was after all misunderstood, but also a sincere contact with at least some of his chief ideas. The Church of Ephesus is ennobled by the fact that its people had had St. Paul in their midst (Eph. 12). If we may claim this attitude for Antioch as well, we see in this age a transformation in the circles which had honored Peter as *the* Apostle and the Twelve as *the* Apostles of the Lord (Gospel of Matthew, cf. p. 752). The authority of St. Paul, which after the controversy with St. Peter had been deeply shaken, is at the very least completely rehabilitated. When Ignatius in his letter to the Romans (ch. 4) places Peter and Paul side by side, this is because of the especial connection of both of them with Rome, perhaps in imitation of I Clem. 5. In other respects he represents the typical point of view of post-apostolic, ecclesiastical Christianity, since the Apostles appear to

[69] [*Translator's Note.* Unless the canonical Ephesians be the first; cf. E. J. Goodspeed, *The Meaning of Ephesians.* Goodspeed (*New Solutions of New Testament Problems,* pp. 21-28), sees in the letter corpus of Revelation (to *seven* churches with a covering encyclical) another example of Pauline influence, though of course not so significant. Goodspeed believes that the canonical Ephesians used all the Pauline letters. Mr. John Knox has recently argued that Ignatius used even Philemon in his own epistles to the Ephesians and Romans.]

[70] It is important that he not merely takes over various concepts and copies various passages, but that he imitates the rhetoric of St. Paul, in an excessive, coarsened and disjointed manner which surpasses even that of the Epistle to the Ephesians. An exact paralleling of the rhetoric of Ignatius and Paul would prove clearly the originality of the latter, would produce new material to prove the spuriousness of the canonical Ephesians, but would also force recognition of the fact that much which is held in common is due to the same standard, i.e. 'Asiatic' rhetoric.

him to be the pattern of the presbytery (Magn. 6; Trall. 2f; Smyrn. 8) and as the prototype of the Church (Magn. 13), and their commandments (Magn. 13; Trall. 7) as unconditionally binding, along with those of the Lord (cf. pp. 673f).

His relation to the Johannine writings has not been fully clarified. That he was acquainted, e.g. with passages such as John 8:29 (Magn. 8); 3:8 (Philad. 7), and others, appears to be beyond doubt. On the other hand one may not explain everything which has a 'Johannine ring' as due to literary influence—it is precisely the common Hellenistic religious language in which both shared. Whether one may speak moreover of an 'Asia Minor' theology of Ignatius still appears very questionable. Yet the most intimate connections with the Christianity of Asia Minor lie before us in the letters, and it is not to be ruled out as impossible that they already existed before Ignatius' last journey.

CHAPTER XXV

Asia Minor

1. *The Provinces.* From Syria we pass on to *Asia Minor,*[1] the broad region bordering on Syria, to which in the apostolic age St. Paul himself had journeyed on numerous occasions, and in which he was able to begin the task of founding important churches. Here we set foot upon soil which became very important for the development of Christianity even in the post-apostolic age, and we are at the same time in the fortunate situation of possessing a number of sources for this region which give us information concerning the progress of Christianity, at least in some degree, and of its destiny, so that here we can see these better than, say, in the provinces of Judaea and Syria, treatment of which has just been concluded.

The whole broad land which we now designate as Asia Minor[2]—a name which came into use only in late antiquity[3]—in the Roman imperial period formed a group of great provinces, of which some were quite important to the whole empire. These provinces, beginning from the south, were: first, *Cilicia,* which, of course, faced the sea and thus Syria as well, while it was divided from the rest of Asia Minor by the high wall of the Taurus over which only a few passes led. The great province of *Galatia,* north of Taurus, bordered on Cilicia, and included a large part of the interior of Asia Minor, while on the east it touched the border province of Cappadocia. Northward from Galatia and Cappadocia, stretched at great length along the shore of the Black Sea, lay the province of *Bithynia-Pontus,* and in the west Asia Minor sloped by gradual stages to the sea in the three districts, Mysia, Lydia, and Caria, which together with a large part of ancient Phrygia made up the very important and rich

[1] At this point the original author's work ends and the editor begins the final part of the work, which he brings to conclusion; on the manner and method of completion, see the editor's preface at the beginning of the book.

[2] Cf. on this matter also J. Weiss, "Kleinasien" in Herzog's *Realenzyklopädie,* 3rd ed., vol. x. [*Translator's Note.* The article is found in English in an abridged form in *The New Schaff-Herzog Encyclopaedia of Religious Knowledge,* i, 314-18; cf. also W. M. Ramsay's article in Hastings' *Dictionary of the Bible,* i, 171f; W. M. Ramsay, *Historical Geography of Asia Minor,* chs. A-E.]

[3] Cf. Orosius, the contemporary of Augustine, *Historia,* 1:2, "Asia regio, vel ut proprie dicam, Asia minor. . . ." ("Asia is a region, or rather, to speak more properly, Asia Minor. . . .").

province of *Asia,* in the narrower sense (*Asia proconsularis*). With Asia Minor, finally, must be included the island of *Cyprus,* which was a separate province whose proconsul had his seat in Paphos.

2. Our *chief sources* for the history of Christianity in Asia Minor are, to enumerate them briefly, as follows: the group of five Johannine writings in our canon—among which the Revelation gives us an especially valuable glance into Asiatic church life; the letters of St. Ignatius of Antioch, and, closely connected with those of the Antiochene bishop, the Epistle of Polycarp of Smyrna to the churches of Philippi in Macedonia; the First Epistle of Peter, which as its salutation shows, has in view the needs and troubles of Asiatic churches, indeed of a rather wide circle; the letter of Pliny the younger, governor of Bithynia-Pontus, to the emperor Trajan, dealing with legal proceedings against Christians which he conducted in his province in the years 112-113 (Pliny, *Epistles* 10:96); finally, the canonical Epistle to the Ephesians, and the Pastoral Epistles as we have them in the canon, must be regarded as writings of men of the Pauline school, unknown to us, who wrote partly under the name of their master and who almost certainly worked in Asia. They may with likelihood be assigned to Asia, more precisely, perhaps, to the province of Asia itself, *Asia proconsularis* (cf. also above, pp. 680-685).

3. Not all of the Asia Minor provinces enumerated above come into consideration in the history of Christianity between 70 and 130. In *Cappadocia* we can discover no traces of Christianity either in the age of Paul or in the decades after him; the province is named only in the very broad salutation of First Peter. In *Galatia,* either in the north or the south of the province (on this question, cf. pp. 297-299) St. Paul did indeed found churches. However, they do not arouse attention otherwise, and the sources for the period after 70 do not disclose anything about them; and yet they are included in the salutation of First Peter. Both the provinces of Cappadocia and Galatia, closed off from the sea, belong to the high plateau in the center of Asia Minor, which is by nature inhospitable and not very fruitful, and makes little impression in history. It was the coastal peoples who were the especial bringers of development, in culture generally as in religious movements and Christianity in particular. But for the most part we hear nothing of Christianity in these more favorably endowed areas, either. This is the precise situation of our sources. In *Cilicia* and *Cyprus,* as St. Paul himself (Gal. 1:21) and the Book of the Acts (which has a very good tradition, 11:19; 13:4-12; 15:39) both give partial testimony, Christianity very early

found a footing, arriving from Jerusalem and Antioch. In our period however we hear nothing more of the churches there. There is only the solitary appearance of a certain Philo, 'deacon from Cilicia,' in the Ignatian epistles (Philad. 11:1).

In this condition of our sources we thus cannot say at all whether the attempted onslaught of *Judaism* against the Gentile Christian churches of Galatia in the time of Paul (cf. pp. 299ff) was repulsed by the Apostle's letter. It must be looked upon as a fact which is important and certainly not without consequences, that Jerusalem or at least the legalistic party in the community there, had attempted to extend its propaganda beyond Antioch into the territory of the oldest Antiochene missionary province, and we cannot know with certainty that it did not have results. One can picture such a thing in various ways: Judaism may have come into dominance in some churches, not in others; it may have attempted to make schisms, separate churches, or new foundations of churches; all sorts of things were possible in this district, and we may without difficulty regard it as conceivable that in Galatia there may have existed Jewish Christian or even Gentile Christian churches which observed the Law. But we do not, as we have said, have any more definite information. We shall further on have to consider the fact that syncretistic, gnostic elements gained entrance into the Galatian churches of St. Paul, as indeed in Phrygian Colossae we have seen a Jewish Christian gnostic movement at work (p. 387).

4. In the letters of St. Paul to the Church of Colossae we have evidence of Christian communities in two neighboring Phrygian cities, Hierapolis and Laodicea (Col. 4:13). All three belonged politically to the province of *Asia*. And here in the rich province of *Asia proconsularis*, so bountifully endowed by nature, we meet that development of Christianity which in the whole range of Christian Asia Minor is the most significant, and which from our sources is the most readily comprehensible. Already in the age of Paul, whether directly or indirectly founded by him, we find Christianity present in Ephesus, the capital of the province and the mother city of Asiatic Christianity; in the three Phrygian cities just named, which lay inland from Ephesus in the valley of the river Maeander; finally in the northwest of the province, in Alexandria Troas, an important harbor and commercial city, near the Hellespont (II Cor. 2:12; Acts 20:5ff). Lastly, an early and comparatively strong situation of Christianity in Asia is manifest from the statement of Paul in I Cor.

16:19, written from Ephesus: at even such an early period St. Paul speaks of 'the churches of Asia' in the plural and mentions, in 16:9, 'the great door' which has been opened for him there. In the decades after the death of Paul, a greater number of Christian churches is attested in cities on the coast and also in the valleys which slope downward to the sea. The sources which especially show us the situation of Christianity in our period are the letters of Ignatius and the seven epistles in Rev. 2 and 3. The most significant, most distinguished, and probably also the greatest church was—and continued to be in our period—that of *Ephesus*, which of course became the metropolis of Christian Asia in later ecclesiastical development; it was here that the archbishop of the province had his seat. Ephesus was politically, and in economic matters equally so, the leading city of the province.[4] Thus the first of the apocalyptic letters goes to Ephesus, and not to Pergamum, the actual and official capital; to the same place is addressed the most important and longest of the epistles of Ignatius, in which the Bishop of Antioch heaps up more and higher expressions of praise and esteem than he does in any of the other letters destined to Asian cities: the Church of Ephesus is rich in numbers (Ign., Eph. 1:3); its fame reaches in the angelic world even to the aeons (Eph. 8:1); Ignatius says that he hopes, by the intercession of the Ephesians, to obtain a share in the glory of the Ephesian Christians at the resurrection of the dead: 'I know who I am and to whom I write. I am condemned, you have received mercy; I am in danger, you are established in safety; you are the passageway for those who are being slain for the sake of God, fellow-initiates with Paul . . . . who in every epistle makes mention of you in Christ Jesus' (11:2 and 12). According to the ancient ecclesiastical tradition, that great unknown leading personality of the post-apostolic age, the Asia Minor John, must have sojourned in Ephesus; but of course his circle of action need not be confined to Ephesus.

North of Ephesus, in a commanding position on a deeply indented arm of the sea, lies *Smyrna*. The city was politically, and economically as well, the rival of Ephesus. But the Christian Church of Smyrna appears to be decidedly inferior to the Ephesian Church and to have begun later to play its great part in history. The apocalyptic epistle which is addressed to Smyrna follows immediately the one addressed to Ephesus, but the order of the epistles, beginning with

[4] On Ephesus and also on most of the other cities named hitherto, cf. the previously cited (p. 297) article by J. Weiss.

Ephesus, is determined geographically: the enumeration of the seven churches proceeds along the coast from south to north, then inland in reverse order. In the epistle itself the church is addressed as one which is in distress and poor (Rev. 2:9). As early as this period, as also later, it had to suffer severely under the pressure of the rich and powerful Jewish community. And, as compared with the Ephesian Church, it was at all times at a disadvantage because it was not of apostolic foundation. And this was sufficiently understood by the church itself, and its Bishop Polycarp has expressed it thus in his letter to the Philippian Church: "Among you the blessed Paul labored . . . . For concerning you he boasts in all the churches who then alone had known God, for we had not yet known him" (11:3).

The third church which is addressed in Rev. 2 is that of *Pergamon*. This city had been at an earlier time the royal city of the Attalid kingdom, and in the Roman period was the official capital of the province of Asia, the seat of the proconsul, besides being the permanent seat and meeting place of the Asiatic council, the κοινὸν τῆς Ἀσίας. Pergamon was famed for the worship of the healing god Asclepius, Ἀσκληπιὸς σωτήρ, who had a much-frequented sanctuary in the city. The expression used in Rev. 2:13, 'the throne of Satan,' refers to this shrine and not to the temple of Augustus or the huge altar of Zeus which has been restored in Berlin.

When we arrive at Pergamon we are in the very interior of the land of Asia Minor, and the other churches which are given letters in the Apocalypse and the Ignatian corpus lay removed from the coast in the hinterland and were connected with the seashore by river valleys and much-traveled commercial highways. Inland from Ephesus in the Maeander valley are situated *Magnesia* on the Maeander (or, more exactly, on its tributary, the Lethaeus), and *Tralles*. Ignatius writes to Christian communities in both places. Still further inland, close one to another, lie the three cities already named, *Colossae*, *Laodicea*, and *Hierapolis*. The Church of *Laodicea* is addressed in Rev. 3:14-22, and is pictured as a rich and self-satisfied congregation. Colossae does not appear again in the sources for our period of time; the city appears to have sunk into complete insignificance, along with Laodicea, a fact to be blamed especially on the great earthquake of the year 65. Hierapolis was much more significant than Colossae; but here also the great earthquake appears to have checked the city's development: from the time of

Nero to that of Hadrian no coins of the city appear. The church there, however, is worthy of our notice: Philip the Evangelist and his prophetic daughters (Acts 21:9) are said to have worked there, and his grave and those of two of his daughters were shown there in the second century; cf. Polycrates of Ephesus, in Eusebius, *H. E.* iii. 31. 3. Also, and probably in the time of Trajan, the early ecclesiastical writer Papias was bishop in Hierapolis. All the churches which lay in the Maeander valley had received Christianity from Ephesus.

In the valley of the Hermus, which empties itself north of the mouth of the Maeander, we find evidence of three churches: one in Sardis, famous in antiquity as the royal capital of Lydia (Rev. 3:1-6), another in Thyatira (Rev. 2:18-29), lying on a tributary of the Hermus, and the third, far inland at Philadelphia (Rev. 3:7-13 and Ign., Philad.).

Finally, the continuance of the Church of Troas, where St. Paul had worked, is known from the Ignatian epistles. When Ignatius stopped in Troas before his departure for Macedonia, he made contact with the church there, which transmitted through him its greeting to brother churches in the letters which he sent to Philadelphia and Smyrna (Philad. 11:2; Smyrn. 12:1).

There are thus, besides Colossae, twelve churches in a relatively narrow compass, whose existence is confirmed. At the same time the sources which give information about the expansion of Christianity in Asia are, on the whole, rather scanty: Ignatius writes only to the churches with which he has come into contact; and the apocalyptist intended to, and could, name but a selected group of churches in Asia, since for stylistic reasons he was confined to the number seven. Another possible hypothesis, that the seven churches of the Revelation of John occupied a sort of preëminence in their district, may easily be upheld because of their arrangement in this section of the book. One can say that the apocalyptist does not name Hierapolis and Colossae, since Laodicea was the leading church, and he is silent about Magnesia, since ecclesiastically it stood in dependence upon Ephesus. But the style (seven candlesticks, seven angels, seven churches) proves to have been actually determinative, since the definite article ('*the* seven churches,' 1:4, 11,20) demands some consideration.

If one glances at the list of names in the Apocalypse and Ignatius, one sees without difficulty that, in the province of Asia, the foundation stones which St. Paul had laid with his missionary work had remained standing, and that upon them there had been further building. For we must regard the Asiatic churches, in their inner as well as external life, as being more firmly established, richer, and more complex.

5. For *Bithynia-Pontus*, the northern province of Asia Minor, we possess an important witness in the letters of Pliny, written in 112. The letter in question was probably sent from the eastern part of this great province; those placed near 10:96 in the collection were dispatched from Amisus. Pliny gives explicit information that Christianity, in the time of his governorship, had attained an expansion which was, to him, already threatening. He reports to the emperor that there were Roman citizens who had confessed being Christians, mentions an anonymous accusation which had come to him, containing the names of 'many people,' and explains to the emperor that 'Many people of every age, of every station, and of both sexes, expose themselves to the danger of the severest accusations and will continue to do so in the future. Not only in the cities, but also in the villages and the country, has the infection of this superstition spread. The temples are already deserted and scarcely attended any more, the solemn sacrifices of the state have not been repeated for a long time, and the sacrificial animals offered for sale find buyers only occasionally.' A very great number of persons may have been brought to trial in accordance with the procedure proposed by Pliny to the emperor. Among the former Christians whom Pliny examined, some declared that they had renounced their Christianity twenty-five years previously. Thus the new faith must have arrived in Bithynia-Pontus before the year 90, and probably it was still earlier—perhaps about 70—that it had penetrated thither. In a comparatively short time then it had had a vigorous development. And several other pieces of evidence indicate that especially in the coastal regions of the Black Sea Christianity had made itself at home and had expanded. Sinope, lying northwest of Amisus, certainly possessed a Christian church: Hippolytus, whose testimony is found in Epiphanius (*Haer.* 42:1), says that the father of the famous heretic Marcion, who removed to Rome about 140, was bishop of Sinope. Two additional sources derive from a later age, yet they permit us to draw an *a posteriori* conclusion as to relationships in the period which we are considering. Perhaps about the year 170 Bishop Dionysius of Corinth wrote several letters, of which Eusebius has preserved a table of contents and fragments. One of

these letters is addressed to 'the Church which dwells as a sojourner in Amastris, together with the churches in Pontus' (Eusebius, *H. E.* iv. 23. 6). In this salutation a metropolitan organization is presupposed for the churches of Pontus, the churches apparently constitute a uniformly organized whole, and the leader among them is the Church of Amastris, situated in the old territory of Paphlagonia. The beginnings of these churches must obviously reach far back before 170, and the metropolitan organization which the salutation of the letter of Dionysius presupposes, argues clearly for a strong and comparatively old Christianity. Lucian's satirical tale, *Alexander*, takes us to a similar neighborhood in Paphlagonia. This prophet and wonder worker lived about 100-170 and practised his arts in his home city Abonuteichus, a not inconsiderable place on the Paphlagonian coast. When opposition on the part of the educated people arose against him and his healing god, Asclepius Glycon, he attempted to intimidate his enemies by saying—according to Lucian's account—that Pontus was full of atheists and Christians who had dared to utter the most abusive slanders against him; his followers, if they wished to be participants in the grace of the god, must drive these people out with stones (*Alexander* 25). If the words were first placed in Alexander's mouth by Lucian, nevertheless they indicate the point of view which Lucian, who wrote the book soon after 180, had regarding the position of Christianity in Pontus.

6. The three churches of Laodicea, Hierapolis, and Colossae, which even in their origin were closely connected with each other, lay in the province of *Phrygia*, the western part of which belonged politically to *Asia proconsularis* and the eastern part to Galatia. In Phrygia we must assume a relatively strong and early development of Christianity, which, as it appears, spread—just as it did in Bithynia-Pontus—beyond the cities and through the lowlands. To be sure, we can only infer this from sources which arose later than 130. The reports may however be grouped together here, since they permit *a posteriori* conclusions regarding our period of time. In the year 155 or 156 the Church of Smyrna gave the Church of Philomelium a report on the persecution in which its bishop, Polycarp, and several members of the church sacrificed their lives: *The Martyrdom of Polycarp*. Philomelium lies on the eastern border of Phrygia, in the so-called *Phrygia paroreios*, and is a rather small inland town. In the churches of Phrygia, soon after 150, Montanus appeared with his preaching, and the movement which began with

him presupposes a fairly large expansion of Christianity not merely in the cities, but in the villages of Phrygia as well. In the history of ancient Montanism there emerge the first Christian village churches which are designated by names: Comane in Phrygia and Ardabau in Mysia, bordering on Phrygia (Apollinaris in Eusebius, *H. E.* v. 16. 7,17).

7. *Paulinism in Asia.* From the survey which we have just made we see that the presence of Christianity in our period of time can be demonstrated for all the provinces of Asia Minor. In certain of them, such as Cappadocia, we can recognize only evanescent and scanty traces, but in others we see at a glance that there has been a somewhat surprising development. It was especially in the *Province of Asia* that we were able to see Christianity as firm and expanding. We return to this province, which is most easily visible to us, and take up the question of whether we can establish the permanent operation of Paul's preaching and spirit in the Christianity of these churches which he founded, whether we can look upon the churches as still 'Pauline' in the period between the death of the Apostle and the journey of Ignatius to Rome. Against this a very important voice is raised; it speaks of a 'destruction of Paul's creation,' of a 'new building on the ruins of the Pauline work.' [5] If we examine the facts, we must declare that this idea is not confirmed by the sources. We know nothing either of a breakdown or of a new foundation. There does not exist the slightest trace of evidence to show that the Church of Ephesus to which the apocalyptist writes is any different from that of St. Paul, and Ignatius expressly confirms this identification when he calls the Ephesians 'fellow-initiates of Paul' (Eph. 12:2). To be sure, the Johannine writings never make mention of Paul (a fact which is not to be wondered at); the author of First Peter speaks in the name of St. Peter to the Christians of Asia Minor, as if this were the regular ecclesiastical jurisdiction and mission field of another 'Apostle.' And if on the other hand the author of the Epistle to the Ephesians actually thought of Ephesus as the destination of his epistle, and the epistles to Timothy presuppose that Ephesus was the permanent jurisdiction of St. Paul, it is not, of course, proved that in actuality the churches of this province had maintained the Pauline tradition. But —to be specific—in what sense had it been maintained? In what way should one think of that continuity which is denied by one

[5] Weizsäcker, *Das Apostolische Zeitalter*, pp. 493-497; Engl. ed., *The Apostolic Age*, ii, 161-166.

party and upheld by the other? How did a destruction ensue? Perhaps the churches in general underwent a cessation of activity. But no trace of such a thing exists. Or were there, perhaps, teachers who were oriented altogether differently, who took the place of Paul, teachers who consciously uprooted the memory of the founder and of his teaching? This is a question which, as soon as it is asked, must be answered in the negative. If, however, the results of the Apostle's work were appropriated by teachers with essentially similar ideas, it is hardly to be assumed that on that account they had bound the churches, so to speak, to the personality and special teaching of the Apostle. The idea of a Pauline school, maintained in orthodoxy, must obviously be abandoned. By the nature of things, exactly that teaching which we are wont to regard as 'specifically Pauline,' such as that of justification by faith and victory over the Law, must recede into the background, in proportion as its occasion, viz. the claims of legalistic Judaism, was a thing of the past. Now this was actually the case in Asia. Likewise the requirement of circumcision was no longer maintained after the Council of the Apostles. In any case we notice no effort in this direction either in the Apocalypse or in the Gospel of John. In one point, to be sure, the demand of Jerusalem appears to have been successful: in Asia Minor the Apostolic Decree was in force; to particularize, there can be no doubt that the use of meat from idolatrous sacrifices belonged, along with unchastity, to the class of great scandals which were forbidden in Christian congregations (Rev. 2:14,20,24f; 3:4). But if St. Paul did not publish the decree (pp. 267ff, 311ff), it is also true that he did not stand opposed in principle to its essential content (I Cor. 10:7f; cf. pp. 311ff, 325f). One can in no wise picture it as a victory of legalistic Judaism and a suppression of the Pauline gospel when the decree is recognized as valid in Asia. And so it also follows that the circumcision of Gentile Christians and the imposition of the whole Law are abandoned. Thus we need not wonder, when—either because of peace concluded or victory won—the wartime phraseology no longer appears. In proportion as the *anti-Judaistic* points of Paulinism receded into the background, the *anti-Judaists* appeared more prominently than ever. St. Paul had, in general, more love and understanding for his abandoned and deluded people than for the 'false brethren' of the circumcision. The struggle with them sets him in motion more vigorously (in Galatians) than does the break with Judaism (in Romans), which was occasioned by a pacific purpose and the hope of a final conversion and understanding. But as the struggle with Judaizers came to be quieted, the struggle with Judaism became more vehement. And so we find, e.g. in the epistles of the Apocalypse and in the Gospel of John, a sharpening of judgment upon the Jews which could not be surpassed in severity and certainly went far beyond that of Paul. The author of the apocalyptic letters, although he is a Jew by birth, as his name and his language show, has yet broken completely with his people: 'Them which say they are Jews, and they are not, but are a synagogue of Satan' (2:9; 3:19); they have forfeited the rights and the title of honor of God's people and lost them to the Christians, to whom have been transferred (1:6,9; 5:10; 20:6) the name of 'holy people,' the 'royal power' and the 'priesthood' (Ex. 19:6). Only an *exactly-reckoned* chosen number from the twelve tribes of Israel (cf. Rom. 11:7), sealed with the seal of God, will escape the judgment (Rev. 7:4-8), while the innumerable multitude of those who are purchased by the blood of the Lamb are *from all peoples and tongues* (5:9f; 7:9—this is one of the ideas of the basic Johannine document; cf. SNT on 7:9), and constitute the nucleus of the Church. The author stands thus, with the fullest self-consciousness, on the ground of the Gentile Christian Church. Still more of course is this the case with the Johannine Gospel, which is permeated with anti-Jewish polemic and calls down a destructive, hopeless judgment upon the 'Jews'; they are simply the 'world,' which remains in darkness and has laid upon itself a double guilt, since in the past it has not received him who came unto his own, and since now it persecutes his own, who are not of the world, with all the world's hatred (cf. e.g. 15:20—16:2; 1:11; 3:20; 3:36; 5:40; 8:23,49; 9:22).

If one wishes to corroborate the 'Paulinism' of these two Asia Minor documents by reference to literary dependence upon the Pauline letters which have been preserved, it is true that one will obtain no overwhelming results.[6] Certainly much contact in details is indicated, although not to the same extent as in Ignatius' case. But one should assume, as a matter of course, that a possible after-effect of St. Paul's ministry would be shown less in a literary way than in the fact that a certain mode of thought and feeling which is characteristic of the personality and activity of Paul, would prove itself to be alive here. And this is actually the case. Thus the same cosmological-Christological viewpoint as that of St. Paul dominates

[6] The list which Holtzmann-Bauer gives in the *Handkommentar* (3rd ed.), iv, p. 412, requires reëxamination: it contains much which is inconclusive.

the Johannine writings. It may be accidental that in Rev. 1:5; 3:14, both the expressions are reminiscent of Col. 1:18,15: the first-born of the dead and of all creatures; in any case, however, the Pauline 'cosmological Christology' of I Cor. 8:5f and Col. 1:15ff is repeated in John (1:2):

> All things came into being through him
> And without him has nothing come into being;
> That which is, is life only in him,
> And this life shone as light to men.

Here we meet[7] even the same precise distinction of expression between the past act of creation (aorist) and the present condition of the world (perfect) as in Col. 1:15f and 17 (on this point cf. pp. 480f). And if the Logos idea lies at the basis of the Pauline theology, then this expression is a proper name in John 1:1 and Rev. 19:13. But certainly the cosmological Christology, indeed even the Logos concept, plays no great rôle in the Gospel, to say nothing of the Apocalypse. In the latter the Logos name is found but once, and then only in the non-pregnant form of 'the Word of God' (19:13). And the Gospel begins, it is true, in the prologue, with the Logos concept, but one cannot say that it enlarges upon the ideas implicit in it or makes further use of them; at any rate, it never returns to the concept, it is only built—to say the very most—on the foundations of this mode of thought. The same thing is true of the idea of the sacrificial death of Christ. One must regard as significant the appearance of the immolated lamb and the idea, repeated several times, of the redemption of Christians by a sacrificial death (Rev. 1:5; 5:9f; 7:14; 14:3f), besides the word of the Baptist on the Lamb of God (John 1:29,36) and the death of Jesus as the paschal lamb (19:37), the view that Jesus was an expiatory sacrifice (I John 2:2; 4:10, ἱλασμός) and that his blood (I John 1:7; 5:6f; Rev. 1:5; 7:14; 19:13) was the specific means of cleansing and redemption—all of which repeats Pauline expressions or stands on an even line of development with them (e.g. I Cor. 5:7; 7:23; Rom. 3:25; 5:9)—even if, on the whole, in the Johannine theology another type of salvation idea replaces the truly 'soteriological' or 'redemption type,' viz. the 'revelation type.'

But in spite of all this there can be no doubt that the Johannine

[7] To be sure, only in the reading which underlies the passage above, which, however, has its point in this phrase: ὃ γέγονεν . . . . ἐστίν—The variation of the translation chosen here from that offered on p. 481 is intentional.

doctrine and religion stand in general on the basis of Pauline ideas and formulae, and that they draw out further the lines laid down by St. Paul. One need call attention only to two important facts of observation: the nearly complete replacement of eschatology by the present realization of salvation (e.g. John 3:17-21; 5:24; I John 3:14) is a continuation of the anticipation of salvation in the Christian community, which is so strongly and keenly stamped upon Paul; the 'being' and 'abiding' in Jesus, of which John speaks so often, appears as an express and conscious repetition of Pauline formulae (e.g. I John 2:6); the manner in which salvation is connected, finally, with the person of Christ and fellowship with him, is a development of Pauline piety and theology; in the idea and experience of the Spirit and his workings, Paul also leads the way for the Fourth Gospel.

The enduring quality of Paulinism in Asia, and the undiminished esteem, the high reverence paid the great Apostle, may be recognized from still other observations. We can hardly place the origin of the Epistle to the Ephesians and the Pastoral Epistles, as well as the writing which we have under the name of First Peter, in any place other than Asia, and more exactly in the province of Asia. Ephesians and the Pastorals bear the name of St. Paul and expound in a more or less modified form the theology of the Apostle as well; and First Peter, although it purports to be written by the head of the primitive Christian circle, at any rate carries on the Pauline piety and theology and possibly stands closer to the true type of Paulinism than does Ephesians. We thus see that after the death of Paul the men of his school were zealous, and exerted themselves effectively, to hold high the authority of their master and to increase widely the effect of his personality and words. And with what inspired words, with what a great sweep of expression, does Ignatius call the Ephesians back to remembrance of their founder and supreme model (Eph. 12:2); in what great measure does Polycarp of Smyrna use the Pauline letters in writing to the Philippians! One sees, however, quite evidently in him, how truly and zealously he—and of course his church as well—continues to preserve the inheritance from his highly honored teacher and theirs. If one holds up before oneself all these observations on the enduring effect of St. Paul and the great esteem felt for him in Asia itself, one cannot very well speak of the destruction of the Pauline mission and a new Johannine foundation.

8. We have just now drawn the *Gospel of John* within the scope of our study. We cannot continue further to picture Asiatic Chris-

tianity in the post-Pauline age without considering somewhat more exactly this contribution—beyond doubt unique and valuable—which Asia made to early Christian literature. We shall not take up here the very difficult question of authorship. We shall deal only generally and in a few brief lines with the character and purpose of the book and the artistic method of its execution, as well as with the piety and world-view which are comprehended in its views of God and Christ.[8]

In our view the work is not in its original form, but has reached us after having been *worked over*. This follows obviously from chapter 21, especially from the conclusion of the chapter. The man who wrote the appendix edited the whole work, and this occurred in fact only after the death of the author. He writes 21:24 in the name of a wider circle which still had known the 'disciple.' From the redactor comes 13:23, in which the disciple is more exactly designated as the one whom Jesus had loved; furthermore, the passages 19:26f, 35; 20:2-10 derive from him; and 1:40ff and 20:24-29 may come from his hand as well. By means of these passages the legend of the Beloved Disciple, which was thus deepened psychologically, gained admission into the gospel itself. The hand of the redactor is to be traced in a long series of passages in the text itself, in sundry comments, developments of the Lord's sayings, and explanations of them; the re-working is especially to be noticed in the farewell speech of Jesus to his disciples (cf. the commentary on chh. 13-17 in SNT), yet in the opening chapters it palpably comes to light: 1:24; 4:2,9b,46,54; 1:6-9,14; 1:20,21a,25; 3:28; 7:41a; 8:24b; 5:34; 3:5f,8c,11c,13c; 6:36-40,44-48; 10:6f,9f,16,18,26-29; 12:39f; 4:20-26,37f; 6:51b-58. It is quite possible, nay probable, that the redactor inserted whole passages, such as perhaps the marriage of Cana, the cripple at the pool of Bethesda, the man born blind, or the raising of Lazarus and the anointing of Jesus. From all this it follows that the basic gospel narrative was much briefer than the book which lies before us. Yet on the other hand the original writing and the redactor stand close to each other; both have forms

[8] The whole problem which the Gospel of John poses finds a good and generally comprehensible treatment in the detailed introduction which Heitmuller, in *SNT,* places before his translation of the gospels; cf. besides, J. Weiss, "Literaturgeschichte des Neuen Testaments" (*Religion in Geschichte und Gegenwart,* iii), especially pp. 2199ff. [*Translator's Note.* E. F. Scott, *The Fourth Gospel,* is still standard, though written some years ago. For a brief bibliography, see F. C. Grant, *The Growth of the Gospels,* pp. 200f. An interesting treatment of the occasion for the gospel is found in E. C. Colwell, "The Fourth Gospel and the Struggle for Respectability," *Jour. of Religion,* xiv (1934), 286-305.]

of piety, religious experience, and religious style which are closely related. The foundation document, fully complete in itself, which ends at 20:30f, tells its story from a Jerusalemite standpoint; of Jesus' Galilean period it gives only the beginning and the end in 4:43—6:71. If the author was a disciple (1:14; 18:15) he was not one of the Galileans who had journeyed with Jesus, but a Jerusalemite, who had seen Jesus only when he came to Jerusalem for the feasts.[9] It is possible that he was John Mark, the man to whom people have been wont to attribute the second Gospel. The redaction of the work certainly took place in Asia, where the original writing also probably had its origin.

In other respects the discords and differences within the Gospel ought not to be exaggerated, for it is certain that, looked at from the point of view of the history of religions, the original author and the redacted work, as we have just pointed out, stand quite close one to the other. Around the author of the original work stood the circle of his disciples, influenced by him, and quite congenial to him in spirit. And it was from this circle, with the consent of a majority, that someone took up the work of redaction and edited the whole work; cf. in 21:24 the testimony of his students to the Disciple.

The whole work of the author (and of the redactor as well) is understandable only if one keeps clearly in mind the fact that not only did he know the *Synoptic Gospels,* but he assumes they are in his readers' hands. The Fourth Gospel is not written as a sort of substitute for the other three, but to supplement them. Only if one keeps this in view can one explain the way in which the baptism of Jesus, for example, or his Galilean ministry, is recounted. These things are simply presupposed as well-known to the readers. It is to be noticed all the more when the gospel diverges quite consciously and obviously from the account of the Synoptists and emphasizes the digression. Such a procedure perhaps lies before us in 18:12f: Jesus is first led before Annas, while in 18:24 the author returns to the synoptic picture and invites the readers to insert in this place the account of the trial before Caiaphas, which was known to him from study of the other gospels, but which the Fourth Gospel itself does not report. But in the very places where the author systematically improves upon the Synoptic presentation, as perhaps in the chronology of the Passion Narrative and in the shifting of the date of Jesus' death, or elsewhere in the further lengthening in the whole

[9] [*Translator's Note.* Cf. B. W. Bacon, *The Gospel of the Hellenists,* pp. 166-175, 196-215, 397-409.]

chronological framework, in 3:24, he does not actually engage in dispute, but he relates affairs as he knows them, he places the cleansing of the Temple at the beginning of the public ministry of Jesus, and with the various journeys of Jesus to Jerusalem he describes a festal cycle—since it can be nothing less than this which is intended. An attack upon the Synoptists on this point is entirely out of the question for him, of course, since the author neither could nor would supplant these older writings from their use in the churches.[10] Certainly there are a great number of things which do not concern him at all, and on this account he does not relate them; but this very fact shows that they nevertheless remain accessible to him and to his readers. Thus his omission of the Last Supper is not to be explained on the ground that he wished to exclude it; he must reckon with the fact that the Eucharist, in spite of his silence, would continue to be celebrated according to the example which the synoptic account had set. In the story of the anointing of Jesus the editor shows himself to be completely dependent upon the synoptic texts, whereas the cleansing of the Temple, the story of the son of the royal official, the feeding, the entrance into Jerusalem, the Passion Narrative and the accounts which follow it, point to a picture which has been only partly influenced by the Synoptists, and on the whole, an independent separate tradition has been preserved. The possession of such independent records would certainly however have been an inducement to the author to write nothing. Thus he must have had an interest in the chronology of the life of Jesus which was lacking in the Synoptists. In offering this chronological framework he simply allowed himself to be led by the necessity of imparting these facts of the case, as they were known to him—without 'tendency' or theology.

How did the Gospel reach its object of edifying and teaching? It is not correct for one to emphasize too strongly this evidential purpose. The author intends to affect the understanding less than the emotions; he does not work with proofs. Instead he intends to produce a strong impression; he is by no means a mere theologian, to a certain degree he is an artist as well. Not only is the material which he has to impart important in making the impression, but the *form of presentation*, the tone of the story and its language, are also of especial importance. This tone is completely unique and has

[10] [*Translator's Note.* It has been suggested by E. J. Goodspeed, *The Formation of the New Testament*, pp. 33-41, that the four-gospel corpus was first collected for the purpose of giving currency to the Fourth Gospel, which found difficulty in maintaining itself alone.]

been effective to this present day. He is not absolutely and universally attractive to all readers; to many the pure naïveté and naturalness of the synoptic picture and its coloring, which is richer in variety, are more sympathetic. Yet the priestly solemnity and sublimity of the Johannine picture make a deep impression upon most people. No one could remain unimpressed by the tone of the prologue: here speaks one who is deeply caught by great, sublime, mysterious matters which he proclaims like a priest and a prophet.[11]

To look at it more precisely, the purposes of the presentation are attained by relatively simple means. A great uniformity of style runs through the whole work. Construction of sentences and connection between sentences are very simple. The sentences are very simply linked to each other by 'and' in homely and popular narrative style, while occasionally they follow one another without any syndeton whatever. Parallelism of members, of similar or contrasting pairs joined together, is a favorite device. In all these features

[11] Here we may attempt to approach the original form of the Johannine prologue, omitting the later redaction to which we have referred above, and to translate it. The attempt was made by J. Weiss and I ought not to withhold it from the wide circle of readers which this book will have.

In the beginning was *He,* the eternal 'Word;'
In God's mind was the 'Word,'
From God's being came the 'Word;'
Thus he was in the beginning with God.

All things came into being through him
And without him has nothing come into being.
That which is, is life only in him,
And this life shone as light to men.

Thus the light shines now in the darkness,
Yet the darkness has never received it.
He is the soul of the world, which first came into being through him,
And yet it has never recognized him.

Once he came to his own,
But his own received him not;
But whoever has willingly received him,
To him has he given power to become God's child.

Then the 'Word' became flesh and dwelt among us,
We saw his glory, that of the only-begotten Son,
Of the Father's fulness, rich in grace and truth;
From his fulness we became rich in grace and by grace.

Moses gave the Law—grace and truth came through Jesus Christ:
No one has seen God at any time,
The only-begotten, God by nature, child of the Father's bosom,
He has revealed him to us.

[*Translator's Note.* Cf. a similar attempt by F. C. Grant, in *The Growth of the Gospels,* p. 220.]

we may be permitted to recognize the influence of the Jewish origin of the author, a result of his Semitic feeling for style, although the last word on this question has by no means been spoken, since similar observations may be made respecting Greek hieratic style as well.

A characteristic way of thinking runs through the *historical narrative* as John presents it to us. Salvation is for him not at all a thing which is entirely—or even predominantly—in the future, but it is already to be apprehended in the present in union with the exalted Christ. For this reason it is in no wise the sole aim of the author to chronicle bare history. To be sure, like Mark he intends to prove from the life of Jesus that he was the Son of God; he now emphasizes more strongly that Jesus in becoming man has not laid aside divine glory (1:14). He intends however to illustrate by the deeds, as well as the words, of Jesus, that for believers he is permanently the source of life. In the Incarnate One he gazes upon the Exalted One, and he animates the portrait of the Exalted One by the picture of the Incarnate. Thus the whole narrative becomes for him a chain of 'signs' and he becomes the expositor of the religious history which he relates. In what sense he interprets the life of Jesus he explains in the prologue; cf. especially 1:18—he who wishes to see God, whom no one has ever seen, may look at the Son; cf. also 14:9—'He who has seen me, has seen the Father.' Thus the author places himself in a position near that of Philo, who makes use of the lives of Abraham, Joseph and Moses, in order to prove ethical truths by them. But as in Philo the history lies at the base and it is taken seriously in its literal sense, along with its deeper import, and thus one would profoundly misunderstand John if one were to deny completely that he had the aim of writing history. The signs and wonders take place as actual occurrences, except that at the same time, as it were behind them, there is placed a deeper meaning. It is for this reason that they are 'signs.' In chapters 9 and 11 the author quite obviously allegorizes, yet his purpose is at the same time completely clear, viz. that of narrating sufficiently and circumstantially the unheard-of wonders which have occurred. And as for the saying about the bread of life—in what connections with the messianic insurrection, the walking on the sea, the demand for signs, does it stand? One sees clearly here that the allegorical interpretation of the story is introduced for the first time, while the group of narratives in the context did not arise from an allegorical motive. The question becomes a vital one when we come to the marriage at Cana. The allegorical sense is so apparent here, the origin of the story so difficult to demonstrate as coming from the doctrinal ideas—diverse enough as they are—which are found in it, and yet the allegorical interpretation of all the separate details leads us into great absurdities. There is quite evidently an apologetic character in the Pilate story; yet it would be too much to maintain that one could explain the course of all its arguments purely by reference to apologetic purposes. On the whole, as we have already made plain, the purpose of John is unmistakably that of telling the story sufficiently and completely, and partly as a supplement to the Synoptics.

The *speeches* of the Gospel display a uniform style, which reminds us quite strongly of the Johannine epistles. The same coloring noticeable in the speeches of Jesus is found also in the words of the Baptist and the prologue. This is at once a proof that the words of Jesus have at least passed through the crucible of the author's mode of thought and have been recast in his own style. In contrast to the richness of the synoptic speeches both in expression and illustration, this style is poor and monotonous. The monotony is heightened still more by the fact that instead of concise sayings or rounded-off groups of sayings, we observe a theme repeatedly contemplated from new angles and drawn out into a longer discourse, without being able to perceive a development; cf. the idea which is continually presented, 'abide in me,' 15:4a,b,5ff. Perhaps the overemphasis and monotony would appear less important if one could succeed with some certainty in separating the re-working from the basic text. But even if one does not attempt to identify the redactional material, yet one can clearly recognize that in many speeches of the Gospel of John, and indeed in its original form, certain underlying words or themes are in their context played upon with variations in a quite simple way. Thus in 15:1-11 there lies at the base an actual parable of the vine and its branches, which is, however, completely allegorized and given a new meaning, and in this way overlaid and concealed. Another metaphor is in 10:1-21, in which the picture of the Good Shepherd is painted in a broad and beautiful form, and then is explained as having two meanings, in vv. 7-10, and more deliberately in vv. 11-18. Since we find parabolic words of Jesus on the good and true shepherd, on the flock, on the lost and sought-for sheep, in existence in the Synoptics as well; since furthermore a saying such as that in 3:3, 'Except a man be born anew, he cannot see the kingdom of God,' has a strongly synoptic ring, one may suppose that John often draws the brief themes of his discourses from the tradition and then twines his own meditations round and round these nuclear words in artistic fashion. To express it figuratively, grains of gold from Jesus' sayings are hammered out by the evangelist and employed as gold foil upon the shrine which he is making. As passages which exhibit parables, possibly from an older tradition, we can name besides the two already mentioned: 3:8,27; 4:36; 8:35; 11:9; 12:24; 16:21; for examples of nuclear words and fundamental themes, cf. also 5:17ff and 6:32f, 35b; and for contacts with sayings in the Synoptics, 2:19; 4:44; 5:8; 12:25f; 13:16 and 15:20; 13:20; 14:31; 16:32; 18:11; 20:23.

But everything which John gives us as sayings of Jesus has in any case passed through his own mind, and in by far the larger part of this material we hear only the evangelist himself speaking. And under the monotone of his words we perceive clearly the strong stream of a mysterious experience rushing along. That is perhaps the highest art of his style, that he understands how to suggest the inexpressible, how to set the minds of his hearers, who have advanced to the stage of believing and knowing, to vibrating in unison with the tones which he sounds, and to expand their inner consciousness with the mystery of their religion. A very important means for attaining this end is to work out strongly the mysterious element in the earthly life of Jesus. That which is obscure in the sayings of Jesus is strongly emphasized by the frequent misunderstandings of his disciples. In a quite deliberate and artistic manner the reader's suspense is aroused by the first silent appearance of Jesus—1:29, 37,39. In 2:24 Jesus confides in no one. One observes further the enigmatical and obscure in the behavior of Jesus, as it is pictured in 7:6,9f. It attains a stronger expression above all in the resurrection narratives: Jesus is unapproachable and untouchable (20:17); only doubting Thomas may handle him, and he bursts out, in the confession which comprises once for all the content of the whole gospel, 'My Lord and my God!' (20:27f). One may observe further the beautiful, deep, rhythmical repetition, 'Peace be with you' in 20:19,21,26, and the mysteriously powerful detail of his breathing upon them (20:22). Elsewhere in the gospel the unapproachableness of Jesus is emphasized; cf. 7:30,44,46; 8:20,59; 9:39; and especially 18:4-9.

Furthermore the portrayal of the Passion must be recognized as quite successful. This Son of God does not passively endure his fate, but goes to it with head held high, in order to fulfil the Scriptures.

His death indeed signifies nothing more than victory made certain, his glorification, his return to the Father (13:31; 16:33; 17:1). Therefore he himself brings about his own death when he incites Judas to betray him (13:27). The portrayal of Jesus' kingly bearing before Annas and Pilate is wonderfully successful. Here the synoptic line is followed, but his royal grandeur is enhanced (as one may observe, e.g. in 18:37ff; observe further the contrast employed in the *Ecce homo*, the silence of Jesus, his final answer in 19:1-11, and finally the lordly τετέλεσται, which replaces Mark's cry from the cross).

The purpose of this portrayal is given by the author of the Gospel—more precisely by the author of the foundation document, but the redactor has let the declaration stand and has accepted it (observe the parallels, 21:25 and 20:30)—at the conclusion of the book itself: Jesus did many other signs for his disciples, which are not noted down in this book. These are written *that thereby you may believe* that Jesus the Christ is *Son of God*, and that by this faith you may have life in his name (20:30f). It is noteworthy that in these words the readers of the book are addressed as 'you.' Use is not made of such an expression as 'all believers' or any similarly general designation which would imply that the work must seek its own reading public; but the readers appear to be a restricted group: the author knows them and they know him. 'In order that you may believe,' says the passage which we have quoted. By this expression it cannot be meant that the readers are not yet converted to faith in Jesus and that this book is to serve that purpose. The book does not bear the character of missionary writing at all; too much knowledge of the person, life and teaching of Jesus is presupposed for this to be the case. It can thus be concerned only with the advancement, deepening, strengthening and enlightening of faith. In the portrayal given by the book we read over and over that the disciples themselves, who from the beginning believe in Jesus, nevertheless constantly 'believe' anew (2:11; 11:15; 13:19). Faith according to the Johannine view is, moreover, not the once-for-all believing reception of glad tidings, but includes an ever new and deepened knowledge and self-abasement: the faithful shall come to recognize truth ever more truly and deeply.

In the passages quoted the content of faith is indicated in a twofold declaration which, however, in essence derives from the same thing: Jesus is the *Christ* and he is the *Son of God*. The former is the honorific title of Jesus, which is emphasized as against Judaism, and since the Gospel, as we shall sufficiently see, comes to some understanding with Judaism, the title bears its original meaning. Yet it has, in spite of 4:22, lost to a great extent its national meaning, and its political meaning is completely lost (cf. especially 18:36, 'My kingdom is not of this world'). Nevertheless the designation appears in the mouth of the Baptist (1:20,25f; 3:28f), of the disciples (1:41; 11:27), and of the Samaritan woman (4:25). In the controversial discourses with the Jews it is also used (cf. 7:26-42). The thread which joins Judaism and Christianity is thus not broken off at this point.[12]

Yet the name which is much more characteristic of John and which lies incomparably nearer his heart is that of the Son of God, which appears also with the more exact designation μονογενής, 'only-begotten,' i.e. the sole one of his kind, the υἱὸς κατ' ἐξοχήν, *par excellence*. The awakening of faith in Jesus as God's Son—that is, according to his own statement and understanding, is the meaning and purpose of the Gospel. And thus in a word the contents of the gospel may be defined as the gospel which begins with the Logos, who is God by nature, and ends with Thomas' confession, 'My Lord and my God.' The religion of John may be described as a faith, which is directed toward Jesus, the Son of God, as mediator of salvation. It is he who has brought the perfect revelation of God, a revelation which is definitive and requires no supplementation. Above the troubled, confused world, which is judged—as in all mysticism—quite pessimistically, dwells God, unapproachable and indeed seen of none, Spirit, Light, Love. Man cannot of himself attain a view of his being; God, who is Love, who first loved us, must reveal himself. This revelation takes place through the Son of God, the glorious spiritual being, God by nature, who dwells in heaven above, and who was with God before all creation, through whom the world was formed. This Logos, this only-begotten, has now become flesh in Jesus Christ, and thereby the perfect revelation of God, not to be surpassed, has been secured; God himself has been made manifest

[12] In this connection it is quite important to observe that the very old designation, Son of Man (cf. above, pp. 126-129), also appears in the Gospel of John, and in a very ancient use as well, which preserves a reminiscence of the heavenly being, his glorification, and his office as judge; cf. 1:51; 3:13f; 5:27; 6:27,53,62; 8:28; 12:23,34; 13:31. If anything is important for the decision of the question, whether and to what extent John stands in immediate connection with primitive Christianity and the Palestinian circle, it is this observation, that he still speaks of the Son of Man. Another very old Messianic designation, which John repeats, is that of the 'holy one of God' (6:69, in Peter's confession; cf. Mark 1:24).

in his Son: 'He that hath seen me hath seen the Father.' On this account the works of Jesus are also God's works, and his deeds God's deeds, and during his earthly life the Son of God gave proof of uninterrupted, superhuman divine knowledge and divine power.

His revelation is completed especially in his *message*, as it is presented by the Gospel. His words are spirit and life (6:63). In the preaching of Jesus throughout the Fourth Gospel it is not the Kingdom of God and its righteousness which have the central position (as in the Synoptics), but it is he himself, the Son of God. He gives testimony before the world, of himself and his nature, which are not of the world. His words remain misunderstood; the deep complaint of all mystics against the world's darkness and lack of understanding, we hear uttered again in the Johannine gospel. Those who can comprehend him, the circle of believers whom he himself has chosen, are only a few, and these are gradually made manifest by the Spirit.

The other revelation which the Son of God presents consists in his *signs*. In these his omnipotence makes itself known; through the outward, obvious happening shine forth divine being and divine glory, the deeds disclose to the knowing and believing ones, by their occurrence; celestial and spiritual happenings. The wonders which the Gospel of John relates are in nearly every case of another sort than those reported by the Synoptists, and even the evangelist's means of portrayal have become partly different and more forceful. In the healing of the ruler's son, it is the coincidence regarding the hour and the working of Jesus' will upon the far-off sick person which is emphasized; in the feeding of the multitude Jesus himself takes the initiative, in the story of the cripple the long duration of the illness is brought into prominence, the blind man is blind from birth, Lazarus' body has already begun to decompose, and the marriage of Cana is a nature-miracle of the most striking kind. Another thing which must not be overlooked is this: the wonders are, for the evangelist, not so much kind actions, not even merely portentous deeds of power (δυνάμεις), but they are in fact 'signs,' revelations of Jesus' godhead and of his δόξα τοῦ θεοῦ ('glory of God'). This comes to the fore most strikingly of all in the three chief miracles which are new to John and have no parallels in the Synoptics. At the marriage of Cana no need is supplied, the man born blind was born blind for the very purpose of making the glory of God manifest to him, and Lazarus must die 'that you may believe,' indeed Jesus rejoices that he had not been present to hinder his death (11:15). In the 'signs' there is thus a characteristic feature of the mystery of Jesus; it is the signs especially which permit his 'glory' to shine through, a glory which is full of grace and truth. And the Son of God has given and bequeathed still another revelation. This is accomplished in *sacrament*. The church in which and for which the gospel was written knows Baptism and the Eucharist. It is in suggestive and exalted words that John speaks of baptism. It is a new generation, a birth from above, and it is by both water and the Spirit; it is a miracle which cannot be comprehended by him who has not experienced it (3:3-13). It is as certain that John's view of baptism, which lies at the base of this, is not characteristic of him alone, as it is that the words have nevertheless a singular delicacy and beauty. In 1:33; 3:22 and 4:2f, baptism is also mentioned, but in those passages nothing new and unique is added. Why the institution of the Eucharist is not related by the evangelist we can by no means discover. But in the long discussion which is appended to the miracle of the feeding, Jesus is obviously speaking about the Lord's Supper (cf. especially the working out of the idea following the question in 6:52). The flesh of the Son of Man is eaten in the Eucharist, his blood is drunk. Yet sacramental religion is not absolutely the last word for John; instead it belongs most clearly to mysticism, i.e. to inner experience. One must read the development of the idea of eating and drinking in connection with the whole sixth chapter.

In John there is surprisingly little concern with the great work which Jesus, according to the Pauline view, accomplished by his *death*. The death is an exaltation; he returns to the Father from whom he came. And at this point appears the Advocate, *the Holy Ghost*. Only with him does the whole truth appear to believers. The revelation of Jesus is the beginning; the Spirit is the end and the climax. Jesus has gone away from the disciples; the Spirit will remain with them for all time (14:17). He will remind them of what Jesus has said (14:26), and still more, he will complete that which Jesus could not say to his own while he was on earth: 'I have yet many things to say unto you, but ye cannot bear them now. Howbeit when he, the Spirit of truth, is come, he shall guide you into all the truth . . . . he taketh of mine, and shall declare it unto you' (16:12-15). And finally, what is perhaps the most important: in the coming of the Spirit, the Father and the Son come to the believer, and they take up their dwelling in him (14:23). Yet the Spirit remains connected with Jesus; from what belongs to Jesus he is to take and proclaim it to those who believe; he speaks that which he has heard and does not speak on his own behalf (16:13f). The mysticism which is here expressed is consciously bound up with the Church and stands under Jesus' influence.

It is clear that a piety which is experienced in the way described here must have views of salvation which are essentially different from those of the earliest Christian circles. Here we again come upon the most conspicuous peculiarity of the Gospel of John. The old eschatology taken over from Judaism is abandoned, except that it is still—without being reconciled at all—retained along with the new views, since it was offered to the faithful by the Church's tradition (cf. 5:28f in this connection), and the Kingdom of God appears only in one passage, which sounds quite ancient in contrast to the context, viz. 3:3,5. Otherwise salvation is shifted from the future to the present, the hope is a secure possession enjoyed in the present, and heaven, hell, judgment and resurrection are gradually and certainly—though not without some traces of the old view—reinterpreted spiritually. The gospel in three places comes to speak in solemn, remarkably brilliant and rather full expression, of the present quality of the expected salvation, viz. in 3:16-21; 5:19-29; 12:44-48. It is not for judgment that the Son has come, but for redemption; therefore he who believes does not come to the judgment, he is already redeemed and has passed from death directly into eternal life. And when he dies he enters into heaven, the eternal world of light; there is the Father's house, in which there are many abiding places; thither has Jesus gone on before, to prepare a place for his own. Jesus will return (this strong hope of ancient Christianity is retained here), not to reign over a kingdom on earth, but to fetch his own people home to the Father, that where he is they may be also (14:2f; cf. also 17:24).

The relation to Christ through the Spirit, of which we have just spoken, is not however the last and highest goal of the Johannine piety. Every connection with Christ is for it also a connection with God, and in God-mysticism the circle of religious experience is completed. It is Jesus himself who in the gospel, especially in the parting discourse, shows the way to the Father. In communion with Christ and the Spirit, union with the Father is attained. The love which the Father has shown toward the Son includes also love for those who cleave to the Son: 'That they may all be one; even as thou, Father, art in me, and I in thee, that they also may be in us . . . . and the glory which thou hast given me I have given unto them; that they may be one, even as we are one; I in them, and thou in me, that they may be perfected into one; that the world may know that they didst send me, and lovedst them, even as thou lovedst me' (17:21ff); 'In that day ye shall know that I am in my Father, and ye in me, and I in you' (14:20). The divine indwelling is timeless, the union with God through Christ takes place here on this earth, in this life, although the perfection of it is marked out for the future and expected only then, when in the blessed vision of God the complete permeation of the believers with the divine nature will take place, since then they will see God face to face, as he is (I John 3:2).

In this God-mysticism, which is very important to the Johannine piety and is the final conclusion of religious experience, something new to us enters into Christianity. For in St. Paul one can perceive mysticism only in the form and experience of the Christ-life and union with Christ. The new experience involves at once a change in the concept of God, namely a far-reaching spiritualization. It is no longer the old God of Judaism, sketched in corporeal form as a king enthroned in heaven above, but it is the All-Inclusive and All-Upholding one, whom John endeavors, by metaphors and concepts, to grasp: God is Spirit and Light and Love and Truth, this God who never rests, but instead works.

The way toward union with Christ and God is described in John by various words. It is at one time *faith*, which leads to 'truth'; of this we have previously heard (cf. alongside 20:31 the famous saying in 3:15, 'everyone who believes on the Son shall not be lost but shall have everlasting life'; cf. also 1:12; 6:47; 7:38; 8:24; 11:25f; 12:44). Faith in the Son is first of all straightforward confidence in Jesus, then further and in an especial sense faith in his divine mission. For he comes from God and reveals the divine life, which man must accept, and in which man must confide; then man experiences *in the present* the blessedness of being a child of God, and the powers of good awake in him. We recognize in the faith of John the strong after-effects of Pauline piety, although the details all receive a different emphasis and religion is experienced somewhat differently, and although—as the Johannine epistles show us especially—the faith has become very strongly anti-gnostic and ecclesiastical.

Most closely contiguous to faith is *knowledge;* one should note the immediate juxtaposition of the two in 6:69 and 17:8 and in I John 4:16. Yet it is certain that knowledge, of which John speaks as often as he does of faith, is regarded in a number of passages as being something different from faith, and deeper. The most conclusive proof of this is the observation that it is never said by Jesus that he has faith in God, while he often says that he has knowledge of God (7:29; 8:55; 17:25). Where the most inward communion, the most complete permeation with the divine nature, are present, there is no longer faith, but gnosis. This 'knowledge' is moreover a concept and an experience which have grown up on the soil of mysticism.

But as in Paul, there is in John a still higher way, which transcends faith and knowledge, and in which the whole richness and blessedness of the experience of God and Christ is linked together: this is *love*. God has loved the world, the Father has loved the Son, the Son loves the Father, Jesus loved his own unto the end, the faithful love God and they love the brethren, they love their Lord so strongly that they are no longer servants but his friends (15:14f). "Beloved, let us love one another: for love is of God; and every one that loveth is begotten of God, and knoweth God. He that loveth not knoweth not God; for God is love. Herein was the love of God manifested in us, that God hath sent his only begotten Son into the world, that we might live through him. Herein is love, not that we loved God, but that he loved us, and sent his Son to be the propitiation for our sins. Beloved, if God so loved us, we also ought to love one another. No man hath beheld God at any time: if we love one another, God abideth in us, and his love is perfected in us" (I John 4:7-12). With this exhibition of the royal way of love we have arrived at the final and highest point of which John can speak. But here as in other passages it must not be overlooked, that the secure framework in which love is enclosed is the Church describing itself, and that accordingly the love of the brethren simply means love for companions in the faith.

Whence comes the form of Christianity which is displayed before us in the Gospel of John and in that First Epistle of John which is closely connected with it? What are the *sources* from which such a great, quiet and yet deep stream has been poured? This is the most difficult but also the most interesting question regarding the gospel which learning has posed, and it is much more important than the other problem (also quite difficult to solve), that of the author and the circumstances of origin of the work. We wish here to collect and develop certain considerations regarding the sources of the gospel in this narrower sense, the presuppositions of its religion and its conception of the person and work of Jesus, considerations of which we have already spoken above.

To begin with the obvious, the author stands within the Christian community and its tradition. Religious forces and viewpoints which were vital in the Church about the turn of the century could affect him. And these were by no means few. We have already seen that the author knows the Synoptics. The recollection of the picture of Jesus which they display is a vivid one for him; for the miracle stories he depends partly upon the synoptic account; various dominical sayings either from the synoptic or some other ecclesiastical tradition are employed by him; Christ, Messiah, the Son of God, the Son of Man, the Kingdom of God, the Kingdom of Christ, and other phrases, are culled by John from the Church's tradition. We may perhaps also say that the supremely prominent place which love occupies in the mysticism of the gospel, and particularly in Jesus' parting discourses, is indeed conditioned by the central position which love has in the preaching of Jesus. Furthermore we have amply seen that Christianity in its Pauline form of coinage corresponds to the most certain and evident presuppositions of the gospel. I intend merely to make this brief reminder: in the Johannine Christ, in the Christ-mysticism, the Pneuma, universalism, freedom from the Law—in all these very important points Paulinism is reëchoed in John. One can, from this point of view, describe John as the greatest of the Pauline school. Yet of course, 'the smell of Palestinian soil which now and again clings to Paulinism has almost completely evaporated,' the rabbinical note is completely lacking, all has become more timeless, quiet, perhaps also more colorless.

Furthermore Judaism belongs to the presuppositions of the Gospel of John. The author is a native Jew. The continual reference to the Old Testament as the great record of divine revelation proves this immediately, and the principal passage which demonstrates the Jewish origin of the author, 4:22 ('salvation comes from the Jews'), is of such character that it is incomprehensible and unlikely in the mouth of one born a Gentile. On the other hand the author in his interior life has separated himself from Judaism to an extent which is quite seldom to be observed in one who is a Jew by birth—incomparably more so than St. Paul. His judgment upon contemporary and future Judaism is fearfully harsh, his Christ repeatedly and solemnly denies to his compatriots any knowledge of the Father (5:38; 7:28; 8:54f; 15:21; 17:25), the Son of God has come to his own people quite in vain, his own received him not (1:11). We have already seen that the author of the gospel is a universalist; the redeeming work of Christ is meant for the 'world,' not the Jews (3:16; 4:42; 8:12; 9:5; 17:21), and apparently he makes the Gentiles appear as the future bearers of the faith, not only in 10:16, in the prophetic words about the sheep which are not of this fold, but also in 12:20ff, where in a very significant, conclusive passage, he introduces the 'Greeks' who were longing to know Jesus.

But even when John rejects and abandons historic Judaism he still remains under the influence of Judaism, often more than is apparent at first glance. Only it is not autochthonous Judaism but the softened and Hellenized Jewish religion of the diaspora, whose chief representative is a somewhat older contemporary of Jesus and Paul, i.e. Philo of Alexandria. Two chief points may be brought out here: the concept of God in John's gospel is strongly philosophical and Alexandrine. God is Spirit, his worship must be in spirit and truth (4:21-24), he is invisible (6:46). The affinity with Philo is especially strong in the application of the Logos doctrine found in the prologue. One thinks further of the dualism between God and the world, spirit and matter, of the dissolution of all historical phenomena into timeless ideas, which comes to light especially in the Johannine treatment of the Old Testament and the events related in it. All that takes place, the far-away past as well as that which takes place at present in the spiritual realm, has along with its outward course of events (which is the only occurrence in the dull eyes of the unknowing) still another mysterious sense which is coördinate and beneath the surface of things: 'All that is transitory is but an allegory.'

If John was under the spell of these decisive influences as a result of the Judaism of the diaspora, still another question is obviously raised: how determinative had the Hellenism of the age become for him, and which of the extremely vital forces in the spiritually and religiously active epoch of later Hellenism impinged immediately upon him? This question cannot be answered with certainty. Hellenism appears as a very essential component in diaspora Judaism itself, and one can never say certainly whether certain emphases and views of John (and of the other leaders of ancient Christianity as well) take their rise from Judaism or directly from Hellenism and its mixture of Greece and the Orient. But it is quite probable that John as well as Ignatius (cf. pp. 767ff above), was touched directly by Hellenism, and to it and not to diaspora Judaism we must refer the dualism in the world-view, certain angles of Johannine mysticism, including rebirth, and the tying up of the sacraments with pneumatic mysticism.

A very intricate question, which shall merely be stated here, and only briefly, concerns the origin of *technical religious language* in John. Here also very different things meet, and though Jewish and Old Testament influence is obvious here, it is not at all the sole determinant.

Thus it is a rich tradition in which John participates. But all the influences which are derived from it do not constitute, after all, the final and highest thing by which we must explain this gospel which is so exceedingly unique. No one who reads this writing with open eyes and a receptive mind, who associates with it that epistle which is most closely connected with the gospel (viz. First John), can fail to gain the impression that here a very great, unique and peculiarly valuable personality is speaking, a personality which gives testimony to what he has experienced in his inmost soul. John has felt inwardly more than it is possible for him to express, and he can set forth only in pictures that which moves him to the depths. In Jesus, the Son of God, and in union with him, he has ascended the heights in the Spirit which bloweth where it listeth, he has experienced contact with God, and his religion is the completion of Christian mysticism, the foundation of which—so far as we can know—was laid by St. Paul, the post-Pauline development of which may be traced in the Epistle to the Ephesians and in Ignatius. What is distinctive in John is his knowledge of how to bind up this highly-wrought mysticism with the Church and its Lord and also with the sacraments of the Church. Because of this the Gospel became in the following age the most powerful writing of Christianity, if we are to judge by its effects.

9. We return now to the Asiatic church, after our lengthy consideration of the Fourth Gospel. Our sources permit us, up to a certain point, a rather accurate glimpse into its destiny. These churches, in the age with which we have to deal, underwent in various places and in various ways oppressions and *persecutions* from without. The native population, as well as the native and Roman magistrates, interfered with them. If we make this observation we must bear in mind that the Province of Asia, as demonstrated, was the land in which the strongest development of Christianity took place. It is obvious that its forward-moving power gave rise to a reaction. The

other thing which we must bear in mind in explaining the persecutions in Asia Minor, especially in Asia itself, is the fact that Asia was the center of emperor-worship. Nowhere else in the Roman empire did the provincials practise so devotedly and earnestly the cult of *diva Roma* and especially of the divinely-honored emperor. It is precisely in Asia that we can recognize from the inscriptions a characteristic, personally colored piety, so to speak, by which the cities and the province gave expression to their admiration of the empire and their thankfulness for belonging to it and standing under the shelter of the emperor, their saviour and god. The frightful, long-enduring period of poverty, disorder, and internal and external war, came to an end with the enthronement of Augustus. Courage to lead the present life, and hope that in the future as well tranquillity, peace and fortune would predominate, a strong feeling that there had been a new creation of the whole world-order, came to expression in the worship of the divinely honored ruler, a cult which Hellenism had taken over from the Orient, and which had been kept up in the kingdoms of the *diadochi*. With respect to this imperial cult, Christianity in Asia came into collision in a number of places with the municipal authorities.[13]

The chief sources which are at our disposal for a picture of the persecution of Christians in the Asiatic provinces, especially in Asia, are the First Epistle of Peter, the letter of Pliny, and the Apocalypse of John.

The sufferings of the Christians of Asia Minor, to whom First Peter is addressed, are not connected with their refusal to worship the emperor. If this were the case, the epistle would certainly express it more clearly, and it would certainly not speak with such friendship and confidence of the emperor and his governors as it does. The emperor must be honored (2:17), he and his governors are the guardians of justice, and one may not resist them with a clear conscience (2:13f). The epistle does not appear to consider in the least the possibility that the government might promote anything which would be contrary to the conscience of Christians. The sufferings which the churches are now undergoing arise from the hatred of the surrounding world, from the suspicion of the heathen population, which slanders the Christians and calls them great criminals and evil-doers (2:12,15; 3:9,16; 4:4,14,16). The Christians were believed to

[13] With what follows, cf. also J. Weiss, "Kleinasien" in Herzog's *Realenzyklopädie* (3rd ed.), x, pp. 539ff ("der Kaiserkultus"), and his commentary on the Revelation of John in SNT, vol. ii; [S. J. Case, *The Evolution of Early Christianity*, pp. 195-238].

be capable of all sorts of evil, and various reports of crimes which they practised circulated among the people. The *nomen ipsum,* the very name of Christian (cf. below, the letter of Pliny) was severely under suspicion. The author is of the confident hope that Christians will succeed in putting the evil reports to shame and silencing them by their blameless behavior (2:12; 3:13; 4:15). But if in spite of all this, suffering is unavoidable, it must be borne; it is a suffering for righteousness, for the sake of Christ's name (3:14; 4:14,16). Perhaps in the last analysis the authorities are also involved in these troubles, inasmuch as the accusations against the Christians are brought before them and they must decide for acquittal or punishment. But the oppression of the Christians does not proceed originally from the authorities, and the state has in no sense organized a persecution. The chief passage from which one may infer an action of the state against Christians is 4:14-19.

Unfortunately it is not clear from the information in the letter to what extent the condemnation went, nor in detail why the prosecution of Christians took place. In 2:14f hope is expressed that the officials will promptly recognize the true state of affairs and acquit the Christians. Behind this hope stands the experience, namely that often (though not always) the authorities did not honor the demands of the populace, and acquitted the Christians. But in this event it cannot have been a case of refusal to worship the emperor—as soon as this was the question, the persevering Christians must have been condemned—but it must have been a case of accusations of crimes which came under the penal law: according to 4:15 the Christians were classed with murderers and thieves. Secret and shameful deeds, a rebellious spirit, intrigues and many other things may have been laid to their account.

The bitter experiences which the Christians had to undergo were something new to them (4:12); their confidence in the officials still appears to be fairly well unbroken. The periods of opposition may thus have been very brief at first. On the other hand it must be observed that according to the salutation the circle of churches which are addressed is large, and that according to 5:7f the danger of martyrdom threatens not only the wide circle of churches for which the writing is intended, but the sword hangs over all Christians wherever they are dispersed in the world. Nevertheless our first observation, viz. that the sufferings were a novelty, will compel us to place the epistle, not toward the end of Domitian's reign or even in the years of Trajan, but perhaps in the period from 81 to 90. To assume that it belongs in the time of Vespasian or Titus is not unlikely in itself, but in other respects we know nothing of legal action against Christians under the first two Flavians.

Oppression of the Asiatic churches, in fact of those situated in the province of Asia, on account of emperor worship, is exhibited first in the *Apocalypse of John*, which—at least in the portions which are important for this question—arose in the time of Domitian. How precisely it came about that the requirement of worshipping the emperor came to be laid upon Christians in his reign, cannot be clearly explained. We do not know, for example, that Domitian commanded, in some special edict, that the provinces pay divine reverence to himself. But it is well known, and trustworthy tradition says that he considered it of great importance that he be designated as 'lord' and 'god' and that these titles were introduced by him into the language of officials, in the correspondence from him and to him. Suetonius, the imperial biographer, relates of Domitian: "At his remarriage with his divorced wife he said that he had summoned her back to his divine abode (*in pulvinar suum*). He also gladly listened, on the day of the great banquet, to the people in the amphitheatre who were shouting, 'Hail to our Lord and our Lady!' (*domino et dominae feliciter!*) . . . . With similar arrogance he availed himself, when he dictated decrees for his private officials (*procuratores*), of the following words: 'Our Lord and God commands as follows' (*dominus et deus noster hoc fieri jubet*). Thus it became the custom thereafter never to address him otherwise, either orally or in writing" (Suetonius, *Domit.* 13). Examples of this usage are given by Martial, *Epigr.* v. 8. 1, *Edictum domini deique nostri* (Edict of our Lord and God), and Dio Chrysostom, *Orat.* 45:1, τὸν ἰσχυρότατον καὶ βαρύτατον καὶ δεσπότην ὀνομαζόμενον καὶ θεὸν παρὰ πᾶσιν Ἕλλησι παὶ βαρβάροις, 'the mightiest and most severe, who also was called lord and god by all Greeks and barbarians.' If indeed this was not an official title, imposed by edict, one must assume absolutely that this attitude to the emperor and the new title were unofficially conferred upon him by a wide group of the population, and that emperor-worship was flourishing. This may be especially conclusive for Asia, the chief seat of the imperial cult, as we have seen. The Asiatic provincial council, the κοινὸν τῆς Ἀσίας, caused games and festivals to be celebrated in a number of cities to the honor of the deceased, divinely-honored emperor, the *divus;* the larger cities had established their own temples and their own sacerdotal organizations for the cult of the Caesars; and the task of the asiarch was to supervise the imperial cult in the whole province, and to lead the games and festivals which the κοινόν gave (cf. also p. 322 above). On such soil and in the presence of such an attitude of the population and the native magistrates, the proconsuls also were forced to be zealous and loyal. Here arose the opportunity of bringing the long-hated Christians before the Roman officials; and if, being led before them, they refused to offer a sacrifice before the emperor's statue, they would of course be condemned.[14]

In the statements of the Apocalypse on the persecutions which had come upon the churches, one must distinguish between those which the Christians had already passed through, and those which were yet to come in the future. The book, or perhaps more exactly the last editor of the book, looks upon a number of blood-witnesses who had already fallen, and upon danger and tribulations which were at present afflicting the churches. Smyrna is warned not to be afraid. Satan will bring certain of the church into imprisonment, yet the affliction of the church will endure for only ten days; but of course bloody martyrdoms may take place and the church must remain faithful even unto death (2:10). In Pergamon, where the throne of Satan stands, the church has remained steadfast and has not denied faith in its Lord, not even in the days when Antipas, the faithful witness of Jesus, was slain in Pergamon (2:13). And the weak church of Philadelphia has, in spite of its limited power, kept the word of the Lord and has not denied his name (3:8,10). In 6:9 also the writer looks back upon a number of martyrdoms which have already taken place: under the heavenly altar are placed the souls of those who were sacrificed for the sake of God's words and the witness which they had. How many there were is not said, and it is also not suggested that they had been slain because of denial of worship to the emperor, i.e. because they had not prayed to the beast. On the contrary: in 20:4, in which the same words are used as in 6:9 and the writer looks upon the same group of blood-witnesses, a difference is clearly made between them and those who have not prayed to the beast and received his mark. The persecution which had already occurred and which was still continuing, in which Antipas had fallen, accordingly has apparently nothing to do with emperor-worship. The sufferings may well be the same as those which, as we have shown, distressed the churches of First Peter: the name of Christian is hated, and serious accusations of all kinds of crimes are

[14] On these points, cf. besides the article "Kleinasien" by J. Weiss, already mentioned, his treatment of emperor-worship in SNT on Rev. 13:12, 2d ed., ii, 658f.

made against them. It is to be observed that according to the Apocalypse, as a matter of fact, not very many condemnations to death had taken place. The great, dreadful slaughters of Christians are still expected to occur in the future. If a single person such as Antipas of Pergamon is referred to by name, it is clear that now is the first time when a few bloody martyrdoms—perhaps only in Pergamon—can have taken place.

But in the future it will be otherwise; persecutions will come. The prophet looks ahead and sees that an innumerable multitude of Christians will be executed; he sees them glorified standing before the throne of God and of the Lamb (7:9-17). Only a small remnant, 144,000, will remain unharmed in the face of violent death (7:3f; 14:1-5). The beast and his helpers will wage in the future a mighty battle against the Lamb and his faithful ones, and the persecution of Christians will extend over the whole earth, not merely over Asia (7:9; 13:7,11-17; 17:14). The faithful will be compelled to worship the beast. All who do not worship the image of the beast will be slain (13:15). The overwhelming majority of Christians, however, will remain steadfast and thus will perish (14:12f; 12:17). The man who writes thus expects, therefore, that the condition of the Christians will become immeasurably worse. It will perhaps be possible for the adversaries, incarnate in the priesthood and magical guild of the second beast, to summon all Christians and demand of them the worship of the first beast, who has risen from the sea. The seer expects thus that all Christians will be brought to the test. It is possible that he expects that an imperial edict will expressly demand of Christians the worship of the emperor, and that he has some information or other of such a plan or believes that he has. It is however more likely that the imminence of the crisis is assumed from popular feeling itself. The provincials in Asia are violently agitated, perhaps incited by the imperial priesthood itself, and it is to be feared that by its demands the Roman officials may be forced to compel the hated Christians to participate in emperor-worship. This insistent demand of the provincials would then compel them to make a legal, governmental ruling. On behalf of this view, according to which enmity against Christians arises in the first instance from the imperial populace and not from state officials, along with other observations which we can make on this matter (cf. above the conclusions from First Peter), one can adduce the evidence of 13:16f, "And he [the second beast, the false prophet] causeth all, the small and the great, and the rich and the poor, and the free and the bond, that there be given them a mark on their right hand, or upon their forehead; and that no man should be able to buy or to sell, save he that hath the mark, even the name of the beast or the number of his name." In this passage (cf. on this point the interpretation in SNT, vol. ii), the reference is neither to imperial money nor to imperial coinage which must, for example, be used in contracts for rent or in sales, but the reference is to a religious 'stigmatization' showing honor of the lord and god, the emperor. The custom, common to many peoples, of branding or scarring oneself with the sign of the god, is extremely old and can be established as existing in very primitive religions. It became active again in the imperial cult and can be proved to have existed in various cults, among others the religion of Mithra. In our passage it is in prospect for the imperial cult, which indeed has united all inhabitants of the province. Those who will not take part in it will incur a civic boycott, which, if it actually is brought about, will have as its consequence not merely the legal and political, but also the physical destruction of those whom it affects. One can recognize in this state of affairs a fanatical temper in the popular mind. And for the Christians a new and very dangerous situation has been created. Previously, along with the Jews, they had been exempted from emperor-worship. The Jews had this privilege, besides freedom from service in the army and the right of not being compelled to appear in court on the Sabbath. The Christians had at first and for a long period thereafter stood under the protection of the Jewish religion; Paul had even had friendly personal relations with certain asiarchs in Ephesus (Acts 19:31). In the period of the Apocalypse, however, a great change appears to have been about to take place: the Christians are to be boycotted by the citizens, and furthermore worship of the emperor is to be demanded of them. How widely these apprehensions came to fulfilment we cannot attempt to say. Nevertheless, in part they became an actuality. That the Christians of Asia had a very difficult position in the midst of the unfriendly population is certain. But the imperial cult demanded its sacrifices as well. Otherwise remembrance of the cruelty of Domitian, the 'second Nero,' would not have survived in the Church (Tertullian, *Apol.* 5:4, *temptaverat et Domitianus, portio Neronis de crudelitate,* "Domitian, a limb of Nero in cruelty, also attacked," i.e. the Christians; and Eusebius, *H. E.,* iii. 17, πολλήν γε μὴν εἰς πολλοὺς ἐπιδειξάμενος ὁ Δομετιανὸς ὠμότητα . . . . τελευτῶν τῆς Νέρωνος θεοεχθρίας τε καὶ θεομαχίας διάδοχον ἑαυτὸν κατεστήσατο, "Domitian, exhibiting a very great cruelty to many people . . . . completing Nero's enmity against God and struggle against God, made himself Nero's worthy successor"). We can learn also from Dio Cassius of the great number of accusations which were raised in Domitian's reign against the Christians on account of 'atheism' and a 'Jewish way of life'; Nerva, so Dio relates, was forced to forbid expressly such denunciations (68:1, καὶ ὁ Νερούας τούς τε κρινομένους ἐπ' ἀσεβείᾳ ἀφῆκε καὶ τοὺς φεύγοντας κατήγαγε . . . . τοῖς δὲ δὴ ἄλλοις οὔτ' ἀσεβείας οὔτ' Ἰουδαϊκοῦ βίου καταιτιᾶσθαί τινας συνεχώρησε, "And Nerva released those on trial for impiety and brought back the fugitives . . . . and he forbade others to accuse certain ones of impiety or a Jewish way of life").

Whether any condemnations of Christians took place in the Asiatic provinces during the short reign of Nerva we do not know. We have, however, at our disposal an especially important source from the reign of Trajan, the *Letter of Pliny* which has already been mentioned above, and the emperor's answer to the governor. We come thus to the territory of another Asiatic province; it is Bithynia-Pontus, no longer Asia, to which the evidence of Pliny's letter is applicable. The state of affairs which may be observed from it is this: Christianity had expanded very widely in the province, and a great number of people had united themselves with it (cf. above, p. 780). This could not of course have happened in secret, and so a number of Christians were reported to Pliny. How much more precisely the accusation was made, Pliny does not say. Probably the simple accusation was sufficient: so and so, listed by name, are Christians. Pliny of course knew, because of his previous official career, that to be a Christian was something punishable, yet he had no clear idea of exactly what procedure ought to be taken against the Christians, since he had never been present at trials of Christians. So he decided to pursue the following course: he asked the accused who were brought before him whether they were Christians. Since, as it appears, all or at least the overwhelming majority, confessed their Christianity, he asked them a second and a third time, threatening them meanwhile with execution. He condemned to death those who were steadfast among them, and quite summarily at that, without the usual procedure in cases of capital crime, by virtue of the administrative power which he possessed as governor (cf. below, p. 813). Those among the accused who possessed Roman citizenship he ordered transported to Rome, that the emperor might pass judgment on them there. This prerogative which Roman citizens had, of appearing before the imperial court, is known to us from St. Paul's trial. As to what precisely was the guilt of the Christians, Pliny did not inquire further. The stubbornness and inflexible obstinacy of the accused, to whom he offered a chance of abjuring their faith, when they might have set themselves free, appeared to him, educated Roman official as he was, as something which in itself deserved severe punishment.

The investigation however went further, and still more types of Christians or of those who had been Christians became known to the governor. An anonymous accusation came to him, which named many people as Christians. Pliny summoned them all to him. Several of them denied glibly: they were not Christians and never had been. At the same time they undertook, in the presence of the governor and in front of his standard, certain actions which true Christians never could have undertaken (*qui sunt re vera Christiani*): they called upon Roman gods, they poured out incense and wine before the statue of the emperor, and cursed Christ, whereupon Pliny released them. Others among those who were enumerated in the accusation as being Christians, denied in a somewhat similar manner: they had at one time been Christians, but had now renounced the religion—some of them three years ago, others a longer period yet, and some even twenty years before. All declared their reverence for the images of the emperor and the gods and reviled Christ. As to the facts of the time when they were Christians they gave quite reassuring information, which is a valuable source for us for the history of early Christian worship. They said that they had been accustomed on a certain day—it is quite obvious that Sunday is meant—to come together before sunrise to sing songs to Christ as to a god, and to bind themselves by a solemn obligation not to commit any crime, but on the contrary to commit no theft, rape, adultery, not to break promises given, and not to embezzle goods which had been entrusted to them. Then they had separated from one another (of course for their daily work) and afterward came together for a common meal. We must think of this meal as being in the evening, the time of day in which the chief meal was then eaten. The common food eaten then was harmless and customary food. We learn here for the first time, but clearly, of the severe charge which people laid against Christians and which the Christian writers of the second century attest repeatedly, viz. that the Christians ate human flesh ('Thyestean feasts'); for Pliny must have asked explicitly, "At your meals did you eat anything abominable or forbidden?" Those examined declared further that the common meal, besides, had been discontinued since the edict promulgated by Pliny, in which in accordance with imperial decree he had forbidden associations. These associations, the clubs (*hetairiai*), had been looked upon with strong disapproval by the Roman government ever since the time of Caesar, since an apparently harmless society could hatch political plots too easily. Among the Greeks of the east there was, along with all their loyalty, still an unquenchable desire for political stump oratory, which was in the blood. For this reason it was only under Trajan that sharper measures were taken against the *hetairiai*. In order to have complete certainty that the information, which had come to him partly from the accused, rested actually on the truth, Pliny had two Christian female slaves, who held the rank of deaconess in the Church, put to the rack. He discovered, however, by this method, nothing which had the appearance of crime or misdeed, but only excessive and perverse superstition (*superstitionem pravam, immodicam*).

When Pliny had carried his investigation to this point he went no further and expressed no judgment, but turned to the emperor. All sorts of doubts had arisen in this educated, enlightened official. The number of Christians was very great (cf. p. 780, above), and so the thing must be considered carefully. That the stubborn confessors of the religion must be condemned appeared clear to him. But he hesitated on three points, and he placed three questions before the emperor. One was whether the various groups of Christians were to be treated differently, whether the adult and the man were to be punished more severely than the wife, the adolescent, and the child. Furthermore, might those who denied their Christianity go free from punishment, or were they also to be punished? And closely joined with this was the third question: was Christianity then, in itself, a punishable offence? Was the 'name,' the fact of being a Christian, in itself sufficient, or must the Christians be convicted of certain crimes which were connected with the name (*nomen ipsum, si flagitiis careat, an flagitia cohaerentia nomini puniantur*)?

The emperor answered the questions of his governor and friend. His answer, which follows immediately after Pliny's questioning letter in the collection of Pliny's epistles, is brief and clear. He approved expressly, on the whole, Pliny's actions hitherto. A universally binding rule by which one could proceed in giving judgment, could not be laid down. The Christians were not to be sought out (*conquirendi non sunt*). The governor was under obligation to search for malefactors in the case of certain great crimes such as robbery and sacrilege, just as among us the supreme power of the state proceeds against certain crimes without waiting for a private accusation on the part of someone who is injured. If the Christians, so the emperor directed further, are accused and convicted of being Christians, they are to be punished (*si deferantur et arguantur, puniendi sunt*). In what way, the emperor does not say. In the whole procedure which we are considering here it is not a case of legal action, trial for a capital crime with judges and jury, in which as a matter of course release or capital punishment (execution, banishment, confiscation of goods) would be the result; rather we are considering, as has been suggested already and as the governor's letter permits us to recognize clearly, an administrative procedure of the police power. In the Roman empire the imperial and native authorities were held responsible for peace and order in their spheres of office; for this reason they were endowed with power to punish, and each one of them could summarily inflict the customary punishments, except the death penalty, without legal proceedings. This procedure was called *coercitio.* We know of the police punishment also, but only for very petty offences; nevertheless, a parallel to the Roman *coercitio* is offered to us in the right of the old Russian administrative authority to banish those suspected or convicted of political crimes. Pliny and the other governors thus had it in their discretion to fix the manner and degree of punishment for the Christians according to circumstances. The emperor decided further that those who denied their Christianity by word and deed should go unpunished, even if the tenor of their past life laid on them strong suspicion of having been Christians (. . . . *ut qui negaverit se Christianum esse idque re ipsa manifestum fecerit, id est supplicando dis nostris, quamvis suspectus in praeteritum, veniam ex poenitentia inpetret,* ". . . . that he who shall deny that he is a Christian and shall make the fact manifest by his actions, i.e. by praying to our gods, although he be suspected of having been one in the past, let him have freedom from punishment"). Sacrifice to the Roman gods was regarded as denial by deed; Trajan makes no explicit statement that incense must be scattered and wine poured out before his own image. On one point only does the emperor correct Pliny's mode of procedure: the governor had received an anonymous accusation and on the basis of it had begun his second investigation. Trajan decides that attention is not to be paid to anonymous reports, which likewise might not be used in other investigations. Otherwise an evil precedent would be set up in violation of contemporary ideas of right.

The rescript of Trajan was intended, above all, merely to judge the single case which had arisen. But the imperial edict, despite its brevity, had great significance in the following age. It became the norm by which, for nearly 150 years, until Decius, the Roman state and its officialdom proceeded. The rescript contained quite clear and simple rules which were, besides, easy to administer; the procedure appeared moderate and, in fact, all too indulgent of the Christians, and the decision of the emperor came quickly to the notice of a wider circle, since the correspondence of Pliny and Trajan was soon edited, and since imperial edicts and rescripts counted as binding law.

The fact of being a Christian, *in itself,* was to be punished administratively, the emperor decided. The denial of the cult of the state is the substance of the matter, and now it is not necessary to convict the Christians of other crimes. The 'name' in itself was sufficient. That which had been allowed the Jews was not to be tolerated in the Christians. In the mind of the Roman government Judaism was merely a national religion and as such had its privileges, while Christianity had no grounds for exemption. Thus one must demand from the Christians what was demanded of all other subjects of the empire: worship of the gods of the Roman state, worship of the emperor. For on these cults rested the unity of the whole realm. To deny these was to transgress against the majesty of the mighty Roman people and to be guilty of atheism.

On the other hand it was decided by the emperor that the Christians were not to be pursued like other criminals, that they might be arraigned only upon definite information which must bear the name of the informer, and that denial by means of sacrifice, without further action, would permit the Christian in question to go scot-free.

Tertullian pointed out that the rescript itself is full of contradictions: "Oh, necessarily confused verdict! He does not want them to be sought out, since they are innocent, and he commands that they be punished because they are guilty, he spares and he rages, he forgives and he condemns" (*Apol.* 2). We can, however, see whence the contradiction arises: Trajan does not intend simply to let Christianity be free, in principle. Yet he and his officials were enlightened and moderate, to this extent: to these Romans the state and its majesty were represented by the gods; to honor them was a patriotic obligation not only for Roman citizens but also for all subjects of the empire; to deny this reverence was sacrilege and *lèse majesté.* And to the emperor as well as to the governors, the stubborn refusal of the Christians to scatter two grains of incense in honor of the majesty of the illustrious Roman people appeared to be an unbelievable wilfulness difficult to be borne (*pertinacia et inflexibilis obstinatio*), which was to be punished with unconditional severity. This reflection might cause the emperor to decide further not to swerve from the position already taken and declare that Christianity was unpunishable: the uncertain position of Christians before the law had existed since Nero, and the direct clash between them and the state had taken place in Domitian's time. Finally, respect for the feelings of provincials may have determined the wording of the rescript for the emperor. It was especially the Greeks of the Asiatic provinces, above all those of Asia itself, who were excessive in their loyalty, who were most strongly devoted to the imperial cult, most hostile to the Christians, since the latter were apparently poor patriots and not friends of the emperor. Thus it might appear politically unwise to oppose this state of mind and protect the Christians.

On the other hand it is clear to the emperor, and it had been proved by many investigations carried on in a manner similar to Pliny's, that the atrocities with which the people charged Christians had in reality never been perpetrated by them. For this reason the emperor decided also that they were not to be sought out by governmental order.

Consideration for the popular temper of mind was, in the Asiatic provinces, a leading motive for the Roman authorities' interference with the Christians. The Apocalypse and Pliny's report show us this. When Eusebius, *H. E.*, iii. 32. 1, says that condemnations of Christians took place under Trajan in a number of cities, in consequence of popular tumults, this account surely corresponds quite closely to the Asiatic situation. And we have a further witness from our period which shows yet once more the wild hatred of the Asiatic population against the Christians. Under Trajan's successor, the emperor Hadrian, the restless anti-Christian population of the province of Asia, gathered in stormy mobs, perhaps at the games, also demanded punishment of the Christians at the hands of the Roman proconsuls, emphasizing their demand by loud appeals and frenzied exclamations. The officials were clearly inclined to indulge the natives. However one proconsul, Serennius Granianus, who must have held office in 123-124, turned to the emperor and reported the true state of affairs to him. Hadrian answered in a rescript, addressed not to Serennius Granianus but to his successor, Minucius Fundanus. The letter of the proconsul is not included, though the imperial answer has been preserved in Justin's *Apology* (ch. 68), and Rufinus' translation of Eusebius (*H. E.*, iv. 9) offers us the original Latin text. Unfortunately the interpretation of the short text cannot be established beyond dispute. According to one view which is presumably correct, the emperor forbids the reception of formless accusations on the part of the agitated mob when they come before the governor and cry, "Down with the Christians!", accusing them of crimes and treason. It is required that the provincials accuse the Christians before the regular tribunals. If such an accusation is made and proved against the Christians, then the governor must decide what punishment is proper (. . . . *ut pro tribunali eos* [the Christians] *in aliquo arguant, hoc eis* [the provincials] *exequi non prohibeo, precibus autem in hoc solis et adclamationibus uti eis non permitto* . . . . *si quis igitur accusat et probat adversum leges quicquam agere memoratos homines, pro merito peccatorum etiam supplicia statues,* ". . . . they may make any charge against them [the Christians] before the tribunal—I do not prohibit them [the provincials] from following such a course; but I do not permit them merely to make supplications and cries of disapprobation . . . . if anyone therefore accuses these people who have been mentioned and proves that they have done anything contrary to the laws, you shall by all means prescribe punishments in proportion to the crimes"). Yet, by Hercules, the governor should take a severe attitude when anyone brings slanderous accusations against the Christians; such a one is to receive the most severe punishment for his baseness. For, as the emperor says in the introductory sentences of the rescript, the innocent must not suffer and slanderers must not have occasion to carry on a predatory existence by preying upon the innocent.

Hadrian has dealt with the question in a very enlightened and cool way if he is to be interpreted as has been suggested. Religion is free; citizens can be prosecuted only for crimes against penal law. Christianity is thereby made substantially free, for if an investigation such as that of Pliny proved no infamous actions on the part of Christians, although it was conducted quite carefully, then provincials can no longer dare to appear with accusations for which they themselves must answer. Unfortunately, however, the interpretation just given is not at all certain, although it rests on the authority of such a historian as Mommsen. We have understood the words *adversum leges quicquam agere* to refer only to such crimes as, e.g. cannibalism, heinous unchastity, conspiracy, revolution and the like. It is nevertheless possible that religious crime also, apostasy from national gods and refusal to sacrifice to tutelary deities of the Roman state, fall under the concept of 'illegal action.' It is certain that in Hadrian's reign, even after the years 123-124, there were actions against the Christians. The Apology addressed by the Christian writer Quadratus to the emperor in 125-126 or perhaps in 129-130 in Athens, indicates this. And in any case Hadrian's rescript endured no longer than his reign. The succeeding emperors and their governors went back to Trajan's more severe decisions.

CHAPTER XXVI

Macedonia and Achaia

(a) *Macedonia*

1. *Foundation.* How Paul came to Macedonia, where he worked in that region and with what results, we have seen previously (cf. pp. 280-286, as well as 353-356, and for the Epistle to the Philippians, 385-387). St. Paul may have founded three churches in the province. The first of these was in Philippi, a Roman military colony and a not unimportant administrative center. The second was in Thessalonica, the capital of Macedonia and the seat of the proconsul, which was at the same time the greatest and most popular city of the province, with a good harbor and extensive trade. We hear least about the third church, which was in Beroea, which lay off the main road but was nevertheless a not insignificant city. Paul had not been able to develop his work as completely as he had intended. He had experienced a multitude of difficulties in three cities which he names, or at least was in danger in them, and had shunned them or been driven from them. But his work continued further, even after he had made Corinth the place of his residence and activity, and he had later had opportunity to return to his Macedonian churches, even though for only a short time. From the Epistle to the Philippians, one of the last documents which we have from the hand of St. Paul, we learn that the Church of Philippi was very dear to him, and that it had held its ground well in situations which were not easy ones.

2. *The Sources.* If now we turn to the sources for the post-Pauline age, we must unfortunately make it plain from the first that according to these sources the Christianity of Macedonia received a strong setback in our period. Only a single, and moreover not a very valuable piece of writing, takes us back to Macedonia, and this piece of literature vouchsafes us information about only one church. It is the *Epistle of Polycarp,* bishop of Smyrna, to the Church of Philippi. The letter purports in the salutation to be written by Polycarp and his presbyters to the Church of Philippi. In fact, however, only Polycarp speaks (cf. the first person singular at the beginning of the composition, 1:1). The occasion of the letter was an earlier note, not preserved to us, which the Philippians had sent to Smyrna. In

this they had reported Ignatius' journey through the city (1:1; 9:1), had requested Polycarp to bestow instruction upon them 'regarding righteousness' (3:1); they had furthermore reported an unseemly happening in their church, an embezzlement which one of their presbyters, Valens by name, aided by his wife, had committed (11:1—12:1); finally they requested that the Smyrnaean church ambassador who should visit the Church of Antioch, lately bereaved of its bishop, might also take with him a letter to the Antiochenes (13:1) and had asked that copies of the letters of St. Ignatius be sent to them (13:2). As an answer to this letter from Philippi, Polycarp's epistle was written; it is in close connection with the Ignatian letters in occasion and time of writing. It was written after Ignatius had sent his letters to the Asiatic churches and after he had come through Philippi on his journey to Rome (cf. pp. 767f above, on the circumstances of origin of Ignatius' epistles).

In its main body (chh. 2-10) the Bishop of Smyrna gives the requested exhortations to righteousness, the proper Christian mode of life, the behavior acceptable to God for the various orders in the Church, defence against heretics—all this is discussed by Polycarp; in 11:1—12:1 he treats of the Valens affair; the conclusion contains further exhortations and an answer to the request of the Philippians for the forwarding of their letter to Antioch and concerning transmission of copies of the Ignatian epistles. The writing exhibits a number of quite definite individual traits, and in it speaks an 'honest shepherd of souls . . . . not especially burdened with his own thoughts,' who everywhere seeks support from and borrows from the trustworthy and acknowledged writings of the Church: not so much from the writings of the Old Testament as from those of Christian origin—the gospels, the Pauline epistles, the letters of John and Peter (First Peter), the Epistle of Clement of Rome.[1]

So appears the chief—indeed the sole—source which gives us information regarding Christianity in Macedonia in the post-Pauline age. What we can learn from this writing—which is not in itself brief—is none too much. For in the main it gives us more of a view of the habits, piety, theology and book-learning of Polycarp, than it does of information about the condition of the church addressed. We can however gather one thing from the letter which we must

[1] Cf. also the translation in *Neutestamentlichen Apokryphen*, pp. 135-138, where the epistle's borrowings are exhaustively collected and are readily recognizable in text and notes. [*Translator's Note*. The most convenient edition in English (with Greek text on opposite pages) is in K. Lake, *The Apostolic Fathers*, i, 9-121.]

bear in mind, namely that Polycarp, as we have just indicated, writes more from his own mind in the main body of the letter, and makes general exhortations without entering into the peculiarities, needs and especial position of the Philippians.

3. Thus unfortunately we can learn little about the size of the *Church of Philippi* and how it was constituted. But it is a Pauline church and its glory is that its beginnings reach back to the first ages of missionary preaching, that it had been founded by St. Paul himself. For this reason Polycarp can write to it, saying, "The firm root of your faith, which has been spoken of from ancient times, still endures today and bears fruit unto our Lord Jesus Christ" (1:2); "Among you the blessed Paul worked, you are praised at the beginning of his epistle; he boasted of you in all the churches which then alone knew God" (11:3); "Neither I nor another like myself may tread in the footsteps of the wisdom of the blessed and glorious Paul, who in person sojourned among you who were then living, and taught the word of truth surely and clearly, who when absent wrote you letters, by which you, if only you will steep yourselves in them, may become edified in the faith which has been given you" (3:1f); "Thus I now exhort you all to obey the word of righteousness and to be patient in every thing, with the patience you have seen with your own eyes, not only in the blessed Ignatius and Zosimus and Rufus, but also in others among yourselves and in Paul himself and the other Apostles" (9:1).

4. The letter gives a number of indications respecting the *church organization* which existed in Philippi, or to express it quite cautiously, which Polycarp presupposes as existing in Philippi.[2] We have seen previously how very strongly and significantly the monarchical episcopate makes its appearance in the Ignatian epistles; and we must assume from the evidence of the Ignatians that it was established in Asia and Syria. Thus it is somewhat strange that Polycarp, who was himself *the* Bishop of Smyrna, presupposes no monarchical episcopate as existing in the Church of Philippi. In no place in the whole letter does he use the title 'bishop' in speaking of Philippi, and in no case does he give the name of a man who may be assumed to be bishop of the Philippians. In 5:3, where he leans most closely upon Ignatius and would have mentioned the bishop if anywhere, he says: "Be subject to the presbyters and deacons as to God and Christ." The situation in the Epistle of Polycarp to the

[2] [*Translator's Note.* On the question of church organization, cf. Streeter, *The Primitive Church.*]

Philippians is similar to that in the Epistle of Ignatius to the Romans. Ignatius also knew of no *single* bishop in Rome. The argument from silence is in both cases rather compelling. At the head of the Church of Philippi stand presbyters. The letter, in chapters 6 and 11, gives information as to the obligations which devolved upon them. Quite evidently, in the circle of these duties, that of managing the church's finances stands out as the most important. For this reason the presbyters are exhorted, in 6:1, to keep themselves free from any covetousness, and not to neglect any widows, orphans or poor. In chapter 11 we learn that Valens, who had been a presbyter in the church, had embezzled the church's money: he had allowed himself to be overcome by avarice and had misused the position which he had occupied in the church. From the wording of this reproach it follows clearly that Valens had to do with the properties of the church. And another thing to be recognized about the activities of the presbyters is that they had certain pastoral tasks. Thus they must look out for the weak and erring, must not be hasty or partisan, but judge kindly and discreetly (6:1). Polycarp says nothing of the important obligations which the presbyters took upon themselves in reference to the worship of the Church, of which Ignatius and First Clement (to be discussed similarly later) speak so amply.

In the Epistle of Polycarp the deacons appear alongside the presbyters. In our other sources these church officials always appear in connection with the bishops, as in the address of the letter which St. Paul addressed to this very church (Phil. 1:1). If Polycarp diverges from this apparently established usage, the reason is perhaps that he at least cannot speak of bishops in the plural when he has in mind the officials of one and the same church. If, accordingly, the leadership of a church lies in the hands of more than one, as is the case in Philippi, Polycarp can speak only of 'presbyters' and he must place the deacons alongside the presbyters. The deacons were the younger assistants who stood by to 'serve' the presbyters in the conduct of their office. In 5:2 the letter gives the model for deacons to follow: they must be blameless before the righteousness of God, as servants of God and not of men; they must not be slanderers, not double-tongued, lovers of money, but on the contrary temperate in all things, merciful, painstaking, living according to the truth of the Lord, who became the servant of all. These are partly admonitions, which recommend to the deacons a quite general zeal in their office and a blameless way of life; but then disinterestedness is desired in particular to be the quality of those who must help the presbyters, since money and gifts to the Church pass through their hands. And furthermore they must not be slanderers; since in pastoral work and visitation they go about a great deal in people's homes, they must have good control over their tongues, and must not bear evil gossip from house to house.

The church must of course be grateful to the presbyters and deacons and recognize the value of their service. At the same time the people have their definite rights as against those of the officers. The proof of this lies in 11:4. There the church is exhorted to be charitable to Valens and his wife and to summon back the erring members. Accordingly they must have had—if not the deciding word—at least an advisory voice and the responsibility of a concurrent vote in the decision of the case.

5. *Heresies.* In the broad exhortations of the epistle, from which we can deduce little, because of its colorless character and generality, polemic against heretics occupies an especial position. We unfortunately do not know how widely the erroneous teaching against which the letter contends is in reality a danger to the Church of Philippi. It is connected with the greater question which confronted us previously: what precisely did the Bishop of Smyrna know in detail about the situation of the Philippian church? Does he not simply assume as existing there the development which he sketches in the chief part of his letter (2-10, and further in 12), and does he not assume this because of the viewpoints which he has gained in his own church? Ignatius on his journey through Asia has encountered the false teachers of Asia Minor and has entered into controversy with them. But the heresy with which he is concerned is one which he has not merely learned to recognize in Asia, but one against which he previously had to work in Antioch. We have already seen what the nature of this heresy was (pp. 763f)—a gnostic docetism, but connected with a secret wisdom of Jewish origin.

We may now as a matter of course entertain the sure expectation that Polycarp contends against essentially the same heretical teachers as did Ignatius. And we shall be able furthermore, with the same certainty, to assume that not only were Antioch and the churches of Asia menaced by Gnosticism, but that it had reached across to Philippi as well. Philippi was not difficult to reach from the coast of Asia, and the churches of Macedonia from the very period of their origin were in communication with the Asiatic churches. Finally Polycarp must also have had opportunity to picture to himself the Church of Philippi; perhaps the Philippians in their lost letter had somehow alluded to the danger of their church, or perhaps the men who delivered the letter had been questioned by Polycarp. The danger in question was certainly not one which had made its appearance today or yesterday. Relying on these considerations, we may at any rate venture to say that the anti-heretical polemic of the Epistle of Polycarp was of importance for the Church of Philippi.

The sections in which Polycarp contends against heresy are comprised, generally speaking, in 6:3—7:2: "So let us now serve him [Christ] with fear and with all reverence, as he himself has commanded, and as the Apostles who announced the gospel to us, and the prophets who have before now announced the advent of the Lord; let us be zealots for righteousness, refraining from scandals, and from the false brethren and those who in hypocrisy bear the name of the Lord, who thus make foolish men confused. For every one who does not confess that Jesus Christ has come in the flesh is an anti-Christ, and he who does not confess the evidence of the Cross is of the devil, and he who twists the words of the Lord to his own desires and says that there is neither resurrection nor judgment, is the first-born of Satan. So let us renounce the foolish babbling of the crowd and the false teachers and let us return to the teaching handed down to us from of old, watching unto prayer and persevering in fasting, beseeching with our supplications the all-seeing God, that he may not lead us into temptation, for as the Lord said, 'The Spirit is willing, but the flesh is weak.' " With this passage one must compare 2:1f, "Wherefore gird up your loins and serve God in fear and in truth, forsake empty foolish babbling and the error of the multitude, believe in him who has raised up our Lord Jesus Christ from the dead and has given him glory and a seat at his right hand, to whom all is subject in heaven and on earth, whom all breath serves, who shall come as judge of the living and the dead, whose blood God will demand of those who are disobedient to him. But he who raised him from the dead will also raise us, if we do according to his will and walk according to his commandment, and love that which he has loved: let us refrain from every unrighteousness," etc. Weak allusions to the hostile presence of the heretics are scattered through other passages of the letter, such as in the introduction (1:2f), the conclusion (12:2) and in 8:1. They are, however, insignificant, and add nothing new to our conclusions about the polemic.

This polemic is not ambiguous in its chief details. The danger appears to the bishop as one which is not insignificant, for a 'multitude' has lapsed into error and has indulged in foolish babbling and false teaching. With respect to its content this teaching is bad Christology. Polycarp is unfortunately not very detailed in his statements, and his expressions can be interpreted variously. What he says in 7:1 can be understood of the doctrine of the two persons, of the indwelling of the heavenly, higher Christ in the human Jesus. Such a Christology is expressly attested to us as existing in early Gnosticism. Cerinthus had held it, and the fight of the First Epistle of John is directed against it. But the words of the Epistle of Polycarp are capable of another interpretation, and the expressions can quite well have been uttered against the quasi-gnostic docetism which is contended against in the letters of Ignatius: Jesus Christ has not come in the flesh, he has not suffered, he has not risen.

And still a second annoyance which the false teachers gave to the men of the church appears in the words of Polycarp: the heretics denied the resurrection and the judgment. Of this Ignatius says nothing. But the fact is not unknown to us from other anti-gnostic polemic. In II Tim. 2:18 we hear of people who say that the resurrection has already taken place; they mean spiritually, mystically, in embracing the faith and in baptism. And they reject completely the primitive Christian-Jewish eschatology with its resurrection of the dead, its universal judgment and its visible Kingdom of God. There is only a salvation which consists in redemption of the Spirit from the world of matter.

In the whole letter one can discern absolutely nothing of menaces or even of a disturbance of the Church on the part of Judaizers. We have already seen that the polemic against Judaistic opponents which we find in St. Paul's Epistle to the Philippians (3:2—4:1) probably did not originally belong to the letter at all (cf. pp. 386f), and that consequently at the time of his Roman imprisonment the Apostle no longer sees any danger from this quarter. But even if the passage in question belongs to the original epistle, one must still ask to what extent this Macedonian church was actually menaced by this danger, and to what extent Paul had merely been uttering a warning. In the Epistle of Polycarp one does not get so much as a glance at Judaism. The heretics against which it inveighs have absolutely nothing to do with Judaism and the Law. And while Ignatius intends to strike at what is objectionable in their Christology by stigmatizing their teaching as Judaizing (cf. above, pp. 763ff), Polycarp does not speak of them in this manner, and never in the whole epistle does he speak of Judaism or anything connected with it.

6. *Paulinism.* One observes on the other hand, from the contents of the letter, that the authority of St. Paul is firmly rooted in Philippi; the Philippians can boast that they are blessed and famous because he had lived among them and taught them the word of truth, and that when he was absent he had written them letters; they may read them, and if they steep themselves in them they will become advanced in the faith delivered to them; no other person who now might write to them could do so with the same results (3:2). In 11:2 a quotation is made from his letters with an express appeal to Paul, and for the glory of the Philippians; allusion is made to the fact that the Apostle had worked among them and had written to them, had praised them in his other letters to all the churches which at that time had known God (cf. also p. 820, above).

And the very great use made of his writings further accords with this estimation of St. Paul. Not only for Polycarp—so we may conclude from our observation—but also for the church which is addressed are the writings of Paul endued with high authority, are loved, honored and read. The circumstances are—to consider it somewhat more carefully—as follows.

Polycarp cites the Old Testament very little. The most obvious quotation is in 10:2, from Tobit 12:9, "Alms rescues from death"; in 11:2, Jer. 5:4 is used in much freer form: "They know not the way or the judgment of the Lord." There are still other allusions here and there to the Old Testament, in language and religious formulae, but they are all quite general, and the brief expressions are completely worked over into the writer's own idiom. From these observations of course one cannot conclude in the slightest that Polycarp or his readers depreciated or discarded the Old Testament as did the Gnostics. The Bishop of Smyrna is however obviously not well acquainted with the sacred scrolls, as he himself expressly says, "I am certain that you are well read in the Holy Scriptures and that nothing escapes you; *to me, of course, this has not been vouchsafed*" (12:1). The meagre Old Testament learning of Polycarp may be due in large part to the fact that he was not Jewish by birth but had come from a Greek family of Asia Minor.

But on the other hand the scant use he makes of Old Testament writings is contrasted strongly with his abundant quotations of Christian literature. Polycarp knows a rather large number of books: not only canonical writings, but also extra-canonical literature such as First Clement, and—it goes without saying—the epistles of Ignatius. Thus he quotes sayings from the Synoptic tradition, he certainly knows First Peter and First John, and the Book of Acts and Epistle to the Hebrews appear to be not unknown to him. The chief position among the Christian writings which Polycarp quotes belongs beyond any doubt to the Pauline epistles: besides Philippians he knows Romans, Galatians, First and Second Corinthians, Ephesians, Colossians, Thessalonians and the Pastorals; in short, the complete collection of Pauline letters as we have them, lies before him; he used them with eagerness and regards them very highly, and supposes that the Philippians do the same. The doctrine of justification with which he begins his composition (1:3) is Pauline: "You know that you have been saved by grace, not by works, but according to the will of God through Jesus Christ."

It is however self-evident that despite this great use made of St. Paul's works, an actual inner assimilation and reproduction of Paulinism does not occur. Polycarp and certainly also the church which he addresses, which had been founded by Paul himself, is in no different position from that of most of the churches and individuals of the post-Pauline age. If one wishes to describe briefly the piety which is expressed in this letter one may say that there has arisen a powerful morality, unfriendly to any mysticism, on the foundation not of the Pauline faith, but of a faith conceived of ecclesiastically (faith=holding steadfastly to the truth and relying upon it). Polycarp represents an entirely different form of faith from that of Ignatius (for example). It will meet us again in a cognate form when we come to consider First Clement. One may add that in Polycarp as in Clement there is a marked feeling for ecclesiastical regulation and for the offices which this regulation brings with it. We shall consider more closely the piety of the Roman church, and for this reason we do not intend to pursue this train of thought further in our discussion of the Epistle of Polycarp, especially since our concern here is with the Philippian church and since we can draw no certain conclusion from the Epistle of Polycarp with respect to the piety of a foreign church.

7. The thick darkness in which the development of Macedonian Christianity lies in the post-Pauline age does not disappear in the following period. *Christian Macedonia*, throughout the second and third centuries, remains an *unknown land* to us. After the letter of Polycarp we hear nothing more of Philippi until the victory of Chris-

tianity under Constantine. And all that we hear of Thessalonica in the same period of time is an indirect mention of the church in a fragment of Melito of Sardis, contained in Eusebius.[3] The passage is as a matter of fact the sole passage in Eusebius' *Church History* in which he mentions the Church of Thessalonica, while that of Philippi does not appear anywhere in his work.

That Christianity in Macedonia appears obscure to us for such a long period of time is due to the fact that no leading men, and especially no active literary men, emerged in that neighborhood. Christianity there is anonymous. And what is true of the Macedonian churches is true also of neighboring Achaia, to which we now return.

(b) Achaia

8. *Corinth and the Rest of the Province.* In Achaia St. Paul, coming thither from Macedonia, had worked for a longer period: Corinth especially had been the scene of his ministry, but he had also worked in Athens, though with scant results. Apparently in his time a church already existed in the eastern port of Corinth, at Cenchreae.

We have already spoken of the significance of Corinth as the greatest city of Greece, as the only actual cosmopolitan city which the country possessed in the Roman period, and of the significance of the Christian church there.[4] St. Paul certainly had great foresight in choosing this city as a place in which to reside for a long period and in gathering together there a church which was to be an important one in his ministry.

In the post-Pauline age we come upon a clear view of Achaia only in the Corinthian church. To this church, about the year 96, an extensive letter is sent from Rome, which bears the title of the First Epistle of Clement, a document which is significant for us as one of the most generally valuable sources for the post-Pauline age. We

[3] *H. E.* iv. 26. 10, . . . ὁ πατήρ σου, καὶ σοῦ τὰ σύμπαντα διοικοῦντος αὐτῷ, ταῖς πόλεσι περὶ τοῦ μηδὲν νεωτερίζειν περὶ ἡμῶν ἔγραψεν, ἐν οἷς καὶ Λαρισαίους καὶ πρὸς Θεσσαλονικεῖς καὶ Ἀθηναίους καὶ πρὸς πάντας Ἕλληνας, "Your father [i. e. Antoninus Pius; Melito addresses the emperor Marcus Aurelius], even when you were ruling all the world for him, wrote to the cities to make no disturbance concerning us [the reference is to a tumult of natives against the Christians, which as we have noted, took place in Asia; cf. Hadrian's rescript, p. 816]; among those whom he addressed were the Larisaeans, the Thessalonians, the Athenians and all the Greeks."

[4] For the ministry of St. Paul in Achaia and Corinth, cf. pp. 291ff above, and for the significance of Corinth see the literature mentioned in note 20, p. 292.

shall find it of interest not merely in the present section, but shall also use it abundantly in our portrayal of the Roman church.

In this piece of literature the Corinthian church is regarded as old and firmly established; its boast is that it had had dealings with the men of the first generation, the Apostles and their friends and associates, and had received letters from St. Paul (47:1-6). At the very beginning of the epistle, where praise is given the Corinthian church of the period before the present disagreeable discord, we are told of many foreign Christians who came to Corinth, for of course the great trading city was visited by many foreigners. In Corinth, Christians who arrived from foreign parts could learn of the glorious and steadfast faith of the church which existed there, could marvel at its thoughtful and gentle piety, could proclaim widely the magnificent style of its hospitality and call the mature and perfect Christian knowledge of the Corinthians blessed (1:2). Since the church was great and distinguished, since it was friendly and people visited it so often, the news of the schism within it had spread widely: not only did Christians speak of the occurrence, but the heathen also, even in Rome, apparently knew the story of the Corinthians' controversy (47:7). For this very reason the church of the capital itself considered it fitting and proper to take a hand in the trouble.

No other church in Achaia beside that of Corinth is explicitly attested in our period. Nevertheless by working backward from the tradition of a later period, we can tell something more of the Christianity of this province in the age which we are studying. It was previously pointed out that the state of Christianity in Macedonia and Achaia is difficult for us to determine, since there are lacking for whole centuries actual leaders in the neighborhood of the local church. This observation must, however, be made with some qualification.

In the second century the Church of Corinth possesses such a man of wide influence in its bishop Dionysius. This man presided over the church probably in the time of Soter, who was Bishop of Rome in the years 166-7 to 174-5. Dionysius must have stood in high esteem even among people far away, since foreign churches came to him with their difficulties and laid controverted questions before him for decision. His letters were collected and after his death circulated widely, but were, however, lost later. This lack is filled to some degree at least by the account of Eusebius, whose sketch of the man and quotations from him in *H. E.* iv. 23 and ii. 25

are our chief and in fact only source for Dionysius' literary activity. Seven church letters were included in the collection which lay before Eusebius. He gives briefly the contents of each, partly, it appears, in Dionysius' own words; and he has given us verbatim four fragments of the epistle to the Romans, which shall concern us further. The church letters of Dionysius were addressed to the Lacedaemonians, Athenians, Nicomedians, to the Church of Gortyna and the other Cretan churches, to the Church of Amastris and the churches of Pontus, to the Church of Cnossus in Crete, and to the Romans.

In Dionysius' writing we discern indeed not only the personal ability of the man, but certainly the authority of the old Church of Corinth as well, a church founded by Paul, whose renown reached to the wide east as far as Asia Minor. The epistles sent by Dionysius to Athens and Lacedaemon, particularly, concern us further at this point. The Church of Athens, of which we know from Eusebius' account, at that time traced its foundation back to St. Paul and named Dionysius the Areopagite as its first bishop. It must however have been quite insignificant in comparison with the Corinthian church, since Dionysius not merely gives it counsels pertaining to its internal life, but also, as it appears, speaks to it in words which are far from mild; Eusebius tells us, " . . . . the letter to the Athenians, in which he exhorts them to faith and to behavior in accordance with the Gospel; he convicts them of wrongdoing, in that they have neglected these things and have nearly fallen away from the Word since the time when their leader Publius had suffered death in the persecutions" (the one under Marcus Aurelius is meant). In a manner corresponding to this Dionysius also wrote to the church in Sparta, and thus considered himself—in comparison with it—as bishop of the leading church of Achaia. Corinth must have occupied such a position from the very beginning. But that there existed in Athens also an ancient Christian church is not to be doubted. There Quadratus had addressed his Apology for the Christians to the emperor Hadrian in the year 125-6 or 129-30. We know absolutely nothing of the church in Sparta; it appears in Dionysius for the first time.

It may be regarded as certain that in the period here considered, Christianity, which had travelled so readily the way of commerce and trade, reached the Greek islands also. Crete at least had Christian churches; Tit. 1:5ff is explicit evidence for an early mission to the great, important and much-visited island, the primitive middle term between orient and occident. Of the letters of Dionysius two are addressed to Cretan recipients, one to the Church of Gortyna and the other churches of Crete, the other to the Church of Cnossus.

9. *Church Organization.* There is little for us to say about what can be learned of Christianity in Achaia; it is not much more than what we know about the churches of Macedonia. Corinth, the leading church, on which such bright light falls in the apostolic age, because of the letters of St. Paul—light such as falls on no other church in the same epoch—in our period largely recedes into the darkness of the century. Nevertheless we shall concern ourselves somewhat more exhaustively with the church when we make use of First Clement, and shall—as we did above in the case of Philippi—take up the question of the Corinthian church and attempt briefly a solution. The letter itself invites this, since it is written to intervene in the disturbed order of the church with a view to settling the disturbance. Of course we must always bear in mind, when we make use of First Clement as a source for the Corinthian church organization, that it is a letter sent from abroad, from Rome to Corinth, that it did not originate in Corinth itself. It is worth while to exercise here the same prudence and reserve which we employed when we studied the Epistle of Polycarp as a source for the Church of Philippi: in First Clement we do not read direct declarations of the Corinthians themselves regarding their church, but only what the Romans presupposed as existing in the sister church, as valid and in use. And we may take for granted, from the material which stands before us in First Clement, that it gives us a picture of the church organization in Rome itself. But of course if the Romans involved themselves, by their exhortations and criticisms, in the internal relations of their sister church, we must therefore conclude that they must have had a clear picture of how things appeared to be arranged in the Corinthian church. There was of course a possibility of the Romans obtaining the necessary insight into these matters; they must, in fact, have had it from the beginning, if in this case they immediately sent exhortations and advice to the Corinthians. We must assume that in both these great churches approximately the same stage of church organization must have been reached, and this stage is obviously different from that which we can observe, say, in Syria and Asia, from the Ignatian epistles.

Unfortunately the accounts which First Clement gives regarding church organization cannot be taken as unequivocal and clear.[5] This is due to the uniqueness of the writing, which intervenes in a still

[5] [*Translator's Note.* Again cf. Streeter, *The Primitive Church,* on these points.]

unsettled controversy within the Corinthian church. The Corinthians of course understood perfectly what the Romans said to them, while at the present time we are able to understand many details only with great difficulty. The situation in point is not different from that of many other early Christian writings, especially the 'epistles.' One needs only to call to mind the many obscurities which of necessity we see in the Pauline letters—difficulties which remain.

First Clement is written for the purpose of helping, by its intervention, in the adjustment of a controversy which has broken out in Corinth. There are two parties in the city. The greater party numerically, which indeed comprises an overwhelming majority in the church, is on one side. It is led by a few men, one or two persons (47:6); they are rash and insolent men, as the Romans picture them (1:1). On the other side stand the officials of the church, who can, however, rely on only a small following. Of these officials a few have been removed (44:6). The majority of the church, with the ringleaders (who are sharply censured by the Romans) at its head, has done this deed. The Romans wish to help in bringing the schism to an end, and therefore at the beginning of the epistle they resolutely range themselves against the majority. They take the part of the deposed officials and hope that they will be restored to their positions, since they have been unjustly supplanted, and their advice is that the ringleader of the controversy, the opponent of the displaced leaders, should voluntarily quit the Corinthian church and go his way in order that quiet may be restored. It is especially chapters 40-58 in which the Romans concern themselves in detail with the schism in Corinth. But despite these relatively broad conclusions, in many points we remain, after all, in the dark. We do not once learn how and from what occasion the opposition to the presbyters and their removal came about, what it was on which the opponents actually relied in their conflict with the presbyters, and how they came to gain so strong an influence over the church. Yet one may perhaps conjecture, in considering such passages as 13:1; 38:1f; 48:5f, that the leaders of the opposition relied on their spiritual gifts or charismata, and that they were prophets, teachers, ascetics. We see in so many places in the evolving church, down to the end of the second century, the progress of this conflict between officialdom and the Spirit, that we might well regard this antithesis as determinative for the situation in Corinth.

If we now turn our attention more closely to the important question as to which ecclesiastical organization can be recognized in

Corinth (and at the same time in Rome as well), it is important that a negative statement be made at the outset. The First Epistle of Clement does not yet know of the monarchical episcopate. This extraordinarily important further development which we have seen in Jerusalem and Palestine, and farther away in Syria and Asia, has not taken place in Corinth, just as it is lacking in Philippi also. It obviously did not prevail in Rome either, as our letter and later sources (the Shepherd of Hermas) indicate, until about 150.

At the head of the church we may apparently recognize church *officials*, in the plural. The epistle customarily designates this group of leaders by the name of elders, presbyters. This designation is repeated four times. In 44:5f it is said, "Blessed are the presbyters who have gone on before [i.e. died], who came to such a fruitful and perfect end, for they need no longer fear that anyone will dislodge them from the place allotted to them"; in 47:6, the Corinthian church is reprimanded thus, "Shameful, beloved, indeed very shameful it is, and unworthy of Christians' way of life, to hear that the distinguished, trustworthy and ancient church of the Corinthians, on account of one or two persons, has rebelled against the presbyters"; in 54:2 advice is given to the effect that a truly noble man filled with sympathy and love would say, "If sedition and strife and schisms take place on my account, I will depart and go my way, whither you will, and do what the church prescribes, in order that the flock of Christ together with its presbyters may live in peace"; in 57:1, finally, the ringleaders of the schism are exhorted: "Now as for you who have begun the schism, submit yourselves to the presbyters." From all these passages just quoted, it is clear that we have to deal here with church officials who are formally installed, who have a definite place in the church and a carefully defined circle of duty, and to them the church owes respect and obedience.

The same men who stand at the head of the church are in other passages of the letter designated by a name which we have encountered on numerous occasions, viz. the title of bishop; and closely linked with bishops are their younger associates and helpers, the deacons. In 42:4f we read: "The Apostles preached in village and city, baptized those who were obedient to the will of God and ordained the first fruits of these, after they had been tested by the Spirit, as bishops and deacons of those who were to believe in the future. This is nothing surprisingly new, since from long ages bishops and deacons have been mentioned in writing. For thus the

Scripture says in one passage: 'I will appoint their bishops in righteousness and their deacons in faith.'"

The very important chapters 40-44, from which we have already been able to draw so many conclusions, give us information as to the ordination and official obligations of presbyters.

Here we are struck by the unusually high valuation of the office, which arises from the fact that its origin is traced back first to the Apostles, and then indirectly through the Apostles to God and Christ. Immediately before the passage just quoted stand the words: "The Apostles received the gospel from Christ, Christ was sent out from God: Christ is thus from God and the Apostles from Christ: both these things took place in proper order according to the will of God. Since, therefore, the Apostles had received their commission, and were filled with certainty by the resurrection of the Lord and strengthened in the Word of God, they went forth in the joyousness of the Holy Ghost to preach the glad tidings of the nearness of the Kingdom of God" (42:1-3). Then follows the just-quoted story of ordination of bishops and deacons by the Apostles. And soon after these statements comes more explicit information about the way in which Clement looks upon the origin of the office and the ordination of presbyters: "Our Apostles knew through our Lord Jesus Christ beforehand that there would arise dissension concerning the name of the episcopate (περὶ τοῦ ὀνόματος τῆς ἐπισκοπῆς). On this account they also, since they knew these things beforehand with complete certainty, appointed those who have been mentioned before, and gave commandment further that when these should fall asleep, other approved men should take over their offices. Thus those who have been appointed by them or later by other approved men with the consent of the whole Church, and who unblameably . . . . have served the flock of Christ . . . . to thrust these men out of their office, we consider unjust" (44:1ff).

That this view, according to which the Apostles sent by God and Christ had appointed the first bishops and deacons in the new churches, cannot be held to be historical, is certain, and needs no further proof. This whole idea underlies the struggle which is often to be observed elsewhere in our period, namely, the concept that everything in the Church which pertains to organization and doctrine can be traced back to the Apostles. But we notice here that already the properly existing church organization is reckoned among those things which are of apostolic origin.

As for the powers of the office, we obtain from this long epistle, unfortunately, only very brief information. The bits of data lie close to each other in the significant chapters 40-44. A very important note appears in 44:4, "It would be reckoned to us as no light sin if we removed those who blamelessly and in a holy manner offered the sacrifices [gifts] of the episcopate" (τοὺς . . . . προσενεγκόντας τὰ δῶρα τῆς ἐπισκοπῆς). This exhortation stands in a broader connection, precisely as do chapters 40-44 which speak of the Old Testament worship and priesthood, and in which it is demanded that just as order prevailed in the cultus organization of the Old Testament, so it shall prevail in that of the New. From this parallelism it may be concluded that we are to look for the 'offering of the gifts' which is here allotted to the presbyter-bishops, in the sphere of cultus. However, the gifts which are offered for the church by the presbyters in divine worship consist of prayers, especially those which accompany the Church's sacrifice, i.e. the Eucharist. The expression, 'service,' which often appears in this context in chapters 40-44 (λειτουργία, 40:2; 44:2f,6), must also refer to this activity of church officials. Certainly the presbyters at Corinth must have exercised still other functions within the church; but the letter says nothing explicitly as to what kind of functions they were. From many statements which we find in other sources we may, however, presume that they had under their control benevolences within the church and general management of finances. At the same time we may remind ourselves of the fact that the gifts of the church were regarded as sacrifices, and that to offer them was pleasing to God.

The presbyters were chosen for their office 'by approved men with the consent of the whole church' (ὑφ' . . . . ἐλλογίμων ἀνδρῶν συνευδοκησάσης τῆς ἐκκλησίας πάσης). With these few words the letter gives an intimation of how the choice and commission of the newly-installed presbyters took place. The 'approved men' are hardly the other members of the college of presbyters. If they were, the letter would express this idea more clearly. But we are to understand the term to apply to a leading group within the church, which included besides the presbyters still other approved men. And if this be correct, we must surely have, ranged alongside the official ministry, prophets and teachers, perhaps also tried and true martyrs (confessors) in the circle of 'approved' men. We shall in like manner see that this wide group of leaders and respected men will meet us in other passages in the epistle.

It does not become very evident from the words of the letter just what, things being so, were the share of the approved ones and the share of the church, in the choice of the presbyter who was about to be installed. According to the language of the epistle it seems most reasonable to assume that the 'approved men' made the actual choice and the church merely confirmed it. But if this is to be assumed also for Rome, which is the place of origin of the letter, nevertheless we must not conclude that in Corinth the approved men merely nominated while the church actually made the choice. This observation leads us to conclude that the Corinthian church deposed its presbyters without any reason other than that it was not content with them.

The office of presbyter was certainly of life tenure in Corinth as in Rome. A removal took place only in special cases; according to the view of the Romans only for unworthy conduct. We have learned above of such a case of gross misconduct in office (p. 821)—in Philippi, where Valens, the presbyter, had embezzled church funds. The power of the church over the presbytery appears to have been conceived of rather more widely in Corinth. But it is impossible to speak more exactly, since we do not know at all precisely why it was that the presbyters in Corinth were removed by the church.

Two passages of the epistle require a more detailed consideration, viz. 1:3 and 21:6. They are similarly constructed, and in the form of a table of ecclesiastical precepts[6] they make exhortations to the various groups within the church. Thus the whole church is divided into leaders (ἡγούμενοι or προηγουμενοι), old men (πρεσβύτεροι), young men (νέοι), women and children. In both passages it is impossible that the old men, the πρεσβύτεροι, are officials, since immediately after them the young men are mentioned. We must undoubtedly interpret the word as referring here to the older, tried and trusted men within the church, who make up a class which is not sharply defined. First Clement thus uses the term 'presbyter' in two ways. At one time it means for him the officials, the presbyters in the narrower sense, but it also refers to the older, upper class (so to speak) in the church, the trusted and approved group of men to whom, as both the passages referred to show plainly, honor is due.

The officials must therefore be meant when the term 'leaders' is used in 1:3 and 21:6. The same term appears in other passages of early Christian literature, e.g. Heb. 13:7,17,24. Here also it signifies an approved and governing group in the church. First Clement demands that one show submission and reverential honor to the

[6] 'Gemeindetafel.'

'leaders.' There is a further question whether the two concepts of presbyter (=official) and leader are simply coincident, or whether the leaders are a wider circle, so that perhaps the approved charismatics also, the prophets, teachers and confessors of the church, are included among them. The second is the more likely hypothesis, for, as 38:1ff and 48:5f prove, First Clement still knows of the great Spirit-filled persons of the Church, who are still evidently to be seen in Hermas, who writes in Rome at a much later date.

On the whole it must be said, when we look back upon the situation as it is pictured here, that much in the church organization which was to be so important for the succeeding age, still remained largely in a state of flux. The variation in terminology proves this. The rules of the church furthermore are still uncertain and are conceived of in various ways, and together with the presbyters the great 'pneumatics' take part in guiding the Church and are honored along with them.

CHAPTER XXVII

Rome

1. *Paul.* We now turn from the east to the west, where the sole church which we can survey is that of Rome. Not that it was actually the only one during the whole period, i.e. until about 130. There was already a Christian church at the time when St. Paul came to Rome, in Puteoli, that significant commercial city with a strongly oriental tinge which lay on the gulf of Naples (Acts 28:14). This notice in the travel document of Acts—more accidental than anything else—is of course for a long period of time the only account we possess of any Christianity in the west outside of Rome. We must assume nevertheless that Christian churches were founded in other parts of Italy as well. It may be assumed with certainty that Ostia, the port of Rome, had one. The beginnings of Christianity in the Rhone valley and in the province of Africa (Carthage) may have taken place in our period also. But the churches of these parts seem first to be attested in sources in the second half of the second century. Thus Rome remains the only church of which we have knowledge in the Latin half of the Roman empire. Rome however is relatively well known to us, and this church taken by itself constitutes a very important counterpart to the Christianity of the east, and as such meets us in a number of pieces of evidence.

We have already had a glance into the church at Rome in considering St. Paul's Epistle to the Romans (cf. pp. 360ff); we have recognized that it originated through unknown missionaries who were connected with the synagogue—from which, however, the Christians soon detached themselves. At the time when Paul wrote his letter to Rome this detachment had already taken place; the majority of the church at that time consisted of those who were Gentiles by birth. And this development may have taken place within fifteen years or so of the time when the church first began. Nevertheless at the time of the Epistle to the Romans, the Jewish Christians, although in the minority, were yet a constituent part of the church which could not be overlooked.

At the close of his life St. Paul had worked in Rome for several years, if not as a free man, yet unhindered (Acts 28:30f). From the epistle which he wrote to the Philippians from Rome we can obtain information which is not insignificant, regarding the composition of the Roman church. In 4:22 Paul says, "All the saints salute you, especially they that are of Caesar's household." These words show us that within the church at Rome there was, as it appears, a well-defined circle made up of people from the imperial palace.[1] We are not to infer that among these were members of the emperor's family, but rather dependents of the imperial household. The latter included —the period is that of Nero's reign!—a number (how many we can hardly say) of slaves and freedmen. The imperial palaces situated on the Aventine were in miniature a copy of the Roman empire or the city of Rome itself. As the empire brought together the greater part of the world's known population, so natives of all possible nations were to be found in the city of Rome,[2] and in the emperor's palace members of all conceivable nations met one another and afforded an example of the syncretism which prevailed in the world at large. Orientals, in fact, had an influential position in the imperial household: Greeks, Egyptians, Syrians, and members of the mixed peoples of Asia Minor. Among the slaves and freedmen of the great imperial household Christianity had found quite early a suitable field for its propaganda. We shall have occasion to speak of the imperial palace again in what follows.

2. *St. Peter* also came to the Roman church in the period when St. Paul was living there. It is a strong and ancient tradition which brings the Apostle to Rome before the end of his life and tells of his death there. That Peter suffered martyrdom, and by crucifixion at that, John 21:18f proves. And before the time of the evangelist I Clem. 5:4 mentions the great example which the Apostle had set by his death. In the course of the second century there appear still more witnesses, such as II Peter 1:14; Dionysius of Corinth in Eusebius, *H. E.* ii. 25. 8; the Muratorian fragment, line 37; and after the end of the second century the witnesses are numerous. That St. Peter had worked in Rome is said as early as I Peter 5:13, where Babylon is to be interpreted as meaning Rome; still more obviously do Papias

[1] [*Translator's Note.* It has of course been denied that Philippians was written in Rome. Arguments for an Ephesian provenance are summarized in A. H. McNeile, *Introduction to the New Testament,* pp. 168-172.]

[2] Martial, *Spectac.* 3, written in the year 80:

Quae tam seposita est, quae gens tam barbara, Caesar,
ex quae spectator non sit in urbe tua, etc.

"What nation so exclusive, so barbarous, from which there is not an onlooker in your city, Caesar?" etc.

in Eusebius iii. 39. 15 and ii. 15. 2, and Ignatius of Antioch in Rom. 4, allude to Peter's sojourn in Rome, to say nothing of the express testimony of Dionysius of Corinth in the passage just mentioned, as well as later writers. The Roman residence and Roman martyrdom of St. Peter mutually support each other. This whole much-discussed question has been dealt with recently by means of an ingenious method which concerns itself with liturgical and archaeological material not hitherto utilized.[3] The period which saw Peter in Rome must have been the last years before his death, and his death must have occurred, as perhaps Paul's did also, in Nero's persecution of the Christians.

3. Herewith we are brought face to face with an event which is quite important and decisive for the history of the primitive Roman church, *the persecution of Christians under Nero.* The chief source for this event is the Roman historian Tacitus, while Suetonius adds a brief account also. Christian tradition speaks of the occurrence in only one place, I Clem. 6, and then only in very general words (cf. below, p. 841, note 5). Suetonius relates in a passage in Nero's biography in which he deals with Nero's more effective police methods and punishments, that he had imposed the death penalty upon the Christians, a class of people with a new superstition which because of its magic was a menace to the commonwealth.[4] Tacitus gives a more detailed report in *Annals,* 15:44, which is our chief source. He connects the Neronian persecution with the great burning of Rome in the year 64. Persistent rumors that Nero had ordered the fire had arisen among the people. All attempts on the part of the emperor to put an end to the story were of no avail. Then the idea of shifting the guilt to others and punishing them with extraordinarily cruel penalties (*quaesitissimis poenis*) occurred to Nero. He chose for this purpose a group of people who were generally hated by the populace for their nefarious deeds—the Christians. These were adherents of a pernicious superstition which had been brought from Judaea to Rome. Several were then seized, and they confessed (*igitur primum correpti qui fatebantur*). On their information it was then possible to seize an exceedingly large crowd of people (*multitudo ingens*), the members of which were of course convicted not of arson but of hatred against the human race (*haud*

[3] H. Lietzmann, *Petrus und Paulus in Rom,* 1915.

[4] Suetonius, *Nero,* 16, *adflicti suppliciis Christiani, genus hominum superstitionis novae ac maleficae,* "The Christians, a race of men with a new and wicked superstition, were visited with punishments."

perinde in crimine incendii, quam odio humani generis convicti sunt). Those who were condemned Nero had executed with mockery and shameful treatment: they were wrapped in skins of wild animals and cast to the dogs, crucified, burned, and even used as torches in the evenings in the emperor's gardens. For this reason there arose the question of whether the Christians had been guilty of serious crimes and had merited the most severe punishment, despite the general sympathy with them. The people came to hold the opinion that the Christians had been executed without regard to the public weal, but in order to gratify the emperor's cruelty.

An explanation of the sentence which we have literally quoted above is essential for understanding Tacitus' passage. *Igitur primum correpti qui fatebantur:* what does this mean? At first glance it may be interpreted to mean that the Christians set fire to the city. But if one considers the intrinsic difficulties which are raised by this interpretation, one sees also that the context of the passage is not favorable to the idea. Tacitus says quite plainly that according to the opinion of the Roman people, with which he agrees, the Christians were innocent of the burning of the city. According to the prevailing view Nero had set the city on fire; the Christians had nothing to do with it, and the trial proved nothing. Thus the object of *fatebantur* must be considered to be something else; one must supply *se Christianos esse* or something similar. The procedure against the accused and those against whom they informed was for the purpose of exposing a disposition of enmity to the whole world, on the part of the Christians. It was certainly on account of their statements regarding their apocalyptic expectations, i.e. the great final judgment, the end of the Roman empire, the condemnation of the Gentiles, that they were executed as haters of the human race and enemies of the governmental and social order. How the information of Suetonius, viz. that the Christians were condemned because of their magic, is to be reconciled with Tacitus' account, is not clear. Yet it is to be observed that both writers speak of the *superstitio* of the Christians. One might easily have connected the 'superstition' of the Christians with secret magic and pernicious witchcraft.

The Neronian persecution, which, as it appears, was confined to Rome, must have interfered seriously with the church there, since it was bloody and widespread. Those condemned belonged to the lower classes, for such punishments as these might be employed only against the rank and file; *honestiores* might not be sewed up in skins and thrown to dogs, crucified, or burnt for a spectacle. Slaves and non-Romans thus must have been numerous in the church. Unfortunately we lack, as we have said before, Christian sources which speak of the Neronian persecution. From I Clem. 6 one merely learns that they must have been executed with severe torture and that their death was made an exhibition.[5]

Under the successors of Nero the Roman church had peace at first, or perhaps one would better say that we know nothing of a persecution under the first two Flavian emperors, Vespasian (69-79) and Titus (79-81).[6]

We have already heard earlier of *trials of Christians under Domitian.* Relatives of Jesus were led before the emperor, but were released by him unharmed (p. 726). We have heard of very severe oppressions connected with denial of worship to the emperor, in the province of Asia. The Revelation of John is the great storm signal of this conflict (pp. 807ff). The following accounts of the situation in Rome lie before us. The historian Dio Cassius says, in his *Roman History,* "In the same year [95] Domitian had many executed, among many others Flavius Clemens, who was consul, although he was his cousin and was married to Flavia Domitilla, who likewise

[5] 6:1f, πολὺ πλῆθος ἐκλεκτῶν . . . . πολλαῖς αἰκίαις καὶ βασάνοις διὰ ζῆλος παθόντες . . . . γυναῖκες Δαναΐδες καὶ Δίρκαι, αἰκίσματα δεινὰ καὶ ἀνόσια παθοῦσαι, "A great multitude of the elect . . . . having suffered many outrages and tortures because of jealousy . . . . women suffering dreadful and profane iniquities as Danaids and Dirces." In the last words the reference appears to be to spectacular executions which took place in the Circus; this harmonizes well with Tacitus' account. Dirce was bound by the two brothers Amphion and Zethos to the horns of a wild bull and dragged to death ('the Farnese bull'). This, then, was imitated in the Circus. We hear elsewhere of such mythological executions. Of course we do not know how Danaids were represented by condemned Christian women. [*Translator's Note.* K. Lake, *ad loc.,* suggests that the text is corrupt here.]

[6] In Christian tradition Nero and Domitian are named as the only persecutors who had executed Christians down to the end of the second century, and Vespasian is expressly excepted from the list of persecutors; cf. Melito in Eusebius, *H. E.,* iv. 26. 9, μόνοι πάντων ἀναπεισθέντες ὑπό τινων βασκάνων ἀνθρώπων τὸν καθ' ἡμᾶς ἐν διαβολῇ καταστῆσαι λόγον ἠθέλησαν Νέρων καὶ Δομετιανός, "The only ones of all who were persuaded by certain slanderous men and who wished to establish the slanderous word against us were Nero and Domitian;" Tertullian, *Apol.* 5:5, *temptaverat et Domitianus, portio Neronis de crudelitate,* 'Domitian, a limb of Nero for cruelty, also attacked,' i.e. the Christians; 5:8, [*leges istae*] . . . . *quas* . . . . *nullus Vespasianus, quamquam Judaeorum debellator* . . . . *impressit,* '[those laws] . . . . which . . . . Vespasian, although he was conqueror of the Jews, never . . . . ordained.' For the Christian author of the Revelation of John, Domitian was *Nero redivivus;* cf. Rev. 13:18 and 17:8f, as well as the comment on these passages in SNT. But despite all this it has not been made a matter of certainty that trials of Christians did not occur under Vespasian and Titus also. The 'good' emperors, such as Vespasian, Trajan, and the Antonines, must not appear in the list of persecutors of Christianity! Yet we know nothing definite regarding Vespasian and the Roman church or any other Christian community, and Titus reigned only very briefly.

was a relative of the emperor. Both were accused of atheism (ἀθεότης), on account of which still many others, who had become perverted to Jewish customs, were condemned, some to death, and others to confiscation of property. Domitilla was however merely banished to Pandateria" (67:14).

Dio's account must be corrected on one important point: it is not a question of Jewish proselytes, at least not of them alone; to a great degree also it was members of the Roman Christian Church who were affected by the persecution. The proof of this which may be adduced is certain and obvious. It consists of the observation that Dio Cassius in his voluminous work systematically and intentionally fails to mention the Christians. And he *must* have known them, since in his age—he wrote under the Severi, and Alexander Severus (222-235), the friend of the Christians, was his patron—they were a quite well-known phenomenon of Roman life. But then we have definite and explicit accounts of Christian writers, who claim that the consul and his wife and many who were executed by Domitian were Christians. In Eusebius' *Chronicle,* which we possess only in the Armenian version, he reports between the fourteenth and fifteenth years of Domitian (ed. J. Karft, 1911, p. 218), "And Bruttius says that many of the Christians suffered martyrdom under Domitian. And Flavia Domitilla also, the niece of Flavius Clemens, the hypatos [consul], fled to the island of Pontia, since she had confessed that she was a Christian." In agreement with this text, which has now been correctly restored, Jerome's *Chronicle* says under the year 2112 from Abraham (ed. R. Helm, 1913, p. 192), *scribit Bruttius plurimos Christianorum sub Domitiano fecisse martyrium, inter quos et Flaviam Domitillam, Flavii Clementis consulis ex sorore neptem in insulam Pontiam relegatam, quia se Christianam esse testata sit,* "Bruttius writes that a very great number of Christians suffered martyrdom under Domitian, among whom was Flavia Domitilla, a grand-daughter of the sister of Flavius Clemens, the consul, who was banished to the island of Pontia because she had testified that she was a Christian." Eusebius tells a corresponding story in his *Church History* (iii. 18. 4). The Roman tradition in Suetonius (*Domitian,* 15:1) approaches the Christian tradition: *denique Flavium Clementem, patruelum suum, contemptissimae inertiae . . . . repente ex tenuissima suspicione, tantum non in ipso ejus consulatu, interemit,* "Finally, he put to death Flavius Clemens, his cousin, a man of the most contemptible laziness . . . . unexpectedly, and on the merest suspicion, but not during his

[Flavius Clemens'] consulate." According to this information, Clement was not executed in his year of office, which fell in 95, but immediately thereafter. The reproach of *contemptissima inertia* may very well be due to the fact that the consul, on account of his Christian faith, refrained as much as possible from taking part in state affairs.

Finally, archaeological research has, in addition to the Christian tradition, furnished us a proof of the highest value: a very ancient Christian cemetery, the *Coemeterium Domitillae,* was a piece of land which at one time belonged to Flavia Domitilla and was given by her to the Roman church.[7] Thereby the Christianity of the wife, at least, is established.

It is thus beyond doubt that the church in Rome was oppressed under Domitian. As to why the condemnations took place we do not have sufficient knowledge. Because of atheism—thus because of apostasy from the ancestral and national gods—says Dio Cassius. But many other questions might have been raised besides this. We might especially think of the crime of *lèse-majesté.* We have already seen with what importance Domitian regarded divine honors to his own person, and how this consciousness which he had of being a Caesar came into collision in Asia with the blunt refusal of Christians to pray to him. Conflicts of this sort would certainly not be absent in Rome, and among those who were condemned there must surely have been some Christians.

In contemporary Christian tradition there is hardly ever any mention of the memory of the Domitianic persecution. Nevertheless the expressions at the beginning of First Clement must refer to it. Here the Roman church excuses itself for not having written sooner to Corinth, because of the misfortunes and hardships that have broken out abruptly and in quick succession (I Clem. 1:1). Perhaps also certain expressions of the Epistle to the Hebrews, such as 12:1-6 and 13:3,13,23, are connected with the experiences of the Roman church under Domitian.

That the Roman church underwent suffering in the short reign of Nerva and later under *Trajan* and *Hadrian* we cannot know certainly; on the position of these emperors with respect to Christianity, cf. pp. 812ff above. Nevertheless we have a Roman writing, the

[7] An exact and extensive description of the catacomb of Domitilla, which the discoverer, de Rossi, could not have given, is found in Orazio Marucchi, *Roma sotteranea cristiana,* nuova serie i, 1909; cf. also N. Müller, "Koimeterien" in Herzog's *Realenzyklopädie,* x (2d ed.), pp. 810f, etc.; English tr. in *Schaff-Herzog,* ii, 480-492.

Shepherd of Hermas, a good part of which arose under Hadrian, though after 130. This book, which was written in the city of Rome, speaks often of persecution and oppression, of steadfastness and denial; cf. Vis. i. 4. 2; ii. 2. 2,7f; ii. 3. 2ff; iii. 6. 5; Simil. i. 5f; vi. 2. 3; viii. 6. 4; viii. 8. 2ff; viii. 10. 2f; and a number of passages in the long ninth similitude: 19:1,3; 21:3; 26:3,6; 28:4. One must assume in the face of the accumulation of testimony here that certainly under Trajan and possibly under Hadrian, condemnations occurred in the Roman community. Because of the Christians' status in the eyes of the law, which we have discussed previously, officials always had the power, and perhaps the duty also, of interfering with the Christians.

4. *Influence of the Christian Community.* The trustworthy points of evidence of the tradition, which have been set down above, which show us that in Domitian's reign relatives of the emperor were accused and condemned on account of Christianity, give us reason to dwell on these facts somewhat longer and to consider them from still another angle. The consul Titus Flavius Clemens was executed in 95, presumably because of Christianity; his wife Flavia Domitilla, who was certainly a Christian woman, was for a similar reason banished to the little isle of Pandateria, which lies west of Cape Misenum, or to the neighboring island of Pontia. In the catacomb of Domitilla, furthermore, there have been found inscriptions the names of which apparently demonstrate connections with the Flavian household, if not with the imperial family itself. From these trustworthy traditions and observations it follows unequivocally that Roman Christianity had *members and protectors in very influential circles* in the city. How did it penetrate into such high places? We may remind ourselves of the passage referred to above in Phil. 4:22, relative to the people from the emperor's house, who are known as a well-defined group, in the generation before the Domitianic trials of Christians. Once it had taken root in the imperial palace Christianity would have grown still further. The way in which it came to the Flavian family can hardly have been otherwise than through slaves and freedmen.

The people from the household of the emperor appear to us, in still another passage from First Clement, as leading and responsible people within the church. In I Clem. 65 there are named three ambassadors of the Roman church who were then being sent with the letter from Rome to Corinth. Of these three one is named Claudius Ephebus, another Valerius Biton, the third Fortunatus. The first two names surprise us. They are double names and their first members, Claudius and Valerius, permit us to conjecture, rather reasonably, a connection with two famous families, the *gens Claudia* and the *gens Valeria*. To the *gens Claudia* belonged the first imperial house, the Julian-Claudian, which died out with Nero in the year 68. Tiberius and Drusus were Claudians, as well as Germanicus, Claudius, Caligula, Britannicus, and Nero, and Suetonius has depicted the renown and nobility of the *gens Claudia* at the beginning of his biography of Tiberius. The *gens Valeria,* likewise very old and highly celebrated, became connected with the *gens Claudia* in the marriage which the emperor Claudius made with Messalina (executed in A. D. 48), a woman of the *gens Valeria*—that famous and proverbially savage amazon, whose deeds Tacitus (*Annal.* 11:2f, 12,26,38), Suetonius (*Claudius,* 26ff), and the poet Juvenal (*Satire* 6:115-135) have portrayed. A good proportion of the slaves of the rich Valerian house came into the palace as a dowry at the time of the nuptials, and among the freedmen of Claudius and his successors are frequently to be found, as the inscriptions show, people bearing the family names of Claudius, Claudia, Valerius, Valeria—freedmen adopt the family names of their masters—and indeed the two gentile names often appear connected with each other on the same stone.[8] It is thus no groundless conjecture to recognize in the two ambassadors whom the Roman church sent to Corinth, perhaps about the year 95, freedmen of the imperial household. They cannot have been members of the two ancient and proud patrician houses, and certainly not of the imperial house itself. It is impossible to assume that they are slaves, because of the form of their names. Moreover they were masters of their own time if they could consent to go on the embassy on behalf of the church of Rome. The people from the emperor's house have thus preserved their honorable position within the Roman church. Two freedmen of the imperial household are exhibited to us here as in leading positions. They were tried and true members of the church: "From their youth to their old age they have lived among us" (I Clem. 63:3); they go abroad as representatives of the church on an important mission.

That the Christian church in Rome had powerful members, or at least protectors of great influence, is also shown irrefutably by the

[8] Cf. the married couple in *Corp. Inscr. Lat.* vi, 8943; *Valeria Hilaria nutrix Octaviae Caesaris Augusti hic requiescit cum Ti. Claudio Fructo viro suo carissimo,* "Valeria Hilaria, nurse of Octavia Caesar Augustus, lies here with Tiberius Claudius Fructus her dearest husband." There are more examples in Lightfoot, *The Apostolic Fathers,* i, "S. Clement of Rome", i. 27f.

letter which Ignatius wrote to the Roman church. Ignatius was, as we have already seen (pp. 767f), condemned in Antioch, and it was to be his fate to be torn to pieces by the wild beasts in the Roman arena. The capital's great spectacles demanded many animals and many men, and from all over the whole empire wild or semi-wild beasts and condemned men were sent to Rome. From Smyrna, by Ephesians who were to be in Rome long before himself, he sent the epistle to the capital. We have considered already the letters sent by Ignatius to Asiatic addresses. How finely and courteously he wrote to these churches, how strongly he praises and appreciates their apparently blameless condition! And yet he understands so well how to give warnings and censures, to fight against heresy in the churches, and to recommend the great means of safety against the heresy in their midst, viz. the safeguard of the threefold ministry. Ignatius quite obviously, although an outsider, feels himself commissioned to speak to the churches about their domestic affairs.

The Epistle to the Romans has a completely different tone; it does not speak of dangers which threaten the church, or give exhortations and warnings against dangers, or speak of bishops, presbyters, and deacons; the content of the Ignatian letter to the Romans is from beginning to end *one* stormy request: "Do not hinder me from being martyred." He adjures the Romans: "If you keep silent concerning me, I shall be a word of God; but if you become inflamed with love for my flesh, I shall again become an empty sound" (2:1); "I die willingly for God, if only you will not hinder me; so I beseech you, do not show me any unseasonable kindness; let it so be that I become the food of beasts, through whom I may participate in God" (4:1); "Speak amicably to the beasts, that thereby they may become my grave" (4:2). These are noteworthy phrases in the Antiochene bishop's writings, highly individual and valuable records of a very original, inner enthusiasm for martyrdom.[9]

What are we to conclude about the Roman church from these words of Ignatius? The Christians in the capital city must have had the opportunity and the power to succeed in gaining at least a mitigation of punishment for condemned comrades in the faith. This may have been accomplished either by a new trial or by a commutation of punishment. In years past the Roman church had often had occasion to interfere successfully in trials of Christians for this very

[9] [*Translator's Note.* Most present-day writers see in St. Ignatius an almost pathological desire for martyrdom; cf. B. H. Streeter, *The Primitive Church,* pp. 168-183; D. W. Riddle, *The Martyrs,* pp. 12, 27f, 60f.]

purpose; Ignatius gives explicit testimony to this: "It is an easy thing for you to do what you will." If the church was in a position so to interfere and if in its determined purpose it had a well-grounded view of the means to be taken to attain its end, and its goal was abrogation or at least commutation of the sentence which had already been passed, one must with good reason conclude that it possessed the means to carry out its intention. Some of its members must have had strong influence with people in key positions, whether in the palace, at the imperial courts of justice, at the prefecture of the city or in the praetorium. It is not to be readily assumed that at that time any higher officials of the state were Christians; the internal and external struggles and dangers were too great for Christians serving as Roman officials. Furthermore the officials were frequently changed, since they were despatched into the provinces. It is better to assume without hesitation that the influence of Christians was from behind the scenes and from the sidelines; it was exercised by slaves and freedmen upon very powerful men and matrons. It is moreover not a groundless assumption that the slaves and freedmen of the palace were the ones who made use of their position.

We can see from an event which took place perhaps sixty or seventy years later in Rome, how we must picture to ourselves the course of these affairs. The Roman writer Hippolytus relates in his *Philosophoumena* (9:12) the changeable destiny of his anti-bishop Calixtus and says in this connection, "Marcia, the favorite among the three hundred women in Commodus' [180-192] harem, who for nine years, down to the very last days of the emperor, had great influence over him, obtained clemency and recall from exile for Christians who had been banished to the Sardinian mines." Behind Marcia, who was not herself a Christian, but who was an avowed friend and protector of the church, stood as her adviser her foster-father, the Roman presbyter, Hyacinth. This man, who according to Hippolytus' account of the affair, travelled in person to Sardinia with the list of the banished and pardoned Christians and released those who had been condemned, was not a slave, but more probably a freedman. This is shown by the ornate, typically Greek name, suitable for a slave (cf., for example, the notorious Narcissus, freedman of Claudius, of whom Tacitus and Suetonius tell us), and furthermore by the express statement of Hippolytus, who says that Hyacinthus was an eunuch. Commodus' successor, Septimius Severus, also had Christian slaves and attendants in the palace. Tertullian

(*To Scapula,* 4) says: "Severus, the father of Antoninus [=Caracalla], showed himself thankful to the Christians, for he sent for Proculus, a Christian, with the surname Torpacion, the guardian of Euodia, who once had healed him with oil, and kept him at his palace to the end of his life. Antoninus also, who was nursed with Christian milk, knew this man [Proculus]." The Christian Prosenes was Severus' chamberlain (*a cubiculo Augusti*), and several freedmen of the house of the Severi appear to have belonged to the church.

In such ways as this—and for once we have clear and explicit confirmation—the Roman Christians in the time of Ignatius may very well have exercised great influence over the fate of their condemned brethren in the faith.

Ignatius, as we have already seen, regards the Roman church with unusually high esteem. This is shown by nearly every sentence of his epistle, and the whole tone of his style exhibits it also. This esteem, however, does not rest merely on the fact that the Roman church is the church of the world's capital and that it 'is easy for it to do what it wishes.' The Church can, according to Ignatius' explicit words, exhibit still other excellences. In the introduction it is called 'president of love' (προκαθημένη τῆς ἀγάπης). This hyperbolic expression, blurted out in Ignatius' best style, refers to the great activity displayed by Rome in deeds of charity. And the best explanation of what Ignatius means here is given by a passage in the letter of the Corinthian bishop Dionysius to the Romans, in the neighborhood of the year 170, and thus about fifty years after Ignatius' correspondence: "For *from of old* you have this custom, of benefitting the brethren in manifold ways, of sending assistance to many churches in various cities, here mitigating the dreadful poverty of the needy, there aiding with support the brethren who have been sent to the mines, as your manner has been *from of old*. Thus you preserve, like true Romans, the Roman custom *inherited from the fathers*" (Eusebius, *H. E.,* iv. 23. 10). That the charity of the Romans was, as these words indicate, zealous in the time of Ignatius, and that even at this early period it did not concern itself merely with poverty in their own church, but instead within a wider circumference helped other churches and individual brethren, is from the testimony of Ignatius indisputable, since it goes back definitely to an earlier age and is connected with relationships transmitted from the past.

The letter of Ignatius prompts us to make a further observation regarding 4:3. We have often noticed previously how highly apostolic foundation and connections were valued in the post-Pauline age. If allusion was made to apostolic foundation and relations of Apostles to the church, Rome could similarly point to two great Apostles who had ministered there and had suffered martyrdom in Rome: Peter and Paul. Ignatius calls to mind this glorious past which the church possessed: "I do not command you as did Peter and Paul; they are free, I have been until now a slave." We are reminded also of I Clem. 5, where Peter and Paul (as in Ignatius, Peter stands before Paul) and their martyrdom are mentioned in a connection which makes their relation to the Roman church quite certain. In the first writing of the post-apostolic age which emanated from Rome (I Clem.) and in the first writing addressed to Rome (Ign., Rom.) the great pair of Apostles is named; and in succeeding ages down to the present time it has been thus on innumerable occasions. And still in the second century, at the beginning of which we stand in our study of Ignatius, the appeal to Peter and Paul had extraordinarily great importance for Rome, the leading church of the west—not merely in its struggle against heresies, but also in the church's internal struggle with the Asiatics, who suffered a great defeat in the paschal controversy in the time of Victor of Rome (189-199).

5. If now we attempt to get a glimpse into the *piety and theology* of the Roman church, to consider this church from within, we must concern ourselves especially with the First Epistle of Clement as the sole piece of literature of undoubted Roman origin. We are, in respect to it, in the fortunate position of possessing a writing which we can date rather accurately—it was written in 95-96 A.D.—which does not proceed from an individual (although of course it has only one *author*), but which is written in the name of the whole church. We can for this reason have firm confidence that we actually have in our hands for our examination a picture of Roman church piety and church theology, and that at least the leading group of the church expresses its mind in this letter. It is proper that the letter should have a certain solemn, official, and documentary character. It is written by the great leading church of the west, addressed to an old, highly esteemed church of the east, the leading church of Achaia. Its treatment of the theme, which centers around a situation created by controversy in Corinth, nevertheless rises far above the necessities of the moment, and paints in broad strokes the ideal picture of Christian life and Christian piety, as these things appear before the mind's eye of the Romans. The writing does not have a

merely accidental or opportune character, but seeks to rise above the needs of the moment and to give a general portrayal of piety. This view is confirmed by a number of observations; we may notice in the first place its artistic (in its own way), planned statement of the case, the universally valid, homiletical character of its expressions. We shall again briefly return to consider this observation. In a carefully arranged and worked out order, supported by detailed Scriptural proofs, the various virtues of true piety are extolled, and the ideal of the Christian way of life is portrayed.

That we are right in ascribing to the epistle a significance transcending its momentary purpose, the epistle itself indicates explicitly in one passage in its conclusion. There (62:1f) expression is given to the proud satisfaction which the Romans had in having sketched the complete ideal of Christian faith and life for the Corinthians in their letter: "Concerning that which is fitting for our religion, which is indispensable for those who wish to lead, piously and righteously, a virtuous life, we have written to you in sufficient detail, brethren. For we have exhausted the themes of faith and repentance and genuine love and self-control and moderation and patience, and have reminded you that by being honorable in righteousness and truth and long-suffering you must be pleasing to Almighty God and that without thinking evil of one another you must maintain concord in love and peace and eager good temper."

If now we attempt to exhibit, in its chief details, the picture of religion as it meets us in this classic document of Roman ecclesiastical piety in the post-Pauline age,[10] the Ignatian epistles, already discussed at some length, commend themselves to us for comparison as a counterpart to First Clement. If one comes to the latter after having read Ignatius, one has a feeling of being transported into a completely different sphere. In the Ignatian writings, as we have

[10] On what follows, cf. A. von Harnack, *Der erste Klemens-Brief: Eine Studie zur Bestimmung des Characters des ältesten Heidenchristentums* (The First Epistle of Clement; a Study toward Determination of the Character of the Earliest Gentile Christianity; *Sitzungsberichte der königl. preuss. Akademie d. Wiss., phil.-hist. Klasse,* 1909, pp. 38-63); W. Wrede, *Untersuchungen zum Ersten Klemens-Briefe* (Researches in the First Epistle of Clement, 1891); Lightfoot, *The Apostolic Fathers,* part i, vol. i (1890), valuable for its treatment of the matter, as well as the commentary on the epistle itself in part i, vol. ii; the discussions of the epistle to be found in H. Windisch, *Taufe und Sünde im ält. Christent. bis auf Origenes* (Baptism and Sin in Ancient Christianity to Origen, 1908), pp. 321-329; and W. Bousset, *Kyrios Christos* (1913), pp. 356-374; translation and short exposition of the letter in E. Hennecke, *Neustamentliche Apokryphen,* and *Handbuch zu den Neutest. Apokr.* (New Testament Apocrypha, and Handbook for the New Testament Apocrypha, 1904). [*Translator's Note.* One might add K. Lake, *The Apostolic Fathers,* i, 3-121.]

observed above (pp. 767ff), we are met by a very strong ecstatic condition, an enthusiastic piety, a piety which, in mysticism and sacrament, is defined in terms which are nearly exclusively Hellenistic; in the Roman letter we find peace, order, temperance, a piety which is quite moralistic and without excesses. To use a metaphor: the building which is erected here is not laid on profoundly deep foundations, yet when one stands inside, the eye loses itself in the awe-inspiring, gathering dusk of halls which vie with heaven in their height; it is, however, erected broadly enough and with sufficient illumination, so that there is room for many and work is provided sufficient for the day and its needs.

The disposition to have absolute order in the church—this is one of the chief traits of the epistle which is conspicuous at first glance. The *strong emphasis upon order,* on mutual self-submission, and on the necessity of obedience, is connected with the occasion of the letter. In Corinth, order within the church has been seriously disturbed, as the beginning of the letter shows. The young men have arisen against the old, the ignorant against those who are held in honor, harmful jealousy has broken out in the church (3:1-4). There are two parties in the church, and the refractory majority is led by rash and shameless people (1:1), by one or two persons (47:6), and has ranged itself against the presbyters, the officers of the church, some of whom have been deposed in the course of the controversy (44:6). It is obvious that in such a situation the letter would stand strongly and resolutely for order, would extol and glorify it. But one can readily notice in the letter's expressions that —far transcending the immediate situation—order belongs to the fixed ideal of piety and church life of the Romans. The author of the letter sees order as prevailing everywhere. There was a fixed order in the Old Testament. Moses had displayed it in God's ordinances; in the Old Covenant it had been decided exactly when, where and by whom the sacrifices should be offered (40f); the priesthood was conferred upon only *one* tribe, a divine mark had been transmitted to the tribe of Levi (43); his peculiar services were prescribed for the high priest, the priests were allotted their places, and the Levites were obliged to perform their respective functions, while for the laity were prescribed things which were fitting for the laity to do (40:5). Only in Jerusalem and then only before the shrine at the altar might there be sacrifices (41:2). He who did anything contrary to the will of God with respect to the cultus suffered death as his fitting fate: this is deep gnosis given in the Old

Testament in order that afterwards Christians might be able to judge for themselves (41:3f).

But peace and order are not confined merely to the revelation and what is laid down in it. All nature, the cosmos above and below, is a complete revelation of peace and order. Thus strongly and clearly, as none other among ancient Christian writers has done, does First Clement sing the praise of the well-ordered creation. Old Testament and Stoicism have had their influence upon him; but that of the latter, already mediated by the liturgy of the Church, has been the stronger. In 20:1-10 stands the beautiful development of the idea, beginning with the heavens which revolve in an orderly manner; then day and night, sun, moon and the chorus of stars are enumerated, the earth and the world beneath, the sea and the ocean, in turn; he speaks further of the seasons, the winds and wells, finally the animals, even the smallest of them, all of which meet together in concord and peace. Therefore there must also be order in the Christians' church, and a table of moral precepts (*Haustafel*) is appended to chapter 20, in which the proper, peaceful, ordered conduct of various groups in the church is depicted.

A strong and, properly speaking, ecclesiastical element is introduced into the epistle by the demand for order. That God is a God of order is shown especially in the peace and good conduct of various groups in the church, which, ranking below the presbyters, pay them honor and treat one another with proper respect. For order has been ordained by God in the present-day church as in the church of the Old Covenant: Christ was sent by God, the Apostles by Christ, both in good order according to the will of God; and the Apostles then went out and preached in village and city and appointed their first-fruits as bishops and deacons for future believers (42:1-4).

In its especial endeavor to establish order and obedience as a chief condition of human success, the letter does not stop at the boundary of the pagan world. It points to the discipline of the Roman army: "Look upon those who take the field for our sovereign, see how precisely, how willingly, how obediently they carry out commands; they are certainly not all generals and colonels and captains and lieutenants, and so forth, but each one in his own place executes what is commanded him by the emperor and the leaders. The great cannot exist without the small, nor the small without the great; there is a certain mixture among all, and there is need of one another" (37:1-4).

It is friendship for the 'world' which is expressed by these and other ideas in the epistle. And this *broad-mindedness* is connected with another significant peculiarity of the writing and the piety which is reflected by it. That is the decided feeling for *moderation*, an unmistakably great temperateness in disposition. There is no extravagance, no ecstasy, absolutely no storming of the gates of heaven, such as is wrought into the very being of the pneumatics. As an example of contrast one may again take Ignatius. Narrowness and fanaticism in the true sense are lacking. The struggle is earnest and determined but it is only against the disturbers in Corinth; nothing must offend against ecclesiastical order. For the rest, clemency (ἐπιείκεια)—one of the favorite words of the letter—is characteristic of its piety. Since the writer sees harmony and order everywhere, even in nature and the pagan world, since he traces everywhere God's will and activity, which provide charitably for all but especially for us who have gained refuge in his sympathy, the writer will of course forbear from condemning harshly and narrowly, from digging moats and erecting walls in one-sided exclusiveness, barriers which include only a small flock of believers and elect and leave all others outside. Apocalyptic gloating which would feast itself upon a mighty slaughter of the nations is far foreign to the trends of thought of the author and his church. Just as in the final prayer of the epistle, which probably is derived from the Roman liturgy, there are petitions for the emperor and the authorities, 'our lords and princes,' just as there it is openly said that God (and not the devil, as in the Revelation of John) has conferred glory and power upon them, just as it is also recognized there that 'we,' the Christians, must subordinate ourselves to the state (60:4—61:1), so in other passages, in the author's own language, lofty examples of ancient love of fatherland and self-sacrifice are held up for emulation: "To give still other examples from pagans, many kings and rulers have delivered themselves up to death in times of pestilence at the behest of oracles which they have received, in order to save their subjects by their own blood; many have wandered far from their home cities, in order to put an end to sedition" (55:1).

Another general observation which can be made regarding the whole epistle from beginning to end is this: that, for the man and the circle which stands in the background of the writing, practical conduct of life and morality make up the kernel and content of the *vita religiosa*. A *strong moralism* runs through all its expressions from the first page to the last. Neither in renunciation of the world nor in enthusiasm, nor in gnosis or mysticism, can one seek and find that which unites the circle of believers and gives it its peculiar character. Even the cultus is far in the background. There must be worship, and established order in it is necessary (chh. 40f), but it can certainly not be by chance that the Eucharist and its celebration are never mentioned in the entire epistle, and that baptism is also strikingly in the background. If one goes through the long development of ideas in the letter one sees quite clearly what it is on which actual Christianity is founded: on its verification in life, in the circles in which the individual lives: love, obedience, humility, chastity, friendship, temperance, clemency, hospitality, sacrifice, purity, peaceableness, forbearance—these are the chief recognizable features of the true Christian way of life. In its opening chapters (1 and 2) the epistle defines the ideal picture of the true, religious church, and there a list is to be found of the following traits: glorious and steadfast faith, rational and gentle piety, magnanimous hospitality, perfect and certain knowledge (of God's commandments), the doing of all things without respect of persons, subordination to the leaders of the church; a reverential attitude on the part of the young; obedience and domesticity on the part of wives; humility, subjection, charity, obedience to the commands of Christ, profound peace, boundless well-doing, a pure will, continual readiness to acknowledge sins, incessant care for the well-being of the whole brotherhood, sincerity and forgiveness, peaceableness, a constantly honorable behavior, fear of God, regard for the commandments of God.

If we are to consider the picture of piety in detail, in accordance with this general description, it is well for us to begin with *faith in God*. For Clement this is the great keynote of religion. God is the Almighty One who has created all things and maintains their order, the Lord and Master, the King, the Father of everyone and everything. The epistle uses a number of names for God, all of which define him more closely in suggestive ways. He is the δεσπότης and the κύριος (cf. here especially the liturgical designations in the great concluding prayer of 59-61). He is the great demiurge (20:11), the demiurge of everything (59:2), the demiurge and father of the aeons (35:3), the demiurge and Lord of all (33:2). Clement is the first who is much given to applying this designation, demiurge, to God; before him it appears only once in Christian literature (Heb. 11:10). God is the Almighty, the Pantokrator (1:1; 32:4; 60:4; 62:2), who created all by his almighty will. The creation of the world is extolled especially in the previously mentioned passage, 20:1-11, and again in 33:2-6. God is the king of aeons, the heavenly King

(61:2). How earnestly this faith is concerned with the will of God is shown by the observation that even the state, the Roman empire and its officialdom, are placed under the lordship and especial care of God (60:4 and 61:1). According to 55:1 it appears as though God had sent his oracles to the heathen as well, for the wonderful self-sacrifice of kings and rulers which is mentioned there was the result of consultation of oracles (χρησμοδοτηθέντες). The designation of God as universal benefactor (εὐεργέτης, 20:11; 59:3) may also be called to attention as being significant.[11]

It is a clear strong monotheism, a pronounced theism, which meets us here. And it is unimpaired as well, because it exhibits no encumbrance such as belief in devils and demons, and even very little admixture with faith in angels. The demons are never mentioned, the devil only once (51:1). One can as a matter of fact see only with difficulty how there can be a place for the devil, if only *one* will orders and guides all things from the depths of the abyss to the extremest heights of heaven. And even the angelic hierarchy obeys perfectly the great One, and there is especially no room for any interference on the part of angels or for occupation of pious fancy with them. God is the Lord and benefactor of spirits, he is surrounded by the myriads of angels which praise him (59:3; 35:5f), but the angels are after all only the celestial household which is a feature of past tradition. First Clement never betrays any consciousness of the idea that any parts of the course of nature or of human destiny are placed under the control of angels. In 29:2, where the angels of the nations are mentioned, we have simply an Old Testament quotation.

If we take up the question, important for the history of religions, of how we are to classify the epistle's faith in God, we must give the following answer. Here we encounter a piety which is strongly influenced by the Old Testament, especially by the Psalms. This is in fact obvious from the quotations made from it. Another and stronger source is popular philosophy of the age and its joyous belief in God. Stoic philosophy, especially, loved to concern itself with ideas of God's control of the world and divine providence. In I Clem. 20 and again in 33 there are expressions which are dependent, as strongly as can be, upon the picture of God and the world which Stoicism sketched. There is little which is peculiarly Christian which is to be discerned in the epistle's faith in God. The mode of expres-

[11] [*Translator's Note*. Lake, i, 110, rejects *εὐεργέτην* in 59:3.]

sion is upon the whole a beautiful coinage of Jewish Hellenism; 'diaspora Judaism plus the Cross,' which has undergone a strong Greek influence, has its expression in him.

And the same observation can be made regarding the use which First Clement makes of the *Holy Scriptures*, the Old Testament.

Considered quite externally, the connections of the epistle with the Old Testament occupy a very large place. The author, and the piety of the circle of which we regard him as the type, live and move in the holy books. The Septuagint's contents and language are very familiar to the author. In no other ancient Christian writing are the connections with the sacred book so extensive as here. By and large the letter is confined to the circle of writings included in the LXX, and there are only a few of its quotations which are not to be found in the Greek Bible, whose origin we cannot determine: 8:3; 17:6; 23:3f; 26:2; 46:2. The use of such apocrypha is, as is well known, not unusual; it is repeated here and there in ancient Christian writings, beginning with St. Paul and continuing until about the end of the second century. In the list of Septuagint writings which First Clement uses, the Psalms and Proverbs, as well as Isaiah and Job, stand out prominently.

The use which First Clement makes of the Scriptures is varied in manner. This is largely the case with his language also; he does not quote verbatim and refer to Old Testament passages, but his speech is permeated with reminiscences and echoes of the LXX. This gives his quotations in many passages a certain elevated hieratic tone; and this certainly must be an effect which is systematically planned. There are also verbatim quotations, introduced by various kinds of citation formulae. They are for the most part verbally exact, but are partly given also in freer form. One sees obviously that the author not only knew where to look for the texts, but that he also had in mind, more or less clearly, a group of quotations. The quotations range in length from short sayings to page-long citations; cf. 3:1; 21:2; 26:3; 30:2; and on the other hand, 16:3-14; 18:2-17; 35:7-12; 57:3-7. It goes without saying that the short quotations are from memory, for the most part, while the long ones are, on the other hand, copied out. There appear conflations of citations in Clement as in other early Christian writers, sometimes altogether intentionally, as in 39:3ff, where various sayings of Job are joined together; in other places the phenomenon is due to a mnemonic linkage of sayings, as in 14:4 or 26:2.

The wider use of the Old Testament which Clement makes is this: he utilizes the book as the great collection of examples, the ethical handbook from which he draws the typical pictures of men well-pleasing to God, and conversely, the frightful images of abominable transgressors, in order to support his paraenesis of virtue by reference to them. Especially in the first part of the writing are to be found compiled long chains of examples from the Old Testament, e.g. chh. 4; 9-11; 16-18. A sub-species of this use of Scripture is the recounting of examples in which a narrative from the Old Testament is reproduced in the author's own words, in free form and circumstantially, as in chapter 12, the story of Rahab of Jericho and the spies, and in chapter 43, the story of Aaron's priesthood. How familiar the author is with his Old Testament material is shown by the observation that occasionally in his narratives and examples he brings in details which go beyond the narrative material of the sacred book itself: the various embellishments, the later Jewish—especially Hellenistic Jewish—constructions upon the narrative material of the Old Testament have not remained foreign to the author's ken; cf. for example 7:6; 11:2, and the detailed procedure which in chapter 43 is ascribed to Moses.

The method which the author applies to the Old Testament strikes us as being, in general, quite acceptable to us. It is simple religious and moral edification which he seeks and finds. He does not pick out from the Old Testament passages which are harsh and difficult to understand, or dead, indifferent sections, in order to transmute dead stone to gold with the magic wand of allegorical interpretation; but he seeks what is by nature and choice kindred to him, the sayings and examples illustrating faith and obedience, confidence, humility, loyalty, peaceableness, and—very important—readiness to repent; as well as sections on the grandeur of God, his omnipresence, his willingness to save, his grace; and finally, the portrayal of the suffering and humble Servant of God. For this reason he can use the quotations from the historical books, the prophets and Psalms, and the wisdom literature, in their simple verbal meaning, without bringing in ingenious significations. If one wishes to see clearly the method of the epistle in this respect—and thus also the method of the author and the circle which he represents—one may compare with it the use of scripture which meets us, e.g., in the so-called Epistle of Barnabas or in Justin's *Dialogue with Trypho the Jew*. Only in occasional and rare details does the author show that he is not completely ignorant of the higher allegorical interpretation as well. One is not to include with these details the fact that he sometimes finds the preëxistent Christ speaking in the Old Testament (as in 16:15 and 22:1), or that he has the prophets foretelling Christ (17:1; 16:2ff; 36). Such employment of the Old Testament was, after all, obviously a matter of general practice in the Church; without it the Holy Scriptures would not be needed by the Christians. However, such a detail as in 12:7, where the red thread which Joshua's spies gave Rahab is taken to refer to Christ and the redeeming power of his blood, belongs indeed to the allegorical interpretation of the Old Testament in the narrow, technical sense.

If one draws the conclusions from these observations which have just now been made briefly, one must say not only that First Clement utilizes the Old Testament to a degree not reached by any early Christian writer before him, but also that he lives in the sacred books, and that he builds up and supports his own piety by means of valuable traits of Old Testament piety. Clement sees the chief points of his religion as already revealed in the Old Testament, and he sees it actually realized in the religious men of the Old Covenant: a conception of Christianity which orients itself to the Old Testament and which is defined in a strongly theistic and moralistic way, points toward the Christianization of the Old Testament (cf. Wrede, *loc. cit.*, p. 99).

In the consideration of this theistic-moralistic conception of religion, as First Clement represents it, of course the question arises quite seriously: what, then, according to the experience and the viewpoint of the author, is the new element in Christianity? What is his experience regarding *Christ and salvation?* And so it must be said that very little of what he possesses, after all hardly anything, can be described as being new.

It is indeed significant that only scanty use is made of the new Christian authorities which are already set up or are in process of formation. The author lives in the Old Testament, he is continually interesting himself in it; the words of Jesus, which tradition must surely have profferred to him in some written form, are hardly at all used. Where he quotes from them (13:2; 46:8), he joins with them quotations from the Old Testament, to which he gives precedence in his arrangement; cf. here 13:1f where it is especially evident. Where he refers to the Lord as an example of inner greatness and dignity, and at the same time of outward humility, he uses no sayings of Jesus in working out the example, but he sees Jesus speaking in the famous prophetic words of Isa. 53:1-12 (16:3-14). Paul's collected letters lay before him, but he quotes formally only from I Corinthians (47:1f), even though of course in other passages the same epistle and the Epistle to the Romans are tacitly utilized. In like manner he uses, without mentioning the source, the Epistle to the Hebrews (especially in ch. 36) and perhaps, as several passages indicate, First Peter also. All this taken together is certainly small in comparison with the citations from the Old Testament and explicit references to Old Testament narratives, the number of which amounts to nearly one hundred, in addition to which there appear allusions and tacit employments of the sacred books.

According to First Clement's religion everything has already been given in the Old Testament, since everything connected with it is timeless. Opportunity was given for all races of men to come to knowledge of God, every generation had the possibility of repenting and turning to God: Noah, Jonah, all the prophets had preached repentance: 7:5—8:1. Christ is only, as it appears, the climax and conclusion of this succession, toward whom the prophets have pointed, whose blood is very valuable to his Father, since, having been shed for the sake of our salvation, it has brought the grace of repentance to the whole world (7:4). It appears that First Clement regards the especial gift of Christianity as having been this extension of salvation to the whole world, but of course the development of the idea just mentioned, which follows in 7:5ff, is treated in such a manner that this especial characteristic of Christianity is, after all, attenuated: "Let us, in spirit, review the generations and recognize that from generation to generation the Lord has given opportunity for repentance to those who have been willing to turn to him" (7:5). How it is that the blood of the Lord has such importance before God the epistle does not say, nor does it in those other few passages in which it speaks of Jesus' sufferings: "Through the blood of the Lord, those who believe in God and hope on him shall participate in redemption (λύτρωσις)" (12:7); "Because of the love which he had for us, our Lord Jesus Christ, according to the will of God, gave his blood for us, and his flesh for our flesh and his soul for our souls" (49:6). We must, however, assume it as a certainty that St. Paul has here influenced the religious language and ideas of the epistle.

Another statement or group of statements refers to the exalted Christ and fixes his continual significance for the community of believers: in 36:1 Christ is called high priest of our offerings, patron and helper of our weakness (τὸν ἀρχιερέα τῶν προσφορῶν ἡμῶν, τὸν προστάτην καὶ βοηθὸν τῆς ἀσθενείας ἡμῶν). These expressions likewise are not original with First Clement, but are derived from a source. It is the liturgy from which they come, as a glance at the passages 59:3; 61:3; 64, shows us. From the liturgy, from prayers or hymns, the other Christological expressions in ch. 36 also appear to have come, insofar as they are not derived directly from the Epistle to the Hebrews. Nevertheless we can still recognize in these ideas which are connected with the exalted Christ something which is characteristically Christian.

In its conception of the person of Christ the epistle holds from beginning to end the point of view which, as far as we can see, is the prevailing one. Christ is preëxistent and he has appeared in flesh; the expressions of ch. 36 and also of 16:2 are instructive on this point: Christ is depicted, in expressions partly taken over from the Epistle to the Hebrews, as the reflection of the divine glory, the Son of God, more glorious than the angels, as the sceptre of divine majesty; and it is said of him that he could have come in ostentation and proud pomp, but that he had come in humility, as Isaiah had prophesied concerning him.

With noteworthy firmness he holds to the primitive Christian eschatology taken over from Judaism. Not that we have portrayed here in detailed form, as it is in the Apocalypse of John (19:11-21), the idea of the warrior Messiah who takes vengeance on his enemies and leads his own into the kingdom of glory. But he adheres strongly and firmly to the idea of the judgment which will come certainly and come soon, and this judgment is connected with the resurrection of the body, a point on which there can be no doubt. Chapters 23-27 contain the chief developments of this idea. Again it is God who does everything and creates all; he hardly thinks of the Messiah in this connection (yet cf. 23:5 and 24:1). And one must not overlook the strong rationalism which carries through the whole section. The resurrection can be proved, according to the view of the author. God, who raised up the Lord Jesus, has given proofs of the future resurrection in the succession of day and night, in the perishing and germination of grains of seed, and finally in a rare but nevertheless a terrestrial occurrence, a phenomenon of natural history, the revivification of the phoenix bird. And the whole discussion of 23-27 comes immediately after the praise of the Creator God, who is a God of order, and who is glorified by Clement in inspired language (ch. 20): "Creation and resurrection, world preservation and world judgment, this is the beginning and end of the great working of God. We ought therefore to fear the All-Seeing One, and to flee wicked appetites, in order that we may be protected by his compassion in the coming judgment" (28:1). Yet the realistic eschatology, which Clement so explicitly confesses, is no longer the solely prevailing conception of salvation. Salvation is clearly beginning to be recognized as a present possession. And we hear the Hellenistic notes—which we have noticed before—of 'life' and 'immortality' which have previously been sounded in Christianity. Quite significant for this point is the section 35:1ff, where present and future possession are joined together: "How blessed and marvelous are the gifts of God, beloved. Life in immortality, splendor in righteousness, truth in freedom of speech, faith in confidence, continence in sanctification. These things we know already. But what are the gifts which are prepared for those who endure to the end? The creator and father of aeons, the All-Holy, alone knows their number and glory."

Finally the views expressed in the letter concerning *justification* and *atonement* correspond to the strong moralism which, as we have seen, permeates the whole epistle. Paulinism is obviously having its after-effects, and in 32:4 use is made of the Pauline formula of justification by faith: "We are not righteous of ourselves, nor through our wisdom or piety or understanding, or through the works which we perfect in purity of heart, but by faith, by means of which Almighty God has justified all from the beginning." But one can see nearly at first glance how true it is that this formula is only a borrowed one, and how little the Pauline religion and theology is a living thing for the author and his circle. For indeed that which is opposed to faith is not the works of the Law, the ἔργα νόμου, but one's own wisdom, piety, insight and works, perfected in purity of heart. And so, alongside the formula 'to be justified by faith' there stand, in other passages of the letter, two which are completely different; one of which, closely akin to the passage just quoted, says 'to be justified by deeds and not by words' (30:3). The other stands in an earlier connection: Abraham, St. Paul's great example of faith, received grace 'on account of his faith and hospitality' (10:7). Lot was saved because of his hospitality and piety (11:1); Rahab, again like Abraham, on account of her faith and hospitality (12:1). It immediately becomes clear from these formulae how little understanding there was in this age of Paul's great struggle for justification by faith; his presuppositions, the Jewish and Judaizing opposition, and also the peculiar experience of St. Paul's converts, were no longer present in Clement's day.

And Clement says quite clearly wherein the substance of faith consists, so far as he is concerned: in obedience. Abraham, who was called the friend of God, was found faithful because he was obedient to the word of God—so we read in 10:1—and the whole significant section, 9:1—12:8, inculcates the importance and glory of obedience to the exalted and majestic will of God. This will of God, however, as the preceding and following chapters (8 and 13) show, is that one repent and be humble without ostentation, arrogance, folly, or anger. God is merciful and it is his will that everyone have help in escaping from his sins; one must only be obedient and submissive to his will and do good works. In the discussion of paths of blessing, which stands in chh. 31-36, obedience and humility and the good works which are done in this attitude of mind stand out as being of the greatest significance.

Repentance, understood in this sense, and the forgiveness of sins by God do not end within the circle of believers. Sin is to be found inside the Church as well, and within it repentance, perfected in obedience and humility, must be used to obtain God's forgiveness. The moralism of the epistle reaches its climax in this group of ideas and experiences. Its author knows well that all Christians are in actuality carried away by the dominating power of sin, but that it is nevertheless possible for those who know the will of God and have received forgiveness of their pre-Christian sins to live in purity. Indeed in the ideal picture of a church, as chapters 1 and 2 sketch it, the significant trait is found: "Full of holy intention, in good eagerness, with pious confidence, you raised your hands aloft to Almighty God and implored him to be gracious to you, if perchance you had sinned involuntarily in anything" (2:3). There are indeed sins, and very serious ones too, which occur involuntarily, or as the epistle in other passages permits us to see, 'by the attacks of the adversary' (51:1). Where Clement draws the line at which he believes that sins which are actually unforgivable begin, we remain uncertain. Since, however, we see that not only does he include intemperance, but also fornication and adultery, within the circle of sins which Christians may commit and yet receive forgiveness (30:1), we must say that he regards forgiveness as possible in the case of nearly every sin conceivable. Nor does he doubt for a moment that the agitators in Corinth, whose conduct he condemns with especial severity, may obtain forgiveness of their sins as soon as they repent, bend the knees of their hearts, submit themselves and consent to obey the presbyters. That this broad-minded view of repentance, in itself healthy through and through, was probably not only the view of the author, but also of the whole church in Rome, follows from the leading passages of the church prayer found at the end of I Clement (chh. 59-61), in which is expressed in very beautiful—one might indeed say unforgettable—form, the consciousness that Christians still require greatly the grace and mercy of God, but that a broken heart and an afflicted spirit are acceptable to him:

We beseech thee, Lord,
Be our helper, and take our part.
Rescue those of us who are in distress,
Pity those who are lowly,
Raise up the fallen,
Show thyself to those who are in need,
Heal the sick,
Those who are erring among thy people
Lead again into the right way.

* * * * *
* * * * *

Compassionate and merciful one,
Forgive us our sins and failings,
Offences and transgressions.
Reckon not all sins to thy servants and handmaidens,
But purify us with the purification of thy truth,
And guide our footsteps,
That we may walk in purity of heart,
And do that which is good and pleasing.

* * * * *
* * * * *

Yea, Lord, let thy face
Shine upon us for salvation in peace,
That we, being stayed by thy strong hand,
And by thine exalted arm, may be preserved from all sin.

6. *Final Summary*. We are at the conclusion of our studies and now we wish merely to draw two observations and conclusions from our consideration of Rome and the church there, conclusions which for the most part follow obviously from the material with which we have hitherto dealt.

Christianity in Rome during our epoch, and in fact throughout the entire second century, exists substantially among the non-Latin, i.e. the Greek and oriental ingredients of the population. The language which the Roman church has used in speaking to those outside has of course been Greek. Still more, we cannot discover that in the church itself, in its own use, especially in divine worship, in preaching and in the liturgy, any language other than Greek has been used. The mode of expression and the style of Clement exhibit in many places the strongly stamped formulae of Greek liturgy and preaching, and the great prayer at the end is original Greek. And similar observations can be made respecting still later writings. It was not until toward the end of the second century that in Rome (and elsewhere in the west, e.g. in Africa), Christianity reached into the Latin-speaking circles and classes. Then arose the earliest translations of the Bible into Latin, then other beloved writings were translated, and at the end of the second century independent Latin literature first makes its appearance in Bishop Victor of Rome and in Tertullian of Carthage. That was an age when, in other spheres as well, in culture, in world literature, in the economic sphere, the west emancipated itself from the overlordship of the east—the age of the African emperor Septimius Severus.

We have often emphasized in the foregoing pages the significance which the great cities of the Mediterranean basin had for ancient Christianity: Jerusalem, Antioch in Syria, Ephesus and Smyrna, Thessalonica, Corinth, to say nothing of Alexandria, whose outlines are now visible in the dawn, and finally Rome—all these have come into our view. From the great cities as central points the new faith expanded along the roads of every-day commerce, first to the smaller cities, and then into the country districts. We can only very occasionally observe Christianity, in the period which we have considered, among the rural people of such provinces as Bithynia-Pontus or Phrygia (cf. above, p. 776 and p. 780). This development which reached out from the large city was, moreover, decisively operative on behalf of an enduring unity. The small churches of the minor cities found unity and support in the churches of the greater cities. From the latter they had received their Christianity, there their members found a friendly reception if they came to the capital on their own business or for the church: it was not in vain that hospitality occupied such a conspicuous place in the circle of early Christian virtues. The great city churches were, furthermore, often of great antiquity; most of those enumerated above were of apostolic foundation, and their church tradition was superior to that of those which were later organized. Ephesus had the undisputed position of leadership among the churches in the province of Asia, as had Antioch in Syria and Corinth in Achaia.

The leading churches, moreover, had interchange and communication not merely with the smaller ones but also with one another; the First Epistle of Clement or the letters and messengers which travelled from Asia to Antioch, when the Church of Antioch was persecuted under Trajan (pp. 818f), give testimony to this fact. By means of the active communication and intercourse, which we can clearly observe, there was possible a very widespread and uniform development of Christianity in the Roman empire among the widely dispersed churches, despite the weak position which Christianity had in the world at the time.

From what we have intimated it becomes clear to us immediately what extraordinary importance the Roman Church must have had for the whole church from the very beginning. In imperial Rome communications from the whole empire sped to a single point. The threads of the political administration of the great empire came together here; the city had a very great supply of commodities of various sorts, which were brought thither from the ends of the earth, and trade in transit from west to east and back again passed through Rome; foreign influence was great there as nowhere else; and even the resident population was made up of members of all known races.[12] The Roman empire was, by and large, the Mediterranean world; and what lay beyond it, such as northern France, Germany, the Danube provinces, Cappadocia, and Armenia, were outposts against Germans and Parthians; Rome was indeed geographically the natural central point of this empire. Our attention has been occasionally arrested in the preceding pages by the great reverence with which the inhabitants of the empire regarded the capital city. A special worship was offered *diva Roma*, and the cult of the emperor was itself in fact a deep reverence on the part of the provinces for the majesty of the ruling people and its ancient city-state.

From this we can understand how the Christian Church in Rome occupied a position which commanded especial esteem, as the church of the Roman city, nearly from the very beginning. The decisions of this church, by the very fact that they came from Rome, the chief

[12] A very fine picture of the greatness and absolutely surpassing significance of imperial Rome is to be found in the famous work of Friedländer, *Darstellungen aus der Sittengeschichte Roms in der Zeit von August bis zum Ausgang der Antonine* (Sketches from the History of Morals in Rome from Augustus to the End of the Antonines, 8th ed., 1910); cf. especially vols. i and ii.

city of the world, easily obtained an authoritative significance. These decisions and the tradition to which the Roman church could appeal had moreover quite unusual importance, since it was here that the two great Apostles, Peter and Paul, had worked, and had suffered the death of martyrdom. And finally the fact must not be overlooked that the Roman church had, so far as we can observe, already felt in a much earlier period the great obligation which was given her along with her leading position, and which she fulfilled. She willingly espoused the cause of the other churches, bestowed counsel and exhortation upon them, practised extensive hospitality and charity, and collected the necessary funds for this work in her own midst.

Thus in the very beginnings of the Roman Church is heralded the leading position which was later to elevate Rome to the headship of the whole Church, and the words spoken by the singer of imperial Rome, Virgil, of the city of Augustus, are fitting for Christian Rome as well:

> Verum haec tantum alias inter caput extulit urbes,
> Quantum lenta solent inter viburna cupressi.[13]

[13] "But in truth this city exalts its head above other cities, just as the cypresses do amid the sprawling viburnum trees."

INDEX TO VOLUME II

Achaia 827ff
Acts, Book of
  Author and date 655f
  Its conception of Baptism 622f
  Its conception of 'apostolic' 685f
  Period of origin 724
Aeons 603f
Alexander, son of Simon of Cyrene 690
Allegory 440, 857f
Almighty-formula 471, 478f 483
Amastris 781
Ananos, high-priest 709
Andronicus 674
Angels 599–603
Anthropology 605–611
Antioch 644, 740, 752, 766
  Later development of the church 766
Antipas of Pergamon 807f
Apocalyptic in Paul 543ff
Apollos
  Missionary activity 661
Apostles
  As missionary leaders 673
  Meaning of the term 674ff
  Marks of an Apostle 677f
  Later Catholic idea 681
  As founders of the ecclesiastical organization 687
Apostolic Council 677
Apostolic Decree 666, 743, 766, 783
Aquila 593, 661
Ardabau 782
Asceticism 566f
Asia 774f
  'Pauline' communities after the death of Paul 782f

Baptism
  Jewish baptism of proselytes 631
  In Paul's teaching 463, 622ff, 630–639
Bar-Kochba 722f
Barnabas 674
  Arrival in Antioch 740
Barnabas, Epistle of 656, 658
Basanitis 716
Basilides 762 n. 44
Beatitudes, The 744f
Beroea 669, 818
Birth of Christ 490f
Bithynia-Pontus 774, 780f
Breaking of the bread 640
Brethren (and relatives) of the Lord 716–719

Cappadocia 774
Cathechumèns 624
Cephas: see Peter
'Children of God' 505
Christ-cult: see Jesus-cult
Christians 730
Christology
  Adoptionist Christology 476
  Son of David Christology 732
  Son of Man Christology 485f
  World-Creator and World-Soul 478–484
  The Heavenly Man 484–488
  The Incarnation 488–491
  Birth 490f 732f
  Death and Resurrection 491–495
  In the Gospel of Mark 697f
  Heretical Jewish-Christian Christology 730–733
  The Genealogies 718 n. 16, 732f
Christ-title 730
Church: see Ecclesia of God
Cilicia 740, 747f
Circumcision 671f, 735
Civil life, Relation of the Christian to 591–594
Claudius Ephebus 844
Clemens, Flavius, 841, 844
Clement, First Epistle of 656, 685
  The address 827
  Church organization in 830–836
  Occasion 831
  Date 849
  Character 850
  Eschatology 860
  Justification and atonement 861
  Faith 862
  Repentance 862
  Church Order 851f
  Broad-mindedness and moderation 852f
  Moralism 853f
  Monotheism 855
  Use of the Scriptures 856–859
  Christ and Salvation 858f
Clopas 726
Colossae 776, 778
Colossians, Epistle to 480f, 588, 620
Comane 782
Communion: see Lord's Supper
Communion of saints 616–622
Community
  Pauline conception of the Christian 615–651
Community of goods 593
Conversion-experience 496f
Conversion-theology 442–445
Corinth
  Lax conditions 648
  Development after Paul 827
  Church order 830–836
I Corinthians
  Address 681
Cosmos 595–599
  Paul's view of 600f
Courage and Loyalty 577–580
Crete 830
Cyprus 775

Damascus 723, 740
Decapolis 716
Demons 855
Dialectic 435f
Dio Cassius 841
Dionysius the Areopagite 829
Dionysius of Corinth 780f, 828f
Divorce: see also Marriage
Docetism 761, 764f
Domitian 841f
Domitilla, Flavia 841f, 844
Dositheus 756f
Doxa 432, 478
Dualism 412, 597f, 607f, 762f
Duties, Lists of: see 'Haustafel'

Ebionites 730–739
  Origin and significance of the name 730f
  Christology 731ff
  Anti-Pauline nomism 735
  Gospel of 736f
Ecclesia of God 616–622
Ecstasy 625
Education 576f
Egypt 741
Egyptians, Gospel of the 658
Election 506ff
Emancipation, Ideas of 584f
Emperor-worship 803f, 806, 842f
Enthusiasm 468, 518ff, 566, 625
Epaphroditus 675
Ephesians, Epistle to 620, 622, 682, 775
  Catholic character 682
  Example of pseudo-apostolic authorship 683f
Ephesus 776f
Erastus 593
Eucharist: see also Lord's Supper
Evodius (Euodios), Bishop of Antioch 766
Exorcism 634f

Faith
  The Pauline conception 424–428
Fornication in Corinth 627
Fortunatus 844

Galatia 774
  Syncretistic-Gnostic elements in the community 776
Galilee 723
Genealogy of Jesus 718 n. 16, 731f
Gentile Christianity
  Relation to the primitive community 723
  Relation to the Old Testament 662f
Gifts of the Spirit 623f
  The Pauline conception 430
Gnosis 738
  Gnostic tendencies in later Jewish Christianity 738
  Samaritan Gnosis 756–763
  Judaistic Docetism 763ff
Gospel 687–703
  Origin of the word 687f
  The earliest Gospel 687–703
Gospels
  Ebionite-Gospel 736f
  Gospel of the Nazarenes 737f

Hadrian 723, 815ff, 843
  His letter to Fundanus 815f
Haggada 438

'Haustafel'
In the Epistle to Colossians 588f
In First Clement 835, 852
Hebrews, Epistle to
Date 656
Purpose 670
Hebrews, Gospel according to the 736
Hegesippus 711, 717
Account of James 712 n. 7
Hellenism 440f, 465f
Heresy 729–739
Heretical Jewish Christianity: Nazarenes and Ebionites 730–739
Heretical Christology 731ff
Samaritan Gnosis 756–766
Polemic of Polycarp, 822–826
Heretics
Jewish prayers against, 708, 729
Hermas, Shepherd of 844
Herod Agrippa I 724
Hierapolis 776, 778
Holiness 563f
House, The church in the 620
Human nature, The Pauline conception of 611–614
Hyacinth, Presbyter 847

Ignatius 764ff
Episcopate 766f
His type of Christianity 767
Antijudaism 767f
Doctrine of redemption 769f
Mysticism 770f
Relation to Paul 771f
Relation to the Johannine writings 773
His own letters 776f
Ignatius, Epistles of 656, 764f, 767, 775
Date 767
Epistle to Romans 846
Incarnation 488–491
Infancy Narrative 725

Jacob of Kaphar Sama 727
Jacob of Kaphar Sicanim 728
James, the Brother of the Lord, 674
Martyrdom 709–712
His Judaism, according to Hegesippus 711f
Influence upon the Syrian churches 740
Relation to Peter 719
Episcopal title 719f
Position in the Book of Acts 724
James, Epistle of 668, 743–751
The address 743f
Destination 745
The readers 745f
Attitude of the author to the Lord 747
Language and style 748f
Date 751
Anti-Gnostic features 751
Jerusalem: see also Primitive Community 776
Destruction 714ff
The Christian community after the year 70 717f
Origin of monarchical episcopate 719f
List of Bishops 721
Revolt of Bar-Kochba 722f
Jesus-cult 741
Jews
Mission among the 660f
Johannine Writings 775
John, Apocalypse of 591, 656, 684, 806–809
Persecution reflected in 806–810
John, Epistles of
Date 656
John, Gospel of
Date 656
Antijudaism 666
Redaction 787f
Relation to the Synoptics 788
Literary form 790f
Narrative material 791
Signs and wonders 791, 796f
The Discourses of Jesus 792f, 796
The element of mystery 793
The Passion Narrative 788, 793f
Purpose of the work 794
Faith 794f
Faith and knowledge 799f
Love 800
Christology 795
Mysticism 796, 798f
Sacraments 797
The Spirit 797
Salvation 798
Its Presuppositions:
Christian 800f
Jewish 801f
Hellenistic 802f
Personal experience 803
John Mark 788
Martyrdom 710
Joy, 506
Judaea 707–739
The Jewish War 726ff
Judaism
Paul's judgment upon 613f
Theory of rejection 663
The Gospel of Matthew and 755f
Judaizers
Paul's conflict with them 666f
Heretical Jewish Christianity 729–739
Judaizing Docetism 763f
Judas Barsabbas 740
Judas' grandsons 752f
Judgment, The Last 540–543, 559f
Junias 674
Justification 428f, 444, 498–504, 632f
Justus, Bishop 721

Kaphar Sama 727
Kaphar Sicanim 728
Knowledge 510f, 556f, 611
Kochaba 716
Kyrios 741 n. 3

Laodicea 776, 778
Law, The
Attitude of Paul 546, 559
Freedom of Christians from the Law 546
Polemic against, in Epistle to Galatians 549
Fulfilment of the Law, according to Paul 551–554
Ebionite observance of 734
In the Epistle of James 747f
Legalism, in the Gospel of Matthew 754
Logos doctrine 479f, 481ff
Lord's Supper
Words of Institution 640f
Pauline conception 639–649
Love 569–573
Lucian 781
His Alexander 781
Luke, Gospel of 656, 664f
Date 656
Infancy Narrative 725, 733
Stories of the Baptist 724

Macedonia 818–827
Maeander 779
Magnesia 779
Maranatha 457
Marcia 847
Marcion 650, 757, 780
Mark, Gospel of
Date 655
Impersonal character 689f
Purpose 690
Proclamation of the Person of Christ 691f
Basic ideas 693f
Parables 695
Polemic against Judaism 663, 695
Importance for Church History 697
Christology 697f
Not a biography 699
Lack of chronological order 700
Absence of character drawing 700f
Indirect characterization 700f
Absence of any fanatical glorification of Jesus 701
Apologetic 701
Sympathetic features 702f
Marriage 581–585
Mary, The mother of Jesus 731
Matthew, Gospel of
Date 656, 751f
Tendency 668f
Used by Ebionite Jewish Christians 736
Partiality for Peter 752
Place of writing 752
Legalism versus lawlessness 753f
Author 754
Attitude toward the Jewish people 755
Meals, in common 648f
Mediation of Christ 472f

Melito of Sardis 827
Menander 756f
His attitude toward Christianity 757
His pessimism 762f
Messiahship 446–452, 733
Messianic beliefs, Jewish 474
Minucius Fundanus 815
Miracles of Jesus 692f
Mission
The mission field of early Christianity 657–660
The mission to Jews 660ff
The mission to Gentiles 662f
Mission of the Disciples 678f
Mission-theology 442–445
Monotheism 412f, 603, 855
Montanus 781
Mystery cult 450, 520f, 637, 646, 741f
Mysticism 463–471, 511ff, 771f

Names of Christ 455–458
As formula in Baptism 635
Nazoraeans 730–739
Origin of the name 730
Their Christology 731f
Their Gospel 736
In Beroea 669
Nero 839f

Onesimus 588
Ostia 837

Panther, Son of (libel of Jesus) 728
Paphos 775
Papias 779
Parousia ('second coming') of Christ 526, 544, 648, 694f
Pastoral Epistles 775
Date of writing 656
Paul
6. Paul the author
His literary directness 399ff
Epistolary forms 401f
Extravagance of style 402–405
Homiletic tone 405f
Artistic form 406–411
Antitheses 411–416
Diatribe 416–418
Dialectic 418f
Didactic exposition 419
Controversial style 419
Paul, The Epistles of
Earliest collection 681–684
Paul's Theology and Religion
1. The theological thinker
Connection between theology and religion 422ff
The eschatological emphasis 445
Knowledge and love 559
The idea of faith 424–428
The idea of the Spirit 430f
Earlier history of the idea 422
Forms of thought 433ff
Dialectic forms 435f
Scripture proof 436–440
Hellenistic elements 440f
Proof from experience 441f
Theology of conversion and of mission 442–445
2. The Faith in Christ
Relation to the historical Jesus 452–455
Eschatological Messianic belief 446ff
The new figure of the Messiah 448–452
The titles of Christ 455–458
The Kyrios-title 458–463
Christ-mysticism 464ff
Its Hellenistic origin 465–471
Faith in Christ and faith in God 471–475
Christological speculation 475–495
Christ's divine Sonship 476ff
Christ the Creator and Soul of the World 478–484
The Heavenly 'Man' 484–488
The Incarnation 488–491
Death and Resurrection 491–495
Cosmis antecedents 492
3. The new relation to God
Experience of conversion 496f
Reconciliation 497f
Justification 428f, 443, 498–504, 541
Children of God 505
Election 506ff
Faith, Love, Knowledge the work of God 508ff
God-mysticism 510–513
4. The new creation
Redemption 429, 442, 514f, 541
Enthusiastic anticipation of perfection 518ff
Death and resurrection with Christ 520–523, 636ff
The new life realized physically 523ff
5. The Christian Hope
The longing for Christ 526
God's victory over the world, 526ff
The dominion of the saints 528f
Eternal Life, Salvation, Glory 529ff
Resurrection of the dead 531–537
Transformation of those who survive 537ff
The Judgment 540–543
Apocalyptic details 543ff
6. Ethics
(1) Norms of the Pauline ethic 546–559
The Law 546–554
The Words and example of the Lord 554ff
The spirit as norm and power 556f
The baptismal commandments 557ff
(2) Motifs of the Pauline ethic 559–569
The eschatological motif 559–563
The religious motif 563f
The motif of fellowship 564ff
The motif of personality 566–569
(3) Particular application of ethical ideals 569–594
Love 569–573
Truth 573f
Self-examination 574ff
Education and training 576f
Courage and loyalty 577–580
Possessions and worldly duties 580–594
7. Conception of the world
The cosmos and Paul's estimate of it 595ff
The angelic world 599–603
The aeons 603ff
Anthropology 605–611
Humanity 611–614
8. Conception of the Community
The Church of God 615–622
Membership in the community and possession of the Spirit 622–629
The Sacraments 629–650
9. After-effects
Paul and Peter 719, 849
Paul and the Ebionites 476ff
Polemic against Paul in the Epistle of James 750
Paul and Ignatius 772
The Pauline heritage in Asia 782–786
Pella 714, 716
Perfection 576, 627
Pergamon 778, 807f
Persecution of Christians
In Asia 803–817
In Rome 839–844
Peter
Peter and Paul 686
Not the founder of the Roman church 838f
Martyr-death 839
Mission-preaching 657f
Rock of the Church and Guardian of the Keys 719, 752
Position in the Book of Acts 724
Visit to Antioch 740

Position in the Gospel of Matthew 751f
Bishop of Antioch 766
Peter, Epistles of
First Epistle 657, 685, 775, 804
Author 657
As source for persecution of Christians in Asia 804f
Date of composition 805
Peter, Gospel of 664
Philadelphia 779, 807
Philemon. Epistle to 405, 588
Philip the Evangelist 779
His prophetic daughters 779
Philippi 818–821
Character of the Christian community 819f
Its organization 820ff
Danger of heresy 822–825
Philo of Alexandria 435, 440, 479 n. 27, 482f, 487f, 608, 610
Philo of Cilicia 776
Philomelium 781
Phrygia 781
Pilate 664
Pliny, Epistle of 775, 810
Trial of Christians in Bithynia 810ff
Trajan's Rescript 812–815
Polycarp, Epistle of 656, 775, 818
Occasion 818f
Date 819
Contents 819
As source for history of the Church in Philippi 819–822
Paulinism 825f
Polemic against heretics 822–825
Religion 826
Posidonius 595
Practice 576f
Prayer, times of 582
Preëxistence 485
Primitive community
Propaganda 666f
Development after the death of Stephen 707
Fidelity to the Law 707
Jewish opposition 707f
The Jewish prayer against heretics 708
Persecutions by process of Law 708
Death of James 709–712
End of the primitive community in Jerusalem 714
Appearance of the 'abomination' 714
Flight of Christians to Pella 716
Second period, following the year 70 717
Monarchical episcopate 719–722
Priscilla 593, 661
Proculus Torpacion 848
Proof from experience in Paul 441f
Puteoli 837

Reconciliation, Pauline doctrine of 497f
Redemption 429, 443, 515
Regeneration 520–523
Resurrection: denials of 533f
Resurrection of Jesus
In the Pauline Christology 491–495
Reward, Ethics of 560–563
Righteousness
The Pauline conception 428–431
Romans, Epistle to
Final doxology 684
Rome 741
Work of Paul 837f
Peter in Rome 838f
Neronian persecution 839f
Trial of Christians under Domitian 841f
Influential circles 844–847
Charitable work of the church 848
Importance of Roman community for the church as a whole 865
Rufus, son of Simon of Cyrene 690

Sabbath-controversy 696
Sacrifice, Christ's death a 449, 645f
Salvation, The history of 425f
Samaria 723, 740, 756
Sardis 779
Satan 602f
Saturninus (Satornilus) 756, 761ff
Sayings of the Lord 554ff, 641f
Scripture proof 436–440
Self-criticism, Christian 574ff
Septuagint 617, 619, 856
Septuagint Greek 431ff
Serennius Granianus, Proconsul 815
Sex, Early Christian attitude toward 580–585
Silas (Silvanus) 416, 674, 740
Simeon, son of Clopas 717, 719, 726
Martyrdom 722
Simon Magus 756
Relation to Christianity 759ff
Doctrine of descent 757f
Identification with Jesus 759f
Pessimism 762f
Antinomism 763
Myth of Helen 763
Sin, Confession of 575
Sin, Relation between the flesh and 606ff
Sinope 780
Slavery, Christian attitude toward 585–590
Smyrna 777
Son of Man 485f
Sonship, Jesus', to God 475–478
Sparta 829
Spirit 463f, 512f, 524, 556f
State, Attitude of Christians toward the 590f
Stephanus 588
Stoics 440, 511, 579, 855
Suetonius 839
Syncretism, Syrian 743
Syria 740
Christian communities in 740

Tacitus 839
Teaching of the Twelve Apostles (Didache) 558, 640, 658, 678
Teleogy 433
Thessalonica 818
Thyatira 779
Timothy 416, 674
Titles of Christ 455–458
Titus 841
Tongues, speaking with 626
Trajan 810–814, 844
Tralles 778
Troas 776, 779
Truth 573f
Twelve, The 673
Identification with the Apostles 673f

Unchastity 580ff
Underworld 596f
Unity of men with God 510f
Universality of the message of Salvation 661f

Valens, presbyter in Philippi 819
Valerius Biton 844
Vespasian 841

Worship
In the Christian community 624

Zacchaeus, bishop of Caesarea 721
Zealots 591, 614
Zebedee, Sons of 718
Zoker 726 n. 34